THE THINGS
THAT MATTER MOST

AN APPROACH TO THE PROBLEMS
OF HUMAN VALUES

615

by

RALPH TYLER FLEWELLING

DIRECTOR OF INTERNATIONAL STUDIES, OLIVE HILL FOUNDATION
SCHOOL OF PHILOSOPHY, THE UNIVERSITY OF
SOUTHERN CALIFORNIA

THE RONALD PRESS COMPANY   •   NEW YORK

Second Printing, December, 1946

PREFACE

This study attempts no formal treatment of ethics. It aims rather to provide the basis for inquiry into practical problems of morals, as one of a larger group designed for college students in General Studies.

To create a more vivid interest, and at the same time to give the student a glimpse of the treatment of moral problems as set forth in the world's great literature, it seemed good to take in a wide diversity of teachings. Such a method would serve as a spur to discussion and inquiry, since that which smacks of biography excites a more living interest. Other equally fascinating historical figures might have been chosen with profit but the number considered necessarily had to be limited. Thus, Socrates was chosen to the elimination of Plato and Aristotle, not only because he was the originator of the movement which they elaborated, but because he presented the essential problems in a simpler form, furnished an alluring personality, and was a formative influence in Western civilization. Of him one modern scholar has written:

> . . . the greatness of Socrates cannot possibly be measured by judging him simply as a theoretical philosopher. What he did was to create a new attitude towards life, which formed the climax to a long and painful ascent towards human freedom, and which can never be transcended by any other. The gospel he preached was the self-mastery and self-sufficiency of the moral character.[1]

Pasteur was chosen as the representative of the scientific idea of value, partly because of the human interest of his researches, which led to the modern conquest of infectious and contagious diseases, and partly because of his heroic devotion to truth. Passing by their military hero Napoleon, the French people voted him to be the greatest Frenchman in history, while Sir William Osler pronounced him the most perfect scientist.

The work is planned to provide for one explanatory or supplementary lecture by the instructor, if he so desires, and two periods of discussion, either open, formal, or with student papers. The leader of the course can easily work out his own preferred method with the material here presented, with the advantage to be obtained

[1] Maier: *Sokrates*, quoted by Werner Jaeger: *Paideia*, II, pp. 24-25. Oxford University Press, New York.

by direct acquaintance of the student with the original writings of the individuals considered. The presence of original sources adds to the diversity of expedients that will suggest themselves to the teacher. The hope has been to raise questions in an arresting and challenging way, rather than to prescribe the thinking of the student, since his own conclusions will be the most lasting in the effect upon him.

Acknowledgment of helpful suggestions are due to my colleagues Dean A. S. Raubenheimer and Professor J. W. Wallbank, under whose supervision the course has passed from the state of experiment to popular and successful standing after some years of testing. Quite particular is the indebtedness to Professors Wilbur Long, Herbert L. Searles, Paul R. Helsel, and Sterling M. McMurrin, whose devoted efforts have been responsible for the success achieved. Thanks are due as well to the Curriculum Committee of the College of Letters, Arts and Sciences for their willingness to allow the experiment, as also to Chancellor R. B. von KleinSmid, of the University of Southern California. In no small way is the author indebted to Mrs. Emma D. Helsel and Mrs. Florence Smith in, the typing of the manuscript; to Dr. Seeley G. Mudd and the Olive Hill Foundation for grant in aid, to my grandson Ralph Hunter Flewelling for the drawing on page 74, and to my wife, Jane Carlin Flewelling, for hours at proofreading.

RALPH TYLER FLEWELLING

Los Angeles, June 1, 1946.

ACKNOWLEDGMENTS

Acknowledgment is made to the following publishers for permission to quote selections from material copyrighted by them:

Cambridge University Press: Arnold's *The Light of Asia*. Cambridge University Press and The Macmillan Company: "The Decree of Athens on Zeno"; Arnold's *Roman Stoicism*. China Institute of Pacific Relations, Shanghai: *Symposium on Chinese Culture*. College of Chinese Studies, Peking: Flewelling's *Reflections on the Basic Ideas of East and West*. The Confraternity of Christian Doctrine: "A Digression on Charity," Chapter 13 of *I Corinthians*. Thomas Y. Crowell Company: Dante's *The Divine Comedy*. Lindsay Drummond, Ltd., London: *Transformation Two*. E. P. Dutton & Company: Rousseau's *Émile* and *The Social Contract;* Watt's *The Spirit of Zen*. Journal of the Franklin Institute: selection from the paper of E. C. Kemble. Harcourt, Brace & Company: Mumford's *The Condition of Man*. Harvard University Press: Boethius' *The Consolation of Philosophy*. Heinneman, London: Naidu, *The Golden Threshold*. Johns Hopkins Press: Turnbull's *Tongues of Fire*. Houghton Mifflin Company: Hawthorne's *Mosses from an Old Manse;* Cabot's *What Men Live By;* Chapman's *Dante;* Longfellow's *Divine Comedy*. Lippincott Company: "Tales of the Mermaid Tavern," Noyes' *Collected Poems*. Little, Brown & Company: Higginson's translation of *The Discourses of Epictetus;* Long's *The Thoughts of Marcus Aurelius*. The Macmillan Company: Nietzsche's *Beyond Good and Evil;* Baker's *Science and the Planned State;* Morley's *Rousseau and His Era;* Flewelling's *Creative Personality;* Windelband's *History of Philosophy;* Browning's *Poetical Works;* Moulton's Modern Reader's Bible, selections from the *Book of Job*. W. W. Norton & Company, Inc.: Max Planck's *The Philosophy of Physics*. Oxford University Press: Bailey's *Epicurus*, and *The Greek Atomists and Epicurus;* Jaeger's *Paideia*. Princeton University Press: Erasmus' *The Praise of Folly*. Random House: Cleanthes' "Hymn" and "Lucretius" from Oates' *The Stoic and Epicurean Philosophers;* Gibbon's *Decline and Fall of the Roman Empire*. Charles Scribner's Sons: Plato's *The Apology* and *The Phaedo,* from Modern Student's Library. Shanghai Book Company: Confucius' *Four Books*. United Newspapers Magazine Corporation: *This Week Magazine,* Compton's "What You and I Need Most." The University of Chicago Press: Goodspeed's *The Apocrypha*. The University of Southern California: *The Personalist:* Flewelling's "Scientific Data and Spiritual Fact."

R. T. F.

CONTENTS

PART III
SIX PROPONENTS OF VALUE

PART IV

SELF-REALIZATION AS VALUE

THE THINGS
THAT MATTER MOST

INTRODUCTION

Plotinus, who lived in the third century after Christ, defined the field of philosophy to be "the things that matter most": *TÒ TIMI-ÓTATON*. With all the changes and developments that have taken place during the centuries since, this definition has a strikingly modern sound. We are still endeavoring to find out what are the things that matter most; in fact it is one of the most conspicuous fields of modern inquiry. There are many opinions as to what is most worth while, and many people who could make a most respectable list of the things that matter. yet show a great hesitancy in seeking them. They are quite sure about what is best for the neighbors, the Hottentots, or the children, but display a remarkable lassitude in seizing these values for themselves.

The world of our time has been fairly obsessed by the idea that the principal values were to come by the way of better education, greater abundance, increasing scientific discovery, without apparently asking a serious question as to whether thereby it is possible to purchase peace of mind, without which nothing matters. An age of great invention, and increased luxury, with goods enough to make everybody comfortable, may suddenly find itself in the most disastrous social and political chaos the world has ever known. Such has been the experience of multitudes in days recently past, that all values of money, physical comfort, and luxury were outclassed by the simple values of the presence or safety of some member of the family caught in the maelstrom of war. Under the spur of such questionings as we are likely to experience, it may be necessary to open the problem of value anew, to discover what is *most* worth while. In this crisis, philosophy, which is supposed to have things to say about the moral values, has on the whole seemed strangely silent, or has lent its assent to the claim that there are no moral values. This teaching seems today inappropriate in the face of what unscrupulous men, armed with the latest inventions, can do to a world which for the most part would like to live in peace, justice, and common well-being. There is serious question as to whether philosophy has any task comparable to that of considering the reality of the things worth while. The present status of the world emphasizes more than ever the fact that, regardless of physical comforts or scientific discoveries, little is to be gained by

3

these, if falling into the hands of evil-minded, unsocial, or avaricious men they are used primarily for the enslavement of others. If we are to face the world of tomorrow successfully, we must meet this question for ourselves, and decide what are the things that matter most. Our answer to the question will determine, not only our own happiness and future, but the future of our world as well.

If in our minds the query should arise, as to why the problem at which men have struggled for so many generations has not yet been solved, and if the further issue appears as to what is the prospect or value of finding an answer, we must remember that it is a question which living men cannot evade, and which is so important that its answer may determine the outcome of individual happiness, the social order, and the succeeding centuries of human history.

. That is a curious trend of human interest which has led us to put so much emphasis on isolating the elements of matter as a means of discovering reality. We have, like children, been chiefly concerned with taking apart the toy of reality in order to discover "what makes it go," only to find that "what makes it go" is not visible. For complete knowledge we have to consider things not as independent parts, but in relationship to other things. It is these very immaterial relationships that present us with intelligent meaning, furnishing the qualities that make things significant and real. Our utmost "real" cannot escape this non-material aspect. This may be exactly the region where we shall find "the things that matter most."

We have, for instance, spent generations isolating the distinct elements in chemistry, but this was only the stepping-stone to, not the end of, inquiry. The chemistry of organism, as it might be called, or of relationship, is a comparatively new field of research. Yet "synthetic" chemistry has in a few short years revolutionized our thought of the nature of substance, by showing us how to spin silk from cornstalks, clothing from sand, and glass into wrapping paper. This progress has not resulted from further isolation of elements, but from the discovery of their relationships, which promises great practical benefits.

A similar situation is to be found in the field of biology. Much effort of past centuries has been spent on discovering new differences of classification, and inventing names for the differences, to the frequent confusion of the student. That work was pioneering and necessary. We now turn our attention, with surprising profit, to the subtle relationships that exist between plants and animals and their environments, of sun, sea, sky, air, and certain "vitamins." We have long known and benefited by the fact that some figs cannot produce without the wasp, that certain flowers demand the bumble-bee, while others are apparently built for the special activities of the honey-bee. In the jungles of South America there is said to be a trumpet flower, some sixteen inches long, the fertilization of which depends upon a single species of moth having a corresponding proboscis. Without these relationships which must be considered a part of nature and reality, these plants could not long exist. Now we are discovering new relationships of staggering significance.

In language we have recorded hundreds of human dialects, but up to the present our most successful approach to common speech seems to be through "Pidgin English." In analysis, in pulling things apart, we certainly have achieved. We now need to turn our attention to synthesis. With taking things apart we seem to have no frontiers left, but with putting them together we are presented with virgin territory in the midst of exclusive nationalisms, racial hatreds, social misunderstandings and injustices, and the bitterness of religious rivalry. In these things that matter most for the peace and prosperity of the world, we have made little more than a beginning.

In the realm of personal life, we have been still slower in finding out what are the things that matter. Geographical exploration has been pushed to the ends of the earth until we know most of the inaccessible places, but we have scarcely begun to disclose the possibilities of the human mind, with its creative powers and its relation to the external world. Not until recently have we come to see the importance of the study of the nature of experience in the interpretation of scientific knowledge. It was Professor Edwin C. Kemble of Harvard who, in addressing the symposium of physicists at the Franklin Institute in December 1937, declared that the direct items of our experience, such as electric and magnetic fields, atoms, electrons, and wave functions, are but mental constructs, and in conclusion declared that the province of the physicist is not the study of the external world, but of the inner world of experience.[1]

One thing is certain, there can be in the future no credible theory of values which does not take into account the very human characteristics of the things that matter most, in the fields of science, of philosophy, and of religion. We are set upon an inquiry into the nature and reality of human values, and we are likely to meet with some who deny altogether the existence of such values. We need to uncover the secrets of man's inner life, the sources of his genius and creativeness, the basis of mental and spiritual experience and insight, the unlocking of his hidden powers, and the relation they bear

[1] *Journal of the Franklin Institute,* Vol. 225, No. 3, March, 1938.

both to the inner and outer worlds. We need to carry the evolution of man up to the climax that his dormant powers foretell, that he may realize his supreme reality in the things that are of utmost importance to his success and happiness. There have been periods when an effort to defend these superior but imponderable actualities would have been considered an attempt at arguing the obvious, but often our minds are so intoxicated with the wine of physical invention and discovery that we think of matter as the only reality. The deeper fires that burn within the mental experience of man, that give inspiration to creative art, literature, social and spiritual achievement, and even to scientific invention, are easily passed over as unreal. Yet these are the determining influences of life, which Dr. Richard Cabot calls "the things men live by." Religion and philosophy are occasionally charged with invalidating preconceptions from which science is assumed to be quite free. Yet science, too, has its sweeping preconceptions beyond the range of proof, hypotheses which are accepted because they are workable and do not conflict with the demands of human thought. The advances of science grow out of synthesis, the relation of fact to fact, "the leap in the dark," through which the mind comes to construct a universe of meanings profitable to human experience. What the atom *is* we do not know except through such activities issuing from such points in space as yield themselves to the measurements of our physical senses. No reputable scientist would think of claiming that these results already obtained are all there is of it. In the field of human values, demonstration in foot-pounds of energy is impossible, but there need not be for that reason any lessening of the assurance of their reality. The current of electricity can be measured by resistances, but love, patriotism, honor, integrity, drive men to acts and accomplishments just as real and, for human experience, even more important. Here lie the influences that change the course of human history, and give meaning to human life. There may have been mental and psychological elements as well as physical that led to Blucher's delay which lost the Battle of Waterloo, caused Hitler's hesitancy at Dunkirk, and the misjudgment of the Japanese Admiral at Midway. Were we to attempt to describe such turning-points in history in terms of chemisms and affinities, we should not get any closer to their meaning. Our accustomed yardstick doesn't apply here, but the values involved are no more invalidated than the current of electricity would be disproved because we could not measure it in a bushel basket. No one would be interested in the number of foot-pounds of energy represented in the love of a little child, and he who would demand the contributing testimony of the lie-detector before trusting the love of his wife or sweetheart would destroy it, because love rests on faith. Yet these are matters of greatest moment to our happiness and success.

Such are the values that give worth and meaning to life, the things by which we live. However we may attempt to ignore them, they continue to be our supreme interests. The finer and immaterial loyalties of our world are superior to the most startling of external facts. The heart of a friend is a possession above rubies, which no wealth can buy. Without it life is left desolate. Patriotism is by some considered a mere sentiment, but for it men leave wives, children, and all besides that they have counted dear, in a voluntary sacrifice for principles. Upon loyalties like these is built the structure of society, and they can never be truly evaluated in terms of fifty dollars a month, hospital service, and a pension. By facts such as these men live and are ready to die, because these immaterial values survive the changing and passing order and are necessary to the preservation of civilization itself. The progress of civilization is not to be altogether measured by advancing discovery, nor by the extent of physical possessions, but rather by the esteem in which men generally hold these finer values.

Even the most obvious facts cannot eventually be separated from judgments of value. Their importance to us lies in making us masters of our environment, adding to the joy of living, and providing insight into the common relations of life. It is for these imponderables that the scientist gives his life and energies in a devotion no less than religious. The absence of these higher motives would impoverish the history of science. Where education is indifferent or hostile to moral and spiritual realities, we have a result like that in yesterday's Germany, knowledge devoted to human destruction. Without righteousness, understanding becomes a menace to society. Facts are clothed with profound moral significance in our world, and science, religion, and philosophy must ultimately be judged by their contribution to human values.

PART I

VALUES DEFINED

"The unconsidered life is not worth living."
—SOCRATES

615

Chapter 1

THE NATURE OF VALUE

Introduction

I
Is There Such a Thing as Value?

II
The Value Underlying Values

III
Human Values in the Role of History

IV
Some Objectives in the Study of Values

Chapter 1

THE NATURE OF VALUE

In the opening lines of Goethe's drama of Faust we have the description of a study-worn student who has taken honors in law, medicine, and theology without finding the satisfaction that he feels should come with the diplomas and the title of Doctor. He is torn between the conflicting impulses either to commit suicide, or to do something devilish. This situation in the life of Faust is not a unique nor even an unusual one. Whoever in life expects external rewards to bring him lasting satisfactions is headed directly toward the frustrated and worn-out feelings of the youthful Faust.

The reason for the Faustian disillusionment was not to be found in his surroundings. One doubts if it was altogether due to the dreariness of the professorial lectures. It was brought about rather by his failure to know the sources of the permanent values of life. The result was not only that he made the worst possible choice, but that the better choices were unrecognized by him, yet his selection of values determined his career. Since his concept of what is worth while is to be the decisive factor in his success or failure, it is essential for the college student to reflect upon the problem of values. To have the fullest information he will need to know how other men in other times have attempted to solve it. From these one may take advice while retaining his own judgment, for, after all, as Socrates has said: "The unconsidered life is not worth living." About any man one needs to know primarily what he most desires. It then requires no crystal-gazer to tell what he will become.

I

Is There Such a Thing as Value?

Whether there is such a thing as value may seem a queer question to ask, but there are those who deny its reality at the same time that they pursue it. Few have had the courage openly to doubt the existence of what all men seek after, and so the reality of values has seldom been directly attacked. Yet in the face of common opinion it is appropriate that in a study devoted to values, we should, first of all, inquire whether their validity can be established. Perhaps no one in the history of literature has discussed more interestingly the reality of values than has Desiderius Erasmus (1446-1536) who in 1516-17 published the classic satire on value under the title: *The Praise of Folly.* He was the leading classical scholar of his time, the beginning of the Renaissance, which produced a remarkable coterie of scholars and great men. The society of his day was characterized by totalitarianism in Church and State. Criticism of men and measures was, under the conditions, highly dangerous to the critic, yet it was essential to the good of society to rebuke often the conduct of the powerful. This could be done with a degree of safety only under the appearance of clownishness. Every court supported its "jester," a half-wit who provided entertainment by his comments on court and courtiers. He was dressed in motley with cap and bells, and he might be a moron or he might pretend to be moronic for the pleasure and support he received. His criticisms passed as jokes. There grew up in Europe a literature of foolishness, such as Brant's *Ship of Fools,* and Erasmus' *Praise of Folly.* There were fraternities of professional fools like those of the Joyous Societies of France. On "All Fools Day" these took over the town, the court, and even parodied the solemn Mass in the Cathedral, taking off the idiosyncrasies of their superiors. However sharp the reproof might be, the victim had to take it in fun, for resentment was an open confession of guilt. Our own successors to the caste of professional "fools" must be sought in the political cartoonists, the circus clown, or the actor on the stage.

Erasmus, travelling from an audience with the Pope at Rome to the England of Henry the Eighth, conceived of a clever pun upon the name of his revered friend and literary collaborator, Sir Thomas More, later to become the author of the famous *Utopia* and, by the road of martyrdom, to be recognized as a saint by the Church. Both men spoke and wrote in Latin, in which language Erasmus' friend was addressed as Morus, which in Latin meant "Fool." Hence it occurred to Erasmus as a clever idea to ridicule the ruling follies of the time with a hint at the name of his brilliant friend under the title *Encomium Moriae,* or *Praise of Folly.* So it came about that on the long journey from Italy on muleback he sketched out the classic bit of irony that called in question the existence of the commonly accepted values.

An attack upon ordinary opinions can best be made indirectly,

as by what Nietzsche called "the transvaluation of values," and
this was the device that Erasmus employed. His essay can be understood only when seen as a satirization of the inconsistencies of
his times by praising them as evidences of wisdom. Such a method
had personal advantages for himself (his friend More was beheaded for entertaining the opinion of the superior authority of
the Pope) and conduced to the toleration of his own message. It
exempted him from the charge of slandering the great and it added
piquancy to his work. Clothed in the spirit of banter, those most
hit by the satire would least admit that it was directed at them,
and others would enjoy fitting the coat on those they deemed deserving of the sarcasm. The interest for us lies in the questions
it raises respecting the nature and existence of values.

The impersonation of Folly is represented as a young woman in
academic gown but with the proverbial cap of the court fool with
long tabs, such as would fit over the ears of a donkey, and each
bearing a tinkling bell at the tip. The argument of the piece could
be briefly summed up in the phrase: "Where ignorance is bliss, 'tis
folly to be wise."

Folly assumes that she will be readily recognized and welcomed
since everybody is a bit of a fool, himself, and so will respond to her
arguments and speeches. It is fitting for her to begin by praising
herself because she is best acquainted with herself, and it is cheaper
than hiring a publicity man. Then others might be unwilling to
"toot her horn" for her, and she can recall many others who are less
deserving of praise than herself. As the Goddess of Folly she addresses her advice to her loyal admirers and faithful subjects "of
whom the number is infinite" and all-embracing, including everybody.

She begins drastically with the assertion that the idea that life
itself is a supreme value is meaningless without the creative power
and presence of folly. Pleasure is the whole desideratum of life,
and pleasure without folly is unthinkable. "To know nothing,"
quoting Sophocles, "affords the happiest life." "Folly is the one
thing that makes fleeting youth linger and keeps ugly old age away."
Children, fools, and the feeble-minded by old age represent the happier portion of society.

After pleasure, she attacks the other commonly assumed values,
such as sex, social entertainment, eating and drinking, friendship,
self-esteem, warlike courage, education, fame, prudence, reputation
for scholarship, and wealth. These are the values everybody seeks,
and they can come only through folly. Foolish people, unscrupulous

people, folks who are willing to accept a reputation for wisdom as a sufficient substitute for the real thing, those who make gain by dishonesty with a get-rich-quick ardor, these often out-distance men of honest ambition. Why then go to the toil and trouble of coming by them in the accepted way? Fortune seems (sometimes) to favor the rasher sort, and even religion, from the standpoint of material profit, can be seen as a sort of folly, lacking in worldly wisdom.

The success of the Erasmian irony depends upon the ambiguity or double meaning lurking in popular concepts of value, such as the apparent effectiveness of flattery and falsehood in getting ahead. What greater honor could there be (no matter how it is brought about, deserved or undeserved) than to be carried in a popular parade, or have a statue in the city square? She sees all values in their least and most popular significance. The fame of great learning is held to be more than offset by the toil of achieving it. Fools frequently get the reputation without the learning. Isn't that reaping the desired result without the work? And with what ease? What more is likely to be asked?

What, further, is the essence of prudence which is so much admired? Is it anything more than the ability to keep with the crowd, to realize which way the wind blows? As to riches, they are often attended by a niggardliness that indicates poverty of mind and spirit. There is a sense in which a king may be the poorest of men. All life may be seen as a sort of fool's paradise as unreal as are the changing costumes of the theatre to indicate the real characters of the actors. Human love can be very disappointing, more so if it is genuine; riches may be merely the result of dishonesty; business success the result of crookedness. Fools often seem to be the most prosperous; cheaters may advance the fastest. According to a shallow casting of accounts folly is the most profitable; largest returns from smallest investment. We hear such arguments from the mouths of cynics every day; arguments against sincere love, honest work, real learning, fair business practice, and even religion, as if the endeavor to be good were an object of contempt.

Erasmus thus represents the popular criticism which seems to undercut and sweep away the validity of most values. While he settles nothing he raises questions that will not down.

II
The Value Underlying Values

From these considerations it will appear that our problem of what matters most cannot be answered in an easy offhand way. It is not so simple as appears on the surface, nor will any superficial solution permanently satisfy. This conviction is deepened as we read the selection from Hawthorne's *Mosses From an Old Manse.* Here the City of Vanity, first pictured by John Bunyan in the world's most famous allegory, *The Pilgrim's Progress,* is set forth by Hawthorne as a modern town characterized by all the activity and movement sought in days of celebration and gaiety. Christian and Faithful in the older story found buffeting and persecution because of their religious sobriety, and Christian was burned at the stake. In the modern Vanity of Hawthorne's parody the same principles still obtain under the show of up-to-dateness and modern "improvements" which are intended to gloss over, though they cannot conceal, the inner hostility to honest living. Modern Vanity, unlike the old one, is abundantly supplied with churches which have no stomach for the unpopularity which would follow a straightforward dealing with the follies of the people. The main interest centers in the Market where all sorts of people are attempting to acquire values by purchase. There are people from all walks of life: princes, presidents, poets, generals, artists, actors, and philanthropists. Here the young man of fortune, for the sake of a good time, reduces himself to disease, rags, and regrets; for a like reason the young girl trades "a heart as clear as crystal" for one that is tawdry and worthless. In the shop where crowns of laurel and myrtle were displayed, soldiers, authors, and statesmen bought these at the expense of slavery, sacrifice, and life. Indeed it seemed that one could have almost anything he might want at the expense of conscience. The politician got what he wanted by selling his constituents "down the river." Everywhere men were bartering away long range benefits for the obvious and the quick returns.

In this way we have brought to our attention a phase of the problem of value most often overlooked by the unthinking: that beneath the external appearance of values there is a deeper one calling for consideration. The wise man not only will look at the surface of things, but will endeavor to find the hidden values underlying appearances.

Is there any difference between possible choices of what we want, or are all desires to be taken at face value, such as common opinion, or the fad of the hour?

There are some who assume that the great universal and all but exclusive value is money, or possessions. Get this, they say, and you can come by all the others—friends, ease, luxury, and success. It was our misfortune once to meet such a man, and with him to be compelled to travel on a small freighter from Port Said to Manila. He boasted that his best friend was his dollar. He had visited the outstanding cities of the world, but all he knew of them was of the various dives wherein we suspect he found his dollars as well as his friends. He had never heard of the leading institutions of the cities he had visited: the universities, the libraries, the art galleries, or even the outstanding architectural or natural features. That his dollar was an unsatisfactory friend was evidenced by his anxiety to be thought well of by his fellow passengers, as evidenced by his continual boasting. That his life was obsessed by fears was indicated by the manner of his leaving the ship at Manila, with the remainder of his passage unused. After all, his friend the dollar had, we suspect, the habit of deserting him when he most needed it; it would not lessen his fears, and it could not return his love. His thought about what was most worth having had reduced his life to a sort of slavery, in which his action was dictated by his fear of discovery. Even slight consideration shows that in all cases our desire for money is based on some simpler want. We desire money, not for what it is in itself, but for the satisfactions it will buy. Money is the medium which we can use to procure food, clothing, dwellings, luxuries, and the paraphernalia of abundant living, and so may symbolize the whole field of material wants. If money had no power to put us in possession of these more basic desires we would feel no incentive to acquire it. The tragedy of King Midas was that the magic with which he was endowed turned whatever he touched into gold. In making such a wish he had not deeply considered the problem, nor even the nature, of value. He could not touch a cup of water to his lips without having both cup and contents instantly solidified into gold. The possession of gold was his ruin because he had almost nothing else. A thousand other things were now denied him without which all his gold was worthless. His life, his existence, his comfort and happiness depended on a multitude of things he had overlooked and which were of far greater moment than gold. It is possible for us, like King Midas, to set our choices in such directions as to gain that which we want, and to lose those things which are of most account. One can gain the whole world and yet lose what is most precious. That is the reason we are setting out on a study of the nature and problem of values. If it is true that values are constituted by our needs and desires, and money is good only in so far as it can satisfy these, there must be a variety of human wants that could be named as possessing worth. Out of the endless array of such desires there must be some that are more important or more satisfying than others. There is little prospect of exhausting the catalogue of mortal wishes, but a few stand out more prominently than the rest and some may be taken as the symbols or representative of many. Many presumed benefits are mutually exclusive. That is, to obtain them we have to deny ourselves other advantages that may be quite as legitimate. To enjoy the privilege of scholarship we choose to give up a certain amount of freedom in other directions. Days and nights are spent in mental toil, because the advantages of an educated man are thought superior to those of the uneducated. A whole rank of lawful wants is set aside in order to achieve better ones. If one accomplishes anything greatly worth working for he has to learn how to do without some advantages. In fact, life is made up of constantly recurring choices between desirable things.

After the desire for money, which as we have seen is given first place not because of intrinsic worth but because it easily provides many other advantages, there is the very human wish for fame or notoriety. We should see, if we went at all deeply into this, that it is essentially a good that has to do with the consciousness of personality, a hope that our personality shall in some way be shown to be outstanding among others. It is the secret of the hold that competitions have over us in every sort of game or contest. In its baser form it is no more than a hunger for notoriety. Frequently, when fame is denied, the individual tries to satisfy his egotism with notoriety, which is a mock fame, a substitute for reality. Men frequently sacrifice money, comfort, the substantial wants in the pursuit of a flair for publicity. This craving ranges all the way from the low level of leadership of the "Alley gang," or "Public Enemy Number One," or the most extravagant liar, or the most popular this or that, up to mention in the society column, presidency of the club, or fraternity, captain of the football team, political office, literary eminence, through a thousand others, to the top wherever that may be considered to be. These ambitions are themselves shot through with varying motives, but as long as they center in mere self-satisfaction they contain a certain common element—the appeal to personal vanity. When we stop to consider this underlying element of much of the world's struggle and effort we shall be close to a clue to the sense of frustration so common in an ambitious age. Only those values which are devoid of personal vanity seem to yield the more permanent and abiding fame.

All of these things for which we are willing to pay a price of money, labor, or striving are in a way to be considered values. Our lives are sure to spend their energies seeking one or another, or

many of them.   In fact what we consider to be desirable has begun
to determine the youngest life.   Under such circumstances the study
of what matters most would seem to be as practical and important
as any that can engage attention.   As we have seen, not all things
sought after are of equal importance, and wisdom of life consists
in knowing how to surrender the lesser in order to arrive at the
greater.   The aims pursued by Public Enemy Number One are
not worthy of comparison with those that spurred the ambition of
George Washington.   There is also a difference to be discerned between the most notorious liar and the most honored saint.

Some advantages after which we struggle are like counterfeit
money—good only in outward appearance—and the possession of
them can yield no satisfaction but only accumulate grief.   There are
counterfeit pleasures, ambitions, and possessions which look bright
at a distance but which, like the fabled Apples of Sodom, turn to
ashes at the touch.   We must evidently keep in mind the deeper values that underlie all surface considerations.

Some values are only transitory.   They cannot long engage any
but infantile intelligences.   We have scarcely achieved them before
we begin to be bored with them, like "jack straws" or "tit-tat-toe."
This is because we find more interest in better and worthier activities.   Evidently if we are to build our ambitions into anything permanently satisfying there is a whole class of achievements that we
need to learn about and others we need to avoid.

Some values are what might be called incidental.   They are like
sugar on the doughnut, legitimate, desirable, but insufficient, apart
from the doughnut itself.   We need substance as well as frosting.
Many things good in themselves and in their places are yet not
worth the devotion of one's life energy.   This class might include
such innocent and health-giving diversions as roller-skating, tap-
dancing, or whistling.   Their worth consists not in themselves, but in
what they contribute to relaxation and recuperation in pursuit of
higher ends.   My grammar school seat-mate died of an overworked
heart in a roller-skating contest.   He was the champion of the
county, but for this honor he gave up what might have been a useful and happy life.   These incidental interests are the legitimate in-
terludes in the serious business of living, nothing more.

Some values may thus become destructive of those that are greater.   We sometimes pay a high price to achieve desires that prevent
us from reaching and satisfying more important needs.   This happens when we allow pleasure or leisure to usurp the place which
should be occupied by attention to real accomplishments.

Some satisfactions are more lasting than others. Easily acquired possessions are usually the least permanent, for laborious application usually builds up larger powers of endurance, intelligence, foresight, and insight. Beware the six-weeks course that promises to fit you for any calling. It is as impossible to build up intellectual acumen in short order as it would be to condition yourself for the football field by a single work-out in the gymnasium. If one is really serious and desires enduring success he must beware the short-cut. The men who take the pains to learn things from the ground up and are thus enabled to take in the most minute and exhausting details are the ones who ultimately reach the front and enjoy real success.

Furthermore, values to be permanent must be such as to command indefinitely our intellectual, moral, and spiritual self-respect. Otherwise we shall sicken with disgust at the things we are doing and suffer from that most common complaint of our modern life, a sense of disappointment and frustration.

Some goods are cumulative. The more we possess of them the greater grows our capacity for enjoying them while they open the way to greater accomplishments, but others in the very acquisition destroy themselves.

We have, for the most part, spoken of external and physical excellencies. These are not, however, the ones that yield the largest returns in happiness, contentment, and peace of mind. The most satisfying goods are inner, mental, moral, and spiritual, those which may definitely be called human. They are the most important because they are the only possessions that lie beyond the touch of misfortune, accident, poverty, or untoward circumstance. If some one asks what they are, the reply must be that they are the achievements and virtues that follow in the train of doing one's best, living up to one's highest ideals. Their importance lies not only in their possession, but also in the fact that they form the inspiration of serious activities. The capacity for this type of achievement is what distinguishes men from the beasts. The animal is capable of physical satisfactions. He knows hunger and thirst and their alleviation. He is conscious of shelter and even of society of his kind. But he lacks powers of reflection. He feels no "ought." Man, on the other hand, is able to reflect on his relation to his world, to learn and to determine the causes of action, to control his impulses in the interest of more abundant living. Man can evaluate his own thoughts, weigh his own motives, reflect on his obligations to others and on theirs toward him. He has in this capacity the source of greater powers of enjoyment than are possible to the beast, and he is continually reminded of these higher capabilities. If he does not live up to them he becomes consciously inferior, inferior to others, inferior to his potentially superior self, and this "inferiority complex," as it is called, deadens in turn his own imaginative and creative genius. Hence come the discontents, despairs, frustrations, and tragedies which spell failure. ⸢Man can never be enduringly happy except through the realization of his highest capacities.⸥ The benefits that follow in the train of doing one's best are moral and spiritual. They are as natural as the air, the earth, and the sun. They are not made by regulations, rules, or human dictation. The demand for them lies in human nature itself. They are the normal functioning of our personalities and the penalties for nonobservance are written into our characters and capacities for self-realization as unavoidably as the law of gravitation, or of momentum, is written into physical nature.

All values are ultimately human. That is, they are created, evaluated, and enjoyed by individuals. They have no existence apart from the service, welfare, and gratification of human beings. The degree of their worth consists in the service they can render in the development of the highest type of experience, and by this fact they must eventually be judged. / If this is true, and how can it be successfully refuted, the intensest values have a most intimate character. Love of the fatherland may seem sentimental, but only traitors, most despicable of all citizens, would sell out their loyalty. To become a Quisling is to be despised by all, including the Quisling himself. Many a bonnie lad has given away his life to the love of a flag, which is the mute but stirring symbol of his country. Friendship is an intangible thing, but once convince a man that he has no friends and he is ready for suicide. How careless we often are of the richest treasures! Love seems but fragile and we often speak slightingly of the human passions that put on the false face of love, but real love is the one power that can enable us to face disaster with a calm spirit, and it is good for life and for death. Perhaps we shall find in these studies that these inner accomplishments are after all the supreme ones, the ones that matter most. This is made plain by Dr. Richard Cabot, who out of his scientific experience as a physician and psychologist has noted the most important elements in human success and health as gathering round man's need for work, play, love, and worship, which he describes as "the things men live by." Certainly his claims cannot be lightly brushed aside. They are altogether in line with our previous considerations.

III

Human Values in the Role of History

The importance of human values cannot be fully appreciated so long as we consider them only in the light of individual prosperity. Human values have made and are making history. Just as the sense of value determines the outcome of the human lives that entertain it, so the general estimates of worth held by large portions of society determine the future of races and nations. Civilizations, historical cultures, even languages are modified or created by prevalent ideas of value. Change the objectives of the people's desires and you change the course of history. Every great movement in education, in art, in architecture, in science, or in religion has depended for its inception upon some concept of worth, whether of freedom, power, commercial supremacy, or domination of other peoples.

The refining of the Greek sense of religion as it broke away from the cruder concepts of animism, that worshipped every unusual tree or stone, and brought sacrifices of food, fruit, or animals, arose from the hope to appease the local gods that they might increase the fertility of flock or field, and ward off drought, famine, and disease. These lesser gods came now to be replaced with deities of wider scope and sympathy, ethereal and universal. Religious reform led to a break from an idol worship localized in grove and hilltop, to the concept of gods who were over all. With the uprush of such an idealistic feeling and conviction came the great artistic age of Greece, bringing a perfection in sculpture that has been the despair of succeeding aeons, and a literature so great as still to survive. Such artistry could be empowered only by the deepest and sincerest convictions of value. It was a time of great insights and of great faith, the essential components of a great age.

In another age, Rome was profoundly moved by the esteem of reason and justice which had received impetus from the introduction of the Stoic philosophy. Such unpurchasable patriots as Cato and Seneca laid the foundations of that impartiality before the law which became the inspiration of Roman organization, and caused the disorderly tribes to welcome a conquest which brought the reliefs of stable government. The Roman Procurator could, for the most part, be depended upon for stricter justice than had been rendered by the tribal and grafting officials that had preceded him. Out of this concept and enthusiasm for equal justice grew the greatness of the Roman Empire.

During the Middle Ages, around the year one thousand, there

swept over Europe a reforming zeal in religion. Men who had been possessed by a worldly cast of mind, obsessed with the notion of the immediate Second Coming of Christ in judgment, released their slaves, endowed the churches and monasteries, and retired to a life of religious devotion. These were the men who laid the foundations for the capitalistic order, for the monasteries soon became dominant with a power which occasionally could dictate to kings. Again, it was the concept of the things worth while that moved them. The manumitted craftsmen founded the Free Cities; industrialism and democracy were in the air. The common people showed their sense of relief by the construction of the Gothic cathedral, dedicated to the Virgin, the mild and gentle lover of the masses, and their protector from the wrath of a stern and theological God. Less idealistic, but springing from a similar sense of release, was the passion of modern business, which kept pace with the democratic spirit in the discovery of the New World, and the development of natural resources hitherto unrealized. Modern business became almost as exacting as religion had been, and was attended by profound convictions respecting the well-being of men and the virtue of free competition. We witness herein the power of an idea to make over a world within a few short generations. The modern effect has in its influence been comparable to the invention of Gothic architecture. The complexity and extent of business organizations has wrought the startling revolutions in transportation and communication, radio, television, travel by automobile and by air, and skyscraper buildings that are in many ways as impressive as the Gothic cathedral. From all this, what could be more apparent than the transforming power of ideas of value let loose upon the world? The form taken by civilization in one case arose from the relationship of religion to the Greek sense of beauty; in another, that equality before the law was the great desideratum of government; in another, the dream of a religion so universal as to gather into its care the least and feeblest of men; in still another, a passion for the mastery of nature and circumstance through which should come eventual freedom from toil and want. What matter if each of these in turn changed virtue into a restricting form because men forgot the sources of their primary inspiration! The gods forgotten, Greek art and architecture and literature declined; the Stoic virtues lost, law was debased to a means of impressing aliens into the Roman Legions, a further instrument of oppression; religion, formalized and written in dead statutes and creeds, lost much of the spiritual inspiration in which it arose. The capacity of free men to work out their own destinies through unhampered competition, once greatly triumphant, threatens to become an autocracy by the few.

This survey of history establishes one thing above another, however—the power of value-concepts to determine civilization and to change the face of the world. Another promise of hope also resides in this fact: the changes that may be wrought through the influence of single individuals. Let Socrates drop the opinion that every man has within himself an inerrant voice of reason in accordance with which he can act and we have as the far-off result the rise of democracy in Europe and America. If perchance, an Augustine, worried over the decline of the Roman Empire, writes a book entitled *The City of God,* we may have eventually the building of an ecclesiastical and spiritual empire strong enough to fend off the Moslem invasions, and lay the foundation of medieval civilization. Abelard entertained the idea of untrammeled academic freedom, the desirability of change from a purely clerical to a secular learning, and drawing thousands of wandering scholars into the fields to hear his lectures, in which he demanded the examination of all opinions, set the pattern of the modern university. John Locke was called upon to formulate the fundamental principles essential to a democracy and the result was the famous Declaration, written into the constitution of the State of Virginia, and later into the Federal constitution of the United States. Even now perhaps more than any other influence, what is commonly termed the "Bill of Rights," is the basic law for the decisions of our Supreme Court. Rousseau preached a new theory of education and a hundred and fifty years later we find his theory an accepted part of American educational practice. Rousseau's *Emile* is required reading for practically all graduates in education. His *New Heloise* furnishes the type for the modern romantic novel, and he set forth an interpretation of liberty which let loose the "Terror" of the French Revolution, and that notion of irresponsible freedom which even yet troubles us.

It would be interesting and valuable to trace the relation of philosophical, religious, and scientific ideas to the various turning points they have made in history. Such a theme might profitably engage some of your future studies. Since this course is too brief to permit extended consideration of this fact of history, let us turn to a single instance observable by all, an instance which involves the future of civilization in our day. We have but recently engaged in a war of values between those who entertained a concept of freedom in the form of democracy, and those who sought security in the form of totalitarianism. These contradictory concepts of value attained a world-wide significance and faced each other with hostile intent among every people. The war-torn world was called upon to decide whether it should be ruled by strictly national and racial, or by world, concepts. We fought for the things we considered most worth while, and the progress of events forced us day by day to stand for the larger interpretation of freedom for all men. This is the concept of value formulated in the Atlantic Charter as the Four Freedoms. We were and are determined that this wider sense of value must prevail. It is of even greater importance than guns and ammunition, for it has to do with that morale, that conviction, that keeps men fighting for a cause even after they are physically defeated. The more universal our concept of the application of freedom, the more powerful our cause shall become, since we know that behind us there is an eternal justice which is mandatory upon all right-minded men. There was never a time in the history of the world when there was more need for morale than now, and we shall have it to the very degree that we are moved by right concepts of what matters most. If we can rightly determine this problem of values, tomorrow may bring in the very conditions of which we dream, but it is necessary for us to have convictions. We cannot drift into a better world which is to be. We must have clear concepts of value and we must be ready to fight for them.

IV

Some Objectives in the Study of Values

It is now our purpose to enter into the nature of values, in order that as free and thinking men and women we may know the direction we are taking and be better able to judge the movements of our times and to direct wisely the course of life. While we ask about the nature of value in an academic way, every reader of these pages has already begun to give his answers in a thousand daily choices, whether consciously or unconsciously. Value is whatever we want, or whatever we can trade for what we want. It is that which is diligently sought as possessing worth or interest. Willingness to undergo some discomforts in order to acquire an education, the time and energy spent to make "the first team," or to become a leader in University activities, or to acquire an automobile, or even a tire, or a partner for the class dance—all these activities proclaim one's concept of what matters louder than words.

As important as these interests may seem in academic life, still we recognize how inadequate they would be as the ideals to which a whole life should be given. The important question remains as to what we will seek in the great world outside the school. Will our dream be of an easy life, self-centered in its enjoyments? Is that a sufficiently broad aim to bring the greatest and most permanent satisfactions? Any man may be the possessor of capacity for great things, and the scope of life is likely to be as wide as his concept of the things that matter most.

We are not compelled, however, to start this investigation *de novo,* or from the beginning. The problem of human desires has been considered from before the dawn of history, as is evidenced in ancient legend. It was symbolized in the Fable of the Sphinx, which was represented as putting a riddle to all passers-by and devouring those who failed in the solution; there is more than an inkling in that riddle as to where the ancients considered the answer to lie. The riddle was: "What animal walks on all fours in the morning, on two at noon, and on three at night?" The solution was, of course, "man," who creeps on all fours in childhood, walks on two legs in manhood, and with a cane in old age. But this was only the superficial interpretation. The Sphinx was fabled to devour the victim who did not discover the secret. Each had to find out for himself the meaning of life, what mattered most, and in finding the solution he would spend life itself. The peculiar problem of everyone is to find and to pursue the things most worth-while. These dreams and ideals which one pursues, make him while he pursues them, and in the end he is what he dreams of being, and wants to be. We spend our lives working at the riddle of existence, ourselves are the answer. Such is the problem of human values.

There are certain guideposts along the way that survive from both the near and the distant past. Every literature under the sun is filled with attempted answers. These solutions are to be found in the great religions and philosophies, in the masterpieces of literature and art, architecture, and music. If we have an open eye and an understanding heart we shall read the clews in all of man's successful works and most of all in the laws of the moral universe.

We shall study and attempt to analyze and estimate the outstanding solutions as they have appeared in human history. We shall try to draw from them such instructions as may promise guidance in our own situation. We shall inquire into the nature and sources of worth, and how it may be achieved. We shall ask what values are lasting. We shall pose the question: which ones have power to lift us over the vicissitudes of misfortune; which will lead to the highest satisfactions, to enduring happiness, to peace of mind, to complete realization of our own powers.

It is not the purpose of this study to go into detailed and exhaustive philosophical or psychological discussion of the subject. More may be gained, perhaps, from a raising of questions than by a presentation of solutions. The main hope is to lead the student himself to the formation of his own ideas, and Socratic-wise to encourage the framing of his own replies. Perchance most of the answers cannot spring from academic or dialectic knowledge, but must eventually be found in life itself; the best we may do may be to call attention to some of the great interpretations which have been sought in the history of the human race. We shall be happy if by this means we can arouse the student's interest and discussion to the consciousness that the problem of human values is a paramount issue.

(For Readings see Chapter 2, page 38.)

Chapter 2

VALUE-CONCEPTS AND ACHIEVEMENT

I
Successful Achievement Must Conform to Nature

II
Achieving a Knowledge of Nature

III
Sense of Value Determines Achievement

IV
The Creative Nature of Values

Chapter 2

VALUE-CONCEPTS AND ACHIEVEMENT

All human efforts are based on some concept of value. One may live to eat, to get rich, to avoid work, to have a good time, to become famous as a college president, as a prize-fighter, as a politician or a football player, as an author or a sword-swallower. Human interest demands some objectives as incentives to action. Whichever one or more we may choose indicates what we consider to be worth while. This idea of what constitutes worth is as present and active an incentive in the hobo who boils his coffee in a tin can in "the jungle" by the railroad tracks, as it is in the head of a great nation. While the latter may have in mind the goal of exercising power over other men and leaving a great name for himself in the nation's history, the hobo may simply have a tremendous allergy for work and may consider the best life to be in line with the least effort.

In any event no one can escape the habit of assessing values, and the estimate we put on different courses of action will dictate the course of achievement as inevitably as the magnetic needle points to the pole.

Moreover, our sense of what is desirable is not something born with us, but is affected by our education, early environment, social relations, associations. By these a man may arrive at new sets of appreciation which may change not only the tenor of his own life but the direction of the society in which he lives. It is this adaptability or flexibility in the consciousness of worth that makes possible those changes in human lives which we admire and praise. So very often the impact and course of a life may be changed by a change of opinion, or a new attitude, or some differing standpoint, a new interest, or a fresh insight. For this reason, because a sense of value dictates the future, it is important for everyone whose life is still before him to enter into an examination of his ideals and to learn what he can of those concepts which have dominated the great leaders of the past.

I

Successful Achievement Must Conform to Nature

Every one who has worked in a gymnasium, or played tennis or football, or engaged successfully in any skilful physical sport has impressed upon him the necessity of coordination. His movements must be rhythmical, they must be in keeping with the natural structure of his body. He must likewise have a mind to the laws of nature such as gravitation, velocity, reaction, and so on. In addition to all this he must recognize certain psychological factors such as the will-to-win, overconfidence, and a host of others. All these factors constitute a harmony within himself and with his world that are necessary for the successful athlete. Only in some such way as this is it possible to achieve the important values of life. We cannot succeed by fighting nature, society, or our surroundings. We are compelled to cooperate in order to succeed.

Values are an ingredient of nature herself. She possesses a character which is in keeping with man's highest interests and is not indifferent to the creation of value. This fact is in the strictest accord with the evolutionary processes of the universe. All living things are committed to progress or improvement. They must cooperate toward some end, a true and normal fulfilment for which they exist, or failing this, they sicken and die by the wastage or neglect of powers which they do not properly use. These facts of nature can never be rightly interpreted as meaning that nature is indifferent to achievements.

The reason for this is that the law of success is incorporated in normal physical functioning. The law of evolution is progress or perish. Whatever is unnatural is ugly, or offensive or weakening or degrading. As we work in unison with and conformity to the purposes of nature, our work becomes easy and we unlock her closer secrets. There could have been no success in the invention of an airplane except by strict observance of the laws of the air, for we cannot impose our wills on nature unless we first ascertain what her will is. Working without regard to law brings nothing but failure; working with law enables us to do what seemed at first impossible.

It is very easy to make a mistake at this point and to overlook a certain undeviating character of the physical universe which furthers exactness, truth, and morality. In man the power of conscious choice introduces a new factor. If Nature in her unconscious processes may be said to be moral, morality in a subject of free

choice has a new significance. One may choose to do the unnatural thing, the act which is not in keeping with the higher character which may be his by the gift of conscious choice. Is nature
indifferent? Then why is it that she deprives of life the man who
eats or drinks with careless impunity? The man of violence finds
himself living in a world of violence that finally worsts him. The
thief raises against himself the opposition of honest men to eventually prevent his thievery. The liar after a time fails not only to
get himself believed, but distorts his own mind to such an atmosphere of falsehood that finally he is deceived by his own lies. The
cheater eventually cheats himself, the betrayer betrays himself, the
murderer kills within himself the sources of happiness and sets
the hand of every man against him. This could not be except for
the fact that we live in a moral world, where only the highest and
best possibilities are in keeping with the natural order. Where the
effort after perfection is the law of life, to reach fullness of living
in human experience is in the truest sense to live according to
nature.

II

Achieving a Knowledge of Nature

If, in order to secure values, it is necessary to cooperate with
nature, the matter of first importance to human destiny is to find
out what nature is, what she will do, and how we can cooperate
with her in such fashion as to produce best results. The attempt
to discover the meaning of the world has been pursued along three
very definite lines. We study the physical universe that we may
learn to cooperate with the physical side of nature. We study philosophy in order to get a consistent and coherent view of the facts
of experience. We prize religion for the interpretations it sets
on such realities as justice, honor, truth, and love, the moral and
spiritual facts of existence. In view of the relation of these facts
to human happiness and social welfare, no wise man is going to
say: There are no values but material values. Even material values
and facts have to be evaluated by human minds and have no meaning apart from such interpretations. We are very conscious of a
world of ponderable matter, of hardness, of force, of activity, of
time. But every one of these, and any others we experience, possess
worth and meaning because they are in some fashion related to
human intelligences. Their reality lies in what they tell us about
ourselves, our neighbors, and the use to which we may put the
physical forces of the world to the betterment of human welfare.

What the scientist tries to do is to gather from the phenomena those facts about the physical world which may help persons to master or understand it and to make beneficial use of this knowledge by foreseeing and controlling the forces of Nature. It is very apparent, then, that the progress and well-being of society demand the utmost freedom for the scientist to investigate physical phenomena and to announce his conclusions. It must not be forgotten, however, that he is forced to work under certain limitations. He is set to find out what he can about the world from the standpoint of its material characteristics. What he will find out will be limited to what he can weigh or measure as an expression of extension or force. His field is every fact which can be thus determined, but it does not necessarily mean that nothing else exists. One might estimate you by measuring your height, your weight, the color of eyes and hair, your speed at running, your dexterity and still know nothing about your most important characteristics, such as your honesty, integrity, patriotism, loyalty to friends, your intellectual endurance, or your fortitude in misfortune. These are the most important things about you as a member of society, the things any employer will want to know. Yet these facts cannot be ascertained by any measurements of force, extension, or ponderability.

How then are we to get at these actualities? One way is to seek the way of common sense, which is to ask, in view of all the facts, What is reasonable? If we live in a world that is assumed to be intelligible we should expect a certain intelligent coherence between facts, this search for coherence in the items of our knowledge is philosophy. As human beings equipped with minds we cannot persistently hold to contradictory or incompatible assumptions. Our intellects call for a certain logical connection between facts. All knowledge has some degree of relation to philosophy. We are disturbed when we are forced to seek some higher synthesis in which the apparent contradictions dissolve. A present case is the effort to ascertain how the wave theory of light and the corpuscular theory can both be true. Both must be true and yet they have appeared contradictory. Philosophy presents a way to the ascertaining of values by seeking a coherent world of thought and of concepts of things.

Neither science nor philosophy alone, or in cooperation, seem able, however, to provide us with all the facts that are of moment to human lives. For you and me the most important field can be touched by neither discipline. There is in every human being a certain hunger for values that can be satisfied only on the level of our subjective nature. As the great scientist-philosopher Pascal once wrote: "The heart has her reasons which the reason cannot understand." However much we may persuade ourselves that there is nothing outside the material universe and our physical satisfactions, there is a loneliness in each of us in our deeper moments which no material compensation can satisfy. Living on the physical level of life does not suffice us, because we feel there is something about us that should be greater and more permanent. Physical enjoyments soon satiate and disgust us. Living for ourselves alone does not satisfy our human nature. We soon learn that we get permanent contentment, not as we receive but as we give. How then are we to arrive at this supreme satisfaction? Whatever way we do arrive will be essentially religious. And this value will be a religious value.

III

Sense of Value Determines Achievement

This brings us to the third point of consideration, which is that these ruling desires become the organizing centers of life. We saw in the beginning how our idea of what matters most would eventually determine the character of our career. If that is true, as I think it must be, and we add to it the fact that the physical universe itself is of such a nature that she works in conformity with whoever works in harmony with her; if further, the disciplines of science, philosophy, and religion enable us in their different fields to judge what is of greatest worth, then we have a most important truth concerning the place of value.

Any sort of aim earnestly pursued becomes an organizing center for the life that seeks it. If there is something we really want we bend our energies in the direction of getting it. We cut off habits and outlooks that we feel would prevent the realization of our ambition. In this respect we make our world and our lives as large, or as small, as our desires. Do we think only in terms of eating and drinking, and ephemeral pleasure? Then our world becomes for us only a vast market or playground. Are we chiefly concerned only with the affairs of our own neighborhood? The gossip of the street, "what will the neighbors think," then becomes for us the substance of life. Are we interested chiefly in the shortcomings of others? Life becomes crabbed, cynical, unlovely, and unlovable, fastened down to the little round of unimportant desires and ambitions. On the other hand, we may send our sympathies out into a whole world of associations and connections that will enlarge life and inevitably make it great. From this center of our commanding interest, all of life organizes itself and the results are as certain as the harvest that follows on the sowing. The fullest life of all can be realized only as we reach the highest functioning of our nature. As we seek these possibilities we find ourselves lifted to a new plane of activity and satisfaction. Just as intellectual pursuits create broader understandings of our world, of other times, other men, other cultures, making possible a new set of satisfactions, so the highest of all, genuine religion, in that meaning of the term used here, brings us to an insight and a sympathy with others, a broader appreciation of the nature of the world of men and things otherwise impossible.

Nature is of such a character that she cooperates in varying degrees as we organize life about our concept of what matters most. As we seek we shall find, as we knock, doors will be opened to us.

IV

The Creative Nature of Value

Perhaps the most important point of all in these reflections lies in the effect of known and noble pursuits on the creative imagination. We cannot feel any great enthusiasm toward a course of activity that is degrading, or contemptible, or that is unworthy of our best. Such courses of action induce feelings of inferiority and fear which the psychologist tells us are deadening to constructive and creative activities. We need for our plan of life to pick out those courses of action for which we can feel a respect, of which we will not be ashamed. The emotional side of our life is strongest and most productive under the spur and inspiration of great and noble objectives. They create ends to which we can enthusiastically give ourselves. There is scarcely anyone of normal capacity who, if he will find a worthy objective which can command his highest powers without respect to ulterior rewards and profits, but may achieve distinction in his chosen work. The more unselfish his aim, the more complete and satisfying will be his reward, for his deepest compensation will be in the work itself, a compensation which neither moth nor rust can corrupt, and which thieves cannot steal.

Such a statement is in strict conformity with the laws of nature and of fact. [For the man who can emotionally love his work has a mind that dwells continually upon the desired and worthy objective. We must then, in seeking a central interest for life, choose an end we can truly respect and love.] This is far more important than the financial return. For the thing we love mixes itself with our very dreams by night, the sleeping hours work out and present solutions to our waking moments, and we come to live and move in the environment of a great and worthy objective. As we sometimes say: "We have it on our heart." Of a worthy aim the mind never tires, never turns away in disgust, but enthusiasm rises with achievement.] The force of the subconscious mind is added to the conscious efforts. He is a wise man who learns to use these subconscious faculties. He "sleeps" on his knottiest problems, for even in slumber the mind is still active, and may deal with questions that have been suggested to it. Here the individual has access to the larger field of acquired knowledge which strained and voluntary attention in some measure hinders, as when the name we *strive* to remember comes suddenly to mind when we cease trying to recall it. The result of these suggestions and solutions from the so-called subconscious will ordinarily be fresher, more spontaneous and original and without the exhaustion that accompanies strained attention, just as the unconscious and involuntary movements of heart and lungs do not carry the weariness of willed and attentive effort. If here in the region of our desires we can achieve a unity within ourselves, and a harmony with our environment and with the universe, we are not likely to be permanently thwarted nor disappointed. The things worth-while, or whatever we conceive to be worth while, consciously or unconsciously become the organizing centers of life.

In the readings that follow we have one of the most famous of satires on the society of the times of the great Humanist, Erasmus (1466-1536). It is based on the generally false choices of the leaders of the social and political order, the mistaking of fraudulent claims for real ones. Erasmus lays bare these false estimates of things worth-while by seeming to agree that after all since nearly everybody runs after folly, folly must be the outstanding good. The fact must be kept in mind that throughout there is a double meaning. He assumes to praise that which he aims to condemn. His purpose is to show how the outcome of life is dictated by the aims, ambitions, and desires which one follows. He holds clearly before us, as in a mirror, the deceptive nature of the things most often sought after as values, and he does it by resort to sarcasm and irony.   The same is true of Hawthorne's essay which attempts to apply to modern conditions the satire of John Bunyan on a previous age, in his famous *Pilgrim's Progress*.   Dr. Cabot lends a modern touch to the consideration of values.

READINGS

(Chapters 1 and 2)

DESIDERIUS ERASMUS: *THE PRAISE OF FOLLY.* Princeton University Press, Princeton, N. J., 1941. Pp. 13-20, 22-51, 68-70, 103-104.

[Folly speaks]—

"[5] You have learned of my family, upbringing, and companions. Now, that it may not look as if I have usurped the name of goddess for myself without good grounds, please give closest attention while I tell how many advantages I bestow on both gods and men, and how broadly my power is displayed. For if, as some one has judiciously observed, this only is to be a god, to help men, and if deservedly they have been admitted to the rank of gods who have shown to mortals the use of wine, or grain, or any other such commodity, why am not I of right named and venerated as the *alpha* of all gods, who single-handed bestow all things on all men?

"In the first place, what can be dearer or more precious than life? And the beginning and first principle of life is owed to whom else but me? Not the spear of 'potent-fathered' Pallas, not the shield of 'cloud-compelling' Jove, procreates the children of men or multiplies their race. Even he, the father of gods and king of men, who shakes all heaven by a nod, is obliged to lay aside his three-pronged thunder and that Titanic aspect by which, when he pleases, he scares all the gods, and assumes another character in the slavish manner of an actor, if he wishes to do what he never refrains from doing, that is to say, to beget children. Now the Stoics believe that they are next-door neighbors to gods. But give me a triple Stoic, or a quadruple one, or, if you will, a Stoic multiplied by six hundred; if for this purpose he will not put off his beard, the ensign of wisdom (though displayed also by goats), yet he will certainly lay by his gravity, smooth his brow, renounce his rock-bound principles, and for a few minutes toy and talk nonsense. In fine, the wise man must send for me, I repeat, if he ever wishes to become a father. . . .

"[6] But let it be accounted a little thing that the seedplot and source of existence are mine, if I do not show that whatever is profitable in any life is also of my giving. For what about it? Can life be called life at all if you take away pleasure? . . . You applaud! I knew that none of you is so wise—or rather so foolish—no, I prefer to say so wise—as to err on that point. Even the famous Stoics do not really

38

scorn pleasure, but they studiously dissemble and attack it in public with a thousand reproaches, only to the end that, with other people scared off, they may enjoy it more liberally.   But let them tell me, by Jove, what part of life is not sad, unpleasant, graceless, flat, and burdensome, unless you have pleasure added to it, that is, a seasoning of folly?   As proof of this, there is extant that lovely tribute to me by Sophocles, who can never be sufficiently praised, 'To know nothing affords the happiest life'; and he would be authority enough, but come, I will open the whole matter, step by step.

"First of all, who does not know the earliest period of a man's life is by far the happiest for him and by far the most pleasant for all about him?   What is it in children, that we should kiss them the way we do, and cuddle them, and fondle them—so that even an enemy would give aid to one of that age—except this enchantment of folly, which prudent nature carefully bestows on the newly born; so that by this pleasure, as a sort of prepayment, they win the favor of their nurses and parents and make these forget the pains of bringing them up.   After this comes adolescence.   How welcome it is in every home!   How well everyone wishes it!   How studiously does everyone promote it, how officiously they lend it the helping hand!   But, I ask, whence comes this grace of youth?   Whence but from me, by whose favor the young know so little —and how lightly worn is that little!   And presently when lads grown larger begin, through experience and discipline, to have some smack of manhood, I am a liar if by the same token the brightness of their beauty does not fade, their quickness diminish, their wit lose its edge, their vigor slacken.   The farther one gets from me, then, the less and less he lives, until *molesta senectus* (that is, irksome old age) arrives, hateful to others, to be sure, but also and more so to itself.

"Old age would not be tolerable to any mortal at all, were it not that I, out of pity for its troubles, stand once more at its right hand; and just as the gods of the poets customarily save, by some metamorphosis or other, those who are dying, in like manner I bring those who have one foot in the grave back to their infancy again, for as long as possible; so that the folk are not far off in speaking of them as 'in their second childhood.'   If anyone would like to know the method of bringing about this alteration, I shall not conceal it.   I lead them to my spring of Lethe—for that stream rises in the Fortunate Isles, and only a little rivulet of it flows in the underworld—so that then and there they may drink draughts of forgetfulness.   With their cares of mind purged away, by gentle stages they become young again.   But now, you say, they merely dote, and play the fool.   Yes, quite so.   But precisely this it is to renew one's infancy.   Is to be childish anything other than to dote and play the fool?   As if in that age the greatest joy were not this, that one knows nothing!   For who does not dread and shun as a prodigy the boy who has a man's wisdom?   As the proverb current among the folk has it, 'I hate a boy of premature wisdom.'   Who could bear to converse or transact business with an old man who should join to his long experience of things, an equal vigor of mind and sharpness of judgment? Hence it is that an old man dotes, thanks to me.

"Yet this dotard of mind, meanwhile, is exempt from those carking cares by which your wise man is distracted. My dotard, too, is still an acceptable pot-companion. He does not feel life's tedium, which a younger constitution can scarce abide. Occasionally, like the old gentleman in Plautus, he goes back to conning those three letters, *a, m, o*— the unhappiest man in the world if he had his wits about him; but meanwhile happy, through my grace, a source of pleasure to his friends, a hail-fellow-well-met. . . .

"These arguments have the strong support of a proverb current among the folk; as they often say, 'Folly is the one thing that makes fleeting youth linger and keeps ugly old age away. And rightly do they bruit it about concerning the people of Brabant, that although time brings prudence to others, the older Brabanters grow the more foolish they are. Yet no other race is more genial than theirs in the ordinary converse of life, and no other race feels so little the misery of old age. Neighbors to the Brabanters, by affinity of temperament as much as by geography, are my Hollanders—for why should I not call mine those who are such eager amateurs of folly that they have won a proverbial name for it, a name they are not ashamed of, but bandy back and forth among themselves?

"Go, foolish mortals, and vainly seek for your Medeas and Circes and Venuses and Auroras, and the unknown fountain in which you may restore your youth! When all the time I alone have that power; I alone use it. In my shop is that miraculous juice with which the daughter of Memnon lengthened the days of her grandfather Tithonus. I am that Venus by whose favor Phaon grew young again so that he might be loved so much by Sappho. Mine are those herbs (if they exist), mine that fountain, mine the spells which not only bring back departed youth but, still better, preserve it in perpetuity. If, then, all of you subscribe to this sentiment, that nothing is better than adolescence or more undesirable than age, I think you must see how much you owe to me, who conserve so great a good and fend off so great an evil. . . .

(Pp. 13-20.)

"[8] But now the time has come when, following the pattern of Homer, we should turn our backs on the heavens and travel down again to earth, where likewise we shall perceive nothing joyous or fortunate except by my favor. First of all, you see with what foresight nature, the source and artificer of the human race, has made provision that this race shall never lack its seasoning of folly. For since, by the Stoic definitions, wisdom is no other than to be governed by reason, while folly is to be moved at the whim of the passions, Jupiter, to the end, obviously, that the life of mankind should not be sad and harsh, put in—how much more of passions than of reason? Well, the proportions run about one pound to half an ounce. Besides, he imprisoned reason in a cramped corner of the head, and turned over all the rest of the body to the emotions. After that he instated two most violent tyrants, as it were in opposition to reason: anger . . . and lust. . . . How much reason is good for, against these twin forces, the ordinary life of men sufficiently reveals when reason—and it is all she can do— shouts out her prohibitions until she is hoarse and dictates formulas of virtue. But the passions simply bid their so-called king go hang himself, and more brazenly roar down the opposition, until the man, tired out as well, willingly yields and knuckles under. . . .

". . . I do not suppose the female sex is so foolish as to become incensed at me for this, that I, a woman and Folly as well, attribute folly to women. For if they rightly consider the matter, they are bound to score up a credit to Folly for this, that in many respects they are better off than men. For one thing, they have the gift of beauty, which with good reason they prefer above all things else. Assisted by it, they wield a tyranny over tyrants themselves. Whence but from the malady of prudence comes that horrendous visage, rough as to skin, with an undergrowth of beard and a suggestion of senility, in men? Whereas the cheeks of women are always bare and smooth, their voice gentle, their skin soft, as if presenting a picture of perpetual youth. Furthermore, what else do they want in life but to be as attractive as possible to men? Do not all their trimmings and cosmetics have this end in view, and all their baths, fittings, creams, scents, as well—and all those arts of making up, painting, and fashioning the face, eyes, and skin? Just so. And by what other sponsor are they better recommended to men than by folly? What is there that men will not permit to women? But for what consideration, except pleasure? And women please by no other thing than their folly. The truth of this no one will deny who has considered what nonsense a man talks with a woman, and what quaint tricks he plays, as often as he has a mind to enjoy the delights of feminine society.

"You have heard, then, about the source whence flows the first and sovereign solace of life. But there are some men, principally old ones, who are topers rather than womanizers, and decree that the highest pleasure lies in bouts of drinking. Whether there can be any general entertainment with no woman present, let others decide. This remains certain: without some relish of folly, no banquet is pleasing. Hence if someone is not present who creates laughter by his real or simulated folly, the revellers send out and get a comedian for hire, or bring in some other silly parasite, who by his jests—that is, foolish gibes—will drive silence and moroseness away from the company. For what avails it to load the belly with all those fine wines, savory dishes, and rare meats, if similarly our eyes and ears, our whole souls, do not batten on laughter, jests, and witticisms? I am the only confectioner of these desserts. Yes, and those other ceremonies of banquets, such as choosing a king by lot, playing at dice, drinking healths, sending the cups around, singing in rounds and relays, dancing, mimicking—the Seven Sages of Greece did not discover these for the solace of mankind; I did. The nature of all this sort of thing is such that the more of folly it has in it, the more it advantages the life of men, which surely ought not to be called life at all if it is unhappy. Yet unhappy it must need be, unless by diversions of this kind you chase away ennui, the brother of unhappiness.

"[9] Yet there are others, perhaps, who do not care for this department of pleasure either, but find satisfaction in the love and familiar society of friends, letting it be known that friendship uniquely deserves to be preferred above all else; as being so necessary a thing that not air, fire, or water is more so; and so delightful that he who would take it from the world would take the sun from the sky; and lastly so honorable (as if honor had something to do with the subject) that the philosophers themselves have not hesitated to name it among the greatest goods. But what if I demonstrate that I am both the stem and the stern of this admired good also? And I shall not demonstrate it by ambiguous syllogisms, sorites, horned dilemmas, or any other sophistical subtleties of that sort; but by crude common sense, as the phrase is, I shall point it out as plainly as if with my finger. Go to! Conniving at your friends' vices, passing them over, being blind to them and deceived by them, even loving and admiring your friends' egregious faults as if they were virtues—does not this seem pretty close to folly? Think a moment of the fellow who kisses the mole on his mistress' neck, or of the other who is delighted by the growth on his little lady's nose, or of the father who says of his cross-eyed son that his eyes twinkle? What is all this, I ask you, but sheer folly? Ay, you all vote—triple and quadruple foolishness! Yet this same foolishness both joins friends and, after joining them, keeps their friendship alive. . . .

"What has been said of friendship applies even better to marriage, which is an indivisible bond of life. Good Lord, what divorces, or worse things, would not happen all over the place, were not the domestic association of man and woman propped up and fostered by flattery, by jesting, by pliableness, ignorance, dissimulation—satellites of mine, remember! Mercy me, how few marriages would come off, if the husband prudently inquired what tricks his seemingly coy and modest little lady had played long before the wedding! And still fewer, though entered upon, would last, did not most of the wife's doings escape her husband's knowledge, through his negligence or stupidity. But these blessings are owed to Folly. She brings it about that the wife pleases the husband, the husband pleases the wife, the household is tranquil, the alliance holds. . . .

"In sum, no society, no union in life, could be either pleasant or lasting without me. A people does not for long tolerate its prince, or a master tolerate his servant, a handmaiden her mistress, a teacher his student, a friend his friends, a wife her husband, a landlord his tenant, a partner his partner, or a boarder his fellow-boarder, except as they mutually or by turns are mistaken, on occasion flatter, on occasion wisely wink, and otherwise soothe themselves with the sweetness of folly.

"[10] Now I am aware that this seems the most that can be said, but you are going to hear what is greater. I ask you: will he who hates himself love anyone? Will he who does not get along with himself agree with another? Or will he who is disagreeable and irksome to himself bring pleasure to any? No one would say so, unless he were himself more foolish than Folly. . . .

"For what is so foolish as to be satisfied with yourself? Or to admire yourself? Yet on the other hand, if you are displeased with yourself, what can you do that is pleasing or graceful or seemly? Take this ingredient from life, and at once the orator, like his style, will be flat and cold, the musician will be as sour as his notes, the actor, with all his mimicry, will be hissed from the stage, the painter as well as his pictures will be cheap, and the poor doctor will famish among his poor medicines. Without self-love, though you may be a handsome Nireus, you will appear like Thersites; you will seem a Nestor, though a Phaon; a sow instead of Minerva, tongue-tied instead of eloquent, a gawk instead of a man of the world. That is how necessary it is to capture your own fancy, and to appreciate your own value by a bit of self-applause, before you can be held in price by others. Finally, since the better part of happiness is to wish to be what you are, why certainly my Philautia reaches that end by a short cut; so that no one is ashamed of his own looks, no one regrets his own temperament, or feels shame for his race, his locality, his profession, or his fatherland. An Irishman does not want to change places with an Athenian, or a Scythian with a dweller in the Fortunate Isles. Oh, the singular foresight of nature, who, in spite of such differences of condition, equalizes all things! Where she has withheld something of her bounties, there she is wont to add a little more self-love; but I have made a foolish saying, for self-love is itself the greatest bounty of nature.

"[11] May I not affirm, indeed, that you will find no great exploit undertaken, no important arts invented, except at my prompting? As, for instance, is not the war the seedplot and fountain of renowned actions? Yet what is more foolish than to enter upon a conflict for I know not what causes, wherein each side reaps more of loss than of gain? As for those who fall, as was said of the Megarians, 'no particulars.' And when armored ranks engage each other and bugles bray with harsh accord, of what use are those wise men, who, exhausted by studies, scarce maintain any life in their thin, cold blood? The day belongs to stout, gross fellows; the littler wit they have, the bolder they are—unless, forsooth, you prefer a soldier like Demosthenes, who, since he agreed with the poetic sentiment of Archilochus, dropped his shield and ran, as cowardly in warfare as he was consummate in eloquence.

But wise planning, they say, is of most importance in war. Yes, on the part of a general, I grant; yet is it military, not philosophical, wisdom. . . .

"But in God's good grace, after everything else, that famous saying of Plato's is trotted out: 'Happy is the state where philosophers are made kings, or whose kings become philosophers!' No, if you consult the historians, you will find, as plain as day, that nowhere have princes been so baneful to commonwealths as where the rule has developed upon some philosophaster or bookish fellow. The Catos, I suggest, give support enough to this point: one of them was always vexing the tranquility of the republic by hare-brained accusations, and the other totally destroyed the liberty of the Roman people, defending it, all the while, as wisely as you please. But to the Catos add your Brutus, your Cassius, the Gracchi, and even Cicero himself, who was no less fatal to the commonwealth of Rome than Demosthenes was to Athens. Then there is Marcus Aurelius—so that we may allow there was once a good emperor, I have just now been able to dig him up—who was vexatious and even hateful to the citizens for the very reason that he was so good a philosopher. I say that we must allow he was a good emperor, yet by leaving behind such a son as his, he certainly harmed the state more than he had benefited it by his good management. For a fact, this whole species of men who give themselves over to the pursuit of wisdom run to unluckiness in most things, and in none so much as in the children they beget; nature ordering it thus, I suggest, that the mischief of wisdom shall not be too generally insinuated into the race. Thus, as we all know, Cicero had a son quite unlike his ancestors, and the wise Socrates had children who 'favored the mother somewhat more than the father,' as one author rather nicely put it; that is, they were fools.

"If it were merely that your wise men approach public affairs precisely 'as asses do a lyre,' it might be borne; but they are no more dexterous in performing any of life's duties. Take your sage to a feast, and he will mar the good cheer either by a morose silence or by conducting a quiz. Invite him to a ball, and you learn how a camel dances. If you carry him to a play, he will dampen the mirth of the audience, and, a modern Cato, he will be forced to walk out of the theater because he cannot put off his gravity. If he engages in conversation, on a sudden it is a case of the wolf in the story. If something is to be bought, or a contract made, if, in short, any of those things without which our daily life could not be carried on must be done, you will say that this wiseacre is no man, but dead wood. Thus he can be of little use to himself, his country, or his family, and all because he is inexpert in everyday matters, and far out of step with general ways of thinking and modes of life among the folk; by the same token he is bound to fall into odium, through the great diversity between his and their lives and minds. For what that passes among mortals everywhere is not full of folly, done by fools in the presence of fools? If some one wishes to set up an opposition to the whole business, I should urge him to imitate

Timon and move to some wilderness, where he may enjoy his wisdom alone.

"[12] But let me get back to what I had outlined. What power was it drew together into civil society those stony, wooden, and wild people, if not flattery? That famed lyre of Amphion and that other of Orpheus mean nothing else than this. When the Roman people were hatching revolutions, what recalled them to civic concord? A philosophical oration, perhaps? No, not that. It was a silly and puerile story made up about the belly and the other members of the body. The tale Themistocles told about a fox and a hedge-hog worked in the same way. What oration by a wise man could have availed so well as did the fictitious white hind of Sertorius, or as the silly object lesson of the Spartan about the two puppies, or the other one about pulling the hair out of horses' tails? I am saying nothing of Minos and Numa, both of whom ruled the foolish multitude by making up fables; for by such toys that great and powerful beast, the people, is to be controlled. Again, what city ever adopted the doctrines of Socrates or the laws framed by Plato or Aristotle? On the other hand, what persuaded the three Decii to give themselves, for their country's sake, to the gods of the underworld? What carried Quintus Curtius into that fissure, if not mere glory—a certain exceedingly lovely siren who, strangely enough, is frowned upon by your wise men. For, as they point out, what is more foolish than for a candidate seeking office to flatter the people, to buy their favor with doles, to court the applause of so many fools, to be pleased by their shouts, to be carried about in parades as if he were a spectacle for the populace, to have his statue in the marketplace? To all these add the adoption of new names, and nicknames; then add those divine honors paid to very sorry fellows, and the deification, at great public ceremonies, of criminal tyrants. This sort of thing is most arrant folly. One Democritus cannot suffice for laughing at it. Who denies this? And yet from this source arise all those memorable exploits of doughty heroes which are extolled by the pens of so many eloquent men. The same foolishness gave rise to cities, by it empires are maintained, along with magistracy, religion, policy, and courts; nor is human life in general anything but a kind of fool's game.

"Let me say a word about the arts. What but a thirst for glory has enlisted the talents of men in the task of inventing and transmitting to posterity all these learned disciplines, which they deem so wonderful? Men who really are among the most foolish have thought that by nights without sleep, and by their sweat, they could purchase fame—I know not what sort of fame, but certainly nothing could be more empty. Yet at any rate you owe these choice blessings of life to Folly, and—what is the cream of the jest—you reap the fruits of a madness you need not share.

"[13] And now, since I have made good my title to renown for courage and resourcefulness, suppose I should lay claim also to prudence?

'But,' someone will say, 'with no more effort you might mix fire and water.' Perhaps so. Still, I shall have good success in this, I am convinced, if only you will lend me, as you have done so far, your ears and minds. And first, if prudence depends upon experience of affairs, to whom does the honor of this attribute belong? To the wise man, who, by reason partly of modesty and partly of faint-heartedness, will attempt no action? Or to the fool, who is not deterred from any enterprise by modesty, of which he is innocent, or by peril, which he never pauses to weigh? The wise man runs to books of the ancients and learns from them a merely verbal shrewdness. The fool arrives at true prudence, if I am not deceived, by addressing himself at once to the business and taking his chances. Homer seems to have seen this, for all that he was blind, when he said, 'Even a fool is wise after a thing is done.' There are two great obstacles to developing a knowledge of affairs—shame, which throws a smoke over the understanding, and fear, which, once danger has been sighted, dissuades from going through with an exploit. Folly, with a grand gesture, frees us from both. Never to feel shame, to dare anything—few mortals know to what further blessings these will carry us!

"Yet if they prefer to have that prudence which consists in the mere discernment of things, then hear, I adjure you, how far they are from it who still vaunt themselves upon the name. For first of all, the fact is that all human affairs, like the Sileni of Alcibiades, have two aspects, each quite different from the other; even to the point that what at first blush (as the phrase goes) seems to be death may prove, if you look further into it, to be life. What at first sight is beautiful may really be ugly; the apparently wealthy may be poorest of all; the disgraceful, glorious; the learned, ignorant; the robust, feeble; the noble, base; the joyous, sad; the favorable, adverse; what is friendly, an enemy; and what is wholesome, poisonous. In brief, you find all things suddenly reversed, when you open up the Silenus. Perhaps this seems too philosophical a saying; but come, with the help of a somewhat fat Minerva (to use an old expression), I shall make it more clear. Who would not avow that the king is a rich and great lord? Yet let the king be unfurnished in goods of the spirit, let him find satisfaction in nothing, and you see in a trice that he is the poorest of men. Suppose that his soul is given over to vices; now he is a vile slave. In like manner one might philosophize concerning others also, but let this one serve as an example.

"But where, one asks, does it all lead? Have patience, and let us carry it further. If a person were to try stripping the disguises from actors while they play a scene upon the stage, showing to the audience their real looks and the faces they were born with, would not such a one spoil the whole play? And would not the spectators think he deserved to be driven out of the theater with brickbats, as a drunken disturber? For at once a new order of things would be apparent. The actor who played a woman would now be seen a man; he who a moment ago appeared young, is old; he who but now was a king, is suddenly an hostler; and he who played the god is a sorry little scrub. Destroy the illusion and any play is ruined. It is the paint and trappings that take the eyes of spectators. Now what else is the whole life of mortals but a sort of comedy, in which the various actors, disguised by various costumes and masks, walk on and play each one his part, until the manager waves them off the stage? Moreover, this manager frequently bids the same actor go back in a different costume, so that he who has but lately played the king in scarlet now acts the flunkey in patched clothes. Thus all things are presented by shadows; yet this play is put on in no other way. . . .

"[15] But aided in part by ignorance, and in part by inadvertence. sometimes by forgetfulness of evil, sometimes by hope of good, sprinkling in a few honeyed delights at certain seasons, I bring relief from these ills; so that men are unwilling to relinquish their lives even when, by the exactly measured thread of the Fates, life is due to relinquish them. The less reason they have for remaining alive, the more they seem to delight in living—so far are they from being stricken with any tedium of life. Surely it is because of my bounty that you everywhere see these old fellows of Nestor's age, with hardly the shape of a man left them, babbling and silly, toothless, white-haired, bald—or better, let me describe them in the words of Aristophanes, 'slovenly, crooked, wrinkled, glabrous, and toothless.' And yet you see them still enjoying life so much and trying to be young so hard that one of them dyes his white hair, another covers his baldness with a wig, another enjoys the use of borrowed teeth, probably taken from the jaw of a pig; another is perishing miserably for love of some girl, and outdoes any adolescent in his amorous absurdities. . . . But the best sport of all is to watch our old women, already moribund with age, so cadaverous that you would think they had come back from their graves, . . . They industriously smear their faces with paint, never getting away from a mirror; they pluck out hairs from the strangest places; . . . they tipple, and mingle with the groups of young women; they write love-letters. These capers are laughed at by everyone, with good reason, as being the silliest in the world. Yet the old ladies are satisfied with themselves, and in the meantime they swim in pleasure and anoint themselves all over with honey; they are happy, in a word, by courtesy of me. And as for the people who find it all too ridiculous, I want them to mull over the question whether it is not better to lead this sort of honeyed life in folly than to look for a rafter, as the phrase goes, suitable for a hanging. Besides, it makes no difference to my fools that such things may be held disgraceful by the crowd, since fools do not feel disgrace, or, if they feel it, they can easily pass it off. If a rock falls on your head, that is bad; but shame, infamy, opprobrium, and curses hurt only so far as they are felt. If one has no sense of them, they are not evils at all. What harm is it if everybody hisses you, so long as you applaud yourself? But to this happy end, only Folly avails.

"[16] And now I seem to hear the philosophers disagreeing with me. But the true unhappiness, they say, is to be engrossed in folly, to err, to be deceived, not to know. Nay, this is to live as a man. Why they call it 'unhappy' I cannot see. It is simply that men are born thus, trained thus, constituted thus; it is the common lot of all. Nothing can be called unhappy if it fulfils its own nature, unless you would conclude that a man ought to be pitied because he cannot fly about with the birds, and cannot run on four feet like the whole family of beasts, and is not armed with horns like a bull. But by the same token one will call the finest horse miserable because he has not learned grammar and does not eat cheesecakes; one will call the bull unhappy because he is such a sorry wrestler. Hence, just as a horse ignorant of grammar is not miserable, a man who is a fool is not unhappy; the reason being that in each case the attribute is consistent with the nature.

"But our logic-choppers have something else to urge. Knowledge of the sciences, they say, is peculiarly the attribute of man; using them as tools, he makes up in his powers for what nature withheld from him. As if this had the least semblance of truth—that nature, which expended so much exact care upon gnats, and upon herbs and flowers, should have fallen asleep over the making of man! So that he has need of sciences—which Theuth, that evil genius of the human race, excogitated for the hurt of man, and which are so far from furthering his happiness that they actually hinder it. To that end they were discovered, according to report, just as that wise king in Plato wittily proves with respect to the invention of letters. Thus the sciences crept in by stealth, along with other banes of human life, and from the very sources whence all evils flow—devils, let us say. Even the name you call them shows this, for 'daemons' means 'those who know.'

"The simple folk of the golden age flourished without any armament of sciences, being guided only by nature and instinct. For what need was there of grammar when all spoke the same language, and had no other aim in speaking but that some one else should understand? What use for dialectic, where there was no battle of opinions ranged in contradiction to each other? What room for rhetoric, when no man cared to make trouble for his neighbor? Wherein was the study of law called for, when folk had not learned the evil ways from which, we must admit, our good laws arose. Then, moreover, they had too much piety to search out, with a profane curiosity, the secrets of nature; to investigate the dimensions, motions, and influences of the stars, or the hidden causes of things; deeming it a sacrilege for mortal man to try to know more than is proper to his station. This madness of inquiring what may lie beyond the sky never entered their heads. But as the pristine simplicity of the golden age little by little slipped away, first the arts were discovered—by evil spirits, as I have told; but they were few in number and accepted by few people. Later on, the superstitution of the Chaldeans and the frivolous curiosity of the Greeks added hundreds of them—mere vexations of the spirit, seeing that a single system of grammar will amply provide continuous torture through a long lifetime.

"And yet among these disciplines the ones that approach nearest to common sense, that is, to folly, are held in highest esteem. Theologians are starved, naturalists find cold comfort, astrologers are mocked, and logicians are slighted. 'The doctor alone is worth all the rest put together.' Within the profession of medicine, furthermore, so far as any member is eminently unlearned, impudent, or careless, he is valued the more, even in the chambers of belted earls. For medicine, especially as now practised by many, is but a subdivision of the art of flattery, no less truly than is rhetoric. Lawyers have the next place after doctors, and I do not know but that they should have first place; with great unanimity the philosophers—not that I would say such a thing myself —are wont to ridicule the law as an ass. Yet great matters and little matters alike are settled by the arbitrament of these asses. They gather goodly freeholds with broad acres, while the theologian, after poring over chestfuls of the great corpus of divinity, gnaws on bitter beans, at the same time manfully waging war against lice and fleas. As those arts are more successful which have the greatest affinity with folly, so those people are by far the happiest who enjoy the privilege of avoiding all contact with the learned disciplines, and who follow nature as their only guide, since she is in no respect wanting, except as a mortal wishes to transgress the limits set for his status. Nature hates counterfeits; and that which is innocent of art gets along far the more prosperously.

"Consider: among the several kinds of living creatures, do you not observe that the ones which live most happily are those which are farthest from any discipline, and which are controlled by no other master than nature? What could be more happy than the bees—or more wonderful? They do not seem to have all of the bodily senses; yet what has architecture discovered that can match their principles of construction? What philosopher has ever framed a republic equal to theirs? The horse, on the other hand, so far as he has senses like to man's, and travels about with companies of men, is also a partaker in human misfortunes. Thus many a horse actually feels shame to be outrun, and for that reason he becomes wind-broken by often racing. Or if the horse courts triumph in the wars, he is stuck through, and 'bites the dust' along with his rider. I need not mention the cruel bits and sharpened spurs, the prison of a stable, the whips, batons, and tie-straps, the rider—in brief, all that tragedy of serfdom to which he exposes himself when he imitates brave men and too zealously endeavors to wreak vengeance upon the enemy. How much more desirable, except for the traps laid by men, the life of flies and birds, living for the moment and solely by the light of nature! And if it happens that birds are shut up in cages and practise making the sounds of human speech, it is marvellous how they decline from their natural beauty and gaiety. At every level of life, what nature has ordained is more happy than what is adulterated by art.

"Therefore I shall never praise enough that cock, who was really Pythagoras: though but one, he had been all things—a philosopher, a man, a woman, a king, a subject, a fish, a horse, a frog, I think even a sponge—and he came to the conclusion that no creature is more miserable than man; for all the others are satisfied with their natural limitations, but man alone strives to go beyond the bounds proper to his station. And among men, in turn, this cock ranked simpletons, on many counts, above the learned and great. That fellow Gryllus was not a little wiser than 'Odysseus of the many counsels,' when he elected to grunt in a sty rather than to expose himself, along with that worthy, to painful mishaps. It seems to me that Homer, the father of nonsense, does not disagree with these sentiments; he more than once applies to all mortals the epithets of 'wretched and calamity-stricken,' and still oftener he calls Ulysses, that pattern of wisdom, 'miserable': whereas he never speaks so of Paris, or Ajax, or Achilles. Why should Ulysses be miserable, except that the wily and resourceful rogue never undertook anything without the advice of Pallas? He was overly wise, and got too far away from the guidance of nature. Hence it appears that among mortals they who are zealous for wisdom are farthest from happiness, being by the same token fools twice over: that is, although they are born men, they then so far forget their own station as to hanker after the life of the immortal gods; and on the example of the Giants, with arts and sciences as their engines they wage war on nature. So also those appear to be least unhappy who approach nearest to the temperament and simplicity of the beasts, nor ever undertake what is beyond man.

"[17] Come, let us not test this with Stoic enthymemes, when we can demonstrate it by a single plain example. By the gods above, is there anything that is better off than that class of men whom we generally call morons, fools, halfwits, and zanies—the most beautiful names I know of! You see, I am telling you what at first blush may seem silly and absurd but is true many times over. For first of all, these folk are free from all fear of death—and this fear, by Jove, is no piddling evil! They are free from tortures of conscience. They are not frightened by tales of ghosts, or scared to death by specters and goblins. They are not tormented by dread of impending evils, and they are not blown up with hope of future good. In short, they are not vexed by the thousand cares to which this life is subject. They do not feel shame or fear, they are not ambitious, they do not envy, they do not love. And finally, if they should approach even more closely to the irrationality of dumb animals they would not sin, according to the writers of theology. I wish you would think over for me, you wise fool, how by night and by day your soul is torn by so many carking cares; I wish you would gather into one heap all the discommodities of your life: then you will begin to understand from how many evils I have delivered my fools. Remember also that they are continually merry, they play, sing, and laugh; and what is more, they bring to others, wherever they may come, pleasure, jesting, sport, and laughter, as if they were created, by a merciful dispensation of the gods, for this one purpose—to drive away the sadness of human life.

"Thus it comes about that, in a world where men are differently affected toward each other, all are at one in their attitude toward these innocents; all seek them out, give them food, keep them warm, embrace them, and give them aid, if occasion rises; and all grant them leave to say and to do what they wish, with impunity. So true it is that no one wishes to hurt them that even wild beasts, by a certain natural sense of their innocence, will refrain from doing them harm. They are indeed held sacred by the gods, especially by me; and not impiously do all men pay such honor to them. Thus kings find such consummate pleasure in my naturals that they cannot eat, or go on a progress, or even pass an hour, without them. The fact is that in some degree they prefer these simpletons to their crabbed wise men, whom yet they support for dignity's sake. That kings have this preference ought not, I suggest, seem remarkable or difficult of explanation: the wise men make a habit of bringing before them only serious matters, and, confident in their learning, will not fear at times 'to grate their tender ears with rasping truths'; but fools furnish the one kind of thing that rulers are glad to get from any quarter and in any shape—jests, japes, laughter, pastime.

"Notice also this estimable gift of fools, that they alone are frank and ingenuous. What is more praiseworthy than truth? Granted that the proverb of Alcibiades in Plato attributes truth to drunkards and children, yet all its merit is peculiarly mine, even as Euripides witnesses; his famous saying has come down to us: 'A fool speaks foolish things.' Whatever a fool has in his heart, that he sets also in his face and utters in his speech. But your wise man has two tongues, as this same Euripides mentions, one used for speaking truth, the other for speaking what he judges most opportune at the moment. Black is turned into white by these men of wisdom; they blow hot and cold with the same breath, and hidden in the breast they have something quite different from what they frame in speech. With all their felicity, indeed, the princes of earth seem to me most unfortunate in this respect, that they have no one to tell them the truth, but are compelled to have toadies instead of friends. But, some one will say, the ears of princes have an antipathy to truth, and for this reason the princes shun wise counsellors, fearing that possibly one more free than the others will stand forth and dare to speak things true rather than pleasant. Yes, by and large, veracity is disliked by kings. And yet a remarkable thing happens in the experience of my fools: from them not only true things, but even sharp reproaches, will be listened to; so that a statement which, if it came from a wise

man's mouth, might be a capital offense, coming from a fool gives rise
to incredible delight. Veracity, you know, has a certain authentic power
of giving pleasure, if nothing offensive goes with it: but this the gods
have granted only to fools. And for more or less the same reasons
women are wont to take vast delight in men of this class, women being
by nature more inclined to pleasure and toys. And however they may
carry on with fools, even if it begins to wax a little too serious, they
pass it off as a joke or a game—for the sex is ingenious, especially in
veiling its own lapses.

"Let me return to the topic of the happiness of fools. After a life
lived out in much jollity, with no fear of death, or sense of it, they go
straight to the Elysian Fields, there to entertain the pious and idle shades
with their jests. Let us go about, then, and compare the lot of the
wise man with that of the fool. Fancy some pattern of wisdom to put
up against him, a man who wore out his whole boyhood and youth in
pursuing the learned disciplines. He wasted the pleasantest time of
life in unintermitted watchings, cares, and studies; and through the
remaining part of it he never tasted so much as a tittle of pleasure;
always frugal, impecunious, sad, austere; unfair and strict toward himself, morose and unamiable to others; afflicted by pallor, leanness, in-
validism, sore eyes, premature age and white hair; dying before his
appointed day. By the way, what difference does it make when a man
of that sort dies? He has never lived. There you have a clear picture
of the wise man.

(Pp. 22-51.)

"[24] You would never believe what sport and entertainment your
mortal manikins provide daily for the gods. These gods, you know, set
aside their sober forenoon hours for composing quarrels and giving ear to
prayers. But after that, when they are well moistened with nectar and
have no desire for the transaction of business, they seek out some prom-
ontory of heaven and, sitting there with faces bent downward, they
watch what mortal men are adoing. There is no show like it, Good God,
what a theater! How various the action of fools! (I may say that now
and then I take a seat alongside the gods of the poets.) Here is a fellow
dying for love of a sweet young thing, and the less he is loved in return,
the more helplessly he is in love. This one marries a dowry, not a wife.
This one prostitutes his own wife. The jealousy of another keeps watch
like Argus. Here is a man in mourning, but mercy me, what fool things
he says and does! Hiring mourners as if they were actors, to play a
comedy of grief! Another man squeezes out a tear at the tomb of his
mother-in-law. This one spends on his belly whatever he can scrape
together by hook or crook, but presently he will be just as hungry again.
Another finds nothing better than sleep and idleness. There are those
who get themselves into a stew working at what is other people's busi-

ness, while they neglect their own. There is also the broker, who accounts himself rich on other people's money, but is on the way to bankruptcy. Another thinks that the happy life consists in living like a pauper in order that his heir may be wealthy. Another, for the sake of a small and uncertain profit, sails the seven seas, exposing his life, which no money could pay for, to the hazard of waves and winds. This one prefers seeking riches in war to passing a safe and quiet life at home. Some decide that they can most conveniently attain to wealth by courting and fawning upon childless old men. There are even those who prefer to do the same to rich old women. Both kinds furnish rare sport to the gods who are spectators, because they are usually cheated by the parties they set out to catch.

"But the most foolish and sordid of all are your merchants, in that they carry on the most sordid business of all and this by the most sordid methods; for on occasion they lie, they perjure themselves, they steal, they cheat, they impose on the public. Yet they make themselves men of importance—because they have gold rings on their fingers. Nor do they lack for flattering friars who admire them and call them Right Honorable in public, with the purpose, surely, that some little driblet from the ill-gotten gains may flow to themselves. Elsewhere you will see certain Pythagoreans, in whose eyes all things are common—to such a degree, in fact, that whatever they light upon that is lying around loose they carry off with a tranquil spirit, as if it passed to them by inheritance. There are others who are rich only in wishes; they build beautiful air-castles and conceive that doing so is enough for happiness. Some delight in passing for wealthy men away from home, though they starve meanly enough in their own houses. One man hastens to put into circulation what money he has; his neighbor hoards his up through thick and thin. This one pushes forward as a candidate for public honors; that one finds his pleasure by his fireside. A good many people bring suits which are destined never to end; once and again they eagerly strive to outdo each other—in enriching the judge who sets the postponements and the advocate who colludes with him. One burns with zeal for revolutions; another is toiling upon his Grand Scheme. This man leaves wife and children at home and sets out on a pilgrimage to Jerusalem, Rome, or the shrine of St. James, where he has no particular business. In sum, if you might look down from the moon, as Menippus did of old, upon the numberless agitations among mortal men, you would think you were seeing a swarm of flies or gnats, quarreling among themselves, waging wars, setting snares for each other, robbing, sporting, wantoning, being born, growing old, and dying. And one can scarce believe what commotions and what tragedies this animalcule, little as he is and so soon to perish, sets agoing. For sometimes a trivial war or a spell of the plague will sweep off and utterly wipe out thousands of them at once.

(Pp. 68-70.)

"To my subject, then. Fortune loves those who are less than discreet, she loves the rasher sort, and the ones who are fond of that saying, 'The die is cast.' But wisdom makes men meticulous, which is why you commonly see that the traffic of wise men is with poverty, hunger, and smoke; you see them living neglected, inglorious, and disliked. You see my fools abounding in money, holding the helms of states, in brief, flourishing every way. For if we esteem it a blessing to please princes and to mingle with such favorites of mine, these gods decked with gems, what is less to the purpose than wisdom? In the eyes of that rank of men, what, indeed, is more damning? If wealth is to be gathered, how much money would a merchant make if, running after wisdom, he should boggle at perjury, should blush to be taken in a lie, should in the least suffer from those inconvenient scruples of the wise touching theft and the taking of usury? Then if anyone sets his heart upon ecclesiastical honors and wealth, an ass or a buffalo will attain to them sooner than a wise man. If you are inclined to a certain sort of pleasure, the girls, a very important part of the human comedy, have given their hearts away to fools; they startle at a wise man and run from him, as from a scorpion. Lastly, whoever makes preparations to live a little more gaily and jovially will first of all shut the wise man out, and will prefer to let in any other animal. Wherever you circulate, in short, among popes, princes, judges, magistrates, friends, enemies, the great, or the humble, everything is done by cash in hand; and as the wise have contempt for cash, it carefully maintains the custom of avoiding them."

(Pp. 103-104.)

HAWTHORNE: *MOSSES FROM AN OLD MANSE*. Houghton Mifflin Company, Boston. Essay entitled "The Celestial Railroad."

"It was late in the day when the train thundered into the ancient city of Vanity, where Vanity Fair is still at the height of prosperity, and exhibits an epitome of whatever is brilliant, gay, and fascinating beneath the sun. As I purposed to make a considerable stay here, it gratified me to learn that there is no longer the want of harmony between the town's people and pilgrims, which impelled the former to such lamentably mistaken measures as the persecution of Christian and the fiery martyrdom of Faithful. On the contrary, as the new railroad brings with it great trade and a constant influx of strangers, the lord of Vanity Fair is its chief patron, and the capitalists of the city are among the largest stockholders. Many passengers stop to take their pleasure or make their profit in the Fair, instead of going onward to the Celestial City. Indeed, such are the charms of the place that people often affirm it to be the true and only heaven; stoutly contending that there is no other, that those who seek further are mere dreamers, and that, if the fabled brightness of the Celestial City lay but a bare mile beyond the gates of Vanity, they would not be fools enough to go thither. Without subscribing to these perhaps exaggerated encomiums, I can truly say that my abode in the city was mainly agreeable, and my intercourse with the inhabitants productive of much amusement and instruction.

"Being naturally of a serious turn, my attention was directed to the solid advantages derivable from a residence here, rather than to the effervescent pleasures which are the great object with too many visitants. The Christian reader, if he had had no account of the city later than Bunyan's time, will be surprised to hear that almost every street has its church, and that the reverend clergy are nowhere held in higher respect than at Vanity Fair. And well do they deserve such honorable estimation; for the maxims of wisdom and virtue which fell from their lips come from as deep a spiritual source, and tend to as lofty a religious aim, as those of the sagest philosophers of old. In justification of this high praise I need only mention the names of the Reverend Mr. Shallow-deep, the Rev. Mr. Stumble-at-truth, and fine old clerical character the Rev. Mr. This-to-day, who expects shortly to resign his pulpit to the Rev. Mr. That-to-morrow; together with the Rev. Mr. Bewilderment, the Rev. Mr. Clog-the-spirit, and, last and greatest, the Rev. Mr. Wind-of-doctrine. The labors of these eminent divines are aided by those of innumerable lecturers, who diffuse such a various profundity, on all subjects of human or celestial science, that any man may acquire an omnigenous erudition without the trouble of even learning to read. Thus literature is etherealized by assuming for its medium the human voice; and knowledge, depositing all its heavier particles, except, doubtless, its gold, becomes exhaled into a sound, which forthwith steals into the ever-open ear of the community. These ingenious methods constitute a sort of machinery, by which thought and study are done to every person's hand without his putting himself to the slightest inconvenience in the matter. There is another species of machine for the wholesale manufacture of individual morality. This excellent result is effected by societies for all manner of virtuous purposes, with which a man has merely to connect himself, throwing, as it were, his quota of virtue into the common stock, and the president and directors will take care that the aggregate amount be well applied. All these, and other wonderful improvements in ethics, religion, and literature, being made plain to my comprehension by the ingenious Mr. Smooth-it-away, inspired me with a vast admiration of Vanity Fair.

"It would fill a volume, in an age of pamphlets, were I to record all my observation in this great capital of human business and pleasure. There was an unlimited range of society—the powerful, the wise, the witty, and the famous in every walk of life; princes, presidents, poets, generals, artists, actors, and philanthropists,—all making their own market at the fair, and deeming no price too exorbitant for such commodities as hit their fancy. It was well worth one's while, even if he had no idea of buying or selling, to loiter through the bazaars and observe the various sorts of traffic that were going forward.

"Some of the purchasers, I thought, made very foolish bargains. For instance, a young man having inherited a splendid fortune, laid out a considerable portion of it in the purchase of diseases, and finally spent all the rest for a heavy lot of repentance and a suit of rags. A very pretty girl bartered a heart as clear as crystal, and which seemed her most valuable possession, for another jewel of the same kind, but so worn and defaced as to be utterly worthless. In one shop there were a great many crowns of laurels and myrtle, which soldiers, authors, statesmen, and various other people pressed eagerly to buy; some purchased these paltry wreaths with their lives, others by a toilsome servitude of years, and many sacrificed whatever was most valuable, yet finally slunk away without the crown. There was a sort of stock or scrip, called Conscience, which seemed to be in great demand, and would purchase almost anything. Indeed, few rich commodities were to be obtained without paying a heavy sum in this particular stock, and a man's business was seldom very lucrative unless he knew precisely when and how to throw his hoard of conscience into the market. Yet as this stock was the only thing of permanent value, whoever parted with it was sure to find himself a loser in the long run. Several of the speculations were of a questionable character. Occasionally a member of Congress recruited his pocket by the sale of his constituents; and I was assured that public officers have often sold their country at very moderate prices. Thousands sold their happiness for a whim. Gilded chains were in great demand, and purchased with almost any sacrifice. In truth, those who desired, according to the old adage, to sell anything, valuable for a song, might find customers all over the Fair; and there were innumerable messes of pottage, piping hot, for such as chose to buy them with their birthrights. A few articles, however, could not be found genuine at Vanity Fair. If a customer wished to renew his stock of youth the dealers offered him a set of false teeth and an auburn wig; if he demanded peace of mind, they recommended opium or a brandy bottle.

"Tracts of land and golden mansions, situated in the Celestial City, were often exchanged, at very disadvantageous rates, for a few years' lease of small, dismal, inconvenient tenements in Vanity Fair. Prince Beelzebub [or Satan] himself took great interest in this sort of traffic, and sometimes condescended to meddle with smaller matters. I once had the pleasure to see him bargaining with a miser for his soul, which, after much ingenious skirmishing on both sides, his highness succeeded in obtaining at about the value of sixpence. The prince remarked with a smile, that he was a loser by the transaction."

CABOT: *WHAT MEN LIVE BY*. Houghton Mifflin Company, Boston, 1914. Pp. xiv-xx.

"Out of the dazzle and welter of modern civilization, which offers a hundred quack remedies for every ill of the soul, work, play, and love emerge as the permanent sources of helpfulness to which parents, educators, and social workers are now turning with confidence, while over their shoulders they glance wistfully toward worship.

" 'Real Life,' then, if it is to mean the nourishing, sustaining, and developing of existence, demands work, play, and love, and so much of the material and spiritual conditions of existence as make these possible.

"Though I came to this belief first from a doctor's point of view, and as the result of search for the essential principles of healing within a special field, I have since come to notice that the special groups of people whom I see as patients are not the only ones who need these great medicines. I notice a growing tendency to center all remedial effort upon the same trio of ends, no matter what sort of trouble is at hand. More satisfying and interesting occupation, more refreshment through art and play, deeper and more intense affection, are the life-preservers which one wants to secure about the blind, the maimed, the invalid, the discharged prisoner, the orphan, the deserted wife, the discouraged, down-at-the-heel family, the neglected or abused child, the alcoholic, the convalescent, the insane, the feeble-minded, the morphinist, the boy who has inherited millions, and the society girl who has got through 'coming out.' In genuine emergencies and for those overdriven in their industrial harness, material relief (food, rest, air, sleep, warmth) may be the first necessity, but unless we can give the vital nourishment which I am now advising, all material relief soon becomes a farce or a poison, just as medicine is in most chronic diseases a farce or a poison. Vitality and resisting power are what we most need, and these must be created for the sick out of the same nourishment which keeps the well people well.

"I made just now a long list of sufferers. Did I mention all who need the essentials of real life? Obviously not, for those who are going right need these life-saving activities as much as those who are going wrong. It is the stake in life given us by our work, our play, and our love that keeps any one from going wrong. The conservative needs them to leaven his conservatism; the radical needs them to hold him down to solid ground. Young and old need them, for by these three principles we are helped to grow up and saved from growing old.

"In this style I was sailing confidently along when one day a friend asked me: 'How do you distinguish Work, Play, and Love from Drudgery, Frivolity, and Lust? You have made saints of your favorites and put halos around their heads, but not every one can see the halos or can believe in them upon your say-so.'

" 'True!' I should answer, 'not on my say-so, but on your own. You believe in them now.' Everybody sees halos and worships saints of some kind, though many have learned to hide the habit even from themselves. Work, play, and love are my saints, and in this book I want to draw their lineaments and make their halos visible to others. The religion of work, or art, and of love is not the strongest or the truest, but it is a good beginning. There one finds outlet for devotion and gropes toward God. One can do all but speak to God. One fails only when it comes to worship, which is to-day so unfashionable a habit that one must be prepared to shock the modern ear and to violate all the scientific properties if one confesses belief in it. Civilization is supposed to have carried us beyond the need of rites and forms and to have fused the demonstrative and emotional side of religion into daily work, play, and affection.

"But this is theory, not observation. As a matter of fact the doctor, social worker, or teacher who believes that all true religion can be woven into work, play, or affection falls into the same fallacy as those who think English composition can be taught by weaving it into the courses in history, science, and philosophy. Experience shows, I think, that vital religion and the ability to write good English are not acquired in this incidental way. Scientists, economists, and historians often write barbarously. We must practice the art of writing as well as incidentally, else we shall duplicate the catastrophe of our public-school system, wherein the conscientious effort to avoid proselyting, to abolish sectarian teaching, and let religion take care of itself, has now brought us perilously near the French secularism.

"There is no originality in my suggestion that we should focus our efforts upon work, play, love, and worship. For though we talk a great deal about 'efficiency,' economics, hygiene, and other matters of secondary importance, at bottom we all know well enough what we need, and what all the paraphernalia of civilization, money, health, and education, are really meant for. If I were not persuaded that, in our right minds, we know the fundamental reasons for all this hurry and bustle, I should not venture to write a reminder. We know where we are traveling, but we need a time-table to remind us of details.

"I do not say that every one *wants* only the ends which I have named. He usually wants fame, riches, wisdom, talents, personal beauty, and an easy time of it generally. He may be too sleepy and comfortable, or too tired and miserable, to want anything but Nirvana or release. Yet, enervated by heat, calloused by routine, steeped in sin, crazed with pain, stupefied by luxury or by grief, still he needs four inexorable blessings.

"The interplay of these four is the end of life, and the sole worthy end, in my creed. This is the fruit of the 'life and liberty' which are guaranteed under our Constitution. This is the goal to be secured through efficient and progressive governmental machinery. This is the end of all education and all moral training. This is the food of the soul in health or in disease, needed by the doctor, the social worker, the teacher, and the statesman, to feed their souls as well as to prevent and to cure social ills. This is our justification for the enormous machinery and the costly ugliness of civilization. This is the essential of that 'more abundant life' which many modern prophets extol without defining.

"Every human being, man, woman, and child, hero and convict, neurasthenic and deep-sea fisherman, needs the blessing of God through these four gifts. With these any life is happy despite sorrow and pain, successful despite bitter failure. Without them we lapse into animalism or below it. If you want to keep a headstrong, fatuous youth from overreaching himself and falling, these must be the elements of strength. When you try to put courage and aspiration into the gelatinous character of the alcoholic or the street-walker, you will fail unless you can give responsibility, recreation, affection, and through them a glimpse of God.

"I do not believe that evolution, revolution, or decadence have power to change these elemental needs. For all I know, we may be this instant in the position of the French court before the Revolution. At this very moment we may be lurching over the smooth bend of a cataract that is to overwhelm us; but if so, it is because we have not enough of that unchanging valor which has preserved us so far, and will reconstitute us after our downfall. For work, play, love, and prayer are open to rich and poor, to young and old; they are of all times and all races in whom character is an ideal.

"On each of these gigantic forces I have particular designs: I want to show the sacredness of work and love; I want to show the accessibility and the universality of play and worship. That despite our secular habits, we are so close to worship that we may at any time abruptly fall into it; that play and art can be closely woven into the fabric of work, till drudgery is reduced to a minimum; that work is our key to the sacredness of material nature, and that affection can be disciplined only by consecration. These are my theses."

(Pp. xiv-xx.)

Questions and Statements for Discussion

(Chapters 1 and 2)

(The Praise of Folly)

1. "Nowhere have princes been so baneful to commonwealths as where the rule has devolved upon some philosophaster or bookish fellow." (P. 44.) This is still a common belief. How does it arise, and is it always true?

2. Evaluate the popularity that springs from flattery. Is there any truth in the assumption that flattery is the basis of social cooperation? If not, what are some necessary elements in social adjustment? (P. 45.)

3. Does prudence mean absence of conviction, or does it consist of a clever "keeping with the crowd"? Is the athlete who rushes in and takes his chances likely to win? What is prudent in such a case?

4. What is wrong with the assumption that scientific knowledge is incompatible with pleasure? (P. 48.)

5. Are the fools described in p. 49 any of them pursuing the things that matter most?

6. "No creature is more miserable than man." Is there any other so capable of happiness? May there be a relation between capacity for happiness and capacity for misery?

7. Do the paradoxes of pp. 52-53 prove the unreality of all human values, or only of some of them? What is the solution?

8. Is there anything to be said in defense of "wisdom" as portrayed on p. 54?

(What Men Live By)

9. Why do not work, play, and love, provide, according to Dr. Cabot, a sufficiently vital nourishment for a normal life?

10. In what sense could work be discussed as value?

11. Discuss the sources of creative genius as described by Cabot.

12. Why is play essential, and what is the test of value in a game?

13. How does the lack of good sportsmanship destroy the value of a game?

14. How does possessiveness interfere with all types of love?

15. What place in successful home life is played by responsibility?

16. Discuss worship as a cure for "staleness." How does it work?

Suggested General Readings for the whole course:

Flewelling: "Three Windows into Reality." *Philosophical Review*, March, 1939.

Urban: *Fundamentals of Ethics.* Henry Holt, New York. Pp. 16-19; 170-175.

Everett: *Moral Values.* Henry Holt, New York. Pp. 188-249.

Cabot: *What Men Live By.* Houghton Mifflin, Boston.

Green: *Prolegomena to Ethics.* Oxford University Press, New York. Sec. 184, pp. 217-219.

Brentano: *The Origin of the Knowledge of Right and Wrong.* Constable, London. Pp. 9-16.

Prall: *A Study in the Theory of Value.* California Publications in Philosophy, Vol. 3.

Urban: *Valuation, Its Nature and Laws.* Unwin, London. Pp. 159ff.

Eaton: *The Austrian Philosophy of Values.* University of Oklahoma Press, Norman, Okla., Chap. VIII, "The Definition of Value"; Chap. IX, "False Values and True Values."

Perry: *The General Theory of Value.* Longmans, Green, New York. Pp. 3-13.

Laird: *The Idea of Value.* Cambridge University Press, New York.

Pringle-Pattison: *The Idea of God.* Oxford University Press, New York. Chap. II, "Kant and the Idea of Intrinsic Value." Pp. 24-45.

Schiller: "Value," article in Hastings' *Encyclopaedia of Religion and Ethics.* Scribner's, New York.

Santayana: *Realms of Being.* (One vol. ed.) Scribner's, New York, 1942. Pp. 152-154.

Bosanquet: *The Value and Destiny of the Individual.* (2 vols.) *The Principle of Individuality and Value.* Macmillan, New York.

Laird: *An Inquiry into Moral Notions.* Columbia University Press, New York.

PART II

FIVE WORLD-CONCEPTS OF HUMAN VALUES

"The great-minded man is prodigal of life, since he knows there are terms on which it is not worth while to live."

—ARISTOTLE

"Religion is belief in the conservation of values."

—HÖFFDING

Foreword

The story is told of Dante, the great poet of the Middle Ages, that, exiled from his native city of Florence, distraught with the cruel turn of personal fortune, he decided to walk from Italy to Paris in order to study philosophy there, and thus to gather some insight into the meaning of life and destiny. He found himself a belated traveller, knocking at the gates of the monastery of Santa Croce, seeking refuge from the night. A surly brother, disturbed from his prayers, or more likely from his slumbers, threw the door suddenly open, and in a gruff voice demanded: "What do you want?" Dante, with a darkness in his soul far deeper than the darkest Italian night, replied in a single word: "Peace!" That was the profoundest answer that could be made, for it was the summation of his deepest wants, and of ours as well.

We must begin the search for values with the question: What do I most desire? Or, we may ask ourselves what is it that we hope eventually to gain in our search for fame, or friends, or wealth, or ease from toil, or want? An examination which is at all profound will disclose that what we want after all could be summed up in that one word of Dante: "Peace!" We want peace of mind, satisfactory adjustment to the world of mental, physical, and spiritual needs, and within our own minds. Nothing that we can acquire can be satisfying unless along with it we can have peace, but with peace we can endure physical discomforts, deprivations of every sort, with equanimity. The external things we seek after we hope will somehow afford us complacency of mind, even if it is no more than that of the defeated man, who is conscious of having done his best for a worthy cause. Only peace can be the ultimate answer to man's search, the one that includes all others.

The following five systems set for us to study are widely separated in time and place, in contrasting cultures and ideas, and yet there is a single thread that binds them together. However disparate their solutions they each seek the answer to this vexing problem of life: How and where shall we be able to find peace? Since peace is the deepest want of our nature, and concerns itself with the profoundest psychological facts, those systems that seek it, directly and professedly, have by that fact some right to be considered expressions of religion.

65

This is as true of Confucianism, which hopes to reach peace by an inward as well as outward harmony which constitutes a man the perfect "gentleman," as it was of Buddha who thought that peace could be had by turning away from all the distractions of an evil world.   Since "the world" had the characteristic of pursuing him into the most secluded retreat, he had then to command the pack of his own evil and disturbing thoughts, imaginings, and desires, to make them run like dogs "at heel," or to lie down and no more distress him.   So he sought peace by a complete and all-absorbing meditation, as free from all contacts with life as he could make it.   A study of Stoic philosophy will show just as surely as Buddhism, this struggle for peace of mind, in the consciousness that man's life is ruled by Reason.   How could a man conduct himself in a world of evil fate and untoward circumstance, sickness and disease, petty tyrants and dictators, and remain unmoved from the life of virtue and reason?   The Stoic thought he caught the answer to that problem in the control of his emotions.   Let not feeling but Reason dictate every act.   To pain he would throw the challenge of being unmoved by it.   Nothing should disturb his peace and equanimity, because the mind could be superior to circumstance.   The Stoic Epictetus, a slave, put on the rack by his cruel owner, who professed to be a Christian, is said to have remarked as the painful cords began to strain: "If you do not look out you will break my leg, so that I cannot serve you."   When the leg was broken, he added: "I told you so."   Then with a Stoic pride in his self-possession he is said to have added: "Could a Christian have done better than that?"   It was a high degree of fortitude, no doubt, but the essential principle was to let nothing disrupt one's inward calm.   Anyone who lived by justice and reason could look with contempt upon both the persecution and the persecutor.   Nothing should move the imperturbable soul that lived by reason.

Epicurus sought peace in a yet different way.   Enjoy the world moderately, was his solution, because our equanimity is disturbed by entertaining desires that cannot be realized.   Tranquillity, he thought, would come with absence of mental desire, and of physical pain.   Since pain could not always be avoided, he invented a system of argumentative reasoning, or dialectic, as it is called.   If the pain is light, "grin and bear it," it is endurable; if it is heavy, it will not last long since it will kill you.   Death is not to be feared, because so long as you live you are not dead, and when you are dead, you will not know it.   As for the anger of the gods, from which it was the purpose of Epicureanism to remove the common dread, they were too busy enjoying themselves (pleasure being the supreme aim of life) to take time out to punish or torture anybody. Thus he tried to make himself believe that he had arrived at peace by arguing away his troubles, and not wanting anything he could not get.

Judaeo-Christianity took another direction but its object was like that of the others, the achievement of peace. This was to come through conformity with the will of a God of righteousness, love, and justice, who creates and sustains the world, both of the present and of the hereafter. One of the most beautiful summations of the Judaeo-Christian system was made by Tolstoi:

> Where there is faith, there is love;
> Where there is love, there is peace;
> Where there is peace, there is God;
> And where there is God, there is no need.

However diverse the solutions may be, these various approaches to the problem of value in different historic times, countries, and civilizations bear the mark of man's common need and endeavor. "What are the things that matter most?" With unanimous voice they all exclaim: "The value that includes all others is peace." Peace of body, peace of mind, peace of soul, harmony in external relations, harmony with the universe, and with what may be behind the universe as the cause of all things, harmony within one's self. these are the things that for human beings are supreme values. We hope to see, in the discussions that follow, how these contrasting efforts have worked out, and to gain some light of our own on the outstanding values of human life.

These systems, with all their diversity, were remarkable also in their contemporancity. It was as if widely separated peoples were moved by a common impulse after the same values. How much they may have influenced each other we cannot say, but there was a world-wide revolt against narrowing superstitions, and demand for new intellectual freedoms. Such a movement of the human spirit would, in the very nature of thought, present everywhere some common characteristics. Beneath the search for and striving after a righteous God there are basic elements of common understanding that have never yet been truly assessed, because men have been more anxious to magnify their differences than to emphasize their common interests. The world was at that time perhaps nearer to universal understandings than it can ever be again, until men can cease the strife for non-essential differences, and honestly devote themselves to impartial righteousness, justice, and truth, with a determination on this basis to understand each other. Men of good-will must face each other with honest purpose and sincere appreciation, for righteousness, justice, love, and truth know no boundaries of nation, race, religion, or sect. Out of a world-hunger of the spirit arose Confucianism in China, Buddhism in India, the religio-philosophic sects in Greece, and that prophetic cult in Israel that culminated in Christianity. These common elements present an interesting episode in a world-wide search to discover what matters most.

Chapter 3

THE "GENTLEMAN" OF CONFUCIUS

I

The Social and Intellectual Background of Confucian Teaching
1. The intensive nature of Chinese Culture
2. The cosmic wheel and its implications
3. The society of Heaven and Earth
4. Ancestor worship

II

The Life of Confucius

III

The Confucian Doctrines
1. "Ancestor Worship"
2. "Filial Piety"
3. "The Golden Mean"
4. The "Princely Man," or Gentleman

    (a) Racial self-satisfaction
    (b) Refinement of manner
    (c) Religious tolerance
    (d) The life of harmony with nature

Chapter 3

THE "GENTLEMAN" OF CONFUCIUS

I

The Social and Intellectual Background of Confucian Teaching

Some orientation is necessary for the understanding of the Confucian concept of value. It is essential to know something of the background of that civilization which made itself vocal through the lips of Confucius. Basically, it was a civilization quite dissimilar to our own, and this different outlook on life is what we must try to comprehend if we are to profit by the Confucian philosophy.

China represents the longest historical life achieved by any nation in recorded time. It was contemporary with the civilizations of Babylon, Egypt, and Persia and of all that lie between. It has existed in an organized form for more than five thousand years. While these five thousand years undoubtedly wrought many changes in her internal order, it may easily be true that the transitions in Chinese life during the past century, or even in the last fifty years, are greater in their significance than those that took place in the previous fifty centuries.

If China was not herself the site of the earliest appearance of civilization, so far as we have any records, she was at least very close to it, and profoundly affected by it. Her history must have been modified by her geographical position behind high mountain ranges, bordering on the widest ocean and yet vulnerable to attack from such as were willing or able to approach her across the deserts of Central Asia. It was from this direction that she was frequently invaded, and usually by people of intrepid daring to whom the desert was a home rather than a handicap. The influx of peoples from the west found her able to meet the succeeding crises in but one way; that was the way of absorption rather than retreat. European history, on the other hand, was the story of warlike tribes crowding each other in successive waves farther and farther west. In China, though some of her people probably found their way to the American hemisphere, there was no possibility of mass migration in that direction. China became like a deep pool in a fast flowing stream, revolving upon itself, increasing in population to the starving point, trying its resources to the limit. Under such crowding only one way of survival was possible, assimilation: to live in harmony both with one's neighbors and in harmony with earth and sea and sky and air from which it was necessary to gain one's living. The concept of harmony became the practical philosophy of the Chinese, and perhaps their great contribution to history.

It is easy to envision a society under such conditions taking on certain marked characteristics. It would profit from the absorption of the daring and adventurous peoples who attacked and entered it. The transfusion of such blood into an older culture would likely favor an early progress in the arts and sciences. It would, further, become a land of traditions as one layer of culture imposed itself upon or was assimilated by another. Places, but not peoples, do not change, and every cave and mountain, river and lake, would inevitably become incrusted with tradition, myth, and legend from an earlier time. Even newcomers would not permanently resist the propitiation of the local gods under conditions of fear or famine, and before long would be identifying themselves with the local population. The rapid assimilation by China of foreign peoples is one of the truisms of history. In the earlier days of Western penetration, so set were the customs and also the costumes, that the foreigner appeared to disturb the harmony of heaven and earth, which seemed to the Chinese so necessary to success. The only way to work and live in China was to adopt the Chinese ways. And this was, and still is, quite easy to do, as those who live in China for a time find difficulty in readapting themselves to the Western manner of life after return home. China seems to be as much an atmosphere of living as it is a place, and there are few who can live there long without absorbing the Chinese state of mind.

The strict limitations of arable land would not only lead to intensive cultivation but would have a tendency to concentrate family life, since it would be more and more difficult for the younger members of the family to find maintenance in new fields. Clinging to the parental shelter intensifies the family life and increases the parental authority. Thus the oldest member of the family, having the highest claim to the patrimony, became the autocrat of the household, and the fathers of families came to rule the village, which was autonomous in itself. The father was held responsible not only for the support of his family but also for any crimes they might commit, since it was held that a good father would not be the parent of an evil son. Within the house the authority was the oldest woman, grandmother or first wife who ruled the other wives, concubines, daughters and daughters-in-law in a way that was frequently akin to slavery. Each woman knew, however, that if she could only live long enough she would succeed to the rule of others and have her day. The most distant relationships were recognized in cases of misfortune, disaster, debt, hunger, clothing, family honor, or even the education of those members who showed promise of intellectual capacity. Under the circumstances it may be argued that the individual became lost in his family, but while this was true it was also true that his reputation was as good as that of his family, and he was surrounded with the security of numbers.

The Chinese merchant takes little pains, in extending credit, to look up your personal accountability, but judges your reliability by your family, your firm, or your institutional connections. If these are good, he is satisfied, and seems to put no limit on the extent of confidence in you. Furthermore you will not be required to settle in full until the ensuing New Year's Day. Then the account must be settled either by you or by your family, for all of them are considered responsible. The Chinese family feels such an accountability for the debts of its members. It is said that frequently the harassed debtor goes about on New Year's Day with a lighted lantern, to bear out the fiction that day has not yet dawned. If he cannot settle he loses "face," and suicide is the appropriate end. Such were the conditions of the Chinese pride of family, his sense of social obligation, his fear of losing "face." Not only must he honor the living, he owed an obligation to ancestors who had honorably borne his name in the past, and had established for him a standing in society, on which he was dependent for life, happiness, and success. This tradition was dramatized and fostered by the system known as "ancestor worship." "Honor thy father and thy mother" has scarcely come so near to being a living commandment as in China.

The crowded, and of necessity regulated, life made imperative an intense and comprehensive system of etiquette, of personal dress and behavior. This fact presents us with the reason why Confucius concerned himself so much with "form," the rites and ceremonies of dress and conduct. Only so, among a crowded people, could appropriate order be obtained. In official life, and especially about the court, it was possible, by failure in dress, and in courtesy, to give offense that would draw severe and even capital punishment. Where such was the case, respect for manners became a matter of meticulous attention. The late Dowager Empress Tsu Tze is said to have stopped all receptions in the Great Hall of the Palace, where the foreign embassies were customarily received, because an American woman was observed fingering the draperies and inquiring about their probable cost. One friend, brought up in the Forbidden City, informed me that he had never seen the Empress, because whenever the Herald announced her approach, the children had immediately to turn their faces to the wall. Peeking would have been promptly and severely punished. Anything like direct contact would have been unthinkable. With the intense congestion of population, inadvertent contact, or undue familiarity, could best be avoided only if one's rank was indicated in his garb. With this apparel went also the accompanying formality which was driven into one from childhood. In the Chinese system, the education of the brightest in each household became the obligation of the whole family, even to the remote cousins, since education was the way to official recognition and promotion that raised the standing of the family. Political preferment came to those who passed the state examinations, and the knowledge of etiquette by such was a matter of supreme importance. With education and good manners, governmental position, next in rank to that of the Emperor, was a possibility for the child of the humblest family. There was more in this than mere form. The ceremonies had a symbolic moral and even religious significance. Each gesture, the tone of the voice, the manner of walk, the grace in kotowing before the Emperor or magistrate, the cut and trimming of the dress, which had to conform to the occasion, all these were officially prescribed. In view of the religious character of such ceremonies, any accidental oversight might mean demotion or disgrace, and wilful disobedience might lead to execution. So from the Emperor down to the lowest official in the state, courtesy became a matter of prime consideration. It was not strange that under such a regime, the Chinese interpretation of "the Gentleman" took on a character never realized to such an extent elsewhere.

Upon the firm basis of the family and village life the Empire was erected. Families and villages governed themselves without interference from the central authority so long as they provided the necessary taxes to province and Empire. The Jeffersonian dictum, that the best governed state was the least governed, came close to being exemplified. The average citizen had little care as to who might be the ruling Emperor so long as the tax was not excessive nor was he moved when one dynasty of rulers was thrown out and another came in. Whoever was Emperor had, however, the obligation of propitiating Heaven, and keeping serene the harmony of Heaven and Earth, for upon this depended the prosperity of the state. Should war, famine, or flood arise, it was taken as direct evidence that the ruler had not satisfactorily performed the sacrifices and that Heaven now indicated that his time was up. He could then be deposed or even executed. A ready illustration is to be found in the career of the last Ming Emperor. Opposite the College of Chinese Studies in Peking, where once stood the Imperial Palace, there still remain the ruins of an ancient temple. In the disorders that preceded the overthrow of his dynasty, the Emperor resorted to this temple, that in this sacred place he might ascertain what was the will of Heaven. As the father of a family in China is held responsible for the acts of his descendants, so the

THE BINARY WHEEL OF YANG AND YIN
With The Eight Trigrams

YANG (Represented by White)		YIN (Represented by Black)
HEAVEN		EARTH
ACTIVE		PASSIVE
LIGHT		DARKNESS
HEAT		COLD
EXPANSION		CONTRACTION
MASCULINE		FEMININE
GOOD		BAD
SUMMER		WINTER
ABOVE		BELOW
FRONT SEAT		BACK SEAT
JOY		DISTRESS
WEALTH		POVERTY
LIFE		DEATH

The Binary Wheel which, derived from India, was substituted by Laõtze for the more ancient Quinary, or five-spoke Wheel, illustrates the cyclical concept of History. Opposites represented eventual balance, and Harmony and History and Life were seen as constant repetitions. The Supreme Unity, having differentiated itself into Heaven and Earth, acts through the rotation of Yang and Yin. The chronological period represented may be the season of the year, or a cycle of thirty years, the period of a life, or of a dynasty. Unbroken lines represent Yang, broken ones, Yin. According to the period in which dates of birth, etc, fell, general success or failure was forecasted.

Emperor, as the father of the nation, was presumed in default of duty if any misfortune befell his people. Famine, pestilence, drought, flood, domestic disorder, or invasion, would be held as springing from his failure to keep the harmony of Heaven and Earth. He himself was assumed to be the Son of Heaven, and if calamities befell the state it could only indicate his impiety. In the attitude of prayer, then, he visited the temple, to decide by the drawing of lots whether Heaven was really angry. The lot being adverse, he went out and committed suicide.

The insistence upon harmony went to extremes. All innovation was frowned upon as discordant and evil. Such changes as occurred in nature were observed as routine and recurring, and were therefore not to be considered innovations. All life, industry, and government were like the rising and setting of the sun, the waxing and waning of the moon, the return of the seasons of the year. What appeared as change was only illusion, the cyclic ebb and flow of what was really an eternally static world. The changes in history and in personal life yielded the same interpretations. One was born, grew in strength, and faded out in old age. Sickness was followed by health, failure by success, poverty by riches as surely as the rise and fall of the tide, the recurrence of night and morning, summer and winter, dry and wet, sweet and sour. These opposites composed the whole reality of life and there was nothing much the individual could do about it except to wait with complacency for the change of fortune that was clearly on the way. If in hardship, one must not be too downcast since better times were coming; if in success, not too overelated because hard times would come again. Life was to follow the Golden Mean, no over-exultation, no over-despair, nothing in excess. Might not this outlook on history and life have been due to conditions of congestion, with a growing opposition to innovation which would make necessary drastic changes, and the upsetting of the common ways? As successive waves of migration swept in from the west, there was nothing to do but to accept them as fate, or the will of Heaven. As the Son of Heaven, the reigning Emperor was held entitled to world-wide empire. The throne was the center of the world, and from it radiated all power and dominion. There were five points of the compass, but the throne represented the place from which all sprang. This they had symbolized in a five-spoked wheel, but when the Buddhists came in with the Binary Wheel, that seemed to them an even more appropriate symbol of life and the Empire with its changing fortune of good and evil. The Buddhists applied it to the calendar, to the various periods of time, months, years, lifetimes, or dynasties, as the case might be, and from it were thought able to foretell lucky days and lucky ventures. Into society of this kind came Confucius, and in it his teaching was exemplified for twenty-five hundred years.

II

The Life of Confucius

Out of such a background, Confucius was born, about 551 B.C. His life was contemporary with that of the prophets Ezekiel and Daniel in Palestine, with Solon and Pythagoras in Greece, and with Buddha in India. In addition to the strong social influences that dominated his life in the customs we have been considering, China at this time was in a state of turmoil, such as seems to have characterized the rest of the civilized world of that age. It was the hour of the break-up of the older feudal system in China, a time when there was continual strife among the small principalities that made up the Empire. The central power was weak and civil war invaded not only the Empire itself but the smaller states as well, while bandits and guerrillas, military leaders, and upstart nobles tried in turn to seize the power. This internal turmoil was destined to have grave effect upon the teachings of Confucius as well as upon the course of his life.

Though he was born in poverty, his father having died when the boy was but three years old, he came of a family originally noble, and could trace his ancestry back through centuries, even as today we know who is his direct living descendant. His relatives were interested in giving him an education, and so he became one of that group of scholars who, as *Ju,* were trained to become counsellors to the ruling officials of the state. Confucius can be best understood in the light of this, his calling, and the political and social conditions which he felt delegated to remedy. Though he has been often charged with being a callous formalist, and a "die-hard" for the old ways, to put that interpretation upon him is to miss the more important elements in his character and teaching. He saw that the essential thing in China was, as strangely like it is today, to bring harmony between discordant factions. To his mind this could best be done by appeal to the great past, when the Empire was in its glory, a time of great traditions and progress. And when we consider the height of civilization which had been previously reached it should have been a spectacle to thrill and inspire the greatest patriotism. In his judgment, if there was ever again to be law and order it must be by the re-introduction of the orderly customs of other days. This lay also in no formal observance of ceremonies, for the observance of ceremonies could be effectual only as it sprang out of the hearts, the inner consciousness, loves, and feelings of the people. Lip-service would never do, and against that he was continually fighting. Failure to appreciate this element in Confucius has led to much misunderstanding of his message. Take, for instance, his description of the Gentleman, the "superior" man, the "princely" man, or the "real" man as the term is variously interpreted. He consistently held that his actions were effective only as they were sincere. For this reason the term "Gentleman" has been chosen in this work, as being as satisfactory as any, though none of them seems quite adequate. We use the term in its highest sense, as used in America to represent the man of good manners, of self-forgetting and invariable courtesy, of unquestionable honesty and integrity, of profound sympathy and simplicity of heart, devoid of egotism, and broadly tolerant, free from vulgarity. Our common expression for such a man is to call him a "Christian Gentleman," sometimes adding, as Confucius surely would have had he lived in our time, "A Gentleman of the Old School," whose like we shall not see again. This seems to be the picture that Confucius attempted to draw of the Gentleman. He would, of course, observe all the formalities of polite intercourse, but he could never do this if his heart, his religious devotion were not in it. The mere formalist would always disclose himself as a boor in fact by some rudeness, some unexpected slip that would give the lie to all his ceremoniousness. To love one's neighbor in truth was, with him, the truest way to strict courtesy. Only the devout man, then, could in Confucius' opinion measure up to the standard. Devoutness included a rightful respect for the past, for the approved institutions of society, for the rules by which men lived, for those customs and laws which made organized society possible. These laws were scarcely enforceable by violence, they must first be written in the hearts of men. If there were self-control and harmony within the person, these would find their outworking in society at large. If the hearts of men were unruly and contentious then there was little hope for the Great Society. He conceived the order of society to spring primarily from the quality of the persons who composed it. His various teachings can be truly interpreted only in the light of this concept. Inner harmony was assisted by having always the right thing, the rhythm and harmony of music, the ritual, to put one in true and proper relations and perspective with his fellow men. The essence of the Confucian ethics has been said to be the search for the best in one's own nature, and steadfast devotion to the ideal. A true and proper understanding of the term "person," would fit exactly Confucius' ideal of the Gentleman. In the pursuit of this ideal, since the individual does not know yet what he may become, let him aim at the impossible: "The true person knows that a thing cannot be done, and yet wants to do it."

So outstanding was Confucius' teaching that he soon gathered about him a band of disciples and was said at one time to have had as many as three thousand studying under him. Since his calling was that of adviser to the rulers of the state, he spent most of his life in wandering from one province to another hoping to be called into council. But his counsel was never crafty, and always honest and straightforward, which among men of plots and counterplots for power and position did not receive the recognition it deserved. Several political appointments he did receive, however, and in these achieved conspicuous success. Duke Ting of the province of Lu, Confucius' birthplace, made him the governor of the city of Chungtu. This Confucius made into a model city. So successful was he in governing that it was said that after three months the butchers no longer adulterated the meat (an easy task in China where the meat is commonly cut into small bits before consumption), lost articles in the streets were not carried off, and visiting strangers felt at home. He was rapidly promoted, first to the office of Public Works, and later to Chief Minister. The growing strength of the province of Lu under Confucius' direction began to alarm the rulers of the neighboring province of Ch'i, so that they began to plot against him. Appointing an inter-provincial conference, the ruler of Ch'i came with a great band of mummers and dancers. This was too much for the gravity of Confucius, who demanded to know the reason for the presence of "these barbarian musicians," when the rulers were celebrating a peace conference, and demanded their dismissal. When musicians and dancers refused to leave, he stepped forward and declared that common people who thus attempted to corrupt their rulers were deserving of death, and the master of ceremonies had them executed. Thus Confucius gained the reputation of being incorruptible. This was not, however, the end of plots against him. Eventually the people of Ch'i made a present to the Duke of Lu, of eighty dancing girls and a hundred and twenty horses, and, so taken up with them was the Duke that he forgot the annual sacrifices to Heaven, which were deemed necessary to ward off calamity from the state. At this sign of weakness on the part of the ruler Confucius departed in disgust.

The remainder of his life was, much of it, given to wandering from state to turbulent state, meeting with many rebuffs and many adventures. He refused to remain in the province of Wei because he discovered himself the subject of military espionage, but later returning, received a letter from the Queen, Nancia, that if he wished to be friends with the King he must call on her. This he did with the most approved chasteness. A little later it fell to his lot to ride in a parade behind the carriage of the King and Queen. To his aversion, the Queen, of loose reputation, drew all the attention of the crowd, whereupon he remarked: "I have never seen people attracted by virtuous scholars as they are by beautiful women." Contemplating a visit to the province of Chin, he learned, before crossing the border, that the reigning Duke had put to death two of his wisest counsellors, and refused to enter, saying: "I have heard that when people disembowel embryos, or kill the young, the unicorn refuses to appear in the countryside; when people drain a pond in order to catch fish, the dragon refuses to bring the *yin* and *yang* principles into harmony (the forerunner of famine or flood); when they snatch birds' nests and break bird eggs, the phoenix declines to come. And why? Because a gentleman avoids those who kill their own kind. If even the birds and beasts avoid the unrighteous, why should I not do the same?"

His complete honesty and untarnished sincerity could not win favor on the part of those who hoped to profit by dishonesty and indirection, and they therefore feared him. At one time, Duke Chao of Ch'i, impressed by his service to the state, proposed to give him a holding of land which would have provided him with the standing he deserved, but a jealous courtier poisoned the mind of the Duke. "The *Ju*," said he, "are bad models to follow. Their doctrines should hardly be applied to the people because of their adherence to the ancient burial customs which are very costly. They make bad rulers because they wander around begging. With the decline of the great imperial dynasty of Chou our rituals and music are largely forgotten, and now this fellow comes proposing their re-instatement. Let us not change the customs of the country again." With such persuasion, the courtier won out.

Confucius finally returned to Lu, his home province, and settled down to teaching and writing. From this work came what are known as the Five Classics: The Book of Songs; The Book of History; The Book of Changes; The Book of Spring and Autumn; The Book of Rites. These form the body of his historic learning, being his comments on events, principles, and customs. The Spring and Autumn chronicles cover the period of the twelve Dukes of Lu from 722 B.C. to 481 B.C. The other Four Books were the work of his disciples.

In his early career Confucius had spent much time in the study of the rites and ceremonies which he held to be largely responsible for the success of the great Chou Empire. He was fond of music and the composer of songs, as the promotion of music seemed to him the way to that inner harmony which was necessary to the true gentleman. We find him playing an instrument and singing or composing songs in the most critical and trying moments of life. His teachings were summarized in four principles: the study of literature, of human conduct, of being true to one's self, and of honesty in human relationships. He denounced four attitudes: arbitrariness of opinion, dogmatism, narrow-mindedness, and egotism. Surely we have here one of the great counsels of human perfection, reminding us of the words of the Jewish prophet: "What doth the Lord require of thee, but to do justly, and to love mercy, and to walk humbly with thy God."

Even the greatness of his life and teaching did not save him from that sense of frustration that comes to every leader of the world's thought. He could not understand why counsels so just should be so unwelcome, for it was difficult for him to understand why the ideals of any man should be less than his own. Visited in his last illness by one of his disciples he sang:

> The mountain is crumbling down
> The pillar is falling.
> The philosopher is passing away.

His wonder at the callousness of the world to his supreme message was then expressed in weeping, as he exclaimed: "The world has long been living in moral chaos, and no ruler has followed me." His judgment on the success of his life was all out of proportion to the facts. He could not see nor know how much greater it was to be than anything he could dream, for his social and moral maxims were to dominate the minds of uncounted millions of men who were to come after him. They were so great that they became formative in Chinese civilization, and came to take a place in the lives of the Chinese from the Emperor down to the last and least of the coolie class. Rare is the Chinese who has not many of his sayings by heart as the directive of social conduct. His sayings, written into The Classics, formed the basis of the civil examinations, to which every Chinese scholar aspired. In the great temple of Confucius or rather in the Halls of Examination adjacent to that temple in Peking, his words are carved in stone, and it was required of successful contestants that they be able to repeat them all from memory. Civil service reform was thus to strike China some millenia before being taken up by our own government. Place in the state was governed by one's success in the examination, and the way was opened for any citizen of brains and persistence to qualify for the highest position short of that of the Emperor. Nowhere in the world has scholarship and the refinements of the true gentleman been held in such favor as in China, and that this is so was due in great measure to the astounding influence of Confucius.

III

The Confucian Doctrines

There have been Chinese mystics, such as Lao-tse, Mo-ti, and Chuang-tse, and it is possible to argue the presence of mysticism on the part of Confucius because of his faith in the rule of the Heavenly Powers. This characteristic is usually lost sight of in the practical realism of his maxims. The influence of this mood makes the average Chinese appear hardheaded and unsentimental to the Westerner. The Chinese has sentiments, but he does not often display them to the public gaze.

1. "ANCESTOR WORSHIP." First among the teachings of Confucius must be considered the reverence for ancestors, which sprang from the peculiar development of family life and led to a high regard for the past. In no other country is such respect paid to age. The older one is, the more he is revered and listened to. The counsel of the old was not only hung upon, but it was slavishly obeyed by the younger generation. Age was placed before wisdom, and to question the advice of the oldest was something like sacrilege. Under such conditions the son would act wisely by imitating most closely his father, or even better, his grandfather, and the golden age of man's achievement seemed inevitably to have been in the past. The effect of such a viewpoint upon invention, initiative, and new enterprise is at once apparent. To attempt anything new would be for the individual

to assume himself to be wiser than his ancestors, and would make him despised by his relatives and neighbors. The discoverer of alcohol received capital punishment for the innovation. Confucius undoubtedly found this hostility to novelty a fixed idea in the minds of his people, and considering it a help to law and order, he took pains to foster the notion.

2. "FILIAL PIETY." Filial piety became naturally one of the main tenets of his teaching. This for two reasons: one was the effect upon the state, just mentioned; the other was to be found in the development of the individual.

As to the *first reason,* we have already seen how the maintenance of public morals lay in the hands of the old men, the father of the family or the elders of the village. If a member of his family committed a crime it was the duty of the father to punish even to the imposition of the death penalty. Only in case he did nothing was the matter taken up by the elders of the village and then might require the extinction of the whole family since all would appear involved in an equal guilt. It was necessary for the village thus to clear itself, for it was assumed that a bad son had behind him a bad father and a bad family. So the teaching of Confucius concerning filial piety was first of all an effort after an orderly government. The family system of China was doubtless the chief source of her long maintained organized history. Not only so, but the system prepared the way for the reception of democracy. Each family enjoyed an autonomy within itself, ruled by its oldest member. This was certain in most cases to be benevolent, as it was dictated by the love of parents for their children. The village was but a replica of the family, for here the communal interests were entrusted to the patriarchs of the village. The families in many instances were so intermarried that the village was indistinguishable from a tribe or clan. Perhaps no nearer approach to democracy could be had under an absolutist government. The Emperor was satisfied, so long as local order was maintained and the requisite revenues were produced at the hand of the provincial governor who was to be seen largely in the light of a tax collector. This family and village autonomy gave to every person, not an outlaw, representation and a large degree of freedom. For this reason, China was, perhaps, of all despotisms the best prepared to enter on a fully representative government. The point of greatest weakness would of course be where local autonomy is swallowed up in the congested population of great cities.

The *second reason* for the teaching of filial piety was, however, individual. Veneration for parents was not only surety for public order, it was likewise the source of that individual self-restraint, reverence, and courtesy which were fundamental to personal character, the character of the superior, or princely man, or perhaps as we in America use the term, the gentleman.

In observance of filial piety the son must not change any of the ways of doing things for three years after the father's death, and must meticulously observe, so far as he could guess them, what the wishes of that father would be. "If the son for three years does not alter from the way of his father, he may be called 'filial' " (*Analects,* Bk. IV, xx). "A youth when at home should be filial, and abroad respectful to his elders" (*ibid.,* I, vi). "He sacrificed to the dead as if they were present. He sacrificed to the spirits as if the spirits were present" (*ibid.,* III, xii). "In serving his parents a son may remonstrate with them, but gently; when he sees they do not incline to follow his advice, he shows an increased degree of reverence, but does not abandon his purpose; and should they punish him, he does not allow himself to murmur" (*ibid.,* IV, xviii).

3. "THE GOLDEN MEAN." The golden mean, nothing in excess, was the outward or formal aspect of the gentleman of Confucius, and he thus defined it: "Where the solid qualities are in excess of accomplishments, we have rusticity; where the accomplishments are in excess of the solid qualities, we have the manners of a clerk. When the accomplishments and the solid qualities are equally blended, we then have the gentleman" (*ibid.,* VI, xvi). Here his great emphasis was upon propriety. Civilized society establishes forms and ceremonies to protect itself from the overweening, the selfish, the greedy. Decorum is necessary in a crowded society. Why do we make our meals at home a sort of sacrament with spotless linen, appropriate dishes, and that height of good taste, a prayer of thanksgiving to the Giver of all good. These may be looked upon as a mere formality. It is possible to snatch food from a common pot, to devour it from the hand, and to crowd the less favored from the dish. Food so eaten satisfies hunger, but it offends certain finer and more essential instincts of the gentleman. Why all this formality? Because the self-restraint of civilization denotes superiority of conduct and is a protection for those who would otherwise be imposed upon. One must not only have regard for his own ap-

petite, but he must eat in such a way as not to disgust and repel others. The formalities of social intercourse are based not on aristocratic feelings, but really upon the democratic principle of common rights. Good table manners may lie at the root of good citizenship. In all his associations, then, the gentleman would exercise self-restraint, and out of it would grow reverence for orderly living, respect for others, and respect for one's self, that gift so necessary to success. Therefore Confucius taught the importance of the golden mean—self-restraint, nothing to excess. "He who aims to be a complete man of virtue in his food does not seek to gratify his appetite, nor in his dwelling-place does he seek appliances of ease" [such as overstuffed furniture?] (*ibid.*, I, xiv). "The gentleman does not set his mind either for anything or against anything. What is right he will follow" (*ibid.*, IV, x). "When agreements are made according to what is right, what is spoken can be made good. When respect is shown according to what is proper, one keeps far from shame and disgrace. When the parties upon whom a man leans are proper persons to be intimate with, he can make them his guides and masters" (*ibid.*, I, xiii).

4. THE "PRINCELY MAN," OR GENTLEMAN. All these teachings are really summed up in the Confucian description of the gentleman.

The gentleman was the possessor of poise. "He feels no discomposure though men take no note of him" (*ibid.*, I, iii). "He is a profound thinker who looks past appearances to the root of the matter" (*ibid.*, II, ii). He is "serious-minded, faithful, sincere and having no friends not equal to himself" (*ibid.*, I, viii). He does not indulge inordinate appetite for food, is careful in his speech, and frequents the company of men of principle (*ibid.*, I, xiv). Though poor he is cheerful, and though rich he loves the rules of propriety (*ibid.*, I, xv, 1). He entertains no depraved thoughts (*ibid.*, II, ii). He is progressive: at fifteen, bent on learning; at thirty, steadfast; at forty, still believing; at fifty, acknowledging the decrees of Heaven; at sixty, open-minded; at seventy, so self-disciplined that he could do anything he wants and still do nothing wrong (*ibid.*, II, iv). He does not do to others what he would not wish others to do to him (*ibid.*, V, xi). He is a man who, in his eager pursuit of knowledge, forgets his food, who, in the joy of its attainment, forgets his sorrows, and who does not perceive that old age is coming on (*ibid.*, VIII, xviii,

2). He seeks to achieve an all-pervading unity within himself (*ibid.*, XV, ii, 3), spends a lifetime in prayer (*ibid.*, VII, xxxiv), and is a good sportsman: in fishing he does not fish with a net, and in hunting he waits for the game to flush.

The gentleman has nine principles which are the subject of thoughtful consideration. "In regard to the use of his eyes, he is anxious to see clearly; in regard to his ears he is anxious to hear distinctly. In regard to his countenance he is anxious that it should be benign. In regard to demeanor, he is anxious that it should be respectful. In regard to his speech, he is anxious that it should be sincere. In regard to the conduct of business, he is anxious that it should be reverently careful. In regard to his doubts, he is anxious to question others. When he is angry, he reminds himself of the difficulties in which unrestrained anger may involve him. When he sees a chance for gain he remembers righteousness" (*ibid.*, XVI, x). Gravity, generosity of soul, sincerity, earnestness, and kindness, these are the marks of a gentleman (*ibid.*, XVII, vi).

How the Confucian picture of the gentleman came to take so leading a part in Chinese thought will seem puzzling to us unless we refer to the graphic nature of his descriptions. What he really does is to present "action patterns" for men to follow, so that those who become acquainted with his teaching naturally compare their conduct with that of his perfect gentleman. There is in it something akin to the ideographic character of the Chinese language, which should by its nature be the language most vividly to motivate to action since it pictures the act. The whole of Chinese life has been affected by the concept of the gentleman. Western ways and manners must in many respects seem crude to the cultured Chinese, and especially American aggressiveness, which, too often, does not hesitate to barge into any situation where its interests are at stake. This race who think of themselves as gentlemen are justly proud of their old civilization, compared with which ours appears to them a mushroom growth. It also tends to make them a bit self-sufficient and self-satisfied even when those qualities are not apparent in their demeanor. The self-restraint required of the gentleman of the Chinese school induces an uncommon refinement of manner, a quiet and unobtrusive demeanor, and a deference to others too often misunderstood by the Westerner. The concept leads also to a great tolerance of contrasting ideas, shown particularly in their welcome to foreign religions. Christianity, Buddhism, Taoism, have at times threatened to become dominant over Confucianism, and all have been met with but sporadic signs of persecution. The attitude of the Chinese gentleman toward family and birthplace has increased the sense of modesty, and relationship to the larger order of things, and reduced his egoism. Out of that very landscape from which he sprang into life he hopes to return. For this reason he seeks to return to the place of his childhood to die, and will go to extremes to have his ashes returned to the dust from which they came. One can occasionally see runners starting out from such a city as Peking, bearing coffins to distant parts of the interior, with "soul chickens" resting in cages on top, so that if in the long journey the soul of the deceased should be inclined to wander away from the body, the roosters who sing their matinals at the most appropriate hour of the morning may call it back. So deep is the Chinese gentleman's feeling for nature and ancestors and his place of birth. All these things go to make up the harmony which the true man seeks within and without, for whatever is strange or unfitting, or inharmonious, cannot be pleasing in the sight of Heaven. He leaves undisturbed the family graves, even when they come to occupy more than half of his tillable field, and within them rest the bones of ancestors beyond memory and beyond history. Thus the concept of the gentleman has given marked characteristics to a great people, from whom, if we are wise, we can learn much. For them, we shall hope most devoutly, the present impact of the West will not be so strong as to remove the finest and most gracious elements. In our cosmopolitan day, a knowledge of human values would be incomplete without some reference to the concepts of Confucius.

READINGS

(Chapter 3)

CONFUCIUS: *THE FOUR BOOKS.* Selections from the translation of James Legge, Shanghai Book Company, Shanghai.

"FILIAL PIETY"

A youth when at home should be filial, and, abroad respectful to his elders. He should be earnest and truthful. He should overflow in love to all, and cultivate the friendship of the good. When he has time and opportunity, after the performance of these things, he should employ them in polite studies. *An.* Bk. I, vi.

While a man's father is alive, look at the bent of his will; when his father is dead, look at his conduct. If for three years he does not alter from the way of his father, he may be called filial. *An.* Bk. I, xi.

Asked what filial piety was, the Master said, "It is not being disobedient" . . . soon after, Fan Ch'ih said, "What did you mean?" . . . That parents, when alive, should be served according to propriety; that when dead, they should be buried according to propriety; and that they should be sacrificed to according to propriety. *An.* Bk. II, v.

The filial piety of nowadays means the support of one's parents. But dogs and horses likewise are able to do something in the way of support; —without reverence, what is there to distinguish the one support from the other? *An.* Bk. II, vii.

In serving his parents, a son may remonstrate with them, but gently; when he sees that they do not incline to follow his advice, he shows an increased degree of reverence, but does not abandon his purpose; and, should they punish him, he does not allow himself to murmur. *An.* Bk. IV, xviii.

While his parents are alive, the son may not go abroad to a distance. If he does go abroad, he must have a fixed place to which he goes. *An.* Bk. IV, xix.

The years of parents may by no means not be kept in the memory, as an occasion at once for joy and for fear. *An.* Bk. III, xxi.

The Duke of Sheh informed Confucius saying, "Among us here are those who may be styled upright in conduct. If their father have stolen a sheep, they will bear witness to the fact." Confucius said, "Among us, in our part of the country, those who are upright are different from this. The father conceals the misconduct of the son, and the son conceals the misconduct of the father. Uprightness is to be found in this." *An.* Bk. XIII, xviii.

"THE GOLDEN MEAN"

When agreements are made according to what is right, what is spoken can be made good. When respect is shown according to what is proper, one keeps far from shame and disgrace. When the parties upon whom a man leans are proper persons to be intimate with, he can make them his guides and masters. *An.* Bk. I, xiii.

The Master said, "He who aims to be a man of complete virtue in his food does not seek to gratify his appetite, nor in his dwelling place does he seek the appliances of ease; he is earnest in what he is doing, and careful in his speech; he frequents the company of men of principle that he may be rectified:—such a person may be said indeed to love to learn." *An.* Bk. I, xiv.

In festive ceremonies, it is better to be sparing than extravagant. In the ceremonies of mourning it is better that there be deep sorrow than a minute attention to observances. *An* Bk. III, iv. 3.

The gentleman, extensively studying all learning, and keeping himself under the restraint of the rules of propriety, may thus likewise not overstep what is right. *An.* Bk. VI, xxv.

Perfect is the virtue, which is according to the Constant Mean! Rare for a long time has been its practice among the people. *An.* Bk. VI, xxvii.

Respectfulness, without the rules of propriety, becomes laborious bustle; carefulness, without the rules of propriety, becomes timidity; boldness, without the rules of propriety, becomes insubordination; straightforwardness without the rules of propriety, becomes rudeness. *An.* Bk. VIII, ii, 1.

There are three principles of conduct which the man of high rank should consider especially important:—that in his deportment and manner he keep from violence and heedlessness; that in regulating his countenance he keep near to sincerity; and that in his words and tones he keep far from lowness and impropriety. *An.* Bk. VIII, iv. 3.

It is by the Rules of Propriety that the character is established. *An.* Bk. VIII, 2.

Shih goes beyond the due mean, and Shang does not come up to it. Which is superior?

The Master said: "To go beyond is as wrong as to fall short." *An.* Bk. XI, xv.

There is nothing more visible than what is secret, and nothing more manifest than what is minute. Therefore the superior man is watchful over himself, when he is alone.

Let the states of equilibrium and harmony exist in perfection, and a happy order will prevail throughout heaven and earth, and all things will be nourished and flourish.

When one cultivates to the utmost the principles of his nature, and exercises them on the principle of reciprocity, he is not far from the path. What you do not like when done to yourself, do not do to others. *The Doctrine of the Mean*, XIII, 3.

The gentleman does what is proper to the station in which he is; he does not desire to go beyond this.

In a position of wealth and honor, he does what is proper to a position of wealth and honor. In a poor and low position, he does what is proper to a poor and low position. Situated among barbarous tribes, he does what is proper to a situation among barbarous tribes. In a position of sorrow and difficulty, he does what is proper to a position of sorrow and difficulty. The gentleman can find himself in no situation in which he is not himself.

In a high situation, he does not treat with contempt his inferiors. In a low situation he does not court the favor of his superiors. He rectifies himself, and seeks for nothing from others, so that he has no dissatisfactions. He does not murmur against Heaven or grumble against men.

Thus it is that the gentleman is quiet and calm waiting for the appointments of Heaven, while the mean man walks in dangerous paths, looking for lucky occurrences.

In archery we have something like the way of the gentleman. When the archer misses the center of the target, he turns round and seeks for the cause of his failure in himself. *The Doctrine of the Mean*, XIV, 1-5.

"THE GENTLEMAN"

Four Characteristics of a Gentleman

In his conduct, he was humble; in serving his superior, he was respectful; in nourishing the people, he was kind; in ordering the people he was just. *An.* Bk. V, xv.

In the Book of Poetry are three hundred pieces, but the design of them all may be embraced in one sentence: "Having no depraved thoughts." *An.* Bk. II, ii.

I do not know how a man without truthfulness is to get on. How can a large carriage be made to go without the cross-bar for yoking the oxen to, or a small carriage without the arrangement for yoking the horses? *An.* Bk. II, xxii.

To see what is right and not to do it is want of courage. *An.* Bk. II, xxiv, 2.

It is only the (truly) virtuous man, who can love, or who can hate others.

If the will be set on virtue, there will be no practice of wickedness.

I have not seen a person who loved virtue, or one who hated what was not virtuous. He who loved virtue would esteem nothing above it. He who hated what is not virtuous, would practice virtue in such a way that he would not allow anything that is not virtuous to approach his person.

Is any one able for one day to apply his strength to virtue? I have not seen the case in which his strength would be insufficient.

The faults of men are characteristic of the class to which they belong. By observing a man's faults, it may be known that he is virtuous. *An.* Bk. IV, vi, vii.

The superior man thinks of virtue; the small man thinks of comfort. The superior man thinks of the sanctions of law; the small man thinks of favors which he may receive. *An.* Bk. IV, xi.

The mind of the superior man is conversant with righteousness; the mind of the mean man is conversant with gain. *An.* Bk. IV, xvi.

Virtue is not left to stand alone. He who practices it will have neighbors. *An.* Bk. IV, xxv.

Some one said, "Yung is truly virtuous, but he is not ready with his tongue."

The Master said, "What is the good of being ready with the tongue? They who encounter men with smartnesses of speech for the most part procure for themselves hatred. I know not whether he be truly virtuous, but why should he show readiness of the tongue?" *An.* Bk. V, iv, 1, 2.

Man is born for uprightness. If a man lose his uprightness, and yet live, his escape from death is the effect of mere good fortune. *An.* Bk. VI, xvii.

The man of virtue makes the difficulty to be overcome his first business, and success only a subsequent consideration:—this may be called perfect virtue. *An.* Bk. VI, xx.

The man of perfect virtue, wishing to be established himself, seeks also to establish others; wishing to be enlarged himself, he seeks also to enlarge others.

To be able to judge of others by what is in ourselves:—this may be called the art of virtue. *An.* Bk. VI, xxviii, 2, 3.

Heaven produced the virtue that is in me. Hwan T'ui—what can he do to me? *An.* Bk. VII, xxii.

Is virtue a thing remote? I wish to be virtuous, and lo! virtue is at hand. *An.* Bk. VII, xxix.

Yen Yuan asked about perfect virtue.

The Master said, "To subdue one's self and return to propriety, is perfect virtue. If a man can for one day subdue himself and return to propriety, all under heaven will ascribe perfect virtue to him. Is the practice of perfect virtue from a man himself, or is it from others?"

Yen Yuan said, "I beg to ask the steps of that process."

The Master replied: "Look not at what is contrary to propriety."

Chung-Kung asked about perfect virtue. The Master said, "It is, when you go abroad, to behave to every one as if you were receiving a great guest; to employ the people as if you were assisting at a great sacrifice; not to do to others as you would not wish done to yourself; to have no murmuring against you in the country, and none in the family."

The Gentleman has neither anxiety nor fear.

"Being without anxiety and fear," said Niu:— "does that constitute what we call the gentleman?"

The Master said, "When internal examination discovers nothing wrong, what is there to be anxious about, what is there to fear ?" *An.* Bk. XII, iv, 1, 2, 3.

Fan Ch'ih said, "I venture to ask how to exalt virtue, to correct cherished evil, and to discover delusions."

The Master said, "Truly a good question !"

"If doing what is to be done be made the first business and success a secondary consideration; is not this the way to exalt virtue? To assail one's own wickedness and not assail that of others; is not this the way to correct cherished evil? For a morning's anger to disregard one's own life, and involve that of his parents; is not this a case of delusion?" *An.* Bk. XII, xxi, 1, 2, 3.

Fan Ch'ih asked about perfect virtue. The Master said, "It is in retirement, to be sedately grave; in the management of business, to be reverently attentive; in intercourse with others, to be strictly sincere. Though a man go among rude, uncultivated tribes, these qualities may not be neglected." *An.* Bk. XIII, xix.

When the love of superiority, boasting, resentments, and covetousness are repressed, this may be deemed perfect virtue? The Master said, "This may be regarded as a difficult achievement." Bk. XIV, ii, 1.

He then added, "But what is the necessity for a complete man of the present day to have all these things? The man, who in the view of gain, thinks of righteousness; who in the view of danger is prepared to give up his life; and who does not forget an old agreement however far back it extends:—such a man may be reckoned a complete man." *An.* Bk. XIV, xiii, 1, 2.

He who does not anticipate attempts to deceive him, nor think beforehand of his not being believed, and yet apprehends these things readily (when they occur) ; is he not a man of superior worth? *An.* Bk. XIV, xxxiii.

The gentleman in everything considers righteousness to be essential. He performs it according to the rules of propriety. He brings it forth in humility. He completes it with sincerity. This is indeed a gentleman.

The gentleman is distressed by his want of ability. He is not distressed by men's not knowing him. *An.* Bk. XV, xvii, xviii.

What the gentleman seeks is in himself. What the mean man seeks is in others. The gentleman is dignified, but does not wrangle. He is sociable but not a partisan.

The gentleman does not promote a man simply on account of his words, nor does he put aside good words because of the man. *An.* Bk. XV, xx, xxi, xxii.

The Master said, "The object of the superior man is truth. Food is not his object. There is plowing:—even in that there is sometimes want. So with learning :—emolument may be found in it. The superior man is anxious lest he should not get truth; he is not anxious lest poverty should come upon him." *An.* Bk. XV, xxxi.

THE FIVE VIRTUES

He who puts on a face of stern firmness, while inwardly he is weak, is like one of the small, mean people:—yea is he not like the thief who breaks through, or climbs over a wall. *An.* Bk. XVII, xii.

Does the gentleman esteem valor? The Master said, "the gentleman holds righteousness to be of highest importance. A man in a superior situation, having valor without righteousness, will be guilty of insubordination; one of the lower people, having valor without righteousness, will commit robbery." *An.* Bk. XVII, xxiii.

Tsze-kung said, "Has the superior man his hatreds also?" The Master said, "He has his hatreds. He hates those who proclaim the evil of others. He hates the man who, being in a low station, slanders his superiors. He hates those who have valor merely, and are unobservant of propriety. He hates those who are forward and determined, and, at the same time, of contracted understanding." *An.* Bk. XVII, xxiv.

A man should say, "I am not concerned that I have no place, I am concerned how I may fit myself for one. I am not concerned that I am not known, I seek to be worthy to be known."

To be poor without murmuring is difficult. To be rich without being proud is easy. *An.* Bk. XIV, xi.

If a man withdraws his mind from the love of beauty, and applies it as sincerely to the love of the virtuous; if in serving his parents, he can exert his utmost strength; if in serving his prince, he can devote his life; if in his intercourse with his friends, his words are sincere:— although men say that he has not learned, I will certainly say that he has. *An.* Bk. I, vii.

The Master said, "At fifteen, I had my mind bent on learning.

At thirty, I stood firm.

At forty, I had no doubts.

At fifty, I knew the decrees of Heaven.

At sixty, my ear was an obedient organ for the reception of truth.

At seventy, I could follow what my heart desired, without transgressing what was right." *An.* Bk. II, iv, 1.

If a man keeps cherishing his old knowledge, so as continually to be acquiring new, he may be a teacher of others. *An.* Bk. II, xi.

Learning without thought is labor lost; thought without learning is perilous. *An.* Bk. II, xv.

The study of strange doctrines is injurious indeed. *An.* Bk. II, xvi.

Shall I teach you what knowledge is? When you know a thing, to hold that you know it; and when you do not know a thing, to allow that you do not know it:—this is knowledge. *An* Bk. II, xvii.

They who know the truth are not equal to those who love it, and they who love it are not equal to those who delight in it. *An.* Bk. VI, xviii.

The leaving virtue without proper cultivation: the not thoroughly discussing what is learned; not being able to move toward righteousness of which a knowledge is gained; and not being able to change what is not good:—these are the things which occasion my solicitude. *An*. Bk. VII, iii.

I do not open up the truth to one who is not eager to get knowledge, nor help out anyone who is not anxious to explain himself. When I have presented one corner of a subject to anyone, and he cannot from it learn the other three, I do not repeat my lesson. *An*. Bk. VII, viii.

The Duke of Sheh asked Tsze-lu about Confucius, and Tsze-lu did not answer him.

The Master said, "Why did you not say to him,—He is simply a man, who in his eager pursuit (of knowledge) forgets his food, who in the joy of its attainments forgets his sorrows, and who does not perceive that old age is coming on?" *An*. Bk. VII, xviii, 1, 2.

When I walk along with two others, they may serve me as my teachers. I will select their good qualities and follow them, their bad qualities and avoid them. *An*. Bk. VII, xxi.

There may be those who act without knowing why. I do not do so. Hearing much and selecting what is good and following it; seeing much and keeping it in memory:—this is the second style of knowledge. *An*. Bk. VII, xxvii.

Learn as if you could not reach your object, and were always fearing also lest you should lose it. *An* Bk. VIII, xvii.

Tsze-chang asked what constituted intelligence. The Master said, "He with whom neither slander that gradually soaks into the mind, nor statements that startle like a wound in the flesh, are successful, may be called intelligent indeed. Yea, he with whom neither soaking slander, nor startling statements, are successful, may be called farseeing." *An*. Bk. XII, vi.

What qualities must a man possess to entitle him to be called a scholar?

He must be thus,—earnest, urgent, and bland: among his friends, earnest and urgent; among his brethren, bland. *An*. Bk. XIII, xxviii.

The scholar who cherishes the love of comfort is not fit to be deemed a scholar. *An*. Bk. XIV, iii.

The determined scholar and the man of virtue will not seek to live at the expense of injuring their virtue. They will even sacrifice their lives to preserve their virtue complete. *An*. Bk. XV, viii.

How the flowers of the aspen-plum flutter and turn! Do I not think of you? But your house is distant. The Master said, "How is it distant?"[1] *An*. Bk. IX, xxx, 1, 2.

You love a man and wish him to live; you hate him and wish him

[1] Hughes: *Chinese Philosophy in Classical Times*, explains that the lover claims his love dwells continually on his beloved, but that her home is too far away for him to go to her.

Confucius declares that if he loved as deeply as he claimed, no distance would be too great to keep him from her.

to die. Having wished him to live, you also wish him to die. This is a case of delusion. (Meaning, real love does not change to hate.)

It may not be on account of her being rich (that you love her), yet you come to make a difference. *An.* Bk. XII, x, 1, 2.

Faithfully admonish your friend, and skillfully lead him on. If you find him impracticable, stop. Do not disgrace yourself. *An.* Bk. XII, xxiii.

The Gentleman on grounds of culture meets with his friends, and by their friendship helps his virtue. *An.* Bk. XII, xxiv.

He who requires much from himself and little from others, will keep himself from being the object of resentment. *An.* Bk. XV, xiv.

The Master said, "The superior man wishes to be slow in his speech and earnest in his conduct."

What I do not wish men to do to me, I also wish not to do to other men. *An.* Bk. V, xi.

The Master angled but did not use a net. He shot,—but not at birds perching. *An.* Bk. VII, xxvi.

The superior man is affable, but not adulatory; the mean man is adulatory, but not affable. *An.* Bk. XIII, xxiii.

The gentleman is easy to serve and difficult to please. If you try to please him in any way which is not accordant with right he will not be pleased. But in his employment of men, he uses them according to their capacity. The mean man is difficult to serve, and easy to please. If you try to please him, even though it be in a way which is not accordant with right, he may be pleased. But in his employment of men, he wishes them to be equal to everything. *An.* Bk. XIII, xxv.

The gentleman has a dignified ease without pride. The mean man has pride without dignified ease.

The firm, the enduring, the simple, and the modest are near to virtue. *An.* Bk. XIII, xxvi, xxvii.

Tsze-kung asked, saying, "Is there one word which may serve as a rule of practice for all one's life?" The Master said, "Is not *RECIPROCITY* such a word? What you do not want done to yourself, do not do to others."

Is he not a man of complete virtue, who feels no discomposure though men take no note of him? *An.* Bk. I, i, 3.

I will not be afflicted at men's not knowing me; I will be afflicted that I do not know men. *An.* Bk. I, xvi.

Where the solid qualities are in excess of accomplishments, we have rusticity; where the accomplishments are in excess of the solid qualities, we have the manners of a clerk. When the accomplishments and the solid qualities are equally blended, we then have the man of virtue. *An.* Bk. VI, xvi.

The Master said, "With coarse rice to eat, with water to drink, and my bended arm for a pillow:—I have still joy in the midst of these things.   Riches and honors acquired by unrighteousness are to me as a floating cloud." *An.* Bk. VII, xv.

It is only he who is possessed of the most complete sincerity that can exist under heaven, who can give its full development to his nature. Able to give its full development to his own nature, he can do the same to the nature of other men.   Able to give its full development to the nature of other men, he can give their full development to the natures of animals and things.   Able to give their full development to the natures of creatures and things, he can assist the transforming and nourishing powers of Heaven and Earth.   Able to assist the transforming and nourishing powers of Heaven and Earth, he may with Heaven and Earth form a ternion. *The Doctrine of the Mean,* xxii.

He who exercises government by means of his virtue may be compared to the north polar star, which keeps its place and all the stars turn towards it. *An.* Bk. II, i.

The Master said, "If the people be led by laws, and uniformity sought to be given them by punishments, they will try to avoid the punishment, but have no sense of shame.

If they be led by virtue, and uniformity sought to be given them by rules of propriety, they will have the sense of shame, and moreover will become good." *An.* Bk. II, iii.

Tsze-chang was learning with a view to official emolument.

The Master said, "Hear much and put aside the points of which you stand in doubt, while you speak cautiously at the same time of the others :—then you will afford few occasions for blame. See much and put aside the things which seem perilous, while you are cautious at the same time in carrying the others into practice :—then you will have few occasions for repentance. When one gives few occasions for blame in his words, and few occasions for repentance in his conduct, he is in the way to get emolument." *An.* Bk. II, xviii, 1, 2.

In hearing litigations I am·like any other body. What is necessary, however, is to cause the people to have no litigations. *An.* Bk. XII, xiii.

Tsze-lu said, "The ruler of Wei has been waiting for you, in order with you to administer the government. What will you consider the first thing to be done?"

The Master replied, "What is necessary is to rectify names."

"So, indeed!" said Tsze-lu. "You are wide of the mark! Why must there be such rectification?"

The Master said, "How uncultivated you are, Yu! A superior man, in regard to what he does not know, shows a cautious reserve.

If names be not correct, language is not in accordance with the truth of things. If language be not in accordance with the truth of things, affairs cannot be carried on to success.

When affairs cannot be carried on to success, proprieties and music will not flourish. When proprieties and music do not flourish, punishments will not be properly awarded. When punishments are not properly awarded, the people do not know how to move hand or foot.

Therefore a superior man considers it necessary that the names he uses may be spoken appropriately, and also that what he speaks may be carried out appropriately. What the superior man requires is just that in his words there may be nothing incorrect." *An.* Bk. XIII, iii, 1-7.

The Master said, "Though a man may be able to recite the three hundred odes, yet if, when intrusted with a governmental charge, he knows not how to act, or if, when sent to any quarter on a mission, he cannot give his replies unassisted, notwithstanding the extent of his learning, of what practical use is it?"

The Master said, "When a prince's personal conduct is correct, his government is effective without the issuing of orders. If his personal conduct is not correct, he may issue orders, but they will not be followed." *An.* Bk. XIII, v, vi.

If good men were to govern a country in succession for a hundred years, they would be able to transform the violently bad, and dispense with capital punishments. *An.* Bk. XIII, xi.

Hsien asked what was shameful. The Master said, "When good government prevails in a state, to be thinking only of salary; and, when bad government prevails, to be thinking, in the same way, only of salary: —this is shameful." *An.* Bk. XIV, i.

Good Family Life Makes a Good State

What is meant by "making the thoughts sincere," is the allowing no self-deception, as when we hate a bad smell, and as when we love what is beautiful. This is called self-enjoyment. Therefore, the superior man must be watchful over himself when he is alone.

There is no evil to which the mean man, dwelling retired, will not proceed, but when he sees a superior man, he instantly tries to disguise himself, concealing his evil, and displaying what is good. The other beholds him, as if he saw his heart and reins:—of what use is his disguise? This is an instance of the saying—"What truly is within will be manifested without." Therefore, the superior man must be watchful over himself when he is alone.

The disciple Tsang said, "What ten eyes behold, what ten hands point to, is to be regarded with reverence!

Riches adorn a house, and virtue adorns the person. The mind is expanded, and the body is at ease. Therefore, the superior man must make his thoughts sincere.

What is meant by, "The cultivation of the person depends on rectifying the mind," may be thus illustrated:—If a man be under the influence of passion, he will be incorrect in his conduct. He will be the same, if he is under the influence of terror, or under the influence of fond regard, or under that of sorrow and distress.

When the mind is not present, we look and do not see; we hear and do not understand; we eat and do not know the taste of what we eat.

This is what is meant by saying that the cultivation of the person depends on the rectifying of the mind.

What is meant by "The regulation of one's family depends on the cultivation of his person," is this:—Men are partial where they feel affection and love; partial where they despise and dislike; partial where they stand in awe and reverence; partial where they feel sorrow and compassion; partial where they are arrogant and rude. Thus it is that there are few men in the world who love and at the same time know the bad qualities of the object of their love, or who hate and yet know the excellence of the object of their hatred.

Hence it is said, in the common adage, "A man does not know the wickedness of his son; he does not know the richness of his growing corn."

This is what is meant by saying that if the person be not cultivated, a man cannot regulate his family.

What is meant by "In order rightly to govern the state, it is necessary first to regulate the family," is this:—It is not possible for one to teach others, while he cannot teach his own family. Therefore, the ruler, without going beyond his family, completes the lessons for the state. There is filial piety:—therewith the sovereign should be served. There is fraternal submission:—therewith elders and superiors should be served. There is kindness:—therewith the multitude should be treated.

In the Announcement to K'ang, it is said, "Act as if you were watching over an infant." If (a mother) is really anxious about it, though she may not hit exactly the wants of her infant, she will not be far from doing so. There never has been a girl who learned to bring up a child, that she might afterwards marry.

From the loving example of one family a whole state becomes loving, and from its courtesies the whole state becomes courteous, while, from the ambition and perverseness of the One man, the whole state may be led to rebellious disorder:—such is the nature of the influence. This verifies the saying, "Affairs may be ruined by a single sentence; a kingdom may be settled by its One man."

Yao and Shun led on the kingdom with benevolence, and the people followed them. Chieh and Chau led on the kingdom with violence, and the people followed them. The orders which these issued were contrary to the practices which they loved, and so the people did not follow them. On this account, the ruler must himself be possessed of the good qualities, and then he may require them in the people. He must not have the bad qualities in himself, and then he may require that they shall not be in the people. Never has there been a man, who, not having reference to his own character and wishes in dealing with others, was able effectually to instruct them.

Thus we see how the government of the state depends on the regulation of the family.

In the Book of Poetry, it is said, "In his deportment there is nothing wrong; he rectifies all the people of the state." Yes; when the ruler, as a father, a son, and a brother, is a model, then the people imitate him.

This is what is meant by saying, "The government of his kingdom depends on his regulation of the family."

What is meant by "The making the whole kingdom peaceful and happy depends on the government of his state," is this:—When the sovereign behaves to his aged, as the aged should be behaved to, the people become filial; when the sovereign behaves to his elders, as the elders should be behaved to, the people learn brotherly submission; when the sovereign treats compassionately the young and helpless, the people do the same. Thus the ruler has a principle with which, as with a measuring square, he may regulate his conduct.

What a man dislikes in his superiors, let him not display in the treatment of his inferiors; what he dislikes in inferiors, let him not display in the service of his superiors; what he hates in those who are before him, let him not therewith precede those who are behind him; what he hates in those who are behind him, let him not therewith follow those who are before him; what he hates to receive on the right, let him not bestow on the left; what he hates to receive on the left, let him not bestow on the right:—this is what is called "The principle with which, as with a measuring square, to regulate one's conduct."

In the Book of Poetry, it is said, "Lofty is that southern hill, with its rugged masses of rocks! Greatly distinguished are you, O grand-teacher Yin, the people all look up to you." Rulers of states may not neglect to be careful. If they deviate to a mean selfishness, they will be a disgrace in the kingdom.

In the Book of Poetry, it is said, "Before the sovereigns of the Yin dynasty had lost the hearts of the people, they could appear before God." Take warning from the house of Yin. The great decree is not easily preserved. This shows that, by gaining the people, the kingdom is gained, and, by losing the people, the kingdom is lost.

On this account, the ruler will first take pains about his own virtue. Possessing virtue will give him the people. Possessing the people will give him the territory. Possessing the territory will give him its wealth. Possessing the wealth, he will have resources for expenditure.

Virtue is the root; wealth is the result.

If he make the root his secondary object, and the result his primary, he will only wrangle with his people, and teach them rapine.

Hence, the accumulation of wealth is the way to scatter the people; and the letting it be scattered among them is the way to collect the people.

And hence, the ruler's words going forth contrary to right, will come back to him in the same way, and wealth, gotten by improper ways, will take its departure by the same.

In the Announcement to K'ang, it is said, "The decree indeed may not always rest on us"; that is, goodness obtains the decree, and the want of goodness loses it.

In the Book of Chu, it is said, "The kingdom of Chu does not consider that to be valuable. It values, instead, its good men."

Duke Wan's uncle, Fan, said, "Our fugitive does not account that to be precious. What he considers precious is the affection due to his parent."

In the Declaration of the duke of Ch'in, it is said, "Let me have but one minister, plain and sincere, not pretending to other abilities, but with a simple, upright, mind; and possessed of generosity, regarding the talents of others as if he himself possessed them, and, where he finds accomplished and perspicacious men, loving them in his heart more than his mouth expresses, and really showing himself able to bear them and employ them:—such a minister will be able to preserve my sons and grandsons and black-haired people, and benefits likewise to the kingdom may well be looked for from him. But if it be his character, when he finds men of ability, to be jealous and hate them; and, when he finds accomplished and perspicacious men, to oppose them and not allow their advancement, showing himself really not able to bear them:—such a minister will not be able to protect my sons and grandsons and black-haired people; and may he not also be pronounced dangerous to the state?"

It is only the truly virtuous man who can send away such a man and banish him, driving him out among the barbarous tribes around, determined not to dwell along with him in the Middle Kingdom. This is in accordance with the saying, "It is only the truly virtuous man who can love or who can hate others."

To see men of worth and not be able to raise them to office; to raise them to office, but not to do so quickly;—this is disrespectful. To see bad men and not be able to remove them; to remove them, but not to do so to a distance:—this is weakness.

To love those whom men hate, and to hate those whom men love:—this is to outrage the natural feeling of men. Calamities cannot fail to come down on him who does so.

Thus we see that the sovereign has a great course to pursue. He must show entire self-devotion and sincerity to attain it, and by pride and extravagance he will fail of it.

Never has there been a case of the sovereign loving benevolence, and the people not loving righteousness. Never has there been a case where the people have loved righteousness, and the affairs of the sovereign have not been carried to completion. And never has there been a case where the wealth in such a state, collected in the treasuries and arsenals, did not continue in the sovereign's possession.

When he who presides over a state or a family makes his revenues his chief business, he must be under the influence of some small, mean man. He may consider this man to be good; but when such a person is employed in the administration of a state or family, calamities from Heaven, and injuries from men, will befall it together, and, though a good man may take his place, he will not be able to remedy the evil. This illustrates again the saying, "In a state, gain is not to be considered prosperity, but its prosperity will be found in righteousness." *The Great Learning,* Chap. VI-X.

The institutions of the Ruler are rooted in his own character and conduct, and sufficient attestation of them is given by the masses of the people. He examines them by comparison with those of the three kings [the traditionally perfect rulers of the past], and finds them without mistake. He sets them up before heaven and earth and finds nothing in them contrary to [nature].

He presents himself with them before spiritual beings, and no doubts about them arise. He is prepared to wait for the rise of a sage a hundred ages after and has no misgivings. [He awaits with calmness the judgment of the ages]. *The Doctrine of the Mean,* XXIX, 3.

It is only the individual possessed of the most entire sincerity that can exist under heaven, who can adjust the great invariable relations of mankind, establish the great fundamental virtues of humanity, and know the transforming and nurturing operations of Heaven and Earth: —shall this individual have any being or anything beyond himself on which he depends?

Call him man in his ideal, how earnest he is! Call him an abyss, how deep is he! Call him Heaven, how vast is he!

Who can know him, but he who is indeed quick in apprehension, clear in discernment, of far-reaching intelligence, and all-embracing knowledge, possessing all heavenly virtue? *The Doctrine of the Mean,* XXXII, 1-3.

MISCELLANEOUS

THREE FRIENDSHIPS

Confucius said, "There are three friendships which are advantageous, and three which are injurious. Friendship with the upright; friendship with the sincere; and friendship with the man of much observation: —these are advantageous. Friendship with the man of specious airs; friendship with the insinuatingly soft; and friendship with the glib-tongued:—these are injurious." *An.* Bk. XVI, iv.

Three Pleasures, Good and Bad

There are three things men find enjoyment in which are advantageous, and three things they find enjoyment in which are injurious.

To find enjoyment in the discriminating study of ceremonies and music; to find enjoyment in speaking of the goodness of others; to find enjoyment in having many worthy friends:—these are advantageous.

To find enjoyment in extravagant pleasures; to find enjoyment in idleness and sauntering; to find enjoyment in the pleasures of feasting:—these are injurious. *An.* Bk. XVI, v.

Three Errors

There are three errors to which they who stand in the presence of a man of virtue and station are liable.

They may speak when it does not come to them to speak:—this is called rashness.

They may not speak when it comes to them to speak:—this is called concealment.

They may speak without looking at the countenance of their superior:—this is called blindness. *An.* Bk. XVI, vi.

Three Sins of Youth, Manhood and Age

Confucius said, "There are three things which the superior man guards against. In youth, when the physical powers are not yet settled, he guards against lust. When he is strong and the physical powers are full of vigor, he guards against quarrelsomeness. When he is old, and the animal powers are decayed, he guards against covetousness." *An.* Bk. XVI, vii.

Three Awes

There are three things of which the gentleman stands in awe.

He stands in awe of the ordinances of Heaven.
He stands in awe of great men.
He stands in awe of the words of the sages.

The mean man does not know the ordinances of Heaven, and consequently

He does not stand in awe of them.
He is disrespectful to great men.
He makes sport of the words of sages.

An. Bk. XVI, viii, 1, 2.

Three Classes of Men

Those who are born with the possession of knowledge are the highest class of men. Those who learn, and so, readily get possession of knowledge, are the next. Those who are dull and stupid and yet compass the learning, are another class to these.

As to those who are dull and stupid and yet do not learn:—they are the lowest of the people. *An.* Bk. XVI, ix.

THREE POINTS OF SELF-EXAMINATION

I daily examine myself on three points:—whether, in transacting business for others, I may not have been faithful; whether in intercourse with friends, I may not have been sincere; whether I may not have mastered and practised the instructions of my teacher. *An.* Bk. I, iv.

THREE TIMES THREE CARES

Confucius said, "The superior man has nine things which are subjects with him of thoughtful consideration. In regard to the use of his eyes, he is anxious to see clearly. In regard to the use of his ears, he is anxious to hear distinctly. In regard to his countenance, he is anxious that it should be benign. In regard to his demeanor, he is anxious that it should be respectful. In regard to his speech, he is anxious that it should be sincere. In regard to his doing of business, he is anxious that it should be reverently careful. In regard to what he doubts about, he is anxious to question others. When he is angry, he thinks of the difficulties (his anger may involve him in). When he sees gain to be got, he thinks of righteousness." *An.* Bk. XVI, x.

FOUR CHARACTERISTICS OF A GENTLEMAN

In his conduct of himself, he is humble.
In his serving his superior, he is respectful.
In nourishing the people, he is kind.
In ordering the people, he is just.

An. Bk. V. xv.

CAUTION

If you had the conduct of the armies of a great state, whom would you have to act with you?

The Master said, "I would not have him to act with me, who will unarmed attack a tiger, or cross a river without a boat, dying without regret. My associate must be the man who proceeds to action full of solicitude, who is fond of adjusting his plans, and then carries them into execution."

SENSE OF MISSION

If Heaven had wished to let this cause of truth perish, then I, a future mortal, should not have got such a relation to that cause. As long as Heaven does not let the cause of truth perish, what can the people of K'wang do to me? *An.* Bk. IX, v, 3.

FLEWELLING: Selections from *REFLECTIONS ON THE BASIC IDEAS OF EAST AND WEST*. College of Chinese Studies, Peking. Chap. III, pp. 33-45.

THE CONTRASTING CONCEPTS OF TIME AND SPACE

Changing the tempo of a musical composition transmutes one of the loveliest of our classics into the syncopated and unlovely "I'm Forever Blowing Bubbles" or the "Humoresque" into "Apple Blossom Time in Normandy." Change the tempo of a civilization and you change completely its character. Yet in the whole realm of philosophy there are no knottier problems than those of Time and Space. These concepts, however held, enter intimately into the life and folkways of a people and go far toward determining the types of their reactions to experience.

At no point does the contrast of Chinese and Western concepts show greater than at this. Because the space-time notions enter so directly into the common assumptions that when they differ, they render one civilization almost unintelligible to another.

Chinese space-time concepts are of a piece with the other notions of their closely co-ordinated system and are synthetic, or involuted. The cyclic idea of time so native to all Oriental thought is theirs, while we with our sense of individualism, of racial destiny, see it strung out in procession, having a beginning, and therefore an end. This idea of time has scarcely been questioned in the Western world until the present. Now we have developed both mathematical and physical concepts to such a degree that our millenia-old notions of time are no longer adequate for the expression of mathematical ideas and we are in the midst of a conceptual revolution regarding both time and space.

This revolution will eventually change our thought of society and will find certain repercussion in the practices of our civilization. An interesting question arises as to whether Occidental and Oriental may find some common meeting-ground in space-time philosophy. A short while ago it would have seemed to imply an inevitable clash, an uncompromisible incompatibility such as Kipling expressed in "East is East, and West is West, and never the twain shall meet," but now the old feeling of certainty is gone. It may be that a compromising tempo will be found that will help to banish the ancient wall of partition between us.

I

THE WESTERN IDEA OF TIME AND SPACE

We must begin by attempting to understand the long regnant notion of the West respecting both time and space.

To the average person, time is a stream that flows, and space is a sort of box in which to put things like a convenient closet where we can thrust the inconvenient. Our classic picture of time is that of the three Fates, one of whom spins the thread of time, one of whom lengthens or stretches it out, and the last of whom snips it off. Snipping it off is our principal preoccupation, for we further picture Time as a short skirted gentleman in a Greek costume with farmer whiskers, scythe in hand, ready to cut down the living.

Our concept of history is in close relation to this. We string out our history in a straight line. The divisions we make in it are predominantly arithmetical. These divisions have no relation whatever to the nature of the events except that of succession which can hardly be called a quality. We speak unconsciously of history by centuries as if the Fifteenth century could be separated with distinctness from the Sixteenth, or as if history came to a dead wall in 1599 and then by some magic the Seventeenth century were born. We attempt to differentiate sharply between the Nineteenth and Twentieth centuries. The result has been a tendency to despise our past, to think of the Nineteenth as somehow inferior to the Twentieth century. . . . This has eventuated in a perversion of historical perspective. It has prevented us from just evaluations. It has led us to think too highly of ourselves, of our own age and its importance in the long roll of history. It has profoundly modified our ideas, and is the warp and woof of our thinking. It approaches close to what might be called the genius of the West, its concept of destiny, its theory of continuous and evolutionary progress toward a goal. It is largely responsible for those ways in which our civilization differs from that of the Orient, but the results have been both good and bad, and we are now facing the possibility of the coming of concepts which can be no less than revolutionary.

II

THE ORIENTAL CONCEPT OF SPACE AND TIME

It would certainly be enlightening if someone in close contact with Chinese thought would take the pains to gather the myths, stories, legends and proverbs which throw an interpretative light on the space-time concept of the Chinese. Without doing that exhaustively, however, we have abundant material for our present purpose to indicate the main differences at this point between East and West. To the Chinese time is not spread out in a long line of definite and successive moments,—it is a revolving wheel. You will note the practical differences that arise out of this contrasting attitude. The Westerner must rush to keep up with time. His eye is set on a far goal. If he does not hurry he will be left behind. Our most burning sarcasm on a business, an institution, educational, social or spiritual, is that it is out of date, belated. The most valuable journal, containing the choicest information does not interest us if the date on the cover indicates that it is a month old.

While the Occidental rushes to keep up with his lengthening line of time, the Oriental on the other hand waits for it to come round to him. His notion is that time is like a wheel. No use to worry about the past! It will soon come back again. There is no use to worry about the future, it will be a repetition of the past. There is considerable logic in this for many problems have ways of solving themselves under the lapse of time. If letters present problems that are too vexatious, put them in your desk unanswered. Presently the problems will have solved themselves, and it will be unnecessary to take the trouble to write at all. There will be nothing to write about.

One effect of this notion of time is revealed in the Chinese treatment of history. To the Chinese, history is not a scale of centuries strung out in unvarying order. It is rather a collection of rolling cycles which have their own individual characteristics, but from which the time element, as we conceive it, number of days, years or centuries, is entirely wanting. He does not count time as a matter of number at all. These cycles of his history are most frequently identified with the rise, flowering, and decadence of Imperial dynasties seen as a whole.

Each dynasty was inaugurated by a change of calendar, with rites and ceremonies that were conducted in the face of the whole Empire, and visibly initiated a new era and a new time. The new Emperor was for the Chinese the beginning of a time, the originator of a cycle, able by decree to pronounce old things to have passed away, and who under the mandate of Heaven had power to make all things new. As time centered in the Emperor, so also did space. Space was the distance away from the Emperor and his seat which was considered to be the center of the universe. There was the place of the Emperor and there were the other four directions, North, South, East and West. These had significance only as they related to the Emperor. To his Empire there were no physical boundaries. All nations were but subsidiaries of the Empire, though some might be negligent about bringing in the tribute. If the King of England sent an embassy with gifts, it could be conceived only in the light of a recognition of the universal over-lordship of the Emperor of China, a token of submission.

III

CONTRASTS ARISING FROM CONTRADICTORY CONCEPTS

The contrasts arising from the contradictory concepts of time and space have already been hinted at. Let us pursue the subject a bit further.   Suppose we, as Westerners, had as overwhelming beliefs these: that tomorrow is certain to be like today; that change is more or less an illusion and rests barely on the surface of things, never able to go deeply into reality.   Suppose that you considered yourself such an integral part of a general situation, a spoke in the revolving wheel of time, that your sole duty was to preserve the general harmony by repeating the past.   Suppose the worst sin you could commit would be disloyalty to that past, deviating in any particular from the thoughts, opinions, and ways of your father.   Suppose it were generally considered to be your sole duty to pass along unsullied the already made reputations of ancestors.   Suppose the only wisdom you could ever hope to have were the wisdom that has already been fully and perfectly achieved, to which nothing could possibly be added. Suppose there could be no result of striving that could bring anything new, or could change in any particular the circular course of history, except as it called down disaster upon you as an individual, or upon your family which would be held accountable for your conduct, even to the death penalty.   Suppose whatever golden age might be, must be considered to lie forever behind you, and could come again only as the cyclic wheel of events brought about its return.   Suppose all this and try to see what difference it would make in your conduct and general attitude toward society.

Once China was the richest, most populous, and most powerful Empire in all the earth.   It has had always a varied succession of ups and downs, but each cycle has witnessed much the same vicissitudes. If the T'angs are ruling today the Sungs are sure to follow them tomorrow.   If the Sungs are now coming in it is certain they will flourish and then decay, and make way for the rising Mongols.   The Mongols being in power will mean that the Mings are already on the way, but these, in turn will give way to the Manchu.   These varying cycles are not, for the common man, cataclysmic.   They affect chiefly the fortunes of a very few of the upper classes, while the lives of ordinary people flow on in the same undisturbed round of their fathers and grandfathers.   This general cycle no individual can disturb nor upset since all things occur by the will of Heaven.   Whoever goes against Heaven only insures his own destruction, be he peasant or Emperor. . It seems easy to see how the cyclic view of time becomes the source of Chinese fatalism.   It binds the individual round with cords stronger than steel.   It saps individualistic effort at its root.   It confines ambition to the routine of family welfare and preservation.   There could be no physical opiate in Chinese life comparable to this wider-scale mental morphia.   This constitutes the present pressing problem of a great people.

The Westerner suggests with a laugh the old adage that history repeats itself, but he does not believe it when he says it.   For him time gone never can return.   It is like the flowing river of Heraclitus, into which no one could step twice. His genius is to think of history as an advance, a growing conquest of new fields of social, intellectual, and spiritual endeavor. No gifts of outward circumstance can long lure him to satisfaction. He finds no home for his soul. However much of wealth, or power, or wisdom are his, he dreams of other worlds to conquer. His is essentially the pilgrim spirit. The musical strain that voices the deepest genius of the Western people is the recurring theme of Richard Wagner's Tannhäuser, *The Pilgrim Chorus*. All our literature tells the same story, from Aeschylus' *Prometheus Bound,* through Dante's *Divine Comedy* and Shakespeare's *Hamlet,* and Goethe's *Faust* to the plays of Ibsen. In fact, it was Homer himself that set the pilgrim pace. The one fatality, the one unbearable condition for the Westerner is that the individual should be turned in upon himself and his own resources alone; to find himself tied to a wheel of fate against which he cannot prevail. This to us constitutes the supreme problem of evil. Our unanswerable Atheism would arise from the belief that the individual is caught in conditions from which it is impossible for him to escape.

To the Chinese mind this is not a problem at all. It is the accepted reality, the will of Heaven.

Enough has now been written to show the deep-lying incompatibilities in the ways of looking at life and destiny which arise out of these contrasting concepts of time and space. Each civilization, East and West, has written them deeply into its social customs, its learning, its laws, its philosophy, its ways of looking at things. To each, the contrasting concept of time held by the other, constitutes the main puzzle of the present generation. As we mentioned in the beginning, the notion of time is the most difficult of all philosophical ideas, because it is the unconscious assumption that backs the whole fabric of thought and society, and only thinkers can orientate themselves into the contrasting systems. This is why it devolves upon philosophy to discover and bring about the readjustment of fundamental ideas which will make possible common understandings between East and West.

IV

NEW CONCEPTS OF SPACE AND TIME

The most significant intellectual event in the Western world since the advancement of the Copernican theory has, perhaps, been the formulation by Einstein of the Theory of Relativity. That and the accompanying incidental changes in scientific thought, introduce concepts into our thinking which are no less than revolutionary in character, and whose outcome cannot at present be fully foreseen. The significant thing is that they bring a revolution in space-time ideas which must eventually revolutionize our thinking in many, if not all fields.

The Oriental, or cyclic, view of time has never been quite unknown in Western philosophy. It has sprung up sporadically through the twenty-five centuries of philosophic history, and has usually been the result of Oriental contacts of some kind. Among the modern philosophers, it was Schelling who conceived of History as the farther and farther Iliad of man's wanderings from God and the ever-repeated Odyssey of his return to God. Afterwards, in grand form, Hegel gave us the Oriental and cyclic philosophy of history, touched with his own individual, Western genius. He was, himself, profoundly influenced by the earlier Spinoza, whose roots were in turn deep set in the Orient, and who in addition to the Oriental background of his birth and education, may have fallen under the more direct influence of Chinese philosophy. Spengler in our own day has resorted to this same cyclic view of history in his well-known book, *The Decline of the West*. In general this view of history has been so foreign to the genius of Western thought and ideas that it has never been able to capture any but a fleeting hold upon Western fancy.

In the meantime there has arisen in the Western world a new space-time concept just at the moment when the old straight line and box-space notions of time and space were breaking down. Philosophy has all along been conscious of the crudeness and inconsistency which lurked in the popular theories of space and time, and from which science for long made no effort to clear itself. Philosophy was unable to get a hearing so long as science clung to the cruder concepts, and was at the same time able to make so many practical advances and discoveries. The dilemma which lurked in the old views has been philosophically apparent since the fourth century B.C. For very long it has been seen that time is to be defined as the form of thought under which we relate events to each other and to ourselves, while space is the form of thought under which we relate objects to each other and to our own experience.

Under the Theory of Relativity, these more refined and logical definitions of space are replacing the earlier and illogical concepts in the realm of science itself, and for the first time since science attempted to separate itself from the domain of philosophy. Science has been made aware of the problem through the work of Einstein, Lorenz, Planck, Millikan and a host of other investigators. It is now seen that neither time nor space has any abstract and independent existence apart from meaning. Time is not a stream that flows irrespective of events, meanings, and of observing minds. Space can likewise no longer be considered an empty box always there to hold things irrespective of meanings, minds, intelligences, and out of all connection with time. The world is now seen as an intricate system of relationships and this in itself might be considered a movement toward the Chinese synthetic type of thinking. These relations are such by reason of their meanings. They have no existence apart from these meanings and the system in which they occur.

The effect of this revolution in thought cannot but be manifold and far-reaching. In the first place, it puts a new dignity upon intelligence. The human mind, thrust into the background as insignificant by a type of materialism under which all things were evaluated by statistics of number and size, is now seen to be much the most important of all created realities. This is because any possible interpretation of the world of matter is dependent upon the reactions of this mind which is a party to the transaction and profoundly modifies all meanings in accordance with its own predilections and capacities.

However, the discovery does not make for the recrudescence of that individualism which has characterized the genius of the West. The reason for this is that it has removed the emphasis from individuality, the mere worship of quantity and number to those of quality, value, and meaning. When meaning, value, and quality become the objects of search, individualism rises into personalism. That is, it seeks the fulfilment of its individual self-expression in a higher range of interests, having mental, moral and spiritual significance. The individual can find the climax of his own achievements in the general good; he dies to individual interests in order that he may begin to live in the higher and the broader aspects of the common welfare. He abrogates the old self-seeking individualism, which sought its own satisfactions at whatever expense of suffering and wrong to others, and finds his inspiration and self-fulfilment in seeking the common good, becoming in the truest sense a person.

Such a time-space concept can be nothing less than revolutionary in its effect, and, whether we wish it or not, it is now in process of realization.

It is apparent that the cyclic view of time is best fitted for a social order of slight variability, whereas the present is an age of lightning-like change. Such a view of time stands today directly in the way of what we consider progress. Making little draft upon individual genius and invention, hostile to change of every sort, it seems quite unfitted to meet the problems of a world of which variation is the marked characteristic. It seems also inadequate to meet the demands of democracy, and is appropriate only to the system which it has built about itself through the centuries of history, that is, a definitely centered autocracy. It could possibly flourish today only as a type of dictatorship, that new species of nationalism which is Europe's despairing answer to the failure of her dream of democracy. But in this modern age such systems must be viewed as the stop-gap expedients of social change which must pass away with the individual genius that has for the moment called them into existence.

They are not fitted for the ever-narrowing world of invention and discovery which is destined to erase more and more the artificial boundaries of nationalism and provincialism.

Neither is it possible to look hopefully upon the Western time-view for the solution of present difficulties. It too has outgrown the shell of its usefulness. Bent too much upon the single devotion to number, enumeration, quantity, it has built upon the basis of a free democracy a machine civilization that is the principal foe of that democracy. Under the impact of this development Western civilization has become self-destructive. It is being crowded out of its original molds by the very force of its own machines. Its ancient watchwords can no longer command allegiance unless they can be raised to the height of a new moral and spiritual conception of democracy.

The newly advanced theory of space-time may be made to provide what both other views have lacked, an opportunity for the development of the individual. The rising concept re-emphasizes what was strong in Western thought before it was strangled by the machine age, namely: the significance, importance, and reality of the person. Man's world is whatever he chooses to make it. He may be master but he cannot rule in hermit-like selfishness. His full self-development can take place only in a society devoted to freedom, to righteousness, and to the common welfare of all men. He must now advance to seize upon this long-neglected heritage or civilization itself will fail.

QUESTIONS AND STATEMENTS FOR DISCUSSION

(*The Analects*)

1. "Is he not a man of complete virtue who feels no discomposure though men take no note of him." (Legge: Four Books, *The Analects*, Bk. I, Chap. I, 3.) P. 94.

2. "The Master said, 'If the people be led by laws, and uniformity sought to be given them by punishments, they will try to avoid the punishment, but have no sense of shame. If they be led by virtue, and uniformity sought to be given by rules of propriety, they will have the sense of shame, and, moreover, will become good." (Bk. II, Chap. III, 1, 2.) P. 95.

3. "Learning without thought is labor lost; thought without learning is perilous." (Bk. II, Chap. XV.) P. 92.

4. "A scholar whose mind is set on truth, and who is ashamed of bad clothes and bad food, is not fit to be discoursed with." (Bk. IV, Chap. IX.) P. 93.

5. "Have no friends not equal to yourself." (Bk. IX, Chap. XXIV.) P. 100.

6. "Fine words and an insinuating appearance are seldom associated with virtue." (Bk. XVII, Chap. XVII.)

7. "I do not open up the truth to one who is not eager to get knowledge, nor help out anyone who is not anxious to explain himself. When I have presented one corner of a subject to anyone, and he cannot from it learn the other three, I do not repeat the lesson." (Bk. VII, Chap. VIII.) P. 93.

8. "From the Son of Heaven down to the mass of the people, all must consider the cultivation of the person the root of everything besides." ("The Great Learning," 6.) P. 96.

9. "There is nothing more visible than what is secret, and nothing more manifest than what is minute. Therefore the superior man is watchful over himself, when he is alone." ("The Doctrine of the Mean," Chap. I, 3.) P. 88.

10. "The superior man is quiet and calm, waiting for the appointments of Heaven, while the mean man walks in dangerous paths, looking for lucky occurrences." (*Ibid.*, Chap. XIV, 4.) P. 89.

11. "It is the way of the superior man to prefer the concealment of his virtue, while it daily becomes more illustrious, and it is the way of the mean man to seek notoriety, while he daily goes more and more to ruin." (*Ibid.*, Chap. XXXIII, 1.)

12. "In archery we have something like the way of the Gentleman When the archer misses the center of the target, he turns about and seeks the causes of his failure in himself." ("The Golden Mean." Chap. XIV, 1-5.) P. 89. Does this action properly distinguish between the gentleman and the boor? What is its relation to personal development?

13. "When internal examination discovers nothing wrong what is there to fear?" (*An.* XII, 4ff.) P. 91. Discuss the sources of fear.
14. Is there any essential difference between the negative Golden Rule of Confucius and the positive one of Jesus? Pp. 90, 94.
15. Discuss relation of family life to the state. How did this concept work in China and is it relevant to American life? Pp. 96-98.
16. Is this a true judgment of the measure of love entertained by the lover who writes: "Do I not think of you? But your house is distant." P. 93.
17. Only the gentleman can love and hate. Pp. 89, 92.
18. Why should the three friendships be considered injurious? P. 100.

Suggested Supplementary Readings:

Lin Yu Tang: *The Wisdom of Confucius.* Modern Library, New York. Pp. 1-35.
Doeblin: *The Living Thoughts of Confucius.* Living Thoughts Library Series, Longmans, Green, New York. Pp. 1-94.
Giles, trans.: *The Sayings of Confucius.* John Murray, London.
Cranmer-Byng: *The Vision of Asia.* Farrar & Rinehart, New York.
Soothill: *The Three Religions of China.* Oxford University Press, New York.
Wilhelm: *Confucius and Confucianism.* Harcourt, Brace, New York.

Chapter 4

THE BUDDHIST RETREAT FROM THE WORLD

Indian Thought and the Life of Gautama Buddha
1. His disillusionment
2. His enlightenment

    (a) The "Four Noble Truths"
    (b) The "Eight-fold Path"

I
Hinayana

1. All things are momentary
2. The goal of existence: cessation of consciousness
3. Method: meditation

II
Mahayana

1. The conception of a Supreme Being
2. The Bodhisattvas
3. Salvation by faith

III
Zen

1. The conquest of desire
2. The illusion of possession
3. The way to knowledge

IV
Some Concluding Remarks

Chapter 4

THE BUDDHIST RETREAT FROM THE WORLD

Introduction

There is certain to be great difficulty in the apprehension by the Western mind of the doctrines and ideas of Buddhism. The whole background of Buddhistic thinking is foreign to Western concepts and ways of life. It is safe to say that Buddhism is to be comprehended by the average Westerner, in its practices rather than in its philosophy. No other system of thought could illustrate more certainly the effect of ideas on history. The contrast between the achievements of Orient and Occident is clearly mirrored in the antitheses between Buddhism and Judaeo-Christianity. The heart of this difference is to be found in the opposing views regarding the value of the person. The Western world tends toward an increasing democracy in the degree that it considers the person of supreme worth. The East gets farther away from democracy the more it disvalues and disclaims personal worth in the search for the All or the Absolute through self-repression.

This study is of special interest in throwing light upon the reasons, not only for the failure of the most highly civilized peoples to make social and scientific progress, but also for the way in which their systems have made them the victims of political tyranny. With the contempt for the individual have come political and social weakness, spiritual deterioration, and an incapacity for union in the defense of obvious rights. Having said this, it is no more than fair to point out the nobler and more attractive features of the Buddhist concept of value. Perchance in viewpoints so divergent from our own there may lie reproof for the weaknesses of our own views of life, as well as new understanding, sympathy, and appreciation.

The study of reality, with which the whole question of values must concern itself, can start from either one of two standpoints: from the nature of the thinking self, or from the nature of the world of objects. The Western world has predominatingly given itself to a consideration of the world of objects. The Oriental world, and particularly India, has given itself to the contemplation of the self as the means to a knowledge of the world. Through self-examination it hopes to discover truth and reality, and to achieve the things that matter most. The Indian motto was similar to that of Socrates as we shall shortly see; *Atmanam vidhi* was the equivalent of the Socratic *Gnothe seauton,* "Know thyself." In our time, both Eastern and Western culture stand at pause, not so much because they have taken opposite roads to determine value, but, it may be, because each has given an overemphasis to an important method. Turning in upon himself, the East Indian has come to disbelief in the reality of the self, and of the material world; while the Occidental, giving himself almost wholly to the pursuit of objective or material reality, has in his latest pronouncements in the field of scientific physics come to disbelieve in the existence of reality as materiality. The Easterner discards selfhood as sin, and the Westerner describes his material atom as "an event in a space-time continuum." In losing the self the East has lost touch with the world of concrete reality, and is incapable of saving itself from foreign rule; in its devotion to materialism the West, strangled by the false worship of power, now struggles to preserve the right of self-rule.

In India we have the example of a people whose main thought may be said to have been spent on the search after the higher values. There first, so far as the effect upon modern thought is concerned, came an eager pursuit of metaphysical reality, that real which lies behind all that we can see and experience, and a determination to discover man's relation to the whole cosmic order. Nor should we think of India as destitute of practical and scientific contributions to civilization. The Western world is under deep debt to India for the very foundations of its citadel of knowledge. From India came the earliest discoveries in mathematics, with the invention of algebra, and, it is also claimed, with the application of algebra to astronomy and geometry. The decimal system with its misnamed "Arabic" numerals was the device by which they made possible a mathematical development never before achieved, a result revolutionary in its scope and benefits. The East Indians made important astronomical discoveries and conceived the sciences of Logic and Grammar. India was also advanced in the arts of medicine, chemistry, and surgery, and particularly through the agency of the Moslem invasions and culture, became the stimulus of European learning and science. After having made so brilliant a beginning, she seems to have settled down to a life of contemplation, fairly symbolized in Buddha's own retreat from the world. What she thus gained from the turn to introspective endeavor also had wide repercussions in the history of human culture. To China she sent the Buddhist mis-

sionaries, who there met with such success as to transfer to it the
seat of power for Buddhism after the cult had faded out in the land
of its birth.   India may have influenced Greece through the Eleatics,
an advanced philosophic sect which held all change to be illusion,
and is often held to have set her mark upon the Greek Plato, with
his doctrine of Ideas from which all created things were held to
emanate.   India doubtless inspired the scientific work of the Pythagoreans, through whom was developed the first Elucidean geometry.
India also might be assumed to have given a turn to Parseeism,
Zoroastrianism, and those other forms of religious thought, which,
like Manichaeism, strongly influenced Christian theology through
the schools of Alexandria.

When and why so powerful and active a civilization was so generally diverted to the task of self-examination, is a question that
may well be asked.   The philosophic expression of Indian spiritual
longings may be assumed to go back more than four thousand
years in the Hymns of the Veda.   What brought about that early
change in the intellectual atmosphere, whether it was mass-migration,
wars, pestilence, disparity between rich and poor, or search for
escape from a life that had grown too troublous and complicated,
who can tell?   At any rate, Buddhism, a late-comer upon the scene,
came into being when social unrest was at its height.   It was a time
of wars, clannish and tribal, and the condition of thought was even
more chaotic.   Into this social situation came Buddhism as a movement of reform.   One characteristic of Indian thought has been its
reluctance to break entirely with old ideas.   The result has been that
it has added the new to the old, adapting but not discarding.   The
original doctrines of Hinduism have been incorporated into those
of a multitude of sects, of which Buddhism is but one.   It exhibits,
therefore, the most striking contrasts.   The most primitive animism
and idol worship thrive in the same community alongside the most
elevated and profound philosophic thought.   Life is held to be such
a sacred thing that not only is the eating of flesh repugnant to her
most devoted souls, but even the killing of vermin is thought a mis-
deed.   On the other hand, her streets have in the past witnessed the
suicide of thousands who have thrown themselves under the car
of the Juggernaut, and her widows have immolated themselves upon
her funeral pyres as a testimony of love for the dead.   Along with
this extreme concern for life as represented in the animals, it was
possible for a band of professional murderers, the Thugs of later
times, to find some kind of social recognition. Yet such a custom
as Suttee, the burning of the widows, was spiritualized and defended

in the noble verse and sentiment of Sarojini Naidu, India's brilliant contemporary woman poet, in such a phrase as this:

Shall the flesh survive when the soul is gone?[1]

This dark background furnished the incentive for the reforming zeal of the Buddha. His sensitive spirit was agonizingly touched by the conditions around him. The contrasts between power and weakness; riotous living and starvation in an overpopulated state; the terrible condition of the "untouchables" brought about by the tyranny of caste; the absence of love in the lowest, and the marked callousness and spiritual pride in the highest; these moved his soul at his first contact with the outside world. He decided to pursue the question of what things matter most with all the energy at his command, but he could do this only along the line of thought which had ruled the generations of the past. His solution, then, will be found to be in keeping with the highest and profoundest thinking of his people. There is a sense in which Buddhism may be considered only a continuation of the other high expressions of Indian thought. Buddha might be expected, following the ideas of those who had gone before, to seek the solution of the woes of the world through contemplation, purification, fasting, prayer, and retreat. Such was the setting for the appearance of Gautama Buddha.

He is known under various names. Now he is called Gautama, which was his birth name; now Buddha, which means the Enlightened One; now Sakyamuni, from his birthplace; now Siddhartha, as the one who has fulfilled the object of his coming. Though his actual existence has been disputed, it is ordinarily assumed that he was born about the middle of the sixth century before Christ. The story of his life was not written for two hundred years afterward. His father was the ruler of a provincial kingdom, who surrounded the young prince Sakyamuni with every pleasure and advantage that wealth could afford. He was brought up delicately, and the attempt was made to keep him from all contact with, or knowledge of, the life of the low and common herd. Suddhodana, the father, desired that his son should be a king rather than a religious recluse. But it had been prophesied that he would abandon the world for religion after having seen an old man, a sick man, a dead man, and a monk. For this reason he was kept in ignorance of the existence of suffering and death. In a period when the usual restrictions to bar such sights from his eyes had been relaxed, he drove forth from the palace and saw on four successive days the fateful objects. This

[1] Translation of a folk song, *The Golden Threshold*, Heinneman, London.

is explained as the action of the gods in outwitting the king who had banned such sights by royal decree.   They assumed these forms which made the young prince acquainted with the facts of old age, illness, and death, as well as the serenity of the monk who had become superior to all such experiences.   Siddhartha immediately announced his intention of becoming a monk in order to find a way of escape from the burden of age, suffering, and death.   Thus in the most natural manner possible his father had prepared the way for an intense revulsion of feeling when at last he did come into contact with the woes of the world.   In the sight of a loathsomely diseased man, of an aged man almost as repellent, and a dead body thrown out by the wayside, Gautama received impressions which not only shocked and disgusted him, but which revolutionized both his ideas and his life.   The sight of a monk in calm and unperturbed contemplation gave him what seemed to be the clue to the better life.   He sought to quiet the storm which had been raised in his mind, in a strictly Indian way, by separating himself from his world of delight, and giving himself wholly to meditation.

Here he found his path laid out before him in the sacred scriptures of his people.   According to the Samkara commentary on the Vedanta Sutras, there were four conditions which these laid down as essential to any man who would become a philosopher.   The first of these was that he must learn to distinguish between that which was only ephemeral and passing and that which was eternal.   Eternal Reality, or Eternal Being, is the supreme belief or Indian philosophy.   The philosophic soul is to be distinguished by its insight into the permanent and eternal.

The second condition demanded a detachment from all personal desires and profit.   To see clearly one must be free from selfish desires, the gratification of the appetites, the lust for profit and power.   Until one could look on the world of experience as a detached and unprejudiced spectator, one would not be in a position to understand it.   Nothing so blinds the average man to truth as the presence of selfish interests.

One can arrive at this high state of detachment, however, only by a change of heart, which was the third essential.   This would mean that there must be a complete change of desires, ambitions, and loves which would create a new set of objectives.   In the train of such self-renunciation and restraint would come the calm poise and balance that would accept the truth however naturally unwelcome it might be.

The fourth condition must be an honest and consuming desire for release from all contaminating and subversive thoughts or feelings, everything that would keep the philosopher back from complete participation in the Eternal. This latter condition would be what is known as the arrival at Nirvana, where even the feeling of separate existence is lost in the Supreme Being.

In this way the philosopher, by the strictest discipline, learns through experience what are the things that matter most, and the Indian answer would undoubtedly be that only the Eternal matters.

Such a reversal of all life's aims and occupations could not come without a profound shock to one who had been raised so tenderly as Buddha. This struck the young Bodisat (candidate for Buddhahood, whether Buddha or any of his followers) as he drove forth from the palace, scene of his careless and voluptuous pleasures, and received his first impressions of suffering, old age, disease, and death. In the face of facts so terrifying he found it impossible to justify the enjoyment of merely sensual desires and was led to make the Great Renunciation. Fleeing the palace by night, prohibited from caressing his son by fear of arousing the wife and child, he made his way into the wilderness. Here he spent six years in ascetic contemplation, endeavoring to reach some peace of mind, to find some solution for the distressing thoughts which tormented him. Sitting under the now famous Bo tree he tried to wrestle out his solution. But he could not find in the way of contemplation the peace of mind which he sought.

The Indian Sage has always placed much dependence for enlightenment, upon the effect of fasting. It is a well-known psychological fact that a state of semi-starvation lends itself to vision and hallucination. Where ideas are considered the supreme values, such a means of producing them would likely be in favor. So, it is said, he reduced himself to living on a single grain of rice a day. A strict limitation of food does undoubtedly clear the mind for thinking, and Mr. Gandhi in our own day practices it in the crises of his political and social career. It may produce clearness of thought in him as well as political pressure upon his opponents. This method, it will be seen, was applied in its extremity by Buddha, and out of it came what is known as the Great Enlightenment.

There was in Indian philosophy a curious premonition of the modern doctrine of change made popular by the teaching of the late Henri Bergson. The theory is that everything is in a state of continuous change, is never the same from moment to moment. If that is true, one has the alternative of assuming that the person who gathers past, present, and future into a synthesis of meaning is the permanent reality, which is Bergson's interpretation, or one can hold that this succession is illusion, the passing having no perma-

nence or reality outside of the eternal. In the face of such a philosophy, the Indian pundit chooses to think that every moment of
existence in a person's life is a new moment, and from moment to
moment constitutes him a new existence. Thus the assertion of
"the chain of being" is arrived at. One is not a single existence,
but a multiplicity of existences, as he changes from hour to hour.
Edwin Arnold has described this condition in *The Light of Asia*:[2]

> Many a house of life
> Hath held me . . . seeking ever him who wrought
> These prisons of the senses, sorrow-fraught;
> Sore was my ceaseless strife!
>
> But now,
> Thou builder of this Tabernacle . . . thou!
> I know thee! Never shalt thou build again
>   These walls of pain,
> Nor raise the roof-tree of deceits, nor lay
>   Fresh rafters on the clay;
> Broken thy house is, and the ridge-pole split!
>   Delusion fashioned it!
> Safe pass I thence, deliverance to obtain.

It is the belief in this ever-shifting chain of causation which mis-
leads the western thinker respecting the doctrines of transmigration
and Nirvana. According to one school of Buddhism, it is only the
existence which happens at the moment of death that has any connection with the new life which (though others interpret more
broadly) seeks embodiment. One's final thought determines the
next stage of being. This explanation seems rather essential to our
understanding of the dialectic involved in the *Sermon of Benares,*
which contains the gist of Buddhistic teaching and in which is explained the content of *The Great Enlightenment: The Four Noble
Truths,* and *The Eight-Fold Path,* by which Buddha arrived at
peace of mind.

By "The Four Noble Truths" Buddha thought to come into possession of the incontrovertible facts of life. These had to be faced.
The situation was akin to that of a Western mystic, Thomas Carlyle,
who in the meditations of his *Sartor Resartus,* arrived at the Everlasting No!, the dismissal of all fears and doubts. The first of these
undisguisable facts was the reality of pain and suffering. The second
was that this suffering has a cause: it was due to some other condition. The third was that this state could be remedied and the pain
obliterated. The fourth noble truth was the manner in which this
suppression could be accomplished. Here, one begins by suppressing
ignorance (complete absence of lust) which, in turn, destroys the

---

[2] Cambridge University Press, Cambridge.

mental complexes (samkaras), which destroys consciousness, which destroys name and form, which destroys the six provinces, which destroys contact, which destroys sensation, which destroys thirst, which destroys attachment, which destroys birth, which destroys old age and death, grief, lamentation and suffering, dejection and despair. Thus the whole flock of miseries are brought to an end.[3]

Such a way to peace represents a thoroughly pessimistic outlook upon life, for the Buddha identifies suffering with existence, and moral values with escape from it. All existence is only suffering. To get rid of pain, one must get rid of consciousness and even of life. If, in accordance with the second noble truth, suffering has a cause, let us ask what that cause may be. Here the answer is indicated as thirst, or desire. We are always wanting something as long as we live. Our desires lead us to unhappiness and frustration. Sakyamuni's answer is like that of the Greek Epicurus, only far more drastic. Epicurus would limit one's desires to one's capacity to obtain. If you can buy only a "jalopy," want only a "jalopy." Buddha would have been more severe. He would have said: "Do not even long after a 'jalopy,' because all desire is a sin and the source of unhappiness." If we think for a moment of the perplexities of recapped tires, broken and disordered mechanism, and financial support, perhaps Buddha's was the greater wisdom. If we want nothing, we cannot be disappointed.

Buddha held, moreover, that we must be more extreme than this. Desire springs from consciousness of the world around us. Here, he held, we put our finger on the deeper truth beneath all our suffering. If we were entirely oblivious to everything we should not suffer. This leads us to the fourth great truth; we can do away with suffering by doing away with consciousness.

By such steps we are brought to "The Eight-Fold Path," the means by which we are utterly to stamp out self-consciousness. These means will seem to some of us to be incongruous with destruction of self-consciousness, though they are highly moral and praiseworthy, and comprise the real values which Buddhism presents to practical life. "The Eight-Fold Path" by which the Buddhist hopes to achieve salvation from himself lies in: right beliefs; right aspirations; right speech; right conduct; right manner of gaining a living; right effort; right-mindedness; and right rapture.

Right belief is important because what we do invariably reflects what we think. Wrong acts spring from wrong beliefs.

[3] Rhadakrishnan, *Indian Philosophy,* The Macmillan Company, London, Vol. I, pp. 410-411.

Right aspiration is the product of a true insight, the longing after self-renunciation; "the hope to live in love with all." The aspirant for sainthood must say: "I bear the burden of all creatures."

Right speech demands that one shall abstain from falsehood, from backbiting, from harsh language, from frivolous talk.

Right effort involves the practice of self-control over all passions, both by inhibiting the evil and sublimating the good, the expulsion of the evil idea by the cultivation of the good, until by analysis and contemplation of evil action one becomes disgusted with it.[4]

The monk who was distracted by the sight of a beautiful woman was directed to say over to himself: "I cannot say whether it is a man or woman that passed this way. I only know that a set of bones is travelling on this road." Perhaps Kipling was thinking of this advice when he wrote his line about "A rag and a bone and a hank of hair."

Right-mindedness calls for purity of heart, and right rapture, the calm of contemplation, which with the Buddhist takes the place of prayer.

The novitiate begins by the contemplation of some object like a clay disk upon which he concentrates his gaze, until he becomes oblivious to the world around him, abandoning all desire, sin, distraction, joy, contact, or difference. By successive steps he becomes unconscious of his consciousness and realizes the actual disappearance of feeling and emotion.[5] Unconscious abstraction completes his retreat from the outside world.

The *Parable of the Sower* is introduced into the required readings to give us Buddha's emphasis upon the life of the spirit; *What Maketh an Outcast* reflects his hostility to the caste system as practised in India, and his gospel of the equality of man. The final exhortation on the meaning of wisdom as a loving relationship toward all men sets the temper of Buddhism as its disciples attempt to practise it.

Buddha's epoch partook of the same characteristics everywhere, in India, in China, in Greece, and in Palestine. There was a common longing on the part of enlightened men to escape from the fears of wrathful gods, ghosts, jinns, poltergeists, and spirits that waited around the corner to snare the unwary. There was a common effort to arrive at a more scientific view of nature, and to discover the smiling face of a benevolent Deity over all and in all.

[4] *Ibid.*, I, 422.
[5] *Ibid.*, I, 426.

Buddha's task ran parallel in meaning, as it did in time, with that of Confucius, the Greek philosophers, the Jewish prophets, and in purpose, with that of Jesus of Nazareth. Buddha seems to have believed that the actual denial of a Supreme Being was better than the faith of his contemporaries in gods whose moral character was of the worst, and whose cultus amounted to a sort of devil-worship and appeasement. Buddha would have appreciated the retort of the New England divine to his compatriot's description of a cruel God: "But your God is my Devil." In the midst of the collapse of creeds and the disintegration of systems Buddha attempted to establish a firm foundation for morality and brotherly love. He aimed to found a system independent of dogma, priest, or sacrifice, which would insist upon a change of heart and the culture of the inner life. A man would inexorably take on the character of his loves, his desires, his pursuits, and his ambitions. This was the law of *Karma* which could in nowise be escaped. His conclusion resembled that of Dante, who saw that the supreme punishment of the wicked man was his own wickedness which forever shut him out of the heaven of heavenly thoughts and the blessedness which only the righteous man can enjoy. In this connection the symbolism of the rotating wheel is of great significance. These rapidly succeeding personalities that compose our lives are determined by the law of *Karma*. What we are this moment will determine what we shall be in the next. We cannot escape the effects of our deeds, because from our own deeds are we born. "My action is my possession." Good deeds were those done with a motive of happiness in the future life; bad deeds were those that sought happiness in the present. Good deeds were those that sought the welfare of others; bad deeds were those which sought welfare for the self. Good acts were characterized by the absence of lust, hate, and delusion. Bad acts were born of false vision, lust, and hatred. So the four sublime moods were those of loving kindness, compassion, cheerfulness, and impartiality. His atheistic tendency apparently arose from his distrust of a God of barter and hate, who could be bought off by gifts and so become a partner in iniquity. He created in his followers a new trust in the strength of righteousness. Thus they were brought to a new and liberating sense of moral freedom which is to be seen in the influence upon the arts, and the amelioration of ancient cruelties between man and man, wherever Buddhist influence became strong.

I

Hinayana

There are many sects in Buddhism, perhaps as many as there are denominations of Christians. There are, however, three main developments under which we may generalize Buddhistic doctrine: Hinayana, Mahayana, and Zen.

Hinayana is commonly held to be the earliest, or pioneer, development of the faith. Recalling the meaning of the Binary Wheel which the Buddhists introduced to China (p. 74) and which played so large a part in Chinese concepts, will help to explain Hinayana. Buddha felt that all humanity was bound to the wheel of fate or consciousness, in which the old is ever dissolving, and the new forever coming into being, or perhaps more strictly, the old is forever repeating itself. This was one of the older concepts of Hindu philosophy which Gautama took over into his own system. Instead of one life then, the individual suffers a succession of lives. He dies only to be reborn, and the condition of his rebirth is dependent upon his previous life. Thus all experience, and life itself, is considered as momentary, something in swift transition. According to Hinayana doctrine, the only escape from this tedious and terrifying succession of lives was to achieve unconsciousness, to obliterate from mind and thought not only the world, but final release was not to be had until one also became unconscious even of himself. The method of accomplishment was by contemplation, like the abstraction that might come by continuous consideration of the end of one's nose. Thus having learned the art of self-hypnotization he was thought to have discovered the way to peace.

II

Mahayana

Mahayana was a later development from this doctrine which made Buddhism more possible and practicable for the multitudes. Gautama had been disgusted with the characteristic idol-worship of his people. Common folk were bound in the dark superstitions of fear of hateful and malevolent deities, and it was a part of his plan to escape these fears. He was not, however, thorough-going enough, or the popular practice was too difficult to overcome, to enable him to clear the superstitions of the people. Buddhism came to tolerate idol worship, which carried over to a considerable extent into his system. It is among the ironies of fate that he who denied the existence of God should himself come to be virtually worshipped as God. He would probably have repudiated the numerous sitting and sleeping Buddhas that encumber the temples if he could have foreseen them. Because of the abuses of idolatry, he refused to assert the existence of God, and his system may in that way be considered agnostic, if not atheistic. One's salvation or damnation, he held, was purely the work of the individual, and the result of his way of living. If, however, there was to be a succession of lives, with an enduring relationship or meaning, there must be some reality outside of, and above, the whole process. This he assumed to be, not a Supreme Person, or God, but a Principle or Law, which he identified as *Karma*. This law punished the wrongdoer by inflicting upon his future life the results of the deeds done in the present. From its judgments none could escape. The rotating wheel was, as someone has said, the symbol of the series of lives determined by the principles of *Karma*. Whether one's next existence was to be that of insect, animal, or saint depended on the manner of life that had preceded. The individual could at last, after thousands of rebirths, by sainthood obtain the release of Nirvana, or complete unconsciousness.

Though Buddha himself came more or less to be deified, he claimed for himself to be no more than the Enlightened One, and he considered the way to enlightenment open to all others. Until they had achieved the heights they were known as Boddhisattvas. Thus it was appropriate to look for many Buddhas and many manifestations of Buddha. One recalls the temple in the Western Hills near Peking, in which there are images of five hundred Buddhas, all possessing different facial expressions as symbolizing different virtues or characteristics of Buddhahood. One indeed, it is customary to point out, as the statue of Marco Polo, among the earliest of Europeans in these parts.

A notable feature of Buddhism, which should not be overlooked, is the amenity which it brought into the field of human relations. It received all its disciples on the basis of equality. There were no degrees of distinction except those of excellence of character. It became the chief opponent of the caste system, which in India had become such a source of suffering and degradation. Perhaps it was due to the power of the caste system in Indian life that Buddhism did not survive in power there, while at the same time it won its victories in the democratic and individualistic atmosphere of China.

III
Zen

In his final accomplishment of the Great Enlightenment, Buddha had received much help from the contemplation of nature. For this reason he and his followers have sought out the wildest and most romantic spots in nature in which to spend their lives in contemplation. The Buddhist temple, or monastery, will, in most cases, be found on some distant and lofty mountain, and, if possible, some spot of natural grandeur. This devotion to nature became a dominating influence in Buddhist art and the source of Zen.

Strong influences in the direction of appreciation for nature were already long supreme in Chinese life when Buddhism entered China, and there can be little doubt that the presence of this element gave it a wider welcome. Emperors, kings, and intellectuals of China had long erected their teahouses and summer places in remote and elevated spots, in order the better to commune with nature and to realize their own harmony in that of heaven and earth. Lacking a mountain one emperor erected a garden beside the palace with miniature mountains, forests, and waterfalls, where he could pray or meditate at sunrise, with some of the suggestions of untamed nature herself around him. It was but normal, therefore, that a naturalistic Buddhism should arise in China. Such a development is represented in the appearance there of Zen Buddhism. It emphasized the conquest of desire, the need for disillusionment respecting all those things after which the world seeks. It stressed the necessity of clearing the mind of all prejudices, opinions, aims, and ideas, before the true knowledge could come in. It called for a catharsis similar to that confession of complete ignorance which Socrates insisted upon as the gateway to wisdom. To do this it was necessary to return to nature, to depend upon natural endowment. Dr. Hu Shih, former Ambassador to the United States, outstanding philosopher and philologist of China, has given us a delightful picture of the Zen theory of education, which is illustrative of the whole system:

> These Zen Buddhists developed a peculiar method of teaching which consisted of two essential steps. The first step is "never to tell anything in too plain language." If a novice asks you what truth is, give him a box on the ear and tell him to hide his shame in the kitchen. Or shout at him a deafening shout. Or tell him that you bought a pair of straw sandals for seventeen cash. If the novice does not understand you, which is usually the case, then tell him to try his luck with some other great master at some other Zen School.

So he takes to travelling, which constitutes the second part of the pedagogical method. He travels from one mountain to another and studies under different masters, who, after the Ninth Century, were employing more or less the same technique in teaching. So he travels on and his experiences are widened and enriched by seeing the beauty and grandeur of nature, by suffering the hardships attendant upon such lonely travellers, by coming into contact with the greatest minds of the age, and by befriending kindred souls troubled by more or less similar problems. Then, some day he hears a chance remark of a barmaid, or the chirping of a bird on yonder tree, or smells the fragrance of a little flower, and all of a sudden, he understands! His experiences seem to have been suddenly correlated, his insight seems to have been deepened without his knowing it, and old problems seem so simple, so easy of solution. Everything seems now so self-evident. He has attained.

And then he travels all the distance back to his first teacher. With tears of gratitude and love he thanks him for never having told him anything. That is Chinese Zen.[6]

The characteristic of Zen was to allow the student to arrive at his own conclusions without dictation from his master. Nature herself was conceived to have a formative influence in any education. This was in line, also, with the belief of Socrates that every man had within the depths of his own soul all the answers. He had only to clear away the fogs of prejudiced opinion, and let that nature which was in him speak, in order to obtain the truth. Taoism also was impregnated with this doctrine of naturalism. One wonders how much Rousseau and Locke, who introduced the idea to the European Enlightenment, may have been indebted to this ancient source. The probabilities are more than strong, for the Enlightenment in Europe had been largely induced by the new contacts with China and India. Socrates may have been influenced from similar Oriental sources. It was not impossible, and it raises most intriguing questions.

Equally important along with this feeling for nature was another element which was fostered by the love of nature, which was detachment. This element was strong in the whole of Oriental philosophy. Zen Buddhism, together with the others, held that a man was inevitably led away from correct conclusions if he was moved by strong desires of possession, or of selfish advantage of any kind. The sure preventative of arriving at truth is an impregnable conviction already arrived at. Love for possession will make the possessor the victim of his possessions. Soon these interests in acquisition come to dictate the life and the activity of the man who acquires.

[6] *Symposium on Chinese Culture*, Sophia H. Chen Zen, ed., art. by Hu Shih, China Institute of Pacific Relations, Shanghai, p. 33.

Thus the very things that should free him and give him liberty become the source of a slavery he can scarcely escape. "Things are in the saddle," as we say. But one can be equally obsessed by ideas and opinions, held so strongly that no new light can penetrate the mind. In this case the individual is more possessed by ideas, outlook, and opinions than the possessor of them. He becomes the slave of false notions and prejudices.

Nor can one achieve great and liberating work, art, ambitions, if they are centered in selfish interests. There must be sense of detachment, disinterestedness in the result before one can make the scientific discovery, realize the philosophic truth, serve the social order, or arrive at true religious practice. This is perhaps the most important truth that Zen has to teach us.

IV

Some Concluding Remarks

There is no purpose in my concluding remarks to derogate from the success and importance of Buddhism. Its great values are to be discovered in the ameliorations it brought to its own times and surroundings. Its doctrine of universal love, exercised toward all creatures, brought great benefits to an age of cruelty and inhumanity. This, linked with a sense of universal brotherhood, made it a powerful modifying influence upon a civilization hitherto committed to a deadening practice of caste. To its ranks, on a basis of equality, it welcomed rich and poor, high and low, learned and ignorant. The practice of this precept was very real in its system. One can travel safely in the remotest parts of the Orient by stopping at the familiar Buddhist temple, from which no one is turned away empty, and general respect for the Buddhist monks will protect him from the attacks of bandits.

To multitudes, moreover, Buddhism brought relief from tragic fear of evil gods who might punish without reason, capricious gods who were the enemies of mankind, and a religion that had no relation to ethical practices and honest intent. It proclaimed the message that every man could work out his own salvation without the mediatory services of priests or gods, and it hoped thereby to exalt human nature and raise the standard of morality. Salvation was to come by the practice of goodness, not by the offering of vain and revolting sacrifices. These values we cannot estimate unless we have been face to face with such social practices as Gautama looked upon. Thus Buddhism has been a mighty civilizing influence. And this has been in many ways; among others, it became the inspiring influence to a new development of art in India, China, and Japan— one of the surest indications of religious realism.

All in all, in its times and in its settings, Buddhism must be considered to have marked a great milestone in the advance of human culture. This progress was not due, however, to its adherence to the principle of escape, which Buddha sought with such fervor, but rather to the advocacy and practice of social abrogation of the system of caste, in which some were highly exalted, and others were considered lower than the animals, the pariah less valuable than the sacred cow. Into such a society came Buddha, himself a Hindu of high birth and blameless life, proclaiming the equality of man, the supreme value of love, the conquest of inner hates, prejudices, and prides. Here, rather than in retreat from the world, lay the conquering power of Buddhism. Beauty of life was likewise enhanced, as it turned from an overdone introspection to the calm voice of nature, and the significance of its message to man. The force of Buddhism lay in its humanism.

These reflections inevitably raise the question of the whole value of escapism as a social principle. Is retreat from the world to be considered an adequate solution for the most pressing problems of the search for values? How does such a system compare in efficiency with that of the Western world, which is what the psychologists would call extrovert? Where does the answer truly lie? The English poet was facing this question when he wrote:

> The world is too much with us late and soon
> Getting and spending, we lay waste our powers.

Do not these words indicate the undertone of failure in our own system which is apparent to all thoughtful men?

The chief barrier to common understanding between East and West lies in what the Oriental would call our self-assertiveness. Seen from the Oriental standpoint, the Western man, who is only a little way from savagery with a young and untried civilization, dares to stand up and question solutions which have been reached by the painstaking and consecrated efforts and thought of a hundred generations. This Western upstart finds fault with nearly everything he sees, while he reaches out for every material benefit in sight, and seeks immediately to replace the old and tried with the strife and tumult of Western ways. What wonder that the long lifetime of a race, bent upon the achievement of peace, should resent this clamorous and untempered youthfulness, and demand that Western civilization await the judgment of time. The self-assertiveness of the West is exactly that egoism which Buddha proclaimed to be the source and sum of all evil. This conceit is, in Indian thought, most surely to be questioned when it is the predominating influence that has brought Western culture and all civilization to the brink of catastrophe, in the proclamation by totalitarianism of superiority of race, and martial power, and the dictation of a world-wide slavery for all but a privileged few. The true answer to the problem raised may lie between the two extremes. Certainly, in his devotion to introspection, to the peace of retreat from the world, the Oriental has laid himself open to the aggressor, and has thereby lost his freedom of action. But, on his part, the Westerner is threatened with becoming the victim of his own aggressiveness, the prey of his own violence, as power is seized by the unscrupulous and immoral. It now appears that there cannot be a true civilization without the moral and spiritual elements which have been too long despised. All the strength of Western civilization lies in its sense of justice, its allegiance with righteousness, its adherence to the principle of equal rights. Without these, it is as weak as water. Under such circumstances it appears possible that neither an introvert nor an extrovert world offers the solution to the pressing problems of modern civilization. If the normal culture of man cannot spring from an escapism which refuses to face a world of reality, it is equally certain that a social order characterized by aggression alone must equally fail. We require the balance provided by attention to the deeper spiritual realities, of which the Western world has so largely tried to divest itself. The words of the popular song:

I don't know where I'm going
But I'm on my way,

have been all too expressive of the breakneck speed and blindness with which the West has been rushing headlong into trouble. Let us make no mistake, our woes cannot be ended merely with the defeat of hostile arms. Victory must be had in the realm of ideas, where the severest battle lies. The ideas that underlie the peace of the future world can be neither wholly extrovert nor introvert.

The hopeful fact in the situation is that neither East nor West is altogether wanting the elements of solution. As the normal person must hold his life in balance between aggression and retreat, so a future civilization must acquire a true balance and proportion. The way is clear that the normal man can cultivate both extroversion and introversion in proper ratio and be stronger by the mingling. How can he overcome such a paradox? He can express his introversion by losing himself and his selfish interests in devotion to the good of others. These are the active virtues for which Buddhism itself calls. But this is extroversion lifted to a new motive, the good of others. It might with equal significance be termed introversion with a new motive, self-discipline without the self in view. The highest self-cultivation lies paradoxically in forgetting selfish ends. This "detachment" from all selfish interests and profits runs like the recurring theme of a fugue through the pages of the Bhagavad-Gita of Hinduism as well as in the literature of Buddhism. A corn of wheat cannot express its highest quality, that of creativity, until it falls into the ground and dies. This in itself is good Buddhistic doctrine. However, there is an obverse to the shield: in seeking the good of others, the self does not destroy but creates a higher selfhood. Dying to the little world of private interests, the person becomes the citizen of a larger world, in which he arrives at the stature of manhood, fullest self-expression. Here alone lies the ending of the conflict between introversion and extroversion in the life of man and in the life of his civilization. The battles fought for selfish interests can yield victories that are in the highest sense only defeats. The battles fought for others are permanent victories even in the presence of momentary defeat.

Much could doubtless be gained if East and West could come together in mutual understanding based upon the principles thus presented. Untempered individualism in the West needs to approach Buddhism by becoming more nearly Christian. Buddhism on its part needs to advance to a new appreciation of the true method of escape from the deadening pursuit of selfish desires. Selfishness, which brings in its train disgust with life, cannot be cured, as the practical tenets of Buddhism teach, by self-repression and retreat from the world alone. The egotistic self dies not by suppression but by being lost in a higher selfhood. The highest development through the love of service is also the way to peace. It calls, not for the extinction of desire, but for desire on the higher level. It calls, not for retreat from the world, but for participation in the world on this loftier plane. Self-sacrifice is dignified, not for its own sake, but by the quality of its purpose and the extent of its self-surrender in the service of other men or of a common and noble cause. Peace and self-realization go together, not in a Nirvana of unconsciousness, but in an all-giving unity with the universe which possesses the characteristics of a Supreme Creative Intelligence.

Karma as an impersonal principle is deadening and enslaving until it is linked with freedom, grace, and forgiveness, through a Divine Being.

Buddhism died out in the place of its birth because it did not sufficiently separate itself from the tragic impersonal forces of a nature theory which characterized the concepts of the religions with which it broke. It can renew itself in an age of confusion only as it revises its doctrine of selfhood to agree with its own ancient respect for the welfare of all creatures.

READINGS

TURNBULL: *TONGUES OF FIRE.* Johns Hopkins Press, Baltimore.
Pp. 172-178; 181-184; 197-198; 200; 206; 227.

—————

BUDDHA'S RENUNCIATION OF THE WORLD

The Bodisat in due course grew to manhood. And the King had
three mansions made, suitable for the three seasons, and he provided
him with forty thousand dancing girls. So the Bodisat like a god
surrounded by troops of houris lived, as the seasons changed, in each
of these mansions in the enjoyment of great majesty. And Yasodhara
was his principal queen.

Now one day the Future Buddha, wanting to go to his pleasance,
ascended his chariot, resplendent as a mansion in the skies, and went
toward the garden. The angels thought: The time for young Siddhattha to attain enlightenment is near; let us show him the Omens!
And they made a son of the gods represent a man wasted by age, with
decayed teeth and grey hair, bent and broken in body.

Then the Bodisat asked his charioteer: What kind of a man is
this whose very hair is not as that of other men? When he heard
his servant's answer, he said: Woe upon birth, since through it decay
must come to every living being! And with agitated heart he turned
back and entered his palace.

Again one day when the Future Buddha, as he went to his pleasance,
saw a man who was ill, he made the same inquiry as before; and then,
with agitated heart turned back.

Once more, when, as he went to his pleasance, he saw a dead man,
he made the same inquiry as before, and then, with agitated heart,
turned back and re-entered his palace.

Once again, when he saw one who had abandoned the world, carefully and decently clad, he asked his charioteer: Friend, what kind
of a man is that? He answered: That is a mendicant friar. And
he described the advantages of renouncing the world. And that day
the Future Buddha, cherishing the thought of renouncing the world,
went on to his pleasance.

At that time Suddhodana the King, who had heard that the wife
of the Bodisat had brought forth a son, sent a message saying: Make
known my joy to my son!

The Future Buddha, hearing this, said: An impediment hath come into being! When the king asked: What did my son say? and heard that saying, he gave command: From henceforth let Rahula (Impediment) be my grandson's name.

But the Bodisat in his splendid chariot rode into the town with great magnificence and exceeding glory and he entered his palace in great splendour and lay on his couch of state. Thereupon women clad in beautiful array, skilful in the dance and song, and lovely as celestial nymphs, brought their instruments of music and ranging themselves in order, danced and sang and played.

But the Bodisat, his heart estranged from sin, took no pleasure in the spectacle and fell asleep. And the women, saying: He for whose sake we were performing is gone to sleep; why should we play any longer? set aside the instruments they held, and lay down to sleep.

The lamps were just burning out when the Bodisat, waking up, saw them with their stage properties laid aside and sleeping, some grinding their teeth, some yawning, some muttering in their sleep, some gaping, and some with their dress in disorder.

To him that magnificent apartment, as splendid as Sakka's heavenly mansion, began to seem like to a charnelhouse of loathsome corpses. Life seemed to him like staying in a house devoured with flames. He gave vent to the solemn utterance; It all oppresseth me! It is intolerable! And his mind turned ardently to the state of those who have renounced the world.

Resolving that very day to accomplish the Great Renunciation, he rose from his couch, went to the door and called: Who is there? Channa, who had been sleeping with his head on the threshold, answered: Sir, it is I.

Then said he: I am resolved today to accomplish the Great Renunciation. Saddle a horse for me! Now after the Bodisat had sent Channa on this errand, he thought: I will just look at my son. And he went to the apartments of his wife and opened her chamber door.

A lamp, fed with sweet-burning oil, was burning dimly in the inner chamber. The mother of Rahula was asleep on a bed strewn with jasmine flowers, resting her hand on the head of her son. Stopping with his foot on the threshold the Bodisat thought: If I lift her hand to take my son, she will awake; that will prevent my going away. I will come back to see him when I become a Buddha. And he left the palace.

The Bodisat adopted the outward signs of an Arahat, and dressed himself in the sacred garb of Renunciation. And he enjoined upon Channa to go and assure his parents of his safety. And Channa did homage to the Bodisat reverently and went.

Now the Bodisat thought: I will perform the uttermost penance. And he brought himself to live on one seed of the oil plant, or one grain of rice a day, and even to fast entirely.[1]

[1] Cf. Luke 4:1-13.

By this fasting, however, he waxed thin as a skeleton; the colour of his body, once fair as gold, grew dark. And one day, when walking up and down, plunged in intense meditation, he was overcome by severe pain; and he fainted and fell.

And he recovered consciousness again and stood up. But he perceived that penance was not the way to Wisdom; and begging through the villages and towns, he collected ordinary food and lived upon it.

His Enlightenment

"The Lord gracious, beautiful to behold, with senses stilled and mind restrained, as one who hath attained the supreme calm of self-conquest, subdued and guarded."

The Udana

Early on the full-moon day in the month of May, the Bodisat had seen five dreams: and considering their purport he had drawn the conclusion: Verily this day I shall become a Buddha. And at the end of the night he washed and dressed himself, and he went early and sat at the foot of the Bodhi-tree,[2] lighting it up with glory.

Then the Bodisat turned his back upon the trunk of the Bodhi-tree, and with his face towards the east, made the firm resolve: My skin and sinews and bones may become arid, and the very blood in my body may dry up; but till I attain to complete insight, this seat I will not leave! And he sat himself down firm and immovable, and not to be dislodged by a hundred thunderbolts.

At that time Mara, the Evil One, thinking: Siddhattha the Prince wanteth to free himself from my dominion, but I will not let him yet get free! went to his hosts, and sounding his war-cry, led them forth to battle.[3]

The angels of the ten thousand worlds continued speaking the praises of the Great Being, but as the army approached and surrounded the Bodhi-tree, not one was able to stay, and they fled each one from the spot, and the Great Being sat there alone.

But Mara said to his host: Friends, there is no other man like Siddhattha, the son of Suddhodana. We cannot give him battle face to face. Let us attack him from behind!

The Great Being looked around and saw that all the angels had fled. Then beholding the hosts of Mara coming thick upon him, he thought: Against me alone this mighty host is putting forth all its energy and strength. Father nor mother are here, nor brother, nor any other relative.

But I have those Ten Perfections, like old retainers, long cherished at my board. It behooveth me then to make the Ten Perfections my

[2] Ficus religiosa; meaning here, on the side, tree of enlightenment.
[3] Cf. Luke 4:1-13.

shield and my sword and to strike a blow with them, that shall destroy this strong array. So he sat meditating on the Ten Perfections.

Then Mara, saying: Thus will I drive away Siddhattha; caused a whirlwind to blow. And immediately such winds rushed together from the four corners of the earth as could have torn down the peaks of mountains half a league, two leagues, three leagues high. But through the majesty of the goodness of the Great Being, they reached him with their power gone, and even the hem of his robe they were unable to shake.

Then saying: I will overwhelm him with water, Mara caused a mighty rain to fall. And the clouds gathered, overspreading one another by hundreds and by thousands, and poured forth rain; and a great flood, overtopping the trees of the forest, approached the Great Being. But it was not able to wet on his robe even the space where a dewdrop might fall.

Then Mara caused a storm of rocks to fall. And mighty mountain peaks came through the air, spitting forth fire and smoke.

Then saying: By this will I terrify Siddhattha, and drive him away! he brought on a thick darkness. And the darkness became fourfold; but before it reached the Future Buddha, it disappeared as darkness disappeareth before the brightness of the sun.

And the angels stood on the edge of the rocks that encircle the world; and stretching forward in amazement, they watched, saying: Lost, lost is Siddhattha the Prince, the glorious and beautiful!

But the army of Mara fled this way and that, so that not even two were left together. Then the heavenly hosts, when they saw that the army of Mara had fled, cried: The tempter is overcome! Siddhattha the Prince hath prevailed!

It was before the sun had set that the Great Being thus put to flight the army of the Evil One. Then, whilst the Bodhi-tree paid him homage by raining its sprigs red like coral upon his priestly robe, he acquired in the first watch of the night the Knowledge of the Past, in the middle watch of the night the Knowledge of the Present, and in the third watch of the night the Knowledge of the Chain of Causation which leadeth to the origin of evil.

And when the Great Being at dawning of the day attained to complete enlightenment the ten thousand worlds became glorious as on a festive day. The blind from birth received their sight; the deaf could hear; cripples could use their limbs; captives went free. Thus in surpassing glory and honour did He attain omniscience, and breathe forth the solemn Hymn of Triumph.[4]

Introduction of the Jataka.

[4] Adapted from Rhys Davids' translation.

THE CHAIN OF CAUSATION

One thing only, the uprooting of sorrow! Buddha.

At that time the Blessed Buddha, having just attained to the Buddhaship, dwelt at Uruvela, on the bank of the river Neranjara, at the foot of the Bodhi-tree, for seven days together enjoying the bliss of emancipation.

Then the Blessed One fixed His mind upon the Chain of Causation:

> From ignorance springeth karma:[5]
> From karma springeth consciousness;
> From consciousness spring name and form;[6]
> From name and form spring the six organs of sense;[7]
> From the six organs of sense springeth contact;
> From contact springeth sensation;
> From sensation springeth desire;
> From desire springeth attachment;
> From attachment springeth existence;
> From existence springeth birth;
> From birth spring old age and death, grief,
>   lamentation, suffering, defection and despair.

Thus doth all this suffering arise. But by the destruction of ignorance all that which issueth therefrom is also destroyed.

Then the Blessed One pronounced this solemn utterance: When the real nature of things becometh clear to the ardent, meditating Brahman, he standeth dispelling the hosts of Mara like the sun that illumineth the sky.

Mahavagga I. i.

THE SERMON AT BENARES

It is in just this way, Ananda, that thou must understand how the whole of this life in religion is concerned with friendship, intimacy, association with whatsoever is lovely and righteous.

Buddha.

The Blessed One was once staying at Benares, at the hermitage called Migadaya. And there He addressed the company of the five Bhikkhus,[8] and said:

There are two extremes, O Bhikkhus, from which he who leadeth the religious life must abstain. What are those two extremes?

One is life of pleasure, devoted to desire and enjoyment; that is

[5] Action and the destiny resulting therefrom.
[6] Individual beings.
[7] The five senses and the mind.
[8] Mendicant friars.

base, ignoble, unspiritual, unworthy, unreal.   The other is a life of mortification; it is gloomy, unworthy, unreal.

The Perfect One, O Bhikkhus, avoiding these extremes, hath discovered the middle path, a path which openeth the eyes, and bestoweth understanding, which leadeth to rest, to knowledge, to enlightenment, to Nirvana.[9]

And what, O Bhikkhus, is that middle path discovered by the Perfect One?   Verily, it is the noble Eightfold Path :[10]

> Right Belief;
> Right Resolve;
> Right Speech;
> Right Conduct;
> Right Occupation;
> Right Effort;
> Right Mindfulness;
> Right Rapture.

This, O Bhikkhus, is that middle path which openeth the eyes, and bestoweth understanding, which leadeth to rest, to knowledge, to enlightenment, to Nirvana!

Now this, O Bhikkhus, is the noble truth concerning suffering: Birth is suffering; decay is suffering; disease is suffering; death is suffering. Presence of objects we hate is suffering; separation from objects we love is suffering; not to obtain what we desire is suffering.   In brief, the clinging to the five elements of existence is suffering.

This, O Bhikkhus, is the noble truth concerning the cause of suffering.   It is the thirst for being which leads to rebirth, together with lust and desire, which finds gratification here and there; the thirst for pleasure, the thirst for power.   This, O Bhikkhus, is the noble truth concerning the extinction of suffering.   Verily, it is the destruction, in which no passion doth remain, of this very thirst; the abandoning, the relinquishing, the deliverance from this thirst: the giving it no room.

Now this, O Bhikkhus, is the noble truth concerning the path which leadeth to the extinction of suffering.   Verily, it is this noble Eightfold Path, to wit:

> Right Belief;
> Right Speech;
> Right Resolve;
> Right Conduct;
> Right Occupation;
> Right Effort;
> Right Mindfulness;
> Right Rapture.

Thus spake the Blessed One, and the company of the five Bhikkhus, glad at heart, rejoiced at His words.

[9] Means literally, *to blowing out of the flame.*
[10] "The numerical statement of things was a mnemonic necessity in an undocumented world."   Wells.

And when the royal chariot wheel of the truth had thus been set rolling onward by the Blessed One, the gods of the earth gave a shout, saying: In Benares, at the hermitage of Migadaya, the supreme wheel of the empire of truth hath been set rolling by the Blessed One,— that wheel which can never be turned back by any god, by Brahma or Mara, or anyone in the universe!

And when they heard the shouts of the gods of the earth, the guardian angels of the four quarters of the globe gave forth a shout saying: In Benares, at the hermitage of Migadaya, the supreme wheel of the empire of truth hath been set rolling by the Blessed One,—that wheel which never can be turned back by any god, by Brahma or Mara, or anyone in the universe!

And thus, in an instant, the sound went up even to the world of Brahma: and the ten-thousand worlds quaked and trembled and shook violently, and an immeasureable bright light appeared in the universe, beyond even the power of the gods.[11]

Dramma-ckka-ppavattana-sutta and Mahavagga I. vi.

THE SERMON OF BENARES EXPLAINED

And what, O priests, is right belief? The knowledge of suffering, the knowledge of the cause of suffering, the knowledge of the extinction of suffering, and the knowledge of the path leading to the extinction of suffering, this is right belief.

And what, O priests, is right resolve? The resolve to renounce sensual pleasure, the resolve to have malice toward none, and the resolve to harm no living creature, this is right resolve.

And what, O priests, is right speech? To abstain from falsehood, to abstain from backbiting, to abstain from harsh language, to abstain from frivolous talk, this is right speech.

And what, O priests, is right conduct? To abstain from destroying life, to abstain from taking what is not given, to abstain from immorality, this is right conduct.

And what, O priests, is right occupation? Whenever a noble disciple, quitting a wrong occupation, gets his livelihood by a right occupation, this is right occupation.

And what, O priests, is right effort? Whenever a priest purposeth, heroically endeavoureth, applieth his mind, and exerteth himself that evil and demeritorious qualities not yet arisen may not arise; that evil and demeritorious qualities already arisen may be abandoned; that meritorious qualities not yet arisen may arise; purposeth, heroically endeavoureth, applieth his mind and exerteth himself for the preservation, retention, growth, increase, development and perfection of meritorious qualities already arisen, this is right effort.

And what, O priests, is right mindfulness? Whenever a priest

[11] From the translation by Davids.

liveth and respecteth the body, the sensations, the mind, the elements of being, observant, strenuous, conscious, contemplative, and hath rid himself of lust and grief, this is right mindfulness.

And what, O priests, is right rapture? Whenever a priest, having isolated himself from sensual pleasures, and from demeritorious traits, entereth upon the first trance which is produced by isolation and characterized by joy and happiness; when, through the subsidence of reasoning and reflection and still retaining joy and happiness, he entereth upon the second trance which is an interior tranquillization and intentness of the thoughts, and is produced by concentration; when, through the paling of joy, indifferent, contemplative, conscious, and in the experience of bodily happiness, he entereth upon the third trance; when through the abandonment of happiness, through the abandonment of misery, through the disappearance of all antecedent gladness and grief, he entereth upon the fourth trance, which hath neither misery nor happiness, but is contemplation refined by indifference, this O priests, is right rapture.[12]

Digha-Nikaya, Sutta 22.

THE PARABLE OF BUDDHA THE SOWER

The Exalted One was once staying on South Hill, at Ekanala, a Brahman village. Now it was time for the ploughing, and Farmer Bharadvaja, the Brahman, had yoked five hundred ploughs. Then the Exalted One, taking robe and bowl, drew near to the ploughing.

Now it was time for Farmer Bharadvaja's distribution of food. And the Exalted One drew near and stood on one side. And Farmer Bharadvaja saw the Exalted One standing there for alms, and said: Now I, O recluse, do plough and sow, and when I have ploughed and sown I eat.

But we see neither Master Gotama's team, nor his plough, nor his ploughshare, nor his goad, nor his oxen. To him the Blessed One made answer: Faith is the seed I sow; penance the rain that watereth it; wisdom is my yoke and plough; the pole is modesty; mindfulness the tie; thoughtfulness my ploughshare and my goad.

Guarded am I in action and in speech; I weed with truth; in kindliness is my salvation; exertion is my ox that never turneth back but beareth onward to Nirvana where it beareth fruit in immortality; whoso this ploughing hath accomplished from all suffering is set free!

Then the Brahman Bharadvaja, having poured rice-milk into a golden bowl, offered it to the Blessed One and said: Let the Blessed One eat of the rice-milk! The venerable Gotama is a ploughman, for He plougheth a ploughing that beareth the fruit of immortality.

Brahman Sutta, Samyutta Nikaya; and Sutta Nipata.

[12] Adapted from Warren's translation.

What Maketh an Outcast

Then the Blessed One, having taken His robes and His bowl, entered Savatthi for alms. And the Blessed One going for alms from house to house went to the house of the Brahman[13] Aggikabharadvaja.

The Brahman saw the Blessed One coming at a distance, and seeing Him said: Stay there, O shaveling! O wretched Samana! O outcast!

The Blessed One answered unto the Brahman: Dost thou know, O Brahman, an outcast, or the things that make an outcast?

Whoso is angry and beareth hatred, is wicked and hypocritical, hath embraced wrong views, is deceitful; whoso harmeth living beings, in whom is no compassion for living beings, him let one know as an outcast.

Whoso destroyeth or layeth siege to villages and towns, and is known as an enemy; whoso appropriateth by theft the property of others; whoso having contracted a debt, runneth away when called upon to pay, saying: There is no debt I owe thee! him let one know as an outcast.

Whoso for his own sake or that of others or for the sake of wealth speaketh falsely when called as a witness, whoso being rich supporteth not mother or father when past their youth, whoso exalteth himself and despiseth others, being mean by his pride, whoso is a provoker and avaricious, hath sinful desires, is shameless in sinning,—him let one know as an outcast!

Not by birth doth one become an outcast, not by birth doth one become a Brahman. By deeds doth one become an outcast, by deeds doth one become a Brahman.[14]

Vasalasutta of the Sutta-Nipata.

What Constituteth Wisdom

Then the Blessed One spake and said: A householder on hearing the Truth hath faith in the Tathagata, and when he hath acquired that faith, full of modesty and pity, he is compassionate and kind to all creatures that have life. He passeth his life in purity and honesty of heart. He liveth a life of chastity. He speaketh truth; from the truth he never swerveth. Faithful and trustworthy, he injureth not his fellowman by deceit. Putting away slander, he abstaineth from calumny.

What he heareth here he repeateth not elsewhere to raise a quarrel against the people here: what he heareth elsewhere he repeateth not here to raise a quarrel against the people there.

Thus he liveth as a binder together of those who are divided, an encourager of those who are friends, a peacemaker, a lover of peace, impassioned for peace. Whatever word is humane, pleasant to the ear, lovely, reaching to the heart, urbane, beloved of the people, such word speaketh he.

[13] The highest or sacerdotal caste, looking down on the others.
[14] Translated by Fausböll.

And he letteth his mind pervade all the quarters of the world, above, below, around and everywhere, doth he continue to pervade with a heart of love, far-reaching, grown great, and beyond measure.

So of all things which have life, there is not one that he passeth by or leaveth aside, but regardeth them all with mind set free, and deep-felt love.   Verily this is the way to a state of union with Brahma.[15]

I & II, Tevigga Sutta, Digha Nikaya.

There are certain subjects for meditation that have been made known by the Blessed One, by Him of knowledge and insight, by the Arahat, the Buddha supreme.   And they are these:

> The idea of the impermanence of every thing and of every being;
> The idea of the absence of any abiding principle in them;
> The idea of the impurity and danger connected with the body;
> The idea of getting rid of evil dispositions;
> The idea of freedom from passion;
> The idea of peace;
> The idea of dissatisfaction with the things of the world;
> The idea of the ecstatic trance;
> The idea of love to all beings;
> The idea of pity for all beings;
> The idea of sympathy with all beings;
> The idea of equanimity in all the changing circumstances of life;
> The idea of death.

Milinda Panha V. 6.

[15] Translation by Davids.

WATTS: *THE SPIRIT OF ZEN.*   E. P. Dutton & Company, New York.
   Pp. 51-52, 57-60.

For life, even as the ordinary humdrum series of daily events, is something essentially ungraspable and indefinable; never for a moment does it remain the same; we can never make it stand still for analysis and definition.   If we try to think of the speed at which time is passing or at which things are changing our minds are set in a whirl, for it is a speed which can never be calculated.   The harder we try to catch hold of the moment, to seize a pleasant sensation, or to define something in a way which will be satisfactory for all time, the more elusive do they become.   It has been said that to define is to kill, and if the wind were to stop for one second for us to catch hold of it, it would cease to be wind.   The same is true of life.   Perpetually things and events are moving and changing; we cannot take hold of the present moment and make it stay with us; we cannot call·back past time or keep forever a passing sensation.   Once we try to do this all we have is a dead memory; the reality is not there, and no satisfaction can be found in it.   If we suddenly realize that we are happy, the more we endeavour to think of some means of preserving our happiness, the faster do we see it slipping away.   We try to define happiness so that we may know how to find it when we are feeling miserable; a man thinks, "I am happy now that I am staying in this place.   Therefore happiness, for me, is to come and stay in this place."   And the next time he is unhappy he tries to apply this definition; he goes to that place again and finds that it does not make him happy; there is only the dead memory of happiness, and the definition does not hold.   For happiness is like Maeterlinck's blue birds—try to capture them and they lose their colour; it is like trying to clutch water in one's hands—the harder one grips, the faster it slips through one's fingers.   Therefore a Zen master when asked, "What is the Tao?" replied immediately, "Walk on!" for we can only understand life by keeping pace with it, by a complete affirmation and acceptance of its magic-like transformations and unending changes.   By this acceptance the Zen disciple is filled with a great sense of wonder, for everything is perpetually becoming new.   The beginning of the universe is now, for all things are at this moment being created, and the end of the universe is now, for all things are at this moment passing away.

(Pp. 51-52.)

[There] is another important aspect of Zen, which may be called "spiritual poverty."   Almost every form of religion has insisted that many possessions are a bar to spiritual progress, but while the Zen monk has certainly the minimum of material possessions, Zen interprets poverty as an attitude of mind rather than a physical condition.   One of the most common ways of trying to fix life into rigid definitions is to qualify something, whether a person, a thing or an idea, with the statement, "This belongs to me." But because life is this elusive and perpetually changing process, every time we think we have really taken possession of something, the truth is that we have completely lost it. All that we possess is our own idea about the thing desired—an idea which tends to remain fixed, which does not grow as the thing grows. Thus one of the most noticeable facts about those obsessed with greed for possessions, whether material goods or cherished ideas, is their desire that things shall remain as they are—not only that their possessions shall remain in their own hands, but also that the possessions themselves shall not change. There are theologians and philosophers who show the greatest concern if anyone questions their ideas about the universe, for they imagine that within those ideas they have at last enshrined ultimate truth, and that to lose those ideas would be to lose the truth. But because truth is alive it will not be bound by anything which shows no sign of life—namely, a conception whose validity is held to depend partly on the fact that it is unchangeable. For once we imagine that we have grasped the truth of life, the truth has vanished, for truth cannot become anyone's property, the reason being that truth *is* life, and for one person to think that he possesses all life is a manifest absurdity. The part cannot possess the whole. Therefore Chuang-Tzu tells the following story:

> Shun asked Ch'eng, saying, "Can one get Tao so as to have it for one's own?"
> "Your very body," replied Ch'eng, "is not your own. How should Tao be?"
> "If my body," said Shun, "is not my own, pray whose is it?"
> "It is the delegated image of Tao," replied Ch'eng. "Your life is not your own. It is the delegated harmony of Tao. Your individuality is not your own. It is the delegated adaptability of Tao. . . . You move, but know not how. You are at rest, but know not why. . . . These are the operation of the laws of Tao. How then should you get Tao so as to have it for your own?"

Just as no person can possess life, so no idea which a person may possess can define it; the idea of possession is illusory, for apart from the fact that all things must eventually pass away into some other form, and can never remain in one place for eternity, at the root of possession lies the desire that things shall not alter in any way, and this is a complete impossibility. If, therefore, life can never be grasped, how can it ever be understood? How can truth be known if it can never be defined? Zen would answer: by not trying to grasp or define it, and this is the fundamental Buddhist ideal of non-attachment, or the Taoist idea of *wu-wei*.

But Buddhism and Taoism go further than saying that nothing can ever be possessed; they declare that those who try to possess are in fact *possessed,* they are slaves to their own illusions about life. Spiritual freedom is just that capacity to be as spontaneous and unfettered as life itself, to be "as the wind that bloweth where it listeth and thou hearest the sound thereof but cannot tell whence it cometh nor whither it goeth." "Even so," said Jesus, "is everyone that is born of the Spirit." But non-attachment does not mean running away from things to some peaceful hermitage, for we can never escape from our own illusions about life; we carry them with us, and if we are afraid of them and wish to escape it means that we are doubly enslaved. For whether we are content with our illusions or frightened of them, we are equally possessed by them, and hence the non-attachment of Buddhism and Taoism means not running away from life but running with it, for freedom comes through complete acceptance of reality. Those who wish to keep their illusions do not move at all; those who fear them run backwards into greater illusions, while those who conquer them "Walk on."

(Pp. 57-60.)

QUESTIONS AND STATEMENTS FOR DISCUSSION

1. "All existence involves suffering.
   "All suffering is caused by indulging in inherently insatiable desires.
   "Therefore all suffering will cease upon the suppressing of all desires." (From *The Four Noble Truths*.)
2. "The blame for the consequences of a person's evil deeds must be placed upon himself, not upon heredity, society, fate, God, or devil."
3. Is the self extinguished, or is a higher self created, through love to all beings, men, and things alike?
4. What, if anything, does the ecstatic abandon in addition to "desire, sin, distractions, discursiveness, joy, hedonic feeling"?
5. "The old is forever repeating itself"; is this possible in a world of change?
6. One must clear the mind of all prejudices, opinions, aims, and ideas, before true knowledge can come in. Every time we think we have really taken possession of something we have really lost it. Discuss these paradoxes. (Watts, *The Spirit of Zen,* pp. 57-60.) Pp. 143-145.
7. "All of a sudden he understands"—What has really taken place?
8. What principle of modern education is implied above?
9. The Sermon of Benares represents certain laudable repressions— is there any other way of achieving value? Are values ever separable from positive action?
10. How is the previous question answered in *The Parable of Buddha the Sower?*
11. Is there a universal law of human society discoverable in the Buddhistic doctrine of "What maketh an outcast"? Are anger, hatred, deceit, violence, and theft as active in social ostracism as social caste?
12. How many constituents of "wisdom" can you name according to Buddhistic doctrine? Are they genuine values?
13. "If we suddenly realize that we are happy, the more we endeavor to think of some means of preserving our happiness, the faster we see it slipping away." (Watts, *The Spirit of Zen,* p. 51.) P. 143.
14. "All that we possess is our own idea about the thing desired— an idea which tends to remain fixed, which does not grow as the thing grows." (*Ibid.,* p. 58.) P. 144.

Suggested Supplementary Readings:

Haydon: *The Legacy of India, "Buddhism."* Pp. 162-184.
Haydon: *The Biography of the Gods.* Macmillan, New York. Chap. VI, pp. 126-165.

Hume: *The World's Living Religions.* Scribner's, New York.
Chap. IV, pp. 59-62.

Soothill: *The Three Religions of China.* Oxford University
Press, New York. Chap. IV, pp. 77-111.

Radhakrishnan: *Indian Philosophy.* Macmillan, New York.
Vol. I, Chaps. VII, X, XI.

Keith: *Buddhist Philosophy.* Clarendon Press, Oxford.

Carpenter: *Buddhism and Christianity.* Doubleday, Doran, New
York.

Cranmer-Byng: *The Vision of Asia.* Farrar & Rinehart, New
York.

Arnold: *The Light of Asia.* Cambridge University Press.

Chapter 5

THE STOIC "LIFE OF REASON"

I
The Origins of Stoicism
1. The search for "ataraxia" and the times that called it forth
2. The "founding fathers": Socrates, Antisthenes, Diogenes, Xenophon, Zeno of Citium

II
The Stoic Definition of Value
1. The supremacy of mind over matter
2. The intrinsic worth of man

III
Stoicism in the Field of History
1. Its relation to Roman ideals: Epictetus, and Marcus Aurelius
2. Its formative influence on Roman law
3. Its impact on Christianity
4. Its contribution to Western Civilization

IV
Stoicism as a "Way of Life"
Conclusion

Chapter 5

THE STOIC "LIFE OF REASON"

We have already mentioned that remarkable movement in human thought which, between the eighth and the third centuries B.C., brought the civilized world to the verge of a new cosmopolitanism. There seems to have been a universal urge to break away from tribal concepts, local superstitions, and narrow nationalisms, to a recognition of unity among all men, to a universal conception of a Supreme Being, and the brotherly relationship which should exist between men of differing races and speech. This was true at least of the leaders of culture. The general movement, which we have witnessed in Chinese Confucianism and in Indian Buddhism, was paralleled and no less remarkable in Greece. Indeed, it would appear on the surface that Greece developed very rapidly from a conglomeration of savage tribes into a people possessing an advanced philosophy, art, and literature. Under the circumstances it is unthinkable that this culture arose within Greece itself uninfluenced from without. The question arises as to where this culture had been in long development before it appeared within Greece. The answer could only be: in Persia, in India, in Egypt; or, less probably, in China. The first three of these must presumably be held as strongly influencing the intellectual development of Grecian culture. As a matter of fact, we know that the streams of influence were many and frequent. If we are to judge by the nature of philosophic doctrine alone, we can hardly avoid the conclusion that the springs of early Greek philosophy were very definitely in Persia and India, while the more popular religious movements known as "the mysteries" were dominated from Egyptian sources. There seems little doubt that this general "enlightenment" that spread over the civilized world sprang from identical sources. The change in intellectual atmosphere marked everywhere a new period in civilization. Up to this time the notions of tribalism, clannishness, race, and nationalism had been dominant. Religious worship had concerned itself with deities that dwelt specifically within tribal boundaries, and would protect their votaries from the warriors and the gods of other tribes. These deities were held to dwell on some local mountain, or within some sacred cave, or tree, or other natural wonder. Now began an era of philosophy, and of world-religion, in which the universal relation of all men became recognized, and the tribal god grew to cosmic proportions. For a few brief centuries cosmopolitanism was in the air.

Wherever the new philosophy went it met with resistance, because it seemed, on the one hand, impious, as neglecting or repudiating the accepted tribal deities; and on the other, as unpatriotic, since the national gods were looked to for protection against foreign enemies. Such was the sentiment which lay behind the execution of Socrates. Confucius, Buddha, Socrates, Zoroaster, the Jewish prophets, and Jesus, were all of them engaged in breaking their people away from tribal and racial conceptions to a belief in one God of all peoples.

In Greece the beginnings of the movement are discernible in Heraclitus of Ephesus, whose philosophy in many respects resembled that of Buddhism. His philosophy of change is more than suggestive of the Buddhistic doctrine of the multiplicity of existences, and the Great Chain of Being. His doctrine of law possesses affinity with the *Karma* of the Buddhists, while from Indian philosophy he may have taken his concept of the *Logos, Nous,* the word, the Divine Wisdom, which is the permanent behind all change.

Upon these specific doctrines the Stoics based their philosophy of value. Whether these doctrines had been transmitted to Heraclitus by Buddhist missionaries, whether they were absorbed from Zoroastrian Persism, or from earlier Hinduism is uncertain, but the results would have been about the same. Heraclitus had, however, achieved a cosmopolitanism which was lacking in the others, and which gave a decided bent to Stoic development.

The great search for the discovery of the real values which characterized the period was aimed at release from the terrible fears of nature and the gods, by which the ruling caste had enslaved the common people. These fears had been intensified by the prevalent ignorance and superstition. The object now was to demonstrate a world of natural law, and a benevolent Deity friendly to the human race. Such terrors had made impossible any peace of mind for the multitudes. These fears were the destroyers of that inner calm which the ancients described in the words *ataraxia,* or *apathia,* meaning thereby the power to remain indifferent to circumstance, the possession of an unperturbed spirit amid the most direful events of a troublous age. Like the

other Greek schools of the time, Stoicism came forth in a world
of political tumult, mental confusion, religious defection, and moral
anarchy.   This world was one of moral degradation.   Men were
denying that there was such a thing as a moral value; that men
could know or do the right; they claimed emancipation from ignorance, announced the death of the gods, the lapse of conscience,
denied the existence of justice in the state, the right of the individual to democracy.   Power to seize the government, power to
seize the goods and even the bodies of their fellow citizens seemed
to many a sufficient justification for tyranny.   Out of this reign
of terror and irresponsibility arose Stoicism as a combative force
against injustice, and a protagonist for the reality of the spiritual
and moral values.   It sought some respite from fear in a day
when human life and liberty were the easy prey of tyrant and
demagogue.   Surrounded by terror and injustice, how could
an honest man live in decency and self-respect?   How could he
become indifferent toward and superior to circumstances?

There were three leading schools of Greek philosophy which
sought to achieve this inner peace, each in its own way.   There
were the Epicureans who were materialists, and thought that
the chief satisfactions of life were physical.   The wise man would,
in their opinion, seize as many of these as he could without cloy-
ing his appetite.   Their motto was: "Eat, drink, and be merry,
for tomorrow we die."   The late Epicureans arrived at this conclusion in spite of the pronounced asceticism of their founder
Epicurus, who thought one should limit his desires to his possible satisfactions.   The chief opponents of the Epicureans were
the Stoics.   While the Epicureans thought matter to be the only
reality, the Stoics held that moral and spiritual achievement,
Mind and Reason, were the realities most worth-while.   Materialism of the Epicurean type invariably disparages man and his
highest qualities.   Throttle down your desires to the time and
the opportunity surely, but since physical matter is the only reality
why worry about moral responsibilities?   Have a good time while
it lasts, for we are a long time dead, and the clods of the valley
will shortly rest sweetly upon the best and the worst of us alike.

There was also the Skeptic school of philosophy, which held
that the reason men felt disturbed in mind was because they
harbored convictions, opinions.   If you would have peace of mind,
said they, refuse to entertain an opinion about anything.   Make
no assertions.   If you have no convictions you have nothing to
quarrel about.   Assume that nothing matters since nothing can

be surely known. Some modern men are known to have arrived at exactly this conclusion, being unwilling to assert their own existence. So complete a skepticism is, of course, untenable with any consistency for anyone who continues to live in harmony with the neighbors and eat three square meals a day. Many notions can be held academically that do not accord with life.

Unlike these other schools, Stoicism stood for the supreme reality and worth of the person, and of Reason, the power of the mind to rise superior to circumstances of every kind. Let a man learn to master himself, they declared, let him be uninfluenced by praise or blame, unmoved by his passions, conforming all his acts and even his thoughts to Reason. In order to do this let him accommodate his will to the will of God, who alone is the supreme Wisdom, and of whom the world of Nature itself is but the incarnation.

Each of these diverse schools claimed Socrates as its founder, which is more of an indication of the greatness of that philosopher's fame than it is of the consistency of his successors. How does all this, you may say, concern us moderns at some two thousand years remove from those times? If we think at all deeply about the matter we shall discover that the attitude of the most unphilosophical man of our acquaintance partakes of the characteristics of some one of these three schools. Each one of us, in our outlook on life, is consciously or unconsciously either Stoic, Epicurean, or Skeptic.

I

The Origins of Stoicism

Diverse legends exist concerning the recognized founder of Stoicism, Zeno of Citium. In this city on the island of Cyprus, Zeno was born in the year 336 B.C., the year that Alexander the Great succeeded to the throne of Macedon, and began his career which was to end in the conquest of the world. Zeno's father was said to have been a merchant of purple, a dye obtained from the shellfish found in that part of the Mediterranean Sea. Perhaps his business was the sale of the cloth treated with this dye, sought after for its rarity and identified with the royal purple of kings. One story relates that his father on his wide journeyings between Egypt and Greece had bought and sent back to the growing boy the Greek philosophical manuscripts which formed an intellectual bent. Another describes him at Athens as a travelling salesman for his father, chancing in the market-place upon a copy of Xenophon's *Memoirs of Socrates,* and, disappointed by the wrecking of a shipload of merchandise, deciding that fate had marked him for philosophy. It is reported that he inquired of the bookseller where he could find a teacher capable of such a philosophy as he had discovered in the *Memoirs.* At that very moment Crates, the Cynic, happened to be passing and was pointed out to the would-be student. Thus it came about that Zeno's first lessons in philosophy came from those who called themselves Cynics, because they despised the world, but who were thus enabled to give an early bias to Stoicism. Zeno's young enthusiasm soon resulted in a book, the title of which was *The Republic,* which was an attack upon Plato's book by the same title. Plato's work was a distinctly aristocratic dream of Utopia, possessing totalitarian features, in which a regimented people should be ruled by a philosopher king. Such a scheme could apply only to a village or city state, small in population, self-contained, and with a strong system of caste. Zeno, in opposition to this, contended for a Republic which should be classless, which should embrace the whole world, should be ruled only by nature, and in which love should be the only master. The growing mind of the young philosopher could not long be contained in the mental mold of his first teacher. It is said that when he attempted to leave Master Crates for Master Stilpo, the Megarian, a physical struggle arose between the two Masters as to whose pupil he should be. Upon this, Zeno rebuked Crates with the assertion that argument in this case would have more force than violence. The cosmopolitanism he had advocated in government now began to influence his personal life, for, after studying for a time with Stilpo, he turned to Polemo, a member of the Platonist school which his early volume had attacked. Though influenced by Platonic doctrines he did not turn Platonist. Indeed, Polemo complained of him: "I see plainly what you are after: You break down my garden wall and steal my teaching which you dress in Phoenician clothes"; an unconscious tribute to Zeno's independence. Stoicism continued to be influenced by Cynic doctrines.

Zeno was thus given the nickname "the Phoenician," which carried the implication of Semitic origin, since Cyprus was largely populated from Phoenicia and he may have been Jewish. At least there is nothing in his teaching out of keeping with the best of Jewish thought. There was not only that confidence in individual judgment and capacity for moral action which characterized Socrates, but there was also the unifying principle and sense of cosmic order that seemed the peculiar gift of the great Jewish prophets. Such an assumption would account for certain elements in the Stoic scheme that are foreign to earlier Greek thought. Stoicism, like Epicureanism and Skepticism, laid claim to Socratic origin, but Zeno outran Socrates in a capacity for reverence. It was this capacity in Stoicism that ennobled the more naturalistic Greek concepts. This gift of reverence was natural to the Semitic mind, but may have been increased and emphasized through many other media. Socrates' disciple, General Xenophon, had fought under Darius, the Persian, and had returned full of enthusiasm for the ways and ideas with which he had come in contact. Persism as it was called, or Zoroastrianism, was replete with the philosophy of the East, with which we have become acquainted through Buddhism. Zoroastrianism had most likely influenced Jewish thought in bolstering the opposition which the Jewish prophets raised against idolatry of every kind, and in their contention for a supreme Deity, purposive and holy, the God and Father of all mankind, with whom, in the struggle of light with darkness, the individual could have conscious relationship. These ideas and many more formed the background for the Stoic philosophy, a belief that Divine Reason was the inner voice of which Socrates had told, that spoke in every man.

II

The Stoic Definition of Value

The moral system of the Stoics was dependent upon their concept of reality. They were first impressed with the necessity of honor, decency, and goodwill, reverence, and freedom for the individual in the fabric of any enduring society. In the business of living these values were far more important than business success, fame, or the overlordship of other men, more real than physical circumstance or objectivity. Hence the correct life would be the life of reason, the search for the possession of these higher reals. But if honesty, justice, decency, and goodwill were things that matter most in human life, it could only be because such is the nature of the world. If such is the nature of the world then Reason is the Supreme Fact. Our morals, our science, our concept of the beautiful, none of them can be abstracted and isolated from nature as a whole. They and we, and all our thoughts, are a part of nature too.

The Stoic task was this: to show that a system of morals must be grounded both in the nature of man and in the nature of the universe. If they did not altogether succeed in this, yet they made the farthest religious advance of any purely philosophical movement, and they helped to found that culture under the protection of whose institutions we now live. They felt that morality as duty could not be maintained unless the world itself and its natural processes were basically moral. Nature must herself favor the good and punish the evil. If there was reason in man there was reason in Nature. If reason was the highest capacity of man it must also be the highest capacity of Nature. Cicero, in his *De Natura Deorum,* quotes Zeno as declaring: "Nothing destitute of consciousness and reason can produce out of itself beings endowed with consciousness and reason."

To the Epicureans the world was the mere product of chance, "a fortuitous concomitance of atoms," but to the Stoic, it contained too much of order, regularity, and reason to be the product of accident. It was rather the product of reason, purpose, and intelligence. The whole universe was infilled with intelligence, and this indwelling intelligence was Reason, or God. Even if we are to trust our senses it must be because we believe intelligence is possible. But we cannot know our world unless it is intelligible, and if it is intelligible it is because there is in it, as its very substance or essence, a Supreme Creative Intelligence. Thus Intelligence, the Supreme value of all, was, to the Stoic, the Supreme Reality or Reason.

In this way they grounded their doctrine of value. To live in accord with nature was to live a life in unison with Reason. Any view of nature as something detached from or hostile to morality was a distortion, a failure to comprehend the true meaning of nature. In man's acquiescence with nature lay his true freedom, his achievement of *apathia.* Thus they would supplant the naturalism of Epicureanism with a higher naturalism of the spirit. This life in accord with Nature, as the means of arriving at the highest values, is well illustrated in the four types of misconduct which they recognized as the cardinal sins. These are set forth by E. Vernon Arnold[1] as *fear, greed, grief,* and *hilarity.* A little reflection will indicate how each of these must be recognized as among the most disintegrating to character. *Fear* is the sin that mistakes a future disadvantage for a future evil, that is,

---

[1] *Roman Stoicism,* Cambridge University Press, Cambridge, England, 1911, p. 331.

it is really a distrust of one's self, and of the ultimate order of things, a disbelief in God and righteousness, and in the power to be true to one's self. *Greed* is the sin in which a future advantage is mistaken for a future good. This sin, by the pursuit of advantages that may be only illusory, tempts to cruelty, anger, revenge, the nursing of ill feeling, which is a transgression of a proper soberness with which the goods of life should be approached. *Grief* is the sin in which the present disadvantage is mistaken for a present evil. Here discontent, vexation, worry, or fretfulness lead to disappointed ambition, self-pity, oversensitiveness, and misanthropy. *Hilarity* is the sin in which a present advantage is mistaken for a present good. Here we have elation, exaltation, excitement, which lead to excesses of eating, drinking, sex, or intolerance. All of these the Stoic considered to be maladies of the soul which were hostile to the life of reason and the highest nature of things.

III

Stoicism in the Field of History

Zeno set up his school in the Painted Porch, or *Stoa,* of Athens, and soon drew great crowds of students to what was the earliest type of the University. While he adhered to the very principles for which the Athenians had executed Socrates, so great was his fame, and so profitable to the tradesmen the crowds he drew to his lectures, that, instead of decreeing for him the poison hemlock, they voted to Zeno a golden crown and a bronze statue. We have embedded in the works of Diogenes Laertius the very words of the public commendation which we find translated for us in Arnold's *Roman Stoicism*:

> Whereas Zeno the son of Mnaseas from Citium has spent many years in this city in the pursuit of philosophy; and has been throughout a good man in all respects; and has encouraged the young men who resorted to him in virtue and temperance; and has sped them on the right path; and has made his own life an example to all men, for it has been consistent with the teaching he has set forth;
>
> Now it seems good to the people of Athens to commend Zeno the son of Mnaseas from Citium, and to crown him with a golden crown (in accordance with the law) for his virtue and temperance, and to build him a tomb on the Ceramicus at the public expense. . . . And the treasurer shall make due allotment of the expense, that all men may see that the people of Athens honor good men both in their lifetime and after their death.[2]

[2] By permission of The Macmillan Company, Cambridge University Department.

Although Stoicism had a lively development in Greek thought, it was destined to influence history chiefly through the social and political concepts of the Roman Empire. In the final days of Athenian independence, three Athenian philosophers were included in the commission that was sent to Rome to secure more lenient terms from their Roman conquerors. One of these was a Stoic and through his presence there for three years, the Romans came to know the Stoic teaching as an indigenous rather than an exotic philosophy, though Panaetius of Rhodes and Posidonius, the teacher of Cicero and of Pompey, were the real founders of Roman Stoicism. The result was eventually that the literature of Stoicism came to be written under Roman auspices. Chief among these were Cleanthes, the Greek author of the "Hymn," Epictetus, the Greco-Roman slave, and Marcus Aurelius, the Roman Emperor.

The principal literary exponent of Stoicism was Epictetus, whose *Discourses* provide us with the Stoic philosophy, and also formed the background for the *Meditations* of Marcus Aurelius. Epictetus was at one time a slave of the Emperor Nero's freedman Epaphroditus. The story is sometimes told, though it seems not altogether consistent in view of the Neronian persecution of the Christians, that this Epaphroditus was a Christian, and that punishing Epictetus and while torturing him, he was warned by the latter that if he persisted he would break his leg. Afterward when the leg had been actually broken, it is said that Epictetus remarked: "There, I told you so," and then added: "Could your Christians have done so well as that?" This story was told to account for the lameness that accompanied Epictetus' later years, when he was known as "the Lame." Through the kindness of Epaphroditus he was sent for training to Musonius Rufus, who had been the teacher of Octavius Caesar at Tarsus, and whom the latter had brought back with him to Rome. In his youth Epictetus is said to have gone about in Socratic fashion "inquiring after men's souls," but that he ceased this practice as the result of many rebuffs and some violence which he was said to have suffered. He seems to have lived an exemplary moral life and to have modified the harsher aspects of Stoicism toward an acknowledgment of the place of human affection. His high and lofty philosophy was unattended by the modesty of self-depreciation, which would have been considered weakness in a Stoic, and was characterized by a superlative egotism and self-righteousness. He lived from A.D. 50 to 130.

The other chief literary exponent of Stoicism was Marcus Aurelius (A.D. 121-180) who ruled as Emperor of Rome from 161 to 180. He was outstanding among Roman Emperors for high moral principles as well as for ability in office. Unless we have regard to the times in which he lived such a statement seems at variance with the facts, for he persecuted the Christians, then the rising opponents of Stoicism, and was responsible for the execution of Justin Martyr. He undoubtedly did this, however, with a clear conscience, for the character of Christianity had been sadly falsified by its enemies. His *Meditations* were disconnected thoughts jotted down during one of his campaigns along the Danube. Firmness of character was to him the supreme good, and to him the universe presents a cosmos, not a chaos. Stoicism was already in decadence, however, and he had lost the belief in immortality that characterized the thinking of Seneca, the early Stoic.

The loftiest expression of Stoic literary genius was to be presented, however, by Cleanthes, the first of Stoic writers to be mentioned. Cleanthes was the immediate follower of Zeno as head of the school at Athens. While Epictetus and Marcus Aurelius were to provide the more extended literature of Stoicism, it remained for Cleanthes to give expression to one of the greatest poems of Hellenistic Greece, *The Hymn to Zeus.* Apart from this production Cleanthes seems to have been of rather ordinary attainments, adding little to the work of Zeno, and characterized by the bigotry of the religious zealot. In spite of his own teaching about the sun as the ruler of the universe, when Aristarchus of Samos anticipated by eighteen centuries the discoveries of Copernicus, by affirming the heliocentricity of the solar system, Cleanthes declared a sort of holy war upon him, calling upon all and sundry to join in persecuting this blasphemous fellow for desecrating the "altar-hearth of the universe."

However, by his famous hymn, Cleanthes did prepare the Stoic mind for that elevation of thought respecting God that may have paved the way for the coming of Christianity and also laid the foundation for an appreciation of Stoic philosophy by Christianity.

It is difficult to overestimate the contribution which Stoicism made to Western civilization, for it must stand in rank next to Judaeo-Christianity itself. The German philosopher Windelband has written of it:

> To the Stoic ethics belongs the glory that in the ripest and highest which the ethical life of antiquity produced, and by means of

which it transcended itself and pointed to the future, attained its
best formulation. The intrinsic worth of the moral personality, the
overcoming of the world in man's overcoming of himself, the subordination of the individual to a divine law of the world, his disposition in an ideal union of spirits by means of which he is raised
far above the bounds of this earthly life, and yet, in connection with
this, the energetic feeling of duty that teaches him to fill vigorously
his place in the actual world . . . all these . . . present one of the
most powerful and pregnant creations in the history of conceptions
of human life.[3]

The moral distance between the life of the profligate Nero and that
of Marcus Aurelius is the measure of the progress of Stoicism in the
conquest of Roman ideals. The contribution of Stoicism to the
glory which was Rome is no less apparent in the institutions that
passed away than in those that survived the collapse of her political
power. The dream of the life of culture, in an ordered society,
under a legal code insuring equal protection without distinction of
race, class, or condition—in fact, the main undergirding of present
civilization is itself the precious gift of Stoicism to the world.

Stoicism has been mentioned as the highest religious achievement
within the realm of philosophy, but beyond estimate was the preparation which it made for Christianity itself. Christianity could
scarcely have gained a foothold without it. Its literature and its
ideas flowed into and helped to form the Christian concept of the
moral life. The contrasts drawn between Paul and Jesus rest upon
the intellectual background of Stoic Tarsus which everywhere influenced the Pauline concepts, for in Paul's day Tarsus, his birthplace, was a center of Stoicism, but Judaism furnished perhaps the
background which brought the two together.

Not the least contribution of Stoicism was the inspiration to modern democracy. In this it worked hand in glove with Christianity. It conceived of slave and freeman, poor and rich, low and
high as being equal before God and the law. The expression of this
theory created the Common Law of the Roman code, the basis of
Western political organization: a force which has so far been too
strong for any but a temporary tyranny, and must eventually become the ruling principle of organized society.

[3] Windelband, *History of Philosophy,* translated by J. H. Tufts, by permission,
The Macmillan Company, New York.

IV
The Inadequacy of Stoicism

It may seem, after such extensive praise, a bit ungenerous to point out the failures of Stoicism. Stoicism professed a complete rationalism and as such it failed. Man is not completely rational. His emotional nature is as much part and parcel of nature as his mind. It was consciousness of failure at this point which opened the way for Christianity.

The rationalism of Stoicism was too complete. An utterly reasonable universe would be one in which no change could take place. It would be forever completed, finished, done. It would not be a place for the growth of moral human beings, a training ground for better achievement and understanding. Hence the Stoic fell into a complacent agreement with a static world. Since this world was already Reason, everything that was, was right. It was the best possible of worlds. In this assumption lay a fatal inconsistency with its own principles of righteousness. A world of social inequity and injustice could not yet be a world of Reason. In their pursuit of imperturbability, or *apathia,* they transgressed the bounds of reason. They not only condemned self-pity but they came in their conflict with emotionalism to condemn pity itself. They thus discarded the one virtue that would have enabled them to redeem society. In this way they were led to an impasse in the problem of evil. There was fate, *moira,* ruling forever in the background, over which God himself had no power. In the last analysis there was no hope and no forgiveness for the world. For life defeated and broken, the sum of whose joys was outweighted by its miseries, there was only Epictetus' *Open Door* of suicide. The inadequacy of his philosophy, the failure of its rationality even, seems disclosed in Zeno's reputed suicide because in a fall he had broken a finger, or in that equally legendary story of Cleanthes who was said to have destroyed himself because he found a toothache unbearable. The reason for this failure, as has already been indicated, lay in the Stoic oversight of the importance of the emotions which are the seat of the creative powers. The early Stoic exercised neither compassion nor forgiveness. Even to the intimates of his own household any display of affection was a fall from the Stoic ideal of perfection. For this reason Stoicism could be perfected only in Judaeo-Christianity, with its doctrine of love.

Conclusion

What in particular is the message of Stoicism for our day? The message seems rather simple but fundamental. The greatness of Stoicism sprang from the doctrine of the supremacy of the individual over the circumstances of life. We need to read anew the legend that the sources of happiness are internal and not dependent on external goods. What we need is not more "dates," more automobiles, more houses and lands, more honors or positions, but a keener appreciation of the things we already have.

Along with the Stoic sense of the innate worth and dignity of the individual, went also a profound sense of the reality of moral responsibility, wherein lies the solution of the problem of value and the triumph of Democracy as well.

READINGS

(Chapter 5)

Selections from *THE DISCOURSES OF EPICTETUS*. Translated from
the Greek by Thomas Wentworth Higginson. Little, Brown & Company, Boston. Bk. I, pp. 5-7, 47-49, 78-79; Bk. II, pp. 114-117, 132-134;
Bk. III, pp. 35-36, 38, 57-59; Bk. IV, pp. 119-120, 140-141, 142-147.

But what says Zeus? "O Epictetus, if it had been possible, I had
made this little body and property of thine free, and not liable to hindrance. But now do not mistake; it is not thy own, but only a finer
mixture of clay. Since, then, I could not give thee this, I have given
thee a certain portion of myself; this faculty of exerting the powers
of pursuit and avoidance, of desire and aversion, and, in a word, the
use of the appearances of things. Taking care of this point, and making
what is thy own to consist in this, thou wilt never be restrained, never
be hindered; thou wilt not groan, wilt not complain, wilt not flatter any
one. How, then? Do all these advantages seem small to thee? Heaven
forbid! Let them suffice thee, then, and thank the gods."

But now, when it is in our power to take care of one thing, and to
apply ourselves to one, we choose rather to take care of many, and to
encumber ourselves with many,—body, property, brother, friend, child,
and slave,—and, by this multiplicity of encumbrances, we are burdened
and weighed down. Thus, when the weather does not happen to be fair
for sailing, we sit in distress and gaze out perpetually. Which way is
the wind? North. What good will that do us? When will the west
wind blow? When it pleases, friend, or when Aeolus pleases; for Zeus
has not made you dispenser of the winds, but Aeolus.

What, then, is to be done?

To make the best of what is in our power, and take the rest as it
occurs.

And how does it occur?

As it pleases God.

What, then, must I be the only one to lose my head?

Why, would you have all the world, then, lose their heads for your
consolation? Why are not you willing to stretch out your neck, like
Lateranus,[1] when he was commanded by Nero to be beheaded? For,

---

[1] Plautius Lateranus, a consul elect, was put to death by the command of Nero,
for being privy to the conspiracy of Piso. His execution was so sudden that he
was not permitted to take leave of his wife and children, but was hurried into a
place appropriated to the punishment of slaves, and there killed by the hand of
the tribune Statius. He suffered in obstinate silence, and without making any
reproach to Statius, who was concerned in the same plot for which he himself was
punished. Tacitus, Ann. xv. c. 60-C.

shrinking a little after receiving a weak blow, he stretched it out again. And before this, when Epaphroditus,[2] the freedman of Nero, interrogated him about the conspiracy, "If I have a mind to say anything," replied he, "I will tell it to your master."

What resource have we, then, upon such occasion? Why, what else but to distinguish between what is *ours,* and what not *ours,*—what is right, and what is wrong? I must die, and must I die groaning too? I must be fettered; must I be lamenting too? I must be exiled; and what hinders me, then, but that I may go smiling, and cheerful, and serene? "Betray a secret." I will not betray it, for this is in my own power. "Then I will fetter you." What do you say, man? Fetter me? You will fetter my leg, but not Zeus himself can get the better of my free will. "I will throw you into prison; I will behead that paltry body of yours." Did I ever tell you that I alone had a head not liable to be cut off? These things ought philosophers to study; these ought they daily to write, and in these to exercise themselves.

. . . . . .

Difficulties are things that show what men are. For the future, in case of any difficulty, remember that God, like a gymnastic trainer, has pitted you against a rough antagonist. For what end? That you may be an Olympic conqueror; and this cannot be without toil. No man, in my opinion, has a more profitable difficulty on his hands than you have, provided you will but use it, as an athletic champion uses his antagonist.

Suppose we were to send you as a scout to Rome. But no one ever sends a timorous scout, who, when he only hears a noise, or sees a shadow, runs back frightened, and says, "The enemy is at hand." So now, if you should come and tell us, "Things are in a fearful way at Rome, death is terrible, banishment terrible, calumny terrible, poverty terrible; run, good people, the enemy is at hand"; we will answer, Get you gone, and prophesy for yourself; our only fault is that we have sent such a scout. Diogenes was sent as a scout before you, but he told us other tidings. He says that death is no evil, for it is nothing base; that calumny is only the noise of madmen. And what account did this spy give us of pain, of pleasure, of poverty? He says that to be naked is better than a purple robe; to sleep upon the bare ground than the softest bed; and gives a proof of all he says by his own courage, tranquility, and freedom, and, moreover, by a healthy and robust body. "There is no enemy near," he says; "all is profound peace." How so, Diogenes? "Look upon me," he says. "Am I hurt? Am I wounded? Have I run away from any one?" This is a scout worth having. But

---

[2] Epaphroditus was the master of requests and freedman of Nero, and the master of Epictetus. He assisted Nero in killing himself, for which he was condemned to death by Domitian. Suetonius in *Vita Neronis,* c. 49; Domit. c. 14.—C.

you come, and tell us one tale after another. Go back and look more
carefully, and without fear.

(Bk. I, pp. 5-7, 47-49, 78-79.)

Consider, you who are going to take your trial, what you wish to
preserve, and in what to succeed. For if you wish to preserve a mind
in harmony with nature, you are entirely safe; everything goes well;
you have no trouble on your hands. While you wish to preserve that
freedom which belongs to you, and are contented with that, for what
have you longer to be anxious? For who is the master of things like
these? Who can take them away? If you wish to be a man of modesty
and fidelity, who shall prevent you? If you wish not to be restrained
or compelled, who shall compel you to desires contrary to your principles; to aversions contrary to your opinion? The judge, perhaps,
will pass a sentence against you, which he thinks formidable; but can
he likewise make you receive it with shrinking? Since, then, desire
and aversion are in your own power, for what have you to be anxious?
Let this be your introduction; this your narration; this your proof;
this your conclusion; this your victory; and this your applause. Thus
said Socrates to one who put him in mind to prepare himself for his
trial: "Do you not think that I have been preparing myself for this
very thing my whole life long?" By what kind of preparation? "I
have attended to my own work." What mean you? "I have done
nothing unjust, either in public or in private life."

But if you wish to retain possession of outward things too, your
body, your estate, your dignity, I advise you immediately to prepare
yourself by every possible preparation; and besides, to consider the disposition of your judge and of your adversary. If it be necessary to
embrace his knees, do so; if to weep, weep; if to groan, groan. For
when you have once made yourself a slave to externals, be a slave
wholly; do not struggle, and be alternately willing and unwilling, but
be simply and thoroughly the one or the other,—free, or a slave; instructed, or ignorant; a gamecock, or a craven; either bear to be beaten
till you die, or give out at once; and do not be soundly beaten first, and
then give out at last.

If both alternatives be shameful, learn immediately to distinguish
where good and evil lie. They lie where truth likewise lies. Where
truth and nature dictate, there exercise caution or courage. Why, do
you think that if Socrates had concerned himself about externals, he
would have said, when he appeared at his trial, "Anytus and Melitus
may indeed kill me, but hurt me they cannot?" Was he so foolish as
not to see that this way did not lead to safety, but the contrary? What,
then, is the reason that he not only disregarded, but defied his judges?
Thus my friend Heraclitus, in a trifling suit about a little estate at
Rhodes, after having proved to the judges that his cause was good,
when he came to the conclusion of his speech, "I will not entreat you,"

said he; "nor be anxious as to what judgment you give; for it is rather you who are to be judged, than I." And thus he lost his suit. What need was there of this? Be content not to entreat; yet do not proclaim that you will not entreat; unless it be a proper time to provoke the judges designedly, as in the case of Socrates. But if you too are pre- paring such a speech as his, what do you wait for? Why do you con- sent to be tried? For if you wish to be hanged, have patience, and the gibbet will come. But if you choose rather to consent, and make your defence as well as you can, all the rest is to be ordered accordingly, with a due regard, however, to the preservation of your own proper character.

For this reason it is absurd to call upon me for specific advice. How should I know what to advise you? Ask me rather to teach you to accommodate yourself to whatever may be the event. The former is just as if an illiterate person should say, "Tell me how to write down some name that is proposed to me"; and I show him how to write the name of Dion; and then another comes, and asks him to write the name, not of Dion, but of Theon. What will be the consequence? What will he write? Whereas, if you make writing your study, you are ready prepared for whatever word may occur; if not, how can I advise you? For if the actual case should suggest something else, what will you say, or how will you act? Remember, then, the general rule, and you will need no special suggestions; but if you are absorbed in externals, you must necessarily be tossed up and down, according to the inclination of your master. Who is your master? Whosoever controls those things which you seek or shun.

(Bk. II, pp. 114-117.)

Wherein consists the Essence of Good.

God is beneficial. Good is also beneficial. It should seem, then, that where the essence of God is, there too is the essence of good. What then is the essence of God,—flesh? By no means. An estate? Fame? By no means. Intelligence? Knowledge? Right reason? Certainly. Here, then, without more ado, seek the essence of good. For do you seek that quality in a plant? No. Or in a brute? No. If, then, you seek it only in a rational subject, why do you seek it anywhere but in what distinguishes that from things irrational? Plants make no volun- tary use of things, and therefore you do not apply the term of *good* to them. *Good,* then, implies such use. And nothing else? If so, you may say that good and happiness and unhappiness belong to mere ani- mals. But this you do not say, and you are right; for, how much soever they have the use of things, they have not the intelligent use, and with good reason; for they are made to be subservient to others, and not of primary importance. Why was an ass made? Was it as being of primary importance? No; but because we had need of a back able to carry burdens. We had need too that he should be capable of locomotion; therefore he had the voluntary use of things added, otherwise he could not have moved. But here his endowments end; for, if an understanding of that use had been likewise added, he would not, in reason, have been subject to us, nor have done us these services, but would have been like and equal to ourselves. Why will you not, therefore, seek the essence of good in that without which you cannot say that there is good in anything?

What then? Are not all these likewise the works of the gods? They are; but not primary existences, nor parts of the gods. But you are a primary existence. You are a distinct portion of the essence of God, and contain a certain part of him in yourself. Why then are you ignorant of your noble birth? Why do not you consider whence you came? Why do not you remember, when you are eating, who you are who eat, and whom you feed? When you are in the company of women, when you are conversing, when you are exercising, when you are disputing, do not you know that it is the Divine you feed, the Divine you exercise? You carry a God about with you, poor wretch, and know nothing of it. Do you suppose I mean some god without you of gold or silver? It is within yourself that you carry him; and you do not observe that you profane him by impure thoughts and unclean actions. If the mere external image of God were present, you would not dare to act as you do; and when God himself is within you, and hears and sees all, are not you ashamed to think and act thus,— insensible of your own nature, and at enmity with God?

We should have all our principles ready for use on every occasion— at dinner, such as relate to dinner; in the bath, such as relate to the bath; in the bed, such as relate to the bed.

> Let not the stealing god of sleep surprise,
> Nor creep in slumbers on thy weary eyes,
> Ere every action of the former day
> Strictly thou dost, and righteously survey.
> What have I done? In what have I transgressed?
> What good, or ill, has this day's life expressed?
> Where have I failed in what I ought to do?
> If evil were thy deeds, repent and mourn;
> If good, rejoice.[3]

We should retain these verses so as to apply them to our use; not merely to say them by rote, as we do with verses in honor of Apollo.

Again, in a fever we should have such principles ready as relate to a fever; and not, as soon as we are taken ill, forget all. Provided I do but act like a philosopher, let what will happen. Some way or other I must depart from this frail body, whether a fever comes or not. What is it to be a philosopher? Is it not to be prepared against events? Do

---

[3] Pythagoras, *Golden Verses*, 40-44. This is Lowe's translation, as quoted by Mrs. Carter, but not precisely as given in Davier's Pythagoras (London, 1707), p. 165.—H.

you not comprehend that you then say, in effect, "If I am but prepared to bear all events with calmness, let what will happen?" Otherwise you are like an athlete, who, after receiving a blow, should quit the combat. In that case, indeed, you might leave off without a penalty. But what shall we get by leaving off philosophy?

What, then; each of us to say upon every difficult occasion, "It was for this that I exercised; it was for this that I trained myself?" God says to you, Give me a proof if you have gone through the preparatory combats according to rule; if you have followed a proper diet and proper exercise; if you have obeyed your master; and after this, do you faint at the very time of action?

Now is your time for a fever. Bear it well. For thirst; bear it well. For hunger; bear it well. Is it not in your power? Who shall restrain you? A physician may restrain you from drinking, but he cannot restrain you from bearing your thirst well. He may restrain you from eating, but he cannot restrain you from bearing hunger well.

(Bk. III, pp. 35-36.)

What occasion is there, then, for fear; what occasion for anger, for desire, about things that belong to others, or are of no value? For two rules we should always have ready,—*that there is nothing good or evil save in the Will;* and *that we are not to lead events, but to follow them.* "My brother ought not to have treated me so." Very true; but he must see to that. However he treats me, I am to act rightly with regard to him; for the one is my own concern, the other is not; the one cannot be restrained, the other may. . . .

(Bk. III, p. 38.)

What advantage does a wrestler gain from him with whom he exercises himself before the combat? The greatest. And just in the same manner I exercise myself with this man. He exercises me in patience, in gentleness, in meekness. I am to suppose, then, that I gain an advantage from him who exercises my neck, and puts my back and shoulders in order; so that the trainer may well bid me grapple him with both hands, and the heavier he is the better for me; and yet it is no advantage to me when I am exercised in gentleness of temper! This is not to know how to gain an advantage from men. Is my neighbor a bad one? He is so to himself, but a good one to me; he exercises my good temper, my moderation. Is my father bad? To himself; but not to me.

"This is the rod of Hermes. Touch with it whatever you please, and it will become gold." No; but bring whatever you please, and I will turn it into *good*. Bring sickness, death, want, reproach, trial for life. All these, by the rod of Hermes, shall turn to advantage. "What will you make of death?" Why, what but an ornament to you; what but a means of your showing, by action, what that man is who knows and follows the will of Nature? "What will you make of sickness?"

I will show its nature. I will make a good figure in it; I will be composed and happy; I will not beseech my physician, nor yet will I pray
to die. What need you ask further? Whatever you give me, I will
make it happy, fortunate, respectable, and eligible.

(Bk. III, pp. 57-59.)

He is free who lives as he likes; who is not subject to compulsion,
to restraint, or to violence; whose pursuits are unhindered, his desires
successful, his aversions unincurred. Who, then, would wish to lead
a wrong course of life? "No one." Who would live deceived, erring,
unjust, dissolute, discontented, dejected? "No one." No wicked man,
then, lives as he likes; therefore no such man is free. And who would
live in sorrow, fear, envy, pity, with disappointed desires and unavail-
ing aversions? "No one." Do we then find any of the wicked exempt
from these evils? "Not one." Consequently, then, they are not free.

If some person who has been twice consul should hear this, he will
forgive you, provided you add, "but you are wise, and this had no reference to you." But if you tell him the truth, that, in point of slavery,
he does not necessarily differ from those who have been thrice sold,
what but chastisement can you expect? "For how," he says, "am I
a slave? My father was free, my mother free. Besides, I am a senator,
too, and the friend of Caesar, and have been twice consul, and have myself many slaves." In the first place, most worthy sire, perhaps your
father too was a slave of the same kind; and your mother, and your
grandfather, and all your series of ancestors. But even were they ever
so free, what is that to you? For what if they were of a generous, you
of a mean spirit; they brave, and you a coward; they sober, and you
dissolute?

"But what," he says, "has this to do with my being a slave?" Is it
no part of slavery to act against your will, under compulsion, and lamenting? "Be it so. But who can compel me but the master of all, Caesar?"
By your own confession, then, you have *one* master; and let not his
being, as you say, master of all, give you any comfort; for then you
are merely a slave in a large family. Thus the Nicopolitans, too, frequently cry out, "By the genius of Caesar we are *free*!"

What is it, then, that makes a man free and independent? For
neither riches, nor consulship, nor the command of provinces nor of
kingdoms, can make him so; but something else must be found. What
is it that keeps any one from being hindered and restrained in penmanship, for instance? "The science of penmanship?" In music? "The
science of music." Therefore in life too, it must be the science of living. As you have heard it in general, then, consider it likewise in particulars. Is it possible for him to be unrestrained who desires any of
those things that are within the power of others? "No." Can he avoid
being hindered? "No." Therefore neither can he be free. Consider,
then, whether we have nothing or everything in our sole power,—or

whether some things are in our own power and some in that of others. What do you mean? When you would have your body perfect, is it in your own power, or is it not? "It is not." When you would be healthy? "It is not." When you would be handsome? "It is not." When you would live or die? "It is not." Your body then is not your own; but is subject to everything that proves stronger than itself. "Agreed." Well; is it in your own power to have an estate when you please, and such a one as you please? "No." Slaves? "No." Clothes? "No." A house? "No." Horses? "Indeed, none of these." Well, if you desire ever so earnestly to have your children live, or your wife, or your brother, or your friends, is it in your own power? "No, it is not."

Will you then say that there is *nothing* independent which is in your own power alone, and unalienable? See if you have anything of this sort. "I do not know." But consider it thus: can any one make you assent to a falsehood? "No one." In the matter of assent, then, you are unrestrained and unhindered. "Agreed." Well, and can any one compel you to exert your aims towards what you do not like? "He can, for when he threatens me with death, or fetters, he thus compels me." If, then, you were to despise dying or being fettered, would you any longer regard him? "No." Is despising death, then, an action in our power, or is it not? "It is." Is it therefore in your power also to exert your aims towards anything, or is it not? "Agreed that it is. But in whose power is my avoiding anything?" This, too, is in your own. "What then if, when I am exerting myself to walk, any one should restrain me?" What part of you can he restrain? Can he restrain your assent? "No, but my body." Ay, as he may a stone. "Be it so. But still I cease to walk." And who claimed that walking was one of the actions that cannot be restrained? For I only said that your exerting yourself towards it could not be restrained. But wherever the body and its assistance are essential, you have already heard that nothing is in your power. "Be this, too, agreed." And can any one compel you to desire against your will? "No one." Or to propose, or intend, or, in short, not to be beguiled by the appearances of things? "Nor this. But when I desire anything, he can restrain me from obtaining what I desire." If you desire anything that is truly within your reach, and that cannot be restrained, how can he restrain you? "By no means." And pray who claims that he who longs for what depends on another will be free from restraint? (Bk. IV, pp. 119-120.)

What say you, philosopher? A tyrant calls upon you to speak some things unbecoming you. Will you say it, or will you not? "Stay, let me consider." Would you consider *now*? And what did you use to consider when you were in the schools? Did you not study what things were good and evil, and what indifferent? "I did." Well, and what were the opinions which pleased us? "That just and fair actions were good; unjust and base ones, evil." Is living a good? "No." Dying, an evil?

"No." A prison? "No." And what did a mean and dishonest speech, the betraying a friend, or the flattering a tyrant, appear to us? "Evils." Why, then, are you still considering, and have not already considered and come to a resolution? For what sort of a consideration is this: "Whether I ought, when it is in my power, to procure myself the greatest good, instead of procuring myself the greatest evil." A fine and necessary consideration, truly, and deserving mighty deliberation! Why do you trifle with us, man? No one ever needed to consider any such point; nor, if you really imagined things fair and honest to be good, things base and dishonest to be evil, and all other things indifferent, would you ever be in such a perplexity as this, or near it; but you would presently be able to distinguish by your understanding as you do by your sight. For do you ever have to consider whether black is white, or whether light is heavy? Do you not follow the plain evidence of your senses? Why, then, do you say that you are now considering whether things indifferent are to be avoided, rather than evils? The truth is, you have no principles; for things indifferent do not impress you as such, but as the greatest evils; and these last, on the other hand, as things of no importance.   (Bk. IV, pp. 140-141.)

"And what is all this to freedom?" It lies in nothing else than this, —whether you rich people approve or not. "And who affords evidence of this?" Who but yourselves? You have a powerful master, and live by his notion and nod, and faint away if he does but look sternly upon you, who pay your court to old men and old women, and say, "I cannot do this or that, it is not in my power." Why is it not in your power? Did you not just now contradict me, and say you were free? "But Aprylla has forbidden me." Speak the truth, then, slave, and do not run away from your masters nor deny them nor dare to assert your freedom, when you have so many proofs of your slavery. One might indeed find some excuse for a person compelled by love to do something contrary to his opinion, even when at the same time he sees what is best without having resolution enough to follow it, since he is withheld by something overpowering, and in some measure divine. But who can bear with you, who are in love with old men and old women, and perform menial offices for them, and bribe them with presents, and wait upon them like a slave when they are sick; at the same time wishing they may die, and inquiring of the physician whether their distemper be yet mortal? And again, when for these great and venerable magistracies and honors you kiss the hands of the slaves of others; so that you are the slave of those who are not free themselves! And then you walk about in state, a praetor or a consul. Do I not know how you came to be praetor; whence you received the consulship; who gave it to you? For my own part, I would not even live, if I must live by Felicio's means, and bear his pride and slavish insolence. For I know what a slave is, blinded by what he thinks good fortune.

"Are you free yourself, then?" you may ask. By Heaven, I wish and pray for it. But I own I cannot yet face my masters. I still pay a regard to my body, and set a great value on keeping it whole; though, for that matter, it is not whole. But I can show you one who was free, that you may no longer seek an example. Diogenes was free. "How so?" Not because he was of free parents, for he was not; but because he was so in himself; because he had cast away all which gives a handle to slavery; nor was there any way of getting at him, nor anywhere to lay hold on him; everything only just hung on. If you took hold on his possessions, he would rather let them go than follow you for them; if on his leg, he let go his leg; if his body, he let go his body; acquaintance, friends, country just the same. For he knew whence he had them, and from whom, and upon what conditions he received them. But he would never have forsaken his true parents, the gods, and his real country (the universe); nor have suffered any one to be more dutiful and obedient to them than he; nor would any one have died more readily for his country than he. He never had to inquire whether he should act for the good of the whole universe; for he remembered that everything that exists belongs to that administration, and is commanded by its ruler. Accordingly, see what he himself says and writes. "Upon this account," said he, "O Diogenes, it is in your power to converse as you will with the Persian monarch and with Archidamus, king of the Lacedemonians." Was it because he was born of free parents? Or was it because they were descended from slaves, that all the Athenians, and all the Lacedemonians, and Corinthians, could not converse with them as they pleased; but feared and paid court to them? Why then is it in your power, Diogenes? "Because I do not esteem this poor body as my own. Because I want nothing. Because this and nothing else is a law to me." These were the things that enabled him to be free.

And that you may not urge that I show you the example of a man clear of incumbrances, without a wife or children or country or friends or relations, to bend and draw him aside, take Socrates, and consider him, who had a wife and children, but held them not as his own; had a country, friends, relations, but held them only so long as it was proper, and in the manner that was proper; submitting all these to the law and to the obedience due to it. Hence, when it was proper to fight, he was the first to go out, and exposed himself to danger without the least reserve. But when he was sent by the thirty tyrants to apprehend Leon,[4] because he esteemed it a base action, he did not even deliberate about it;

---

[4] Socrates, with four other persons, was commanded by the thirty tyrants of Athens to fetch Leon from the isle of Salamis, in order to be put to death. His companions executed their commission; but Socrates remained at home, and chose rather to expose his life to the fury of the tyrants, than be accessory to the death of an innocent person. He would most probably have fallen a sacrifice to their vengeance, if the Oligarchy had not shortly after been dissolved. See Plato's Apology.—C.

though he knew that, perhaps, he might die for it. But what did that signify to him? For it was something else that he wanted to preserve, not his mere flesh; but his fidelity, his honor, free from attack or subjection. And afterwards, when he was to make a defence for his life, does he behave like one having children, or a wife? No, but like a single man. And how does he behave, when required to drink the poison? When he might escape, and Crito would have him escape from prison for the sake of his children, what says he? Does he esteem it a fortunate opportunity? How should he? But he considers what is becoming, and neither sees nor regards anything else. "For I am not desirous," he says, "to preserve this pitiful body; but that part which is improved and preserved by justice, and impaired and destroyed by injustice." Socrates is not to be basely preserved. He who refused to vote for what the Athenians commanded; he who contemned the thirty tyrants; he who held such discourses on virtue and moral beauty,— such a man is not to be preserved by a base action, but is preserved by dying, instead of running away. For even a good actor is preserved as such by leaving off when he ought; not by going on to act beyond his time. "What then will become of your children?" "If I had gone away into Thessaly, you would have taken care of them; and will there be no one to take care of them when I am departed to Hades?"[5] You see how he ridicules and plays with death. But if it had been you or I, we should presently have proved by philosophical arguments that those who act unjustly are to be repaid in their own way; and should have added: "If I escape I shall be of use to many; if I die, to none." Nay, if it had been necessary we should have crept through a mousehole to get away. But how should we have been of use to any? Where must they have dwelt? If we were useful alive, should we not be of still more use to mankind by dying when we ought and as we ought? And now the remembrance of the death of Socrates is not less, but even more useful to the world than that of the things which he did and said when alive.

(Bk. IV, pp. 142-147.)

[5] Plato, *Crito*, i, 15.—H.

THE THOUGHTS OF MARCUS AURELIUS. Translated by George
Long. Little, Brown & Company, Boston, 1920. Bks. I, II, and III,
pp. 85-120.

I

1. From my grandfather Varus (I learned) good morals and the
government of my temper.

2. From the reputation and remembrance of my father, modesty
and a manly character.

3. From my mother, piety and beneficence, and abstinence, not only
from evil deeds, but even from evil thoughts; and further, simplicity in
my way of living, far removed from the habits of the rich.

4. From my great-grandfather, not to have frequented public schools,
and to have had good teachers at home, and to know that on such things
a man should spend liberally.

5. From my governor, to be neither of the green nor of the blue
party at the games in the Circus, nor a partisan either of the Parmu-
larius or the Scutarius at the gladiators' fights; from him too I learned
endurance of labor, and to want little, and to work with my own hands,
and not to meddle with other people's affairs, and not to be ready to
listen to slander.

6. From Diognetus, not to busy myself about trifling things, and
not to give credit to what was said by miracle-workers and jugglers
about incantations and the driving away of daemons and such things;
and not to breed quails (for fighting), nor to give myself up passionately to such things; and to endure freedom of speech; and to have become intimate with philosophy; and to have been a hearer, first of
Bacchius, then of Tandasis and Marcianus; and to have written dialogues
in my youth; and to have desired a plank bed and skin, and whatever
else of the kind belongs to the Grecian discipline.

7. From Rusticus I received the impression that my character required improvement and discipline; and from him I learned not to be
led astray to sophistic emulation, nor to writing on speculative matters,
nor to delivering little hortatory orations, nor to showing myself off as
a man who practices such discipline or does benevolent acts in order
to make a display; and to abstain from rhetoric, and poetry, and fine
writing; and not to walk about in the house in my outdoor dress, nor to
do other things of the kind; and to write my letters with simplicity, like
the letter which Rusticus wrote from Sinuessa to my mother; and with
respect to those who have offended me by words, or done me wrong,
to be easily disposed to be pacified and reconciled, as soon as they have
shown a readiness to be reconciled; and to read carefully, and not to

be satisfied with a superficial understanding of a book, nor hastily to give my assent to those who talk overmuch; and I am indebted to him for being acquainted with the discourses of Epictetus, which he communicated to me out of his own collection.

8. From Apollonius I learned freedom of will and undeviating steadiness of purpose; and to look to nothing else, not even for a moment, except to reason; and to be always the same, in sharp pains, on the occasion of the loss of a child, and in long illness; and to see clearly in a living example that the same man can be both most resolute and yielding, and not peevish in giving his instruction; and to have had before my eyes a man who clearly considered his experience and his skill in expounding philosophical principles as the smallest of his merits; and from him I learned how to receive from friends what are esteemed favors, without being either humbled by them or letting them pass unnoticed.

9. From Sextus, a benevolent disposition, and the example of a family governed in a fatherly manner, and the idea of living conformably to nature; and gravity without affectation, and to look carefully after the interests of friends, and to tolerate ignorant persons, and those who form opinions without consideration: he had the power of readily accommodating himself to all, so that intercourse with him was more agreeable than any flattery; and at the same time he was most highly venerated by those who associated with him; and he had the faculty both of discovering and ordering, in an intelligent and methodical way, the principles necessary for life; and he never showed anger or any other passion, but was entirely free from passion, and also most affectionate; and he could express approbation without noisy display, and he possessed much knowledge without ostentation.

10. From Alexander the grammarian, to refrain from fault-finding, and not in a reproachful way to chide those who uttered any barbarous or solecistic or strange-sounding expression; but dexterously to introduce the very expression which ought to have been used, and in the way of answer or giving confirmation, or joining in an inquiry about the thing itself, not about the word, or by some other fit suggestion.

11. From Fronto I learned to observe what envy and duplicity and hypocrisy are in a tyrant, and that generally those among us who are called Patricians are rather deficient in paternal affection.

12. From Alexander the Platonist, not frequently nor without necessity to say to any one, or to write in a letter, that I have no leisure; nor continually to excuse the neglect of duties required by our relation to those with whom we live, by alleging urgent occupations.

13. From Catulus, not to be indifferent when a friend finds fault, even if he should find fault without reason, but to try to restore him to

his usual disposition; and to be ready to speak well of teachers, as it is reported of Domitius and Athenodotus; and to love my children truly.

14. From my brother Severus, to love my kin, and to love truth, and to love justice; and through him I learned to know Thrasea, Helvidius, Cato, Dion, Brutus, and from him I received the idea of a polity in which there is the same law for all, a polity administered with regard to equal rights and equal freedom of speech, and the idea of a kingly government which respects most of all the freedom of the governed; I learned from him also consistency and undeviating steadiness in my regard for philosophy; and a disposition to do good, and to give to others readily, and to cherish good hopes, and to believe that I am loved by my friends; and in him I observed no concealment of his opinions with respect to those whom he condemned, and that his friends had no need to conjecture what he wished or did not wish, but it was quite plain.

15. From Maximus I learned self-government, and not to be led aside by anything; and cheerfulness in all circumstances, as well as in illness; and a just admixture in the moral character of sweetness and dignity, and to do what was set before me without complaining. I observed that everybody believed that he thought as he spoke, and that in all that he did he never had any bad intention; and he never showed amazement and surprise, and was never in a hurry, and never put off doing a thing, nor was perplexed nor dejected, nor did he ever laugh to disguise his vexation, nor, on the other hand, was he ever passionate or suspicious. He was accustomed to do acts of beneficence, and was ready to forgive, and was free from all falsehood; and he presented the appearance of a man who could not be diverted from right, rather than of a man who had been improved. I observed, too, that no man could ever think that he was despised by Maximus, or ever venture to think himself a better man. He had also the art of being humorous in an agreeable way.

16. In my father I observed mildness of temper, and unchangeable resolution in the things which he had determined after due deliberation; and no vainglory in those things which men call honors; and a love of labor and perseverance; and a readiness to listen to those who had anything to propose for the common weal; and undeviating firmness in giving to every man according to his deserts; and a knowledge derived from experience of the occasions for vigorous action and for remission. And I observed that he had overcome all passion for boys; and he considered himself no more than any other citizen; and he released his friends from all obligation to sup with him or to attend him of necessity when he went abroad, and those who had failed to accompany him, by reason of any urgent circumstances, always found him the same. I observed too his habit of careful inquiry in all matters of deliberation,

and his persistency, and that he never stopped his investigation through being satisfied with appearances which first present themselves; and that his disposition was to keep his friends, and not to be soon tired of them, nor yet to be extravagant in his affection; and to be satisfied on all occasions, and cheerful; and to foresee things a long way off, and to provide for the smallest without display; and to check immediately popular applause and all flattery; and to be ever watchful over the things which were necessary for the administration of the empire, and to be a good manager of the expenditure, and patiently to endure the blame which he got for such conduct; and he was neither superstitious with respect to the gods, nor did he court men by gifts or by trying to please them, or by flattering the populace, and never any mean thoughts or action, nor love of novelty. And the things which conduce in any way to the commodity of life and of which fortune gives an abundant supply, he used without arrogance and without excusing himself; so that when he had them, he enjoyed them without affectation, and when he had them not, he did not want them. No one could ever say of him that he was either a sophist or a (home-bred) flippant slave or a pedant; but every one acknowledged him to be a man ripe, perfect, above flattery, able to manage his own and other men's affairs. Besides this, he honored those who were true philosophers, and he did not reproach those who pretended to be philosophers, nor yet was he easily led by them. He was also easy in conversation, and he made himself agreeable without any offensive affectation. He took a reasonable care of his body's health, not as one who was greatly attached to life, nor out of regard to personal appearance, nor yet in a careless way, but so that through his own attention he very seldom stood in need of the physician's art or of medicine or external applications. He was most ready to give without envy to those who possessed any particular faculty, such as that of eloquence or knowledge of the law or of morals, or of anything else; and he gave them his help, that each might enjoy reputation according to his deserts; and he always acted conformably to the institutions of his country, without showing any affectation of doing so. Further, he was not fond of change nor unsteady, but he loved to stay in the same places, and to employ himself about the same things; and after his paroxysms of headache he came immediately fresh and vigorous to his usual occupations. His secrets were not many, but very few and very rare, and these only about public matters; and he showed prudence and economy in the exhibitation of the public spectacles and the construction of public buildings, his donations to the people, and in such things, for he was a man who looked to what ought to be done, not to the reputation which is got by a man's acts. He did not take the bath at unseasonable hours; he was not fond of building houses, nor curious about what he ate, nor about the texture and color of his clothes, nor about the beauty of his slaves. His dress came from Lorium, his villa on the coast, and from Lanuvium generally. We know how he behaved to the toll-collector at Tusculum who asked his pardon; and such was all his behavior. There was in him nothing harsh, nor implacable, nor violent, nor, as one may say, anything carried to the sweating point; but he examined all things severally, as if he had abundance of time, and without confusion, in an orderly way, vigorously and consistently. And that might be applied to him which is recorded of Socrates, that he was able both to abstain from, and to enjoy, those things which many are too weak to abstain from, and cannot enjoy without excess. But to be strong enough both to bear the one and to be sober in the other is the mark of a man who has a perfect and invincible soul, such as he showed in the illness of Maximus.

17. To the gods I am indebted for having good grandfathers, good parents, a good sister, good teachers, good associates, good kinsmen and friends, nearly everything good. Further, I owe it to the gods that I was not hurried into any offence against any of them, though I had a disposition which, if opportunity had offered, might have led me to do something of this kind; but, through their favor, there never was such a concurrence of circumstances as put me to the trial. Further, I am thankful to the gods that I was not longer brought up with my grandfather's concubine, and that I preserved the flower of my youth, and that I did not make proof of my virility before the proper season, but even deferred the time; that I was subjected to a ruler and a father who was able to take away all pride from me, and to bring me to the knowledge that it is possible for a man to live in a palace without wanting either guards or embroidered dresses, or torches and statues, and suchlike show; but that it is in such a man's power to bring himself very near to the fashion of a private person, without being for this reason either meaner in thought, or more remiss in action, with respect to the things which must be done for the public interest in a manner that befits a ruler. I thank the gods for giving me such a brother, who was able by his moral character to rouse me to vigilance over myself, and who at the same time pleased me by his respect and affection; that my children have not been stupid nor deformed in body; that I did not make more proficiency in rhetoric, poetry and the other studies, in which I should perhaps have been completely engaged, if I had seen that I was making progress in them; that I made haste to place those who brought me up in the station of honor, which they seemed to desire, without putting them off with hope of my doing it some other time after, because they were then still young; that I knew Apollonius, Rusticus, Maximus; that I received clear and frequent impressions about living according to nature, and what kind of a life that is, so that, so far as depended on the gods, and their gifts, and help, and inspirations, nothing hindered me from forthwith living according to nature, though I still fall short of it through my own fault, and through not observing the admonitions of the gods, and, I may almost say, their direct instructions; that my

body has held out so long in such a kind of life; that I never touched either Benedicta or Theodotus, and that, after having fallen into amatory passions, I was cured, and, though I was often out of humor with Rusticus, I never did anything of which I had occasion to repent; that, though it was my mother's fate to die young, she spent the last years of her life with me; that, whenever I wished to help any man in his need, or on any other occasion, I was never told that I had not the means of doing it; and that to myself the same necessity never happened, to receive anything from another; that I have such a wife, so obedient, and so affectionate, and so simple; that I had abundance of good masters for my children; and that remedies have been shown to me by dreams, both others, and against blood-spitting and giddiness . . . ; and then, when I had an inclination to philosophy, I did not fall into the hands of any sophist, and that I did not waste my time on writers (of histories), or in the resolution of syllogisms, or occupy myself about the investigations of appearances in the heavens; for all these things require the help of the gods and fortune.

Among the Quadi at the Granua.

II

1. Begin the morning by saying to thyself, I shall meet with the busybody, the ungrateful, arrogant, deceitful, envious, unsocial. All these things happen to them by reason of their ignorance of what is good and evil. But I who have seen the nature of the good that it is beautiful, and of the bad that it is ugly, and the nature of him who does wrong, that it is akin to me, not (only) of the same blood or seed, but that it participates in (the same) intelligence and (the same) portion of the divinity, I can neither be injured by any of them, for no one can fix on me what is ugly, nor can I be angry with my kinsman, nor hate him. For we are made for co-operation, like feet, like hands, like eyelids, like the rows of the upper and lower teeth. To act against one another, then, is contrary to nature; and it is acting one against one another to be vexed and to turn away.

2. Whatever this is that I am, it is a little flesh and breath, and the ruling part. Throw away thy books; no longer distract thyself: it is not allowed; but as if thou wast now dying, despise the flesh; it is blood and bones and a network, a contexture of nerves, veins, and arteries. See the breath also, what kind of a thing it is; air, and not always the same, but every moment sent out and again sucked in. The third, then, is the ruling part; consider thus: Thou art an old man; no longer let this be a slave, no longer be pulled by the strings like a puppet to unsocial movements, no longer be either dissatisfied with the present lot, or shrink from the future.

3. All that is from the gods is full of providence. That which is from fortune is not separated from nature or without an interweaving and involution with the things which are ordered by providence. From thence all things flow; and there is besides necessity, and that which is for the advantage of the whole universe, of which thou art a part. But that is good for every part of nature which the nature of the whole brings, and what serves to maintain this nature. Now the universe is preserved, as by the changes of the elements so by the changes of things compounded of the elements. Let these principles be enough for thee; let them always be fixed opinions. But cast away the thirst after books, that thou mayest not die murmuring, but cheerfully, truly, and from thy heart thankful to the gods.

4. Remember how long thou hast been putting off these things, and how often thou hast received an opportunity from the gods, and yet dost not use it. Thou must now at last perceive of what universe thou art a part, and of what administrator of the universe thy existence is an efflux, and that a limit of time is fixed for thee, which if thou dost not use for clearing away the clouds from thy mind, it will go and thou wilt go, and it will never return.

5. Every moment think steadily as a Roman and a man to do what thou hast in hand with perfect and simple dignity, and feeling of affection, and freedom, and justice, and to give thyself relief from all other thoughts. And thou wilt give thyself relief if thou doest every act of thy life as if it were the last, laying aside all carelessness and passionate aversion from the commands of reason, and all hypocrisy, and self-love, and discontent with the portion which has been given to thee. Thou seest how few the things are, the which if a man lays hold of, he is able to live a life which flows in quiet, and is like the existence of the gods; for the gods on their part will require nothing more from him who observes these things.

6. Do wrong to thyself, do wrong to thyself, my soul; but thou wilt no longer have the opportunity of honoring thyself. Every man's life is sufficient. But thine is nearly finished, though thy soul reverences not itself, but places thy felicity in the souls of others.

7. Do the things external which fall upon thee distract thee? Give thyself time to learn something new and good, and cease to be whirled around. But then thou must also avoid being carried about the other way; for those too are triflers who have wearied themselves in life by their activity, and yet have no object to which to direct every movement, and, in a word, all their thoughts.

8. Through not observing what is in the mind of another a man has seldom been seen to be unhappy; but those who do not observe the movements of their own minds must of necessity be unhappy.

9. This thou must always bear in mind, what is the nature of the whole, and what is my nature, and how this is related to that, and what kind of a part it is of what kind of a whole, and that there is no one who hinders thee from always doing and saying the things which are according to the nature of which thou art a part.

10. Theophrastus, in his comparison of bad acts—such a comparison as one would make in accordance with the common notions of mankind—says, like a true philosopher, that the offences which are committed through desire are more blamable than those which are committed through anger. For he who is excited by anger seems to turn away from reason with a certain pain and unconscious contraction; but he who offends through desire, being overpowered by pleasure, seems to be in a manner more intemperate and more womanish in his offences. Rightly, then, and in a way worthy of philosophy, he said that the offences which are committed with pleasure are more blamable than those which are committed with pain; and on the whole the one is more like a person who has been first wronged and through pain is compelled to be angry; but the other is moved by his own impulse to do wrong, being carried towards doing something by desire.

11. Since it is possible that thou mayest depart from life this very moment, regulate every act and thought accordingly. But to go away from among men, if there are gods, is not a thing to be afraid of, for the gods will not involve thee in evil; but if indeed they do not exist, or if they have no concern about human affairs, what is it to me to live in a universe devoid of gods or devoid of providence? But in truth they do exist, and they do care for human beings, and they have put all the means in man's power to enable him not to fall into real evils. And as to the rest, if there was anything evil, they would have provided for this also, that it should be altogether in a man's power not to fall into it. Now that which does not make a man worse, how can it make a man's life worse? But neither through ignorance, nor having the knowledge but not the power to guard against or correct these things, is it possible that the nature of the universe has overlooked them; nor is it possible that it has made so great a mistake, either through want of power or want of skill, that good and evil should happen indiscriminately to the good and the bad. But death certainly, and life, honor and dishonor, pain and pleasure,—all these things equally happen to good men and bad, being things which make us neither better nor worse. Therefore they are neither good nor evil.

12. How quickly all things disappear,—in the universe the bodies themselves, but in time the remembrance of them. What is the nature of all sensible things, and particularly those which attract with the bait of pleasure or terrify by pain, or are noised abroad by vapory fame; how worthless, and contemptible, and sordid, and perishable, and dead

they are,—all this it is the part of the intellectual faculty to observe. To observe too who these are whose opinions and voices give reputation; what death is, and the fact that, if a man looks at it in itself, and by the abstractive power of reflection resolves into their parts all the things which present themselves to the imagination in it, he will then consider it to be nothing else than an operation of nature; and if any one is afraid of an operation of nature, he is a child. This, however, is not only an operation of nature, but it is also a thing which conduces to the purposes of nature. To observe too how man comes near to the Deity, and by what part of him, and when this part of man is so disposed.

13. Nothing is more wretched than a man who traverses everything in a round, and pries into the things beneath the earth, as the poet says, and seeks by conjecture what is in the minds of his neighbors, without perceiving that it is sufficient to attend to the daemon within him, and to reverence it sincerely. And reverence of the daemon consists in keeping it pure from passion and thoughtlessness, and dissatisfaction with what comes from gods and men. For the things from the gods merit veneration for their excellence; and the things from men should be dear to us by reason of kinship; and sometimes even, in a manner, they move our pity by reason of men's ignorance of good and bad; this defect being not less than that which deprives us of the power of distinguishing things that are white and black.

14. Though thou shouldest be going to live three thousand years, and as many times ten thousand years, still remember that no man loses any other life than this which he now lives, nor lives any other than this which he now loses. The longest and shortest are thus brought to the same. For the present is the same to all, though that which perishes is not the same; and so that which is lost appears to be a mere moment. For a man cannot lose either the past or the future: for what a man has not, how can any one take this from him? These two things then thou must bear in mind; the one, that all things from eternity are of like forms and come round in a circle, and that it makes no difference whether a man shall see the same things during a hundred years, or two hundred, or an infinite time; and the second, that the longest liver and he who will die soonest lose just the same. For the present is the only thing of which a man can be deprived, if it is true that this is the only thing which he has, and that a man cannot lose a thing if he has it not.

15. Remember that all is opinion. For what was said of Cynic Monimus is manifest: and manifest too is the use of what was said, if a man receives what may be got out of it as far as it is true.

16. The soul of man does violence to itself, first of all, when it becomes an abscess, and, as it were, a tumor on the universe, so far as it can. For to be vexed at anything which happens is a separation of our-

selves from nature, in some part of which the natures of all other things are contained.   In the next place, the soul does violence to itself when it turns away from any man, or even moves towards him with the intention of injuring, such as are the souls of those who are angry.   In the third place, the soul does violence to itself when it is overpowered by pleasure or by pain. Fourthly, when it plays a part, and does or says anything insincerely and untruly. Fifthly, when it allows any act of its own and any movement to be without an aim, and does anything thought-lessly and without considering what it is, it being right that even the smallest things be done with reference to an end; and the end of ra-tional animals is to follow the reason and the law of the most ancient city and polity.

17. Of human life the time is a point, and the substance is in a flux, and the perception dull, and the composition of the whole body subject to putrefaction, and the soul a whirl, and fortune hard to divine, and fame a thing devoid of judgment. And, to say all in a word, everything which belongs to the body is a stream, and what belongs to the soul is a dream and vapor, and life is a warfare and a stranger's sojourn, and after-fame is oblivion. What then is that which is able to conduct a man? One thing, and only one, philosophy. But this consists in keep-ing the daemon within a man free from violence and unharmed, superior to pains and pleasures, doing nothing without a purpose, nor yet falsely and with hypocrisy, not feeling the need of another man's doing or not doing anything; and besides, accepting all that happens, and all that is allotted, as coming from thence, wherever it is, from whence he him-self came; and finally, waiting for death with a cheerful mind, as being nothing else than a dissolution of the elements of which every being is compounded. But if there is no harm to the elements themselves in each continually changing into another, why should a man have any appre-hension about the change and dissolution of all the elements? For it is according to nature, and nothing is evil which is according to nature.

This is Carnuntum.

OATES: *THE STOIC AND EPICUREAN PHILOSOPHERS.* Modern Library, Random House, New York.

CLEANTHES' HYMN TO ZEUS

O God most glorious, called by many a name,
Nature's great King, through endless years the same;
Omnipotence, who by thy just decree
Controllest all, hail Zeus, for unto thee
Behoves all creatures in all lands to call.
We are thy children, we alone of all
On earth's broad ways that wander to and fro,
Bearing thine image wheresoe'er we go.
Wherefore with songs of praise thy power I will forth show.
Lo! yonder Heaven, that round the earth is wheeled,
Follows thy guidance, still to thee doth yield
Glad homage; thine unconquerable hand
Such flaming minister, the levin brand,
Wieldeth, a sword two-edged, whose deathless might
Pulsates through all that nature brings to light;
Vehicle of the universal Word, that flows
Through all, and in the light celestial glows
Of stars both great and small. A King of Kings
Through ceaseless ages, God, whose purpose brings
To birth, whate'er on land or in the sea
Is wrought, or in high heaven's immensity;
Save what the sinner works infatuate.
Nay, but thou knowest to make the crooked straight:
Chaos to thee is order: in thine eyes
The unloved is lovely, who didst harmonize
Things evil with things good, that there should be
One Word through all things everlastingly.
One Word—whose voice alas! the wicked spurn;
Insatiate for the good their spirits yearn:
Yet seeing see not, neither hearing hear
God's universal law, which those revere,
By reason guided, happiness who win.
The rest, unreasoning, diverse shapes of sin
Self-prompted follow: for an idle name
Vainly they wrestle in the lists of fame:
Others inordinately riches woo,
Or dissolute, the joys of flesh pursue.
Now here, now there they wander, fruitless still,
Forever seeking good and finding ill.
Zeus, the all-bountiful, whom darkness shrouds,
Whose lightning lightens in the thunder-clouds;

Thy children save from error's deadly sway:
Turn thou the darkness from their souls away:
Vouchsafe that unto knowledge they attain;
For thou by knowledge art made strong to reign
O'er all, and all things rulest righteously.
So by thee honored, we will honor thee,
Praising thy works continually with songs,
As mortals should; nor higher meed belongs
E'en to the gods, than justly to adore
The universal law for evermore.

QUESTIONS AND STATEMENTS FOR DISCUSSION
(*Epictetus*)

1. "What then is to be done? To make the best of what is in our power, and take the rest as it naturally happens." (*Epictetus*, Bk. I, Chap. I.) Discuss the cogency of the Stoic doctrine not to worry over things not within our power. Is it best, as he says, "to stretch out your neck for the blow"?

2. "Difficulties are the things that show what men are." (Bk. I, Chap. XXIV.) How are difficulties to be viewed? The meaning of "profitable difficulties"?

3. What is the drift of the discussions on the limitations of freedom? (P. 165.) Where alone are we free? Epictetus declares: "The body is but a finer mixture of clay"—but Zeus says: "I have given thee a portion of myself—this faculty of exerting powers of pursuit and avoidance, of desire and aversion." With what does Epictetus connect freedom? Is freedom a supreme value?

4. Why does good lie alongside truth, so that the just man need not be intimidated by false judgments?

5. What do you think of the expression: "Where the essence of God is, there too is the essence of Good"? Could this be reversed with equal truth: Where the essence of Good is, there is the essence of God?

6. "There is nothing good or evil, save in the will." (P. 168.)

7. "No wicked man lives as he likes." True or false? Why? (P. 169.)

8. What constitutes slavery? (Pp. 169-170.)

9. "Socrates was preserved by dying instead of running away." In what sense could this be true? (Pp. 172-173.)

(*The Thoughts of Marcus Aurelius*)

10. Discuss the negative character of Marcus Aurelius' background as described in *The Meditations* I:1-15.

11. Why are wrong acts committed from desire more blameworthy than those which involve pain? II:10.

12. Does the picture drawn in II:17, disclose the full duty of man?

13. "Never value anything as profitable to thyself which shall compel thee to break thy promise, to lose thy self-respect, to hate any man, to suspect, to curse, to act the hypocrite, to desire anything which needs walls and curtains." III:7.

Suggested Supplementary Readings:

Hyde: *Five Great Philosophies of Life.*   Macmillan, New York,
Chap. II, pp. 66-109.
Arnold: *Roman Stoicism.*   Cambridge University Press, Cam-
bridge, England.
Gummere: *Seneca the Philosopher and His Modern Message.*
Marshall-Jones, Boston.
Bevan: *Later Greek Religion.*   E. P. Dutton, New York.

Chapter 6

THE EPICUREAN "LIMITATION OF DESIRES"

I
The Life of Epicurus

II
The Development of Greek Science

III
The Epicurean Formula

1. "Right belief concerning the gods"
2. "Right knowledge respecting death"
3. "Elaboration of pleasure; the simple life"
4. "The conquest of pain"

IV
The Modern Significance of Epicurus

1. The right to skepticism
2. The scientific standpoint
3. The impetus to democracy
4. The oversight in the Epicurean doctrine of values

Chapter 6

THE EPICUREAN "LIMITATION OF DESIRES"

The rise of philosophy in Greece had been a distinct effort after freedom. The all-prevalent idolatry was the basis of cultivated fears by which the ruling class of tyrants and priests had kept in subjection the slaves and the unenlightened. This subordination had been brought about through the teaching that natural phenomena such as earthquakes, volcanic eruptions, thunder and lightning, tornado, and tide were the acts of superhuman beings who thus wreaked their vengeance upon hapless men who might quite innocently incur their wrath. The only way to turn this aside was by obedience to the ruling families who claimed descent from the gods and by liberal offerings at temples and shrines. From the seventh century B.C. on, there seems to have been a world-wide struggle at release from these fears which are the characteristic of paganism and which differentiate it from religion. The effort to throw off this dread by replacing it with concepts of a benign, rational, and spiritual Supreme Being was the impelling source which gave rise to the world-philosophies and religions which we are considering from the standpoint of their concept of value.

Nowhere was the movement away from what we might call "these pagan fears," quite so complete as in the development of Western civilization. At the same time it must be admitted that the inspiration of the movement came from Oriental sources such as Parseeism, Pythagoreanism, Hinduism, Buddhism, and Judaism, culminating for Western civilization in Christianity.

Epicureanism was a part of the individualistic scientific progress. It must be understood indeed by its opposition to the prevalent worship of the gods and its effort in place thereof to set up scientific criteria that would explode the old superstitions of fear.

Epicurus felt that the aim of the practical philosophers of his time, *apathia,* or indifference, could never be achieved until men became aware of the undeviating character of the forces of nature and their divorcement from all divine purposes. He hoped to divest the minds of men of the fear of capricious gods by an appeal to a world of natural law.

Note the similarity of effort between Buddhism, Stoicism, and

Epicureanism at this point.   Each one of these systems was, after its own lights, an effort after emancipation; Buddha by declaring the dark side of human experience illusion, the Stoic by appeal to a supreme and lawfully acting Reason, Epicurus by a consideration of the scientific nature of reality.

Epicurus' place in the progress of the West must be seen then in what he and the later Epicureans did for the advancement of science.   The whole movement, which began at least with the early "nature" philosophers, was to seek the causes behind natural phenomena instead of assuming them to result from the anger of the gods. That this scientific spirit arose and became dominant in the Western world was in very great measure due to the work of Epicurus and his followers.   In that it sought out individual causes in the series of phenomena and turned away from Pagan superstitions it, along with Stoicism, helped to further the cause of freedom, science, and democracy.

I

The Life of Epicurus

Epicurus was born in 352-351 B.C., whether near Athens or on the Island of Samos is not known.   His family seems to have moved about a good deal.   They migrated from Attica to Samos when that island was opened to Greek settlement and later evacuated when the Greeks were moved out.   This was but a token of the rover's life which beset Epicurus himself, who lived at times in various cities of Asia Minor, and at Mitylene, or the Island of Lesbos, before settling down to teach in Athens.   His father was a schoolmaster and his mother, Bailey tells us, was a sort of fake priestess going about pronouncing incantations and thereby professedly warding off disease and ill-luck.   Epicurus as a lad is said to have assisted her as an acolyte.   Such a beginning—with the possible conflict in his own home between intelligence and superstition, the schoolmaster and the priestess, an early disillusionment respecting the mysticism of his mother—would very naturally prepare the mind of the boy for a repudiation of all mysticism and religion.   At the same time the questions raised in his mind may have been an impelling influence to philosophy.   His success in Lampsacus, a city of Asia Minor, seems to have encouraged him to move his "school" along with his pupils to a place outside Athens which became known as "Epicurus' Garden."   Over the entrance was said to have been inscribed these sentences :

Stranger, here if you please, you may abide in a good condition; here the Supreme Good is Pleasure; the steward of this homely cottage is hospitable, humane, and ready to receive you; he shall afford you barley broth, and pure water of the spring, and say, friends, are you not well entertained? For these gardens do not invite hunger, but satisfy it; nor increase your thirst with drinks, while they should extinguish it, but wholly overcome it with a natural and grateful liquor.

Here he gathered about him a community of disciples who lived holding all things in common, achieving with apparent success what centuries later failed in the Brook Farm experiment of the Concord Transcendentalists. The inclusion of women in the community group became a scandal in the eyes of other philosophers, especially of the Stoics, and probably led to the tales of profligacy, which became associated with the names Epicurean and Epicurus. Epicurus himself was not an epicure. He was most abstemious in his own life, declaring barley bread and spring water would amply supply the need for food. If one disliked these he needed only to go without long enough and they would be as welcome as the richest viands. However, his materialism, his dependence upon the senses, his anti-religious attitude, and his emphasis on pleasure as the true end of life laid a foundation of practice in his disciples which the Master's asceticism was incapable of preventing. There is no doubt that in later Epicureanism the charge of profligacy was often well-founded.

Epicureanism was introduced at Rome at least contemporaneously with Stoicism and by the time of the Caesars there must have been many Epicurean "clubs" or societies. Piso, the father-in-law of Julius Caesar, was an Epicurean and there has been preserved to us the wording of the invitation that was extended to him to join an Epicurean society. This invitation was written by Philodemus of Gadara, the Latin poet-philosopher, and has been translated by Richard Garnett, the late librarian of the British Museum. It runs:

Tomorrow, dearest Piso, one will come
To lead thee to a philosophic home,
Where Epicurus' Disciples, we
Observe our Master's anniversary.
Song have we, and sincerity of soul,
But look not, Piso, for the Chian bowl,
Or sumptuous dishes, or aught exquisite
Except thine own urbanity and wit.

The assumption that the Piso of the invitation was Calpurnius Piso Censorinus, seems not illogical in view of the fact that his villa, unearthed in Herculaneum in the eighteenth century, was found to contain eighteen hundred papyri devoted to the literature of Epicureanism. The Piso family was numerous, noble, and active in Roman political life, tracing their ancestry back to the ancient Roman king. Numa Pompilius (715-673 B.C.) It is easy to confuse individual members of the clan because of similarity of names.

II
The Development of Greek Science

Greek science took its rise from the Milesian philosophers of Asia Minor, who sought a knowledge of natural phenomena by the observance of nature herself. This, as has been already mentioned, was a liberating movement to escape the superstitions that had held the world in bondage. There were Thales, Anaximander, and Anaximenes, who held respectively that water, void, and air were the primary substances from which all things were made. These early Milesians were called philosophers but would today be more strictly called physicists. Those who followed them show the influence of Persian, Hindu, and Buddist thought, and most of them, perhaps, had been in contact with Oriental philosophy, if indeed, as some have claimed, the ideas of Indian philosophy were not first introduced into Greece through migrations from India that took place in prehistoric times. As early as the seventh century B.C. Zoroaster had proclaimed a non-idolatrous and spiritual faith, and the Greeks had long known something of the culture of the Persian Empire. Heraclitus was in all probability thus influenced, and prepared the way for later developments by affirming that all things were in constant change. After him came Leucippus, the originator in Western thought of the concepts of atomism, and he had studied with the Magi, or Persian wise men, and very likely may have met the Indian Gymnosophs, this being another name for philosophers. To Democritus of Greece was given the honor of making atomism a going concern, and setting forth a concept of the atom which has lasted in modern science down almost to the present without important changes. The atoms were conceived as the tiniest possible particles of matter, invisible, indivisible, similar, and of which all things were composed. The differences of quality given to the senses were held to be due merely to the conformation or density of these particles. Thus was formed the basis for a materialistic philosophy of reality, and upon this Epicurus seized as a means of denying the existence of Divine purpose in the world-order. Epicurus' interest in science was plainly but a means of offsetting the prevalent superstition, as he indicates in his Principal Doctrines:

A man cannot dispel his fear about the most important matters if he does not know what is the nature of the universe but suspects the truth of some mythical story. So that without natural science it is not possible to attain our pleasures unalloyed.

There is no profit in securing protection in relation to men, if things above and things beneath the earth and indeed all in the boundless universe remain matters of suspicion.[1]

By the study of physical science alone can the tranquility of the mind be fully and permanently secured: freed from the possibility of great fears for the future, and pleasurably occupied in the search for scientific truth, which will confirm its freedom, it may peacefully rest in the contemplation of the pleasures of the body, past, present, and future, and so attain its own characteristic "imperturbability" (*ataraxia*). There will then be but little room left, even as there is little inclination, for vain desires: 'through love of true philosophy every disturbing and troublesome desire is ended.' And the result is a happy and useful life: 'we must laugh and philosophize at the same time and do our household duties and employ our other faculties, and never cease proclaiming the sayings of the true philosophy.'[2]

Had Epicurus been a modern and writing about religion, he would have based his reasoning on the same considerations that moved Lewis Browne in *This Believing World,* in which fear is assumed to be the ground of religion. If it really were, no intelligent man could be sincerely religious. Genuine religion rests in love of goodness and in faith in eternal righteousness, in which love and faith are regenerative and creative principles, whereas fear is destructive of high motives, and disintegrating to personality. In the slang of today, Epicurus had two "pet peeves." His hostility to these two fears arose out of his belief that they were the two destroyers of peace in the human heart. The first of these was fear of the gods, and the second was the fear of death. For the cultivation of these fears he held religion responsible.

The chief disquietude of the human mind he believed arose from the terrible dread of the gods inculcated by the ruling caste, and intensified by ignorance and superstition. The common man was always anticipating some everlasting misery, and Epicurus held that peace of mind could only come as men were delivered from these terrors. His whole interest in science, as he expressed it in a letter to Pythocles, was that by a knowledge of natural phenomena one could reach peace of mind and a certain confidence. Freedom of the soul from all disturbance thus became for him the whole aim of life, as by avoiding pain and fear "the whole tempest of the soul is

[1] Bailey, *Epicurus,* Oxford University Press, New York, p. 97.
[2] Bailey, *The Greek Atomists and Epicurus,* Oxford University Press, New York, p. 505.

dispersed." He did not deny the *existence* of the gods, but rather their *malevolence*. Since they had achieved supreme blessedness, they would not take pleasure in afflicting mortals, or putting it another way, they would not disturb their own calm by disturbing others. "Believe that God is a being immortal and blessed . . . and do not assign to him anything alien to his immortality or ill-suited to his blessedness," was his advice in a letter to Menoeceus.

By the search for pleasure as the end of life, Epicurus did not favor the pleasures of profligacy, but only freedom from pain in the body and forebodings in the mind. In a strangely paradoxical way, this advocate of self-gratification as the aim of life removed the zest from pleasure by making it wholly negative, for, as merely the absence of pain, it is emptied of pleasurable content.

The Epicurean hostility to religion was primarily based upon the misuse of religion. He felt it necessary to fight the worship of the gods as popularly practised in order to defend the gods. He was really set against false concepts of the gods, and these false concepts were identified with religion, much as some people of our own day do not distinguish between religion and theology. It is no act of piety, wrote Lucretius, to turn with covered head to a stone, and approaching every altar to fall prone on the ground with outspread hands before the statues of the gods, sprinkling the altars with the blood of beasts, and adding vow to vow, but rather to be able to look on all the world with a mind of peace. One is reminded of the fury with which the Jewish prophet assailed the priesthood of his time for pouring rivers of bestial blood upon their altars, when all that piety required was "to do justly, to love mercy, and to walk humbly with God." The Epicurean horror at this false religion is well illustrated in the beginning of Lucretius' great poem on nature. When he condemns religion he means the kind of religion exhibited in such a superstitious abomination as that perpetrated in Aulis when, in order to secure calm seas for his military expedition, King Agamemnon propitiated the gods by murdering his own daughter Iphigenia on the altar of sacrifice. Against all such religion the Epicurean was the avowed and rightful enemy.

In general, Lucretius' contribution to Epicurean literature was original only in its literary expression. The poem on *Nature* seems to have been almost wholly a reproduction in verse of the now lost *Larger Epitome,* written by Epicurus himself, whom Lucretius worshipped almost as a divinity. But it does show literary, if not philosophical, genius. The really new idea he advanced over those of Epicurus, Democritus, and Leucippus was through an emendation of the atomic theory which they had taught.   Lucretius asserted a creative "swerve" in the falling atoms which he held responsible for all the qualities and diversities of the whole of creation.   As previously stated, his only interest in science was to substitute natural -law for the belief in magic, and he did this largely by wishful thinking, scientific imagination instead of scientific investigation.   In each case he sought to displace purpose and will by some clever creation of the imagination.   Nevertheless, while some of his scientific claims were absurd, some did in a remarkable way find confirmation in modern science.

His outlook on life was essentially pessimistic and uncreative, because he magnified his disbeliefs, and his despair was shown in many ways.   The whole of life, he declared, was only a struggle in the dark, and he praised "the good old times" with all the fervor of a twentieth century pessimist.   The age is enfeebled, he writes, and the earth, once bounteous in food, is now so exhausted that it can produce only pigmies in comparison with the bulk of huge beasts that once roamed the earth.   In the good old days there was abundance of corn, and "joyous" vineyards, but now men wear out their plows on fields that scarcely feed the plowman.   The present farmer shakes his head and compares existing poverty with past opulence, not understanding how everything is wasting away and going to oblivion. The futility and frustration of life is described in words appropriate to our automobile civilization, when he pictures the Roman householder driving his mules in headlong haste as if going to a fire, and, once he reaches the door of his own house he begins to yawn and falls asleep, or hastens back to town, trying all the time to flee from himself, a self he can never escape.   He runs forever after what is not present, and despises whatever is, because life has slipped from his grasp, unfinished and unsatisfying.

Lucretius expanded the doctrine of evolution which he had received from earlier Greek philosophy, and gave it such outstanding literary expression that it became the vehicle by which the scientific spirit was, in some measure at least, carried into the life of the Renaissance.   However faulty his conclusions, he strengthened the spirit of protest against religious superstition, and gave impetus to the coming scientific age.   The atomism of Leucippus, Democritus, and Epicurus was thus saved to the world as a scientific concept, little changed in the recent Daltonian atom, and waiting until the late morning of the twentieth century to be superseded by the new concept of the atom as immaterial force, "an event in a space-time continuum."

III

The Epicurean Formula

The Epicurean formula for achieving the good life was known as "The Quadruple Remedy." This is more than suggestive of the "Four Noble Truths" of Buddha because both start off in the same way with "right beliefs." With this the comparison breaks down.

The first remedy for the ills of life with Epicurus was right belief respecting the gods. This consisted not in a complete atheism or denial of the existence of deities. It was rather an assertion of their kindliness. Since they must be assumed to have achieved the good life, which is one of pleasure or *ataraxia,* it must be believed that anger, the will to trouble other people, is foreign to their nature. One has nothing then to fear from the gods.

The second element of the "Quadruple Remedy" was true knowledge regarding death. This doctrine is beautifully illuminated in other parts of his teaching.

> Death is nothing to us: for that which is dissolved is without sensation; and that which lacks sensation is nothing to us. *Principal Doctrines II.*

From Charlton's translation of 1656 we have these expressions regarding death:

> Death doth nothing concern us because while we are, death is not; and when death is, we are not.

and again:

> And this reasoning moreover, causeth, that we shall not be frustrated of Pleasure even then, when Death shall take us by the hand, and shew us the period of all these mortall things, insomuch as we shall therby attain to the perfect, and so delectable End of a very Good Life, rising from the table of the World as Guests well satisfied with the Good Entertainments of life, and having duly performed all these Duties, which to perform, we received life. (Charlton's translation and spelling, London (1656) p. 109).

The third of the "Quadruple Remedies" was to be the elaboration of pleasures. He asserts that the limit of pleasure comes with the removal of all that is painful. If, this being achieved, you attempt still further to increase your pleasure you destroy it. Bread and water fulfil the satisfaction of hunger and in doing that are quite as effective as luxurious dishes. If you go beyond the satisfaction of bodily needs you bring discomfort, pain, and disease. The wise man then will limit his desires to the needs of simple satisfaction. He

will be happy with whatever he has. He will require only absence
of pain in body and mind. Since most of our unhappiness springs
from wanting things impossible or difficult to obtain we will strictly
limit our desires to our simplest needs.

The fourth of the "Quadruple Remedies" had to do with the conquest of pain. This consisted, as in the case of Buddha, very largely
in thinking it away. One is advised to endure pain with equanimity
because if it is acute it must soon end (with the death of the sufferer) and if it is light and continues it is overbalanced by other pleasures. Epicurus was ridiculed by his opponents for being so blind
to the meaning of his own philosophy of pleasure as to declare "that
one could be happy though on the rack." This would seem to call
for all the fortitude of a thoroughgoing Stoic, rather than for an
Epicurean whose ideal is the life of painless pleasure.

IV

The Modern Significance of Epicurus

Does Epicureanism hold anything of significance for our modern
age? Much in many ways. First of all because it epitomizes so
much of the modern spirit and outlook. It has for more than two
thousand years represented that opposition to idealism and the spiritual which has found such general expression in our own time.
This opposition more than anything else has kept idealism to its feet
and kept off a reign of fanaticism. Is there then a value and a right
to skepticism?—that skepticism which questions traditions, common
beliefs, the "wisdom" of the past, things which many consider the
fundamental assurances? Surely there is but one answer the present day can give that question in the light of modern science. For
science has made its prime discoveries by ignoring traditions as if
they were but old wives' fables. Out of this consistent questioning
has grown the knowledge which has given us a new world. A reverent skepticism is as essential to progress as a reverent faith. To
each generation things can be known only at first hand, only as they
are examined anew, only as the rising generation wrests its truth
from its own experience. Epicureanism, because it fostered the spirit
of inquiry, has been the stalwart mother of science, and has established the right of a reverent skepticism, but please note the qualify-
ing adjective, *reverent*. To the Epicurean skepticism we are indebted
for the prevalence of the scientific view so prominent in our age.

The establishment of the scientific view thus wrought into the
fabric of modern life is really the counterbalance needed to make

faith effective.   Untempered faith is misleading—for faith must ever be self-justifying, must always be able to give an account of itself.   On the other hand, a skepticism which merely enters a general denial of everything is only weakness and futility.   Thus out of faith and a reverent skepticism, the conflict between belief on the one hand, and unbelief on the other, grows the scientific spirit.

But the right to question old opinion brought other benefits in its train.   One of these was the right of individual belief, individual examination of the facts, which has fostered the spirit of democracy at the same time it was establishing the right of skepticism.   These were great gains in the growth of democracy.

What of the relation of Epicureanism to the general problem of value?   Does it show us the way to the supreme values?   We must admit it does not.   Its tale of human happiness does not run deeply enough to take in man's higher and distinctive nature.   Human beings, using that term in its truest sense, can never be satisfied with food and drink, or lack of physical suffering which the Epicurean pictured as the supreme goal and satisfying value of life.   Having all these things in the highest degree one may be damned with a sense of frustration and futility to the point of desiring suicide.   Struggle, hardship, pain, and suffering are as essential to our satisfaction and our profoundest happiness as are ease and pleasure.   In fact these latter are of little worth to us except as they are by-products of our toil and pain.   The reason is that our deepest satisfactions are not physical but rather spiritual.   For the thrill of victory, or the proud possession of a ribbon, the athlete rushes into physical disaster with a cheer.   For love of country, of freedom, of righteousness, men have faced death, and agony worse than death, with jubilant hearts.   In the loss of things physical man rises to the heights of spiritual self-conquest, and fulfils the call of destiny.   We have fallen upon a time in the world's history when perhaps the present generation sees this truth more clearly than any other in human history.   By the same token, the way may be opened to a higher social achievement than has ever before been known.   But Epicureanism will not form its chief inspiration.   To those values, which we now discover to be so essential to peace, Epicureanism was oblivious or indifferent.

To this generation it remains to add to the scientific spirit that appreciation of spiritual values which alone can provide convincing power.   To you of the rising generation it may be given to discover the solution of the problem of the things that matter most where Epicureanism fell short.

READINGS

BAILEY: *EPICURUS*. Oxford University Press, New York. Pp. 95-105, 107-119, 133-139.

———✦———

IV

PRINCIPAL DOCTRINES

I. The blessed and immortal nature knows no trouble itself nor causes trouble to any other, so that it is never constrained by anger or favour. For all such things exist only in the weak.

II. Death is nothing to us: for that which is dissolved is without sensation; and that which lacks sensation is nothing to us.

III. The limit of quantity in pleasures is the removal of all that is painful. Wherever pleasure is present, as long as it is there, there is neither pain of body nor of mind, nor of both at once.

IV. Pain does not last continuously in the flesh, but the acutest pain is there for a very short time, and even that which just exceeds the pleasure in the flesh does not continue for many days at once. But chronic illnesses permit a predominance of pleasure over pain in the flesh.

V. It is not possible to live pleasantly without living prudently and honourably and justly, [nor again to live a life of prudence, honour, and justice] without living pleasantly. And the man who does not possess the pleasant life, is not living prudently and honourably and justly, [and the man who does not possess the virtuous life, cannot possibly live] pleasantly.

VI. To secure protection from men anything is a natural good, by which you may be able to attain this end.

VII. Some men wished to become famous and conspicuous, thinking that they would thus win for themselves safety from other men. Wherefore if the life of such men is safe, they have obtained the good which nature craves; but if it is not safe, they do not possess that for which they strove at first by the instinct of nature.

VIII. No pleasure is a bad thing in itself: but the means which produce some pleasures bring with them disturbances many times greater than the pleasures.

IX. If every pleasure could be intensified so that it lasted and influenced the whole organism or the most essential parts of our nature, pleasures would never differ from one another.

X. If the things that produce the pleasures of profligates could dispel the fears of the mind about the phenomena of the sky and death and its pains, and also teach the limits of desires (and of pains), we should never have cause to blame them : for they would be filling themselves full with pleasures from every source and never have pain of body or mind, which is the evil of life.

XI. If we were not troubled by our suspicions of the phenomena of the sky and about death, fearing that it concerns us, and also by our failure to grasp the limits of pains and desires, we should have no need of natural science.

XII. A man cannot dispel his fear about the most important matters if he does not know what is the nature of the universe but suspects the truth of some mythical story. So that without natural science it is not possible to attain our pleasures unalloyed.

XIII. There is no profit in securing protection in relation to men, if things above and things beneath the earth and indeed all in the boundless universe remain matters of suspicion.

XIV. The most unalloyed source of protection from men, which is secured to some extent by a certain force of expulsion, is in fact the immunity which results from a quiet life and the retirement from the world.

XV. The wealth demanded by nature is both limited and easily procured; that demanded by idle imaginings stretches on to infinity.

XVI. In but few things chance hinders a wise man, but the greatest and most important matters reason has ordained and throughout the whole period of life does and will ordain.

XVII. The just man is most free from trouble, the unjust most full of trouble.

XVIII. The pleasure in the flesh is not increased, when once the pain due to want is removed, but is only varied : and the limit as regards pleasure in the mind is begotten by the reasoned understanding of these very pleasures and of the emotions akin to them, which used to cause the greatest fear to the mind.

XIX. Infinite time contains no greater pleasure than limited time, if one measures by reason the limits of pleasure.

XX. The flesh perceives the limits of pleasure as unlimited and unlimited time is required to supply it. But the mind, having attained a reasoned understanding of the ultimate good of the flesh and its limits and having dissipated the fears concerning the time to come, supplies us with the complete life, and we have no further need of infinite time : but neither does the mind shun pleasure, nor, when circumstances begin to bring about the departure from life, does it approach its end as though it fell short in any way of the best life.

XXI. He who has learned the limits of life knows that that which removes the pain due to want and makes the whole of life complete is easy to obtain; so that there is no need of actions which involve competition.

XXII. We must consider both the real purpose and all the evidence of direct perception, to which we always refer the conclusions of opinion; otherwise, all will be full of doubt and confusion.

XXIII. If you fight against all sensations, you will have no standard by which to judge even those of them which you say are false.

XXIV. If you reject any single sensation and fail to distinguish between the conclusion of opinion as to the appearance awaiting confirmation and that which is actually given by the sensation or feeling, or each intuitive apprehension of the mind, you will confound all other sensations as well with the same groundless opinion, so that you will reject every standard of judgment. And if among the mental images created by your opinion you affirm both that which awaits confirmation and that which does not, you will not escape error since you will have preserved the whole cause of doubt in every judgment between what is right and what is wrong.

XXV. If on each occasion instead of referring your actions to the end of nature, you turn to some other nearer standard when you are making a choice or an avoidance, your actions will not be consistent with your principles.

XXVI. Of desires, all that do not lead to a sense of pain, if they are not satisfied, are not necessary, but involve a craving which is easily dispelled, when the object is hard to procure or they seem likely to produce harm.

XXVII. Of all the things which wisdom acquires to produce the blessedness of the complete life, far the greatest is the possession of friendship.

XXVIII. The same conviction which has given us confidence that there is nothing terrible that lasts forever or even for long, has also seen the protection of friendship most fully completed in the limited evils of this life.

XXIX. Among desires some are natural (and necessary), some natural (but not necessary), and others neither natural nor necessary, but due to idle imagination.

XXX. Wherever in the case of desires which are physical, but do not lead to a sense of pain, if they are not fulfilled, the effort is intense, such pleasures are due to idle imagination, and it is not owing to their own nature that they fail to be dispelled, but owing to the empty imaginings of the man.

XXXI. The justice which arises from nature is a pledge of mutual advantage to restrain men from harming one another and save them from being harmed.

XXXII. For all living things which have not been able to make compacts not to harm one another or be harmed, nothing ever is either just or unjust; and likewise too for all tribes of men which have been unable or unwilling to make compacts not to harm or be harmed.

XXXIII.   Justice never is anything in itself, but in the dealings of men with one another in any place whatever and at any time it is a kind of compact not to harm or be harmed.

XXXIV.   Injustice is not an evil in itself, but only in consequence of the fear which attaches to the apprehension of being unable to escape those appointed to punish such actions.

XXXV.   It is not possible for one who acts in secret contravention of the terms of the compact not to harm or be harmed, to be confident that he will escape detection, even if at present he escapes a thousand times.   For up to the time of death it cannot be certain that he will indeed escape.

XXXVI.   In its general aspect justice is the same for all, for it is a kind of mutual advantage in the dealings of men with one another: but with reference to the individual peculiarities of a country or any other circumstances the same thing does not turn out to be just for all.

XXXVII.   Among actions which are sanctioned as just by law, that which is proved on examination to be of advantage in the requirements of men's dealings with one another, has the guarantee of justice, whether it is the same for all or not.   But if a man makes a law and it does not turn out to lead to advantage in men's dealings with each other, then it no longer has the essential nature of justice.   And even if the advantage in the matter of justice shifts from one side to the other, but for a while accords with the general concept, it is none the less just for that period in the eyes of those who do not confound themselves with empty sounds but look to the actual facts.

XXXVIII.   Where, provided the circumstances have not been altered, actions which were considered just, have been shown not to accord with the general concept in actual practice, then they are not just. But where, when circumstances have changed, the same actions which were sanctioned as just no longer lead to advantage, there they were just at the time when they were of advantage for the dealings of fellow-citizens with one another; but subsequently they are no longer just, when no longer of advantage.

XXXIX.   The man who has best ordered the element of disquiet arising from external circumstances has made those things that he could akin to himself and the rest at least not alien: but with all to which he could not do even this, he has refrained from mixing, and has expelled from his life all which it was of advantage to treat thus.

XL.   As many as possess the power to procure complete immunity from their neighbours, these also live most pleasantly with one another, since they have the most certain pledge of security, and after they have enjoyed the fullest intimacy, they do not lament the previous departure of a dead friend, as though he were to be pitied.

(Pp. 95-105.)

V

FRAGMENTS

A.

Vatican Collection

"Epicurus' Exhortation"

IV.   All bodily suffering is negligible: for that which causes acute pain has short duration, and that which endures long in the flesh causes but mild pain.

VII.   It is hard for an evil-doer to escape detection, but to obtain security for escaping is impossible.

IX.   Necessity is an evil, but there is no necessity to live under the control of necessity.

[X.   Remember that you are of mortal nature and have a limited time to live and have devoted yourself to discussions on nature for all time and eternity and have seen 'things that are now and are to come and have been'.]

XI.   For most men rest is stagnation and activity madness.

XIV.   We are born once and cannot be born twice, but for all time must be no more.   But you, who are not (master) of to-morrow, postpone your happiness: life is wasted in procrastination and each one of us dies without allowing himself leisure.

XV.   We value our characters as something peculiar to ourselves, whether they are good and we are esteemed by men, or not; so ought we to value the characters of others, if they are well-disposed to us.

XVI.   No one when he sees evil deliberately chooses it, but is enticed by it as being good in comparison with a greater evil and so pursues it.

XVII.   It is not the young man who should be thought happy, but an old man who has lived a good life.   For the young man at the height of his powers is unstable and is carried this way and that by fortune, like a headlong stream.   But the old man has come to anchor in old age as though in port, and the good things for which before he hardly hoped he has brought into safe harbourage in his grateful recollections.

XVIII.   Remove sight, association, and contact, and the passion of love is at an end.

XIX.   Forgetting the good that has been he has become old this very day.

XXI.   We must not violate nature, but obey her; and we shall obey her if we fulfil the necessary desires and also the physical, if they bring no harm to us, but sternly reject the harmful.

XXIII.   All friendship is desirable in itself, though it starts from the need of help.

XXIV.   Dreams have no divine character nor any prophetic force, but they originate from the influx of images.

XXV.   Poverty, when measured by the natural purpose of life, is great wealth, but unlimited wealth is great poverty.

XXVI.   You must understand that whether the discourse be long or short it tends to the same end.

XXVII.   In all other occupations the fruit comes painfully after completion, but in philosophy pleasure goes hand in hand with knowledge; for enjoyment does not follow comprehension, but comprehension and enjoyment are simultaneous.

XXVIII.   We must not approve either those who are always ready for friendship, or those who hang back, but for friendship's sake we must even run risks.

XXIX.   In investigating nature I would prefer to speak openly and like an oracle to give answers serviceable to all mankind, even though no one should understand me, rather than to conform to popular opinions and so win the praise freely scattered by the mob.

[XXX.   Some men throughout their lives gather together the means of life, for they do not see that the draught swallowed by all of us at birth is a draught of death.]

XXXI.   Against all else it is possible to provide security, but as against death all of us mortals alike dwell in an unfortified city.

XXXII.   The veneration of the wise man is a great blessing to those who venerate him.

XXXIII.   The flesh cries out to be saved from hunger, thirst, and cold.   For if a man possess this safety and hope to possess it, he might rival even Zeus in happiness.

XXXIV.   It is not so much our friends' help that helps us as the confidence of their help.

XXXV.   We should not spoil what we have by desiring what we have not, but remember that what we have too was the gift of fortune.

[XXXVI.   Epicurus' life when compared to other men's in respect of gentleness and self-sufficiency might be thought a mere legend.]

XXXVII.   Nature is weak towards evil, not towards good: because it is saved by pleasures, but destroyed by pains.

XXXVIII.   He is a little man in all respects who has many good reasons for quitting life.

XXXIX.   He is no friend who is continually asking for help, nor he who never associates help with friendship.   For the former barters kindly feeling for a practical return and the latter destroys the hope of good in the future.

XL.   The man who says that all things come to pass by necessity cannot criticize one who denies that all things come to pass by necessity: for he admits that this too happens of necessity.

XLI.   We must laugh and philosophize at the same time and do our household duties and employ our other faculties, and never cease proclaiming the sayings of the true philosophy.

XLII.   The greatest blessing is created and enjoyed at the same moment.

XLIII.   The love of money, if unjustly gained, is impious, and, if justly, shameful; for it is unseemly to be merely parsimonious even with justice on one's side.

XLIV.   The wise man when he has accommodated himself to straits knows better how to give than to receive: so great is the treasure of self-sufficiency which he has discovered.

XLV.   The study of nature does not make men productive of boasting or bragging nor apt to display that culture which is the object of rivalry with the many, but high-spirited and self-sufficient, taking pride in the good things of their own minds and not of their circumstances.

XLVI.   Our bad habits, like evil men who have long done us great harm, let us utterly drive from us.

XLVII.   I have anticipated thee, Fortune, and entrenched myself against all thy secret attacks.   And we will not give ourselves up as captives to thee or to any other circumstance; but when it is time for us to go, spitting contempt on life and on those who here vainly cling to it, we will leave life crying aloud in a glorious triumph-song that we have lived well.

XLVIII.   We must try to make the end of the journey better than the beginning, as long as we are journeying; but when we come to the end, we must be happy and content.

LI.   You tell me that the stimulus of the flesh makes you too prone to the pleasures of love.   Provided that you do not break the laws or good customs and do not distress any of your neighbours or do harm to your body or squander your pittance; you may indulge your inclination as you please.   Yet it is impossible not to come up against one or other of these barriers: for the pleasures of love never profited a man and he is lucky if they do him no harm.

LII.   Friendship goes dancing round the world proclaiming to us all to awake to the praises of a happy life.

LIII.   We must envy no one: for the good do not deserve envy and the bad, the more they prosper, the more they injure themselves.

LIV.   We must not pretend to study philosophy, but study it in reality: for it is not the appearance of health that we need, but real health.

LV.   We must heal our misfortunes by the grateful recollection of what has been and by the recognition that it is impossible to make undone what has been done.

LVI-LVII.   The wise man is not more pained when being tortured (himself, than when seeing) his friend (tortured): (but if his friend does him wrong), his whole life will be confounded by distrust and completely upset.

LVIII. We must release ourselves from the prison of affairs and politics.

LIX. It is not the stomach that is insatiable, as is generally said, but the false opinion that the stomach needs an unlimited amount to fill it.

LX.—Every man passes out of life as though he had just been born.

LXI. Most beautiful too is the sight of those near and dear to us, when our original kinship makes us of one mind; for such sight is a great incitement to this end.

LXII. Now if parents are justly angry with their children, it is certainly useless to fight against it and not to ask for pardon; but if their anger is unjust and irrational, it is quite ridiculous to add fuel to their irrational passion by nursing one's own indignation, and not to attempt to turn aside their wrath in other ways by gentleness.

LXIII. Frugality too has a limit, and the man who disregards it is in like case with him who errs through excess.

LXIV. Praise from others must come unasked: we must concern ourselves with the healing of our own lives.

LXV. It is vain to ask of the gods what a man is capable of supplying for himself.

LXVI. Let us show our feeling for our lost friends not by lamentation but by meditation.

LXVII. A free life cannot acquire many possessions, because this is not easy to do without servility to mobs or monarchs, yet it possesses all things in unfailing abundance; and if by chance it obtains many possessions, it is easy to distribute them so as to win the gratitude of neighbours.

LXVIII. Nothing is sufficient for him to whom what is sufficient seems little.

LXIX. The ungrateful greed of the soul makes the creature everlastingly desire varieties of dainty food.

LXX. Let nothing be done in your life, which will cause you to fear if it becomes known to your neighbour.

LXXI. Every desire must be confronted with this question: what will happen to me, if the object of my desire is accomplished and what if it is not?

LXXIII. The occurrence of certain bodily pains assists us in guarding against others like them.

LXXIV. In a philosophical discussion he who is worsted gains more in proportion as he learns more.

LXXV. Ungrateful towards the blessings of the past is the saying, 'Wait till the end of a long life.'

LXXVI. You are in your old age just such as I urge you to be, and you have seen the difference between studying philosophy for one-self and proclaiming it to Greece at large: I rejoice with you.

LXXVII. The greatest fruit of self-sufficiency is freedom.

LXXVIII. The noble soul occupies itself with wisdom and friend-ship: of these the one is a mortal good, the other immortal.

LXXIX. The man who is serene causes no disturbance to himself or to another.

LXXX. The first measure of security is to watch over one's youth and to guard against what makes havoc of all by means of pestering desires.

LXXXI. The disturbance of the soul cannot be ended nor true joy created either by the possession of the greatest wealth or by honour and respect in the eyes of the mob or by anything else that is associated with causes of unlimited desire.

(Pp. 109-119.)

(Fragments from Uncertain Sources)

ON PHILOSOPHY

LIV. Vain is the word of a philosopher which does not heal any suffering of man. For just as there is no profit in medicine if it does not expel the diseases of the body, so there is no profit in philosophy either, if it does not expel the suffering of the mind.

PHYSICS

LV. Nothing new happens in the universe, if you consider the infinite time past.

LVI. We shall not be considering them any happier or less de-structible, if we think of them as not speaking nor conversing with one another, but resembling dumb men.

LVII. Let us at least sacrifice piously and rightly where it is customary, and let us do all things rightly according to the laws not troubling ourselves with common beliefs in what concerns the noblest and holiest of beings. Further let us be free of any charge in regard to their opinion. For thus can one live in conformity with nature. . . .

LVIII. If God listened to the prayers of men, all men would quickly have perished: for they are forever praying for evil against one another.

ETHICS

LIX. The beginning and the root of all good is the pleasure of the stomach; even wisdom and culture must be referred to this.

LX. We have need of pleasure when we are in pain from its ab-sence: but when we are not feeling such pain, though we are in a con-dition of sensation, we have no need of pleasure. For the pleasure which arises from nature does not produce wickedness, but rather the longing connected with vain fancies.

LXI.   That which creates joy insuperable is the complete removal of a great evil. And this is the nature of good, if one can once grasp it rightly, and then hold by it, and not walk about babbling idly about the good.

LXII.   It is better to endure these particular pains so that we may enjoy greater joys. It is well to abstain from these particular pleasures in order that we may not suffer more severe pains.

LXIII.   Let us not blame the flesh as the cause of great evils, nor blame circumstances for our distresses.

LXIV.   Great pains quickly put an end to life; long-enduring pains are not severe.

LXV.   Excessive pain will bring you to death.

LXVI.   Through love of true philosophy every disturbing and troublesome desire is ended.

LXVII.   Thanks be to blessed Nature because she has made what is necessary easy to supply, and what is not easy unnecessary.

LXVIII.   It is common to find a man who is (poor) in respect of the natural end of life and rich in empty fancies. For of the fools none is satisfied with what he has, but is grieved for what he has not. Just as men with fever through the malignance of their (disease) are always thirsty and desire the most injurious things, so too those whose mind is in an evil state are always poor in everything and in their greed are plunged into ever-changing desires.

LXIX.   Nothing satisfies the man who is not satisfied with a little.

LXX.   Self-sufficiency is the greatest of all riches.

LXXI.   Most men fear frugality and through their fear are led to actions most likely to produce fear.

LXXII.   Many men when they have acquired riches have not found the escape from their ills but only a change to greater ills.

LXXIII.   By means of occupations worthy of a beast abundance of riches is heaped up, but a miserable life results.

LXXIV.   Unhappiness comes either through fear or through vain and unbridled desire: but if a man curbs these, he can win for himself the blessedness of understanding.

LXXV.   It is not deprivation of these things which is pain, but rather the bearing of the useless pain that arises from vain fancies.

LXXVI.   The mean soul is puffed up by prosperity and cast down by misfortune.

LXXVII.   (Nature) teaches us to pay little heed to what fortune brings, and when we are prosperous to understand that we are unfortunate, and when we are unfortunate not to regard prosperity highly, and to receive unmoved the good things which come from fortune and to range ourselves boldly against the seeming evils which it brings: for all that the many regard as good or evil is fleeting, and wisdom has nothing in common with fortune.

LXXVIII. He who least needs tomorrow, will most gladly go to meet tomorrow.

LXXIX. I spit upon the beautiful and those who vainly admire it, when it does not produce any pleasure.

LXXX. The greatest fruit of justice is serenity.

LXXXI. The laws exist for the sake of the wise, not that they may not do wrong, but that they may not suffer it.

LXXXII. Even if they are able to escape punishment, it is impossible to win security for escaping: and so the fear of the future which always presses upon them does not suffer them to be happy or to be free from anxiety in the present.

LXXXIII. The man who has attained the natural end of the human race will be equally good, even though no one is present.

LXXXIV. A man who causes fear cannot be free from fear.

LXXXV. The happy and blessed state belongs not to abundance of riches or dignity of position or any office or power, but to freedom from pain and moderation in feelings and an attitude of mind which imposes the limits ordained by nature.

LXXXVI. Live unknown.

LXXXVII. We must say how best a man will maintain the natural end of life, and how no one will willingly at first aim at public office.

(Pp. 133-139)

Selections from *"EPICURUS' MORALS."* Collected partly out of Marcus Antoninus, Plutarch, Cicero, and Seneca, and faithfully Englished (by Walter Charlton), London 1656. (First edition of the first English translation, p. 101.)[1]

CHAPTER XVIII, Section vii.

Now, as for what we said, of the *Immensity of such Riches as are coveted upon the suggestion of vain Opinions;* the Reason of it is this, that when Nature is satisfied with Little, vain Opinion ushering in Desire, alwaies engageth the Mind to think of something, which it doth not possesse, and, as if it were really needfull, converts and fixeth the Desire wholly and entirely upon it. Whence it comes, that to him, who is not satisfied with a little, nothing can ever be enough: but still the more wealth he possesseth, the more he conceives himself to want.

Section viii.

Wherefore, seeing there can never be want of a Little, the Wise man, doubtlesse, while he possesseth that little, ought to account it very great Riches: because therein is no want, whereas other riches, though great in esteem, are really very small, because they want multiplication to infinity. Whence it follows, that he who thinks not his own Estate, how small soever, sufficiently ample; though he should become Lord of the whole World, will ever be miserable. For, Misery is the companion of Want; and the same vain opinion, which first perswaded him that his own Estate was not sufficient, will continue to perswade him that one World is not sufficient, but that he wants more and more to infinity.

Section ix.

Have you, then, a design to make anyone Rich indeed? Know, that the way is not by adding to his Riches, but by Detracting from his Desires. For, when having cut off all vain and superfluous desires from his breast, he shall so compose himself to the praescripts of Nature, as to covet no more than she needs and requires: then at length shall he find himself to be a Rich man in reality, because he shall then find that Nothing is wanting to him. Hereupon may you also inculcate this maxim to him; *If you live according to Nature, you shall never be poor: but if according to Opinion, you shall never be rich. Nature desires little, Opinion infinite.*

CHAPTER XIX, Section xi.

And this Reasoning moreover, causeth, that we shall not be frustrated of Pleasure even then, when Death shall take us by the hand, and shew us the period of all these mortall things, insomuch as we shall therby attain to the perfect, and so delectable End of a very Good Life, rising

---

[1] Spelling, capitalization, and punctuation follow the archaisms of the original English edition.

from the table of the World as Guests well satisfied with the Good Entertainments of life, and having duly performed all those Duties, which to perform, we received life.

CHAPTER XXII, Section v.

We said, that *Death* (accounted the King of Terrors, and most horrid of all Evills) *doth nothing concerne us,* because, while we are, Death is not; and when Death is, we are not; so that he, who profoundly considers the matter, will soone conclude that Death doth concerne neither the Living nor the Dead; not the Living, because it toucheth them not, not the Dead because they are not.

LUCRETIUS: *ON NATURE.* Oates: *THE STOIC AND EPI-
CUREAN PHILOSOPHERS.* Random House, New York. Pp. 70-72,
96-97, 113-114, 115-116, 135-136.

=—≋—=

"When human life to view lay foully prostrate upon earth crushed
down under the weight of religion, who showed her head from the quarters of heaven with hideous aspect lowering upon mortals, a man of
Greece[1] ventured first to lift up his mortal eyes to her face and first to
withstand her to her face. Him neither story of gods nor thunderbolts
nor heaven with threatening roar could quell: they only chafed the more
the eager courage of his soul, filling him with desire to be the first to burst
the fast bars of nature's portals. Therefore the living force of his soul
gained the day: on he passed far beyond the flaming walls of the world
and traversed throughout in mind and spirit the immeasurable universe;
whence he returns a conqueror to tell us what can, what cannot come
into being; in short on what principle each thing has its powers defined,
its deepset boundary mark. Therefore religion is put under foot and
trampled upon in turn; us his victory brings level with heaven.

"This is what I fear herein, lest haply you should fancy that you
are entering on unholy grounds of reason and treading the path of
sin; whereas on the contrary often and often that very religion has given
birth to sinful and unholy deeds. Thus in Aulis the chosen chief-
tains of the Danai, foremost of men, foully polluted with Iphianassa's
blood the altar of the Trivian maid.[2] Soon as the fillet encircling her
maiden tresses shed itself in equal lengths adown each cheek, and soon
as she saw her father standing sorrowful before the altars and beside
him the ministering priests hiding the knife and her countrymen at
sight of her shedding tears, speechless in terror she dropped down on her
knees and sank to the ground. Nor aught in such a moment could it
avail the luckless girl that she had first bestowed the name of father
on the king. For lifted up in the hands of the men she was carried
shivering to the altars, not after due performance of the customary
rites to be escorted by the clear-ringing bridal song, but in the very
season of marriage, stainless maid mid the stain of blood, to fall a sad
victim by the sacrificing stroke of a father, that thus a happy and prosperous departure might be granted to the fleet. So great the evils to
which religion could prompt!

"You yourself some time or other overcome by the terror-speaking
tales of the seers will seek to fall away from us. Ay indeed for how
many dreams may they now imagine for you, enough to upset the cal-
culations of life and trouble all your fortunes with fear! And with

[1] The reference is to Epicurus, who is devoutly praised by Lucretius in his
poem. Cf. especially the opening lines of Bks. III, V, and VI.
[2] Here follows Lucretius' famous account of the sacrifice of Iphigenia by her
father Agamemnon at Aulis that the Greek ships might sail on their expedition
against Troy.

good cause; for if men saw that there was a fixed limit to their woes, they would be able in some way to withstand the religious scruples and threatenings of the seers. As it is, there is no way, no means of resisting, since they must fear after death everlasting pains. For they cannot tell what is the nature of the soul, whether it be born or on the contrary find its way into men at their birth, and whether it perish together with us when severed from us by death or visit the gloom of Orcus and wasteful pools or by divine decree find its way into brutes in our stead, as sang our Ennius who first brought down from delightful Helicon a crown of unfading leaf, destined to bright renown throughout Italian clans of men. And yet with all this Ennius sets forth that there are Acherusian quarters, publishing it in immortal verses; though in our passage thither neither our souls nor bodies hold together, but only certain idols pale in wondrous wise. From these places he tells us the ghost of everliving Homer uprose before him and began to shed salt tears and to unfold in words the nature of things. Wherefore we must well grasp the principle of things above, the principle by which the courses of the sun and moon go on, the force by which every thing on earth proceeds, but above all we must find out by keen reason what the soul and the nature of the mind consist of, and what thing it is which meets us when awake and frightens our minds, if we are under the influence of disease; meets and frightens us too when we are buried in sleep; so that we seem to see and hear speaking to us face to face them who are dead, whose bones earth holds in its embrace. Nor does my mind fail to perceive how hard it is to make clear in Latin verses the dark discoveries of the Greeks, especially as many points must be dealt with in new terms on account of the poverty of the language and the novelty of the questions. But yet your worth and the looked-for pleasure of sweet friendship prompt me to undergo any labour and lead me on to watch the clear nights through, seeking by what words and in what verse I may be able in the end to shed on your mind so clear a light that you can thoroughly scan hidden things.

"This terror then and darkness of mind must be dispelled not by the rays of the sun and glittering shafts of day, but by the aspect and the law of nature;[3] the warp of whose design we shall begin with this first principle, nothing is ever gotten out of nothing by divine power. Fear in sooth holds so in check all mortals, because they see many operations go on in earth and heaven, the causes of which they can in no way understand, believing them therefore to be done by power divine. For these reasons when we shall have seen that nothing can be produced from nothing, we shall then more correctly ascertain that which we are seeking, both the elements out of which every thing can be produced and the manner in which all things are done without the hand of the gods."

(Pp. 70-72)

[3] These lines are frequently repeated by Lucretius and give obviously the clue to his rational and scientific mode of attack.

"Again if all motion is ever linked together and a new motion ever springs from another in a fixed order and first-beginnings do not by swerving make some commencement of motion to break through the decrees of fate, that cause follow not cause from everlasting, whence have all living creatures here on earth, whence, I ask, has been wrested from the fates the power by which we go forward whither the will leads each, by which likewise we change the direction of our motions neither at a fixed time nor fixed place; but when and where the mind itself has prompted? For beyond a doubt in these things his own will makes for each a beginning and from this beginning motions are welled through the limbs. See you not too, when the barriers are thrown open at a given moment, that yet the eager powers of the horses cannot start forward so instantaneously as the mind itself desires? The whole store of matter through the whole body must be sought out, in order that stirred up through all the frame it may follow with undivided effort the bent of the mind; so that you see the beginning of motion is born from the heart, and the action first commences in the will of the mind and next is transmitted through the whole body and frame. Quite different is the case when we move on propelled by a stroke inflicted by the strong might and strong compulsion of another; for then it is quite clear that all the matter of the whole body moves and is hurried on against our inclination, until the will has reined it in throughout the limbs. Do you see then in this case that, though an outward force often pushes men on and compels them frequently to advance against their will and to be hurried headlong on, there yet is something in our breast sufficient to struggle against and resist it? And when too this something chooses, the store of matter is compelled sometimes to change its course through the limbs and frame, and after it has been forced forward, is reined in and settles back into its place. Wherefore in seeds too you must admit the same, admit that besides blows and weights there is another cause of motions, from which this power of free action has been begotten in us, since we see that nothing can come from nothing. For weight forbids that all things be done by blows through as it were an outward force; but that the mind itself does not feel an internal necessity in all its actions and is not as it were overmastered and compelled to bear and put up with this, is caused by a minute swerving of first-beginnings at no fixed part of space and no fixed time.

"Nor was the store of matter ever more closely massed nor held apart by larger spaces between; for nothing is either added to its bulk or lost to it. Wherefore the bodies of the first-beginnings in time gone by moved in the same way in which now they move, and will ever hereafter be borne along in like manner, and the things which have been wont to be begotten will be begotten after the same law and will be and will grow and will wax in strength so far as is given to each by the decrees of nature. And no force can change the sum of things; for there is nothing outside, either into which any kind of matter can escape out of the universe or out of which a new supply can arise and burst into the universe and change all the nature of things and alter their motions.

"And herein you need not wonder at this, that though the first-beginnings of things are all in motion, yet the sum is seen to rest in supreme repose, unless where a thing exhibits motions with its individual body. For all the nature of first things lies far away from our senses beneath their ken. . . ."

(Pp. 96-97.)

"With good reason therefore all things perish, when they have been rarefied by the ebb of particles and succumb to blows from without, since food sooner or later fails advanced age, and bodies never cease to destroy a thing by thumping it from without and to overpower it by aggressive blows. In this way then the walls too of the great world around shall be stormed and fall to decay and crumbling ruin. Yes, and even now the age is enfeebled and the earth exhausted by bearing scarce produces little living creatures, she who produced all races and gave birth to the huge bodies of wild beasts. For methinks no golden chain let down to earth from heaven above the races of mortal beings, nor did the sea and waves which lash the rocks produce them, but the same earth bare them which now feeds them out of herself. Moreover she first spontaneously of herself produced for mortals goodly corn-crops and joyous vineyards; of herself gave sweet fruits and glad pastures; which now-a-days scarce attain any size when furthered by our labour: we exhaust the oxen and the strength of the husbandmen; we wear out our iron, scarcely fed after all by the tilled fields; so niggardly are they of their produce and after so much labour do they let it grow. And now the aged ploughman shakes his head and sighs again and again to think that the labours of his hands have come to nothing; and when he compared present times with times past, he often praises the fortunes of his sire and harps on the theme, how the men of old rich in piety comfortably supported life on a scanty plot of ground, since the allotment of land to each man was far less of yore than now. The sorrowful planter too of the exhausted and shrivelled vine impeaches the march of time and wearies heaven, and comprehends not that all things are gradually wasting away and passing to the grave, quite forspent by age and length of days."

(Pp. 113-114.)

"Thou, father, [meaning Epicurus] art discoverer of things, thou furnishest us with fatherly precepts, and like as bees sip of all things in the flowery lawns, we, O glorious being, in like manner feed from out thy pages upon all the golden maxims, golden I say, most worthy ever of endless life. For soon as thy philosophy issuing from a god-like intellect has begun with loud voice to proclaim the nature of things, the terrors of the mind are dispelled, the walls of the world part asunder, I see things in operation throughout the whole void: the divinity of the gods is revealed and their tranquil abodes which neither winds do shake nor clouds drench with rains nor snow congealed by sharp frosts harms with hoary fall: an ever cloudless ether o'ercanopies them, and they laugh with light shed largely round. Nature too supplies all their wants and nothing ever impairs their peace of mind. But on the other hand the Acherusian quarters are nowhere to be seen, though earth is no bar to all things being descried, which are in operation underneath our feet throughout the void. At all this a kind of godlike delight mixed with shuddering awe comes over me to think that nature by thy power is laid thus visibly open, is thus unveiled on every side.

"And now since I have shown what-like the beginnings of all things are and how diverse with varied shapes as they fly spontaneously driven on in everlasting motion, and how all things can be severally produced out of these, next after these questions the nature of the mind and soul should methinks be cleared up by my verses and that dread of Acheron be driven headlong forth, troubling as it does the life of man from its inmost depths and overspreading all things with the blackness of death, allowing no pleasure to be pure and unalloyed. For as to what men often give out that diseases and a life of shame are more to be feared than Tartarus, place of death, and that they know the soul to be of blood or it may be of wind, if haply their choice so direct, and that they have no need at all of our philosophy, you may perceive for the following reasons that all these boasts are thrown out more for glory's sake than because the thing is really believed. These very men, exiles from their country and banished far from the sight of men, live degraded by foul charge of guilt, sunk in a word in every kind of misery, and whithersoever the poor wretches are come, they yet do offer sacrifices to the dead and slaughter black sheep and make libations to the gods' Manes and in times of distress turn their thoughts to religion much more earnestly. Wherefore you can better test the man in doubts and dangers and mid adversity learn who he is; for then and not till then the words of truth are forced out from the bottom of his heart: the mask is torn off, the reality is left. Avarice again and blind lust of honours which constrain unhappy men to overstep the bounds of right and sometimes as partners and agents of crimes to strive night and day with surpassing effort to struggle up to the summit of power—these sores of life are in no small measure fostered by the dread of death. For foul scorn and pinching want in every case are seen to be far removed from a life of pleasure and security and to be a loitering so to say before the fates of death. And while men driven on by an unreal dread wish to escape far away from these and keep them far from them, they amass wealth by civil bloodshed and greedily double their riches piling up murder on murder; cruelly triumph in the sad death of a brother and hate and fear the tables of kinsfolk. Often likewise from the same fear envy causes them to pine: they make moan that before their very eyes he is powerful, he attracts attention, who walks arrayed in gorgeous dignity, while they are wallowing in darkness and dirt. Some wear themselves to death for the sake of statues and a name. And often to such a degree through dread of death does hate of life and of the sight of daylight seize upon mortals, that they commit self-murder with a sorrowing heart, quite forgetting that this fear is the source of their cares, this fear which urges men to every sin, prompts this one to put all shame to rout, another to burst asunder the bonds of friendship, and in fine to overturn duty from its very base; since often ere now men have betrayed country and dear parents in seeking to shun the Acherusian quarters. For even as children are flurried and dread all things in the thick darkness, thus we in the daylight fear at times things not a whit more to be dreaded than what children shudder at in the dark and fancy sure to be. This terror therefore and darkness of mind must be dispelled not by the rays of the sun and glittering shafts of day, but by the aspect and law of nature."

(Pp. 115-116.)

"If, just as they are seen to feel that a load is on their mind which wears them out with its pressure, men might apprehend from what causes too it is produced and whence such a pile, if I may say so, of ill lies on their breast, they would not spend their life as we see them now for the most part do, not knowing any one of them what he means and wanting ever change of place as though he might lay his burden down. The man who is sick of home often issues forth from his large mansion, and as suddenly comes back to it, finding as he does that he is no better off abroad. He races to his country-house, driving his jennets in headlong haste, as if hurrying to bring help to a house on fire; he yawns the moment he has reached the door of his house, or sinks heavily into sleep and seeks forgetfulness, or even in haste goes back again to town. In this way each man flies from himself (but self from whom, as you may be sure is commonly the case, he cannot escape, clings to him in his own despite), hates too himself, because he is sick and knows not the cause of the malady; for if he could rightly see into this, relinquishing all else each man would study to learn the nature of things, since the point at stake is the condition for eternity, not for one hour, in which mortals have to pass all the time which remains for them to expect after death.

"Once more what evil lust of life is this which constrains us with such force to be so mightily troubled in doubts and dangers? A sure term of life is fixed for mortals, and death cannot be shunned, but meet it we must. Moreover we are ever engaged, ever involved in the same pursuits, and no new pleasure is struck out by living on; but whilst what we crave is wanting, it seems to transcend all the rest; then, when it has been gotten, we crave something else, and ever does the same thirst of life possess us, as we gape for it open-mouthed. Quite doubtful it is what fortune the future will carry with it or what chance will bring us or what end is at hand.   Nor by prolonging life do we take one tittle from the time past in death nor can we fret anything away, whereby we may haply be a less long time in the condition of the dead.   Therefore you may complete as many generations as you please during your life; none the less however will that everlasting death await you; and for no less long a time will he be no more in being, who beginning with to-day has ended his life, than the man who has died many months and years ago."

(Pp. 135-136.)

QUESTIONS AND STATEMENTS FOR DISCUSSION

(*Epicurus*)

1. "The wealth demanded by nature is both limited and easily procured; that demanded by idle imaginings stretches on to infinity." (Charlton, trans., Chap. xviii, sections vii, viii, ix: Bailey, section xv.)

2. "It is not possible to live pleasantly without living prudently and honourably and justly, nor again to live a life of prudence, honour, and justice without living pleasantly. And the man who does not possess the pleasant life, is not living prudently, honourably and justly, and the man who does not possess the virtuous life, cannot possibly live pleasantly." (Bailey, v.)

3. "The just man is most free from trouble, the unjust most full of trouble." (xvii.)

4. "Injustice is not an evil in itself, but only in consequence of the fear which attaches to the apprehension of being unable to escape those appointed to punish such actions." (xxxiv.)

5. "No one who sees evil deliberately chooses it, but is enticed by it as being good in comparison with a greater evil and so pursues it." (*Fragments:* Vatican Collection, xvi.)

6. "He is no friend who is continually asking for help, nor he who never associates help with friendship. For the former barters kindly feeling for a practical return, and the latter destroys the hope of good in the future." (xxxix.)

7. "The man who says that all things come to pass by necessity cannot criticize one who denies that all things come to pass by necessity; for he admits that this too happens of necessity." (xl.)

8. "The greatest blessing is created and enjoyed at the same time." (xlii.)

9. "We must envy no one; for the good do not deserve envy, and the bad, the more they prosper, the more they injure themselves." (liii.)

10. "Nothing is sufficient for him to whom what is sufficient seems little." (lxviii.)

11. "Let nothing be done in your life, which will cause you to fear if it becomes known to your neighbor." (lxx.)

12. "The greatest fruit of self-sufficiency is freedom." (lxxvii.)

13. "The disturbance of the soul cannot be ended, nor true joy created, either by the possession of the greatest wealth, or by honor or respect in the eyes of the mob, or by anything else that is associated with causes of unlimited desire." (Oates, lxxxi.)

14. With respect to Lucretius' argument concerning fear as the basis of religion—can fear ever be the basis of genuine goodness? Is there a different element in Judaeo-Christianity such as love of

goodness which is the basis of true religion? (Oates: *The Stoic and Epicurean Philosophers.*)

15. Does knowledge of the laws of nature remove all fears?
16. Does the argument that "the beginning of motion is born in the heart" and commences in the will contradict Lucretius' own theory of a mechanical universe?
17. Is the argument that the earth is declining because there are now no longer dinosaurs or mammoths convincing?
18. Is fear of death the main incentive to the search for wealth and honors? (The same fear according to Lucretius causes sin and righteousness if we identify the latter with religion.)

Suggested Supplementary Readings:

Bailey: *The Greek Atomists and Epicurus.* Oxford University Press, New York.

Bailey: *Epicurus.* Oxford University Press, New York.

Benn: *The Greek Philosophers.* Smith Wilder, Boston. Chap. XI.

More: *Hellenistic Philosophies.* Princeton University Press, Princeton, N. J. Chap. II.

Hyde: *Five Great Philosophies of Life.* The Macmillan Company, New York.

Chapter 7

JUDAEO-CHRISTIAN "UNITY WITH THE DIVINE"

The Law and the Prophets

I
Jewish Emphasis of Value

1. Job's contention
   (a) Natural calamity not the anger of God
   (b) Personal integrity better than success
   (c) In God's will is peace
2. The reply of "Wisdom" to Epicureanism
3. The cosmopolitanism of the Prophets

II
Christian Emphasis of Value

1. Emphasis on the all-inclusiveness of God
2. Re-interpretation of the term "the Holy"
3. The intrinsic worth of man

III
Universal Aspects

1. Possibility of union with the Divine
2. The perfect society, ethical
3. Self-realization the supreme value

IV
The Unrecognized Basis of Democracy

Chapter 7

JUDAEO-CHRISTIAN "UNITY WITH THE DIVINE"

The Law and the Prophets

In the general period we have been considering, the movement of thought from East to West could scarcely pass over Palestine, which was the natural route between Egypt and the mighty empires of Asia, without leaving its impress upon the culture of the people of Israel. Their home on the hills of Judah was like a fortress in enemy country, pressed on either side by insistent foes. The position was something like that of modern Belgium, a battleground for opposing powers. As a military power Israel was usually at the mercy of her enemies, in the greater battle of ideas she was destined to take a leading place in history, perhaps even greater than that of intellectual Greece, as she has topped all in her concept of religion. However isolationist the Jews tried to be, they could not altogether resist the impact of foreign ideas. These came with Judaea's conquerors, as when she was subdued by Alexander, or more strictly by his generals, and again when she was carried captive to Babylon, having already been enslaved in Egypt, where her great lawgiver Moses was trained to the Egyptian priesthood. If in no other way her leading thinkers were compelled to meet and refute notions abhorrent to the Jewish religious sense, concepts to which Judaism was continually exposed through contact with surrounding peoples.

Their most important teachings were alluded to as "The Law and the Prophets." The heart of what was known as the Mosaic Law was contained in the Ten Commandments, the Jewish rules of conduct. The Wisdom Literature, as it was called, fell under the same designation as a part of The Law. The writings on Wisdom were philosophical discussions on the good life, and perhaps in most cases represented the Jewish refutation of widely current non-Jewish philosophies, such as are attempted in *Job* and in *The Wisdom of Solomon*. The Prophets were those great teachers who broke with their contemporaries to condemn wrong social and religious practices, and to castigate dependence upon magic and ritual, and often as well upon heathen political entanglements, to which their people were continually tempted by their idolatrous neighbors. Jewish ideas did not come out into their clear setting until the international upheavals of the eighth and succeeding centuries B.C. had caused the mass expulsion from Palestine of Northern Israel. This was followed later by the exile to Babylon of the leading citizens of the southern kingdom of Judah. Their greatest literature began with the captivity which had forced upon them new world-views, and had made archaic the desire for national isolationism. Nothing could here be gained by a discussion of literary dates, about which there is much diversity of opinion among scholars. Aside from the Ten Commandments, which were basic to Jewish religious thought, the works cited are those that came after the captivity, or between the eighth century and the Christian era. Of these, the *Book of Job* may be the oldest, after *Isaiah*. Job's problem was similar to that of Epicurus in some respects. It was how to be happy though unfortunate, but Job's conclusions are poles apart from those of the Greek hedonist. Job finds peace of mind in a consciousness of right conduct, in his belief that righteousness is the norm of life and the rule of the universe, which he finds confirmed in his own heart by "the vision of God."

To the *Book of Job,* then, we turn for the high-water mark of Jewish literature and philosophy, and the Judaeo-Christian concept of value. This comes to us with special interest in following immediately after our study of the skeptical efforts of Epicureanism to solve the problem of human happiness. For Job is also a skeptical work, but it presses through the shallow and easy conclusions of Epicureanism to a profounder view of the meaning of life and value. The Jewish God, like the Greek deities, was conceived as an angry and jealous rewarder of those who brought in the sacrifices, and a punisher of the negligent. He was the God of the thunder and the storm. If one fell into misfortune or disaster it was a sign of divine displeasure. This kind of teaching was favored by the priestly and ruling elements to bring the common people into line just as in Greece. Like the divinities of the Greeks, also the Jewish Jahweh was a strictly national God, who was thought to take special care of the Jewish people as a race, and who was naturally hostile to the Gentiles. These were the ideas attacked by the unknown author of the *Book of Job,* the profoundest drama of literature.

Job meets the problem of a cruel and irresponsible God in a deeper way than did Confucius, Buddha, the Stoics, or the Epicureans. He sought neither the Confucian shell of indifference, nor Buddhistic isolationism, nor Stoic wishful thinking, nor the Epicurean appeal to the inevitableness of natural law. All these positions he sees and transcends. He is positive and constructive where

they are negative and passive. He demands that we shall not only
discover the smiling countenance behind the severe and unaccountable acts of God or of Natural Law, but that we shall press on to the
discovery of a positive and creative good lurking within all things
evil.   Above all he proclaims the right of every person to free access
to this Divinity without the interference of institutions or traditions.
He was Stoical in his belief in the power of the human spirit to sur-
mount obstacles and to rise supreme to every circumstance, he was
Epicurean in his refusal to be bound by religious tradition, and in his
assertion of the right of skepticism.   He does not ignore, deny, or
avoid the problem raised by suffering but shows the way to transform it into value by means of self-conquest.

I
The Jewish Emphasis of Value

We do not often realize the debt we owe to the singing lines of
this supreme bit of literature, The Book of Job. No other poet
who ever lived has been so commonly quoted in daily life. His
words have entered into natural speech wherever the Bible is known.
Sorrow continues to find resignation in the lines, "The Lord gave,
and the Lord hath taken away," and frustration fondly dreams of a
place where "the wicked cease from troubling and the weary are at
rest."   Despair still reminds itself in Job's words that "man is
born to trouble as the sparks fly upward," and that his days are
"swifter than a weaver's shuttle."   And then there is that supreme
assurance to all sufferers: "He knoweth the way that I take; when
He hath tried me, I shall come forth as gold."   These and a hundred
other beautiful figures of speech are repeated wherever English is
spoken, an unrecognized testimonial to the vitality of this ancient
document.

The opening scene of the drama is laid in heaven. Among the
sons of God comes the Adversary, Satan, from "walking to and fro
in the earth."   Satan is the cynic who believes no one is any better
than he ought to be and who delights in showing everybody up. His
only concept of value is the selfish one. He thinks no one religious
except as he hopes to get some personal profit from it. To this attitude God addresses himself with the question whether Satan has
noticed the blameless life of Job. Satan's reply is a sneer, "Does
Job serve God for naught?" Take away his wealth, his position,
his family, and his health and he will turn around and curse you.
This is the *motif* of the drama. All values are commercial, there is

no such thing as disinterested goodness. This is what the drama sets out to disprove. At the same time the suggestion is made that misfortunes are allowed by the Almighty simply to test men and to bring out their higher qualities. So Satan is permitted to afflict Job.

Upon a day a servant comes running to tell him that while his servants were plowing with the beasts in the field, mountain bandits have swooped down and carried them all away. This one has not finished his story before another comes to say that lightning has fallen and consumed both the sheep and the shepherds. Lightning was supposed to be Jehovah's special weapon of displeasure. While this messenger is yet speaking another bears the news that the Chaldeans have fallen upon the camels and driven them away. Before this tale of disaster is ended another servant runs to tell him that his sons and daughters lie dead in the ruins of their home that has been destroyed by a cyclone. The answer Job returns to all this calamity is, "The Lord gave and the Lord hath taken away."

Satan is permitted a still deeper test lest there be any room for doubt. Leprosy was the one disease which in that time was considered the supreme evidence of Divine wrath. Outside every eastern city was the mound on which was deposited the city garbage, the offal, and the leprous. Here, separated from all men, this former judge and ruler of the city crouched in the dust and filth, abhorred of all for fear of contamination, cast off by his wife who gave him the sardonic advice to "curse God and die." Menials whose fathers he would not have trusted with the dogs that watched his flocks passed by, mocking. His tale was on every lip and soon spread to other lands which brought old friends to visit him as much out of curiosity as of love. In accordance with Oriental courtesy they remain silent before him for seven days and nights, waiting for him to speak the first word. Finally he begins to curse the day of his birth and to lay his sorrows before them. Versed in the prevailing theology, they explain to him that his troubles are doubtless due to the anger of God at his sins. But Job is not conscious of having done anything wrong. Let God try and show him wherein his wrong-doing lay. But his friends are inexorable. His suffering *must* be the result of his sin. So they defend their concept of God until the truth breaks over him that they are doing it for fear they themselves might fall into Divine disfavor and have houses and lands and health taken away from them. In other words their religion was as shallow as their friendship and pursued in the interests of prosperity. It was of the very kind that Satan had railed against. This was Job's moment of heartbreak. He can no longer trust his friends to be honest with

him for fear of the God of their theology. His last and only appeal
is to the Creator himself. God answers him out of a whirlwind, a
storm that terrifies the friends who in the storm are not now so sure
of their own righteousness. Their evident terror before the tempest
refutes all they have said, but Job is undisturbed. He has endured so
much that he would even welcome death itself as a good. He hears a
voice from the tumult commanding him to stand on his feet like a
man and face the supreme terror.   Then in one of the sublimest
passages of literature God is represented as showing him how small
is his place in the vastness of the universe in which his individual
suffering is only as an ugly dream in the night.   The ways of the
Eternal involve such infinity that for man in his limited knowledge
they are past finding out.   Let him trust God for the final results.
He may never be happy but out of his suffering he can come into a
deeper joy, the joy of a man who has been true to himself.   In his
sense of righteousness and conscious devotion to the will of God is to
be found his reward, his peace, a joy that the world of time and
circumstance did not give him and cannot take away.

Job did not blink the hard aspects of the problem thrust upon him,
which was: Evil is real, yet God is good; how can they be reconciled?
Honesty may be the only virtue left him but he will stand by this
even in the face of the Almighty.   Though the prosperity of the
wicked be but temporary, though a little knuckling to the theology of
his friends, a little compromise with his convictions would bring a
return of the prosperity his friends worshipped, what could restore
to him the "years that the locust had eaten"?   There were gifts no
turn of fortune could bring back.   The renewed possession of flocks
and herds, and servants and greetings in the market, and those high
human honors of which he had been deprived, could no longer bring
happiness.   He had seen through all the hollowness of these goods.
There was in his heart the realization that the deepest values were
not after all material.   There was the broken love of a wife that was
worse than death, since it was only a love of his social position, not
of him.   There were the silenced voices of his children, the memory
of whose cradle-songs wrung his heart.   There were the highest
worldly honors which he had supposed would stand against any fate,
now shown to be as ephemeral as the passing cloud.   What can the
empty years bring to fill again the dashed cup of life?   The only
value that survives the storm of life is the one that springs from the
consciousness of his good endeavor, his attempt at unity with the
Divine will.   Out of this springs joy in the very midst of all unhappiness, a joy that is not for sale in the marketplace, cannot be pur-

chased with gold and honors, and is not dependent on the flattery of friends or the feigned respect of those who bowed to his gold and his position instead of doing reverence to his integrity as a man. And so he clings to the witness of his own heart as true in spite of tradition and, so clinging, learns the blessedness of Divine fellowship. In God's will is his peace. One can, with all happiness burned out, yet learn to trust, to serve, to be faithful, to find joy in a new world of sympathy. When upon his ash-heap, lonely and disconsolate, this truth breaks in upon him, Job exclaims, "I have heard of Thee hitherto with the hearing of the ear, but now mine eye seeth Thee." To see God is for Job the supreme value.

The *Wisdom of Solomon* is of particular interest to our study because it gives us the current Jewish idea of Epicureanism. It is addressed "to the rulers of the land" who had, by abandoning Judaism and adopting the popular and fashionable Epicureanism, been able to curry favor with the Roman government and society and thus to win advancement for themselves. Indeed there is nothing inherently impossible in the idea that it might have been addressed to Tiberias Alexander himself, a Jew who had been made prefect of Egypt by the Emperor Nero, and who responded by a bitter persecution of his own people. The author was evidently an Alexandrian Jew, with a knowledge of Greek language, literature, and philosophy, who was able to disclose the insufficiency of the Epicurean treatment of life. At the same time he was probably able to profit by the Stoic criticisms of Epicurus.

False philosophies, he commented, blind the mind and separate men from the truth, "for the holy spirit of instruction will flee from deceit." Ultimate justice will overtake the liar because there is honesty in the cosmic order. "A lying mouth destroys the soul," or as we would put it more modernly, lying disintegrates the selfhood or personality. Death, which the Epicurean attempts to whistle away, is not made by God, who is discoverable only in the living, but death is created by wrong thoughts, evil living, a spending of life on things that can have but a momentary existence. For the righteous alone is there immortality: "Uprightness is immortal."

Our author recounts the pessimism which haunts the pleasure of the Epicurean, the consciousness that it is about to end. The only justification the hedonist can allege for giving himself over to the desires of the flesh is the fact that they cannot last. He takes his fling *because* "life is short and miserable." The reason we are admonished to "Eat, drink, and be merry," is because "tomorrow, we die." "The breath in our nostrils is smoke, and reason is a spark in the beating of our hearts." The men of that age had no notion of the relation of the brain to thought, but considered it a spark struck off by the beating of the heart. When this spark was quenched, the body turned to ashes, and the soul passed away like smoke through the nostrils.

The result of this grim pessimism was that the Epicurean turned to the unsatisfying life of pleasure:

> Let us not miss the spring flowers:
> Let us crown ourselves with rose-buds before they wither.

Even an English Epicurean, Robert Herrick, could not write:

> Gather ye rosebuds while ye may,
> Old Time is still a-flying:

without feeling constrained to raise with it the spectre of despair:

> And this same flower that smiles today
> Tomorrow will be dying.

Pleasure is never adequate in and of itself, nor for its own sake. On the lower level there is always the sad aftermath; the end of pleasure. It is only as we lift our pleasures into the higher ranges of experience that they can become permanent and partake of immortality. All achievements, all ambitions, all loves, including that between men and women, must gather persistence through a common relationship to undying purposes and aims. It is not insignificant that lovers feel the necessity of declaring eternal allegiance to each other, for it is only as we lift our lives into the larger relations beyond time that we can pass beyond death and the range of death. Lesser attachments are not only doomed to transiency, but to disgust and hate.

At one other point was the Epicurean shallow and contradictory in his concept of death. Not only is the brooding fear of death intensified by the emphasis upon the present pleasure, but removing the fear of angry gods does not remove the ill. Do his best, the average mortal is possessed by a horror of extinction. He earnestly endeavors not only to prolong his days, but to build up something that may memorialize him after he has passed from the scene. This fear of extinction is a basic fact. In this he is faced by one of two alternatives. He may, following the advice of *Wisdom*, lift his life to the level of transcendence over death by deserving immortality, or he may resort to the device of Hindu and Buddhist, preparing for extinction in this life by the extinction of all pleasure and, even more, the extinction so far as it can be achieved, of consciousness

itself. By the time such a state of mind is reached it would seem
to make little difference whether one lived or died. Such an attitude would seem more logical, at any rate, than the Epicurean aggra-
vation of one's own fears of death, by the emphasis of transient
pleasure. The difficulty in the belief in extinction lies in that something, inherent in self-consciousness, which makes it impossible to
conceive of personal extinction. All methods that waive the fact
of immortality are like the resort of the frightened child in the
dark repeating, "I am not afraid! I am not afraid!" while all the
time his fears increase. The Epicurean consciousness of failure at
this point is shown by Epicurus' own efforts to empty his philosophy
of pleasure of all pleasurable content. In spite of himself he was
but half-persuaded of his own doctrine;

> Just when we are safest, there's a sunset touch,
> A fancy from a flower-bell, someone's death,
> A chorus-ending from Euripides,

which brings all the dark brood of questions back.

The Alexandrian rightly discovers in this the source of the
Epicurean hatred of religion. Obsessed with the recklessness of
pleasure-seeking as the end of life, the Epicureans turn to the persecution of the upright, who are for them like ghosts at their feasts
of joy. The upright were the Puritan kill-joys of that distant time,
at whom they sneered for calling themselves "the children of the
Lord." He is a reproof to our thoughts, say they, and even to see
him "makes us tired." He isn't like other folks, and we are bored.
He declares the end of the upright is happy, and he looks on us as
counterfeits.

> So they reasoned, but they went astray,
> For their wickedness blinded them,
> And they did not . . .
> . . . .
> . . . . . recognize the prize of blameless souls;

for the prize of blameless souls is immortality.

As to the Epicurean concept of death, the writer of *Wisdom*
holds that it is the gift of the devil, the natural result of confin-
ing the aims of life to the perishing pleasures of the flesh. For the
man who lives after an immortal purpose, an eternal end.

> There is no Death! What seems so is transition:
> This life of mortal breath
> Is but a suburb of the life elysian,
> Whose portal we call Death.

Or as Alfred Noyes has so beautifully put it :

Death was but a change of key in Life, the Golden melody.[1]

Because the keynote of life has been the search for the things most worth-while, the permanent values, and their hope has been full of immortality, God has set eternity in their hearts and rejoices to find them worthy of himself. And so, these pilgrims of eternity shall rule peoples and judge nations in days to come.

As we turn from the *Wisdom* literature to that of the prophets, we encounter a different spirit. Instead of philosophy and reason we find great emphasis upon the intuitional side of thought. The Prophets are not primarily interested in intellectualism. In fact, the great eighth century prophet Amos was a countryman from the desert so shocked by the profligacy of the capital that he felt it necessary to reprimand both King and courtier for their manner of living. He went on to declare the doom of the nation unless there was repentance and reformation. In passages of great power he marshalled the surrounding nations before the tribunal of God for their crimes against God and man, and while his shocked hearers were rejoicing in reproofs that singled out their political neighbors he turned suddenly on the sins of Israel, the drunken luxury of the great, the shameless dress, the wide differences between the rich and the poor, selling a man into slavery for the price of a pair of shoes, a priesthood caught in the general corruption, and afraid to speak out. Out of such conditions he declared political downfall inevitable. The prophets were not, as we often think, interested in foretelling events, but rather in predicting the results of unrighteous and ill-advised courses of action. They were interested in world affairs and international relations. They were super-patriots who in their anxiety for the future of the nation were ready to denounce political and social evil. It had been assumed that Jahweh, the national God, would under all conditions protect the Jews from every foe, since his worship would die out if they ceased nationally to exist. Both Judah and Israel were caught in that mighty storm of the nations when the whole world was breaking up. The sages and the priests would have it that the way to escape national doom was by the propitiation of Jahweh with sacrifices in the temple, or by the political way of appeasement. The prophet placed all his hope in righteousness of conduct, that value that would survive if all else was lost. Before the coming of exile the prophetic exhortation was

[1] "Tales of the Mermaid Tavern," *Collected Poems*, Vol. II, copyright by Alfred Noyes, 1913, by permission, J. B. Lippincott Co., New York.

all concerned with social reform, an ethical clean-up.   When at last the people had been deported by their conquerors, the prophets sought to bring a message of comfort, the sufferings of Israel would become the means of restoring the world.

II
The Christian Emphasis of Value

The prophetic movement produced some of the greatest literature of the Bible, and it is significant that Jesus of Nazareth was reckoned among the prophets by the charges that brought about his crucifixion. It was as an opponent of the established priestly order and, from the Roman standpoint, as a political agitator that he came to his death. Yet he had offered no campaign, no revolutionary acts beyond the utterance of ideas.   He brought no urge to violence, but only the exhortation to love, to righteousness, to justice among men.   The purity of his life made him a horror to the profligate and degenerate Roman-Jewish governors of his time, to whom his doctrine of the intrinsic worth of individuals, as voiced in the Parables of Lost Things, marked him as a dangerous radical who threatened the foundations of Roman rule.   No fact is perhaps more amazing than the fear which seizes dictators in the face of ideas.   The religious people of the time were no less disturbed by his doctrine that the inner voice to which they had refused attention was the voice and presence of the Eternal God.   Jesus took pains also to emphasize the great point of prophetic teaching, the universality of God, who is no respecter of persons, but the lover and supporter of all men, of all races, conditions, and beliefs.

Asked to epitomize the Law (the Ten Commandments) and the Prophets in a phrase or two, Jesus declared: "Thou shalt love the Lord thy God with all thy heart, and with all thy soul, and with all thy mind.   This is the first and great commandment.   And the second is like unto it, Thou shalt love thy neighbor as thyself." These two commandments were not intended to displace the Ten Commandments, but to illuminate them.   These may be taken as the inner heart of religion, a counsel of human perfection.   They are further illustrated in the Sermon on the Mount, which includes the Beatitudes, and the Lord's Prayer.   His concept of the intrinsic worth of men and women is set forth in the Parables of Lost Things, of which two are here given, the Parable of the Lost Son, and the Parable of the Lost Sheep.

The conflict in Judaism between the narrower conception of

God as a national Deity, granting special favors to a chosen people and refusing them to all others, who indicated anger by the withdrawal of prosperity, and the conception on the other hand of God as the lover of all men, indicates the difference between the priestly writings of the Old Testament and those of the Jewish prophets. Significantly enough, prophetism in Judah coincided in time with these other systems we have considered, as a movement away from idolatrous practice and belief. Christianity was a continuance and completion of the Jewish prophetic movement. The new emphasis moved in two parallel directions. One was an emphasis upon the universality of God, as against the narrower tribal concept, the other was a re-emphasis upon the intrinsic value of the person, of all persons, for in Christ there was to be neither Jew nor Gentile, bond nor free. A kingdom was dreamed of in terms of universal brotherhood, inner ties that were to bind in one all races upon the face of the earth.

The concept of the holiness of God was further amplified by giving it a more universal and a more human meaning. The priestly idea of the Divine holiness had been a barrier of separation between God and the individual. Human nature was considered corrupt and always unworthy. Though this characteristic has often followed down through into Christian theology, the emphasis which Christianity was intended to set was close to the Greek concept and in line with prophetism: it exalted the divinity of man, even to the extent of identifying God with the highest human achievement in the person of the Man of Nazareth. In this way Christianity gave a divine sanction to democracy and emphasized the intrinsic value and sanctity of human beings. Every one, bond or free, Jew or Gentile, had within him a spark of divinity, potentially at least, and the possibility of realizing himself as a son of God. The divine spirit in God and the divine spirit in man were identical wherever one should find them. These broader and more universal interpretations were embryonic in the Jewish prophets themselves, and found their later expression in the teachings of Jesus.

III

Universal Aspects

Let us inquire into the resulting doctrines of the life of value as seen from the Judaeo-Christian outlook. These may be briefly summarized as, *first:* a belief in the possibility of union with the Divine. This is a far cry from the paganism which looked with fear upon the gods as sinister influences whose wrath must be appeased. The sublimer and nobler motives of a man's inner consciousness are seen as the direct inspiration and indwelling of Divinity by obedience to which alone man can realize his highest selfhood and destiny. The Divine is not far off in the heavens that we may bring Him down, nor in the depths that we may call Him forth. He is present in the unescapable self. "If I ascend into heaven He is there. If I make my bed in Hell, lo, He is there! Though I take the wings of the morning and dwell in the uttermost parts of the earth, even there shall He be with me and His right hand shall hold me."

> "Closer is He than breathing,
> Nearer than hands or feet."

The *second* of these doctrines is merely the completion of the first. The nature of the perfect social state is mirrored in the ethical nature of man. Since man has the possibility of communion with Divinity, the perfect social state will be characterized by righteousness. There will be in the perfect society to bind it together a common desire for justice. Such, for instance, was the pact made in the cabin of the Mayflower by the Pilgrim Fathers. They conceived the will of God to be the governing constitution of the new colony. The state was to be theocratic, and the Jewish laws as set forth in the Old Testament were, so far as they could be accommodated to modern settings, to be the law of the land. For a brief period the theocratic state existed in Plymouth Colony in greater completeness probably than ever in Judaea.

The *third* of the universal assumptions became basic to all. It was the notion that self-fulfilment was itself of supreme worth, and that the highest manhood could be realized only through unity with God. At this point Christianity completes and fulfils the concept which had been advocated by Jewish prophecy but which had not been, nor is it now, generally accepted. This concept was that every person, regardless of race, creed, color, descent, or education, possessed an intrinsic and inalienable worth because of what he might become. As he realized his unity with the Divine he himself became a fragment of Divinity, and therefore of supreme value.

IV

The Unrecognized Basis of Democracy

It is quite impossible to overemphasize the importance of this last concept, for it is the basis of democracy as well as of religion. Western democracy has grown out of the Judaeo-Christian concept

of man.   Here lies the hope for the future of a world torn with
strife between Democracy and Totalitarianism.   Let us try to grasp
the universality of its application.   If every person is of value in-
trinsically, the good life, happiness, peace, *ataraxia,* can be achieved
only as each is given opportunity and permitted and encouraged to
realize his highest possibilities.   The good society is menaced if
within its bounds any one is denied by any means the right to his
highest self-expression.   The right of each to "life, liberty, and the
pursuit of happiness" becomes then a supreme right and the basis
of democracy.

READINGS

Selections from the *BOOK OF JOB*. From Moulton's translation, Modern Reader's Bible, by permission of The Macmillan Company, New York.

DRAMATIS PERSONAE

Job, from the Land of Uz
Eliphaz, the Temanite ⎫
Bildad, the Shuhite ⎬ Three friends of Job
Zophar, the Naamathite ⎭

JOB: [Cursing the day of his birth][1]

Let the day perish wherein I was born;
And the night which said, There is a man child conceived!

Let that day be darkness;
Let not God regard it from above,
Neither let the light shine upon it!
Let darkness and the shadow of death claim it for their own;
Let a cloud dwell upon it;
Let all that maketh black the day terrify it!

. . . .

Why died I not from the womb?

. . . .

For now I should have lien down and been quiet;
I should have slept; then had I been at rest,
With kings and counsellors of the earth,
Which built solitary piles for themselves [the pyramids];
Or with princes that had gold,
Who filled their houses with silver.

. . . .

There the wicked cease from troubling;
And there the weary be at rest.
There the prisoners are at ease together;
They hear not the voice of the taskmaster.
The small and great are there;
And the servant is free from his master.

[1] Parts in brackets by the editor.

THE DEBATE

Eliphaz: [Job *must* be wicked, since he is unfortunate]
    Is not thy fear of God thy confidence,
      And thy hope the integrity of thy ways?
    Remember, I pray thee, who ever perished, being innocent?
    Or where were the upright cut off?

    According as I have seen, they that plow iniquity,
    And sow trouble, reap the same.
      By the breath of God they perish,
      And by the blast of his anger are they consumed.
. . . .
    Shall mortal man be just before God?
    Shall a man be pure before his Maker?

. . . .

Eliphaz, continuing: [All pain is for correction]

    Behold, happy is the man whom God correcteth:
    Therefore despise not thou the chastening of the Almighty.
    For he maketh sore, and bindeth up;
    He woundeth, and his hands make whole.
    He shall deliver thee in six troubles;
    Yea, in seven there shall no evil touch thee.
    In famine he shall redeem thee from death;
      And in war from the power of the sword.
    Thou shalt be hid from the scourge of the tongue;
      Neither shalt thou be afraid of destruction when it cometh.
    At destruction and dearth thou shalt laugh:
      Neither shalt thou be afraid of the beasts of the earth.
    For thou shalt be in league with the stones of the field;
      And the beasts of the field shall be at peace with thee.
    And thou shalt know that thy tent is in peace;
      And thou shalt visit thy fold and shalt miss nothing.
    Thou shalt know also that thy seed shall be great,
      And thine offspring as the grass of the earth.
    Thou shalt come to thy grave in full age,
      Like as a shock of corn cometh in its season.
    Lo, this, we have searched it, so it is;
      Hear it, and know thou it for thy good.

Job: [Disappointed in human friendship]

. . . .
    To him that is ready to faint kindness should be shown by his
    friend;

Even to him that forsaketh the fear of the Almighty.
  My brethren have dealt deceitfully as a brook,
  As the channel of brooks that pass away;
  Which are black by reason of the ice,
  And wherein the snow hideth itself:
  What time they wax warm, they vanish:
  When it is hot, they are consumed out of their place.
The paths of their way are turned aside,
They go up into the waste and perish.
The caravans of Tema looked,
The companies of Sheba waited for them;
They were ashamed because they had hoped;
They came thither and were confounded.
[They perished of thirst because the dry brook held no water]
. . . .

JOB, continuing: [All he had asked was sympathy]
  Did I say, Give unto me?
. . . .·. . . . .
Is there not a time of service to man upon earth?
And are not his days like the days of an hireling?
                    [Sunset at last?]
  As a servant that earnestly desireth the shadow,
  And as an hireling that looketh for his wages,
  So am I made to possess months of vanity,
  And wearisome nights are appointed to me.
  When I lie down, I say, When shall I arise?
  But the night is long;
  And I am full of tossings to and fro
  Unto the dawning of the day.
  My flesh is clothed with worms and clods of dust;
  My skin closeth up and breaketh out afresh.
  My days are swifter than a weaver's shuttle,
  And are spent without hope.
. . . .
  If I have sinned, what can I do unto thee, O thou Watcher of men?
  Why hast thou set me (up) as a mark for thee,
  So that I am a burden to myself?
  And why dost thou not pardon my transgression,
  And take away mine iniquity?
  For now shall I lie down in the dust;
  And thou shalt seek me diligently, but I shall not be!

BILDAD: ["Rubbing it in"; no doubt but pain is the result of sin]

. . . .
If thou wert pure and upright, surely now He would awake for thee,
And make the habitation of thy righteousness prosperous.
. . . .
Can the rush grow up without mire?
Can the flag grow without water?
   Whilst it is yet in its greenness, and not cut down,
   It withereth before any other herb.
So are the paths of all that forget God;
And the hope of the godless man shall perish.
. . . .
Behold, God will not cast away a perfect man,
Neither will he uphold the evil-doers.
   He will yet fill thy mouth with laughter,
   And thy lips with shouting.
   They that hate thee shall be clothed with shame,
   And the tent of the wicked shall be no more.

JOB: [But between man and God who shall be judge?]

How can a man be just with God?
If he be pleased to contend with him,
He cannot answer him one of a thousand.
He is wise in heart and mighty in strength:
Who hath hardened himself against him and prospered?
Which removeth the mountains and they know it not,
When he overturneth them in his anger.
Which shaketh the earth out of her place,
And the pillars thereof tremble.
Which commandeth the sun and it riseth not;
And sealeth up the stars.
Which alone stretcheth out the heavens,
And treadeth upon the waves of the sea.
. . . .
Lo, he goeth by me, and I see him not:
He passeth on also, but I perceive him not.
. . . .
If we speak of the strength of the mighty,
Lo, he is there!
And if of judgment,
Who will appoint me a time?
   Though I be righteous, mine own mouth shall condemn me:
   Though I be perfect, it shall prove me perverse.
. . . .
If the scourge slay suddenly,

He will mock at the trial of the innocent.
The earth is given into the hand of the wicked:
He covereth the faces of the judges thereof.
If it be not HE,
WHO then is it?

ZOPHAR: [If Job only had a good philosophy, or wisdom, or theology]

Should not the multitude of words be answered?
And should a man full of talk be justified?
. . . .
For thou sayest, My doctrine is pure,
And I am clean in thine eyes.
   But Oh that God would speak,
   And open his lips against thee;
   And that he would shew thee the secrets of wisdom.
. . . .
   Know therefore that God exacteth of thee
   Less than thine iniquity deserveth.

JOB: [But wisdom must not shut its eyes to the facts]

The tents of robbers prosper,
And they that provoke God are secure.
. . . .
   Will ye speak unrighteously for God,
   And talk deceitfully for him?
. . . .

              [And life is so short]

Man that is born of a woman
Is of few days and full of trouble;
He cometh forth like a flower, and is cut down,
He fleeth also as a shadow and continueth not.
. . . .
   Look away from him, that he may rest,
   Till he shall accomplish, as an hireling, his day.
For there is hope of a tree, if it be cut down,
That it will sprout again,
And that the tender branch thereof will not cease;
Though the root thereof wax old in the earth,
And the stock thereof die in the ground,
Yet through the scent of water it will bud,
And put forth boughs like a plant.
But man dieth, and wasteth away:
Yea, man giveth up the ghost, and where is he?
As the waters fail from the sea,
And the river decayeth and drieth up,

So man lieth down and riseth not;
Till the heavens be no more. . . .
His sons come to honor, and he knoweth it not;
And they are brought low, but he perceiveth it not. . . .

ELIPHAZ: [You are altogether too bold in God's presence]

. . . .
. . . Thou doest away with fear,

[And art lacking in reverence]

. . . .
The wicked man travaileth with pain all his days.

JOB: [Show me!]
I have heard many such things:
Miserable comforters are ye all.

. . . .
I also could speak as ye do;
If your soul were in my soul's stead.

[Light from darkness at last]

They have gaped upon me with their mouth;
They have smitten me upon the cheek reproachfully:
They gather themselves together against me.
God delivereth me to the ungodly,
And casteth me into the hands of the wicked.
I was at ease, and he brake me asunder;
Yea, he hath taken me by the neck, and dashed me to pieces:

. . . .
My face is foul with weeping,
And on my eyelids is the shadow of death;
Although there is no violence in my hands,
And my prayer is pure.
   O earth, cover not thou my blood
   And let my cry have no resting place.

[First landing place]

Even now, *behold, my Witness is in heaven,*
And He that voucheth for me is on high.

. . . .
Oh that my words were written!
Oh that they were inscribed in a book!
That with an iron pen and lead
They were graven in the rock forever!

[Second landing place]

For *I know that my Vindicator liveth,*
And that He shall stand up at the last upon the earth;

And after my skin hath been thus destroyed,
Yet without my flesh shall I see God!
Whom I shall see on my side,
And mine eyes shall behold, and not another.

ZOPHAR: (interrupting)

. . . .
Knowest thou not this of old time,
Since man was placed upon earth,
That the triumphing of the wicked is short,
And the joy of the godless but for a moment?

. . . .

JOB:

Wherefore do the wicked live,
    Become old, yea, wax mighty in power?
Their seed is established with them in their sight,
    And their offspring before their eyes.
Their houses are safe from fear,
    Neither is the rod of God upon them.

. . . .
They spend their days in prosperity,
    And in a moment they go down to Sheol.
Yet they said unto God, "Depart from us,
    For we desire not the knowledge of thy ways.
What is the Almighty that we should serve him?
    And what profit should we have if we pray unto him?"

ELIPHAZ: (interrupting)

Lo, their prosperity is not in their hand:
The counsel of the wicked is far from me.

JOB:

How oft is it that the lamp of the wicked is put out?
That their calamity cometh upon them?
That God distributeth sorrows in his anger?
That they are as stubble before the wind,
And as chaff that the storm carrieth away?

BILDAD: (interrupting)

God layeth up his iniquity for his children.

JOB:

Let H'm recompense it unto himself, that he may know it.
Let his own eyes see his destruction.

ZOPHAR: (interrupting)

Shall any (one) teach God knowledge?

JOB:

. . . .

The evil man is spared in the day of calamity.

ELIPHAZ: [Grows personal]

. . . .

Is not thy wickedness great?
Neither is there any end to thine iniquities.
   For thou hast taken pledges of thy brother for nought,
And stripped the naked of their clothing.
   Thou hast not given water to the weary to drink,
   And thou hast withholden bread from the hungry.
. . . .

Thou hast sent widows away empty,
And the arms of the fatherless have been broken.
. . . .

Wilt thou keep the old way
Which wicked men have trodden?
. . . .

Who said unto God, Depart from us;
And, What can the Almighty do for us?
Yet he filled their houses with good things:
But the counsel of the wicked is far from me.
The righteous see it, and are glad;
And the innocent laugh them to scorn.
   [The argument here is in danger of cutting off its own head, for
the alleged shortcomings are foreign to Job's character, and only
surmised from his misfortunes]

JOB: [The appeal to heaven]

. . . .
Oh that I knew where I might find Him,
That I might come even to his seat!
   I would order my cause before him,
   And fill my mouth with arguments.
   I would know the words which he would answer me,
   And understand what he would say unto me.
Would he contend with me in the greatness of his power?
Nay, but he would give heed unto me;
There the upright might reason with him:
So should I be delivered forever from my judge (critic).
Behold I go forward,

But he is not there;
And backward,
But I cannot perceive him;
On the left hand when he doth work,
But I cannot behold him;
He hideth himself on the right hand,
That I cannot see him.
    [Third landing place. Job has found a philosophy at last]
But *He knoweth the way that I take;*
When He hath tried me I shall come forth as gold.

. . . .
Till I die I will not put away mine integrity from me.
. . . .

    [This wisdom or philosophy is better than miner's treasures]
Surely there is a mine for silver,
And a place for gold which they refine.
Iron is taken out of the earth,
And brass is molten out of the stone.
Man setteth an end to darkness,
And searcheth out to the furthest bound
The stones of thick darkness and of the shadow of death.
He breaketh open a shaft away from (the sojourn of men).
  They are forgotten of the foot that passeth by;
  They hang afar from men, they swing to and fro.
As for the earth, out of it cometh bread;
And underneath it is turned up as it were by fire.
The stones thereof are the place of sapphires,
And it hath dust of gold.
That path no bird of prey knoweth,
Neither hath the falcon's eye seen it:
The proud beasts have not trodden it,
Nor hath the fierce lion passed thereby.
He putteth forth his hand upon the flinty rock;
He overturneth the mountains by the roots.
He cutteth out passages among the rocks;
And his eye seeth every precious thing.
He bindeth the streams that they trickle not;
And the thing that is hid he bringeth forth to light.
But where shall wisdom be found?
And where is the place of understanding?
Man knoweth not the price thereof;
Neither is it found in the land of the living.
The deep saith, It is not in me:
And the sea saith, It is not with me.
It cannot be gotten for gold,

Neither shall silver be weighed for the price thereof.
It cannot be valued with the gold of Ophir,
With the precious onyx, or the sapphire.
    Gold and glass cannot equal it,
    Neither shall it be valued with pure gold.
    No mention shall be made of coral or of crystal:
    Yea, the price of wisdom is above rubies.
    The topaz of Ethiopia shall not equal it,
    Neither shall it be valued with pure gold.
Whence then cometh wisdom?
And where is the place of understanding?

. . . .

Behold the fear of the Lord, that is wisdom:
    And to depart from evil is understanding.

Voice out of the Whirlwind:
    [Who is this prating about wisdom?]
    Who is this that darkeneth counsel by words without knowledge?
    Gird up now thy loins like a man;
    For I will demand of thee, and declare thou unto me.
    Where wast thou when I laid the foundations of the earth?
    ———Declare if thou hast understanding———
    Who determined the measures thereof, if thou knowest?
    Or who stretched the line upon it?
    Whereupon were the foundations thereof fastened?
    Or who laid the corner stone thereof;
    When the morning stars sang together,
    And all the sons of God shouted for joy?
    Or who shut up the sea with doors,
    When it brake forth and issued out of the womb;
        When I made the cloud the garment thereof,
        And thick darkness the swaddling band for it,
        And prescribed for it my decree,
        And set bars and doors,
        And said, "Hitherto shalt thou come, and no further;
        And here shall thy proud waves be stayed?"

. . . .

    Hast thou entered into the springs of the sea?
    Or hast thou walked in the recesses of the deep?
    Have the gates of death been revealed unto thee?
    Or hast thou seen the gates of the shadow of death?
    Hast thou comprehended the breadth of the earth?
    ———Declare if thou knowest it all———

. . . .

    Doth the hawk soar by thy wisdom,
    And stretch her wings toward the south?

> Doth the eagle mount up at thy command,
> And make her nest on high?
>
> . . . .
>
> Shall he that cavilleth contend with the Almighty?
> He that argueth with God, let him answer.

JOB: Behold I am of small account (wherewith shall I answer.)

VOICE out of the Whirlwind:

> Gird up thy loins now like a man:
> I will demand of thee, and declare thou unto me.

JOB:

> I know that thou canst do all things,
> And that no purpose of thine can be restrained.
>
> . . . .
>
> . . . I have uttered that which I understood not,
> Things too wonderful for me, which I knew not.
>
> . . . .
>
> *I had heard of thee by the hearing of the ear;*
> *But now mine eye seeth thee:* [knowledge of God, the Supreme
>   Value]
> Wherefore I abhor myself, and repent
> In dust and ashes.

THE WISDOM OF SOLOMON. Translated from *The Apocrypha* by
Edgar J. Goodspeed. University of Chicago Press, Chicago. Pp.
102-106. (Used by special permission.)

I

1 LOVE UPRIGHTNESS, YOU WHO JUDGE THE LAND,
   Think of the Lord with goodness,
   And seek him with sincerity of heart.
2 For he is found by those who do not try him,
   And is manifested to those who do not disbelieve him.
3 For crooked reasonings separate from God,
   And when his power is tested, it exposes fools.
4 For wisdom cannot enter a deceitful soul,
   Or live in a body in debt to sin.
5 For the holy spirit of instruction will flee from deceit,
   And will rise and leave at unwise reasoning,
   And be put to confusion at the approach of wrong.
6 For wisdom is a kindly spirit,
   And will not acquit a blasphemer of what he says,
   For God is a witness of his heart,
   And a truthful observer of his mind,
   And a hearer of his tongue.
7 For the spirit of the Lord fills the world,
   And that which embraces all things knows all that is said.
8 Therefore no one who utters what is wrong will go unobserved,
   Nor will justice, in its investigation, pass him by.
9 For there will be an inquiry into the designs of the ungodly,
   And the sound of his words will reach the Lord,
   To convict him of his transgressions.
10 For a jealous ear hears everything,
   And the sound of grumbling is not hidden.
11 So beware of useless grumbling,
   And spare your tongue from slander;
   For no secret word goes for naught,
   And a lying mouth destroys the soul.
12 Do not invite death by the error of your life,
   Or incur destruction by the work of your hands;
13 For God did not make death,
   And he does not enjoy the destruction of the living.
14 For he created everything to exist,
   And the generative forces of the world are wholesome,
   And there is no poisonous drug in them,
   And the kingdom of Hades is not on earth.
15 For uprightness is immortal.

II

1 They thought him their friend, and softened,
And made an agreement with him,
For they are fit to belong to his party.
For they did not reason soundly, but said to themselves,
"Our life is short and miserable,
And there is no cure when man comes to his end,
And no one has been known to return from Hades.

2 For we were born at a venture,
And hereafter we shall be as though we had never existed,
Because the breath in our nostrils is smoke,
And reason is a spark in the beating of our hearts;

3 When it is quenched, the body will turn to ashes,
And the spirit will dissolve like empty air.

4 And in time our name will be forgotten,
And no one will remember what we have done,
And our life will pass away like the traces of a cloud,
And be scattered like mist
Pursued by the sun's rays
And overcome by its heat.

5 For our life is a fleeting shadow,
And there is no way to recall our end
For it is sealed up and no one can bring it back.

6 So come, let us enjoy the good things that exist,
And eagerly make use of the creation as we did in our youth.

7 Let us have our fill of costly wine and perfumes,
And let us not miss the spring flowers.

8 Let us crown ourselves with rosebuds before they wither;

9 Let none of us miss his share in our revelry;
Everywhere let us leave the signs of our gladness;
For this is our portion and this our lot.

10 Let us oppress the upright poor;
Let us not spare the widow,
Or respect the venerable gray head of the aged.

11 But let our strength be our law of uprightness,
For weakness is proved useless.

12 Let us lie in wait for the upright, for he inconveniences us
And opposes our doings,
And reproaches us with our transgressions of the Law,
And charges us with sins against what we have been taught;

13 He professes to possess knowledge of God,
And calls himself a child of the Lord;

14 We have found him a reproof of our thoughts,
He is wearisome to us even to see,

15 For his life is not like others,
    And his ways are strange.
16 He considers us counterfeit,
    And avoids our ways as unclean.
    He calls the end of the upright happy,
    And boasts that God is his father.
17 Let us see whether what he says is true,
    And let us test what will happen at his departure.
18 For if the upright man is a son of God, he will help him,
    And save him from the hands of his adversaries.
19 Let us test him with insults and torture,
    So that we may learn his patience,
    And prove his forbearance.
20 Let us condemn him to a shameful death,
    For he will be watched over, from what he says!"
21   So they reasoned, but they went astray,
    For their wickedness blinded them,
22 And they did not know God's secrets,
    Or hope for the reward of holiness,
    Or recognize the prize of blameless souls.
23 For God created man for immortality,
    And made him the image of his own eternity,
24 But through the devil's envy death came into the world,
    And those who belong to his party experience it.

III

1 But the souls of the upright are in the hand of God,
    And no torment can reach them.
2 In the eyes of foolish people they seemed to die,
    And their decease was thought an affliction,
3 And their departure from us their ruin,
    But they are at peace.
4 For though in the sight of men they are punished,
    Their hope is full of immortality,
5 And after being disciplined a little, they will be shown great
      kindness.
    For God has tried them,
    And found them worthy of himself.
6 He has tested them like gold in a furnace,
    And accepted them like the sacrifice of a whole burnt offering.
7 They will shine out, when he visits them,
    And spread like sparks among the stubble.
8 They will judge nations and rule peoples,
    And the Lord will reign over them forever.

THE TEN COMMANDMENTS. Deuteronomy 5:7-31.

7 Thou shalt have none other gods before me.

8 Thou shalt not make thee any graven image, or any likeness of anything that is in heaven above, or that is in the earth beneath. or that is in the waters beneath the earth:

9 Thou shalt not bow down thyself unto them, nor serve them: for I the Lord thy God am a jealous God, visiting the iniquity of the fathers upon the children unto the third and fourth generation of them that hate me,

10 And shewing mercy unto thousands of them that love me and keep my commandments.

11 Thou shalt not take the name of the Lord thy God in vain: for the Lord will not hold him guiltless that taketh his name in vain.

12 Keep the sabbath day to sanctify it, as the Lord thy God hath commanded thee.

13 Six days thou shalt labour, and do all thy work:

14 But the seventh day is the sabbath of the Lord thy God: in it thou shalt not do any work, thou, nor thy son, nor thy daughter, nor thy manservant, nor thy maidservant, nor thine ox, nor thine ass, nor any of thy cattle, nor thy stranger that is within thy gates; that thy manservant and thy maidservant may rest as well as thou.

15 And remember that thou wast a servant in the land of Egypt, and that the Lord thy God brought thee out thence through a mighty hand and by a stretched out arm: therefore the Lord thy God commanded thee to keep the sabbath day.

16 Honour thy father and thy mother, as the Lord thy God hath commanded thee; that thy days may be prolonged, and that it may go well with thee, in the land which the Lord thy God giveth thee.

17 Thou shalt not kill.

18 Neither shalt thou commit adultery.

19 Neither shalt thou steal.

20 Neither shalt thou bear false witness against thy neighbour.

21 Neither shalt thou desire thy neighbour's wife, neither shalt thou covet thy neighbour's house, his field, or his manservant, or his maidservant, his ox, or his ass, or any thing that is thy neighbour's.

ISAIAH 1:1-20.

"The Great Arraignment."

"Hear, O heavens, and give ear, O earth, for the Lord hath spoken: I have nourished and brought up children, and they have rebelled against me.

"The ox knoweth his owner, and the ass his master's crib: but Israel doth not know, my people doth not consider. Ah sinful nation, a people laden with iniquity, a seed of evil-doers, children that deal corruptly: they have forsaken the Lord, they have despised the Holy One of Israel, they are estranged and gone backward. Why will ye be still stricken, that ye revolt more and more? The whole head is sick, and the whole heart faint. From the sole of the foot even unto the head there is no soundness in it; but wounds, and bruises, and festering sores: they have not been closed, neither bound up, neither mollified with oil. Your country is desolate; your cities are burned with fire; your land, strangers devour it in your presence, and it is desolate, as overthrown by strangers. And the daughter of Zion is left as a booth in a vineyard, as a lodge in a garden of cucumbers, as a besieged city. Except the Lord of hosts had left unto us a very small remnant, we should have been as Sodom, we should have been like unto Gomorrah.

"Hear the word of the Lord, ye rulers of Sodom; give ear unto the law of our God, ye people of Gomorrah. To what purpose is the multitude of your sacrifices unto me? saith the LORD: I am full of the burnt offerings of rams, and the fat of fed beasts; and I delight not in the blood of bullocks, or of lambs, or of he-goats. When ye come to appear before me, who hath required this at your hand, to trample my courts? Bring no more vain oblations; incense is an abomination unto me; new moon and sabbath, the calling of assemblies,—I cannot away with iniquity and the solemn meeting. Your new moons and your appointed feasts my soul hateth: they are a trouble unto me; I am weary to bear them. And when ye spread forth your hands, I will hide mine eyes from you: yea, when ye make many prayers, I will not hear: your hands are full of blood.

"Wash you, make you clean; put away the evil of your doings from before mine eyes; cease to do evil: learn to do well; seek judgment, relieve the oppressed, judge the fatherless, plead for the widow. Come now, and let us reason together, saith the Lord: though your sins be as scarlet, they shall be as white as snow: though they be red like crimson, they shall be as wool. If ye be willing and obedient, ye shall eat the good of the land: but if ye refuse and rebel, ye shall be devoured with the sword: for the mouth of the Lord hath spoken it.

"How is the faithful city become an harlot! she that was full of judgment! righteousness lodged in her, but not murderers. Thy silver is become dross, thy wine mixed with water. Thy princes are rebellious, and companions of thieves; every one loveth gifts, and followeth after rewards: they judge not the fatherless, neither doth the cause of the widow come unto them.   Therefore saith the Lord, the LORD of hosts, the Mighty One of Israel, Ah, I will ease me of mine adversaries, and avenge me of mine enemies: and I will turn my hand upon thee, and thoroughly purge away thy dross, and will take away all thy alloy: and I will restore thy judges as at the first, and thy counsellors as at the beginning: afterward thou shalt be called The City of Righteousness, the faithful city.   Zion shall be redeemed with judgment, and her converts with righteousness.   But the destruction of the transgressors and the sinners shall be together, and they shall be ashamed of the oaks which ye have desired, and ye shall be confounded for the gardens that ye have chosen.   For ye shall be as an oak whose leaf fadeth, and as a garden that hath no water.   And the strong shall be as tow, and his work as a spark; and they shall both burn together and none shall quench them."

THE BIBLE: *THE SERMON ON THE MOUNT—THE BEATI-
TUDES.* Matthew 5:1-20; 6:5-34; 7:1-27.

"And seeing the multitudes, he went up into the mountain: and when
he had sat down, his disciples came unto him: and he opened his mouth
and taught them, saying:

> "Blessed are the poor in spirit:
> For theirs is the kingdom of heaven.

"Blessed are they that mourn: for they shall be comforted. Blessed
are the meek: for they shall inherit the earth. Blessed are they that
hunger and thirst after righteousness: for they shall be filled. Blessed
are the merciful: for they shall obtain mercy. Blessed are the pure in
heart: for they shall see God. Blessed are the peacemakers: for they
shall be called sons of God. Blessed are they that have been persecuted
for righteousness' sake: for theirs is the kingdom of heaven. Blessed
are ye when men shall reproach you, and persecute you, and say all
manner of evil against you falsely, for my sake. Rejoice, and be exceeding glad: for great is your reward in heaven: for so persecuted they the
prophets which were before you.

> "Ye are the salt of the earth.

"But if the salt have lost its savour, wherewith shall it be salted: it
is thenceforth good for nothing, but to be cast out and trodden under
foot of men.

> "Ye are the light of the world.

"A city set on a hill cannot be hid. Neither do men light a lamp and
put it under the bushel, but on the stand; and it shineth unto all that are
in the house. Even so let your light shine before men, that they may
see your good works, and glorify your Father which is in heaven.

> "Think not that I came to destroy the law or the prophets:
> I came not to destroy, but to fulfil.

"For verily I say unto you, Till heaven and earth pass away, one jot
or one tittle shall in nowise pass away from the law, till all things be
accomplished. Whosoever therefore shall break one of these least commandments, and shall teach men so, shall be called least in the kingdom of
heaven: but whosoever shall do and teach them, he shall be called great
in the kingdom of heaven.

"For I say unto you, that except your righteousness shall exceed the
righteousness of the scribes and Pharisees, ye shall in no wise enter into
the kingdom of heaven. Ye have heard that it was said to them of
old time, Thou shalt not kill; and whosoever shall kill shall be in danger
of the judgment: but I say unto you, that every one who is angry

with his brother shall be in danger of the judgment; and whosoever shall say to his brother, *Raca,* shall be in danger of the council; and whosoever shall say, Thou fool, shall be in danger of the hell of fire.   If therefore thou art offering thy gift at the altar, and there rememberest that thy brother hath aught against thee, leave there thy gift before the altar, and go thy way, first be reconciled to thy brother, and then come and offer thy gift.   Agree with thine adversary quickly, whiles thou art with him in the way; lest haply the adversary deliver thee to the judge, and the judge deliver thee to the officer, and thou be cast into prison: verily I say unto thee, Thou shalt by no means come out thence, till thou have paid the last farthing.   Ye have heard that it was said, Thou shalt not commit adultery: but I say unto you, that every one that looketh on a woman to lust after her hath committed adultery with her already in his heart.   And if thy right eye causeth thee to stumble, pluck it out, and cast it from thee: for it is profitable for thee that one of thy members should perish, and not thy whole body be cast into hell.   And if thy right hand causeth thee to stumble, cut it off, and cast it from thee: for it is profitable for thee that one of thy members should perish, and not thy whole body go into hell.   It was said also, Whosoever shall put away his wife, let him give her a writing of divorcement: but I say unto you, that every one that putteth away his wife, saving for the cause of fornication, maketh her an adulteress: and whosoever shall marry her when she is put away committeth adultery.   Again, ye have heard that it was said to them of old time, Thou shalt not forswear thyself, but shalt perform unto the Lord thine oaths: but I say unto you, Swear not at all; neither by the heaven, for it is the throne of God; nor by the earth, for it is the footstool of his feet; nor by Jerusalem, for it is the city of the great King; neither shalt thou swear by thy head, for thou canst not make one hair white or black. But let your speech be, Yea, yea; Nay, nay: and whatsoever is more than these is of the evil one.   Ye have heard that it was said, an eye for an eye, and a tooth for a tooth: but I say unto you, Resist not him that is evil: but whosoever smiteth thee on thy right cheek, turn to him the other also.   And if any man would go to law with thee, and take away thy coat, let him have thy cloke also.   And whosoever shall compel thee to go one mile, go with him twain.   Give to him that asketh thee, and from him that would borrow of thee turn not thou away.   Ye have heard that it was said, Thou shalt love thy neighbour, and hate thine enemy: but I say unto you, Love your enemies, and pray for them that persecute you; that ye may be sons of your Father which is in heaven: for he maketh his sun to rise on the evil and the good, and sendeth rain on the just and the unjust.   For if ye love them that love you, what reward have ye? do not even the publicans the same? And if ye salute your brethren only, what do ye more than others? do not even the Gentiles the same?   Ye therefore shall be perfect, as your heavenly Father is perfect.

"Take heed that ye do not your righteousness before men, to be
    seen of them:
Else ye have no reward with your Father which is in heaven.

"When therefore thou doest alms, sound not a trumpet before thee,
as the hypocrites do in the synagogues and in the streets, that they may
have glory of men. Verily I say unto you, They have received their
reward. But when thou doest alms, let not thy left hand know what thy
right hand doeth; that thine alms may be in secret: and thy Father
which seeth in secret shall recompense thee. And when ye pray, ye
shall not be as the hypocrites: for they love to stand and pray in the
synagogues and in the corners of the streets, that they may be seen of
men. Verily I say unto you, They have received their reward. But
thou, when thou prayest, enter into thine inner chamber, and having
shut thy door, pray to thy Father which is in secret, and thy Father
which seeth in secret shall recompense thee. And in praying use not
vain repetitions, as the Gentiles do: for they think that they shall be
heard for their much speaking. Be not therefore like unto them: for
your Father knoweth what things ye have need of, before ye ask him."

The Lord's Prayer

"After this manner therefore pray ye:

"Our Father which art in heaven:
    Hallowed be thy name,
    Thy kingdom come,
    Thy will be done,
As in heaven, so on earth.

Give us this day
Our daily bread.
And forgive us our debts,
As we also have forgiven our debtors.

And bring us not into temptation,
But deliver us from the evil one."

For if ye forgive men their trespasses, your heavenly Father will also
forgive you. But if ye forgive not men their trespasses, neither will
your Father forgive your trespasses. Moreover when ye fast, be not,
as the hypocrites, of a sad countenance: for they disfigure their faces,
that they may be seen of men to fast. Verily I say unto you, They have
received their reward. But thou, when thou fastest, anoint thy head,
and wash thy face; that thou be not seen of men to fast, but of thy
Father which is in secret: and thy Father, which seeth in secret, shall
recompense thee.

"Lay not up for yourselves treasures upon the earth,
    Where moth and rust doth consume,
    And where thieves break through and steal:
But lay up for yourselves treasures in heaven,
    Where neither moth nor rust doth consume,
    And where thieves do not break through nor steal.

For where thy treasure is, there will thy heart be also. The lamp of the body is the eye: if therefore thine eye be single, thy whole body shall be full of light; but if thine eye be evil, thy whole body shall be full of darkness; if therefore the light that is in thee be darkness, how great is the darkness! No man can serve two masters: for either he will hate the one, and love the other; or else he will hold to one, and despise the other. Ye cannot serve God and mammon. Therefore I say unto you, be not anxious for your life, what ye shall eat, or what ye shall drink; nor yet for your body, what ye shall put on. Is not the life more than the food, and the body than the raiment? Behold the birds of the heaven, that they sow not, neither do they reap, nor gather into barns; and your heavenly Father feedeth them. Are not ye of much more value than they? And which of you by being anxious can add one cubit unto his stature? And why are ye anxious concerning raiment? Consider the lilies of the field, how they grow; they toil not, neither do they spin: yet I say unto you, that even Solomon in all his glory was not arrayed like one of these. But if God doth so clothe the grass of the field, which today is, and tomorrow is cast into the oven, shall He not much more clothe you, O ye of little faith? Be not therefore anxious, saying, What shall we eat? or, What shall we drink? or, Wherewithal shall we be clothed?—for after all these things do the Gentiles seek—for your heavenly Father knoweth that ye have need of all these things. But seek ye first his kingdom, and his righteousness; and all these things shall be added unto you. Be not therefore anxious for the morrow: for the morrow will be anxious for itself. Sufficient unto the day is the evil thereof."

"Judge not:
    That ye be not judged.

For with what judgment ye judge, ye shall be judged: and with what measure ye mete, it shall be measured unto you. And why beholdest thou the mote that is in thy brother's eye, but considerest not the beam that is in thine own eye? Or how wilt thou say to thy brother, Let me cast out the mote out of thine eye; and lo, the beam is in thine own eye? Thou hypocrite, cast out first the beam out of thine own eye; and then shalt thou see clearly to cast out the mote out of thy brother's eye.

"Give not that which is holy unto the dogs,
    Neither cast your pearls before the swine:
    Lest haply they trample them under their feet,
And turn and rend you.

Ask, and it shall be given you;
Seek, and ye shall find;
Knock, and it shall be opened unto you:
For every one that asketh receiveth,
And he that seeketh findeth,
And to him that knocketh it shall be opened.

"Or what man is there of you, who, if his son shall ask him for a loaf, will give him a stone; or if he shall ask for a fish, will give him a serpent? If ye then, being evil, know how to give good gifts unto your children, how much more shall your Father which is in heaven give good things to them that ask him?

"All things therefore whatsoever ye would that men should do unto you, even so do ye also unto them: for this is the law and the prophets."

"Enter ye in by the narrow gate.

For wide is the gate, and broad is the way, that leadeth to destruction, and many be they that enter in thereby. For narrow is the gate, and straitened the way, that leadeth unto life, and few be they that find it.

"Beware of false prophets,
Which come to you in sheep's clothing,
But inwardly are ravening wolves.

"By their fruits ye shall know them. Do men gather grapes of thorns, or figs of thistles? Even so every good tree bringeth forth good fruit; but the corrupt tree bringeth forth evil fruit. A good tree cannot bring forth evil fruit, neither can a corrupt tree bring forth good fruit. Every tree that bringeth not forth good fruit is hewn down, and cast into the fire. Therefore by their fruits ye shall know them.

"Not every one that saith unto me, Lord, Lord, shall enter into the kingdom of heaven; but he that doeth the will of my Father which is in heaven. Many will say to me in that day, Lord, Lord, did we not prophesy by thy name, and by thy name cast out devils, and by thy name do many mighty works? And then will I profess unto them, I never knew you: depart from me, ye that work iniquity. Every one therefore which heareth these words of mine, and doeth them, shall be likened unto a wise man, which built his house upon the rock: and the rain descended, and the floods came, and the winds blew, and beat upon that house; and it fell not: for it was founded upon the rock. And every one that heareth these words of mine, and doeth them not, shall be likened unto a foolish man, which built his house upon the sand: and the rain descended, and the floods came, and the winds blew, and smote upon that house; and it fell: and great was the fall thereof."

PARABLES OF LOST THINGS, or The Value of the Individual.

THE LOST SHEEP. Luke 15.

1 Then drew near unto him all the publicans and sinners for to hear him.

2 And the Pharisees and scribes murmured, saying, This man receiveth sinners, and eateth with them.

3 And he spake this parable unto them, saying,

4 What man of you, having an hundred sheep, if he lose one of them, doth not leave the ninety and nine in the wilderness, and go after that which is lost, until he find it?

5 And when he hath found it, he layeth it on his shoulders, rejoicing.

6 And when he cometh home, he calleth together his friends and neighbours, saying unto them, Rejoice with me; for I have found my sheep which was lost.

7 I say unto you, that likewise joy shall be in heaven over one sinner that repenteth, more than over ninety and nine just persons, which need no repentance.

THE LOST COIN.

8 Either what woman having ten pieces of silver, if she lose one piece, doth not light a candle, and sweep the house, and seek diligently till she find it?

9 And when she hath found it, she calleth her friends and her neighbours together saying, Rejoice with me; for I have found the piece which I had lost.

10 Likewise, I say unto you, there is joy in the presence of the angels of God over one sinner that repenteth.

THE PRODIGAL SON.

11 And he said, A certain man had two sons:

12 And the younger of them said to his father, Father, give me the portion of goods that falleth to me. And he divided unto them his living.

13 And not many days after the younger son gathered all together, and took his journey into a far country, and there wasted his substance with riotous living.

14 And when he had spent all, there arose a mighty famine in that land; and he began to be in want.

15 And he went and joined himself to a citizen of that country; and he sent him into his fields to feed swine.

16 And he would fain have filled his belly with the husks that the swine did eat: and no man gave unto him.

17 And when he came to himself, he said, How many hired servants of my father's have bread enough and to spare, and I perish with hunger!

18 I will arise and go to my father, and will say unto him, Father, I have sinned against heaven, and before thee,

19 And am no more worthy to be called thy son: make me as one of thy hired servants.

20 And he arose, and came to his father. But when he was yet a great way off, his father saw him, and had compassion and ran, and fell on his neck, and kissed him.

21 And the son said unto him, Father, I have sinned against heaven, and in thy sight, and am no more worthy to be called thy son.

22 But the father said to his servants, Bring forth the best robe, and put it on him; and put a ring on his hand, and shoes on his feet;

23 And bring hither the fatted calf, and kill it; and let us eat, and be merry:

24 For this my son was dead, and is alive again; he was lost, and is found. And they began to be merry.

25 Now his elder son was in the field: and as he came and drew nigh to the house, he heard music and dancing.

26 And he called one of the servants, and asked what these things meant.

27 And he said unto him, Thy brother is come; and thy father hath killed the fatted calf, because he hath received him safe and sound.

28 And he was angry, and would not go in; therefore came his father out, and intreated him.

29 And he answering said to his father, Lo, these many years do I serve thee, neither transgressed I at any time thy commandment: and yet thou never gavest me a kid, that I might make merry with my friends:

30 But as soon as this thy son was come, which hath devoured thy living with harlots, thou hast killed for him the fatted calf.

31 And he said unto him, Son, thou art ever with me, and all that I have is thine.

32 It was meet that we should make merry, and be glad: for this thy brother was dead, and is alive again: and was lost, and is found.

A DIGRESSION ON CHARITY. I Corinthians 13:1-13. By special
permission of the Roman Catholic Confraternity of Christian Doctrine.

And I point out to you a yet more excellent way. If I should speak
with the tongues of men and of angels, but do not have charity, I have
become as sounding brass or a tinkling cymbal. And if I have prophecy
and know all mysteries and all knowledge, and if I have all faith so
as to remove mountains, yet do not have charity, I am nothing. And
if I distribute all my goods to feed the poor, and if I deliver my body
to be burned, yet do not have charity, it profits me nothing.

Charity is patient, is kind; charity does not envy, is not pretentious,
is not puffed up, is not ambitious, is not self-seeking, is not provoked;
thinks no evil, does not rejoice over wickedness, but rejoices with the
truth; bears with all things, believes all things, hopes all things, endures
all things.

Charity never fails, whereas prophecies will disappear, and tongues
will cease, and knowledge will be destroyed. For we know in part and
we prophesy in part; but when that which is perfect has come, that
which is imperfect will be done away with. When I was a child I spoke
as a child, I felt as a child, I thought as a child. Now that I have become a man, I have put away the things of a child. We see now through
a mirror in an obscure manner, but then face to face. Now I know in
part, but then I shall know even as I have been known. So there abide
faith, hope, and charity, these three; but the greatest of these is charity.

QUESTIONS AND STATEMENTS FOR DISCUSSION

1. Does the speech of Eliphaz (All pain is for correction), and the attendant argument, convince you of the truth of the saying: "Be good and you will be happy"? In what sense could it be true?

2. What can be said for the consciousness of being right as a supreme value; i.e., as conforming to the Cosmic order as expressed in the words: "My Witness is in Heaven," and "I know that my Vindicator Liveth"?

3. What weight has Job's final argument: "I shall come forth as gold"? Does "seeing God" imply something more than the philosophy of Eliphaz (All pain is for correction), like joyous conformity to the Divine Will?

4. "Wisdom cannot enter a deceitful soul. Or live in debt to sin." (*Wisdom of Solomon,* 4.) Why not?

5. "Their wickedness blinded them." (*Ibid.,* II, 21.) Is this statement sustained in modern experience? If so, why?

6. What did Isaiah consider to be the things that matter most?

7. Are the "Ten Commandments" (Deuteronomy 5:7-21) still acceptable norms of conduct in civilized society, or could we do with less? Which ones would you omit?

8. "The meek shall inherit the earth." (Matthew 5:5.) In what sense?

9. Discuss the relation to the problem of values, of Matthew 6:19f.

10. "Everyone that asketh receiveth, and he that seeketh findeth." (Matthew 7:8.) In what sense, if any, is this true?

11. Discuss the discrepancy between "saying" and "doing" expressed in Matthew 7:20-22. Why are the "doers" building on secure foundations?

12. Can you discover the reason (Luke 15:17-32) for the father's reward of the Prodigal son? Which boy was now more likely to represent the higher loyalty? Why?

13. Is there an incipient democracy expressed in Luke 15:1-16 which has been a powerful incentive to free government where Judaeo-Christianity has prevailed?

14. In the light of Corinthians 13:1-13, how can the bestowal of charity to feed the poor be thus nullified? Is there any weakness of this kind lurking in organized charity?

Suggested Supplementary Readings:

Isaiah. Chap. 1-66.
Job. As translated by Genung: *The Epic of the Inner Life.* Riverside Press, Cambridge, or Moulton: Modern Reader's Bible, Macmillan, New York.
The Psalms.

Maimonides: *Guide to the Perplexed,* Bks. II, III.
The Gospel of John.
St. Exupery: *Flight to Arras.*   Reynal & Hitchcock, New York.
Pratt: *Can We Keep the Faith?*   Yale University Press, New Haven.
Flewelling: *The Reason in Faith.*   Abingdon Press, New York.
Flewelling: *Christ and the Dramas of Doubt.*   Abingdon Press, New York.
Job: Chaps. V, VI, VII, VIII.
Carrel: "Prayer."   *The Reader's Digest,* March, 1941.   Pp. 107-122, 123-125.

PART III

SIX PROPONENTS OF VALUE

" 'Value' is the word I use for the intrinsic reality of
an event."
—ALFRED NORTH WHITEHEAD.

Foreword

Any choice of six proponents of value must in the nature of the case appear arbitrary. It is not proposed to pick the six greatest characters of history, nor the six men who have most influenced the world. We are bound by the restrictions of a college course, and in the consideration of values we must seek as wide a diversity as our time will allow. Furthermore, it is advisable to choose such as will provide the more vivid and interesting illustrations for our purposes. There is no claim that equally good selections of other sextets might not be made, or perhaps better ones. Another consideration had to be included. Since this is intended as an elementary and general course, it seemed desirable to lean toward the side of literature rather than to that of philosophy, into which we should have been deeply plunged by the study of such intellectual leaders as Plato and Aristotle. Perhaps the absence of these two will be partly supplied by the study of their forerunner and inspirer, their spiritual father, Socrates.

Boethius is included, partly because he was the cultural bridge between the ancient and medieval worlds, partly because of his relation to the curriculum of. the modern university, but more especially for his clear-sighted description of "the things that matter most," his faith which was duly demonstrated in his own life and martyrdom.

Dante appears, not only because he is the supreme literary representative of Medievalism, ignorance of whose *Divina Commedia* is inexcusable in a cultured man, but also because he was the prophet of modern democracy in letters, in society, in State, and in Church.

About Rousseau there might be doubt, because there are many respects in which he might seem to come utterly short of greatness. Nevertheless, when we ponder on his influence in contemporary life, a consideration of his work appears necessary to the understanding of three leading movements of our day. Rousseau, for good or ill, became the initiator of the modern romantic novel in *La Nouvelle Héloise*, the leader of "progressive education" in *Émile*, and the spokesman of modern democratic theory in *Du Contrat Social*. Much as we may despise him we need to know him if we are to know the deep undercurrent of our own age.

Much the same may be said of Nietzsche, the evil genius of Totalitarianism, who is worshipped from opposite sides as Lord or Devil, but whose sane and insane lucubrations have done much toward producing a social and political impasse in world history. Even though we consider him a "Devil's Advocate," we must yet take account of him, if for no other reason than to avoid betrayal by his specious reasoning which so often tempers the common speech.

Since it was important to recognize the place of science in common thought, and in relation to values, Louis Pasteur was chosen as the man most generally accorded the supreme place in modern science, as discoverer and as proponent of values.

Chapter 8

THE SOCRATIC DEPENDENCE ON SELF-KNOWLEDGE

I

The Life of Socrates

II

Confession of Ignorance the Gateway to Knowledge
1. Partial acceptance by modern educators of the Socratic theory
2. The Socratic method in modern courts of law

III

The Affirmations of the Inner Life
1. Upset of traditional religion
2. The principle of freedom

IV

Self-Knowledge and the Maintenance of Democratic Ideals
1. Man the key to wisdom
2. The moral nature of the universe

V

The Influence of the Socratic Ideals on European Civilization
1. The Socratic break with tradition
2. Authority of the "Inner Voice"
3. The correlated freedom
4. Self-control as the basis of democracy
5. Reverence for law
6. Preparation for Christianity

Chapter 8

THE SOCRATIC DEPENDENCE ON SELF-KNOWLEDGE

Socrates must be seen as the child of his time; notwithstanding, there was a permanence about his work that bears a message and a significance to our own age. For our present civilization must date back in good part to him as its spiritual father. Ours is a Socratic as well as a Judaeo-Christian civilization, and has in these late years engaged in a titanic struggle to determine whether that which was begun in the far-off days of Socrates should be perpetuated or cast aside. That the interest in Socrates is perennial is evidenced by a recent volume aimed to "debunk" the reputation of a man who lived approximately twenty-five hundred years ago.

Our information concerning Socrates comes both from his enemies and from his friends. The two chief informants were his pupils: one, Xenophon, a General of an army of Greek mercenaries under Cyrus the Persian, the other, Plato, most famous of all literary philosophers, for whom a course is named in every extended college philosophy program. These were his friends and admirers. On the other side we have the Athenian poet Aristophanes, who in the comedy *The Clouds* has given us a notion of how Socrates was looked upon by his competitors and opponents in his day and society. If we are to say that his students were prejudiced in his favor, we must also admit a prejudice in his enemies as well, and, since the friends of a man are certain to be his best interpreters, we can better trust the picture that Xenophon and Plato have drawn. There are two of these works by Xenophon, *The Memorabilia,* or Memoirs, and *The Symposium,* or Banquet. Plato's accounts have been written in the famous series known as the *Dialogues of Plato.* Toward the latter part of his life, while he continued to put speeches into the mouth of Socrates, Plato may have been using the master's reputation to carry his own ideas.

The time at which Socrates appeared was, as we have previously noted, that period at which European civilization was trying to throw off the bondage of dark superstition and pagan practice and to arrive at broader and more cosmopolitan views. They were seeking to free themselves from fear of the forces of nature, and to arrive at a philosophy of government and of human relations. The

way had been prepared for Socrates by the earlier Greek philosophers, and it was upon their foundation that he built. As intelligent
men had ridded themselves of the fear of capricious deities who
appeared in storm and tornado, in thunder and lightning, a new set
of philosophers came forth who were distinguished by the boldness
of their disbeliefs. These were the Sophists. They drew men away
from a superstitious credulity to their own stupid incredulity. And
Socrates was trained in the school of the Sophists. The Sophists
were in particularly bad odor, first, because they took money for
their teaching; second, because they were indifferent to the prevailing religion; third, because they trained young men by the art
of dialectic to defend themselves in the courts so successfully as to
make "the worse appear the better reason." As these young men
were rich and idle, bent principally upon their own pleasure and
indifferent to the laws, the common opinion of Athenians regarding
them was not high.

In the comedy of Aristophanes, as indeed at the trial of Socrates
who was condemned to death by the Athenians, the charges made
against him were in general the charges which would have been
preferred against any of the Sophists. The accusations were inept
in great part because, though Socrates retained the method of argument he had learned from the Sophists, his ideas had been revolutionized by a remarkable conversion that had occurred on the field
of the Hoplites, where he was engaged in the annual military
training.

I
The Life of Socrates

Socrates was born about 470 B.C. and was put to death in
399 B.C. His father, Sophroniscus, had been a stone-cutter and his
mother, Phaenarete, was a midwife. The stone-cutter's trade was
not, in Athens, considered a high calling, even if in the hands of
the artisan it had become an art. The name of Phidias the sculptor
is now one of the great names of all time, but any ambitious society lad of Athens would have felt the calling of a Phidias as
far beneath him. Plato, Socrates' great pupil, ranked the philoso-
pher-king, the righteous warrior, first in social standing, and poets
and artists sixth in the scale, followed only by the farmers, dema-
gogues, and tyrants. So the artists and architects of the famed
buildings of the Acropolis would be considered humble members
of society. Legend has it that Socrates himself was the sculptor

of the draped figures of the "Graces" which appeared in relief
on the frieze of the Parthenon. Reference to it by Aristophanes
in the comedy *The Clouds* would seem to give it historic verification. There may have been playful reference to himself in
the role of sculptor that led Socrates to assert that he was the
child of Daedalus, the mystical carver of wooden images. But
revolution was in the air and in the mercantilism which followed
on the Persian Wars, skilled artisans were rising in the social scale.

Xanthippe, Socrates' wife, was the most notorious nag and
scold of all time. When rallied by Xenophon at the banquet as to
why he had married her, Socrates replied that a horseman did
not pick out the most easily broken colt, but rather one with the
highest spirits and a hard mouth on which to exercise his skill
of horsemanship. This he accounted for by saying: "having
designed to converse with all sorts of people, I believed I should
find nothing to disturb me in their conversation or manners, being
once accustomed to bear the unhappy temper of Xanthippe" (Xenophon: *Banquet;* Works, p. 605). Once when Socrates, according to his custom, was discoursing to a handful of disciples on
the street outside the door, Xanthippe is said to have launched
a bucket of kitchen slops upon him, whereupon he remarked that
where there was so much thunder one must expect some rain.
He characterized his work as that of an intellectual midwife,
which was not so much teaching people what they did not already
know as helping them to realize the truth of which they were
already more or less aware in the depths of their own being. This
he aimed to accomplish by directing at them certain leading questions, after the manner of the Sophists, at the end of which the
man, confused by questioning, reduced to a confession of complete ignorance, cleared of his opinionativeness, would produce
from his own inner consciousness and reasoning the correct answer.
Since the conclusion would seem to be his own, he would be all
the more surely convinced. The manner of cross-questioning
became known as the *Socratic Method,* while the capacity assumed
to be possessed by every man to find an answer in his own consciousness was named the *Socratic Principle.* Socrates himself
had constant resort to this inner consciousness which we would
perhaps call conscience, but which he called his "genius" or
daimonion. He also referred to himself in his famous defense
as "the gadfly of Athens." This was a reference to his habit
of going about the city engaging in conversation anyone who
would argue with him and asking these same people leading and

inconvenient questions, that is, showing up their ignorance. In this manner he pricked the bubble of many a pompous pretext and lost the friendship of the pretentious. These included some of the politicians of the day, as well as some who presumed to literary fame or social position, or even to others of his own social class who laid claim to superior artistic skill. It is not without significance that it was exactly from these classes that the charges came which eventuated in his execution.

The period in which Socrates lived was one of social turbulence and change, brought about by the wars with Persia, by the social and economic invasion from the East, and even more by the introduction of new cultures and new ideas which shook the world that had been, out of its condition of complacency. The age was one in which the old tribal organization was breaking up. Power was slipping from the hands of the large landowners and the establishment of a currency of exchange had made possible the coming to wealth of the commercial and artisan classes. The vastness of the totalitarian empires of the East was as yet unknown to the little Greek city-states in which the tribal condition and outlook had preserved the notion of democracy.

This notion was emphasized in the Greek mind by the ominous appearance on their horizon of so great an autocrat as Xerxes, with his threat to reduce them to utter slavery. From this they had been saved only by force of circumstances and the self-forgetting bravery of the Greeks who fought "the long-haired Medes at Marathon."

But the democracy that was now displacing the tribal autocracy was only partially democratic. A large portion of society was made up of slaves. So long as there was not a common coinage or currency of exchange, the landowner with his slaves was the only independent and financially self-contained member of society. With money came commerce and exchange of goods. Skilled workmen came into prominence as providing the basis of commerce. With commerce arose the growth and power of the cities and the city-state. But what democracy was known existed only for the smaller group of privileged people. By political connivance, groups of citizens were able to seize and maintain the power, as when the Thirty Tyrants ruled Athens. Democracy became oligarchy.

In the beginning Socrates seems to have been something of a radical. As a stone-cutter, that would be natural to one of his social standing. He had studied with the Sophists who were bent on the upset of existing institutions, defiance to old traditions and customs. He became profoundly interested in the new scientific learning of the time which was divesting his world of the traditional gods presumed to fight the tribal battles and who were supposed to play as favorites those who did homage to them. The new science had received a unique impetus in the concepts of Leucippus and Democritus, who held that all physical reality was made up of indivisible and invisible atoms. Such a science could not escape a tendency toward individualism and democracy, since all wholes were but collections of individual parts, each of equal importance. With his Sophist training, his scientific interest, and the rising importance of the class from which he sprang, it was but natural that the young Socrates should ally himself with the forces of liberalism. It was his misfortune, however, to see this liberalism which had promised so much for democracy turn under his very hand and eye into the worst form of oligarchy. On one notable occasion it fell to his lot to preside at the Athenian council at which it was proposed to condemn to death the eight generals who were charged with abandoning their armies.

It was designed to pass judgment by popular acclaim without trial, legal complaint, or defense, and Socrates aroused the wrath of the *demos* by refusing to put the question as being unconstitutional. Whether this or some earlier event or many events influenced his attitude, there is evidence of a wide change of sentiment on his part, a turning perhaps to the inner resources of his own mind and spirit, a refusal to participate further in political events, and a growing sympathy for, and association with, the Athenian upper classes, from which it was essential that his discipleship come if he were to be a teacher of men. Much of this must be read between the lines, much of it may be debatable, some may be legendary. However, the Socrates ridiculed by Aristophanes, friend of conservatism, is lampooned as a scientist trying in his "think-shop" to determine by the size of a flea's foot how many flea-feet there are in a flea jump, and to determine the source of the gnat's "hum." He is represented in this early comedy *The Clouds,* as displacing the ancient "Thunderer," Zeus, with the clouds which themselves produce thunder, lightning, and rain through natural rather than supernatural means. Above all, he is represented as using the Sophistic method of teaching the young men how to escape the laws of Athens by arguments which made the worse appear the better reason. All these were charged against the early Socrates, first advanced by Aristophanes, and revived at the trial of the old man of seventy, as being most likely to secure his conviction.

In the comedy *The Clouds,* Phidippides had overplayed the races, and between his gambling ventures and the support of a stable had all but ruined his father, Speucippus, who had heard that Socrates taught men so to argue in the courts as to be able to avoid the payment of their debts.   In his desperation he is represented in the comedy as attempting to put the young man into Socrates' school to become expert in debt repudiation.

Indicative of the low social standing of Socrates in early life is the ridicule underlying the remark of the young social climber Phidippides to his lower-class father, that if he enters Socrates' "thought factory" he will be socially ostracized by "the Knights," the gay young men who might be called the "Hollywood Set" of ancient Athens.

We have some inkling of change in the Socratic social standing in later plays of Aristophanes and in the late friendliness which seems to have developed between the sculptor-philosopher and the dramatist.   In *The Birds* (lines 1258-1294) Aristophanes harks back to the old days when "men went dirty like Socrates, and carried shillelaghs," and again where reference may be made to an acquired refinement in Socrates by referring to him (lines 1547-1578) as the "unwashed Socrates" who in the marsh "evokes the souls of men."

At least there seems to be an unexplained social difference between the despised stone-cutter and the Socrates who travels in the circle of Pericles, Phidias, and Aspasia, and fights in the ranks of the socially highest class Hoplites.   An effort to account for the apparent change in fortune is discoverable in the mythical introduction of Myrto, a rich widow, as his second wife, in the face of Plato's description of Xanthippe and her children in the dungeon of his execution.   But the changed social status may be accounted for quite naturally by the striking figure, the popular teaching, and the profound respect he had gained by his character, his life, and his philosophy, and an improved financial standing.

II

Confession of Ignorance the Gateway to Knowledge

Our modern theories of education have pretty generally accepted a part of the Socratic theory of education. They are favorable to the thought that education does not consist of pouring information into the minds of students, but rather of educing or drawing out the student's own powers by cultivating his own interests to self-expression. To this extent Socrates may be named the forerunner of the latest educational theory. But equally important with this in the mind of Socrates was the conviction with which the mind of the student must be imbued, that as yet he knew nothing. The whole purpose of the Socratic dialectic was to convince the student that hitherto his thought on a given subject had been superficial and hence only prejudiced opinion. So long as one thought himself wise, nothing could be done for him. The admission of ignorance was the first and necessary step to knowledge. Having forced from the learner the confession of ignorance and brought him to the position of listening to the argument in an unprejudiced spirit, then, and only then, did Socrates feel that it was possible for the pupil to find within himself the answer to his questions.

In fact, the Socratic method took so strong a hold upon Western civilization that to this day it is the practice of our own law courts, in bringing out the truth, to submit the witness to cross-examination in which leading questions are adroitly asked, which are likely to involve the disingenuous witness in contradictions which he has not foreseen and which will upset his direct testimony. The practice is exactly that of the Socratic method.

III

The Affirmations of the Inner Life

Implementing the Socratic Method was the Socratic Principle. Out of his Sophistic training Socrates had arrived at a profound agnosticism, if not atheism. His scientific studies had persuaded him that natural causes lay behind natural phenomena. This had led to a discarding of the belief in the potency of idols and of the old Greek gods. In truth, the Sophists had gone so far with their agnosticism that they declared there was no way of affirming truth about anything. Whatever one wished to be true, or was for his interest, or would afford him pleasure, could be assumed as true since there was no way of discovering absolute truth. Now that the gods were gone and could not longer be held as being displeased with human actions, one was to do whatever was for his profit to do. In other words, the old moral sanctions under the new scientific way of thinking seemed altogether wiped out.

There is little doubt that this was Socrates' concept as a young man.   As we have seen, one point of Aristophanes' caricature of Socrates in his comedy *The Clouds* hangs on this interpretation, and there must have been some truth in it or the force of the satire would not have been understood by the Athenians, who witnessed the play.   Socrates is represented as having forsaken belief in the old gods and to be praying to the forces of nature.   The clouds are reckoned as producing the thunder in the place of Zeus, the Thunderer; and Socrates is characterized as praying to the "Great Vortex."   The maintenance of Zeus and the worship of Athena and of the other gods and goddesses was conceived by the common people as identified with the welfare of Athens.   Fear of these deities was the means that kept the large slave population in subjection.   To teach the nonexistence of these powers, or rather to dissociate the forces of nature from these powers, was held treason against the state.   To teach this sort of thing to the young was thought to cultivate in them disrespect for rulers, parents, and the laws, and so Socrates was charged with corrupting the youth.

What Socrates was really trying to get at was dependence upon the testimony of the inner life.   He had been faced by a great question in his career as a Sophist, a question which would not down.   Were there no criteria by which courses of action could be judged right or wrong?   If the old standards laid down by the pagan religion, which demanded obedience to the gods, were gone, what would remain?   Absorbed in this question, Socrates remained standing on the training field, it is said, throughout a whole night while his soldier companions lay in their blankets to watch him in ridicule.   Out of this trance he emerged with a great affirmation; every man bore within himself the consciousness of right and wrong.   One could never do evil without feeling the wrongness within himself.   He need not go to the priest or inquire in the temple about the taboos as to whether any given course of action might be doubtful.   The question was a moral question, and he had only to inquire of his own soul.   His discovery was of a piece with the phrase of Robert Louis Stevenson in the Christmas Sermon: "to keep friends with one's self."

> To be honest, to be kind, to earn a little and to spend a little less: to make upon the whole, a family happier for his presence; to renounce when that shall be necessary and not be embittered; to have a few friends and those without capitulation; above all upon the same grim condition, to keep friends with one's self; this is a task for all that a man has of fortitude and delicacy.

Thus it was that Socrates arrived at the great and liberating principle of freedom. There is no just law against the good man or of which he may be afraid. Neither law of God nor of man. This inner witness of the spirit also is the gift of every man, "the light that lighteth every man that cometh into the world." In this discovery of Socrates we have the true basis of education and democracy. It is not necessary to consult the law, the magistrate, the priest, the institution, or even public opinion. Look within! *gnothe seauton*! Know thyself!

If the conversion that took place on the training field of the Hoplites was important, as disclosing to Socrates the democratic principle of the access to truth and right action, which is God's gift to every human being, there was a second conversion, even more important, which took place to complement and complete his philosophy of value. Of this conversion as well as of the first we have his own description. One day (*Phaedo* 97c), as he heard someone reading from a book of Anaxagoras, that it is mind which is the ordering principle and cause of everything, he was impressed with the insight that here at last was the ultimate origin of all causation, and he thought he had found a teacher after his own heart. So moved was he that he would not have sold his hopes "for a great sum of money" and rushed off to buy for himself the books Anaxagoras had written, reading them with breathless interest. On reading, he found this marvellous hope swept away since the author was disclosed as making no use of mind at all. Anaxagoras, after laying down so profound a principle, failed to profit by it and resorted to the old method of mechanical explanation, as if the posture of Socrates sitting on his cot in the Athenian jail was to be explained by the bones in his body and the joints in his legs instead of by his determination to obey the law of Athens, and by his refusal to escape. If these sinews and bones could have been consulted they would long ago have reached Megara or Boeotia, moved by their opinion of what is best. Existence itself he saw to be shot full of meaning and to be self-explanatory only on the basis of an indwelling and overshadowing intelligence. He had reached the first great insight of philosophy, that personality is the ultimate and important reality, for the ultimate cause can be no other than a causal intelligence exercised by a person human or divine.[1]

In refusing escape from the toils of his judges he had "chosen

---

[1] In this connection a most important comment is to be found in Duncan, *The Phaedo of Plato*, pp. 117-175.

the nobler and better part," and here truly was the seat of causation. Existence at this point is self-explanatory, self-caused, since no one could say that any external circumstance had dictated Socrates' decision. Here is disclosed the center of a true metaphysics of reality, the source of democracy, the basis of morality, and the heart of theism. If it was much to learn the necessity to "know one's self," it was still greater to realize the spiritual independence which came in the wake of such knowledge.

IV

Self-Knowledge and the Maintenance of Democratic Ideals

Gnothe seauton, "Know thyself," was the motto over the entrance to the famous oracle of Apollo at Delphi, where Socrates had been pronounced the wisest of men; this not because of what he knew, but because while others were ignorant and did not know it, he knew that he did not know. Thus he was in the way to higher knowledge. Not only was Socrates profoundly affected by contact with the oracle, whose words had been reported by Chaerephontes, but the motto of which I have spoken became the principle of his life. It was the acceptance of this precept that turned him from the observance of natural phenomena as the way to knowledge, to the observation of man himself as the key to wisdom. To the scientific emphasis placed upon the importance of every step in the natural processes, Socrates now added the concept of man himself as a necessary and nonnegligible part of that nature. Every man had a *daimonion,* or inner consciousness which would infallibly warn him against immoral action. If this is true, certain corollaries emerge. *First:* ethics is grounded in the nature of the universe and man, and the immoral man is an unnatural man, from whom nature herself will demand inevitable accounting. *Second:* since every man bears this witness within himself, every man, slave or free, must be seen as possessing an intrinsic value which society and government cannot overlook. This is of the very essence of freedom and the spirit of democracy. It raises the moral question as the most important for man to solve, and it assumes that every citizen has within his inner consciousness, the power to answer it by obeying the laws. The most precious amalgam of the state then is good-will. Without it the state will perish.

And last of all, since the integrity of personality is self-sustaining and self-accountable, we have the basis for a belief in immortality. Immortality appears self-evident to Socrates, because he discovers within himself that higher reality which, while using the world of matter, is not dependent upon it. The soul is immortal because its very essence is eternal, a capacity to be unmoved by the world of time and sense.

V

The Influence of Socratic Ideals on European Civilization

It is not easy to sum up the influence of so great a life as that of Socrates. One will either seem to fall short of full justice or to be extravagant in statement. Socrates was chiefly an innovator—a man who cast into the field of thought seed that could only ripen later and must be tended and harvested by other hands. A multitude of other men and institutions must needs make possible the results we here attribute to Socrates. Socraticism was germinal to the whole development of Western civilization, but of itself alone could not have found fulfillment. It was, *first* of all, a break with tradition. Socratic teaching was as unique as the man was himself peculiar. He broke with the traditional gods and directed attention to the divinity which is in every man. *Second:* he proclaimed the unquestionable authority of this inner voice as against all others, be they the fulminations of oracle, priest, tyrant, or demagogue. *Third:* the correlative of this was to lay down the new dream of democracy in which men listening to the higher voices of their own spirits should learn to live the life of reason and self-control, become conscious of the presence within them of an unconquerable soul, and should thus be free. *Fourth:* he taught the power of self-mastery which alone can implement democracy and make it workable. *Fifth:* he went to his death in order to demonstrate his respect for the laws of society. Though he felt himself unjustly condemned, he refused to save his life because to do so would seem to give sanction to law-breaking. *Sixth:* his teaching and discipleship prepared the Greek and Roman worlds for the introduction of Christianity: first, by the engendered respect for law which through the Stoic teaching had come both to dominate Roman administration and to make it agreeable to conquered peoples; this provided protection for the first missionaries and a peaceable state of society in which they could labor; second, in the mental and spiritual preparation by the philosophic sects which made ready the soil of the field of thought. Stoicism had carried the movement of civilization far, but it produced a loveless and callous world. Judaeo-Christianity brought in the lacking elements, whose absence was obvious as soon as it appeared. Stoicism survived in Christianity, which was able to absorb its best features and to go on to something better, and Judaism formed the amalgam that made their union possible.

In this manner the life and teachings of Socrates wove themselves into the warp and woof of Western society and in the light of them our civilization still lives.

READINGS

(Chapter 8)

DIALOGUES OF PLATO. Selections from Socrates' Defense at his
Trial, from *THE APOLOGY.* Modern Student's Library, Oxford
University Press, New York (by permission). Pp. 3-5, 6-9, 16-22, 25-27,
28, 29, 30, 31, 33.

=⟨⟩=

"I will begin at the beginning, and ask what is the accusation which
has given rise to the slander of me, and in fact has encouraged Meletus
to prefer this charge against me. Well, what do the slanderers say?
They shall be my prosecutors, and I will sum up their words in an
affidavit: 'Socrates is an evil-doer, and a curious person, who searches
into things under the earth and in heaven, and he makes the worse appear the better cause; and he teaches the aforesaid doctrines to others.'
Such is the nature of the accusation: it is just what you have yourselves seen in the comedy of Aristophanes, who has introduced a man
whom he calls Socrates, going about and saying that he walks in air,
and talking a deal of nonsense concerning matters of which I do not
pretend to know either much or little—not that I mean to speak dis-
paragingly of any one who is a student of natural philosophy. I should
be very sorry if Meletus could bring so grave a charge against me.
But the simple truth is, O Athenians, that I have nothing to do with
physical speculations. Very many of these here present are witnesses
to the truth of this, and to them I appeal. Speak then, you who have
heard me, and tell your neighbours whether any of you have ever known
me hold forth in few words, or in many, upon such matters. . . . You
hear their answer. And from what they say of this part of the charge
you will be able to judge of the truth of the rest.

"As little foundation is there for the report that I am a teacher,
and take money; this accusation has no more truth in it than the other.
Although, if a man were really able to instruct mankind, to receive
money for giving instruction would, in my opinion, be an honour to
him. There is Gorgias of Leontium, and Prodicus of Ceos, and Hippias
of Elis, who go the round of the cities, and are able to persuade the
young men to leave their own citizens by whom they might be taught
for nothing, and come to them whom they not only pay, but are thankful
if they may be allowed to pay them. . . . 'But [Socrates,] what is the
origin of these accusations which are brought against you; there must
have been something strange which you have been doing? All these
rumours and this talk about you would never have arisen if you had been
like other men: tell us, then, what is the cause of them, for we should be

sorry to judge hastily of you.' Now I regard this as a fair challenge, and I will endeavour to explain to you the reason why I am called wise and have such an evil fame. . . . Men of Athens, this reputation of mine has come of a certain sort of wisdom which I possess. If you ask me what kind of wisdom, I reply, wisdom such as may perhaps be attained by man, for to that extent I am inclined to believe that I am wise; whereas the persons of whom I was speaking have a super-human wisdom, which I may fail to describe, because I have it not myself; and he who says that I have, speaks falsely, and is taking away my character. . . . I will refer you to a witness who is worthy of credit; that witness shall be the God of Delphi—he will tell you about my wisdom, if I have any, and of what sort it is. You must have known Chaerephon; he was early a friend of mine and also a friend of yours, for he shared in the recent exile of the people, and returned with you. Well, Chaerephon, as you know, was very impetuous in all his doings, and he went to Delphi and boldly asked the oracle to tell him whether . . . any one was wiser than I was, and the Pythian prophetess answered, that there was no man wiser. Chaerephon is dead himself; but his brother, who is in court, will confirm the truth of what I am saying.

"Why do I mention this? Because I am going to explain to you why I have such an evil name. When I heard the answer, I said to myself, What can the god mean? and what is the interpretation of his riddle? for I know that I have no wisdom, small or great. What then can he mean when he says that I am the wisest of men? And yet he is a god, and cannot lie; that would be against his nature. After long consideration, I thought of a method of trying the question. I reflected that if I could only find a man wiser than myself, then I might go to the god with a refutation in my hand. I should say to him, 'Here is a man who is wiser than I am; but you said that I was the wisest.' Accordingly I went to one who had the reputation of wisdom, and observed him—his name I need not mention; he was a politician whom I selected for examination—and the result was as follows: When I began to talk with him, I could not help thinking that he was not really wise, although he was thought wise by many, and still wiser by him-self, and thereupon I tried to explain to him that he thought himself wise, but was not really wise; and the consequence was that he hated me, and his enmity was shared by several who were present and heard me. So I left him, saying to myself, as I went away: Well, although I do not suppose that either of us knows anything really beautiful and good, I am better off than he is,—for he knows nothing, and thinks that he knows; I neither know nor think that I know. In this latter particular, then, I seem to have slightly the advantage of him. Then I went to another who had still higher pretensions to wisdom, and my conclusion was exactly the same. Whereupon I made another enemy of him, and of many others besides him.

"Then I went to one man after another, being not unconscious of the enmity which I provoked, and I lamented and feared this: but necessity was laid upon me,—the word of God, I thought, ought to be considered first. And I said to myself, Go I must to all who appear to know, and find out the meaning of the oracle. And I swear to you, Athenians, by the dog I swear!—for I must tell you the truth—the result of my mission was just this: I found that the men most in repute were all but the most foolish; and that others less esteemed were really wiser and better. I will tell you the tale of my wanderings and of the 'Herculean' labours, as I may call them, which I endured only to find at last the oracle irrefutable. After the politicians, I went to the poets; tragic, dithyrambic, and all sorts. And there, I said to myself, you will be instantly detected; now you will find out that you are more ignorant than they are. Accordingly, I took them some of the most elaborate passages in their own writings, and asked what was the meaning of them—thinking that they would teach me something. Will you believe me? I am almost ashamed to confess the truth, but I must say that there is hardly a person present who would not have talked better about their poetry than they did themselves. Then I knew that not by wisdom do poets write poetry, but by a sort of genius and inspiration; they are like diviners or soothsayers who also say many fine things, but do not understand the meaning of them. The poets appeared to me to be much in the same case; and I further observed that upon the strength of their poetry they believed themselves to be the wisest of men in other things in which they were not wise. So I departed, conceiving myself to be superior to them for the same reason that I was superior to the politicians.

"At last I went to the artisans. I was conscious that I knew nothing at all, as I may say, and I was sure that they knew many fine things; and here I was not mistaken, for they did know many things of which I was ignorant, and in this they certainly were wiser than I was. But I observed that even the good artisans fell into the same error as the poets;—because they were good workmen they thought that they also knew all sorts of high matters, and this defect in them overshadowed their wisdom; and therefore I asked myself on behalf of the oracle, whether I would like to be as I was, neither having their knowledge nor their ignorance, or like them in both; and I made answer to myself and to the oracle that I was better off as I was.

"This inquisition has led to my having many enemies of the worst and most dangerous kind, and has given occasion also to many calumnies. And I am called wise, for my hearers always imagine that I myself possess the wisdom which I find wanting in others: but the truth is, O men of Athens, that God only is wise; and by his answer he intends to show that the wisdom of men is worth little or nothing; he is not speaking of Socrates, he is only using my name by way of illustration, as if he said, He, O men, is the wisest, who, like Socrates, knows that his wisdom is in truth worth nothing. And so I go about the world, obedient to the god, and search and make inquiry into the wisdom of any one, whether citizen or stranger, who appears to be wise; and if he is not wise, then in vindication of the oracle I show him that he is not wise; and my occupation quite absorbs me, and I have no time to give either to any public matter of interest or to any concern of my own, but I am in utter poverty by reason of my devotion to the god.

"There is another thing:—young men of the richer classes, who have not much to do, come about me of their own accord; they like to hear the pretenders examined, and they often imitate me, and proceed to examine others; there are plenty of persons, as they quickly discover, who think that they know something, but really know little or nothing; and then those who are examined by them instead of being angry with themselves are angry with me: This confounded Socrates, they say; this villainous misleader of youth! and then if somebody asks them, Why, what evil does he practise or teach? they do not know, and cannot tell; but in order that they may not appear to be at a loss, they repeat the ready-made charges which are used against all philosophers about teaching things up in the clouds and under the earth, and having no gods, and making the worse appear the better cause; for they do not like to confess that their pretence of knowledge has been detected—which is the truth; and as they are numerous and ambitious and energetic, and are drawn up in battle array and have persuasive tongues, they have filled your ears with their loud and inveterate calumnies. And this is the reason why my three accusers, Meletus and Anytus and Lycon, have set upon me; Meletus, who has a quarrel with me on behalf of the poets; Anytus, on behalf of the craftsmen and politicians; Lycon, on behalf of the rhetoricians: and as I said at the beginning, I cannot expect to get rid of such a mass of calumny all in a moment. . . .

"Some one will say: And are you not ashamed, Socrates, of a course of life which is likely to bring you to an untimely end? To him I may fairly answer: There you are mistaken: a man who is good for anything ought not to calculate the chance of living or dying; he ought only to consider whether in doing anything he is doing right or wrong—acting the part of a good man or of a bad. Whereas, upon your view, the heroes who fell at Troy were not good for much, and the son of Thetis above all, who altogether despised danger in comparison with disgrace; and when he was so eager to slay Hector, his goddess mother said to him, that if he avenged his companion Patroclus, and slew Hector, he would die himself—'Fate,' she said, in these or the like words, 'waits for you next after Hector'; he, receiving this warning, utterly despised danger and death, and instead of fearing them, feared rather to live in dishonour, and not to avenge his friend. 'Let me die forthwith,' he replies, 'and be avenged of my enemy, rather than abide here by the beaked ships, a laughing-stock and a burden of the earth.' Had Achilles any thought of death and danger? For wherever a man's place is, whether the place which he has chosen or that in which he has been placed by a commander, there he ought to remain in the hour of danger; he should not think of death or of anything but of disgrace. And this, O men of Athens, is a true saying.

"Strange, indeed, would be my conduct, O men of Athens, if I who, when I was ordered by the generals whom you chose to command me at Potidaea and Amphipolis and Delium, had remained where they placed me, like any other man, facing death—if now, when, as I conceive and imagine, God orders me to fulfill the philosopher's mission of searching into myself and other men, I were to desert my post through fear of death, or any other fear; that would indeed be strange, and I might justly be arraigned in court for denying the existence of the gods, if I disobeyed the oracle because I was afraid of death, fancying that I was wise when I was not wise. For the fear of death is indeed the pretence of wisdom, and not real wisdom, being a pretence of knowing the unknown, and no one knows whether death, which men in their fear apprehend to be the greatest evil, may not be the greatest good. Is not this ignorance of a disgraceful sort, the ignorance which is the conceit that a man knows what he does not know? And in this respect only I believe myself to differ from men in general, and may perhaps claim to be wiser than they are:—that whereas I know but little of the world below, I do not suppose that I know: but I do know that injustice and disobedience to a better, whether God or man, is evil and dishonourable, and I will never fear or avoid a possible good rather than a certain evil. And therefore if you let me go now, and are not convinced by Anytus, who said that since I had been prosecuted I must be put to death; (or if not that I ought never to have been prosecuted at all); and that if I escape now, your sons will all be utterly ruined by listening to my words—if you say to me, Socrates, this time we will not mind Anytus, and you shall be let off, but upon one condition, that you are not to enquire and speculate in this way any more, and that if you are caught doing so again you shall die;— if this was the condition on which you let me go, I should reply: Men of Athens, I honour and love you; but I shall obey God rather than you, and while I have life and strength I shall never cease from the practice and teaching of philosophy, exhorting any one whom I meet and saying to him after my manner: You, my friend,—a citizen of the great and mighty and wise city of Athens,—are you not ashamed of heaping up the greatest amount of money and honour and reputation, and caring so little about wisdom and truth and the greatest improvement of the soul, which you never regard or heed at all. And if the person with whom I am arguing, says: Yes, but I do care; then I do not leave him or let him go at once; but I proceed to interrogate and examine and cross-examine him, and if I think that he has no virtue in him, but only says that he has, I reproach him with undervaluing the greater, and overvaluing the less. And I shall repeat the same words to everyone whom I meet, young and old, citizen and alien, but especially to the citizens, inasmuch as they are my brethren. For know that this is the command of God; and I believe that no greater good has ever happened in the state than my service to the God. For I do nothing but go about persuading you all, old and young alike, not to take thought for your persons or your properties, but first and chiefly to care about the greatest improvement of the soul. I tell you that virtue is not given by money, but that from virtue comes money and every other good of man, public as well as private. This is my teaching, and if this is the doctrine which corrupts the youth, I am a mischievous person. But if any one says that this is not my teaching, he is speaking an untruth. Wherefore, O men of Athens, I say to you, do as Anytus bids or not as Anytus bids, and either acquit me or not; but whichever you do, understand that I shall never alter my ways, not even if I have to die many times.

"Men of Athens, . . . I have something more to say, at which you may be inclined to cry out; but I believe that to hear me will be good for you, and therefore I beg that you will not cry out. I would have you know, that if you kill such an one as I am, you will injure yourselves more than you will injure me. Nothing will injure me, not Meletus nor yet Anytus —they cannot, for a bad man is not permitted to injure a better than himself. I do not deny that Anytus may, perhaps, kill him, or drive him into exile, or deprive him of civil rights; and he may imagine, and others may imagine, that he is inflicting a great injury upon him: but there I do not agree. For the evil of doing as he is doing—the evil of unjustly taking away the life of another—is greater far.

"And now, Athenians, I am not going to argue for my own sake, as you may think, but for yours, that you may not sin against the God by condemning me, who am his gift to you. For if you kill me you will not easily find a successor to me, who, if I may use such a ludicrous figure of speech, am a sort of gadfly, given to the state by God; and the state is a great and noble steed who is tardy in his motions owing to his very size, and requires to be stirred into life. I am that gadfly which God has attached to the state, and all day long and in all places am always fastening upon you, arousing and persuading and reproaching you. You will not easily find another like me, and therefore I would advise you to spare me. I dare say that you may feel out of temper (like a person who is suddenly awakened from sleep), and you think that you might easily strike me dead as Anytus advises, and then you would sleep on for the remainder of your lives, unless God in his care of you sent you another gadfly. When I say that I am given to you by God, the proof of my mission is this :—if I had been like other men, I should have not neglected all my own concerns or patiently seen the neglect of them during all these years, and have been doing yours, coming to you indi- vidually like a father or elder brother, exhorting you to regard virtue; such conduct, I say, would be unlike human nature. If I had gained anything, or if my exhortations had been paid, there would have been some sense in my doing so; but now, as you will perceive, not even the impudence of my accusers dares to say that I have ever exacted or sought pay of any one; of that they have no witness. And I have a sufficient witness to the truth of what I say—my poverty.

"Some one may wonder why I go about in private giving advice and busying myself with the concerns of others, but do not venture to come forward in public and advise the state. I will tell you why. You have heard me speak at sundry times and in divers places of an oracle or sign which comes to me, and is the divinity which Meletus ridicules in the indictment. This sign, which is a kind of voice, first began to come to me when I was a child; it always forbids but never commands me to do anything which I am going to do. This is what deters me from being a politician. And rightly, as I think. For I am certain, O men of Athens, that if I had engaged in politics, I should have perished long ago, and done no good either to you or to myself. And do not be offended at my telling you the truth: for the truth is, that no man who goes to war with you or any other multitude, honestly striving against the many lawless and unrighteous deeds which are done in a state, will save his life; he who will fight for the right, if he would live even for a brief space, must have a private station and not a public one.

"I can give you convincing evidence of what I say, not words only, but what you value far more—actions. Let me relate to you a passage of my own life which will prove to you that I should never have yielded to injustice from any fear of death, and that 'as I should have refused to yield' I must have died at once. I will tell you a tale of the courts, not very interesting perhaps, but nevertheless true. The only office of state which I ever held, O men of Athens, was that of senator: the tribe Antiochis, which is my tribe, had the presidency at the trial of the generals who had not taken up the bodies of the slain after the battle of Arginusae; and you proposed to try them in a body, contrary to law, as you all thought afterwards; but at the time I was the only one of the Prytanes who was opposed to the illegality, and I gave my vote against you; and when the orators threatened to impeach and arrest me, and you called and shouted, I made up my mind that I would run the risk, having law and justice with me, rather than take part in your injustice because I feared imprisonment and death. This happened in the days of the democracy. But when the oligarchy of the Thirty was in power, they sent for me and four others into the rotunda, and bade us bring Leon the Salaminian from Salamis, as they wanted to put him to death. This was a specimen of the sort of commands which they were always giving with the view of implicating as many as possible in their crimes; and then I showed, not in word only but in deed, that, if I may be allowed to use such an expression, I cared not a straw for death, and that my great and only care was lest I should do an unrighteous or unholy thing. For the strong arm of that oppressive power did not frighten me into doing wrong; and when we came out of the rotunda the other four went to Salamis and fetched Leon, but I went quietly home. For which I might have lost my life, had not the power of the Thirty shortly afterwards come to an end. And many will witness to my words. . . .

"I do believe that there are gods, and in a sense higher than that in which any of my accusers believe in them. And to you and to God I commit my cause, to be determined by you as is best for you and me."

[The vote is taken and is adverse]

"There are many reasons why I am not grieved, O men of Athens, at the vote of condemnation. I expected it, and am only surprised that the votes are so nearly equal; for I had thought that the majority against me would have been far larger; but now, had thirty votes gone over to the other side, I should have been acquitted. And I may say, I think, that I have escaped Meletus. I may say more; for without the assistance of Anytus and Lycon, any one may see that he would not have had a fifth part of the votes, as the law requires, in which case he would have incurred a fine of a thousand drachmae.

"And so he proposes death as the penalty. And what shall I propose on my part, O men of Athens? Clearly that which is my due. And what is my due? What return shall be made to the man who has never had the wit to be idle during his whole life; but has been careless of what the many care for—wealth, and family interests, and military offices, and speaking in the assembly, and magistracies, and plots, and parties. Reflecting that I was really too honest a man to be a politician and live, I did not go where I could do no good to you or to myself; but where I could do the greatest good privately to every one of you, thither I went, and sought to persuade every man among you that he must look to himself, and seek virtue and wisdom before he looks to his private interests, and look to the state before he looks to the interests of the state; and that this should be the order which he observes in all his actions. What shall be done to such an one? Doubtless some good thing, O men of Athens, if he has his reward; and the good should be of a kind suitable to him. What would be a reward suitable to a poor man who is your benefactor, and who desires leisure that he may instruct you? There can be no reward so fitting as maintenance in the Prytaneum, O men of Athens, a reward which he deserves far more than the citizen who has won the prize at Olympia in the horse or chariot race, whether the chariots were drawn by two horses or by many. For I am in want, and he has enough; and he only gives you the appearance of happiness, and I give you the reality. And if I am to estimate the penalty fairly, I should say that maintenance in the Prytaneum is the just return.

". . . And if I say exile (and this may possibly be the penalty which you will affix), I must indeed be blinded by the love of life, if I am so irrational as to expect that when you, who are my own citizens, cannot endure my discourses and words, and have found them so grievous and odious that you will have no more of them, others are likely to endure me. No indeed, men of Athens, that is not very likely. And what a life should I lead, at my age, wandering from city to city, ever changing my place of exile, and always being driven out! For I am quite sure that wherever I go, there, as here, the young men will flock to me; and if I drive them away, their elders will drive me out at their request; and if I let them come, their fathers and friends will drive me out for their sakes.

"Some one will say: Yes, Socrates, but cannot you hold your tongue, and then you may go into a foreign city, and no one will interfere with you? Now I have great difficulty in making you understand my answer to this. If I tell you that to do as you say would be a disobedience to the God, and therefore that I cannot hold my tongue, you will not believe that I am serious; and if I say again that daily to discourse about virtue, and of those other things about which you hear me examining myself and others, is the greatest good of man, and that the unexamined life is not worth living, you are still less likely to believe me. . . ."

[After the Sentence]

". . . You think that I was convicted because I had no words of the sort which would have procured my acquittal—I mean, if I had thought fit to leave nothing undone or unsaid. Not so; the deficiency which led to my conviction was not of words—certainly not. But I had not the boldness or impudence or inclination to address you as you would have liked me to do, weeping and wailing and lamenting, and saying and doing many things which you have been accustomed to hear from others, and which, as I maintain, are unworthy of me. I thought at the time that I ought not to do anything common or mean when in danger: nor do I now repent of the style of my deference; I would rather die having spoken after my manner, than speak in your manner and live. For neither in war nor yet at law ought I or any man to use every way of escaping death. Often in battle there can be no doubt that if a man will throw away his arms, and fall on his knees before his pursuers, he may escape death; and in other dangers there are other ways of escaping death, if a man is willing to say and do anything. The difficulty, my friends, is not to avoid death, but to avoid unrighteousness; for that runs faster than death. I am old and move slowly, and the slower runner has overtaken me, and my accusers are keen and quick, and the faster runner, who is unrighteousness, has overtaken them. And now I depart hence condemned by you to suffer the penalty of death,—they too go their ways condemned by the truth to suffer, the penalty of villainy and wrong; and I must abide by my award—let them abide by theirs. . . .

"Friends, who would have acquitted me, I would like also to talk with you about the thing which has come to pass, while the magistrates are busy, and before I go to the place at which I must die. Stay then a little, for we may as well talk with one another while there is time. You are my friends, and I should like to show you the meaning of this event which has happened to me. O my judges—for you I may truly call judges—I should like to tell you of a wonderful circumstance. Hitherto the divine faculty of which the internal oracle is the source has constantly been in the habit of opposing me even about trifles, if I was going to make a slip or error in any matter; and now as you see there has come upon me that which may be thought, and is generally believed to be, the last and worst evil. But the oracle made no sign of opposition, either when I was leaving my house in the morning, or when I was on my way to the court, or while I was speaking, at anything which I was going to say; and yet I have often been stopped in the middle of a speech, but now in nothing I either said or did touching the matter in hand has the oracle opposed me. What do I take to be the explanation of this silence? I will tell you. It is an intimation that what has happened to me is a good, and that those of us who think that death is an evil are in error. For the customary sign would surely have opposed me had I been going to evil and not to good. . . .

"Wherefore, O judges, be of good cheer about death, and know of a certainty, that no evil can happen to a good man, either in life or after death. He and his are not neglected by the gods; nor has my own approaching end happened by mere chance. But I see clearly that the time had arrived when it was better for me to die and be released from trouble; wherefore the oracle gave no sign. For which reason, also, I am not angry with my condemners, or with my accusers; they have done me no harm, although they did not mean to do me any good; and for this I may gently blame them.

"Still I have a favour to ask of them. When my sons are grown up, I would ask you, O my friends, to punish them; and I would have you trouble them, as I have troubled you, if they seem to care about riches, or anything, more than about virtue; or if they pretend to be something when they are really nothing,—then reprove them, as I have reproved you, for not caring about that for which they ought to care, and thinking that they are something when they are really nothing. And if you do this, both I and my sons will have received justice at your hands.

"The hour of departure has arrived, and we go our ways—I to die, and you to live. Which is better God only knows."

DIALOGUES OF PLATO: THE DEATH OF SOCRATES, from *THE PHAEDO.* Modern Student's Library, Oxford University Press, New York (by permission). Pp. 147-151, 203, 204, 205-207, 228, 229-233.

PERSONS OF THE DIALOGUE

PHAEDO, who is the narrator of the
Dialogue to
ECHECRATES of Phlius
SOCRATES
ATTENDANT OF THE PRISON

APOLLODORUS

SIMMIAS
CERES
CRITO

SCENE:—The Prison of Socrates

PLACE OF THE NARRATION—Phlius

SECTION 57

Echecrates. Were you yourself, Phaedo, in the prison with Socrates on the day when he drank the poison?

Phaedo. Yes, Echecrates, I was.

Ech. I should so like to hear about his death. What did he say in his last hours? We were informed that he died by taking poison, but no one knew anything more; for no Phliasian ever goes to Athens now, and it is a long time since any stranger from Athens has found his way hither; so that we had no clear account.

Phaed. Did you not hear of the proceedings at the trial?

Ech. Yes; some one told us about the trial, and we could not understand why, having been condemned, he should have been put to death, not at the time, but long afterwards. What was the reason of this?

Phaed. An accident, Echecrates: the stern of the ship which the Athenians send to Delos happened to have been crowned on the day before he was tried.

Ech. What is this ship?

Phaed. It is the ship in which, according to Athenian tradition, Theseus went to Crete when he took with him the fourteen youths, and was the saviour of them and of himself. And they are said to have vowed to Apollo at the time, that if they were saved they would send a yearly mission to Delos. Now this custom still continues, and the whole period of the voyage to and from Delos, beginning when the priest of Apollo crowns the stern of the ship, is a holy season, during which the city is not allowed to be polluted by public executions; and when the vessel is detained by contrary winds, the time spent in going and returning is very considerable. As I was saying, the ship was crowned on the day before the trial, and this was the reason why Socrates lay in prison and was not put to death until long after he was condemned.

Ech. What was the manner of his death, Phaedo? What was said or done? And which of his friends were with him? Or did the authorities forbid them to be present—so that he had no friends near him when he died?

Phaed. No; there were several of them with him.

Ech. If you have nothing to do, I wish that you would tell me what passed, as exactly as you can.

Phaed. I have nothing at all to do, and will try to gratify your wish. To be reminded of Socrates is always the greatest delight to me, whether I speak myself or hear another speak of him.

Ech. You will have listeners who are of the same mind with you, and I hope that you will be as exact as you can.

Phaed. I had a singular feeling at being in his company. For I could hardly believe that I was present at the death of a friend, and therefore I did not pity him, Echecrates; he died so fearlessly, and his words and bearing were so noble and gracious, that to me he appeared blessed. I thought that in going to the other world he could not be without a divine call, and that he would be happy, if any man ever was, when he arrived there; and therefore I did not pity him as might have seemed natural at such an hour. But I had not the pleasure which I usually feel in philosophical discourse (for philosophy was the theme of which we spoke). I was pleased, but in the pleasure there was also a strange admixture of pain; for I reflected that he was soon to die, and this double feeling was shared by us all; we were laughing and weeping by turns, especially the excitable Apollodorus—you know the sort of man? . . .

Phaed. I will begin at the beginning, and endeavour to repeat the entire conversation. On the previous days we had been in the habit of assembling early in the morning at the court in which the trial took place, and which is not far from the prison. There we used to wait talking with one another until the opening of the doors (for they were not opened very early); then we went in and generally passed the day with Socrates. On the last morning we assembled sooner than usual, having heard on the day before when we quitted the prison in the evening, that the sacred ship had come from Delos; and so we arranged to meet very early at the accustomed place. On our arrival the jailer who answered the door, instead of admitting us, came out and told us to stay until he called us. "For the Eleven," he said, "are now with Socrates; they are taking off his chains, and giving orders that he is to die to-day." He soon returned and said that we might come in. On entering we found Socrates just released from chains, and Xanthippe, whom you know, sitting by him, and holding his child in her arms. When she saw us she uttered a cry and said, as women will: "O Socrates, this is the last time that either you will converse with your friends, or they with you." Socrates turned to Crito and said: "Crito, let some one take her home." Some of Crito's people accordingly led her away, crying out and beating herself. And when she was gone, Socrates, sitting up on the couch, bent and rubbed his leg, saying, as he was rubbing: How singular is the thing called pleasure, and how curiously related to pain, which might be thought to be the opposite of it; for they are never present to a man at the same instant, and yet he who pursues either is generally compelled to take the other; their bodies are two, but they are joined by a single head. And I cannot help thinking that if Aesop had remembered them, he would have made a fable about God trying to reconcile their strife, and how, when he could not, he fastened their heads together; and this is the reason why when one comes the other follows: as I know by my own experience now, when after the pain in my leg which was caused by the chain, pleasure appears to succeed. . . .

"When I was young, Cebes, said he, I was wonderfully eager for the knowledge that is called natural science. It seemed to me marvellously contrived for knowing the causes of each thing—why it comes to be, why it perishes, and why it exists. And I would constantly turn my mind this way and that—first on inquiries such as this, namely whether, as some maintained, it is when the elements of heat and cold take on a sort of putrefaction that living things assimilate nourishment? And again whether we must dismiss all these and hold that it is the brain which gives rise to the perceptions of hearing and sight and smell, and that out of these materials would come memory and opinion, and out of memory and opinion, having reached a state of rest, knowledge comes into being? Again, I would inquire into the processes of decay in these things and into the changes of the heavens and the earth till in the end I seemed to myself hopelessly unfit for this sort of study. . . .

"One day, however, I heard some one reading from a book of Anaxagoras, as he said, and saying that it is mind which is the ordering principle and the cause of everything. Here at last was a cause which I welcomed. It seemed to me in a way to be good—the principle that mind is the cause of everything—and I thought that, if this were true, then this mind, as the principle of order, would bring everything in order, and dispose each as it is best for it to be. It would follow that if any one should wish to find the cause in respect of each particular thing—how it comes into being or perishes or exists—what he must find out about it is how it is best for it to exist or to possess any other quality or activity. I thought, too, as a consequence of this theory, that a man in studying himself or any other object need look for no other principle but that of what is the best and most desirable. He would necessarily also know what is the worse in each case, since the knowledge of the better and the worse is the same. Now, as I pondered over these things, I was delighted to think that I had found in Anaxagoras a teacher after my own heart of the cause in relation to things. I thought he would tell me first whether the earth is flat or round, and, when he did so, would go on to explain the cause and necessity, on the principle of the better and because it was better for it to be such. Further, if he should say that it is in the centre of the universe he would go on to explain how it was better that it should be in the centre. If he should demonstrate this I was ready to ask for no other sort of cause. I was ready to make the like investigation about the sun and the moon and the stars, as to the speed of their motions in relation to each other, their turnings in their courses, and their other attributes—inquiring in what respect it was better that each of them should so act and be acted upon. I should never have thought that he, holding as he did that they had been set in order by mind, would import any other cause into them, than that it is best that they should be as they are. I thought, therefore, that in assigning a cause to each of them individually, and collectively to all, he would go on to demonstrate the best for each of them and the good which is common to all. I would not have sold my hopes for a great sum of money. In all haste I got the books and proceeded to read them as quickly as I could, so that as soon as possible I might know the greatest good and the less good.

"Well, my friend, it was truly a marvellous hope from which I was swept away, when on going forward with my reading I found a man making no use of mind at all, and not looking to it for causes as regards the ordering of the world, but finding the causes in various sorts of air and ether and water and many other absurdities. He seemed to me to be in a very similar position to a man who should say that Socrates does all that he does by mind, and then when trying to explain the causes of each of my acts should begin by saying that this is the cause that I am sitting here now—namely, that my body is composed of bones and sinews, and the bones together with the muscles and the skin which is the covering of them all, and should then go on to say that, as the bones swing in their joints, the sinews by relaxation and contraction cause my limbs to be capable of bending, and that is the cause of my sitting here with my legs doubled up. Again, he would assign similar causes for my talking with you—voices and currents of air and sensations of hearing and a thousand such things—ignoring the real causes, namely that as the Athenians thought it better to condemn me, so I thought it better to sit here and juster to remain and abide whatever judgment they should decree. Yes, by the dog, I fancy these sinews and bones would long ago have been in the region of Megara or Boeotia, moved by their opinion of what is best, if I had not thought it juster and nobler not to escape and run away, but to make good to the city whatever judgment it may ordain. But to call such things causes is too absurd. If you should say that without having such things—that is bones and sinews and the organs which I have— I should not have been able to do what I decided upon, you would be right. But to say that because of these organs I do what I do (and that too while I am guided by mind in my actions) and not from my choice of the best, would show a great and inveterate slackness of thought. It means being unable to distinguish that the real cause is quite different from that without which the cause would never be a cause."

[After an extended discussion of immortality]

"Wherefore, Simmias, seeing all these things, what ought not we to do that we may obtain virtue and wisdom in this life? Fair is the prize, and the hope great!

"A man of sense ought not to say, nor will I be very confident, that the description which I have given of the soul and her mansions is exactly true. But I do say that, inasmuch as the soul is shown to be immortal, he may venture to think, not improperly or unworthily, that something of the kind is true. The venture is a glorious one, and he ought to comfort himself with words like these, which is the reason why I lengthen out the tale. Wherefore, I say, let a man be of good cheer about his soul, who having cast away the pleasures and ornaments of the body as alien to him and working harm rather than good, has sought after the pleasures of knowledge; and has arrayed the soul, not in some foreign attire, but in her own proper jewels, temperance, and justice, and courage, and nobility, and truth—in these adorned she is ready to go on her journey to the world below, when her hour comes. You, Simmias and Cebes, and all other men, will depart at some time or other. Me already, as a tragic poet would say, the voice of fate calls. Soon I must drink the poison; and I think that I had better repair to the bath first, in order that the women may not have the trouble of washing my body after I am dead.

"When he had done speaking, Crito said: And have you any commands for us, Socrates—anything to say about your children, or any other matter in which we can serve you?

"Nothing particular, Crito, he replied: only, as I have always told you, take care of yourselves; that is a service which you may be ever rendering to me and mine and to all of us, whether you promise to do so or not. But if you have no thought for yourselves, and care not to walk according to the rule which I have prescribed for you, not now for the first time, however much you may profess or promise at the moment, it will be of no avail.

"We will do our best, said Crito: And in what way shall we bury you?

"In any way that you like; but you must get hold of me, and take care that I do not run away from you. Then he turned to us, and added with a smile:—I cannot make Crito believe that I am the same Socrates who have been talking and conducting the argument: he fancies that I am the other Socrates whom he will soon see, a dead body —and he asks, How shall he bury me? And though I have spoken many words in the endeavour to show that when I have drunk the poison I shall leave you and go to the joys of the blessed,—these words of mine, with which I was comforting you and myself, have had, as I perceive, no effect upon Crito. And therefore I want you to be surety for me to him now, as at the trial he was surety to the judges for me: but let the promise be of another sort; for he was surety for me to the judges that I would remain, and you must be my surety to him that I shall not remain, but go away and depart; and then he will suffer less at my death, and not be grieved when he sees my body being burned or buried.   I would not have him sorrow at my hard lot, or say at the burial, Thus we lay out Socrates, or, Thus we follow him to the grave or bury him; for false words are not only evil in themselves, but they infect the soul with evil.   Be of good cheer then, my dear Crito, and say that you are burying my body only, and do with that whatever is usual, and what you think best.

"When he had spoken these words, he arose and went into a chamber to bathe; Crito followed him and told us to wait.   So we remained behind, talking and thinking of the subject of discourse, and also of the greatness of our sorrow; he was like a father of whom we were being bereaved, and we were about to pass the rest of our lives as orphans. When he had taken the bath his children were brought to him—(he had two young sons and an elder one); and the women of his family also came, and he talked to them and gave them a few directions in the presence of Crito; then he dismissed them and returned to us.

"Now the hour of sunset was near, for a good deal of time had passed while he was within.   When he came out, he sat down with us again after his bath, but not much was said.   Soon the jailer, who was the servant of the Eleven, entered and stood by him, saying:—To you, Socrates, whom I know to be the noblest and gentlest and best of all who ever came to this place, I will not impute the angry feelings of other men, who rage and swear at me, when, in obedience to the authorities, I bid them drink the poison—indeed, I am sure that you will not be angry with me; for others, as you are aware, and not I, are to blame. And so fare you well, and try to bear lightly what must needs be— you know my errand.   Then bursting into tears he turned away and went out.

"Socrates looked at him and said: I return your good wishes, and will do as you bid.   Then turning to us, he said, How charming the man is: since I have been in prison he has always been coming to see me, and at times he would talk to me, and was as good to me as could be, and now see how generously he sorrows on my account.   We must do as he says, Crito; and therefore let the cup be brought, if the poison is prepared: if not, let the attendant prepare some.

"Yet, said Crito, the sun is still upon the hill-tops, and I know that many a one has taken the draught late, and after the announcement has been made to him, he has eaten and drunk, and enjoyed the society of his beloved; do not hurry—there is time enough.

"Socrates said: Yes, Crito, and they of whom you speak are right in so acting, for they think that they will be gainers by the delay; but I am right in not following their example, for I do not think that I should gain anything by drinking the poison a little later; I should only be ridiculous in my own eyes for sparing and saving a life which is already forfeit.   Please then to do as I say, and not to refuse me.

"Crito made a sign to the servant, who was standing by; and he went out, and having been absent for some time, returned with the jailer carrying the cup of poison. Socrates said: You, my good friend, who are experienced in these matters, shall give me directions how I am to proceed. The man answered: You have only to walk about until your legs are heavy, and then to lie down, and the poison will act. At the same time he handed the cup to Socrates, who in the easiest and gentlest manner, without the least fear or change of colour or feature, looking at the man with all his eyes, Echecrates, as his manner was, took the cup and said: What do you say about making a libation out of this cup to any god? May I, or not? The man answered: We only prepare, Socrates, just so much as we deem enough. I understand, he said: but I may and must ask the gods to prosper my journey from this to the other world—even so—and so be it according to my prayer. Then raising the cup to his lips, quite readily and cheerfully he drank off the poison. And hitherto most of us had been able to control our sorrow; but now when we saw him drinking, and saw too that he had finished the draught, we could no longer forbear, and in spite of myself my own tears were flowing fast; so that I covered my face and wept, not for him, but at the thought of my own calamity in having to part from such a friend. Nor was I the first; for Crito, when he found himself unable to restrain his tears, had got up, and I followed; and at that moment, Apollodorus, who had been weeping all the time, broke out in a loud and passionate cry which made cowards of us all. Socrates alone retained his calmness: What is this strange outcry? he said. I sent away the women mainly in order that they might not misbehave in this way, for I have been told that a man should die in peace. Be quiet then, and have patience. When we heard his words we were ashamed, and restrained our tears; and he walked about until, as he said, his legs began to fail, and then he lay on his back, according to the directions, and the man who gave him the poison now and then looked at his feet and legs; and after a while he pressed his foot hard, and asked him if he could feel; and he said, No; and then his leg, and so upwards and upwards, and showed us that he was cold and stiff. And he felt them himself, and said: When the poison reaches the heart, that will be the end. He was beginning to grow cold about the groin, when he uncovered his face, for he had covered himself up, and said—they were his last words—he said: Crito, I owe a cock to Asclepius; will you remember to pay the debt? The debt shall be paid, said Crito; is there anything else? There was no answer to this question; but in a minute or two a movement was heard, and the attendants uncovered him; his eyes were set, and Crito closed his eyes and mouth.

"Such was the end, Echecrates, of our friend; concerning whom I may truly say, that of all the men of his time whom I have known, he was the wisest and justest and best."

QUESTIONS AND STATEMENTS FOR DISCUSSION

1. The charges against Socrates—an evil-doer because he is curious, convincing, and teaches his doctrines to others. What can be said for any cause that fears scientific truth and discovery?
2. On what basis did the Delphic Oracle pronounce Socrates the wisest of men? Could that basis be the criterion of wisdom today?
3. Would a wise man likely be hated today? Can you give examples?
4. What was the Socratic concept of the source of creative genius?
5. Discuss the sources of professional jealousy as exposed in the charge of corrupting the Athenian youth.
6. "A man who is good for anything ought not to calculate the chances of living or dying; he ought only to consider whether in doing anything, he is doing right or wrong—acting the part of a good man or a bad." Compare with the Epicurean doctrine that pleasure is the sole good.
7. "No one knows whether death, which men in their fear apprehend to be the greatest evil, may not be the greatest good." Is there any evil worse than death?
8. What did Socrates mean by the "improvement of the soul"?
9. "Nothing will injure me, not Meletus nor yet Anytus—they cannot, for a bad man is not permitted to injure a better than himself."
10. "You have heard me speak . . . of a sign which comes to me . . . which is a kind of voice . . . it always forbids but never commands me to do anything which I am going to do." Is this a common psychological experience? How does it relate itself to personality and character?
11. Was Socrates justified in vetoing the illegal condemnation of the Generals as against majority opinion? On what ground?
12. "I believe in the gods, and in a sense higher than that in which any of my accusers believe in them." How can this statement be verified?
13. "Unrighteousness runs faster than death."
14. "No evil can happen to a good man either in life or after death." Compare this optimistic view with Buddha's doctrine of the tragic character of life and death, and the Christian standpoint.

Suggested Supplementary Readings:

Seven Ages, by "The Gentleman with a Duster." Putnam's, New York.
Jaeger: *Paideia.* University of Wisconsin Press, Madison, Wis. Pp. 367-373.
Socratic Discourses of Plato and Xenophon. Everyman's Library, E. P. Dutton. New York.

Benn: *The Greek Philosophers*. Smith Elder, London. Chap.
IV, pp. 94-143.
Winspear: *Who Was Socrates?* University of Wisconsin Press,
Madison, Wis.
Aristophanes: "The Clouds," *The Complete Greek Drama*. Ran-
dom House, New York. Vol. II.

Chapter 9

BOETHIUS ON THE VALUE OF THE PHILOSOPHIC LIFE

I
The Life and Influence of Boethius

II
His Doctrine of the Unconquerable Self
1. Through self-knowledge
2. By reason of the inner sources of happiness

III
Persons as Ultimate Realities or Values
1. As rational
2. As free
3. As superior to time
4. As both immanent and transcendent
5. As Divine in nature

IV
His Solution of the Problem of Suffering and Evil

Chapter 9

BOETHIUS ON THE VALUE OF THE PHILOSOPHIC LIFE

I

The Life and Influence of Boethius

For the present study we go back to the early twilight of the so-called Dark Ages. Anitius Manilius Severinus Boethius was born in A.D. 480 and suffered martyrdom in 524 or 525. Note how young he was, for his youth was all out of proportion to the longevity of his achievements. He was a patrician of aristocrats, as his family tree rooted in the days of the early Roman Republic and had borne on its branches the high names of Consuls, Senators, and Emperors. His wife, the daughter of the later Symmachus, came from a line equally famous in history. At the time of his death he had achieved the highest political honors, had not only been Consul, but had enjoyed the unique privilege of delivering the oration at the induction of his two sons into the Consulate. Roman culture was now swifty declining. A century had passed since the first sack of Rome under the invasion of Attila, and the Gothic Theodoric was Emperor. Theodoric was, all things considered, a good ruler. He held a friendly attitude toward culture, and a strong hand for law and order. Boethius served under him in the Empire and as Chancellor had been especially helpful in the finances of the state. Yet within two short years of the height of his influence we find him imprisoned at Colvenzano, between Milan and Pavia, and shortly thereafter he was executed on the charge of treason. There has been much argument over the reasons for his sudden fall, into which we cannot go, except that it appears plausible that Theodoric, being an Arian or Unitarian Christian, was fearful of the Old Roman Party, which was Trinitarian. Boethius from the older aristocracy would naturally be sympathetic with this party which had much power in the Latin portion of the Empire, and was favorable to the head of the Eastern Empire. At this moment trouble was looming from the Emperor of the Eastern half of the divided Empire who would naturally seek the help of the Old Roman Party. Because of his aristocratic connections in Rome it was easy to suspect Boethius of collusion with the Eastern Emperor.

There is slight room for suspicion that Boethius was involved in conspiracy against Theodoric. The Roman Senate, ever zealous of its powers, was in almost constant intrigue with the head of the Eastern Empire to resume the rule he continued to claim over both East and West. When such a plot in the Senate, headed up by the Senator Albinus, was suspected, Boethius rushed to his defense, presuming perhaps on his own influence with Theodoric. In a bold and naive enthusiasm he declared: "If Albinus be criminal, the Senate and myself are all guilty of the same crime. If we are innocent, Albinus is equally entitled to the protection of the laws." As it turned out, there was turpitude either in Albinus or the Senate and, though Boethius bravely defended them, the Senators could save themselves only by the sacrifice of Boethius. The Senate, now safe, passed a sentence of confiscation and death against him. He may have been innocent of wrong, but his sympathies led him to betrayal by the men he tried to save. This was the beginning of a persecution of the Old Roman Party by the Emperor, which led to the martyrdom not only of Boethius but of his father-in-law, Symmachus, and indirectly to the death of Pope John. Theodoric, after the manner of the most modern dictator, apparently deemed it wise to take time by the forelock and purge him in advance of any possible trouble. But tradition has it that, overcome with deep remorse at the savage slaughter of an incorruptible and faithful servant, Theodoric died shortly afterward. Thus, as in later times, care was taken to remove the best and brightest members of society in the interests of dictatorship. Boethius was the afterglow of the already belated sunset of Roman culture. Civilization was destined for a long time to turn hungry eyes in the direction of this afterglow for the little light that was to be had.

About A.D. 725 Lúitprand, King of the Lombards, built at Pavia a mausoleum for him in the church of Saint Pierre-au-Ciel-d'Or which had been recently erected. This was the mausoleum Dante mentions as having seen. Already Boethius was recognized for his greatness both as man and as scholar. The church of Saint Pierre was later destroyed and the body moved to the Cathedral. In 1884 he was canonized, so he is now known as St. Severinus.

It is difficult to visualize the fate that overwhelmed western Europe. Successive waves of barbarian invasion destroyed the landmarks of the earlier culture. In Britain it was saved only by remoteness, and then chiefly in the insignificant island of Iona in the Irish Sea, where the candle of the Monastery of St. Columba still lighted the darkness. For centuries, except in this spot, Greek and Latin became largely unknown. When finally order began to emerge from chaos it was to men who owed their education or their inspiration to this monastery that Charlemagne and his successors appealed for a revival of learning and the establishment of schools. Such men were Alcuin of York and Scotus Erigena. But there was little of the literature of erudition available and no one capable of producing more. There were Martianus Capella's *Encyclopaedia,* Cassiodorus' *Seven Liberal Arts,* and the works of Boethius, most important of all. Having spent eighteen years in the schools of Athens, Boethius had translated from the Greek certain portions of Aristotle's *Logic,* and a commentary on Porphyry's commentary on Aristotle, known as the *Isagoge,* and he established the seven liberal arts by gathering from available sources, in addition to the *Rhetoric, Logic,* and *Grammar* of Aristotle, such systematic treatments as the *Arithmetic* of Nicomachus, the *Geometry* of Euclid, the *Music* of Pythagoras, the *Astronomy* of Ptolemy, and the *Mechanics* of Archimedes. These studies were known as the Trivium and Quadrivium. They provided the body of learning for the new schools. Thus was formed the curriculum of the early university to which we even yet do lip-service, at least, by calling a division of the University the department of liberal arts. But Boethius' influence did not end merely by placing his mark on the future of university life. He exercised an equally great influence on literature. The earliest literary efforts of the new civilization which made the common languages of the people, English, French, and Italian, began with translations into the common tongue of Boethius' work *The Consolation of Philosophy.* In England both Alfred the Great and Chaucer translated it, as also in a later century did Queen Elizabeth, in 1593. In Normandy Jean de Meung, author of the first French novel *Romaunt de la Rose,* issued a French version. *The Consolation* was translated into Old High German in the eleventh century by Notker Labao or his pupils. Later in Italy the same task was performed by Dante. Everywhere the version of Boethius' work betokened the appearance of a literary language of the common people, and indicated the humanistic, individualistic, and liberalizing tendencies that existed in the Boethian philosophy.

Out of his treatment of the Aristotelian *Logic* sprang the

countless discussions of medieval theology, which divided the
Christian world into Nominalist and Realist, Dominican and Fran-
ciscan, and finally into Catholic and Protestant. To indicate the
extent of Boethius' authority among the scholars of the Middle
Ages it is only necessary to turn to the common writings of the
time. The *Chartularium Parisiensis,* for instance, contains the
decrees, statutes, and correspondence from the beginning of the
University of Paris. One turns to the record for the year 1259
and finds the Masters of Paris supplicating St. Louis, King of
France, to secure from the Pope the removal of the ban of exile
and punishment from one William of St. Amore, who had out-
raged the conservatives of the day by writing a book, *Novis-
simorum Temporum,* or, in other words, *The Peril of These Latter
Times.* The correspondence between the brothers and the King
was almost wholly a quotation from the writings of Boethius, the
brothers citing Boethius as a reason for the release of William,
the King answering back with quotations against it. Boethius
was necessary to every gentleman's library and an illuminated
manuscript of *The Consolation* was essential to the rich patron
of learning to establish his love of enlightenment. Boethius' work
on music remained the textbook on music at Oxford into the
eighteenth century. Rand[1] calls attention to the remark of an
Oxford professor who declared that Boethius was no more useful
to a modern musician than is Newton's *Principia* to a modern
dancer; and then dryly adds: "We can only admire that stalwart
Oxonian conservatism that prescribed Boethius on *Music* for so
many centuries." Boethius gave an impetus to modern languages
by refusing to translate Aristotle literally, endeavoring rather to
make it living and generally intelligible and thus, as one author
said, "he became the first to teach us barbarian." This was the
touch of the modern in him that caused his influence to leap the
Dark Ages and the Middle Ages, to inspire and liberalize modern
learning, and become the bridge from classicism to modernism.

We have seen how to Boethius was given the primary task
of prescribing the curriculum of studies for the universities which
sprang up in the twelfth and following centuries. That is but a
small portion of the story. Without his work, Aristotle would
have been entirely lost to the West from the sixth to the twelfth
centuries and the whole concept of liberal education would have
been different. The spirit of the modern university rests in its
belief in secular learning, and it was Boethius' influence which

---

[1] *Founders of the Middle Ages,* Harvard University Press, Cambridge.

kept it from being wholly and narrowly theological. Without him there could scarcely have been the university system that eventuated, nor that revival of letters which came with renewed acquaintance with the lost work of Aristotle possessed by the Moslems. It was through Boethius that Aristotle became acceptable to Christian culture, though Aristotelian scientific writings came in with the Mohammedan invasions. All this was essential to the scientific renaissance of which we reap the fruitage in our own day. Viewed from this standpoint Boethius more than any other might be deemed the far-off father of the modern spirit, the founder of secular learning.

II
His Doctrine of the Unconquerable Self

Boethius has been frequently called the last of the ancients. It would be equally appropriate to call him the first of the moderns, for he foreshadowed in a remarkable way the progress of contemporary thought.

The first of these modern characteristics is discoverable in his attitude toward personality, which breathes the full spirit of democracy. He believed with all his soul in the intrinsic worth of the individual as possessing a value within himself which should not be surrendered to prince, power, potentate, or organized society. He had none of that apologetic for humanity which characterized Plotinus, who said he was ashamed that he had a body, nor, on the contrary, of those moderns who are ashamed to admit, or yet who deny, that they have souls. Whatever was human seemed valuable and significant to Boethius. He did not dream of measuring men against mountains of matter, nor against the vastness of the sidereal universe, and then declaring that man with his ways and thoughts was insignificant. If it had been his privilege to stand within the dome of the great new telescope on Mt. Palomar, to catch glimpses of the newly apparent vastnesses within and beyond the galactic system, he would doubtless have been moved to sing a paean to that Power which is over all and in all. He would not have drawn the conclusion that the starry systems of atomic dust were more important than the understanding mind which can invent and train upon them an instrument only less wonderful than they. As he could not have conceived a telescope without an organizing mind behind it, he could not have envisaged an infinitely more complex and orderly universe as an accident of chaos. One man, in the integrity of his selfhood, hoping nothing, fearing nothing, could jubilantly face a world of misfortune and evil, because the springs of triumph or failure were from within.

Here he had a glimpse of the best modern psychology when he declared: "If thou expectest to be cured, thou must discover thy wound" (*Consolation* I, iv, 5). Note how completely this saying is in line with modern thought which holds that the cure of the complexes of fear which enslave the human mind depends upon revealing to the victim the sources of dread in some shock or fright registered in the realm of the subconscious. If we are not to be overcome by untoward circumstances we must first be masters of ourselves. We cannot afford to give hostages to friend or enemy, nor to be so desirous of success, honor, comfort, or pleasure that we surrender one whit of our self-respect. To be more solicitous to hold the good-will of a friend, or to receive some external reward than to keep friends with myself, is to sell myself into a slavery which renders me no longer free. There is no loyalty in the proper sense, superior to loyalty to one's self.

> This above all, to thine own self be true,
> And it must follow as the night the day,
> Thou canst not then be false to any man.

One might as truly reverse the Shakespearian dictum to make it read: Thou canst not be false to any man without betraying thyself. The uncertainty that dogs our decisions, the weaknesses that keep us back from bold enterprises and the development of the genius with which we are endowed spring from the fear complexes. These are the fears of appearing ridiculous, of making an obvious mistake, of what the neighbors will say, of revealing the darker depths of our own souls, or disclosing the meanness of our motives, or revealing our ignorance or false pretensions. These are the fears that keep us back from success and they can be cured only by honest self-examination. Until we arrive at the determination to be what we are without pretense or bluff, we are not in a position to make the most and best of ourselves. Should we succeed in deceiving those around us, which for any length of time is impossible, we have yet to live with ourselves, and life is not worth living if we must always hate ourselves. Consciousness of being less than our best produces the inevitable inferiority complexes which inflict upon us diffidence of manner, self-distrust, and fear, which rob us of initiative, originality, and creative imagination. The hunger after rewards and opinions that are not deserved, pretense to gifts that are not possessed, con-

sciousness of evil motives enslaves one to fear of discovery. As
Boethius put it:

> For nothing hope nor fear thou harm
> So their weak wrath thou shalt disarm,
> But he whom hope or terror takes,
> Being a slave his shield forsakes.
>
> *(Consolation* I, iv, 15.)

This was the condition on which Boethius based the invulner-
ability of the self. The sentiment is as true as life, and Boethius
proved it in his own conduct.

A second element in his doctrine of the unconquerable self
was his discovery that the springs of happiness are within:

> Wherefore, O mortal man, why seek for your felicity abroad,
> which is placed within yourselves? . . . I will briefly show thee the
> center of thy chiefest happiness. Is there anything more precious to
> thee than thyself? Possess that which neither thou wilt ever wish to
> lose nor fortune can take away.
>
> *(Consolation* II, iv, 75.)

It is easy for men, lured by external prosperity, to build their
lives on an assumption directly contrary to the doctrine of Boethius.
It is easy to think that people can be made happy by external possession—another hundred thousand, a high-powered automobile,
election or appointment to honors, one's picture in the newspapers,
another academic degree, applause before the footlights, ability
to jump higher or farther than others, to become "the world's
fastest human," or a hundred other things for which we may
legitimately strive. But these of themselves do not give happiness.
Bitter enemies will filch your purse, jealous colleagues will depreciate your reputation, or even seek to appropriate to themselves
your renown. The athletic record will be discounted and perhaps
rejected altogether. Where, then, can one find happiness? Here
is the answer: in achievements honestly wrought, in an inner consciousness of worth, in satisfaction at doing things that need to be
done, in the knowledge that your work has been of benefit to the
world. And what of failure? Here, too, one need not be devoid
of happiness, the happiness of having tried sincerely and having
done his best. With these inner possessions we can face success
without being spoiled, and we can face failure and still know joy.
Without these inner assurances one cannot be happy with any
success, for deep in his heart he will fear exposure of his true
self, and will stand revealed to himself as something of a cheat
and a hypocrite.

III

Persons as Ultimate Realities or Values

Such considerations have prepared us for Boethius' doctrine that persons are the ultimate value. We see how our own personalities offer the supreme sources of happiness and worth. Boethius further bolstered this concept by certain philosophical considerations. These, in order, were:

1. Reasoning, thinking being is superior to unreasoning being. The amazing thing about the Palomar telescope is not so much that there is a vast physical universe around us; the astounding thing is the facility of the human mind to devise the instrument and to interpret correctly that which it discloses. The subject seeing and knowing is superior to the object seen and known. To depreciate man the words of the Psalmist are often quoted:

> When I consider Thy heavens, the work of Thy fingers, the moon and the stars which Thou hast ordained; what is man that Thou art mindful of him, and the son of man that Thou visiteth him?

Too often we have left the quotation unfinished and have not stayed for an answer, for the remainder reads:

> Thou hast made him a little lower than the angels and hast crowned him with glory and honor . . . Thou hast put all things under his feet.
>
> *(Psalms* 8:3-6.)

To be known is much, but to be the knower is superior and constitutes the individual a partner in creation. Persons rather than things are the supreme realities in the universe.

2. This superiority of man over the physical universe is further emphasized by his freedom. While he does not make the laws of nature, his understanding enables him to utilize these laws in a way that nature unassisted could never do. She could not produce a neon light, an automobile, an airplane, a radio, or television. These are as much the creation of man as a planet. No matter who denies the fact of freedom, everyone knows that it is a fact.

3. Personality is disclosed as the ultimate reality by its command of time. Because he can gather past, present, and future into one unity of meaning, man can exercise freedom in a creative way, follow plans and purposes which he creates. He can thus devise even beyond the limit of this earthly life and project himself into the future even as today we profit by the thinking of Boethius fifteen centuries ago.

4. This ability of man to express himself, his character, his

thoughts, his dreams in his creations makes them personal and unique. He can thus be said to be immanent in his works, while at the same time he transcends them by ability to perform many more and better. It appears that these two terms, immanence and transcendance, are not, as often supposed, contradictory, but complementary terms. Where they come together you find what is meant by personality. Their co-existence implies the presence of a person human or Divine.

5. This creative power in man was seen by Boethius to transform him into a potential partner with nature, and to disclose human powers themselves as a portion of Divinity, the ultimately Real.

Only within the present time has there been a general turning to a recognition of the knower as important to knowledge and to a reasonable theory of reality. If we listen to but one of the many voices in modern advanced physics, we shall see how strangely modern was Boethius. The voice is that of Edwin C. Kemble, Professor of Physics at Harvard University:

> My fundamental point is that the puzzles of quantum theory have originated for the most part in the notion that its constructs are, or should be, direct reflections of the realities of the external world. I assert that the province of the physicist is not the study of an external world, but the study of a portion of the inner world of experience.[2]

IV

His Solution of the Problem of Suffering and Evil

The final point in the Boethian philosophy of value concerned the problem of evil. This type of thought has frequently been charged with failure to face the problem and yet it is the only system which really offers a clue to its explanation. Idealism frequently attempts to meet the problem of suffering by asserting that it does not exist. Materialism sets to weeping and declares the existence of evil is a sign there is no God, mind, purpose, or world order. It can only whistle while passing through the graveyard of existence, saying, "Eat, drink, and be merry, for tomorrow we die." Boethius presented no such easy or disquieting solution. He held that evil and suffering, in so far as they are the experiences of individuals, are real, but he would dissent from the conclusion that the problem cannot be solved. Boethius did not expect to solve it for the whole human race, nor for all time. What he did see was the reality of solving it in his own life. He could

[2] Bulletin of the Franklin Institute, Vol. 225, No. 3, March, 1938.

transform his suffering and the wrongs done him into superior values, as he caused them to work in him a keener sense of justice, a profounder belief in his fellows, those graces of character which go to make up the superior person. He perceived that the problem could be met only in the place where it occurs, in personal experience. He proved by his own life the possibility of making pain yield the higher treasures of character. He could so live that none of these things should have power over him. Nothing which the world calls misfortune could turn him aside from the true goal of character, love, honesty, integrity, serviceableness, and sacrifice. As disasters increased they represented only the refining of the gold of character and this to him was the supreme value, and the purpose for which the worlds were made. Gibbon writes of him: "Reason had informed him of the precarious condition of her gifts; experience had satisfied him of their real value; he had enjoyed them without guilt, he might resign them without a sigh, and calmly disdain the impotent malice of his enemies, who had left him happiness, since they had left him virtue."[3]

Every man must carve out his own victory and his own kingdom in the hard-won conquest of a soul. Boethius found and lived this personal solution. First of all, there had been the loss of emoluments and honors which until now he had not fully appreciated, but which, taken away, had disclosed a finer set of values which were imperishable, and which neither misfortune nor even death could take away. There had been that thrilling moment when he stood before the people inducting his own sons as joint consuls over the Roman people, a moment perhaps unique in Roman history. But this was not the greatest value. Better than this were other unfading treasures of which he had been too unmindful—the affection of his noble father-in-law, Symmachus, and the love and constancy of his faithful wife. The storm of disaster that had swept over him had taken away, it was true, a crowd of sycophants and flatterers, who had courted him for what they might get out of him; these were gone, but his true friends remained untouched, tried as by fire, and more dear to him than ever. And finally, he had come into a new and better appreciation of philosophy and religion, because they had lightened the darkness of his dungeon and led him into the presence of the Eternal, and shown him to be the friend of God and God his friend— which was, after all, the supreme discovery.

[3] Edward Gibbon, *The Decline and Fall of the Roman Empire*, Random House, Modern Library, New York.

READINGS

(Chapter 9)

BOETHIUS: *THE CONSOLATION OF PHILOSOPHY*. Translated by H. F. Stewart. Harvard University Press, Cambridge. Pp. 129-143, 183, 189-197, 243-247, 305-333, 357-361.

⟨knot ornament⟩

The First Book of Boethius

I

I that with youthful heat did verses write,
Must now my woes in doleful tunes indite.
My work is framed by Muses torn and rude,
And my sad cheeks are with true tears bedewed:
For these alone no terror could affray
From being partners of my weary way.
The art that was my young life's joy and glory
Becomes my solace now I'm old and sorry;
Sorrow has filched my youth from me, the thief!
My days are numbered not by time but Grief.
Untimely hoary hairs cover my head,
And my loose skin quakes on my flesh half dead.
O happy death, that spareth sweetest years,
And comes in sorrow often called with tears.
Alas, how deaf is he to wretch's cries;
And loath he is to close up weeping eyes;
While trustless chance me with vain favours crowned,
That saddest hour my life had almost drowned:
Now she hath clouded her deceitful face,
My spiteful days prolong their weary race.
My friends, why did you count me fortunate?
He that is fallen, ne'er stood in settled state.

I

While I ruminated these things with myself, and determined to set forth my woeful complaint in writing, methought I saw a woman stand above my head, having a grave countenance, glistening clear eye, and of quicker sight than commonly Nature doth afford; her colour fresh and bespeaking unabated vigour, and yet discovering so many years, that she could not at all be thought to belong to our times; her stature uncertain and doubtful, for sometime she exceeded not the common height of men, and sometime she seemed to touch the heavens with her head, and if she lifted it up to the highest, she pierced the very heavens, so that she could not be seen by the beholders; her garments were made of most fine threads with cunning workmanship into an ever-during stuff, which (as I knew afterward by her own report) she had woven with her own hands. A certain duskishness caused by negligence and time had darkened their colour, as it is wont to happen when pictures stand in a smoky room. In the lower part of them was placed the Greek letter Π, and in the upper Θ, and betwixt the two letters, in the manner of stairs, there were certain degrees made, by which there was a passage from the lower to the higher letter: this her garment had been cut by the violence of some, who had taken away such pieces as they could get. In her right hand she had certain books, and in her left hand she held a sceptre.

This woman, seeing the poetical Muses standing about my bed, and suggesting words to my tears, being moved for a little space, and inflamed with angry looks: "Who," saith she, "hath permitted these tragical harlots to have access to this sick man, which will not only not comfort his grief with wholesome remedies, but also nourish them with sugared poison? For these be they which with the fruitless thorns of affections do kill the fruitful crop of reason, and do accustom men's minds to sickness, instead of curing them. But if your flattery did deprive us of some profane fellow, as commonly it happeneth, I should think that it were not so grievously to be taken for in him our labours should receive no harm. But now have you laid hold of him who hath been brought up in Eleatical and Academical studies? Rather get you gone, you Sirens pleasant even to destruction, and leave him to my Muses to be cured and healed."

That company being thus checked, overcome with grief, casting their eyes upon the ground, and bewraying their bashfulness with blushing, went sadly away. But I, whose sight was dimmed with tears, so that I could not discern what this woman might be, so imperious, and of such authority, was astonished, and, fixing my countenance upon the earth, began to expect with silence what she would do afterward. Then she coming nigher, sat down at my bed's feet, and beholding my countenance sad with mourning, and cast upon the ground with grief, complained of the perturbation of my mind with these verses.

II

Alas, how thy dull mind is headlong cast
In depths of woe, where, all her light once lost,
She doth to walk in utter darkness haste,
While cares grow great with earthly tempests tost.
He that through the opened heavens did freely run,
And used to travel the celestial ways,
Marking the rosy splendour of the sun,

And noting Cynthia's cold and watery rays;
He that did bravely comprehend in verse
The different spheres and wandering course of stars,
He that was wont the causes to rehearse
Why sounding winds do with the seas make wars,
What spirit moves the world's well-settled frame,
And why the sun, whom forth the east doth bring,
In western waves doth hide his falling flame,
Searching what power tempers the pleasing Spring
Which makes the earth her rosy flowers to bear,
Whose gift it is that Autumn's fruitful season
Should with full grapes flow in a plenteous year,
Telling of secret Nature every reason,
Now having lost the beauty of his mind
Lies with his neck compassed in ponderous chains;
His countenance with heavy weight declined,
Him to behold the sullen earth constrains.

II

"But it is rather time," saith she, "to apply remedies, than to make complaints." And then looking wistfully upon me: "Art thou he," saith she, "which, being long since nursed with our milk, and brought up with our nourishments, wert come to man's estate? But we had given thee such weapons as, if thou haddest not cast them away, would have made thee invincible. Dost thou not know me? Why dost thou not speak? Is is shamefastness, or insensibleness that makes thee silent? I had rather it were shamefastness, but I perceive thou art become insensible." And seeing me not only silent but altogether mute and dumb, fair and easily she laid her hand upon my breast saying: "There is no danger; he is in a lethargy, the common disease of deceived minds; he hath a little forgot himself, but he will easily remember himself again, if he be brought to know us first. To which end, let us a little wipe his eyes, dimmed with the cloud of mortal things." And having thus said, with a corner of her garment she dried my eyes which were wet with tears.

III

Then fled the night and darkness did me leave,
Mine eyes their wonted strength receive,
As when swift Corus spreads the stars with clouds
And the clear sky a veil of tempest shrouds
The sun doth lurk, the earth receiveth night,
Lacking the boon of starry light;
But if fierce Boreas, sent from Thrace, make way
For the restoring of the day,
Phoebus with fresh and sudden beams doth rise,
Striking with light our wondering eyes.

III

In like manner, the mists of sadness dissolved, I came to myself and recovered my judgment, so that I knew my Physician's face; wherefore casting mine eyes upon her somewhat stedfastly, I beheld my nurse Philosophy, in whose house I had remained from my youth, and I said: "O Mistress of all virtues, for what cause art thou come from heaven into this our solitary banishment? Art thou come to bear me company in being falsely accused?"

"Should I," saith she, "forsake thee, my disciple, and not divide the burden, which thou bearest through hatred of my name, by partaking of thy labour? But Philosophy never thought it lawful to forsake the innocent in his trouble. Should I fear any accusations, as though this were any new matter? For dost thou think that this is the first time that Wisdom hath been exposed to danger by wicked men? Have we not in ancient times before our Plato's age had oftentimes great conflicts with the rashness of folly? And while he lived, had not his master Socrates the victory of an unjust death in my presence, whose inheritance, when afterward the mob of Epicures, Stoics, and others (every one for his own sect) endeavoured to usurp, and as it were in part of their prey, sought to draw me to them, exclaiming and striving against them; they tore the garment which I had woven with my own hands, and having gotten some little pieces of it, thinking me to be wholly in their possession, departed. Some of whom, because certain signs of my apparel appeared upon them, were rashly supposed to be my familiar friends, and condemned accordingly through the error of the profane multitude.

But if thou hast not heard of the flight of Anaxagoras, the poison of Socrates, nor the torments of Zeno, because they are foreign examples; yet thou mayest have heard of Canius, of Seneca, of Soranus, whose memory is both fresh and famous, whom nothing else brought to their overthrow but that they had been instructed in our school and were altogether disliking to the humours of wicked men; wherefore thou hast no cause to marvel, if in the sea of this life we be tossed with boisterous storms, whose chiefest purpose is to displease the wicked; of which though there be an huge army, yet it is to be despised, because it is not governed by any captain, but is carried up and down by fantastical error without any order at all. And if at any time they assail us with great force, our captain retireth her band into a castle, leaving them occupied in sacking unprofitable baggage. And from above we laugh them to scorn for seeking so greedily after most vile things, being safe from all their furious assault, and fortified with that defence which aspiring folly cannot prevail against. . . .

"Understandest thou these things," saith she, "and do they make impression in thy mind? Art thou 'like the ass, deaf to the lyre'? Why weepest thou? Why sheddest thou so many tears? Speak out; hide

not thy thoughts.   If thou expectest to be cured, thou must discover
thy wound."

(Pp. 129-143.)

The Second Book of Boethius

II

If Plenty as much wealth should give, ne'er holding back her hand
As the swift winds in troubled seas do toss up heaps of sand,
Or as the stars in lightsome nights shine forth on heaven's face,
Yet wretched men would still accuse their miserable case.
Should God, too liberal of His gold, their greedy wishes hear,
And with bright honour them adorn; yet all that nothing were,
Since ravenous minds, devouring all, for more are ready still.
What bridle can contain in bounds this their contentless will,
When filled with riches they retain the thirst of having more?
He is not rich that fears and grieves, and counts himself but poor.

(P. 183.)

. . . .

IV

To which I answered: "The things which thou reportest are true,
O nurse of all virtues, and I cannot deny the most speedy course of my
prosperity.   But this is that which vexeth me most, when I remember it.
For in all adversity of fortune it is the most unhappy kind of misfortune to have been happy."   "But," quoth she, "thou canst not justly
impute to the things themselves that thou art punished for thy false
opinion.   For if this vain name of casual felicity moveth thee, let us
make accompt with how many and how great things thou aboundest.
Wherefore, if that which in all thy revenues of fortune thou esteemest
most precious doth still by God's providence remain safe, and untouched, canst thou, retaining the best, justly complain of misfortune?

But thy father-in-law, Symmachus (that most excellent ornament
of mankind) liveth in safety, and for the obtaining of which thou
wouldst willingly spend thy life, that man wholly framed to wisdom
and virtues, being secure of his own, mourneth for thy injuries.   Thy
wife liveth, modest in disposition, eminent in chastity, and, to rehearse
briefly all her excellent gifts, like her father.   She liveth, I say, and
weary of her life reserveth her breath only for thee.   In which alone
even I must grant that thy felicity is diminished, she consumeth herself
with tears and grief for thy sake.

What should I speak of thy children, which have been Consuls, in
whom already, as in children of that age, their father's or grandfather's
good disposition appeareth?   Wherefore, since the greatest care that
mortal men have is to save their lives, O happy man that thou art, if
thou knowest thine own wealth, who still hast remaining those things

which no man doubteth to be dearer than life itself? And therefore cease weeping. Fortune hath not hitherto showed her hatred against you all, neither art thou assailed with too boisterous a storm, since those anchors hold fast which permit neither the comfort of the time present nor the hope of the time to come to be wanting."

"And I pray God," quoth I, "that they may hold fast, for so long as they remain, howsoever the world goeth we shall escape drowning. But thou seest how great a part of our ornaments is lost." "We have gotten a little ground," quoth she, "if thy whole estate be not irksome unto thee. But I cannot suffer thy daintiness, who with such lamentation and anxiety complaineth that something is wanting to thy happiness. For who hath so entire happiness that he is not in some part offended with the condition of his estate? The nature of human felicity is doubtful and uncertain, and is neither ever wholly obtained, or never lasteth always. One man hath great revenues, but is contemned for his base lineage. Another's nobility maketh him known, but, oppressed with penury, had rather be unknown. Some, abounding with both, bewail their life without marriage. Some other, well married but wanting children, provideth riches for strangers to inherit. Others, finally, having children, mournfully bewail the vices which their sons or daughters are given to. So that scarce any man is pleased with the condition of his fortune. For there is something in every estate, which without experience is not known, and being experienced doth molest and trouble. Besides that, those which are most happy are most sensible, and unless all things fall out to their liking, impatient of all adversity, every little cross overthrows them, so small are the occasions which take from the most fortunate the height of their happiness. How many are there, thinkest thou, which would think themselves almost in Heaven if they had but the least part of the remains of thy fortune? This very place, which thou callest banishment, is to the inhabitants thereof their native land. So true it is that nothing is miserable but what is thought so, and contrariwise, every estate is happy if he that bears it be content. Who is so happy that if he yieldeth to discontent, desireth not to change his estate? How much bitterness is mingled with the sweetness of man's felicity, which, though it seemeth so pleasant while it is enjoyed, yet can it not be retained from going away when it will. And by this it appeareth how miserable is the blessedness of mortal things, which neither endureth alway with the contented, nor wholly delighteth the pensive.

Wherefore, O mortal men, why seek you for your felicity abroad, which is placed within yourselves? Error and ignorance do confound you. I will briefly show thee the centre of thy chiefest happiness. Is there anything more precious to thee than thyself? I am sure thou wilt say, nothing. Wherefore, if thou enjoyest thyself, thou shalt possess that which neither thou wilt ever wish to lose nor fortune can take away. And that thou mayst acknowledge that blessedness cannot consist in these casual things, gather it thus. If blessedness be the chiefest good of nature endued with reason, and that is not the chiefest good which may by any means be taken away, because that which cannot be taken away is better, it is manifest that the instability of fortune cannot aspire to the obtaining of blessedness. Moreover, he that now enjoyeth this brittle felicity, either knoweth it to be mutable or no. If not, what estate can be blessed by ignorant blindness? And if he knoweth it, he must needs fear lest he lose that which he doubteth not may be lost, wherefore continual fear permitteth him not to be happy. Or though he should lose it, doth he think that a thing of no moment? But so it were a very small good which he would be content to lose. And because thou art one whom I know to be fully persuaded and convinced by innumerable demonstrations that the souls of men are in no wise mortal, and since it is clear that casual felicity is ended by the body's death, there is no doubt, if this can cause blessedness, but that all mankind falleth into misery by death. But if we know many who have sought to reap the fruit of blessedness, not only by death, but also by affliction and torments, how can present happiness make men happy, the loss of which causeth not misery?

IV

Who with an heedful care
Will an eternal seat prepare,
Which cannot be down cast
By force of windy blast,
And will the floods despise,
When threatening billows do arise,
He not on hills must stand,
Nor on the dangerous sinking sand.
For there the winds will threat,
And him with furious tempests beat,
And here the ground too weak
Will with the heavy burden break.
Fly then the dangerous case
Of an untried delightful place,
And thy poor house bestow
In stony places firm and low.
For though the winds do sound,
And waves of troubled seas confound:
Yet thou to rest disposed
In thy safe lowly vale inclosed,
Mayst live a quiet age,
Scorning the air's distempered rage.

. . . .

(Pp. 189-197.)

The Third Book of Boethius

V

But can kingdoms and the familiarity of kings make a man mighty?
Why not, when their felicity lasteth always? But both former and
present times are full of examples that many kings have changed their
happiness with misery. O excellent power, which is not sufficient to
uphold itself! And if this strength of kingdoms be the author of blessedness, doth it not diminish happiness and bring misery, when it is in
any way defective? But though some empires extend themselves far,
there will still remain many nations out of their dominions. Now,
where the power endeth which maketh them happy, there entereth the
contrary which maketh them miserable, so that all kings must needs
have less happiness than misery. That Tyrant, knowing by experience
the dangers of his estate, signified the fears incident to a kingdom,
by the hanging of a drawn sword over a man's head. What power
is this, then, which cannot expel nor avoid biting cares and pricking
fears? They would willingly have lived securely, but could not, and
yet they brag of their power. Thinketh thou him mighty whom thou
seest desire that which he cannot do? Thinketh thou him mighty who
dareth not go without his guard; who feareth others more than they fear
him; who cannot seem mighty, except his servants please? For what
should I speak of kings' followers, since I show that kingdoms themselves
are so full of weakness? Whom the power of kings often standing, but
many times falling, doth overthrow. Nero compelled Seneca, his familiar friend and master, to make choice of his own death. Antonius
called Papinianus, who had been long a gallant courtier, to be cut in
pieces with his soldiers' swords. Yet they would both have renounced
their power, yea Seneca endeavoured to deliver up his riches also to
Nero, and to give himself to a contemplative life. But their very greatness drawing them to their destruction, neither of them could compass
that which they desired. Wherefore what power is this that the possessors fear, which when thou wilt have, thou are not secure, and when
thou wilt leave, thou canst not avoid? Are we the better for those friends
which love us not for our virtue but for our prosperity? But whom
prosperity maketh our friend, adversity will make our enemy. And
what plague is able to hurt us more than a familiar enemy?

V

Who would be powerful, must
His own affections check,
Nor let foul reins of lust
Subdue his conquered neck.
For though the Indian land
Should tremble at thy beck,

And though thy dread command
Far Thule's isle obey,
Unless thou canst withstand
And boldly drive away
Black care and wretched moan,
Thy might is small or none.

. . . .

(Pp. 243-247.)

The Fourth Book of Boethius

II

"Oh!" quoth I. "How great things dost thou promise! And I doubt not but thou canst perform them, wherefore stay me not now that thou hast stirred up my desires." "First then," quoth she, "that good men are always powerful, and evil men of no strength, thou mayst easily know, the one is proved by the other. For since that good and evil are contraries, if it be convinced that goodness is potent, the weakness of evil will be also manifest; and contrariwise if we discern the frailty of evil, we must needs acknowledge the firmness of goodness. But that our opinions may be more certainly embraced, I will take both ways, confirming my propositions, sometime from one part, sometime from another.

There be two things by which all human actions are effected, will and power, of which if either be wanting, there can nothing be performed. For if there want will, no man taketh anything in hand against his will, and if there be not power, the will is in vain. So that, if thou seest any willing to obtain that which he doth not obtain, thou canst not doubt but that he wanted power to obtain what he would." "It is manifest," quoth I, "and can by no means be denied." "And wilt thou doubt that he could, whom thou seest bring to pass what he desired?" "No." "But every man is mighty in that which he can do, and weak in that which he cannot do." "I confess it," quoth I. "Dost thou remember then," quoth she, "that it was inferred by our former discourses that all the intentions of man's will doth hasten to happiness, though their courses be divers?" "I remember," quoth I, "that that also was proved." "Dost thou also call to mind that blessedness is goodness itself, and consequently when blessedness is sought after, goodness must of course be desired?" "I call it not to mind, for I have it already fixed in my memory." "Wherefore all men both good and bad without difference of intentions endeavour to obtain goodness." "It followeth," quoth I. "But it is certain that men are made good by the obtaining of goodness." "It is so." "Wherefore good men obtain what they desire." "So it seemeth." "And if evil men did obtain the goodness they desire, they could not be evil." "It is true."

"Wherefore since they both desire goodness, but the one obtaineth it and the other not, there is no doubt but that good men are powerful, and the evil weak." "Whosoever doubteth of this," quoth I, "he neither considereth the nature of things, nor the consequence of thy reasons." "Again," quoth she, "if there be two to whom the same thing is proposed according to nature, and the one of them bringeth it perfectly to pass with his natural function, but the other cannot exercise that natural function but after another manner than is agreeable to nature, and doth not perform that which he had proposed, but imitateth the other who performeth it: which of these two wilt thou judge to be more powerful?" "Though I conjecture," quoth I, "at thy meaning, yet I desire to hear it more plainly." "Wilt thou deny," quoth she, "that the motion of walking is agreeable to the nature of men?" "No," quoth I. "And makest thou any doubt that the function of it doth naturally belong to the feet?" "There is no doubt of this neither," quoth I. "Wherefore if one that can go upon his feet doth walk, and another who hath not this natural function of his feet endeavoureth to walk by creeping upon his hands, which of these two is deservedly to be esteemed the stronger?" "Infer the rest," quoth I, "for no man doubteth but that he which can use that natural function is stronger than he which cannot." "But," quoth she, "the good seek to obtain the chiefest good, which is equally proposed to bad and good, by the natural function of virtues, but the evil endeavour to obtain the same by divers concupiscences, which are not the natural function of obtaining goodness. Thinkest thou otherwise?" "No," quoth I, "for it is manifest what followeth. For by the force of that which I have already granted, it is necessary that good men are powerful and evil men weak."

"Thou runnest before rightly," quoth she, "and it is (as physicians are wont to hope) a token of an erected and resisting nature. Wherefore, since I see thee most apt and willing to comprehend, I will therefore heap up many reasons together. For consider the great weakness of vicious men, who cannot come so far as their natural intention leadeth and almost compelleth them. And what if they were destitute of this so great and almost invincible help of the direction of nature? Ponder likewise the immense impotency of wicked men. For they are no light or trifling reward which they desire, and cannot obtain: but they fail in the very sum and top of things: neither can the poor wretches compass that which they only labour for nights and days: in which thing the forces of the good eminently appear. For as thou wouldst judge him to be most able to walk who going on foot could come as far as there were any place to go in: so must thou of force judge him most powerful who obtaineth the end of all that can be desired, beyond which there is nothing. Hence that which is opposite also followeth, that the same men are wicked and destitute of all forces. For why do they follow vices, forsaking virtues? By ignorance of that which is good? But what is more devoid of strength than blind ignorance?

Or do they know what they should embrace, but passion driveth them headlong the contrary way? So also intemperance makes them frail, since they cannot strive against vice. Or do they wittingly and willingly forsake goodness, and decline to vices? But in this sort they leave not only to be powerful, but even to be at all. For they which leave the common end of all things which are, leave also being. Which may perhaps seem strange to some, that we should say that evil men are not at all, who are the greatest part of men: but yet it is so. For I deny not that evil men are evil, but withal I say that purely and simply they are not.

For as thou mayest call a carcase a dead man, but not simply a man, so I confess that the vicious are evil, but I cannot grant that they are absolutely. For that is which retaineth order, and keepeth nature, but that which faileth from this leaveth also to be that which is in his own nature. But thou wilt say that evil men can do many things, neither will I deny it, but this their power proceedeth not from forces but from weakness. For they can do evil, which they could not do if they could have remained in the performance of that which is good. Which possibility declareth more evidently that they can do nothing. For if, as we concluded a little before, evil is nothing, since they can only do evil, it is manifest that the wicked can do nothing." "It is most manifest." "And that thou mayest understand what the force of this power is; we determined a little before that there is nothing more powerful than the Sovereign Goodness." "It is true," quoth I. "But He cannot do evil." "No." "Is there any then," quoth she, "that think that men can do all things?" "No man, except he be mad, thinketh so." "But yet men can do evil." "I would to God they could not," quoth I. "Since therefore he that can only do good, can do all things, and they who can do evil, cannot do all things, it is manifest that they which can do evil are less potent. Moreover, we have proved that all power is to be accounted among those things which are to be wished for, and that all such things have reference to goodness, as to the very height of their nature. But the possibility of committing wickedness cannot have reference to goodness. Wherefore it is not to be wished for. Yet all power is to be wished for; and consequently it is manifest, possibility of evil is no power. By all which the power of the good and the undoubted infirmity of evil appeareth. And it is manifest that the sentence of Plato is true: that only wise men can do that which they desire, and that the wicked men practise indeed what they list, but cannot perform what they would. For they do what they list, thinking to obtain the good which they desire by those things which cause them delight; but they obtain it not, because shameful action cannot arrive to happiness.

II

The kings whom we behold
In highest glory placed,
And with rich purple graced,
Compassed with soldiers bold;
Whose countenance shows fierce threats,
Who with rash fury chide,
If any strip the pride
From their vainglorious feats;
He'll see them close oppressed
Within by galling chains.
For filthy lust there reigns
And poisoneth their breast,
Wrath often them perplexeth
Raising their minds like waves,
Sorrow their power enslaves
And sliding hope them vexeth.
So many tyrants still
Dwelling in one poor heart,
Except they first depart
She cannot have her will.

III

Seest thou then in what mire wickedness wallows, and how clearly honesty shineth? By which it is manifest that the good are never without rewards, nor the evil without punishments. For in all things that are done that for which anything is done may deservedly seem the reward of that action, as to him that runneth a race, the crown for which he runneth is proposed as a reward. But we have showed that blessedness is the selfsame goodness for which all things are done. Wherefore this goodness is proposed as a common reward for all human actions, and this cannot be separated from those who are good. For he shall not rightly be any longer called good, who wanteth goodness; wherefore virtuous manners are not left without their due rewards. And how much so ever the evil do rage, yet the wise man's crown will not fade nor wither. For others' wickedness depriveth not virtuous minds of their proper glory. But if he should rejoice at anything which he hath from others, either he who gave it, or any other might take it away. But because every man's virtue is the cause of it, then only he shall want his reward when he leaveth to be virtuous. Lastly, since every reward is therefore desired because it is thought to be good, who can judge him to be devoid of reward, which hath goodness for his possession? But what reward hath he? The most beautiful and the greatest that can be. For remember that *corollarium* which I presented thee with a little before, as with a rare and precious jewel, and infer thus.

Since that goodness itself is happiness, it is manifest that all good men even by being good are made happy. But we agreed that happy men are gods. Wherefore the reward of good men, which no time can waste, no man's power diminish, no man's wickedness obscure, is to become gods. Which things being so, no wise man can any way doubt of the inseparable punishment of the evil. For since goodness and evil, punishment and reward, are opposite the one to the other, those things which we see fall out in the reward of goodness must needs be answerable in a contrary manner in the punishment of evil. Wherefore as to honest men honesty itself is a reward, so to the wicked their very wickedness is a punishment. And he that is punished doubteth not but that he is afflicted with the evil. Wherefore if they would truly consider their own estate, can they think themselves free from punishment, whom wickedness, the worst of all evils, doth not only touch but strongly infect? But weigh the punishment which accompanieth the wicked, by comparing it to the reward of the virtuous. For thou learnedst not long before that whatsoever is at all is one, and that unity is goodness, by which it followeth that whatsoever is must also be good. And in this manner, whatsoever falleth from goodness ceaseth to be, by which it followeth that evil men leave to be that which they were, but the shape of men, which they still retain, showeth them to have been men: wherefore by embracing wickedness they have lost the nature of men. But since virtue alone can exalt us above men, wickedness must needs cast those under the desert of men, which it hath bereaved of that condition. Wherefore thou canst not account him a man whom thou seest transformed by vices. Is the violent extorter of other men's goods carried away with his covetous desire? Thou mayest liken him to a wolf. Is the angry and unquiet man always contending and brawling? Thou mayest compare him to a dog. Doth the treacherous fellow rejoice that he hath deceived others with his hidden frauds? Let him be accounted no better than a fox. Doth the outrageous fret and fume? Let him be thought to have a lion's mind. Is the fearful and timorous afraid without cause? Let him be esteemed like to hares and deer. Is the slow and stupid always idle? He liveth an ass's life. Doth the light and unconstant change his courses? He is nothing different from the birds. Is he drowned in filthy and unclean lusts? He is entangled in the pleasure of a stinking sow. So that he who, leaving virtue, ceaseth to be a man, since he cannot be partaker of the divine condition, is turned into a beast.

III

The sails which wise Ulysses bore,
And ships which in the seas long time did stray
The eastern wind drave to that shore
Where the fair Goddess Lady Circe lay,

Daughter by birth to Phoebus bright,
Who with enchanted cups and charms did stay
Her guests, deceived with their delight
And into sundry figures them did change,
Being most skilful in the might
And secret force of herbs and simples strange;
Some like to savage boars, and some
Like lions fierce, which daily use to range
Through Libya, in tooth and claw become.
Others are changed to the shape and guise
Of ravenous wolves, and waxing dumb
Use howling in the stead of manly cries.
Others like to the tiger rove
Which in the scorched Indian desert lies.
And though the winged son of Jove
From these bewitched cups' delightful taste
To keep the famous captain strove,
Yet them the greedy mariners embraced
With much desire, till turned to swine
Instead of bread they fed on oaken mast.
Ruined in voice and form, no sign
Remains to them of any human grace;
Only their minds unchanged repine
To see their bodies in such ugly case.
O feeble hand and idle art
Which, though it could the outward limbs deface,
Yet had no force to change the heart.
For all the force of men given by God's arm
Lies hidden in their inmost part.
The poisons therefore which within them swarm
More deeply pierce, and with more might,
For to the body though they do no harm,
Yet on the soul they work their spite."

IV

Then said I, "I confess and perceive that thou affirmest not without
cause that the vicious, though they keep the outward shape of men,
are in their inward state of mind changed into brute beasts. But I
would have had them whose cruel and wicked heart rageth to the harm
of the good, restrained from executing their malice." "They are restrained," quoth she, "as shall be proved in convenient place. But
yet if this liberty which they seem to have be taken away, their punishment also is in great part released. For (which perhaps to some may
seem incredible) evil men must necessarily be more unhappy when they
have brought to pass their purposes than if they could not obtain what
they desire. For if it be a miserable thing to desire that which is evil,

it is more miserable to be able to perform it, without which the miserable will could not have any effect. Wherefore since everyone of these hath their peculiar misery, they must of force be oppressed with a threefold wretchedness, whom thou seest desire, be able, and perform wickedness." "I grant it," quoth I, "but earnestly wish that they may soon be delivered from this misery, having lost the power to perform their malice." "They will lose it," quoth she, "sooner than perhaps either thou wouldst, or they themselves suppose. For in the short compass of this life there is nothing so late that any one, least of all an immortal soul, should think it long in coming; so that the great hope and highest attempts of the wicked are many times made frustrate with a sudden and unexpected end, which in truth maketh their misery to be in some measure.

For if wickedness make men miserable, the longer one is wicked, the more miserable he must need be; and I should judge them the most unhappy men that may be, if death did at least not end their malice. For if we have concluded truly of the misery of wickedness, it is manifest that the wretchedness which is everlasting must of force be infinite." "A strange illation," quoth I, "and hard to be granted; but I see that those things which were granted before agree very well with these." "Thou thinkest aright," quoth she, "but he that findeth difficulty to yield to the conclusion must either show that something which is presupposed is false, or that the combination of the propositions makes not a necessary conclusion; otherwise, granting that which went before, he hath no reason to doubt of the inference. For this also which I will conclude now will seem no less strange, and yet followeth as necessarily out of those things which are already assumed." "What?" quoth I. "That wicked men," quoth she, "are more happy being punished than if they escaped the hands of justice. Neither do I now go about to show that which may come into every man's mind, that evil customs are corrected by chastisement, and are reduced to virtue by the terror of punishment, and that others may take example to avoid evil, but in another manner also I think vicious men that go unpunished to be more miserable, although we take no account of correction and pay no regard to example." "And what other manner shall this be," quoth I, "besides these?" "Have we not granted," quoth she, "that the good are happy, and the evil miserable?" "We have," quoth I. "If then," quoth she, "something that is good be added to one's misery, is he not happier than another whose misery is desolate and solitary, without any participation of goodness?" "So it seemeth," quoth I. "What if there be some other evil annexed to this miserable man who is deprived of all goodness, besides those which make him miserable, is he not to be accounted much more unhappy than he whose misery is lightened by partaking of goodness?" "Why not?" quoth I. "But it is manifest that it is just that the wicked be punished, and unjust that they should go unpunished." "Who can deny that?" "But neither will any man deny this," quoth she, "that whatsoever is just, is good, and contrariwise, that whatsoever is unjust, is evil." "Certainly," I answered. "Then the wicked have some good annexed when they are punished, to wit, the punishment itself, which by reason of justice is good, and when they are not punished, they have a further evil, the very impunity which thou hast deservedly granted to be an evil be- cause of its injustice." "I cannot deny it." "Wherefore the vicious are far more unhappy by escaping punishment unjustly, than by being justly punished." "This followeth," quoth I, "out of that which hath been concluded before.

But I pray thee, leavest thou no punishments for the souls after the death of the body?" "And those great too," quoth she. "Some of which I think to be executed as sharp punishments, and others as merciful purgations. But I purpose not now to treat of those. But we have hitherto laboured that thou shouldest perceive the power of the wicked, which to thee seemed intolerable, to be none at all, and that thou shouldest see, that those whom thou complainedst went un- punished, do never escape without punishment for their wickedness. And that thou shouldest learn that the licence which thou wishedst might soon end, is not long, and yet the longer the more miserable, and most unhappy if it were everlasting. Besides, that the wicked are more wretched being permitted to escape with unjust impunity, than being punished with just severity. Out of which it followeth that they are then more grievously punished, when they are thought to go scot-free."

"When I consider thy reasons," quoth I, "I think nothing can be said more truly. But if I return to the judgments of men, who is there that will think them worthy to be believed or so much as heard?" "It is true," quoth she, "for they cannot lift up their eyes accustomed to darkness, to behold the light of manifest truth, and they are like those birds whose sight is quickened by the night, and dimmed by the day. For while they look upon, not the order of things, but their own affections, they think that licence and impunity to sin is happy. But see what the eternal law establisheth. If thou apply thy mind to the better, thou needest no judge to reward thee: thou hast joined thyself to the more excellent things. If thou declinest to that which is worse, never expect any other to punish thee: thou hast put thyself in a miserable estate; as if by turns thou lookest down to the miry ground, and up to heaven, setting aside all outward causes, by the very law of sight thou seemest sometime to be in the dirt, and sometime present to the stars. But the common sort considereth not these things. What then? Shall we join ourselves to them whom we have proved to be like beasts? What if one having altogether lost his sight should like-wise forget that he ever had any, and should think that he wanted nothing which belongeth to human perfection: should we likewise think them blind, that see as well as they saw before? For they will not grant that neither, which may be proved by as forcible reasons, that they are more unhappy that do injury than they which suffer it." "I would," quoth I, "hear these reasons." "Deniest thou," quoth she, "that every wicked man deserveth punishment?" "No." "And it is many ways clear that the vicious are miserable?" "It is true," quoth I. "If then," quoth she, "thou wert to examine this cause, whom wouldest thou appoint to be punished, him that did or that suffered wrong?" "I doubt not," quoth I, "but that I would satisfy him that suffered with the sorrow of him that did it." "The offerer of the injury then would seem to thee more miserable than the receiver?" "It followeth," quoth I. "Hence therefore, and for other causes grounded upon that principle that dishonesty of itself maketh men miserable, it appeareth that the injury which is offered any man is not the receiver's but the doer's misery." "But now-a-days," quoth she, "orators take the contrary course. For they endeavour to draw the judges to commiseration of them who have suffered any grievous afflictions; whereas pity is more justly due to the causers thereof, who should be brought, not by angry, but rather by favourable and compassionate accusers to judgment, as it were sick men to a physician, that their diseases and faults might be taken away by punishments; by which means the defenders' labour would either wholly cease, or if they had rather do their clients some good, they would change their defence into accusations. And the wicked themselves, if they could behold virtue abandoned by them through some little rift, and perceive that they might be delivered from the filth of sin by the affliction of punishments, obtaining virtue in exchange, they would not esteem of torments, and would refuse the assistance of their defenders, and wholly resign themselves to their accusers and judges. By which means it cometh to pass, that in wise men there is no place for hatred. For who but a very fool would hate the good? And to hate the wicked were against reason. For as faintness is a disease of the body, so is vice a sickness of the mind. Wherefore, since we judge those that have corporal infirmities to be rather worthy of compassion than of hatred, much more are they to be pitied, and not abhorred, whose minds are oppressed with wickedness, the greatest malady that may be."

· · · · · · · · · · · · · · ·

(Pp. 305-333.)

VII

"Perceivest thou now what followeth of all that we have hitherto said?" "What?" quoth I. "That," quoth she, "all manner of fortune is good." "How can that be?" quoth I. "Be attentive," quoth she; "since that all fortune, be it pleasing or unpleasing, is directed to the reward or exercise of the good, and to the punishment and direction of the wicked, it is manifest it is all good, since all is just or profitable."

"Thy reason is very true," quoth I, "and if I consider Providence and Fate, which thou didst explicate a little before, thy opinion is well grounded. But if thou pleasest let us account it among those which thou not long since supposest incredible." "Why?" quoth she. "Because men commonly use to say and repeat that some have ill fortune." "Shall we," quoth she, "frame our speech to the vulgar phrase, lest we seem to have as it were forsaken the use of human conversation?" "As it pleaseth thee," quoth I. "Dost thou not think then that that is good which is profitable?" "Yes," quoth I. "But that fortune which either exerciseth or correcteth is profitable?" "It is true," quoth I. "It is good then?" "Why not?" "But this is the estate of them who being either virtuous strive with adversity, or forsaking vices betake themselves to the way of virtue." "I cannot deny it," quoth I. "Now, what sayest thou to that pleasing fortune which is given in reward to the good, doth the common people account it bad?" "No, but judgeth it exceeding good, as it is indeed." "And what of the other which, being unpleasing, restraineth the evil with just punishment, doth not the people think it good?" "Nay," quoth I, "they think it the most miserable that can be." "Look then," quoth she, "how, following the people's opinion, we have concluded a very incredible matter." "What?" quoth I. "For it followeth," quoth she, "out of that which is granted, that all their fortune, whatsoever it be, who are either in the possession or increase or entrance of virtue, is good: and theirs, which remain in vices, the worst that may be." "This," quoth I, "is true, though none dare say so." "Wherefore," quoth she, "a wise man must be no more troubled when he is assaulted with adversity, than a valiant captain dismayed at the sound of an alarum. For difficulties are the matter by which the one must extend his glory, and the other increase his wisdom. For which cause virtue is so called, because it hath sufficient strength to overcome adversity. For you, that are proficients in virtue, are not come hither to be dissolute with dainties or to languish in pleasures. You skirmish fiercely with any fortune, lest either affliction oppress you or prosperity corrupt you. Stay yourselves strongly in the mean! For whatsoever cometh either short, or goeth beyond, may well contemn felicity, but will never obtain any reward of labour. For it is placed in your power to frame to yourselves what fortune you please. For all that seemeth unsavoury either exerciseth or correcteth or punisheth."

(Pp. 357-361.)

(Consolation)

1. What view of modern psychology is forecasted in the expression: "If thou expectest to be cured thou must discover thy wound"? *(Consolation*, p. 143.)

2. Discuss the import of the sayings (pp. 189-215, 183): "Why seek for your felicity abroad when it is placed within yourselves," and "He is not rich that fears and grieves."

3. Will these statements hold water: "As to honest men, honesty is itself a reward, so to the wicked, their wickedness is a punishment"? Pp. 315-320.) "Wicked men are more happy being punished, than if they escaped the hands of justice." (Pp. 323-333.)

4. Can you recall any illustrations from history or life when the following statement was true: "The increase of honour undeservedly obtained hath thrown some headlong into their deserved destruction"? (Pp. 345-353.)

5. When Boethius is faced with the choice of Poetry or Philosophy as his comforter, which does he choose? Why? (This is of interest in comparison with Dante's experience.)

6. Explain: ". . . in wise men there is no place for hatred." (P. 333.)

7. Evaluate: ". . . it is necessary that good men are powerful and evil men weak." (P. 309.) This is an interesting point of view in anticipating Nietzsche's *Will to Power* and "strength" philosophy. See Chapter 12.

8. In the light of *Consolation*, p. 325 (". . . least of all an immortal soul" and ". . . the wretchedness which is everlasting must of force be infinite"), compare the metaphysical solution of the problem of evil offered by the Stoics with that of Boethius. Which seems to you more authentic?

9. (God) "Who beholding from his high turret of providence seeth what is fitting for everyone, and applieth that which he knoweth to be most convenient." (P. 347.) How in terms of this doctrine of Divine Providence can you explain and defend the tragic death of Boethius and of Socrates? How did Boethius defend it?

10. In terms of the above quotation and doctrine, how would Boethius defend, say, the kiss of Judas, the original Quisling? (P. 351.) Are we to act on similar principles?

11. What does Boethius mean by, and how does he sustain, the statement: ". . . all manner of fortune is good"? (P. 357.)

12. How could Nero, who took pleasure in murdering his mother, be said to be "unhappy" in his pleasure? (P. 211.) Compare with the statement (pp. 323-333): "Wicked men are more happy being punished, than if they escaped the hands of justice."

13. What incidents in the life of Boethius, following his own conscience, led to his death? (Pp. 143-155.)

Suggested Supplementary Readings:

Rand: *Founders of the Middle Ages.* Harvard University Press, Cambridge. Pp. 135-180.

Duckett: *Gateway to the Middle Ages.* Macmillan, New York. Pp. 147-169.

Chapter 10

DANTE, THE VOICE OF FREEDOM

I
The Times and Problems of Dante

II
His Theme: How to Achieve the Value Happiness

III
His Assumption: The Cosmic Nature of Love

IV
His Method: Self-Mastery . . . and Freedom

V
Self-Mastery and Democracy

Chapter 10

DANTE, THE VOICE OF FREEDOM

No better prologue or introduction to the spirit and mood of Dante's work could be had than that of the Sonnets with which Henry Wadsworth Longfellow introduced his translation of the various sections of *The Divine Comedy*,[1] the first two of which follow.

Oft have I seen at some cathedral door
A laborer, pausing in the dust and heat,
Lay down his burden, and with reverent feet,
Enter, and cross himself, and on the floor
Kneel to repeat his paternoster o'er;
Far off the noises of the world retreat;
The loud vociferations of the street
Become an undistinguishable roar.
So, as I enter here from day to day,
And leave my burden at this minster gate,
Kneeling in prayer, and not ashamed to pray,
The tumult of the time disconsolate
To inarticulate murmurs dies away,
While the eternal ages watch and wait.

. . . .

I enter and I see thee in the gloom
Of the long aisles, O poet saturnine!
And strive to make my steps keep pace with thine.
The air is filled with some unknown perfume;
The congregation of the dead make room
For thee to pass; the votive tapers shine;
Like rooks that haunt Ravenna's groves of pine
The hovering echoes fly from tomb to tomb.
From the confessionals I hear arise
Rehearsals of forgotten tragedies,
And lamentations from the crypts below;
And then a voice celestial, that begins
With the pathetic words, "Although your sins
As scarlet be," and ends with "as the snow."

[1] Houghton Mifflin Company, Boston.

334

I

The Times and Problems of Dante

Dante was born in Florence in 1265 of a noble family, the Alighieri, and was well supplied with the education of his day. It is said that he learned how to ride, hunt, fence, dance, and write love-poetry, the accomplishments of a gentleman of that time. In a great work (*Medieval Culture*[2]), Vossler, the German scholar, has painted Dante's physical characteristics as being of athletic build with all the violent contradictions of his nature written on his face: a heavy and sensuous underlip, projecting chin, mouth drawn down at the corners, hollowed cheeks, deep-set eyes, the aquiline nose of a dreamer, and depressed eyebrows indicating capacity for stern criticism, dark hair and skin, stooped shoulders, and refinement and correctness of dress combined with cosmopolitan manners. He came under the tutelage of the famous Brunetto Latini whom he describes as "the first master in refining Florentines who taught men how to make themselves great." He was married about 1291 to Gemmi dei Donati, a daughter of a noble house which gave him connections with Corso Donati, one of the most powerful of Florentine politicians. His extended education and brilliance of speech led Dante into participation in the political life of Florence where he held various public offices.

A popular uprising led to an exclusion from public affairs of all the feudal families except such members as should enroll themselves in some one of the labor or professional guilds. Though he must, as a noble, have felt it beneath him, Dante enrolled with the apothecaries and physicians in order to be eligible to the highest political honors. His first political speech is said to have been made with the aim of softening the asperities of that law. Perhaps enrollment with a labor guild may have caused him to be despised by his own social class at the same time that it failed to ingratiate him with the tradesmen and laborers. Then he married into the most feudal family of them all. As one of the six Priors of the city he was sent on a disastrous embassy to the Pope.

Florence, and particularly the party Dante represented, were in critical need of the support of Pope Boniface XIII and Dante was an unanimous choice for the embassy. "If I go who remains; if I remain who goes," he declared. Before life was done with him, however, he learned the lesson of humility the hard way and out of

[2] Harcourt, Brace and Company, New York.

his troubles became something more than a party man, namely, a citizen of the world.

During his absence from Florence, power was seized by his enemies, and he was exiled from the city in 1302. Within two months after the decree of banishment he was condemned to be burned alive if he ever returned to Florence. In 1316, the decree was annulled on condition of his paying a fine and doing penance, which he refused, saying in a letter whose authenticity is uncertain:

> This is not the way for me to return to my country; but if another can be found that shall not derogate from the fame and honor of Dante, that will I take with no lagging steps. But if by no such way Florence is to be entered, then Florence I shall never enter. And what then! Can I not everywhere behold the mirrors of the sun and stars? Contemplate the sweetest truths under any sky, without first giving myself up inglorious, nay, ignominious, to the populace and the city of Florence? And bread, I trust, shall not fail me.[3]

His years of exile were years of wandering. It is both affirmed and denied that he visited the Universities of Bologna and Paris for the study of philosophy. After that he spent much time in Verona as the guest of the Can Grande della Scala. He found refuge finally at Ravenna, where he dragged out his last days and was buried. James Russell Lowell thus paraphased the inscription on his tomb there:

> The rights of Monarchy, the Heavens, the Stream of Fire, the Pit,
> In vision seen, I sang as far as to the Fates seemed fit;
> But since my soul, an alien here, hath flown to nobler wars,
> And happier now, hath gone to seek its Maker 'mid the stars,
> Here am I, Dante, shut, exiled from the ancestral shore,
> Whom Florence, the of all least-loving mother bore.

Dante's problem was twofold. The first issue concerned his public life and activity; his duty to the question of freedom in the state, the separation of church and state. The second problem was how out of the apparent wreckage of a career, which had promised such brilliant success, to make some salvage, to find himself, and to achieve both success and peace. It might not be inappropriate here to remark that, except for the apparently disastrous circumstances that befell him, and the solution which Dante found and expressed in the immortal Comedy, we should not even know his name.

The age in which he lived was the tempestuous period of struggle between Church and State. Dante, a good churchman in belief and feeling, thought himself constrained, both in the interests of political

---

[3] Letter to a Florentine friend.

freedom and the purity of the Church, to fight on the side of the State. His judgment in political affairs was, as seen by the professional politician, poor, being dictated somewhat by sentiment and conscience rather than by policy, so that, to use the language of the street, he showed a capacity for always betting on the wrong horse. The actual results of his influence on the Florentine state itself may be written off as a dead loss. However, his failure to impress his own city was a factor in making him a citizen of the world, the prophet and forerunner of democracy. He was the morning star that ushered in Italian independence.

His personal difficulties and the manner in which he met them have given us not only an example of heroic living but one of the world's most priceless pieces of literature. Written in the speech of the common people, it was the beginning and became the standard of Italian as a written language. In choosing the vulgar tongue as the vehicle of his great poem he followed the practice of the Provençal poets who wrote their love-songs in Italian because the ladies did not understand Latin, the language of scholars. He thus opened to the less cultured a literature, and prepared the way for democratic and popular education. The effect in bringing about the unity of Italy cannot be measured.

Dante's poem is called *The Divine Comedy* to distinguish it from tragedy, because, however much of the tragic may fill its pages, he wished the world to understand that it had a happy outcome. His career fell into three periods, each of which was signalized by a great literary production. The period of boyhood closed with the death of Beatrice, his boyish sweetheart; the second period of active public life was ended with his expulsion from Florence; the third period was that of his exile. His youthful passion for Beatrice which ennobled and enriched his life with pure ideals was told in the *Vita Nuova*, or *The New Life*, which has been called the world's sweetest love-story. The tale of the years after her death, when he fell into wild excesses, and fulfilled his stormy political career, was told in the *Convivio*, or *Banquet*. Last of all, after years of exile came his great effort, *The Divine Comedy*. The result might in one respect be compared to Milton's *Paradise Lost*. Milton wrote for the purpose of justifying the ways of God, but his principal hero turned out to be Satan. Dante set out to picture Heaven, and by far the greatest part of his work is the description of Hell. This was probably due to the fact that he knew more about the latter, having experienced a living Hell in his frustrated career. The children of the street are said to have pointed him out as the man who had been in Hell. It is at this point that *The Divine Comedy* begins. The poet finds himself in middle life in the midst of a dark wood, faced by the stalking beasts of lust, pride, and avarice which bar his way to peace. Lust is symbolized in the leopard of incontinence, pride by the lion of violence, and avarice, the sin of old age, is symbolized in the wolf. Past these deadly beasts which represent the evil forces of his own life he could not have come but for the friendly guidance of Virgil.

II

His Theme: How to Achieve the Value Happiness

Dante thus disclosed to his friend Can Grande the object of writing *The Divine Comedy:*

> The aim of the whole and the individual parts is to bring those who are living in this life out of a state of misery and to guide them into a state of happiness.

But the book everywhere is the mirror of Dante's own state of mind. He is talking out loud, displaying his own weaknesses, and how they are to be overcome. We might well give a modern title to the work as "How to be happy though unfortunate," which is of interest to everyone. The story is told that when Dante, fairly crazed with grief and disappointment, sought to journey to Paris in the hope that the study of philosophy would help him to solve his problems, he stopped one stormy night at the monastery of Santa Croce for shelter, and that he might leave in the care of the monks one of his priceless manuscripts. One, Brother Hilario, disturbed from his prayers, came grumpily to the door, swung it open and growled, "What do you want?" It is said that the forlorn Dante answered in a single word, "Peace." Is not this the same old *ataraxia* which was sought by Stoic and Epicurean, by Confucian and Buddhist? Yes, for after all, peace is what we hope to achieve by all our ambitions whether for wealth, fame, or learning. We entertain the hope that our striving is to eventuate in peace. Therefore it is of the utmost importance that Dante should have attempted to tell us how, out of extreme earthly disaster, and the sacrifice of his ambitions, he arrived at this most sought gift. Dante did not come to the answer easily, nor shall we. He had to work it out through suffering and misery, through the collapse of many earthly hopes. It was gathered up by single steps, as up the steep slope of Purgatory he climbed, cutting off one by one his evil habits of envy, of malice, of scorn for others, of pride and pretense, of low and vulgar ideas, and out of his pain began the cultivation of happier habits. There is no other way. And so he came at long last to this truth and, let us hope, to this experience which he expressed in these words: "In God's will is our peace."

III

His Assumption: The Cosmic Nature of Love

It may seem strange, if you have dipped at all into this remarkable book, and especially if you have read the terrific descriptions of the Inferno and the punishments there, to be told that Dante believed that the principle of love is the one force which rules the whole universe, as he says: "The love that moves the world and all the stars." How you immediately ask, "Can you get an eternal and all-pervasive love out of such a situation?" We shall become aware of what the poet is driving at, perhaps, if we recall the fact of the beneficent law of causation, by which we can accomplish whatever seems right and good to us. If we need a fire to warm us, it is possible to make one. But children and fools frequently burn themselves. Would you ban the beneficence of fire to make it impossible that fire should ever be abused? The farmer, in order to grow the kind and quantity of crops he needs for his family, chooses carefully the seed that will best serve his purpose. We may consider it a beneficent law which provides that he shall get back in harvest the same kind of seed that he sows. These laws of nature seem on the whole to be necessary to a well-ordered world. Men must reap what they sow. It would be a sorry affair for the farmer if he were to sow wheat and never know but that his harvest would be one entirely of thistles. We would not think it reasonable for a man, who insisted upon sowing his field full of weeds, to complain because he did not get a harvest of wheat. If there is to be such a thing as a moral world, men must as surely know what to depend upon in the field of ethics as in the wheatfield. There is an inexorable law in the moral and spiritual realm which demands that we reap the reward of our deeds. No one can abrogate it, no one can escape it. And this law is a beneficent one. It is as much the task of love to protect the good man in his harvest of good deeds as it is to prevent the evil man from suffering for his evil deeds. It is really a law of the supremest love, which we all recognize when we deplore injustice of any kind. The child and even the fool is able to cease from burning himself, and the evil man is not compelled to his evil deeds. The trouble is that too many people think they can do wrong and get by with it. And then because they do not see the immediate effects of their misdeeds, or because the effects are not what they had expected, they have an idea they are getting off scot-free. But such is never the case. "Whatsoever a man soweth that shall he also reap." It is no kindness to any man to hide this fact of life from him. The fine illustration of how this works is shown in the poem itself. There is one song that permeates the universe. It is expressed in the Italian words *Amore! Amore! Amore!* It is the rhythm and beat to which all the stars and worlds move. But the effect of this song is different in different places. In the *Paradiso* it thrills the heavenly host, because love is the natural atmosphere in which they live. Even in Purgatory this song is one of hope for those who are travelling toward the life of love, being a source of inspiration which enables them to strive all the harder to achieve the object of a good life. But that song which is the joy of *Paradiso* and the hope of Purgatory is the punishment of the people of the *Inferno*. To these people who have trained their lives to the consideration of hatred and malice, of evil thoughts and suspicion, a place of universal love would be the worst kind of torment. The gates of heaven do not need to be barred against them because they would be worse than bored by it. The suffering they have brought upon their own lives is the atmosphere in which they have lived and which they have created. We get what we want in this life and what we pay for. That is a law of supreme love which ordains that "whatsoever a man soweth that shall he also reap."

IV

His Method: Self-Mastery . . . and Freedom

I am sure all this will seem very reasonable and even scientific fact the more we consider it. We are like builders working at a house of life, and we are going to live in the very house we build. If we love, we shall be loved. If we are anxious to learn, we shall become learned. If we hope to get a living without working for it, we must not complain if at long last the people from whom we have sponged give up in despair and turn to more likely subjects for their charity. Every good and perfect work that we complete builds in us capabilities of doing something greater, every weakness indulged leaves us weaker and less capable. Under such conditions there is only one way to the good life, and that is the way of self-mastery. Dante expressed this truth when, near the end of the *Purgatorio,* Virgil takes leave of the poet, turning him over to the guidance of Beatrice into the *Paradiso,* saying: "Thee over thyself I crown and mitre." He has achieved self-mastery at last, the inner unity, and with it both peace and freedom.

V
Self-Mastery and Democracy

Not only did Dante point the way to individual freedom; his work had formidable repercussions in the later liberation of his people through allegiances afterward unhappily lost. There must be certain, as yet undisclosed, reasons for the breadth of his acclaim as the voice of freedom. We shall not understand this until we comprehend clearly the relations that exist between the principle of self-mastery and the larger society of democratic government. The same conditions of self-restraint which are essential to individual freedom are necessary to its citizens in any democracy that is long to survive. We have had this truth driven home to us by the pounding surf of an all-out sea of war. Whether democracy shall ultimately survive depends upon the suppression of greed for special privileges, for private comforts, and, in the last analysis, for the means of life and for life itself. The strength of a republic lies in the fortitude and good will of its individual members, their honesty, integrity, allegiance to high principles, and subordination of personal desires to the common good. If all citizens were men of good will there would be no necessity for police. We would be well governed because self-governed. If men are of evil will, bent on breaking the laws, no police power, however great, will be strong enough fully to restrain them.

It becomes apparent, then, how dependent a democratic society is upon the Dantean principle of self-restraint. Its strength is in direct ratio to its love for and achievement of righteousness and justice. As these prevail, it is the most powerful of all political organizations; as these are wanting, it becomes the weakest. All the forces, therefore, that work for the training in, and respect for, morals, the democratic state should foster. Everything that degrades or lowers public sensitiveness to right, the democratic state will strive to prohibit for the sake of its own preservation. There should be unlimited freedom to do right, never such freedom to do wrong. Wide attacks upon the morality of its weaker and unthinking citizens by promulgating the use of narcotics, such as opium, morphine, and alcohol, or the weakening of personal integrity by gambling and lottery, must be considered detrimental to the survival

of democracy. To these subversive influences must be added all
unjust gains and privileges, and whatever arrays one class of
society against another.

For more than a hundred and fifty years the American Republic
has exemplified the power of a self-restraining people to manage
their own affairs. If the time should come when even a powerful
minority shall turn to ways of avarice and injustice, the doom of
the American experiment in political freedom will have been sealed.
It is a basic law in the nature of human values that we are really
free only to do right, and that any lapse into evil ways is a lapse
into mental, moral, and political slavery.

To an age that considered freedom to be the gift of an autocracy
or an institution rather than the willing acts of free men; who
thought that damnation or liberty came from above, Dante established the principle that both punishment and freedom were from
within. Perhaps there is no other message more needed in the
world of today.

***

Dante

The main theme of Dante is love, and gathers about his supreme
boyhood passion for Beatrice, which becomes the symbol of a
universal principle, everywhere prevalent in the universe and destined ultimately to triumph. He clings to this principle in spite of
all appearances to the contrary, and endeavors to account for the
existence of hatred, evil, and death as shadows of a Divine benevolence. The first great shock that comes to him is the loss of Beatrice
which is mirrored in the love sonnets of his *Vita Nuova* or *The
New Life.* The second period of his career was characterized by
his political activities, a time of early advancement and of social and
personal excesses, ending with banishment from Florence. The
story of this period is told in his *Convivio* or *The Banquet.* The
beginning of the *Divina Commedia* finds him in banishment, faced
by the specters of frustration and failure, struggling to discover
some valid principle on which to base a system of real values and
justify existence.

His theological concepts were the common Christian concepts
of his time which had been profoundly modified from those of
Zoroastrianism through the medium of Mohammedanism which in
the preceding centuries had stirred the intellectual life of Europe.
Therefore he believed in a literal Hell of physical suffering, fire
and ice and torment. His work, written in the common or vulgar

tongue, not only did much to create Italian as a literary language but also to fasten common beliefs respecting Hell, Purgatory, and Heaven in the popular mind. It is not without significance that his description of Hell with its various compartments follows the order and content[4] of that in the Moslem Bible, or Koran, and goes far beyond the assumptions discoverable in the Christian Scriptures. Christendom in Dante's day entertained a profound respect for Islamic learning. To meet this intellectual invasion Thomas Aquinas, born forty years earlier than Dante, had rewritten Christian theology in a reinterpretation of Aristotle to make the Aristotelian philosophy, the mainstay of Islamic-Judaic scholars, accord with Christian thought. It was Dante who gave the Aquinian concepts to the popular mind, but it was perhaps inevitable that he should build on prevalent ideas that had been derived partly from Zoroaster, partly from Manichaeism, partly from the Koran, and give them a Christian meaning.

We find Dante, then, in middle life seeking the way to the understanding of ultimate values, and of course to ultimate explanations. In this forest of defeated hopes he is faced by the three wild beasts of lust, represented in the leopard, violence, represented in the lion, and avarice, represented in the world. These are the personal shortcomings in his character which prevent him from discovery of the true way of understanding until the spirit of Virgil, the great Latin poet, essays to lead him at last to the confines of that Heaven of which Beatrice is the symbol. Thus the purity and unselfishness of his love for Beatrice becomes his guiding ideal by which he understands and conforms himself to the Divine love.

The Divine Comedy is divided into three parts, each with thirty-three cantos with the exception of the first, which contains thirty-four, because of an introductory canto. Altogether they make up a complete one hundred and each section closes with a reference to the stars. The first five cantos describe Dante's situation, his meeting with Virgil, and his experiences in the opening circles of Hell.

[4] See Asin, *Islam and the Divine Comedy.*

READINGS

DANTE: *THE DIVINE COMEDY, INFERNO.* Cantos I-III; Canto V; Canto VII, lines 118-134; Canto XV, lines 55-97; Canto XXIII, lines 58-72, 91-104, 111-129; Canto XXXIII, lines 113-155. Translated by Cary, T. Y. Crowell Company, New York.

CANTO I

In the midway of this our mortal life,
I found me in a gloomy wood, astray
Gone from the path direct: and e'en to tell,
It were no easy task, how savage wild
That forest, how robust and rough its growth,   5
Which to remember only, my dismay
Renews, in bitterness not far from death.
Yet to discourse of what there good befell,
All else will I relate discovered there.
　　How first I entered it I scarce can say,   10
Such sleepy dulness in that instant weighed
My senses down, when the true path I left;
But when a mountain's foot I reached, where closed
The valley that had pierced my heart with dread,
I looked aloft, and saw his shoulders broad   15
Already vested with that planet's beam,
Who leads all wanderers safe through every way.
　　Then was a little respite to the fear,
That in my heart's recesses deep had lain,
All of that night, so pitifully past: 20
And as a man, with difficult short breath,
Forespent with toiling, 'scaped from sea to shore,
Turns to the perilous wide waste, and stands
At gaze; e'en so my spirit, that yet failed
Struggling with terror, turned to view the straits,   25
That none hath past and lived. My weary frame
After short pause recomforted, again
I journeyed on over that lonely steep,
The hinder foot still firmer. Scarce the ascent
Began, when, lo! a panther, nimble, light,   30
And covered with a speckled skin, appeared;
Nor, when it saw me, vanished, rather strove

344

To check my onward going ; that ofttimes,
With purpose to retrace my steps, I turned.
   The hour was morning's prime, and on his way   35
Aloft the sun ascended with those stars,
That with him rose when Love divine first moved
Those its fair works : so that with joyous hope
All things conspired to fill me, the gay skin
Of that swift animal, the matin dawn   40
And the sweet season.   Soon that joy was chased,
And by new dread succeeded, when in view
A lion came, 'gainst me, as it appeared,
With his head held aloft and hunger-mad,
That e'en the air was fear-struck.   A she-wolf   45
Was at his heels, who in her leanness seemed
Full of all wants, and many a land hath made
Disconsolate ere now.   She with such fear
O'erwhelmed me, at the sight of her appalled,
That of the height all hope I lost.   As one,   50
Who, with his gain elated, sees the time
When all unwares is gone, he inwardly
Mourns with heart-gripping anguish ; such was I,
Haunted by that fell beast, never at peace,
Who coming o'er against me, by degrees   55
Impell'd me where the sun in silence rests.
   While to the lower space with backward step
I fell, my ken discern'd the form of one
Whose voice seem'd faint through long disuse of speech.
When him in that great desert I espied,   60
"Have mercy on me," cried I out aloud,
"Spirit! or living man! whate'er thou be."
   He answered : "Now not man, man once I was,
And born of Lombard parents, Mantuans both
By country, when the power of Julius yet   65
Was scarcely firm.   At Rome my life was past,
Beneath the mild Augustus, in the time
Of fabled deities and false.   A bard
Was I, and made Anchises' upright son
The subject of my song, who came from Troy,   70
When the flames prey'd on Ilium's haughty towers.
But thou, say wherefore to such perils past
Return'st thou? wherefore not this pleasant mount
Ascendest, cause and source of all delight ?"
   "And art thou then that Virgil, that well-spring,   75
From which such copious floods of eloquence
Have issued ?"   I with front abash'd replied.
"Glory and light of all the tuneful train!

May it avail me, that I long with zeal
Have sought thy volume, and with love immense   80
Have conn'd it o'er. My master thou, and guide!
Thou he from whom alone I have derived
That style, which for its beauty into fame
Exalts me. See the beast, from whom I fled.
O save me from her, thou illustrious sage!   85
For every vein and pulse throughout my frame
She hath made tremble." He, soon as he saw
That I was weeping, answer'd, "Thou must needs
Another way pursue, if thou wouldst 'scape
From out that savage wilderness. This beast,   90
At whom thou criest, her way will suffer none
To pass, and no less hindrance makes than death:
So bad and so accursed in her kind,
That never sated is her ravenous will,
Still after food more craving than before.   95
To many an animal in wedlock vile
She fastens, and shall yet to many more,
Until that Greyhound come, who shall destroy
Her with sharp pain. He will not life support
By earth nor its base metals, but by love,   100
Wisdom, and virtue, and his land shall be
The land 'twixt either Feltro. In his might
Shall safety to Italia's plains arise,
For whose fair realm, Camilla, virgin pure,
Nisus, Euryalus, and Turnus fell.   105
He, with incessant chase, through every town
Shall worry, until he to hell at length
Restore her, thence by envy first let loose.
I, for thy profit pondering, now devise
That thou mayst follow me; and I, thy guide,   110
Will lead thee hence through an eternal space,
Where thou shalt hear despairing shrieks, and see
Spirits of old tormented, who invoke
A second death; and those next view, who dwell
Content in fire, for that they hope to come,   115
Whene'er the time may be, among the blest,
Into whose regions if thou then desire
To ascend, a spirit worthier than I
Must lead thee, in whose charge, when I depart,
Thou shalt be left: for that Almighty King,   120
Who reigns above, a rebel to His law
Adjudges me; and therefore hath decreed
That, to His city, none through me should come.

He in all parts hath sway; there rules, there holds
His citadel and throne. O happy those,   125
Whom there He chooses!" I to him in few:
"Bard! by that God, whom thou didst not adore,
I do beseech thee (that this ill and worse
I may escape) to lead me where thou said'st,
That I Saint Peter's gate may view, and those   130
Who, as thou tell'st, are in such dismal plight."
    Onward he moved, I close his steps pursued.

CANTO II

Now was the day departing, and the air,
Imbrown'd with shadows, from their toils released
All animals on earth; and I alone
Prepared myself the conflict to sustain,
Both of sad pity, and that perilous road,   5
Which my unerring memory shall retrace.
    O Muses! O high genius! now vouchsafe
Your aid. O mind! that all I saw has kept
Safe in a written record, here thy worth
And eminent endowments come to proof.   10
    I thus began: "Bard! thou who art my guide,
Consider well, if virtue be in me
Sufficient, ere to this high enterprise
Thou trust me. Thou hast told that Silvius' sire,
Yet clothed in corruptible flesh, among   15
The immortal tribes had entrance, and was there
Sensibly present. Yet if Heaven's great Lord,
Almighty foe to ill, such favor show'd
In contemplation of the high effect,
Both what and who from him should issue forth,   20
It seems in reason's judgment well deserved;
Sith he of Rome and of Rome's empire wide,
In Heaven's empyreal height was chosen sire:
Both which, if truth be spoken, were ordain'd
And 'stablish'd for the holy place, where sits   25
Who to great Peter's sacred chair succeeds.
He from this journey, in thy song renown'd,
Learn'd things, that to his victory gave rise
And to the papal robe. In after-times
The Chosen Vessel also travelled there,   30
To bring us back assurance in that faith
Which is the entrance to salvation's way.
But I, why should I there presume? or who
Permits it? not Aeneas I, nor Paul.
Myself I deem not worthy, and none else   35

Will deem me. I, if on this voyage then
I venture, fear it will in folly end.
Thou, who art wise, better my meaning know'st,
Than I can speak." As one, who unresolves
What he hath late resolved, and with new thoughts   40
Changes his purpose, from his first intent
Removed ; e'en such was I on that dun coast,
Wasting in thought my enterprise, at first
So eagerly embraced. "If right thy words
I scan," replied that shade magnanimous,   45
"Thy soul is by vile fear assail'd, which oft
So overcasts a man, that he recoils
From noblest resolution, like a beast
At some false semblance in the twilight gloom.
That from this terror thou mayst free thyself,   50
I will instruct thee why I came, and what
I heard in that same instant, when for thee
Grief touch'd me first. I was among the tribe,
Who rest suspended, when a dame, so blest
And lovely I besought her to command,   55
Call'd me ; her eyes were brighter than the star
Of day ; and she, with gentle voice and soft,
Angelically tuned, her speech address'd :
'O courteous shade of Mantua ! thou whose fame
Yet lives, and shall live long as nature lasts !   60
A friend, not of my fortune but myself,
On the wide desert in his road has met
Hindrance so great, that he through fear has turn'd.
Now much I dread lest he past help have stray'd,
And I be risen too late for his relief,   65
From what in heaven of him I heard. Speed now,
And by thy eloquent persuasive tongue,
And by all means for his deliverance meet,
Assist him. So to me will comfort spring.
I, who now bid thee on this errand forth,   70
Am Beatrice ; from a place I come
Revisited with joy. Love brought me thence,
Who prompts my speech. When in my Master's sight
I stand, thy praise to him I oft will tell.'
      "She then was silent, and I thus began :   75
'O lady ! by whose influence alone
Mankind excels whatever is contain'd
Within that heaven which hath the smallest orb,
So thy command delights me, that to obey,
If it were done already, would seem late.   80
No need hast thou further to speak thy will :

Yet tell the reason, why thou art not loth
To leave that ample space, where to return
Thou burnest, for this centre here beneath.'
     "She then : 'Since thou so deeply wouldst inquire,   85
I will instruct thee briefly why no dread
Hinders my entrance here.   Those things alone
Are to be fear'd whence evil may proceed ;
None else, for none are terrible beside.
I am so framed by God, thanks to His grace !   90
That any sufferance of your misery
Touches me not, nor flame of that fierce fire
Assails me.   In high Heaven a blessed Dame
Resides, who mourns with such effectual grief
That hindrance, which I send thee to remove,   95
That God's stern judgment to her will inclines.
To Lucia, calling, her she thus bespake :
'Now doth thy faithful servant need thy aid,
And I commend him to thee.'   At her word
Sped Lucia, of all cruelty the foe,   100
And coming to the place, where I abode
Seated with Rachel, her of ancient days,
She thus address'd me : "Thou true praise of God !
Beatrice ! why is not thy succour lent
To him, who so much loved thee, as to leave   105
For thy sake all the multitude admires ?
Dost thou not hear how pitiful his wail,
Nor mark the death, which in the torrent flood,
Swoln mightier than a sea, him struggling holds ?"
Ne'er among men did any with such speed   110
Haste to their profit, flee from their annoy,
As, when these words were spoken, I came here,
Down from my blessed seat, trusting the force
Of thy pure eloquence, which thee, and all
Who well have mark'd it, into honor brings.'   115
     "When she had ended, her bright beaming eyes
Tearful she turn'd aside ; whereat I felt
Redoubled zeal to serve thee.   As she will'd,
Thus am I come : I saved thee from the beast,
Who thy near way across the goodly mount   120
Prevented.   What is this comes o'er thee then ?
Why, why dost thou hang back ? why in thy breast
Harbour vile fear ? why has not courage there,
And noble daring ; since three maids, so blest,
Thy safety plan e'en in the court of Heaven ;   125
And so much certain good my words forebode ?"
     As florets, by the frosty air of night

Bent down and closed, when day has blanch'd their leaves
Rise all unfolded on their spiry stems;
So was my fainting vigor new restored, 130
And to my heart such kindly courage ran,
That I as one undaunted soon replied:
"O full of pity she, who undertook
My succour! and thou kind, who didst perform
So soon her true behest! With such desire 135
Thou hast disposed me to renew my voyage,
That my first purpose fully is resumed.
Lead on: one only will is in us both.
Thou art my guide, my master thou, and lord."
So spake I; and when he had onward moved, 140
I enter'd on the deep and woody way.

CANTO III

"Through me you pass into the city of woe:
Through me you pass into eternal pain:
Through me among the people lost for aye.
Justice the founder of my fabric moved:
To rear me was the task of Power divine, 5
Supremest Wisdom, and primeval Love.
Before me things create were none, save things
Eternal, and eternal I endure.
All hope abandon, ye who enter here."
Such characters, in color dim, I mark'd 10
Over a portal's lofty arch inscribed.
Whereat I thus: "Master, these words import
Hard meaning." He as one prepared replied:
"Here thou must all distrust behind thee leave;
Here be vile fear extinguish'd. We are come 15
Where I have told thee we shall see the souls
To misery doom'd, who intellectual good
Have lost." And when his hand he had stretch'd forth
To mine, with pleasant looks, whence I was cheer'd,
Into that secret place he led me on. 20
Here sighs, with lamentations and loud moans,
Resounded through the air pierced by no star,
That e'en I wept at entering. Various tongues,
Horrible languages, outcries of woe,
Accents of anger, voices deep and hoarse, 25
With hands together smote that swell'd the sounds,
Made up a tumult, that forever whirls
Round through that air with solid darkness stain'd,
Like to the sand that in the whirlwind flies.

I then, with error yet encompast, cried: 30
"O master! what is this I hear? what race
Are these, who seem so overcome with woe?"
    He thus to me: "This miserable fate
Suffer the wretched souls of those, who lived
Without or praise or blame, with that ill band   35
Of angels mix'd, who nor rebellious proved,
Nor yet were true to God, but for themselves
Were only. From his bounds Heaven drove them forth
Not to impair his lustre; nor the depth
Of Hell receives them, lest the accursed tribe   40
Should glory thence with exultation vain."
    I then: "Master! what doth aggrieve them thus,
That they lament so loud?" He straight replied:
"That will I tell thee briefly. These of death
No hope may entertain: and their blind life   45
So meanly passes, that all other lots
They envy. Fame of them the world hath none,
Nor suffers; Mercy and Justice scorn them both.
Speak not of them, but look, and pass them by."
    And I, who straightaway look'd, beheld a flag,   50
Which whirling ran around so rapidly,
That it no pause obtain'd: and following came
Such a long train of spirits, I should ne'er
Have thought that death so many had despoil'd.
    When some of these I recognized, I saw   55
And knew the shade of him, who to base fear
Yielding, abjured his high estate. Forthwith
I understood, for certain, this the tribe
Of those ill spirits both to God displeasing
And to His foes. These wretches, who ne'er lived,   60
Went on in nakedness, and sorely stung
By wasps and hornets, which bedew'd their cheeks
With blood, that, mix'd with tears, dropp'd to their feet,
And by disgustful worms was gather'd there,
    Then looking further onwards, I beheld   65
A throng upon the shore of a great stream:
Whereat I thus: "Sir! grant me now to know
Whom here we view, and whence impell'd they seem
So eager to pass o'er, as I discern
Through the blear light?" He thus to me in few: 70
"This shalt thou know, soon as our steps arrive
Beside the woeful tide of Acheron."
    Then with eyes downward cast, and fill'd with shame,
Fearing my words offensive to his ear,
Till we had reach'd the river, I from speech   75

Abstain'd. And lo! toward us in a bark
Comes on an old man, hoary white with eld,
Crying, "Woe to you, wicked spirits! hope not
Ever to see the sky again. I come
To take you to the other shore across,   80
Into eternal darkness, there to dwell
In fierce heat and in ice. And thou, who there
Standest, live spirit! get thee hence, and leave
These who are dead." But soon as he beheld
I left them not, "By other way," said he,   85
"By other haven shalt thou come to shore,
Not by this passage; thee a nimbler boat
Must carry." Then to him thus spake my guide:
"Charon! thyself torment not: so 'tis will'd,
Where will and power are one: ask thou no more."   90
     Straightway in silence fell the shaggy cheeks
Of him, the boatman o'er the livid lake,
Around whose eyes glared wheeling flames. Meanwhile
Those spirits, faint and naked, color changed,
And gnash'd their teeth, soon as the cruel words   95
They heard. God and their parents they blasphemed,
The human kind, the place, the time, and seed,
That did engender them and give them birth,
     Then all together sorely wailing drew
To the curst strand, that every man must pass   100
Who fears not God. Charon, demoniac form,
With eyes of burning coal, collects them all,
Beckoning, and each, that lingers, with his oar
Strikes. As fall off the light autumnal leaves
One still another following, till the bough   105
Strews all its honours on the earth beneath;
E'en in like manner Adam's evil brood
Cast themselves, one by one, down from the shore,
Each at a beck, as falcon at his call.
     Thus go they over through the umber'd wave;   110
And ever they on the opposing bank
Be landed, on this side another throng
Still gathers. "Son," thus spake the courteous guide,
"Those who die subject to the wrath of God
All here together come from every clime   115
And to o'erpass the river are not loth:
For so Heaven's justice goads them on, that fear
Is turn'd into desire. Hence ne'er hath past
Good spirit. If of thee Charon complain,
Now mayst thou know the import of his words."   120
     This said, the gloomy region trembling shook

So terribly, that yet with clammy dews
Fear chills my brow. The sad earth gave a blast,
That, lightening, shot forth a vermilion flame,
Which all my senses conquer'd quite, and I   125
Down dropp'd, as one with sudden slumber seized.

    . . . . . .

CANTO V

From the first circle I descended thus
Down to the second, which, a lesser space
Embracing, so much more of grief contains,
Provoking bitter moans. There Minos stands
Grinning with ghastly feature: he, of all   5
Who enter, strict examining the crimes,
Gives sentence, and dismisses them beneath,
According as he foldeth him around:
For when before him comes the ill-fated soul
It all confesses; and that judge severe   10
Of sins, considering what place in Hell
Suits the transgression, with his tail so oft
Himself encircles, as degrees beneath
He dooms it to descend. Before him stand
Always a numerous throng; and in his turn   15
Each one to judgment passing, speaks, and hears
His fate, thence downward to his dwelling hurl'd.
"O thou! who to this residence of woe
Approachest!" when he saw me coming, cried
Minos, relinquishing his dread employ,   20
"Look how thou enter here; beware in whom
Thou place thy trust; let not the entrance broad
Deceive thee to thy harm." To him my guide:
"Wherefore exclaimest? Hinder not his way
By destiny appointed; so 'tis will'd,   25
Where will and power are one. Ask thou no more."
    Now 'gin the rueful wailings to be heard.
Now am I come where many a plaining voice
Smites on mine ear. Into a place I came
Where light was silent all. Bellowing there groan'd   30
A noise, as of a sea in tempest torn
By warring winds. The stormy blast of Hell
With restless fury drives the spirits on,
Whirl'd round and dash'd amain with sore annoy.
When they arrive before the ruinous sweep,   35
There shrieks are heard, there lamentations, moans,
And blasphemies 'gainst the good Power in Heaven.
I understood, that to this torment sad

The carnal sinners are condemn'd, in whom
Reason by lust is sway'd. As, in large troops   40
And multitudinous, when winter reigns,
The starlings on their wings are borne abroad;
So bears the tyrannous gust those evil souls.
On this side and on that, above, below,
It drives them: hope of rest to solace them   45
Is none, nor e'en of milder pang. As cranes,
Chanting their dolorous notes, traverse the sky,
Stretch'd out in long array; so I beheld
Spirits, who came loud wailing, hurried on
By their dire doom. Then I: "Instructor! who   50
Are these, by the black air so scourged?" "The first
'Mong those, of whom thou question'st," he replied,
"O'er many tongues was empress. She in vice
Of luxury was so shameless, that she made
Liking be lawful by promulged decree,   55
To clear the blame she had herself incurr'd.
This is Semiramis, of whom 'tis writ,
That she succeeded Ninus her espoused;
And held the land, which now the Soldan rules.
The next in amorous fury slew herself,   60
And to Sicheus' ashes broke her faith:
Then follows Cleopatra, lustful queen."
    There mark'd I Helen, for whose sake so long
The time was fraught with evil; there the great
Achilles, who with love fought to the end.   65
Paris I saw, and Tristan; and beside,
A thousand more he show'd me, and by name
Pointed them out, whom love bereaved of life.
    When I had heard my sage instructor name
Those dames and knights of antique days, o'erpower'd   70
By pity, well-nigh in amaze my mind
Was lost; and I began: "Bard! willingly
I would address those two together coming,
Which seem so light before the wind." He thus:
"Note thou, when nearer they to us approach.   75
Then by that love which carries them along,
Entreat; and they will come." Soon as the wind
Sway'd them toward us, I thus framed my speech:
"O wearied spirits! come, and hold discourse
With us, if by none else restrain'd." As doves   80
By fond desire invited, on wide wings
And firm, to their sweet nest returning home,
Cleave the air, wafted by their will along;
Thus issued, from that troop where Dido ranks,

They, through the ill air speeding: with such force   85
My cry prevail'd, by strong affection urged.
   "O gracious creature and benign! who go'st
Visiting, through this element obscure,
Us, who the world with bloody stain imbrued;
If, for a friend the King of all, we owned,   90
Our prayer to him should for thy peace arise,
Since thou hast pity on our evil plight.
Of whatsoe'er to hear or to discourse
It pleases thee, that will we hear, of that
Freely with thee discourse, while e'er the wind,   95
As now, is mute. The land, that gave me birth,
Is situate on the coast, where Po descends
To rest in ocean with his sequent streams.
   "Love, that in gentle heart is quickly learnt,
Entangled him by that fair form, from me   100
Ta'en in such cruel sort, as grieves me still:
Love, that denial takes from none beloved,
Caught me with pleasing him so passing well,
That, as thou seest, he yet deserts me not.
Love brought us to one death: Caina waits   105
The soul, who spilt our life." Such were their words:
At hearing which, downward I bent my looks,
And held them there so long, that the bard cried:
"What art thou pondering?" I in answer thus:
"Alas! by what sweet thoughts, what fond desire   110
Must they at length to that ill pass have reach'd!"
   Then turning, I to them my speech address'd,
And thus began: "Francesca! your sad fate
Even to tears my grief and pity moves.
But tell me; in the time of your sweet sighs,   115
By what, and how Love granted, that ye knew
Your yet uncertain wishes?" She replied:
"No greater grief than to remember days
Of joy, when misery is at hand! That kens
Thy learn'd instructor. Yet so eagerly   120
If thou art bent to know the primal root,
From whence our love gat being, I will do
As one, who weeps and tells his tale. One day,
For our delight we read of Lancelot,
How him love thrall'd. Alone we were, and no   125
Suspicion near us. Oft-times by that reading
Our eyes were drawn together, and the hue
Fled from our alter'd cheek. But at one point
Alone we fell. When of that smile we read,
The wished smile, rapturously kiss'd   130

By one so deep in love, then he, who ne'er
From me shall separate, at once my lips
All trembling kiss'd. The book and writer both
Were love's purveyors. In its leaves that day
We read no more." While thus one spirit spake,   135
The other wail'd so sorely, that heart-struck
I, through compassion fainting, seem'd not far
From death, and like a corpse fell to the ground.

[Dante is thus conducted through the deepening circles of Hell where
the punishments endured are exactly such as the sinner has brought on
himself, that is, by his wrong-doing, each has been making the particular
type of Hell he has to endure.]

. . . . . .

CANTO VII

. . . The good instructor spake: "Now seest thou, son!
The souls of those, whom anger overcame.
This too for certain know, that underneath   120
The water dwells a multitude, whose sighs
Into these bubbles make the surface heave,
As thine eye tells thee wheresoe'er it turn.
Fix'd in the slime, they say: 'Sad once were we,
In the sweet air made gladsome by the sun,   125
Carrying a foul and lazy mist within:
Now in these murky settlings are we sad."
Such dolorous strain they gurgle in their throats,
But word distinct can utter none." Our route
Thus compass'd we, a segment widely stretch'd   130
Between the dry embankment, and the core
Of the loath'd pool, turning meanwhile our eyes
Downward on those who gulp'd its muddy lees;
Nor stopp'd, till to a tower's low base we came.

[Here Dante runs across his old teacher, Brunetto Latini, "who taught
the Florentines how to become great," and questions him.]

. . . . . .

CANTO XV

. . . "If thou," he answered, "follow but thy star,   55
Thou canst not miss at last a glorious haven;
Unless in fairer days my judgment erred.
And if my fate so early had not chanced,
Seeing the heavens thus bounteous to thee, I

Had gladly given thee comfort in thy work.   60
But that ungrateful and malignant race,
Who in old times came down from Fiesole,
Ay and still smack of their rough mountain-flint,
Will for thy good deeds show thee enmity.
Nor wonder; for amongst ill-savor'd crabs   65
It suits not the sweet fig-tree lay her fruit.
Old fame reports them in the world for blind,
Covetous, envious, proud. Look to it well:
Take heed thou cleanse thee of their ways. For thee,
Thy fortune hath such honor in reserve,   70
That thou by either party shalt be craved
With hunger keen: but be the fresh herb far
From the goat's tooth. The herd of Fiesole
May of themselves make litter, not touch the plant,
If any such yet spring on their rank bed,   75
In which the holy seed revives, transmitted
From those true Romans, who still there remain'd,
When it was made the nest of so much ill."
     "Were all my wish fulfill'd," I straight replied,
"Thou from the confines of man's nature yet   80
Hadst not been driven forth; for in my mind
Is fix'd, and now strikes full upon my heart
The dear, benign, paternal image, such
As thine was, when so lately thou didst teach me
The way for man to win eternity: 85
And how I prized the lesson, it behoves,
That, long as life endures, my tongue should speak.
What of my fate thou tell'st, that write I down;
And, with another text to comment on,
For her I keep it, the celestial dame,   90
Who will know all, if I to her arrive.
This only would I have thee clearly note:
That, so my conscience have no plea against me,
Do Fortune as she list, I stand prepared.
Not new or strange such earnest to mine ear.   95
Speed Fortune then her wheel, as likes her best;
The clown his mattock; all things have their course."

                    * * * * * *

CANTO XXIII

[The Circle of the deceitful]

. . . There in the depth we saw a painted tribe,
Who paced with tardy steps around, and wept,
Faint in appearance and o'ercome with toil.   60

Caps had they on, with hoods, that fell low down
Before their eyes, in fashion like to those
Worn by the monks in Cologne. Their outside
Was overlaid with gold, dazzling to view,
But leaden all within, and of such weight.   65
That Frederick's compared to these were straw.
Oh, everlasting wearisome attire!
    We yet once more with them together turn'd,
To leftward, on their dismal moan intent.
But by the weight opprest, so slowly came   70
The fainting people, that our company
Was changed, at every movement of the step.

                . . . . . .

"They walk unmantled by the cumbrous stole?"
    Then thus to me: "Tuscan, who visitest
The college of the mourning hypocrites,
Disdain not to instruct us who thou art."
    "By Arno's pleasant stream," I thus replied,   95
"In the great city I was bred and grew,
And wear the body I have ever worn.
But who are ye, from whom such mighty grief,
As now I witness, courseth down your cheeks?
What torment breaks forth in this bitter woe?"   100
    "Our bonnets gleaming bright with orange hue,"
One of them answered, "are so leaden gross,
That with their weight they make the balances
To crack beneath them."

                . . . . . .

    "O Friars!" I began, "your miseries—"
But there brake off, for one had caught mine eye,
Fixed to a cross with three stakes on the ground:
He, when he saw me, writhed himself, throughout
Distorted, ruffling with deep sighs his beard.   115
And Catalano, who thereof was 'ware,
Thus spake: "That pierced spirit, whom intent
Thou view'st, was he who gave the Pharisees
Counsel, that it were fitting for one man
To suffer for the people. He doth lie   120
Transverse; nor any passes, but him first
Behoves make feeling trial how each weighs.
In straits like this along the foss are placed
The father of his consort, and the rest
Partakers in that council, seed of ill   125
And sorrow to the Jews." I noted then,
How Virgil gazed with wonder upon him,

Thus abjectly extended on the cross
In banishment eternal.

[In Canto XXXIII we have the description of those who have betrayed others under pretense of kindness. Among these he notes Fra
Alberigo de Manfredi, who had invited his enemies to a dinner with the
proposed objective of making peace and then feasted them with poisoned
food. Alberigo introduces him to the ghost of another sinner, Branca
Doria, whose body, may we say, lives in Florence while his spirit already
suffers in Hell.]

CANTO XXXIII

. . . . .

"Say who thou wast, if thou wouldst have mine aid;
And if I extricate thee not, far down
As to the lowest ice may I descend."   115
    "The Friar Alberigo," answered he,
"Am I, who from the evil garden pluck'd
Its fruitage, and am here repaid, the date
More luscious for my fig."—"Hah!" I exclaim'd,
"Art thou, too, dead?" "How in the world aloft   120
It fareth with my body," answer'd he,
"I am right ignorant. Such privilege
Hath Ptolomea, that oft-times the soul
Drops hither, ere by Atropos divorced.
And that thou mayst wipe out more willingly   125
The glazed tear-drops that o'erlay mine eyes,
Know that the soul, that moment she betrays,
As I did, yields her body to a fiend
Who after moves and governs it at will,
Till all its time he rounded; headlong she   130
Falls to this cistern. And perchance above
Doth yet appear the body of a ghost,
Who here behind me winters. Him thou know'st,
If thou but newly art arrived below.
The years are many that have passed away,   135
Since to this fastness Branca Doria came."
    "Now," answer'd I, "methinks thou mockest me,
For Branca Doria never yet hath died,
But doth all natural functions of a man,
Eats, drinks, and sleeps, and putteth raiment on."   140
    He thus: "Not yet unto that upper foss
By th' evil talons guarded, where the pitch
Tenacious boils, had Michel Zanche reach'd,
When this one left a demon in his stead
In his own body, and of one his kin,   145

Who with him treachery wrought. But now put forth
Thy hand, and ope mine eyes." I oped them not.
Ill manners were best courtesy to him.
   Ah Genoese! men perverse in every way
With every foulness stain'd, why from the earth   150
Are ye not cancel'd? Such an one of yours
I with Romagna's darkest spirit found,
As, for his doings, even now in soul
Is in Cocytus plunged, and yet doth seem
In body still alive upon the earth.   155

[At the bottom at the farthest from Heaven lies Lucifer, Satan, or
Beelzebub himself, frozen into the sea of ice. The meaning of this is that
his very hatred has frozen him off from the rest of the universe, his only
companions being such other betrayers as Judas Iscariot, Brutus, and
Cassius. From this terrible place they are able to escape only by great
exertion.

Chapman, whose translation follows, writes: "I have prefaced the
'Purgatorio' with the last twelve lines of the 'Inferno' and have followed
it immediately with 'Purgatorio,' the two Cantos being parts, as it were,
of the same Movement."]

CANTO XXXIV

· · · · · ·

[1]There is a place as far above Hell's ground
   As Satan's tomb from its enclosing wall,
Where sights exist no more, but only sound—
   The sound of water from a rocky edge   130
That wears its downward way from ledge to ledge
   In slow descent,—a dreamy waterfall.
And through this secret stair my Lord and I
   Were climbing in the little river's course,
He first, I next. Our thoughts were in the sky,   135
   While up and on we toiled with unabated force;
Till I beheld, as through an open door,
   The heavenly wonders of Eternity,
And, stepping forth, we saw the stars once more.

[1] Chapman, *Dante, Inferno,* Canto XXXIV, lines 127-139, Houghton Mifflin
Company, Boston, pp. 38-43.

CHAPMAN: *DANTE, PURGATORIO,* Canto I, lines 1-126; Canto II, lines 127-140. Houghton Mifflin Company, Boston.

CANTO I

Now for a course upon a happier Sea,
Leaving those cruel waters far behind,
   My bark shakes out her sail of poesy;
And I shall sing the region where Man's mind
   Purges itself for passage to the skies,   5
And sins dissolve from eyes with weeping blind.
   O may dead Poetry herself arise!
Ye Muses, give me back my earlier years.
   While your Calliope her voice supplies,
Sustaining my weak, quavering note with hers   10
   That taught the impious Magpies how to fly.
The tender hue the Persian sapphire wears
   Was gathering in the Zenith's purity,
And poured into my eyes a new delight,
   As, leaving that dead air I saw the sky: 15
It gave me back my spirit and my sight.
   Venus was hung above the laughing East,
Veiling a constellation with her light
   That soothes at dawn the wakeful lover's breast,
When, turning toward the Southern Pole, my gaze   20
   Fell on four stars whose light had never blest
The human eye, since Adam saw their rays.
   O vacant, empty, widowed northern sky!
Those heavens seemed to glory in the blaze
   Which *thou* shalt lack through all eternity.   25
I cast my eyes to northward and, behold,
   The Bear was gone! And, turning round, I see
A single figure like a saint of old,
   Whose gentle aspect on our coming shone
And wrought in us such deference untold   30
   As scarce a father merits from a son.
Long was his beard and dashed with streaks of snow;
   As the hair also, glistening and fine-spun,
That fell in double lists upon his chest below.
   The rays of the four brilliant stars behind   35
Were fringing his pale visage with a glow,
   As if the sun himself against him shined.

'And who are ye,' he questioned, 'that have fled
   The eternal jail and crossed the river blind?'—
With stately motion of his reverent head.—   40

'Who was your guide? What lamp illumed your trail
In issuing from the darkness of the dead
    That broods forever o'er the lower vale?
Are the laws broken yonder in the abyss,
    Or do new counsels in the sky prevail   45
That ye, the damned, invade my boundaries?'
    My Master seized me, and with words and signs
And hands abased my brow and bent my knees
    In reverence: then answered, 'The designs
That bring me are not mine. From heaven came down   50
    A lady who through constant prayer inclines
My fate to succor this man as he journeys on.
    But since thou hast a wish for ampler news,
According to thy will it shall be done;
    For nought that thou canst ask may I refuse.   55
This man has not yet drawn his latest breath,
    Though nigh it was, and little was to choose,
When folly fetched him to the brink of death:
    And I was sent to save him, as I say,
And lead him o'er the road he traveleth   60
    With me for guide;—there was no other way.
Under my eye the wicked he hath seen,
    And now those other spirits he must survey
Who purge their sins beneath thy discipline.
    Our tale of pilgrimage I'll not repeat: 65
From heaven above there falls a force divine
    That drew us on and finds us at thy feet.
Ah, give him gracious welcome, honored Sir!
    He seeks for Freedom. Liberty is sweet:
They know it well who give their lives for Her,—   70
    As thou, at Utica, in earth's despite
Didst drop the mortal dress without a tear
    Which at the Judgment Day shall shine so bright.
Unbroken are the edicts of the sky;
    This man still lives, and I, from Minos free,   75
Dwell in that Circle where the longing eyes
    Of thy chaste Marcia yet appeal to thee
To hold her as thine own. Oh, sainted heart,
    In her love's name we claim thy sympathy!
Then, upward through thy realm let us depart.   80
    I'll bear our thanks to her,—if thou dost deign
To be remembered in that void inert.'

    'So much of heaven in her eyes did reign,'
He said, 'that while on earth I did her will;
    But here, beneath the laws of this domain,   85

Those eyes have lost their power for good or ill.
        If, as thou say'st, a lady there on high
Guides you and guards you, ye may pass my sill.
        It is enough : nor needs there flattery.
Go then, and look thou gird this fellow here   90
        With a smooth rush drawn from the marsh nearby :
And wash his face from every soilure clear ;
        For 'twere not meet with film-beclouded eye
To go before the Sky's Prime Minister.
        Around the isle, amid the oozy flow,   95
The shelving ledges circle towards the sea.
        Where the waves beat their stem the rushes grow ;
No other plant hath pliability
        To take the surge and bend before the blow.'
He spoke and vanished. Then I silently   100
        Drew toward my Leader's side and kept my eyes
        Fastened upon him only, till he said,
'Follow my footsteps closely where the plain
        Slants downward toward its wide extremities.'

The dawn her winning battle did maintain   105
        Against the routed mists, that fled before
The matin trembling of the distant seas :
        We trudged along the solitary shore
Like men who, after wandering far afield,
        Recover a lost track, and stray no more ;   110
And came to where the hoarfrost would not yield,
        But sparred against the Sun and blindly wept,
Half vanquished, 'neath the shade that was its shield.
        The Master stretched his open palms and swept
The greensward tenderly beside our path ;   115
        Whereat I guessed the art of that adept,
And turned my tear-stained cheeks to meet the bath,
        While he, my native color to restore,
Laved from my face the Inferno's aftermath.
        And soon we stood upon a lonely shore   120
Whose seas no ship had furrowed in all time
        Captained by men whom hope of home upbore.
And here he stooped and from the reedy slime
        He drew and cinctured me with a green ring.
O marvel !—As he plucked the humble thing   125
        Another sprouted where it grew before.

CANTO II
· · · · · ·

Like travelers, whose journey fills their mind,
   We paced the strand at sunrise by the sea;
Our hearts pressed on, our bodies lagged behind.
   And lo, as when in rosy mystery,
At dawn Mars glimmers in the vaporous floor   15
   Of ocean's westering immensity,
Even so, I saw (and trust to see once more)
   A glow that came so nimbly through the haze
That nought e'er ran so fast on land or shore.
   For when I turned a moment from the rays   20
To ask my Duke a question, and looked back,
   'Twas larger, brighter, nearer on my gaze.
One brightness shone aloft, above its track;
   Then, by degrees, another from below.

[Up the slopes of Purgatory repentant sinners climb divesting themselves on the various circles of the seven sins: Pride, Envy, Anger,
Gloominess, Avarice, Gluttony, and Incontinence. As they reach the final
upward circle of Purgatory, Virgil turns over his leadership to a more
heavenly guide, Beatrice, but before doing so issues his farewell;]

PURGATORIO: Cary's translation, p. 293.

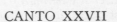

CANTO XXVII
· · · · · ·

And now as glimmering dawn appeared, that breaks   110
More welcome to the pilgrim still, as he
Sojourns less distant on his homeward way,
Darkness from all sides fled, and with it fled
My slumber; whence I rose, and saw my guide
Already risen. "That delicious fruit,   115
Which through so many a branch the zealous care
Of mortals roams in quest of, shall this day
Appease thy hunger." Such the words I heard
From Virgil's lip; and never greeting heard,
So pleasant as the sounds. Within me straight   120
Desire so grew upon desire to mount,
Thenceforward at each step I felt the wings
Increasing for my flight. When we had run
O'er all the ladder to its topmost round,
As there we stood, on me the Mantuan fix'd   125
His eyes, and thus he spake: "Both fires, my son,
The temporal and eternal, thou hast seen;

And art arrived, where of itself my ken
No further reaches. I, with skill and art,
Thus far have drawn thee. Now thy pleasure take   130
For guide. Thou hast o'ercome the steeper way,
O'ercome the straiter. Lo! the sun, that darts
His beam upon my forehead: lo! the herb,
The arborets and flowers, which of itself
This land pours forth profuse. Till those bright eyes   135
With gladness come, which, weeping, made me haste
To succor thee, thou mayst or seat thee down,
Or wander where thou wilt. Expect no more
Sanction of warning voice or sign from me,
Free of thy own arbitrement to chuse,   140
Discreet, judicious. To distrust thy sense
Were henceforth error. I invest thee then
With crown and mitre, sovereign o'er thyself."

[After departing from Virgil, Dante wanders in the Earthly Paradise,
but is unfit to accept Beatrice's guidance into the Heavenly Paradise until
fully absolved from his sin through drinking the waters of Lethe and
Eunoe.]

CANTO XXVIII
. . . . . .

"The water, thou behold'st, springs not from vein,
Restored by vapor, that the cold converts;
As stream that intermittently repairs
And spends his pulse of life; but issues forth   130
From fountain, solid, undecaying, sure:
And, by the Will Omnific, full supply
Feeds whatsoe'er on either side it pours;
On this, devolved with power to take away
Remembrance of offence; on that, to bring   135
Remembrance back of every good deed done.
From whence its name of Lethe on this part;
On the other, Eunoe: both of which must first
Be tasted, ere it work; the last exceeding
All flavors else."   140

[Prepared now by further instruction from Beatrice he sings:]

CANTO XXXIII
. . . . . .

. . . Were further space allowed,
Then, Reader! might I sing, though but in part,
That beverage, with whose sweetness I had ne'er   135
Been sated. But, since all the leaves are full,

Appointed for this second strain, mine art
With warning bridle checks me. I return'd
From the most holy wave, regenerate,   140
E'en as new plants renew'd with foliage new,
Pure and made apt for mounting to the stars.

[In the *Paradiso* we have Heaven described as a great revolving circle
about the unmoved Center, the Eternal Light like the concentric leaves of
a rose, described in the closing lines of the poem as:]

[1]. . . like a wheel

In even motion, by the love impelled,
That moves the sun in heaven and all the stars.   135

[1] *Paradiso,* Canto XXXIII, lines 133-135, Cary's translation.

QUESTIONS AND STATEMENTS FOR DISCUSSION

(Purgatorio)

1. Discuss the symbolism of the leopard, the lion, and the she-wolf: Morning (Spring and Lust); hunger-mad Pride; Greed (full of wants); *Purgatorio*, Canto I: lines 35-48, 94-95.

2. Note the author's state of mind: uncertainty of purpose (II: 40-41), the inhibition of fear (46-49) (starts at shadows); dependence on the love of Beatrice (53ff); and arrival at the first round of self-assurance (87-88): "Those things alone are to be feared whence evil may proceed." In what sense could this be a true platform for fearlessness? Recall Socrates' *Apology:* "No evil can befall a good man, either here or hereafter."

3. Canto III pictures the anteroom to the Inferno where sins of passion are punished, and the upper hall of Hell where malice receives its reward. How could the establishment of Hell as a place of segregation for the wicked be considered (lines 5-6) "the task of power Divine, supremest wisdom, and primeval love?"

4. Is there a logical connection between the lines III:9: "Abandon hope, all ye who enter here," and lines 15-16: "The souls to misery doomed who intellectual good have lost"? By "intellectual good" is meant the knowledge of God. Is there a relation between hope and belief?

5. Discuss the status of those men near the portal who are so weak and vacillating that neither God nor the Devil desires them (III: 34-38). In this connection read, if possible, and compare Browning's characters in "The Statue and the Bust" (Works, Vol. I, p. 434, Macmillan, 1901), where it would seem that even wrong-doing is preferable to life-long contemplation of evil.

> "The sin I impute to each frustrate ghost
> Is—the unlit lamp and the ungirt loin,
> Though the end in sight was a vice I say.
> You of the virtue (we issue join),
> How strive you? *De te fabula.*

Can such a position be justified?

6. Why are the condemned not loth to recross the river (*Purg.*, III: 115-117)? Who are most likely to be the chosen associates of the evil-minded?

7. What seems to be wrong in Paolo's and Francesca's absorption in each other to the exclusion of all other interests (V:104-105)? Romantic love, as represented by Dante, is found only where Christianity flourishes. How does it differ from mere infatuation, or selfish desire? Why is genuine love spiritually centered?

8. Francesca quotes Boethius' words: "No greater grief than to re-

member days of joy, when misery is at hand" (V:118-119). Alfred Musset in a poem, *La Solitude,* denies it. What do you think?

9. What principle of punishment is set forth by Dante in the lines (*Purg.,* VII: 117-134) : "Sad once were we in the sweet air . . . now in these murky settings we are sad"? Is such punishment just, natural, vengeful, or unavoidable?

10. Who was Bruno Latini, and what the force of his words: "Follow but thy star, thou canst not miss at last a glorious haven" (XV:55-56)? Connect this saying with that of lines 84-85.

11. Note "the academic procession" (XXIII:58-72, 91-104, 110-129) of hypocrites under the pressure of caps and hoods, gilded outside, but loaded with lead. Is there a real drawback to the enjoyment of undeserved honors or fraudulent degrees? Specify.

12. Alberigo, imprisoned in the Sea of Ice, along with Satan, the Arch-Fiend, invited men to a feast of reconciliation and poisoned them. What, first, is the significance of the Sea of Ice; second, of Branca Doria being in Hell while he is still living (XXXIII: 113-115). Why is betrayal congealing to human relationships? Private or public? (The "scrap of paper"—Pearl Harbor).

13. In the *Purgatorio,* Canto I: line 114 and following, is a description of the preparation of Dante for a "brighter world." Note the symbolic girding with a reed as a mark of humility, and the washing of the face with "the dews of heaven," and discuss the relation of humility to learning. Why must the mind (symbolized by the face) be cleansed of evil before it can go on to appreciation of the good?

14. Relate the statement (XXVII:142-143) : "I invest thee then with crown and mitre, sovereign o'er thyself," with the problem of free-will, freedom, and democracy.

(Paradiso)

15. Unravel the concept of the unmoved center of the wheel as the symbol of God, as Unmoved Mover of the Universe (*Paradiso,* Canto XXXIII: lines 133-135).

Suggested Supplementary Readings:

Flewelling: "Dante's Treatment of Personality." *The Personalist.* Vol. III, No. 1, pp. 31-38.

Asin: *Islam and the Divine Comedy.* E. P. Dutton, New York.

Dinsmore: *The Teachings of Dante.* Houghton Mifflin, Boston. Pp. 3-35.

Translations of *The Divine Comedy* by Fletcher, Norton, Longfellow, Cary.

Gilbert: *Dante's Conception of Justice.* Duke University Press, Durham, N. C.

Carpenter: *The Spiritual Message of Dante.* Harvard University Press, Cambridge.

Papini: *Dante Vivo.* Translated by Broadus and Benedetti. Macmillan, New York.

Norton: *The Divine Comedy.* Houghton Mifflin, Boston. Pp. 41-45.

Chapter 11

ROUSSEAU AND THE DEMOCRATIC WAY OF LIFE

I
The French Scene in the Era of Rousseau
1. Autocracy and liberalism
2. Impact of voyages and discoveries
3. The Encyclopaedists
4. English influences

II
The Rousseauan Unconventionalism, Psychopathic

III
The Dynamic Results of Rousseau's Concepts
1. The *Social Contract* and the political order
2. *Émile* and the new education
3. *La Nouvelle Héloïse* and literary romanticism

IV
Influence of Rousseau in Contemporary Thought

Chapter 11

ROUSSEAU AND THE DEMOCRATIC WAY OF LIFE

Two other persons could scarcely be found in the field of literature to present such likenesses and such striking contrasts as Rousseau and Dante. Both men spent much time in exile, both were dependent upon others for support, both were frustrated in their main desires, both exerted a vast influence on an age beyond their own. But the contrasts are even greater. Dante was distinguished by orderly self-control, an unyielding integrity; Rousseau was weak in his social relations and at times despicable. Nevertheless, this man, weak in so many respects, managed to weave himself into the texture of modern civilization as few have done. If it is proper to call Dante "the voice of the ten silent centuries," it might, without too great disparity, be said that Rousseau became the spokesman of the noisy nineteenth century.

By ascribing to him an interest in the democratic way of life is not meant to imply that he gave his open assent to democracy as a political form of organization. In fact, he believed democracy impossible except for very small political units in which every citizen should have equal share in making the laws. But the stress he placed on the value and validity of inner feeling made him the unwitting contributor to what we now call democracy. We find Rousseau emphasizing and exploiting inner feeling as a means of reaching the supreme values in human society.

He was the child of his age not by acquiescence but by rebellion and reaction, and has had no little part in the revolutionary temper of our times. Guerard speaks of him as heading up all the great tendencies of the nineteenth century, whether it be revivalism, romanticism, democracy, or socialism, and resisted today as much as ever, a favor we do not accord the dead.[1] How can so broad a statement be justified? On the surface these movements seem to be widely diverse, for one aspect of romanticism is frequently drawn up in conflict with another aspect without any suspicion on the part of either of their common basic hypothesis. In the final confessions of his *Reveries* (p. 39) he begins by writing: "All the strange ideas which pass through my head

[1] *The Life and Death of an Ideal,* Charles Scribner's, Sons, New York, p. 277.

will equally find place." Such a decision rests upon the assumption that every thought and impulse, being natural, contains a mandatory character. If this is true, then important truths may be as various and as contradictory as the impulses of men. Rousseau's age, working on this principle, was strong for private confessions, intimate journals. In religion it took the form of introspection, public confession, the exercises of "class" and prayer-meetings, conclusions of personal righteousness based on "inner feelings" that attended such avowals and confessions. Sometimes the "confessions" reached the point of grotesqueness and untruthfulness in order to exaggerate the feeling. This was the heart of revivalism, which must be considered a part of the romantic movement. Its kinship with Rousseau is illustrated in Rousseau's own *Confessions,* which go beyond the truth both in exaggerating his depravity and also in emphasizing his goodness. His goodness is held to be established once for all by his public confession. The *Confessions* were, according to his own statements, intended as a justification for his despicably weak life. Romanticism was a revolt against the excessive formality of the day as shown by the hollowness and hypocrisy of French court life.

But the spirit of romanticism is also present in a Herbert Spencer, who could "not carelessly let die" the scientific thoughts that were uttered in him as the expression of the Unknowable. The trouble with the Unknowable seems, then, as everywhere, to have been a capacity for uttering contradictions. We have a modern survival of this in the common assertion of the lawfulness of all "natural" impulses. The modern romantic novel lives and grows under the same theory. Whether we like it or not, the influence of Rousseau is still to be reckoned with.

Jean Jacques Rousseau was born of French parents in Geneva, Switzerland, in 1712, whither his ancestors had migrated in the sixteenth century. His father was a watch-maker of roving disposition, independence, and pugnacity, who, at least for one long interval, left his family and worked at his profession in Constantinople. Rousseau's mother died a week after his birth and his bringing up fell into the hands of his father and sisters. But when the lad was ten, the father, because of a brawl which had drawn the attention of the authorities, and threatened with what he thought an injustice, fled Geneva and the boy was taken in by a relative, and later placed with a country parson for education. Young Rousseau's passionate and untamed disposition led him into all sorts of difficulties, made it impossible to keep his friends or the respect of his acquaintances, and set his hand against the world at large. His life was that of a weak voluptuary, stirred with an occasional flash of genius, yet with a feeble intent toward goodness and decency that was continually in peril. In fact, he insisted on being credited with decency if he had contemplated it.

I

The French Scene in the Era of Rousseau

The scene into which Rousseau emerged was ripe for him. Louis XIV, the Grand Monarch, had died in 1715, three years after Rousseau's birth, and the nation was in the heyday of absolutism, profligacy, baroque architecture, unrefined magnificence, pompous splendor, artificiality, and decadent elegance. Two contrasting ideas were already at war in the social order, both resulting from the discovery of the New World and the succeeding voyages which brought untold wealth and plunder to Europe and a knowledge of new refinements in elegance previously unknown. In Rousseau's time these successive enrichments and exploitations had gone on so long that society flattered itself that the conditions created were eternal. At the same time there was a steady undermining of morality and frightful discrepancies between the conditions of the upper and lower classes. The chorus of acclaim for this artificial society was so general and so uninterrupted that Rousseau's first notable effort at literature hit like a thunderbolt and made him famous over night.

One of Rousseau's most consistent and lasting friends was Diderot, the editor of the famous *Encyclopédie,* who had in his writings offended the King's favorite, Madame Pompadour, and was therefore imprisoned in the fortress of Vincennes some five miles or so from Paris. Here Rousseau went daily in company with Madame Diderot. On one such occasion he called Diderot's attention to the offer of a prize by the Dijon Academy for the best essay on the subject: "Whether the recovery of the sciences and the arts had contributed to purify or corrupt morals." Diderot declared that Rousseau was for taking the affirmative until he was reminded that he could more likely win by taking the opposite side of which few others would think. Rousseau claimed it as an impulse original with himself which came at a moment of great enlightenment. At any rate, taking the opposite side of every question became, if it had not already been, the temperament of Rousseau. Thus the direct attack was made upon the sophistication of the age by the affirmation that the recovery of the sciences and arts, that is, civilization, was a corrupter of morals.   Rousseau was from the moment anathema to many.

The voyages of discovery and trade had started a movement opposite to the dream of sophistication and elegance by which Rousseau was to profit in a constructive way.   The French *voyageur* had extravagant tales to tell of the happiness and freedom of the American savage.   The experience of the early French *voyageurs* had been with the Indians of the Five Nations of New York and Canada, who lived a somewhat settled life with farms and orchards. They were supposed to live an idyllic life, close to nature, without government of restrictive kind.   In fact, many Frenchmen had fled from the *lettres cachet* and Bastille of Louis' irresponsible government to the American forest.   These facts afforded an indubitable background for Rousseau's assumption that happiness and the perfect society could be found by a return to nature. Rousseau was a countryman at heart who suffered from a sense of inferiority in the city.   The pot of liberalism had been stewing in many ways.   Forces opposed to political autocracy, often suppressed, had found their place in the great French *Encyclopédie*. The movement toward political freedom had received much impetus from England, particularly through the work of Voltaire. In this the influence of John Locke was outstanding, and Voltaire's admiration and praise for English institutions in his *English Letters* had drawn wide attention in France.   Locke's political creed was written into the famous Bill of Rights in the constitution of Virginia and later into the Federal Constitution.   In fact, what there was of importance in the *Contrat Social,* or in the education of *Émile,* was inspired by the work of Locke.   All France, in enthusiasm for America, was tending toward democracy.   It only needed a bit of shaking to precipitate democratic ideals, and Rousseau, with all his shortcomings, was the man destined to give the necessary jolt.

II

The Rousseauan Unconventionalism, Psychopathic

The psychopathic conditions which had obtained in European society were themselves not the result of Rousseau's work.   He was only a spokesman, or one of the spokesmen, for that revolt against the tyranny of form and pretense which had become insupportable.   Not only was there the overbearing arrogance of financial and political autocracy; there were similar usurpations in the world of religion and of intellect. The prevalence of a sterile Deism and the exaltation of an unbending dependence upon Reason, or rationalism had frozen out the spontaneities of life and replaced them with a gilded hypocrisy in religion and an over-weening smugness in the realm of the intellect. No wonder that the gathering storm would reach extremes of fury. Out of it came what was essentially a psychopathic orgy. Men began to consult their feelings, their emotions, rather than their reason. The reflective processes were held in abeyance while passions were indulged—the passions of the French Revolution, of romanticism in literature, of revivalism in religion, of social democracy in governmental theory, of humanism in education.

The high priest in this upset was the morally weak and tarnished psychopathic Rousseau. After the Dijon prize was awarded him he found himself thrust in a new role. Up to this time he had been elegant and fastidious in dress, aping that of the court. He now traded his powdered wig for a disheveled one and resorted to plainness and untidiness to carry out the suddenly earned reputation of a man who sought to get "back to nature" and to be ruled only by elemental instincts. Through the influence of the Duke of Luxembourg, his play *Le Divin du Village* was given before the King, and Rousseau appeared there amid the elegance of the best-dressed court in Europe in rusty clothes, disheveled wig, and unshaven face to draw the amused attention of the royal retinue. His attempt to be "different" added to his sense of confusion and inferiority. There was doubtless much claptrap and vulgarity about him and much of this was to express itself in the Reign of Terror which ushered in the outward revolution, which was the late aftermath of a long suppression of human emotions and instincts.

III

The Dynamic Results of Rousseau's Concepts

The results of Rousseau's concept of the return to nature were operative in three general directions characterized by his three main literary efforts. His *Nouvelle Héloïse*, the *New Heloise*, marks the modern revival of romanticism in literature. His *Émile;* the education of a *Savoyard Vicar*, which affected little in its day, has become the prevailing theory of education; his *Contrat social*, or *The Social Contract*, became the Bible of the Revolution and the moving ideology of modern democratic movements.

These tendencies in literature, education, and government were grounded on belief in the supreme validity of personal feeling. This is testified by the existence of Rousseau's own personal *Confessions,* in which he endeavors to lay bare all of his inner experiences, even the most intimate. He held it a fault to hold back anything of sentiment or feeling, even when it would injure friends and intimates. Such a situation can arise only when there is a conviction that these intimacies are important, that they bear a validity quite apart from their meaning. They appear as a part of the state of nature. To withhold anything is to betray the supreme values. We witness this psychopathic condition occasionally in criminals who are eager to confess even crimes of which they are not guilty. But these "confessions" often lie dangerously close to pride in evil deeds and even boastfulness. They become means by which the individual calls undeserved attention to himself and can easily feed the egotism which springs from a sense of inferiority.

It can thus be seen how apt a Rousseauan civilization like ours is to become the subject of abuse. If we look for the worst features we find their reflections in many Romantic novels of our own time, in which without reserve our literary men hasten to make public the most intimate of their experiences, so that what is called literature in our time often smells of the brothel, the operating room, and the insane ward.

Rousseau summed up his definition of education in the phrase: "Those who can best endure the good and evil of life are the best educated." To this end he considered it essential that a man should be educated as a man. He must live in an artificial society, created by contract, and yet he must live comformably to his own nature. Left to himself he would become the worst and most selfish of all monsters. By far the best part of the child's education must be imparted by the mother, who begins his adaptation to society and social obligation, thus helping him to the solution of the conflict between his natural wants and the general good of his associates. Thus he concludes the best social institutions are the ones best fitted to make a man unnatural in the sense that he exchanges his independence for dependence.

This position seems, at first blush, to negate any concept of education by nature, but when it is seen how the individual must adapt himself to the wills of others in his environment, it appears in the good Epicurean sense that "he can be free only as he wants that which is obtainable." That man is truly free who desires what he is able to perform; therefore freedom, not power, is the greatest good.   To strike the happy balance so that the child will want only that which he ought to have is for Rousseau the source of all educational rules.

For the fullest freedom, then, the individual must accommodate himself to the needs of society which can, according to his judgment, be best accomplished through the independence that comes to the man who has mastered a trade.   Possession of the skill of the artisan raises him, because of this independence, to the status . of a man.   This status of independence is, in Rousseau's judgment, more important than technical learning, for "there are more mistaken notions in the Academy of Science than in a whole tribe of American Indians."   Presumably the Indian would not be at a loss to take care of himself in an environment in which the Academician would perish.

This limitation of desires has further repercussions upon his life, because goodness or badness is influenced by the extent of lawfulness of his needs.   As we multiply our wants we multiply our dependence upon others and suffer the temptation to fulfill them illegitimately.   It is the fewness of his needs, the narrow limits within which he can compare himself with others, that makes a man really good; what makes him really bad is a multiplicity of needs and dependence on the opinions of others.   The importance of this self-contained attitude is illustrated by the fact that all our acts must be brought before the tribunal of selfhood: "The man who thinks he is enjoying the fruits of his vices is no less tormented by them than if they had not been successful."

Last of all comes the description of the completely educated *Émile:*

> What then is required for the proper study of men? A great wish to know men, great impartiality of judgment, a heart sufficiently sensitive to understand every human passion, and calm enough to be free from passion. If there is any time in our life when this study is likely to be appreciated, it is this that I have chosen for Émile; before this time men would have been strangers to him; later on he would have been like them. Convention, the effects of which he already perceives, has not yet made him its slave, the passions, whose consequences he realises, have not yet stirred his heart. He is a man; he takes an interest in his brethren; he is a just man and he judges his peers. Now it is certain that if he judges them rightly he will not want to change places with any one of them, for the goal of all their anxious efforts is the result of prejudices which he does not share, and that goal seems to him a mere dream. For his own part, he has all he wants within his reach. How should he be

dependent on any one when he is self-sufficing and free from prejudice? Strong arms, good health, moderation, few needs, together
with the means to satisfy those needs, are his. He has been brought
up in complete liberty and servitude is the greatest ill he understands. He pities these miserable kings, the slaves of all who obey
them; he pities these false prophets fettered by their empty fame;
he pities these rich fools, martyrs to their own pomp; he pities these
ostentatious voluptuaries, who spend their life in deadly dullness
that they may seem to enjoy its pleasures. He would pity the very
foe who harmed him, for he would discern his wretchedness beneath
his cloak of spite. He would say to himself, "This man has yielded
to his desire to hurt me, and this need of his places him at my
mercy."

One step more and our goal is attained. Selfishness is a dangerous tool though a useful one; it often wounds the hand that uses it,
and it rarely does good unmixed with evil. When Émile considers
his place among men, when he finds himself so fortunately situated,
he will be tempted to give credit to his own reason for the work of
yours, and to attribute to his own deserts what is really the result
of his good fortune. He will say to himself: "I am wise and other
men are fools." He will pity and despise them and will congratulate
himself all the more heartily; and as he knows he is happier than
they, he will think his deserts are greater. This is the fault we have
most to fear, for it is the most difficult to eradicate. If he remained
in this state of mind, he would have profited little by all our care;
and if I had to choose, I hardly know whether I would not rather
choose the illusions of prejudice than those of pride.

Great men are under no illusion with respect to their superiority;
they see it and know it, but they are none the less modest. The more
they have, the better they know what they lack. They are less vain
of their superiority over us than ashamed by the consciousness of
their weakness, and among the good things they really possess, they
are too wise to pride themselves on a gift which is none of their
getting. The good man may be proud of his virtue for it is his own,
but what cause for pride has the man of intellect?[2]

The resulting benefits to education of Rousseau's theory cannot be denied. though he was quite impractical in his presentation
of it. Humane education has come to mean a training which has
regard to the nature and sensibilities of the person to be educated,
an inner and constructive development within the individual. It
may be carried to excess if it overlooks the Rousseauan doctrine of
conformation of the individual to the needs of the social environment.

The opening sentence of the *Contrat social* was a stroke of
genius, for it immediately arrests the attention of every reader.
"Man is born free; and everywhere he is in chains," is an imme-

[2] *Émile,* Everyman's Library, E. P. Dutton & Company, New York, Book IV,
pp. 206-207.

diate and direct challenge to the existing social order. Later we
learn that the chains are self-forged, due to the necessity of the
individual to live in a world of men. Though his first impulse
is to look out for himself alone, and belong to himself alone,
Rousseau discloses that in a stricter sense he belongs to society.
He alienates his liberty for some benefit to be gained. But Jean
Jacques speaks to an age which is blind to the contractual nature
of social organization. Society is looked upon as the property and
privilege of its rulers. "Force made the first slaves and their
cowardice perpetuated their condition. Are, then, the strongest
to rule the others?" He shows that the strongest are never strong
enough to rule the many indefinitely unless they transform their
strength into right, and obedience is not of force but of duty.
Force itself never creates right, and, since no man has natural
authority over his fellows, legitimate authority is established by
convention. The slave sells himself for subsistence, but even at
that he has no right to deliver over his children to slavery. To
renounce liberty is to renounce being a man, but such a course
is incompatible with man's nature.

Majority rule, then, is founded on such a convention: a general
agreement of all to abide by the will of the majority. How a
man may unite himself with all and yet retain his freedom and
obey himself alone is the problem which is only solved by resort
to the social contract. He wills to will the way of the majority.
"Each one puts his person and all his power under the supreme
direction of the general will." Since one individual cannot contract for his children, there must be new submission of the contract to each passing generation.

The establishment of the civil state works fundamental changes
in man himself as he passes from the rule of individual instinct to
rule by social justice. His faculties, however, are stimulated and
developed as he surrenders unlimited right to get whatever he can,
and thereby gains civil liberty and the right to lawful and social
possession. His civil liberty is bounded by the general will, and
his moral liberty makes him master of himself.

Upon such a suppositional contract rests the right of the state
to establish law and the power of life and death over the individual. Every malefactor by attacking the general right becomes
a rebel and a traitor, making the preservation of the state inconsistent with his own. The state, in self-preservation of the common
good, may rightly take his life. Law then becomes the means by

which right-minded keepers of the social contract are protected from the encroachments of the anti-social.

In the political field, likewise, we need to guard against the Rousseauan extreme by remembering that freedom, democracy, is an affair of reason, of realism as well as one of feeling and sentiment. Democracy as a protection of rights we can all feel and understand. What is not so easy of understanding by the flag-waver and emotionalist is a true consideration of the responsibility involved. *The Social Contract* switched the doctrine of sovereignty from the divine right of kings to that of the divine right of the governed. It is weak in its forgetfulness of the fact that it cannot be implemented by wild and reckless attention to the feelings, but only by a reasonable restraint and self-control. Rousseau was all for freedom without obligation.

IV

Influence of Rousseau in Contemporary Thought

It would be difficult to overestimate the influence of Rousseau in contemporary thought. We might very truly be said to be living in the Rousseauan century. Politically, Rousseau, more perhaps than any other one man, unless it be the Englishman John Locke, fostered the democratic movement. There is no doubt that his work was the main inspiration of the French Revolution, but also, alas, of its excesses and weaknesses. In fact, the attitude of life practised by Rousseau has written itself upon our century and may be seen as the picture and symbol of our own times, and may be one reason why democracy has been discredited and compelled to fight for its very existence. Take, for instance, Rousseau's theory of sovereignty. In *The Social Contract,* the sovereignty is assumed to reside in the people. This seems, and is, a correct and basic principle of democracy, government by the governed. Why is this democratic principle questioned today, after so long a trial? One ventures to say not because it is less true now than when Rousseau first expressed it. It is rather because it is attended by the moral weakness that characterized Rousseau's own conduct. Our democracy, with true Rousseauan sentimentality, has emphasized the rights of the citizen to the full enjoyment of himself, with very slight emphasis upon the responsibilities, self-restraint, and sacrifices which alone make a working democracy possible. Other influences were dominant in the days of the establishment of the American Republic, such as the religious interest and belief, which helped to keep men morally in line, respect for rulers, and a general *camaraderie* possible only in small communities and frontier situations, which made class distinctions of little account if not impossible. These conditions have been changing rapidly in the last half century, and we are becoming more and more the victims of the Rousseauan sentimentality. We want to do whatever we feel like doing rather than what we ought to do. Hence when situations become intolerable, we pass laws. Then while we expect the laws to be enforced against our neighbors, we have little stomach for obeying them ourselves and think we should be the exception. Too many of our citizens are thus willing to break the laws, in the breaking of which they think they will not be detected, or with the purpose of which they disagree, or which they would apply to others. The measure of the strength of democracy lies in the law-abiding character of its citizens when there are no police in the immediate vicinity. This strength is not based on personal sentiment but rather on the broader basis of reason with which too many of us are impatient. This impatience was characteristic of Rousseau, as it is likewise of the romantic spirit generally.

In the matter of the Rousseauan literary romanticism, a like tendency may be noted. This flair for telling all without respect to delicacy of feeling, inner integrity, or even decency, has come not only to distinguish our fiction, but is prevalent in many other directions. One best seller after another vies with the latest in indecency. Only the appeal to vulgarity is assumed to be sufficiently potent to induce sales. A similar situation holds for the cinema and theatre. Our journalism is too slightly concerned to tell the truth, but primarily to represent or misrepresent facts in a sensational way. At all costs we must have a "story." We have here again the practice of romanticism in which feeling is more important than fact. Nor is the same temper wanting from the ranks of professional religion, in which the appeal is primarily to the emotions and the force and power of religion is judged, not by ethical achievements, but rather by inner sentiment, the "feeling" of holiness or happiness or exultation induced by the size of the crowd in attendance. The same romantic temper is displayed in the psychological advice "to let ourselves go" for fear of inhibitions, until the question arises whether one is ever called upon to deny any impulse which may for the moment move him. In education *Émile* has become the master pattern, but little improved upon during the last century and a half—a picture of

the latest progressive scholar. Here the feelings of the pupil are
to be the chief criteria of what he should study. Before he has
had any opportunity to learn distinctions between one course and
another, he is called upon to say which he would like best to do.
These unwelcome facts form the dark side of the Rousseauan
practices. We should not blink the weaknesses because there is
an honorable place for sentiment in literature without which it
becomes impotent, nor because the principle of governmental
sovereignty in the people is still a sound basis for political organization, nor because the newer intellectual processes have brought
a welcome liberation from much that was bad in the past. Let us
freely recognize the benefits that followed in the train of Rousseauan doctrine, but let us beware of those debilitations in our
modern civilization which in Rousseau's own life and conduct
served to undo the best that he had done.

These shortcomings are the menace as well as the impetus to
democracy. If men will not govern themselves, but will be ruled
only by force from without, they must be prepared to endure the
threat of dictatorship. Because measures are decided by sentiment rather than realism, the best safeguards of democracy are
in danger of overthrow. Because men, in a weak sentimentalism,
prefer to be led by pleasant lies rather than unpleasant truths they
are ill-prepared to meet the future. Because of romanticism in
religion, institutions which should have been most realistic of all
in the face of condemnation of human wickedness, have confused
the issues between right and wrong and have been stricken with
moral paralysis. Yet with all this Morley could write of the work
of Rousseau:

> He alone had the gift of the golden mouth. It was in Rousseau
> that polite Europe first hearkened to strange voices and faint rever-
> berations from out of the vague and cavernous shadow in which com-
> mon people move . . . the race owes something to one who helped to
> state the problem, writing up in letters of flame, at the brutal feast
> of Kings and the rich, that civilization is as yet only a mockery.[3]

Let us remember the weaknesses as well as the strengths of the
romantic spirit.

[3] Morley, *Rousseau and His Era,* by permission, The Macmillan Company, New
York, 1923, I, 7.

READINGS

(Chapter 11)

ROUSSEAU: *THE SOCIAL CONTRACT*. Everyman's Library, Edited by Ernest Rhys. E. P. Dutton & Company, New York. Bk. I, Chap. I, p. 5; Chap. II, pp. 6-7; Chap. III, pp. 8-9; Chap. IV, pp. 9-10; Chaps. V, VI, VIII; Bk. II, Chap. V, pp. 30-31; Chap. VI, pp. 32-34.

BOOK I

CHAPTER I

SUBJECT OF THE FIRST BOOK

Man is born free; and everywhere he is in chains. One thinks himself the master of others, and still remains a greater slave than they. How did this change come about? · I do not know. What can make it legitimate? That question I think I can answer.

If I took into account only force, and the effects derived from it, I should say: "As long as a people is compelled to obey, and obeys, it does well; as soon as it can shake off the yoke, and shakes it off, it does still better; for, regaining its liberty by the same right as took it away, either it is justified in resuming it, or there was no justification for those who took it away." But the social order is a sacred right which is the basis of all other rights. Nevertheless, this right does not come from nature, and must therefore be founded on conventions. Before coming to that, I have to prove what I have just asserted.

CHAPTER II

THE FIRST SOCIETIES

The most ancient of all societies, and the only one that is natural, is the family: and even so the children remain attached to the father only so long as they need him for their preservation. As soon as this need ceases, the natural bond is dissolved. The children, released from the obedience they owed to the father, and the father, released from the care he owed his children, return equally to independence. If they remain united, they continue so no longer naturally, but voluntarily; and the family itself is then maintained only by convention.

This common liberty results from the nature of man. His first law is to provide for his own preservation, his first cares are those which he owes to himself; and, as soon as he reaches years of discretion, he is the sole judge of the proper means of preserving himself, and consequently becomes his own master.

The family then may be called the first model of political societies: the ruler corresponds to the father, and the people to the children; and all, being born free and equal, alienate their liberty only for their own advantage. The whole difference is that, in the family, the love of the father for his children repays him for the care he takes of them, while, in the State, the pleasure of commanding takes the place of the love which the chief cannot have for the peoples under him.

Grotius denies that all human power is established in favour of the governed, and quotes slavery as an example. His usual method of reasoning is constantly to establish right by fact. It would be possible to employ a more logical method, but none could be more favourable to tyrants.

It is then, according to Grotius, doubtful whether the human race belongs to a hundred men, or that hundred men to the human race; and, throughout his book, he seems to incline to the former alternative, which is also the view of Hobbes. On this showing, the human species is divided into so many herds of cattle, each with its ruler, who keeps guard over them for the purpose of devouring them.

As a shepherd is of a nature superior to that of his flock, the shepherds of men, *i.e.* their rulers, are of nature superior to that of the peoples under them. Thus, Philo tells us, the Emperor Caligula reasoned, concluding equally well either that kings were gods, or that men were beasts.

The reasoning of Caligula agrees with that of Hobbes and Grotius. Aristotle, before any of them, had said that men are by no means equal naturally, but that some are born for slavery, and others for dominion.

Aristotle was right; but he took the effect for the cause. Nothing can be more certain than that every man born in slavery is born for slavery. Slaves lose everything in their chains, even the desire of escaping from them: they love their servitude, as the comrades of Ulysses loved their brutish condition. If then there are slaves by nature, it is because there have been slaves against nature. Force made the first slaves, and their cowardice perpetuated the condition. . . .

CHAPTER III

THE RIGHT OF THE STRONGEST

The strongest is never strong enough to be always the master, unless he transforms strength into right, and obedience into duty. Hence the right of the strongest, which, though to all seeming meant ironically, is really laid down as a fundamental principle. But are we never to have an explanation of this phrase? Force is a physical power, and I fail to see what moral effect it can have. To yield to force is an act of necessity, not of will—at the most, an act of prudence. In what sense can it be a duty?

Suppose for a moment that this so-called "right" exists. I maintain that the sole result is a mass of inexplicable nonsense. For, if force creates right, the effect changes with the cause: every force that is greater than the first succeeds to its right. As soon as it is possible to disobey with impunity, disobedience is legitimate; and, the strongest being always in the right, the only thing that matters is to act so as to become the strongest. But what kind of right is that which perishes when force fails? If we must obey perforce, there is no need to obey because we ought; and if we are not forced to obey, we are under no obligation to do so. Clearly, the word "right" adds nothing to force: in this connection, it means absolutely nothing.

Obey the powers that be. If this means yield to force, it is a good precept, but superfluous: I can answer for its never being violated. All power comes from God, I admit; but so does all sickness: does that mean that we are forbidden to call in the doctor? A brigand surprises me at the edge of a wood: must I not merely surrender my purse on compulsion; but, even if I could withhold it, am I in conscience bound to give it up? For certainly the pistol he holds is also a power.

Let us then admit that force does not create right, and that we are obliged to obey only legitimate powers. In that case, my original question recurs.

CHAPTER IV

SLAVERY

Since no man has a natural authority over his fellow, and force creates no right, we must conclude that conventions form the basis of all legitimate authority among men.

If an individual, says Grotius, can alienate his liberty and make himself the slave of a master, why could not a whole people do the same and make itself subject to a king? There are in this passage plenty of ambiguous words which would need explaining; but let us confine ourselves to the word *alienate*. To alienate is to give or to sell. Now, a man who becomes the slave of another does not give himself; he sells himself, at the least for his subsistence: but for what does a people sell itself? A king is so far from furnishing his subjects with their subsistence that he gets his own only from them; and, according to Rabelais, kings do not live on nothing. Do subjects then give their persons on condition that the king takes their goods also? I fail to see what they have left to preserve.

It will be said that the despot assures his subjects civil tranquility. Granted; but what do they gain, if the wars his ambition brings down upon them, his insatiable avidity, and the vexatious conduct of his ministers press harder on them than their own dissensions would have done? What do they gain, if the very tranquility they enjoy is one of their miseries? Tranquility is found also in dungeons; but is that enough to make them desirable places to live in? The Greeks imprisoned in the cave of the Cyclops lived there very tranquilly, while they were awaiting their turn to be devoured.

To say that a man gives himself gratuitously, is to say what is absurd and inconceivable.; such an act is null and illegitimate, from the mere fact that he who does it is out of his mind. To say the same of a whole people is to suppose a people of madmen; and madness creates no right.

Even if each man could alienate himself, he could not alienate his children: they are born men and free; their liberty belongs to them, and no one but they has the right to dispose of it. Before they come to years of discretion, the father can, in their name, lay down conditions for their preservation and well-being, but he cannot give them irrevocably and without conditions: such a gift is contrary to the ends of nature, and exceeds the rights of paternity. It would therefore be necessary, in order to legitimize an arbitrary government, that in every generation the people should be in a position to accept or reject it; but. were this so, the government would be no longer arbitrary.

To renounce liberty is to renounce being a man, to surrender the rights of humanity and even its duties. For him who renounces everything no indemnity is possible. Such a renunciation is incompatible with man's nature; to remove all liberty from his will is to remove all morality from his acts. . . .

CHAPTER V

THAT WE MUST ALWAYS GO BACK TO A FIRST CONVENTION

Even if I granted all that I have been refuting, the friends of despotism would be no better off. There will always be a great difference between subduing a multitude and ruling a society. Even if scattered individuals were successively enslaved by one man, however numerous they might be, I still see no more than a master and his slaves, and certainly not a people and its ruler; I see what may be termed an aggregation, but not an association; there is as yet neither public good nor body politic. The man in question, even if he has enslaved half the world, is still only an individual; his interest, apart from that of others, is still a purely private interest. If this same man comes to die, his empire, after him, remains scattered and without unity, as an oak falls and dissolves into a heap of ashes when the fire has consumed it.

A people, says Grotius, can give itself to a king. Then, according to Grotius, a people is a people before it gives itself. The gift is itself a civil act, and implies public deliberation. It would be better, before examining the act by which a people gives itself to a king, to examine that by which it has become a people; for this act, being necessarily prior to the other, is the true foundation of society.

Indeed, if there were no prior convention, where, unless the election were unanimous, would be the obligation on the minority to submit to the choice of the majority? How have a hundred men who wish for a master the right to vote on behalf of ten who do not? The law of majority voting is itself something established by convention, and presupposes unanimity, on one occasion at least.

CHAPTER VI

THE SOCIAL COMPACT

I suppose men to have reached the point at which the obstacles in the way of their preservation in the state of nature show their power of resistance to be greater than the resources at the disposal of each individual for his maintenance in that state. That primitive condition can then subsist no longer; and the human race would perish unless it changed its manner of existence.

But, as men cannot engender new forces, but only unite and direct existing ones, they have no other means of preserving themselves than the formation, by aggregation, of a sum of forces great enough to overcome the resistance. These they have to bring into play by means of a single motive power, and cause to act in concert.

This sum of forces can arise only where several persons come together: but, as the force and liberty of each man are the chief instruments of his self-preservation, how can he pledge them without harming his own interests, and neglecting the care he owes to himself? This difficulty, in its bearing on my present subject, may be stated in the following terms—

"The problem is to find a form of association which will defend and protect with the whole common force the person and goods of each associate, and in which each, while uniting himself with all, may still obey himself alone, and remain as free as before." This is the fundamental problem of which the *Social Contract* provides the solution.

The clauses of this contract are so determined by the nature of the act that the slightest modification would make them vain and ineffective; so that, although they have perhaps never been formally set forth, they are everywhere the same and everywhere tacitly admitted and recognized, until, on the violation of the social compact, each regains his original rights and resumes his natural liberty, while losing the conventional liberty in favour of which he renounced it.

These clauses, properly understood, may be reduced to one—the total alienation of each associate, together with all his rights, to the whole community; for, in the first place, as each gives himself absolutely, the conditions are the same for all; and, this being so, no one has any interest in making them burdensome to others.

Moreover, the alienation being without reserve, the union is as perfect as it can be, and no associate has anything more to demand: for, if the individuals retained certain rights, as there would be no common superior to decide between them and the public, each, being on one point his own judge, would ask to be so on all; the state of nature would thus continue, and the association would necessarily become inoperative or tyrannical.

Finally, each man, in giving himself to all, gives himself to nobody; and as there is no associate over whom he does not acquire the same right as he yields others over himself, he gains an equivalent for everything he loses, and an increase of force for the preservation of what he has.

If then we discard from the social compact what is not of its essence, we shall find that it reduces itself to the following terms—

"Each of us puts his person and all his power in common under the supreme direction of the general will, and, in our corporate capacity, we receive each member as an indivisible part of the whole."

At once, in place of the individual personality of each contracting party, this act of association creates a moral and collective body, composed of as many members as the assembly contains votes, and receiving from this act its unity, its common identity, its life and its will. This public person, so formed by the union of all other persons, formerly took the name of city,[1] and now takes that of *Republic* or *body politic;* it is called by its members *State* when passive, *Sovereign* when active, and *Power* when compared with others like itself. Those who are associated in it take collectively the name of *people,* and severally are called *citizens,* as sharing in the sovereign power, and *subjects,* as being under the laws of the State. But these terms are often confused and taken one for another: it is enough to know how to distinguish them when they are being used with precision. . . .

[1] The real meaning of this word has been almost wholly lost in modern times; most people mistake a town for a city, and a townsman for a citizen. They do not know that houses make a town, but citizens a city. The same mistake long ago cost the Carthaginians dear. I have never read of the title of citizens being given to the subjects of any prince, not even the ancient Macedonians or the English of today, though they are nearer liberty than any one else. The French alone everywhere familiarly adopt the name of citizens, because, as can be seen from their dictionaries, they have no idea of its meaning; otherwise they would be guilty in usurping it, of the crime of *lèse majesté:* among them, the name expresses a virtue, and not a right. When Bodin spoke of our citizens and townsmen, he fell into a bad blunder in taking the one class for the other. M. d'Alembert has avoided the error, and, in his article on Geneva, has clearly distinguished the four orders of men (or even five, counting mere foreigners) who dwell in our town, of which two only compose the Republic. No other French writer, to my knowledge, has understood the real meaning of the word citizen.

CHAPTER VIII

THE CIVIL STATE

The passage from the state of nature to the civil produces a very remarkable change in man, by substituting justice for instinct in his conduct, and giving his actions the morality they had formerly lacked. Then only, when the voice of duty takes the place of physical impulses and right of appetite, does man, who so far had considered only himself, find that he is forced to act on different principles, and to consult his reason before listening to his inclinations. Although, in this state, he deprives himself of some advantages which he got from nature, he gains in return others so great, his faculties are so stimulated and developed, his ideas so extended, his feelings so ennobled, and his whole soul so uplifted, that, did not the abuses of this new condition often degrade him below that which he left, he would be bound to bless continually the happy moment which took him from it forever, and, instead of a stupid and unimaginative animal, made him an intelligent being and a man.

Let us draw up the whole account in terms easily commensurable. What man loses by the social contract is his natural liberty and an unlimited right to everything he tries to get and succeeds in getting; what he gains is civil liberty and the proprietorship of all he possesses. If we are to avoid mistake in weighing one against the other, we must clearly distinguish natural liberty, which is bounded only by the strength of the individual, from civil liberty, which is limited by the general will; and possession, which is merely the effect of force or the right of the first occupier, from property, which can be founded only on a positive title.

We might, over and above all this, add, to what man acquires in the civil state, moral liberty, which alone makes him truly master of himself; for the mere impulse of appetite is slavery, while obedience to a law which we prescribe to ourselves is liberty. But I have already said too much on this head, and the philosophical meaning of the word liberty does not now concern us. . . .

BOOK II

. . . . . .

CHAPTER V

THE RIGHT OF LIFE AND DEATH

The question is often asked how individuals, having no right to dispose of their own lives, can transfer to the Sovereign a right which they do not possess. The difficulty of answering this question seems to me to lie in its being wrongly stated. Every man has a right to risk his own life in order to preserve it. Has it ever been said that a man who throws himself out of the window to escape from a fire is guilty of suicide? Has such a crime ever been laid to the charge of him who perishes in a storm because, when he went on board, he knew of the danger?

The social treaty has for its end the preservation of the contracting parties. He who wills the end wills the means also, and the means must involve some risks, and even some losses. He who wishes to preserve his life at others' expense should also, when it is necessary, be ready to give it up for their sake. Furthermore, the citizen is no longer the judge of the dangers to which the law desires him to expose himself; and when the prince says to him: "It is expedient for the State that you should die," he ought to die, because it is only on that condition that he has been living in security up to the present, and because his life is no longer a mere bounty of nature, but a gift made conditionally by the State.

The death penalty inflicted upon criminals may be looked on in much the same light: it is in order that we may not fall victims to an assassin that we consent to die if we ourselves turn assassins. In this treaty, so far from disposing of our own lives, we think only of securing them, and it is not to be assumed that any of the parties then expects to get hanged.

Again, every malefactor, by attacking social rights, becomes on forfeit a rebel and a traitor to his country; by violating its laws he ceases to be a member of it; he even makes war upon it. In such a case the preservation of the State is inconsistent with his own, and one or the other must perish; in putting the guilty to death, we slay not so much the citizen as an enemy. The trial and the judgment are the proofs that he has broken the social treaty, and is in consequences no longer a member of the State. Since, then, he has recognized himself to be such by living there, he must be removed by exile as a violator of the compact, or by death as a public enemy; for such an enemy is not a moral person, but merely a man; and in such a case the right of war is to kill the vanquished. . . .

CHAPTER VI

LAW

By the social compact we have given the body politic existence and life; we have now by legislation to give it movement and will. For the original act by which the body is formed and united still in no respect determines what it ought to do for its preservation.

What is well and in conformity with order is so by the nature of things and independently of human conventions. All justice comes from God, who is its sole source; but if we knew how to receive so high an inspiration, we should need neither government nor laws. Doubtless, there is a universal justice emanating from reason alone;

but this justice, to be admitted among us, must be mutual. Humanly speaking, in default of natural sanctions, the laws of justice are ineffective among men: they merely make for the good of the wicked and the undoing of the just, when the just man observes them towards everybody and nobody observes them towards him. Conventions and laws are therefore needed to join rights to duties and refer justice to its object. In the state of nature, where everything is common, I owe nothing to him whom I have promised nothing; I recognize as belonging to others only what is of no use to me. In the state of society all rights are fixed by law, and the case becomes different.

But what, after all, is a law? As long as we remain satisfied with attaching purely metaphysical ideas to the word, we shall go on arguing without arriving at an understanding; and when we have defined a law of nature, we shall be no nearer the definition of a law of the State.

I have already said that there can be no general will directed to a particular object. Such an object must be either within or outside the State. If outside, a will which is alien to it cannot be, in relation to it, general; if within, it is part of the State, and in that case there arises a relation between whole and part which makes them two separate beings, of which the part is one, and the whole minus the part the other. But the whole minus a part cannot be the whole; and while this relation persists, there can be no whole, but only two unequal parts; and it follows that the will of one is no longer in any respect general in relation to the other.

But when the whole people decrees for the whole people, it is considering only itself; and if a relation is then formed, it is between two aspects of the entire object, without there being any division of the whole. In that case the matter about which the decree is made is, like the decreeing will, general. This act is what I call a law.

When I say that the object of laws is always general, I mean that law considers subjects *en masse* and actions in the abstract, and never a particular person or action. Thus the law may indeed decree that there shall be privileges, but cannot confer them on anybody by name. It may set up several classes of citizens, and even lay down the qualifications for membership of these classes, but it cannot nominate such and such persons as belonging to them; it may establish a monarchical government and hereditary succession, but it cannot choose a king, or nominate a royal family. In a word, no function which has a particular object belongs to the legislative power.

On this view, we at once see that it can no longer be asked whose business it is to make laws, since they are acts of the general will; nor whether the prince is above the law, since he is a member of the State; nor whether the law can be unjust, since no one is unjust to himself; nor how we can be both free and subject to the laws, since they are but registers of our wills.

We see further that, as the law unites universality of will with universality of object, what a man, whoever he be, commands of his own motion cannot be a law; and even what the Sovereign commands with regard to a particular matter is no nearer being a law, but is a decree, an act, not of sovereignty, but of magistracy.

I therefore give the name "Republic" to every State that is governed by laws, no matter what the form of its administration may be: for only in such a case does the public interest govern, and the *res publica* rank as a *reality*. Every legitimate government is republican;[2] what government is I will explain later on.

Laws are, properly speaking, only the conditions of civil association. The people, being subject to the laws, ought to be their author: the conditions of the society ought to be regulated solely by those who come together to form it. But how are they to regulate them? Is it to be by common agreement, by a sudden inspiration? Has the body politic an organ to declare its will? Who can give it the foresight to formulate and announce its acts in advance? Or how is it to announce them in the hour of need? How can a blind multitude, which often does not know what it wills, because it rarely knows what is good for it, carry out for itself so great and difficult an enterprise as a system of legislation? Of itself the people wills always the good, but of itself it by no means always sees it. The general will is always in the right, but the judgment which guides it is not always enlightened. It must be got to see objects as they are, and sometimes as they ought to appear to it; it must be shown the good road it is in search of, secured from the seductive influences of individual wills, taught to see times and spaces as a series, and made to weigh the attractions of present and sensible advantages against the danger of distant and hidden evils. The individuals see the good they reject; the public wills the good it does not see. All stand equally in need of guidance. The former must be compelled to bring their wills into conformity with their reason; the latter must be taught to know what it wills. If that is done, public enlightenment leads to the union of understanding and will in the social body: the parts are made to work exactly together, and the whole is raised to its highest power. This makes a legislator necessary.

---

[2] I understand, by this word, not merely an aristocracy or a democracy, but generally any government directed by the general will, which is the law. To be legitimate, the government must be, not one with the Sovereign, but its minister. In such a case even a monarchy is a Republic. This will be made clearer in the following book.

ROUSSEAU: *EMILE*. Translated by Barbara Foxley. Everyman's Library, Edited by Ernest Rhys. E. P. Dutton & Company, New York. Bk. I, pp. 5-7, 9; Bk. II, pp. 47-48; Bk. III, pp. 158-159, 167; Bk. IV, pp. 174-175, pp. 206-207.

BOOK I

God makes all things good; man meddles with them and they become evil. He forces one soil to yield the products of another, one tree to bear another's fruit. He confuses and confounds time, place, and natural conditions. He mutilates his dog, his horse, and his slave. He destroys and defaces all things; he loves all that is deformed and monstrous; he will have nothing as nature made it, not even man himself, who must learn his paces like a saddle-horse, and be shaped to his master's taste like the trees in his garden.

Yet things would be worse without this education, and mankind cannot be made by halves. Under existing conditions a man left to himself from birth would be more of a monster than the rest. Prejudice, authority, necessity, example, all the social conditions into which we are plunged, would stifle nature in him and put nothing in her place. She would be like a sapling chance sown in the midst of the highway, bent hither and thither and soon crushed by the passers-by.

Tender, anxious mother,[1] I appeal to you. You can remove this young tree from the highway and shield it from the crushing force of social conventions. Tend and water it ere it dies. One day its fruit will reward your care. From the outset raise a wall round your child's soul; another may sketch the plan, you alone should carry it into execution.

Plants are fashioned by cultivation, man by education. If a man were born tall and strong, his size and strength would be of no good to him till he had learnt to use them; they would even harm him by

[1] The earliest education is most important and it undoubtedly is woman's work. If the author of nature had meant to assign it to men he would have given them milk to feed the child. Address your treatises on education to the women, for not only are they able to watch over it more closely than men, not only is their influence always predominant in education, its success concerns them more nearly, for most widows are at the mercy of their children, who show them very plainly whether their education was good or bad. The laws, always more concerned about property than about people, since their object is not virtue but peace, the laws give too little authority to the mother. Yet her position is more certain than that of the father, her duties are less trying; the right ordering of the family depends more upon her, and she is usually fonder of her children. There are occasions when a son may be excused for lack of respect for his father, but if a child could be so unnatural as to fail in respect for the mother who bore him and nursed him at her breast, who for so many years devoted herself to his care, such a monstrous wretch should be smothered at once as unworthy to live. You say mothers spoil their children, and no doubt that is wrong, but it is worse to deprave them as you do. The mother wants her child to be happy now. She is right, and if her method is wrong, she must be taught a better. Ambition, avarice, tyranny, the mistaken foresight of fathers, their neglect, their harshness, are a hundredfold more harmful to the child than the blind affection of the mother. Moreover, I must explain what I mean by a mother and that explanation follows.

preventing others from coming to his aid;[2] left to himself he would die of want before he knew his needs.   We lament the helplessness of infancy; we fail to perceive that the race would have perished had not man begun by being a child.

We are born weak, we need strength; helpless, we need aid; foolish, we need reason.   All that we lack at birth, all that we need when we come to man's estate, is the gift of education.

This education comes to us from nature, from men, or from things. The inner growth of our organs and faculties is the education of nature, the use we learn to make of this growth is the education of men, what we gain by our experience of our surroundings is the education of things.

Thus we are each taught by three masters.   If their teaching conflicts, the scholar is ill-educated and will never be at peace with himself; if their teaching agrees, he goes straight to his goal, he lives at peace with himself, he is well-educated.

Now of these three factors in education nature is wholly beyond our control, things are only partly in our power; the education of men is the only one controlled by us; and even here our power is largely illusory, for who can hope to direct every word and deed of all with whom the child has to do.

Viewed as an art, the success of education is almost impossible, since the essential conditions of success are beyond our control.   Our efforts may bring us within sight of the goal, but fortune must favour us if we are to reach it.

What is this goal?   As we have just shown, it is the goal of nature. Since all three modes of education must work together, the two that we can control must follow the lead of that which is beyond our control.   Perhaps this word Nature has too vague a meaning.   Let us try to define it.

Nature, we are told, is merely habit.   What does that mean?   Are there not habits formed under compulsion, habits which never stifle nature?   Such, for example, are the habits of plants trained horizontally.   The plant keeps its artificial shape, but the sap has not changed its course, and any new growth the plant may make will be vertical. It is the same with a man's disposition; while the conditions remain the same, habits, even the least natural of them, hold good; but change the conditions, habits vanish, nature reasserts herself.   Education itself is but habit, for are there not people who forget or lose their education and others who keep it?   Whence comes this difference?   If the term nature is to be restricted to habits conformable to nature we need say no more.

We are born sensitive and from our birth onwards we are affected

[2] Like them in externals, but without speech and without the ideas which are expressed by speech, he would be unable to make his wants known, while there would be nothing in his appearance to suggest that he needed their help.

in various ways by our environment. As soon as we become conscious of our sensations we tend to seek or shun the things that cause them, at first because they are pleasant or unpleasant, then because they suit us or not, and at last because of judgments formed by means of the ideas of happiness and goodness which reason gives us. These tendencies gain strength and permanence with the growth of reason, but hindered by our habits they are more or less warped by our prejudices. Before this change they are what I call Nature within us.

Everything should therefore be brought into harmony with these natural tendencies, and that might well be if our three modes of education merely differed from one another; but what can be done when they conflict, when instead of training man for himself you try to train him for others? Harmony becomes impossible. Forced to combat either nature or society, you must make your choice between the man and the citizen, you cannot train both.

The smaller social group, firmly united in itself and dwelling apart from others, tends to withdraw itself from the larger society. Every patriot hates foreigners; they are only men, and nothing to him. This defect is inevitable, but of little importance. The great thing is to be kind to our neighbors. Among strangers the Spartan was selfish, grasping, and unjust, but unselfishness, justice, and harmony ruled his home life. Distrust those cosmopolitans who search out remote duties in their books and neglect those that lie nearest. Such philosophers will love the Tartars to avoid loving their neighbor.

The natural man lives for himself; he is the unit, the whole, dependent only on himself and on his life. The citizen is but the numerator of a fraction, whose value depends on its denominator; his value depends upon the whole, that is, on the community. Good social institutions are those best fitted to make a man unnatural, to exchange his independence for dependence, to merge the unit in the group, so that he no longer regards himself as one, but as a part of the whole, and is only conscious of the common life. . . .

Our inner conflicts are caused by contradictions. Drawn this way by nature and that way by man, compelled to yield to both forces, we make a compromise and reach neither goal. We go through life, struggling and hesitating, and die before we have found peace, useless alike to ourselves and to others.

There remains the education of the home or of nature; but how will a man live with others if he is educated for himself alone? If the twofold aims could be resolved into one by removing the man's self-contradictions, one great obstacle to his happiness would be gone. To judge of this you must see the man full-grown; you must have noted his inclinations, watched his progress, followed his steps; in a word you must really know a natural man. When you have read this work, I think you will have made some progress in this inquiry.

What must be done to train this exceptional man! We can do

much, but the chief thing is to prevent anything being done. To sail against the wind we merely follow one tack and another; to keep our position in a stormy sea we must cast anchor. Beware, young pilot, lest your boat slip its cable or drag its anchor before you know it.

In the social order where each has his own place a man must be educated for it. If such a one leave his own station he is fit for nothing else. His education is only useful when fate agrees with his parents' choice; if not, education harms the scholar, if only by the prejudices it has created. In Egypt, where the son was compelled to adopt his father's calling, education had at least a settled aim; where social grades remain fixed, but the men who form them are constantly changing, no one knows whether he is not harming his son by educating him for his own class.

In the natural order men are all equal and their common calling is that of manhood, so that a well-educated man cannot fail to do well in that calling and those related to it. It matters little to me whether my pupil is intended for the army, the church, or the law. Before his parents chose a calling for him nature called him to be a man. Life is the trade I would teach him. When he leaves me, I grant you, he will be neither a magistrate, a soldier, nor a priest; he will be a man. All that becomes a man he will learn as quickly as another. In vain will fate change his station, he will always be in his right place. "Occupavi te, fortuna, atque cepi; omnes-que aditus tuos interclusi, ut ad me aspirare non posses." The real object of our study is man and his environment. To my mind those of us who can best endure the good and evil of life are the best educated; hence it follows that true education consists less in precept than in practice. We begin to learn when we begin to live; our education begins with ourselves, our first teacher is our nurse. . . .

BOOK II

. . . . . .

Is it nature that carries men so far from their real selves? Is it her will that each should learn his fate from others and even be the last to learn it; so that a man dies happy or miserable before he knows what he is about? There is a healthy, cheerful, strong, and vigorous man; it does me good to see him; his eyes tell of content and well-being; he is the picture of happiness. A letter comes by post; the happy man glances at it, it is addressed to him, he opens it and reads it. In a moment he is changed, he turns pale and falls into a swoon. When he comes to himself he weeps, laments, and groans, he tears his hair, and his shrieks re-echo through the air. You would say he was in convulsions. Fool, what harm has this bit of paper done you? What limb has it torn away? What crime has it made you commit? What change has it wrought in you to reduce you to this state of misery?

Had the letter miscarried, had some kindly hand thrown it unto the fire, it strikes me that the fate of this mortal, at once happy and unhappy, would have offered us a strange problem. His misfortunes, you say, were real enough. Granted; but he did not feel them. What of that? His happiness was imaginary. I admit it; health, wealth, a contented spirit, are mere dreams. We no longer live in our own place, we live outside it. What does it profit us to live in such fear of death, when all that makes life worth living is our own?

Oh, man! live your own life and you will no longer be wretched. Keep to your appointed place in the order of nature and nothing can tear you from it. Do not kick against the stern law of necessity, nor waste in vain resistance the strength bestowed on you by heaven, not to prolong or extend your existence, but to preserve it so far and so long as heaven pleases. Your freedom and your power extend as far and no further than your natural strength; anything more is but slavery, deceit, and trickery. Power itself is servile when it depends upon public opinion; for you are dependent on the prejudices of others when you rule them by means of those prejudices. To lead them as you will, they must be led as they will. They have only to change their way of thinking and you are forced to change your course of action. Those who approach you need only contrive to sway the opinions of those you rule, or of the favourite by whom you are ruled, or those of your own family or theirs. Had you the genius of Themistocles,[3] viziers, courtiers, priests, soldiers, servants, babblers, the very children themselves, would lead you like a child in the midst of your legions. Whatever you do, your actual authority can never extend beyond your own powers. As soon as you are obliged to see with another's eyes you must will what he wills. You say with pride, "My people are my subjects." Granted, but what are you? The subject of your ministers. And your ministers, what are they? The subjects of their clerks, their mistresses, the servants of their servants. Grasp all, usurp all, and then pour out your silver with both hands; set up your batteries, raise the gallows and the wheel; make laws, issue proclamations, multiply your spies, your soldiers, your hangmen, your prisons, and your chains. Poor little men, what good does it do you? You will be no better served, you will be none the less robbed and deceived, you will be no nearer absolute power. You will say continually, "It is our will," and you will continually do the will of others.

There is only one man who gets his own way—he who can get it single-handed; therefore freedom, not power, is the greatest good. That man is truly free who desires what he is able to perform, and

[3] "You see that little boy," said Themistocles to his friends, "the fate of Greece is in his hands, for he rules his mother and his mother rules me, I rule the Athenians and the Athenians rule the Greeks." What petty creatures we should often find controlling great empires if we traced the course of power from the prince to those who secretly put that power in motion.

does what he desires. This is my fundamental maxim. Apply it to childhood, and all the rules of education spring from it. . . .

BOOK III

. . . . . .

The man and the citizen, whoever he may be, has no property to invest in society but himself, all his other goods belong to society in spite of himself, and when a man is rich, either he does not enjoy his wealth, or the public enjoys it too; in the first case he robs others as well as himself; in the second he gives them nothing. Thus his debt to society is still unpaid, while he only pays with his property. "But my father was serving society while he was acquiring his wealth." Just so; he paid his own debt, not yours. You owe more to others than if you had been born with nothing, since you were born under favourable conditions. It is not fair that what one man has done for society should pay another's debt, for since every man owes all that he is, he can only pay his own debt, and no father can transmit to his son any right to be of no use to mankind. "But," you say, "this is just what he does when he leaves me his wealth, the reward of his labour." The man who eats in idleness what he has not himself earned, is a thief, and in my eyes, the man who lives on an income paid him by the state for doing nothing, differs little from a highwayman who lives on those who travel his way. Outside the pale of society, the solitary, owing nothing to any man, may live as he pleases, but in society either he lives at the cost of others, or he owes them in labour the cost of his keep; there is no exception to this rule. Man in society is bound to work; rich or poor, weak or strong, every idler is a thief.

Now of all the pursuits by which a man may earn his living, the nearest to a state of nature is manual labour; of all stations that of the artisan is least dependent on Fortune. The artisan depends on his labour alone, he is a free man while the ploughman is a slave; for the latter depends on his field where the crops may be destroyed by others. An enemy, a prince, a powerful neighbour, or a law-suit may deprive him of his field; through this field he may be harassed in all sorts of ways. But if the artisan is ill-treated his goods are soon packed and he takes himself off. Yet agriculture is the earliest, the most honest of trades, and more useful than all the rest, and therefore more honourable for those who practice it. I do not say to Émile, "Study agriculture," he is already familiar with it. He is acquainted with every kind of rural labour, it was his first occupation, and he returns to it continually. So I say to him, "Cultivate your father's lands, but if you lose this inheritance, or if you have none to lose, what will you do? Learn a trade."

"A trade for my son! My son a working man! What are you thinking of, sir?" Madam, my thoughts are wiser than yours; you want to make him fit for nothing but a lord, a marquis, or a prince; and some day he may be less than nothing. I want to give him a rank which he cannot lose, a rank which will always do him honour; I want to raise him to the status of a man, and, whatever you may say, he will have fewer equals in that rank than in your own.

The letter killeth, the spirit giveth life. Learning a trade matters less than overcoming the prejudices he despises. You will never be reduced to earning your livelihood; so much the worse for you. No matter; work for honour, not for need; stoop to the position of a working man, to rise above your own. To conquer Fortune and everything else, begin by independence. To rule through public opinion, begin by ruling over it.

Remember I demand no talent, only a trade, a genuine trade, a mere mechanical art, in which the hands work harder than the head, a trade which does not lead to fortune but makes you independent of her. In households far removed from all danger of want I have known fathers carry prudence to such a point as to provide their children not only with ordinary teaching but with knowledge by means of which they could get a living if anything happened. These far-sighted parents thought they were doing a great thing. It is nothing, for the resources they fancy they have secured depend on that very fortune of which they would make their children independent; so that unless they found themselves in circumstances fitted for the display of their talents, they would die of hunger as if they had none. . . .

Since all our errors arise in our judgment, it is clear, that had we no need for judgment, we should not need to learn; we should never be liable to mistakes, we should be happier in our ignorance than we can be in our knowledge. Who can deny that a vast number of things are known to the learned, which the unlearned will never know? Are the learned any nearer truth? Not so, the further they go the further they get from truth, for their pride in their judgment increases faster than their progress in knowledge, so that for every truth they acquire they draw a hundred mistaken conclusions. Every one knows that the learned societies of Europe are mere schools of falsehood, and there are assuredly more mistaken notions in the Academy of Sciences than in a whole tribe of American Indians.

The more we know, the more mistakes we make; therefore ignorance is the only way to escape error. Form no judgments and you will never be mistaken. This is the teaching both of nature and reason. We come into direct contact with very few things, and these are very readily perceived; the rest we regard with profound indifference. A savage will not turn his head to watch the working of the finest machinery or all the wonders of electricity. "What does that matter to me?" is the common saying of the ignorant; it is the fittest phrase for the wise.

Unluckily this phrase will no longer serve our turn. Everything matters to us, as we are dependent on everything, and our curiosity naturally increases with our needs.   This is why I attribute much curiosity to the man of science and none to the savage.   The latter needs no help from anybody; the former requires every one, and admirers most of all.

You will tell me I am going beyond nature.   I think not.   She chooses her instruments and orders them, not according to fancy, but necessity.   Now a man's needs vary with his circumstances.   There is all the difference in the world between a natural man living in a state of nature, and a natural man living in society.   Émile is no savage to be banished to the desert, he is a savage who has to live in the town. He must know how to get his living in a town, how to use its inhabitants, and how to live among them, if not of them.

In the midst of so many new relations and dependent on them, he must reason whether he wants to or no.   Let us therefore teach him to reason correctly. . . .

BOOK IV

. . . . . .

Self-love is always good, always in accordance with the order of nature.   The preservation of our own life is specially entrusted to each one of us, and our first care is, and must be, to watch over our own life; and how can we continually watch over it, if we do not take the greatest interest in it?

Self-preservation requires, therefore, that we shall love ourselves above everything, and it follows directly from this that we love what contributes to our preservation.   Every child becomes fond of its nurse; Romulus must have loved the she-wolf who suckled him.   At first this attachment is quite unconscious; the individual is attracted to that which contributes to his welfare and repelled by that which is harmful; this is merely blind instinct.   What transforms this instinct into feeling, the liking into love, the aversion into hatred, is the evident intention of helping or hurting us.   We do not become passionately attached to objects without feeling, which only follow the direction given them; but those from which we expect benefit or injury from their internal disposition, from their will.   Those we see acting freely for or against us, inspire us with like feelings to those they exhibit towards us.   Something does us good, we seek after it; but we love the person who does us good; something harms us and we shrink from it, but we hate the person who tries to hurt us.

The child's first sentiment is self-love, his second, which is derived from it, is love of those about him; for in his present state of weakness he is only aware of people through the help and attention received from them.   At first his affection for his nurse and his governess is mere habit.   He seeks them because he needs them and because he is happy when they are there; it is rather perception than kindly feeling. It takes a long time to discover not merely that they are useful to him, but that they desire to be useful to him, and then it is that he begins to love them.

So a child is naturally disposed to kindly feeling because he sees that every one about him is inclined to help him, and from this experience he gets the habit of a kindly feeling towards his species; but with the expansion of his relations, his needs, his dependence, active or passive, the consciousness of his relations to others is awakened, and leads to the sense of duties and preferences. Then the child becomes masterful, jealous, deceitful, and vindictive. If he is not compelled to obedience, when he does not see the usefulness of what he is told to do, he attributes it to caprice, to an intention of tormenting him, and he rebels. If people give in to him, as soon as anything opposes him he regards it as rebellion, as a determination to resist him; he beats the chair or table for disobeying him. Self-love, which concerns itself only with ourselves, is content to satisfy our own needs; but selfishness, which is always comparing self with others, is never satisfied and never can be; for this feeling, which prefers ourselves to others, requires that they should prefer us to themselves, which is impossible. Thus the tender and gentle passions spring from self-love, while the hateful and angry passions spring from selfishness. So it is the fewness of his needs, the narrow limits within which he can compare himself with others, that makes a man really good; what makes him really bad is a multiplicity of needs and dependence on the opinions of others. It is easy to see how we can apply this principle and guide every passion of children and men towards good or evil. True, man cannot always live alone, and it will be hard therefore to remain good; and this difficulty will increase of necessity as his relations with others are extended. For this reason, above all, the dangers of social life demand that the necessary skill and care shall be devoted to guarding the human heart against the depravity which springs from fresh needs.

Man's proper study is that of his relation to his environment. So long as he only knows that environment through his physical nature, he should study himself in relation to things; this is the business of his childhood; when he begins to be aware of his moral nature, he should study himself in relation to his fellow-men; this is the business of his whole life, and we have now reached the time when that study should be begun.

As soon as a man needs a companion he is no longer an isolated creature, his heart is no longer alone. All his relations with his species, all the affections of his heart, come into being along with this. His first passion soon arouses the rest. . . .

It is our own passions that excite us against the passions of others; it is our self-interest which makes us hate the wicked; if they did us no harm we should pity rather than hate them. We should readily forgive their vices if we could perceive how their own heart punishes those vices. We are aware of the offence, but we do not see the punishment; the advantages are plain, the penalty is hidden. The man who thinks he is enjoying the fruits of his vices is no less tormented by them than if they had not been successful; the object is different, the anxiety is the same; in vain he displays his good fortune and hides his heart; in spite of himself his conduct betrays him; but to discern this, our own heart must be utterly unlike his.

We are led astray by those passions which we share; we are disgusted by those that militate against our own interests; and with a want of logic due to these very passions, we blame in others what we fain would imitate. Aversion and self-deception are inevitable when we are forced to endure at another's hands what we ourselves would do in his place.

What then is required for the proper study of men? A great wish to know men, great impartiality of judgment, a heart sufficiently sensitive to understand every human passion, and calm enough to be free from passion. If there is any time in our life when this study is likely to be appreciated, it is this that I have chosen for Émile; before this time men would have been strangers to him; later on he would have been like them. Convention, the effects of which he already perceives, has not made him its slave, the passions, whose consequences he realizes, have not yet stirred his heart. He is a man; he takes an interest in his brethren; he is a just man and he judges his peers. Now it is certain that if he judges them rightly he will not want to change places with any one of them, for the goal of all their anxious efforts is the result of prejudices which he does not share, and that goal seems to him a mere dream. For his own part, he has all he wants within his reach. How should he be dependent on any one when he is self-sufficing and free from prejudice? Strong arms, good health,[4] moderation, few needs, together with the means to satisfy those needs, are his. He has been brought up in complete liberty and servitude is the greatest ill he understands. He pities these miserable kings, the slaves of all who obey them; he pities these false prophets fettered by their empty fame; he pities these rich fools, martyrs to their own pomp; he pities these ostentatious voluptuaries, who spend their life in deadly dullness that they may seem to enjoy its pleasures. He would pity the very foe who harmed him, for he would discern his wretchedness beneath his cloak of spite. He would say to himself, "This man has yielded to his desire to hurt me, and this need of his places him at my mercy."

One step more and our goal is attained. Selfishness is a dangerous tool though a useful one; it often wounds the hand that uses it, and it rarely does good unmixed with evil. When Émile considers his place

[4] I think I may fairly reckon health and strength among the advantages he has obtained by his education, or rather among the gifts of nature which his education has preserved for him.

among men, when he finds himself so fortunately situated, he will be tempted to give credit to his own reason for the work of yours, and to attribute to his own deserts what is really the result of his good fortune. He will say to himself, "I am wise and other men are fools." He will pity and despise them and will congratulate himself all the more heartily; and as he knows he is happier than they, he will think his deserts are greater. This is the fault we have most to fear, for it is the most difficult to eradicate. If he remained in this state of mind, he would have profited little by all our care; and if I had to choose, I hardly know whether I would not rather choose the illusions of prejudice than those of pride.

Great men are under no illusion with respect to their superiority; they see it and know it, but they are none the less modest. The more they have, the better they know what they lack. They are less vain of their superiority over us than ashamed by the consciousness of their weakness, and among the good things they really possess, they are too wise to pride themselves on a gift which is none of their getting. The good man may be proud of his virtue for it is his own, but what cause for pride has the man of intellect?

Questions and Statements for Discussion

(*The Social Contract*)

1. "Man is born free; and everywhere he is in chains. One thinks himself the master of others, and still remains a greater slave than they." (*The Social Contract*, Bk. 1, Chap. 1, p. 5.) Is this striking statement true or has it ever been strictly true?
2. "Force made the first slaves and their cowardice perpetuated the condition." (Bk. I, Chap. II, p. 7.)
3. "Conventions form the basis of all legitimate authority among men." (Bk. I, Chap. IV, p. 9.) Is there in history any example of a contract by which the common people have abdicated certain rights in the interest of government? Directly or by implication?
4. "He who wishes to preserve his life at others' expense should also, when it is necessary, be ready to give it up for their sake." (Bk. II, Chap. V, p. 30.)

(*Émile*)

5. "Those who can best endure the good and evil of life are the best educated." (*Émile*, Bk. I, p. 9.)
6. "Power itself is servile when it depends upon public opinion." (Bk. II, p. 47.) Is this sentence conformable with a belief in democracy?
7. "That man is truly free who desires what he is able to perform, and does what he desires." (Bk. II, p. 48.) How does the problem of moral values apply at this point?
8. "Man in society is bound to work; rich or poor, weak or strong, every idler is a thief." (Bk. III, p. 158.) What could be the meaning of "idler" to justify this expression?
9. "The more we know the more mistakes we make; therefore ignorance is the only way to escape error." (Bk. III, p. 167.) If under such conditions "ignorance is bliss," is it "folly to be wise"?
10. "Man's proper study is that of his relation to his environment. So long as he only knows that environment through his physical nature, he should study himself in relation to things; . . . when he begins to be aware of his moral nature, he should study himself in relation to his fellow-men." (Bk. IV, p. 175.)
11. "The man who thinks he is enjoying the fruits of his vices is no less tormented by them than if they had not been successful." (Bk. IV, p. 206.)
12. What type of education is most likely to yield happiness: the "practical" which promises a larger salary, or the humanistic-cultural which widens the area of satisfaction and adaptation to circumstance? Treat this under the aspect of the fact that the sources

of happiness are primarily internal, secondarily external and environmental.

———

Suggested Supplementary Readings:

Höffding: *Jean Jacques Rousseau and His Philosophy.* Yale University Press, New Haven, Chap. III, pp. 22-101.

Morley: *Rousseau and His Era.* Macmillan, New York.

Charpentier: *Rousseau Child of Nature.*

Guerard: *The Life and Death of an Ideal.* Scribner's, New York.

Lemaitre: *Jean Jacques Rousseau.*

Babbitt: *Rousseau and Romanticism.*

Carrère: *Degeneration in the Great French Masters.*

Hendel: *Citizen of Geneva.* Oxford University Press, New York.

Chapter 12

NIETZSCHE AND "THE WILL TO POWER"

I
Life, Philosophy, and Influence

II
The Will to Power

III
The Transvaluation of Values

IV
Eternal Recurrence

V
Summary

Chapter 12

NIETZSCHE AND "THE WILL TO POWER"

We have arrived at one of the most difficult of tasks, the consideration and evaluation of the work of Frederic Nietzsche. The obstacles that meet us are manifold. Some of them spring from the disconnected nature of the Nietzschean writings—the fact that they are in great measure loose meditations that mirror the inner and changing experiences of a lifetime. We must take into account the truth that toward the end they are little more than the ravings of a man in advanced stages of insanity. We are beset by the fact that there are contradictions which cannot be explained in any rational manner even though scores of Nietzsche devotees rise up to declare that when Nietzsche used the term "white" he meant "black," and when he wrote "black" he really meant "white." Though he has at times been unfairly attacked, nothing in modern apologetics can exceed the intellectual contortionism and naïveté of many of Nietzsche's disciples who are bound to exalt him into the role of a prophet and almost of a divinity—a role to which he himself aspired when he signed his letters *The Crucified One,* a Valhalla which seems to fit certain characters too often and into which Mr. Hitler once seemed inclined to edge. This psychological contradiction with all its childishness is pointed out by Eric T. Bell in his book on *Numerology,*[1] as accentuated by Nietzsche in giving to his autobiography the title *Ecce Homo,* the words of Pontius Pilate at the trial of Jesus, "Behold the Man"; he thus sought to identify himself with the teacher whom he reviled. Perhaps the most formidable difficulty of all lies in the political significance which the Nietzschean gospel acquired in contemporary history, owing to the fact that Nietzsche was granted a place of honor in the Nazi scriptures and raised to the dignity of spiritual father of the Third Reich.

The grave threat to democracy and world-order contained in the Nietzschean writings was pointed out as early as 1917 by the writer in a little book entitled *Philosophy and the War*[2]: a work that seemed extreme by 1925, but later appeared justified.

[1] Wilkins and Williams, Baltimore, 1933, p. 49.
[2] Abingdon Press, New York.

In the light of late events the statements there seem mild in comparison with the facts. The greatest difficulty now is for the decent-minded to discuss Nietzsche's statements with detachment In the first case, one is so influenced by the philosophy and the literary freshness of his writing that he may swallow everything, hook, line, and sinker, shutting his eyes to the patent contradictions, and the vileness of the morals, or on the other hand, one may be moved by a burning indignation against a madman who apotheosizes evil, and worships violence as a God. Non-partisanship is all but impossible; any judgment will be charged with feeling,

I
Life, Philosophy, and Influence

Nietzsche was born October 15, 1844 in the Prussian province of Saxony in Röchen, where his father was parson of the village church. He came from a family of theologians, both on his father's and his mother's side, and though of humble birth, and moved by an inferiority complex, he labored to persuade himself or the world that he was descended from a noble Polish family (*Ecce Homo:* Why I am so Wise, section 3, p. 8). But he was neither Polish nor noble. His father died when the lad was about five years of age and the young boy fell into the care of his mother and sister, who proceeded to adore the only son in the family and to spoil him. The natural outcome of such adulation was an aroused contempt for women. He was lovingly surrounded by five of them, grandmother, mother, sister, and two aunts, and upon them he was utterly dependent. It may have been a sense of unrequited obligation that led him to react to this loving solicitude by writing in *Zarathustra*[3] "Thou goest to women? Do not forget thy whip." During his youth he seems to have had few friendships and to have been very much of a prig. This latter impression is heightened by his early photographs. He could scarcely have been a normal boy. At the age of twenty he matriculated in theology and philosophy at the University of Bonn, where he remained only one year, having apparently failed in his attempt to "be one of the boys." This was to be accomplished by a successful effort at drunkenness and debauchery which was required in the initiation into the leading fraternity. The role of profligate

[3] I, Chap. XVIII, p. 81, Modern Reader's Library, Giant Edition used throughout.

did not fit one of his tender training, though it was sufficient, apparently, to give him the disease that afterward culminated in insanity and death. From Bonn he went to the University of Leipsic where he met Ritschl, the great German scholar, and discovered the philosophy of Schopenhauer, which marked him for its own. He also made friends of two other scholars, Erwin Rohde and Paul Deussen, who became distinguished and remained friendly to the end. Before he had completed his doctoral thesis at Leipsic, he was called to a professorship at Basle, but his neurotic and egotistic disposition unfitted him for serious work. He was soon out of it and launched on a desultory literary career. He was possessed of an insane fear of ridicule, and a decided feeling of inferiority, which made him bitterly jealous of friends who succeeded where he seemed to fail. For example, his early acquaintance with Wagner inspired him to the writing of his first book, *The Birth of Tragedy,* but Wagner's later success turned him to hate and bitterness and led him to attack the musician insultingly in *Human, All Too Human.*

His life became more and more completely given over to a sense of bitterness and frustration. He was compelled to assume the cost of printing his own books which drew no attention, that reward so necessary to one of his disposition, until he was so far gone in insanity that he could not know about the fame he finally achieved. He died in Wiemar in 1900.

In spite of his disdain for Rousseau, Nietzsche was Rousseau's intellectual offspring, the final flowering of that sensationalism and romanticism which erected feeling into a supreme value. It was, as we have seen, a rebellion against all forms, conventions, and regulations. On such terms, however, society soon turns to anarchy in which the most violent gangster, the most unscrupulous villain, becomes the ruler and reduces all others to submission. He may begin with much mouthing of the terms of democracy, since he aims to be an accomplished liar, but he ends with being a dictator. This lawlessness in Nietzsche has made unusual appeal to society in a time which was breaking away from much of the formalism of the past, but some formality is a necessity in a crowded world. However much we may object to conventions, they are like the walls of our gardens, a means of protecting the person in his individual rights. Modes of decency are necessary where men must live in close proximity. I pause at the door to send up my card not merely because it is the fashion. The intent is to give my prospective host an opportunity to decline the interview, or to receive me in such manner as accords with his comfort or preoccupation.   This is a protection for myself as well as for him.   When one begins war on the conventions, he needs to do it with discrimination lest he destroy that which protects himself. Failure to take into account this fact was the weakness of Nietzsche. He made personal feeling the arbiter of social action.

With the apotheosis of Nietzsche by the late Nazi government, we have the full round of this movement, which is a determination to be ruled only by one's personal desires.   To this end it is necessary to destroy conventions and replace them with a new ideology in order to justify selfishness, violence, and murder.   Such a gospel can be come at only by what Nietzsche calls a transvaluation of all values, whereby it is presumed right for me, or my clique, or my party, to rob and destroy, but wrong for those who are despoiled to resist, or even to resent it.   (See references to *The Genealogy of Morals* and *Beyond Good and Evil,* Chap. I, sections 2, 4, in the Required Readings.)   This way of thinking accounts for that strange psychology which possesses the totalitarian to characterize as perfidy, hypocrisy, and betrayal the slightest efforts at defense on the part of those whom he perfidiously attacks.   This sort of gospel grows on the soil of that ego-insanity which hopes to take its freedom without responsibility or obligation.   Nor is this spirit confined to nationalities.   Everywhere it forms the dark menace to our civilization, is present in our modern culture to an alarming degree, and is the unclean spirit which must tear violently at the structure of society before it can be cast out.

II

The Will to Power

A fostered tradition arose in Germany for the division of culture into two varieties known respectively as the Dionysian and the Apollonian.   The Dionysian is so called from the ancient Greek cult of that name, and is used to indicate a free rein given to violence, power, unrestrained license, and bestiality.   The Apollonian culture is that of Socrates, Plato, and the teachers of morality and self-restraint.   Psychologically, it might be considered a natural offshoot of a sense of inferiority in the finer arts of social intercourse.   We are tempted to despise, and we affect to scorn, gifts which we ourselves do not possess.   This human tendency goes far in accounting for Nietzsche and his egotistic doctrines.   If one hasn't brains, let him boast of brawn, or vice versa.   If one cannot be master in the more delicate and gentler arts, let him make a showing as the alley bully, or the head of the Gashouse Gang. Thus we arrive at the doctrine of "the will to power" as possessing supreme value. By "will to power," Nietzsche meant the power of violence, physical force, and compulsion as pictured in his "blonde beast" (*Genealogy of Morals*, section 11), a being that would recognize no rights in others, observe no decencies. Stamina or grit, the fortitude to take punishment in overriding all opposition, was by him called spiritual and moral strength. It had no relation either to justice or righteousness. No treachery was base if it could succeed, no lie false if it would increase social or political ascendancy.

It is possible from Nietzsche's own writings to disprove everything one may say of his teaching, for he continually contradicted himself. He must be estimated, then, as much by the results of his teachings as by the teachings themselves. He declared the worth of any life to be measured by its worthlessness to others, that is, by the supremacy of its selfishness (*Beyond Good and Evil*, sections 1-2). He affected at different times to praise uniqueness and individuality, but what he really worshipped was his own eccentricity, the eccentricity of irresponsible egotism. Perhaps it was what he referred to as "the egoism of noble souls" which led him in his autobiography to give to the first three chapters the headings: "Why I am so Wise," "Why I am so Clever," and "Why I Write such Excellent Books." Integrity, purity, and sincerity were in their place applauded, but again he referred thereby only to his own opinions. He praised delicacy, subtlety, but by them he meant adroitness in falsehood and deceit. He favored greatness, but this he did not distinguish from brutality. The will to power was the will of the most successful gangster, who would know neither mercy nor tolerance.

It is apparent, then, that "the will to power" cannot be practised by men in general, else society would be one grand Donnybrook Fair. Such a condition Nietzsche's teaching did much to bring about in one corner of Europe. It would delegate power to the strong—those who can seize it. These are the supermen, and their presence is held of such value that the great masses of society must for their sakes be reduced to abject physical and mental slavery. The existence of common or "herd" men is justified only by their support of the rulers of violence. Any raising of the average of intelligence is looked upon as a weakness, as it may interfere with the rule of the supermen. What the "will to power" fails to take into account is the strength for resistance which righteousness brings, and the super-power with which the sense of justice arms its devotees.   The principal fact about the doctrine of the "will to power" is its self-betrayal.

III
The Transvaluation of Values

If we are to justify the so-called Dionysian virtues of trickery, falsehood, deceit, and violence, it can only be by a complete reversal of what we commonly understand by morality.   Nietzsche thus set out to make immorality moral.   Since power can in his system be delegated to a few supermen only, there will have to be two codes of conduct, one for the superman and another for the herd, one for the tyrant and one for the man who has to "knuckle."   The superman is restrained by no special responsibilities or obligations.   He answers to no one for his conduct.   If it appears profitable to his interests to deceive, to break treaties, to destroy, to murder, he is bound by no scruples.   It will never do, however, to attempt to put this shoe on the other foot.   While the superman will meticulously demand that other men keep their promises to him and will exact the direst penalties for every failure, he is free to break every promise, if thereby he can gain more power.   The moral code of keeping promises is for the herd-man but does not apply to his oppressor.   This is exactly what Nietzsche means by the transvaluation of values.   We do wickedly that righteousness may survive.

The greatest detriment to such a dream of society is the existence of Christianity, the doctrine of universal love, integrity, and justice. In the capacity of the superman, both Nietzsche and his follower Hitler were pleased to assume the role of antichrist.   Christianity is the great leveller, since it teaches the intrinsic worth of every man, and his right to justice.   It is the main strength of democracy and must survive if democracy is to remain.

IV
Eternal Recurrence

If you are able to recall what was said in an earlier chapter concerning the Binary Wheel of Buddhism and the peculiarities springing out of the cyclic theory of history, you are prepared to understand the doctrine of "eternal recurrence," which both Nietzsche and his devotees have claimed to be the great Nietzschean discovery. There can be no doubt of its antithesis to all that which we prize in individualism and Western democracy, and which has but slowly fought its way to freedom and scientific advance. Tyranny has always attempted to provide a philosophy for its injustices by an appeal to some general principle which it assumes to be more important than justice and freedom for the individual. There are those who consider themselves to be above the law. They only can tell what is good for the rest of us. This is always the doctrine of authoritarianism and it refers itself to some absolute principle. Hence it should occasion no surprise to discover Nietzsche bolstering totalitarianism with a fling at Orientalism. He does this by advocating the doctrine of eternal recurrence. Just why he should have considered it *his* discovery does not appear, for any man of average intelligence would know better, and he was of more than average intelligence. It is only the ancient cyclic theory of East Indian philosophy, known and taught for thousands of years and imported into Greek and German thought long before Nietzsche.

The cyclic concept is, however, a convenient revolutionary doctrine for the upset of the existing order, because it makes revolution appear as the natural expectation and inevitable sequence of time. Whatever *is,* is looked upon as about to pass away. In Nietzsche's case it may have been due to a misunderstanding of physics. He fought the notion of indefinite evolutionary progress, that characteristic product of Western individualistic thinking. To this end he held that the doctrine of the transference of energy, or the second law of thermodynamics, forbade creation or uniqueness of any kind. Hence he said nothing new can arise, there is only an unending cycle of growth and decay. This was inconsistent with what he taught about the superman and the death of Christianity, but inconsistency never worried Nietzsche. If the gods are dead, there would be nothing more certain, by the law of eternal recurrence than that they would sometime be back again in the saddle. If eternal recurrence is the law, the superman has been here before, and will as surely be again superseded by Christianity when the wheel of time turns around again. No greater opiate to progress and action can be imagined than that offered by the cyclic theory. Beside it Christianity is the true revolutionary. The cyclic supposition is exactly the one which through many centuries has induced men to put up with things as they are, to submit to authority,

because one could not successfully break outside the wheel of fate:
whatever has been, must recur again; why worry? It was exactly
the contrasting Judaeo-Greek-Christian concepts which in Western
society have created the drive toward a new and better day, and
made possible the dream of a true superman.

V
Summary

The advocates of Nietzsche hold an unfair advantage over anyone who attempts criticism, since in spite of his plain words and
meanings in one place it is possible to draw out some exactly opposite statement to be found in another. If one quotes his exhortation to lust, rapine, and murder as the approved virtues of the superior man, it is equally easy to point out that here or there he
praises goodness. If one enters complaint that he *was* antichrist,
as indeed he claimed to be, his adorers appear with his praise of the
Christian virtues as an evidence of his religious sincerity. If one
quotes passages in which he praises violence and war as the supreme
values, his defenders will cite a passage in which he opposes war,
and will tell you that you do not understand him. His disciples set
forth as his great discovery the law of eternal recurrence, yet he can
be quoted just as explicitly as declaring that nothing recurs. He is
followed with equal enthusiasm by both religionists and anti-relig-
ionists, each partisan drawing forth the doctrines that please his
own interpretations and ignoring the others.

Why, then, should we not leave this madman to stew in his own
insanity as a negligible factor in world attention. Because, speaking
exactly, he is not a negligible factor in world history. The beauty
of his literary diction, the power of his intellectual images, the mixture of reason, truth, and morality, along with their contradiction
and denial, do in many minds lead directly to an abrogation of all
moral standards. We have in Nietzsche a gospel of selfishness
which beguiles many minds who do not wish to listen to the voice
of duty and decency, but are looking for the justification of an
anti-social and immoral way of life. This gospel is to be found in
Nietzsche. That is the strength of its present appeal to people who
are dissatisfied with moral and spiritual claims inherent with duties
to their fellow men, above all for men who are dissatisfied with
themselves, but will not take the hard road of social responsibility.
They seek to be beguiled into selfishness and Nietzsche provides the
authority and excuse.

It is not enough then to judge Nietzsche merely by the charm of his writings, to assume that his praise of wickedness is offset by praise of good. We must judge his doctrine by its effect on history which has been unmitigatedly evil. In the quiet of his cell this ineffective philosopher, incapable of earning his own living, could speak of being above good and evil. But as Professor Brinton[4] has justly pointed out, not above effective action "on the part of an Italian Socialist hack writer, nor above an Austrian paper-hanger." For them this gospel coincided with their own evil purposes. There is little use to contend that Nietzsche never intended anything of the kind, nor that he would have been undoubtedly opposed to them if he were now on the scene.

Nietzsche cannot be absolved of responsibility for his portion of the recent assault on civilization, in furnishing the charter and excuse for World War in such words as these, from *The Twilight of the Idols* (section 38) :

> Democracy has in all ages been the form under which.organizing strength has perished. . . . Liberalism, or the transformation of mankind into cattle. . . . Modern democracy is the historic form of the decay of the state. . . . The two opposing parties, the Socialist and the National—or whatever they may be called in the countries of Europe—are worthy of each other; envy and laziness are the motives in each of them. . . . The equality of souls before God, this lie, this screen for the *rancunes* of all the base minded, this anarchist bomb of a concept, which has become the last revolution, the modern idea and principle of the whole social order—this is Christian dynamite.

Another quotation, from *The Genealogy of Morals,* discloses the Nietzschean relation to the general situation, and both sound like the ravings of Hitler who merely echoed them :

> The future of German culture rests with the sons of Prussian officers. . . . Peace and letting other people alone—this is not a policy for which I have any respect whatever. . . . Ye shall love peace as a means to new wars—and the short peace more than the long.

Surely, if any demonstration of the possible results of philosophy upon the practical affairs of men were needed, one would be forced to go no farther than Nietzsche to establish the fact. "The evil that men do lives after them," while the good is often "interred with their bones."

[4] *Nietzsche,* Harvard University Press, p. 106.

READINGS

Chapter 12

NIETZSCHE: *BEYOND GOOD AND EVIL.* The Macmillan Company, New York. Chap. I, sections 1, 2, 4, 13. Chap. II, sections 36, 44; Chap. III, sections 61, 62; Chap. V, sections 202, 203; Chap. VI, sections 210, 211, 212; Chap. VII, section 221; Chap. IX, sections 257, 259, 260, 265.

CHAPTER I

PREJUDICES OF PHILOSOPHERS

1

The Will to Truth, which is to tempt us to many a hazardous enterprise, the famous Truthfulness of which all philosophers have hitherto spoken with respect, what questions has this Will to Truth not laid before us! What strange, perplexing, questionable questions! It is already a long story; yet it seems as if it were hardly commenced. Is it any wonder if we at last grow distrustful, lose patience, and turn impatiently away? That this Sphinx teaches us at last to ask questions ourselves? *Who* is it really that puts questions to us here? *What* really is this "Will to Truth" in us? In fact we made a long halt at the question as to the origin of this Will—until at last we came to an absolute standstill before a yet more fundamental question. We inquired about the *value* of this Will. Granted that we want the truth: *why not rather* untruth? And uncertainty? Even ignorance? The problem of the value of truth presented itself before us—or was it we who presented ourselves before the problem? Which of us is the Œdipus here? Which the Sphinx? It would seem to be a rendezvous of questions and notes of interrogation. And could it be believed that it at last seems to us as if the problem had never been propounded before, as if we were the first to discern it, get a sight of it, and *risk raising* it. For there is risk in raising it, perhaps there is no greater risk.

2

"*How could* anything originate out of its opposite? For example, truth out of error? or the Will to Truth out of the will to deception? or the generous deed out of selfishness? or the pure sun-bright vision of the wise man out of covetousness? Such genesis is impossible; whoever dreams of it is a fool, nay, worse than a fool; things of the

417

highest value must have a different origin, an origin of *their own*—in
this transitory, seductive, illusory, paltry world, in this turmoil of
delusion and cupidity, they cannot have their source. But rather in
the lap of Being, in the intransitory, in the concealed God, in the 'Thing-
in-itself'—*there* must be their source, and nowhere else!"—This mode
of reasoning discloses the typical prejudice by which metaphysicians of
all times can be recognised, this mode of valuation is at the back of
all their logical procedure; through this "belief" of theirs, they exert
themselves for their "knowledge," for something that is in the end
solemnly christened "the Truth." The fundamental belief of metaphysicians is *the belief in antitheses of values.* It never occurred even
to the wariest of them to doubt here on the very threshold (where doubt,
however, was most necessary); though they had made a solemn vow:
"de omnibus dubitandum." For it may be doubted, firstly, whether
antitheses exist at all; and secondly, whether the popular valuations
and antitheses of value upon which metaphysicians have set their seal,
are not perhaps merely superficial estimates, merely provisional perspectives, besides being probably made from some corner, perhaps from
below—"frog perspectives," as it were, to borrow an expression current
among painters. In spite of all the value which may belong to the true,
the positive, and the unselfish, it might be possible that a higher and
more fundamental value for life generally should be assigned to pretence, to the will to delusion, to selfishness, and cupidity. It might even
be possible that *what* constitutes the value of those good and respected
things, consists precisely in their being insidiously related, knotted, and
crocheted to these evil and apparently opposed things—perhaps even
in being essentially identical with them. Perhaps! But who wishes to
concern himself with such dangerous "Perhapses"! For that investigation one must await the advent of a new order of philosophers, such
as will have other tastes and inclinations, the reverse of those hitherto
prevalent—philosophers of the dangerous "Perhaps" in every sense of
the term. And to speak in all seriousness, I see such new philosophers
beginning to appear.

4

The falseness of an opinion is not for us any objection to it: it is
here, perhaps, that our new language sounds most strangely. The question is, how far an opinion is life-furthering, life-preserving, species-
preserving, perhaps species-rearing; and we are fundamentally inclined
to maintain that the falsest opinions (to which the synthetic judgments
a priori belong), are the most indispensable to us; that without a recognition of logical fictions, without a comparison of reality with the purely
imagined world of the absolute and immutable, without a constant coun-
terfeiting of the world by means of numbers, man could not live—that
the renunciation of false opinions would be a renunciation of life, a

negation of life. *To recognize untruth as a condition of life:* that is certainly to impugn the traditional ideas of value in a dangerous manner, and a philosophy which ventures to do so, has thereby alone placed itself beyond good and evil.

13

Psychologists should bethink themselves before putting down the instinct of self-preservation as the cardinal instinct of an organic being. A living thing seeks above all to *discharge* its strength—life itself is *Will to Power;* self-preservation is only one of the indirect and most frequent *results* thereof. In short, here, as everywhere else, let us beware of *superfluous* teleological principles!—one of which is the instinct of self-preservation (we owe it to Spinoza's inconsistency). It is thus, in effect, that method ordains, which must be essentially economy of principles.

CHAPTER II

THE FREE SPIRIT

36

. . . The question is ultimately whether we really recognise the will as *operating,* whether we believe in the causality of the will; if we do so—and fundamentally our belief *in this* is just our belief in causality itself—we *must* make the attempt to posit hypothetically the causality of the will as the only causality. "Will" can naturally only operate on "will"—and not on "matter" (not on "nerves," for instance) :—in short, the hypothesis must be hazarded, whether will does not operate on will wherever "effects" are recognised—and whether all mechanical action, inasmuch as a power operates therein, is not just the power of will, the effect of will. Granted, finally, that we succeeded in explaining our entire instinctive life as the development and ramification of one fundamental form of will—namely, the Will to Power, as *my* thesis puts it; granted that all organic functions could be traced back to this Will to Power, and that the solution of the problem of generation and nutrition—it is one problem—could also be found therein: one would thus have acquired the right to define *all* active force unequivocally as *Will to Power.* The world seen from within, the world defined and designated according to its "intelligible character"—it would simply be "Will to Power," and nothing else.

44

Need I say expressly after all this that they will be free, *very* free spirits, these philosophers of the future—as certainly also they will not be merely free spirits, but something more, higher, greater, and fundamentally different, which does not wish to be misunderstood and mistaken? But while I say this, I feel under *obligation* almost as much to them as to ourselves (we free spirits who are their heralds and forerunners), to sweep away from ourselves altogether a stupid old prejudice and misunderstanding, which, like a fog, has too long made the conception of "free spirit" obscure. In every country of Europe, and the same in America, there is at present something which makes an abuse of this name: a very narrow, prepossessed, enchained class of spirits, who desire almost the opposite of what our intentions and instincts prompt—not to mention that in respect to the *new* philosophers who are appearing, they must still more be closed windows and bolted doors. Briefly and regrettably, they belong to the *levellers,* these wrongly named "free spirits"—as glib-tongued and scribe-fingered slaves of the democratic taste and its "modern ideas": all of them men without solitude, without personal solitude, blunt honest fellows to whom neither courage nor honourable conduct ought to be denied; only, they are not free, and are ludicrously superficial, especially in their innate partiality for seeing the cause of almost *all* human misery and failure in the old forms in which society has hitherto existed—a notion which happily inverts the truth entirely! What they would fain attain with all their strength, is the universal, green-meadow happiness of the herd, together with security, safety, comfort, and alleviation of life for every one; their two most frequently chanted songs and doctrines are called "Equality of Rights" and "Sympathy with all Sufferers"—and suffering itself is looked upon by them as something which must be *done away with.* We opposite ones, however, who have opened our eye and conscience to the question how and where the plant "man" has hitherto grown most vigorously, believe that this has always taken place under the opposite conditions, that for this end the dangerousness of his situation had to be increased enormously, his inventive faculty and dissembling power (his "spirit") had to develop into subtlety and daring under long oppression and compulsion, and his Will to Life had to be increased to the unconditioned Will to Power:—we believe that severity, violence, slavery, danger in the street and in the heart, secrecy, stoicism, tempter's art and devilry of every kind,—that everything wicked, terrible, tyrannical, predatory, and serpentine in man, serves as well for the elevation of the human species as its opposite:—we do not even say enough when we say *this much;* and in any case we find ourselves here, both with our speech and our silence, at the *other* extreme of all modern ideology and gregarious desirability, as their antipodes perhaps? What wonder that we "free spirits" are not exactly the most communicative spirits? that we do not wish to betray in every respect *what* a spirit can free itself from, and *where* perhaps it will then be driven? And as to the import of the dangerous formula, "Beyond Good and Evil," with which we at least avoid confusion, we *are* something else than *"libres-penseurs," "liberi pensatori,"* "free thinkers," and whatever these honest advocates of "modern ideas" like to call themselves.   Having been at home, or at least guests, in many realms of the spirit; having escaped again and again from the gloomy, agreeable nooks in which preferences and prejudices, youth, origin, the accident of men and books, or even the weariness of travel seemed to confine us; full of malice against the seductions of dependency which lie concealed in honours, money, positions, or exaltation of the senses; grateful even for distress and the vicissitudes of illness, because they always free us from some rule, and its "prejudice," grateful to the God, devil, sheep, and worm in us; inquisitive to a fault, investigators to the point of cruelty, with unhesitating fingers for the intangible, with teeth and stomachs for the most indigestible, ready for any business that requires sagacity and acute senses, ready for every adventure, owing to an excess of "free will"; with anterior and posterior souls, into the ultimate intentions of which it is difficult to pry, with fore-grounds and backgrounds to the end of which no foot may run; hidden ones under the mantles of light, appropriators, although we resemble heirs and spendthrifts, arrangers and collectors from morning till night, misers of our wealth and our full-crammed drawers, economical in learning and forgetting, inventive in scheming; sometimes proud of tables of categories, sometimes pedants, sometimes night-owls of work even in full day; yea, if necessary, even scarecrows—and it is necessary nowadays, that is to say, inasmuch as we are the born, sworn, jealous friends of *solitude,* of our own profoundest midnight and mid-day soli-tude:—such kind of men are we, we free spirits! And perhaps *ye* are also something of the same kind, ye coming ones? ye *new* philosophers?

CHAPTER III

THE RELIGIOUS MOOD

61

The philosopher, as *we* free spirits understand him—as the man of the greatest responsibility, who has the conscience for the general de-velopment of mankind,—will use religion for his disciplining and edu-cating work, just as he will use the contemporary political and economic conditions.   The selecting and disciplining influence—destructive, as well as creative and fashioning—which can be exercised by means of re-ligion is manifold and varied, according to the sort of people placed under its spell and protection.   For those who are strong and inde-pendent, destined and trained to command, in whom the judgment and skill of a ruling race is incorporated, religion is an additional means for overcoming resistance in the exercise of authority—as a bond which binds rulers and subjects in common, betraying and surrendering to the former and conscience of the latter, their inmost heart, which would fain escape obedience.   And in the case of the unique natures

of noble origin, if by virtue of superior spirituality they should incline to a more retired and contemplative life, reserving to themselves
only the more refined forms of government (over chosen disciples or
or members of an order), religion itself may be used as a means for obtaining peace from the noise and trouble of managing *grosser* affairs,
and for securing immunity from the *unavoidable* filth of all political
agitation.   The Brahmins, for instance, understood this fact.   With
the help of a religious organization, they secured to themselves the
power of nominating kings for the people, while their sentiments
prompted them to keep apart and outside, as men with a higher and
super-regal mission.   At the same time religion gives inducement and
opportunity to some of the subjects to qualify themselves for future
ruling and commanding: the slowly ascending ranks and classes, in
which, through fortunate marriage customs, volitional power and delight in self-control are on the increase.   To them religion offers sufficient incentives and temptations to aspire to higher intellectuality, and
to experience the sentiments of authoritative self-control, of silence, and
of solitude.   Asceticism and Puritanism are almost indispensable means
of educating and ennobling a race which seeks to rise above its hereditary
baseness and work itself upward to future supremacy.   And finally,
to ordinary men, to the majority of the people, who exist for service
and general utility, and are only so far entitled to exist, religion gives
invaluable contentedness with their lot and condition, peace of heart,
ennoblement of obedience, additional social happiness and sympathy,
with something of transfiguration and embellishment, something of
justification of all the commonplaceness, all the meanness, all the semi-
animal poverty of their souls.   Religion, together with the religious
significance of life, sheds sunshine over such perpetually harassed
men, and makes even their own aspect endurable to them; it operates
upon them as the Epicurean philosophy usually operates upon sufferers
of a higher order, in a refreshing and refining manner, almost *turning*
suffering *to account,* and in the end even hallowing and vindicating it.
There is perhaps nothing so admirable in Christianity and Buddhism
as their art of teaching even the lowest to elevate themselves by piety
to a seemingly higher order of things, and thereby to retain their satisfaction with the actual world in which they find it difficult enough to
live—this very difficulty being necessary.

62

To be sure—to make also the bad counter-reckoning against
such religions, and to bring to light their secret dangers—the cost is
always excessive and terrible when religions do *not* operate as an educational and disciplinary medium in the hands of the philosopher, but
rule voluntarily and *paramountly,* when they wish to be the final end,
and not a means along with other means.   Among men, as among
all other animals, there is a surplus of defective, diseased, degenerating,

infirm, and necessarily suffering individuals; the successful cases, among men also, are always the exception; and in view of the fact that man is *the animal not yet properly adapted to his environment,* the rare exception. But worse still. The higher the type a man represents, the greater is the improbability that he will *succeed;* the accidental, the law of irrationality in the general constitution of mankind, manifests itself most terribly in its destructive effect on the higher orders of men, the conditions of whose lives are delicate, diverse, and difficult to determine. What, then, is the attitude of the two greatest religions above-mentioned to the *surplus* of failures in life? They endeavour to preserve and keep alive whatever can be preserved; in fact, as the religions *for sufferers,* they take the part of these upon principle; they are always in favour of those who suffer from life as from a disease, and they would fain treat every other experience of life as false and impossible. However highly we may esteem this indulgent and preservative care (inasmuch as in applying to others, it has applied, and applies also to the highest and usually the most suffering type of man), the hitherto *paramount* religions—to give a general appreciation of them—are among the principal causes which have kept the type of "man" upon a lower level—they have preserved too much *that which should have perished.* One has to thank them for invaluable service; and who is sufficiently rich in gratitude not to feel poor at the contemplation of all that the "spiritual men" of Christianity have done for Europe hitherto! But when they had given comfort to the sufferers, courage to the oppressed and despairing, a staff and support to the helpless, and when they had allured from society into convents and spiritual penitentiaries the broken-hearted and distracted: what else had they to do in order to work systematically in that fashion, and with a good conscience, for the preservation of all the sick and suffering, which means, in deed and in truth, to work for *the deterioration of the European race?* To *reverse* all estimates of value—*that* is what they had to do! And to shatter the strong, to spoil great hopes, to cast suspicion on the delight in beauty, to break down everything autonomous, manly, conquering, and imperious—all instincts which are natural to the highest and most successful type of "man"—into uncertainty, distress of conscience, and self-destruction; forsooth, to invert all love of the earthly and of supremacy over the earth, into hatred of the earth and earthly things—*that* is the task the Church imposed on itself, and was obliged to impose, until, according, to its standard of value, "unworldiness," "unsensuousness," and "higher man" fused into one sentiment. If one could observe the strangely painful, equally coarse and refined comedy of European Christianity with the derisive and impartial eye of an Epicurean god, I should think one would never cease marvelling and laughing; does it not actually seem that some single will has ruled over Europe for eighteen centuries in order to make a *sublime abortion* of man? He, however, who, with opposite requirements (no longer Epicurean) and with some divine hammer in his hand, could approach this almost voluntary degeneration and stunting of mankind, as exemplified in the European Christian (Pascal, for instance), would he not have to cry aloud with rage, pity, and horror: "Oh, you bunglers, presumptuous pitiful bunglers, what have you done! Was that a work for your hands? How you have hacked and botched my finest stone! What have *you* presumed to do!"—I should say that Christianity has hitherto been the most portentous of presumptions. Men, not great enough, nor hard enough, to be entitled as artists to take part in fashioning *man;* men, not sufficiently strong and far-sighted to *allow,* with sublime self-constraint, the obvious law of the thousandfold failures and perishings to prevail; men, not sufficiently noble to see the radically different grades of rank and intervals of rank that separate man from man:—*such* men, with their "equality before God," have hitherto swayed the destiny of Europe; until at last a dwarfed, almost ludicrous species has been produced, a gregarious animal, something obliging, sickly, mediocre, the European of the present day.

CHAPTER V

THE NATURAL HISTORY OF MORALS

202

Let us at once say again what we have already said a hundred times, for people's ears nowadays are unwilling to hear such truths—*our* truths. We know well enough how offensively it sounds when any one plainly, and without metaphor, counts man amongst the animals; but it will be accounted to us almost a *crime,* that it is precisely in respect to men of "modern ideas" that we have constantly applied the terms "herd," "herd-instincts," and such like expressions. What avail is it? We cannot do otherwise, for it is precisely here that our new insight is. We have found that in all the principal moral judgments Europe has become unanimous, including likewise the countries where European influence prevails: in Europe people evidently *know* what Socrates thought he did not know, and what the famous serpent of old once promised to teach—they "know" to-day what is good and evil. It must then sound hard and be distasteful to the ear, when we always insist that that which here thinks it knows, that which here glorifies itself with praise and blame, and calls itself good, is the instinct of the herding human animal: the instinct which has come and is ever coming more and more to the front, to preponderance and supremacy over other instincts, according to the increasing physiological approximation and resemblance of which it is the symptom. *Morality in Europe at present is herding-animal morality;* and therefore, as we understand the matter, only one kind of human morality, beside which, before which, and after which many other moralities, and above all *higher* moralities, are or should be possible. Against such a "possibility," against such a "should be," however, this morality defends itself with all its strength; it says obstinately and inexorably: "I am morality itself and nothing else is morality!" Indeed, with the help of a religion which has humoured and flattered the sublimest desires of the herding-animal, things have reached such a point that we always find a more visible expression of this morality even in political and social arrangements: the *democratic* movement is the inheritance of the Christian movement. That its *tempo,* however, is much too slow and sleepy for the more impatient ones, for those who are sick and distracted by the herding-instinct, is indicated by the increasingly furious howling, and always less disguised teeth-gnashing of the anarchist dogs, who are now roving through the highways of European culture. Apparently in opposition to the peacefully industrious democrats and Revolution-ideologues, and still more so to the awkward philosophasters and fraternity-visionaries who call themselves Socialists and want a "free society," those are really at one with them all in their thorough and instinctive hostility to every form of society other than that of *autonomous* herd (to the extent even of repudiating the notions "master" and "servant"—*ni dieu ni maître,* says a socialist formula); at one in their tenacious opposition to every special claim, every special right and privilege (this means ultimately opposition to *every* right, for when all are equal, no one needs "rights" any longer); at one in their distrust of punitive justice (as though it were a violation of the weak, unfair to the *necessary* consequences of all former society); but equally at one in their religion of sympathy, in their compassion for all that feels, lives, and suffers (down to the very animals, up even to "God"—the extravagance of "sympathy for God" belongs to a democratic age); altogether at one in the cry and impatience of their sympathy, in their deadly hatred of suffering generally, in their almost feminine incapacity for witnessing it or *allowing* it; at one in their involuntary beglooming and heart-softening, under the spell of which Europe seems to be threatened with a new Buddhism; at one in their belief in the morality of *mutual* sympathy, as though it were morality in itself, the climax, the *attained* climax of mankind, the sole hope of the future, the consolation of the present, the great discharge from all the obligations of the past; altogether at one in their belief in the community as the *deliverer,* in the herd, and therefore in "themselves."

203

We, who hold a different belief—we, who regard the democratic movement, not only as a degenerating form of political organization, but as equivalent to a degenerating, a waning type of man, as involving his mediocrising and depreciation: where have *we* to fix our hopes? In *new philosophers*—there is no other alternative: in minds strong and original enough to initiate opposite estimates of value, to transvalue and invert "eternal valuations"; in forerunners, in men of the future, who in the present shall fix the constraints and fasten the knots which will compel millenniums to take *new* paths. To teach man the future of humanity as his *will,* as depending on human will, and to make preparation for vast hazardous enterprises and collective attempts in rearing and educating, in order thereby to put an end to the frightful rule of folly and chance which has hitherto gone by the name of "history" (the folly of the "greatest number" is only its last form) —for that purpose a new type of philosophers and commanders will some time or other be needed, at the very idea of which everything that has existed in the way of occult, terrible, and benevolent beings might look pale and dwarfed. The image of such leaders hovers before *our* eyes:—is it lawful for me to say it aloud, ye free spirits? The conditions which one would partly have to create and partly utilize for their genesis; the presumptive methods and tests by virtue of which a soul should grow up to such an elevation and power as to feel a *constraint* to these tasks; a transvaluation of values, under the new pressure and hammer of which a conscience should be steeled and a heart transformed into brass, so as to bear the weight of such responsibility; and on the other hand the necessity for such leaders, the dreadful danger that they might be lacking, or miscarry and degenerate:—these are *our* real anxieties and glooms, ye know it well, ye free spirits! these are the heavy distant thoughts and storms which sweep across the heaven of *our* life. There are few pains so grievous as to have seen, divined, or experienced how an exceptional man has missed his way and deteriorated; but he who has the rare eye for the universal danger of "man" himself *deteriorating,* he who like us has recognized the extraordinary fortuitousness which has hitherto played its fame in respect to the future of mankind— a game in which neither the hand, nor even a "finger of God" has participated!—he who divines the fate that is hidden under the idiotic unwariness and blind confidence of "modern ideas," and still more under the whole of Christo-European morality— suffers from an anguish with which no other is to be compared. He sees at a glance all that could still *be made out of man* through a favourable accumulation and augmentation of human powers and arrangements; he knows with all the knowledge of his conviction how unexhausted man still is for the greatest possibilities, and how often in the past the type man has stood in presence of mysterious decisions and new paths:—he knows still better from his painfulest recollections on what wretched obstacles promising developments of the highest rank have hitherto usually gone to pieces, broken down, sunk, and become contemptible. The *universal degeneracy of mankind* to the level of the "man of the future"—as idealized by the socialistic fools and shallow-pates—this degeneracy and dwarfing of man to an absolutely gregarious animal (or as they call it, to a man of "free society"), this brutalising of man into a pigmy with equal rights and claims, is undoubtedly *pos-*

sible! He who has thought out this possibility to its ultimate conclusion knows *another* loathing unknown to the rest of mankind—and perhaps also a new *mission!*

CHAPTER VI

WE SCHOLARS

210

Supposing, then, that in the picture of the philosophers of the future, some trait suggests the question whether they must not perhaps be sceptics in the last-mentioned sense, something in them would only be designated thereby—and *not* they themselves. With equal right they might call themselves critics; and assuredly they will be men of experiments. By the name with which I ventured to baptize them, I have already expressly emphasized their attempting and their love of attempting: is this because, as critics in body and soul, they will love to make use of experiments in a new, and perhaps wider and more dangerous sense? In their passion for knowledge, will they have to go further in daring and painful attempts than the sensitive and pampered taste of a democratic century can approve of?—There is no doubt: these coming ones will be least able to dispense with the serious and not unscrupulous qualities which distinguish the critic from the sceptic: I mean the certainty as to standards of worth, the conscious employment of a unity of method, the wary courage, the standing-alone, and the capacity for self-responsibility; indeed, they will avow among themselves a *delight* in denial and dissection, and a certain considerate cruelty, which knows how to handle the knife surely and deftly, even when the heart bleeds. They will be *sterner* (and perhaps not always towards themselves only) than humane people may desire, they will not deal with the "truth" in order that it may "please" them, or "elevate" and "inspire" them—they will rather have little faith in *"truth"* bringing with it such revels for the feelings. They will smile, those rigorous spirits, when any one says in their presence: "that thought elevates me, why should it not be true?" or: "that work enchants me, why should it not be beautiful?" or: "that artist enlarges me, why should he not be great?" Perhaps they will not only have a smile, but a genuine disgust for all that is thus rapturous, idealistic, feminine, and hermaphroditic; and if any one could look into their inmost hearts, he would not easily find therein the intention to reconcile "Christian sentiments" with "antique taste," or even with "modern parliamentarism" (the kind of reconciliation necessarily found even amongst philosophers in our very uncertain and consequently very conciliatory century). Critical discipline, and every habit that conduces to purity and rigour in intellectual matters, will not only be demanded from themselves by these philosophers of the future; they may even make a display thereof as their special adornment—nevertheless they will not want to be called critics on that account. It will seem to them no small indignity to philosophy to have it decreed, as is so welcome nowadays, that "philosophy itself is criticism and critical science—and nothing else whatever!" Though this estimate of philosophy may enjoy the approval of all Positivists of France and Germany (and possibly it even flattered the heart and taste of *Kant:* let us call to mind the titles of his principal works), our new philosophers will say, notwithstanding, that critics are instruments of the philosopher, and just on that account, as instruments, they are far from being philosophers themselves! Even the great Chinaman of Köningsberg was only a great critic.

211

I insist upon it that people finally cease confounding philosophical workers, and in general scientific men, with philosophers—that precisely here one should strictly give "each his own," and not give those far too much, these far too little. It may be necessary for the education of the real philosopher that he himself should have once stood upon all those steps upon which his servants, the scientific workers of philosophy, remain standing, and *must* remain standing: he himself must perhaps have been critic, and dogmatist, and historian, and besides, poet, and collector, and traveller, and riddle-reader, and moralist, and seer, and "free spirit," and almost everything, in order to traverse the whole range of human values and estimations, and that he may *be able* with a variety of eyes and consciences to look from a height to any distance, from a depth up to any height, from a nook into any expanse. But all these are only preliminary conditions for his task; this task itself demands something else—it requires him *to create values.* The philosophical workers, after the excellent pattern of Kant and Hegel, have to fix and formalise some great existing body of valuations—that is to say, former *determinations of value,* creations of value, which have become prevalent, and are for a time called "truths"— whether in the domain of the *logical,* the *political* (moral), or the *artistic.* It is for these investigators to make whatever has happened and been esteemed hitherto, conspicuous, conceivable, intelligible, and manageable, to shorten everything long, even "time" itself, and to *subjugate* the entire past: an immense and wonderful task, in the carrying out of which all refined pride, all tenacious will, can surely find satisfaction. *The real philosophers, however, are commanders and law-givers;* they say: "Thus *shall* it be!" They determine first the Whither and Why of mankind, and thereby set aside the previous labour of all philosophical workers, and all subjugators of the past— they grasp at the future with a creative hand, and whatever is and was becomes for them thereby a means, an instrument, and a hammer. Their "knowing" is *creating,* their creating is a law-giving, their will to truth is

—*Will to Power.*—Are there at present such philosophers? Have there ever been such philosophers? *Must* there not .be such philosophers some day? . . .

212

It is always more obvious to me that the philosopher, as a man *indispensable* for the morrow and the day after the morrow, has ever found himself, and *has been obliged* to find himself, in contradiction to the day in which he lives; his enemy has always been the ideal of his day. Hitherto all those extraordinary furtherers of humanity whom one calls philosophers—who rarely regarded themselves as lovers of wisdom, but rather as disagreeable fools and dangerous interrogators —have found their mission, their hard, involuntary, imperative mission (in the end however the greatness of their mission), in being the bad conscience of their age. In putting the vivisector's knife to the breast of the very *virtues of their age,* they have betrayed their own secret; it has been for the sake of a *new* greatness of man, a new untrodden path to his aggrandisement. They have always disclosed how much hypocrisy, indolence, self-indulgence, and self-neglect, how much false-hood was concealed under the most venerated types of contemporary morality, how much virtue was *outlived;* they have always said: "We must remove hence to where *you* are least at home." In face of a world of "modern ideas," which would like to confine every one in a corner, in a "specialty," a philosopher, if there could be philosophers nowadays, would be compelled to place the greatness of man, the conception of "greatness," precisely in his comprehensiveness and multifariousness, in his all-roundness; he would even determine worth and rank according to the amount and variety of that which a man could bear and take upon himself, according to the *extent* to which a man could stretch his responsibility. Nowadays the taste and virtue of the age weaken and attenuate the will; nothing is so adapted to the spirit of the age as weakness of will: consequently, in the ideal of the philosopher, strength of will, sternness and capacity for prolonged resolution, must specially be included in the conception of "greatness"; with as good a right as the opposite doctrine, with its ideal of a silly, renouncing, humble, selfless humanity, was suited to an opposite age— such as the sixteenth century, which suffered from its accumulated energy of will, and from the wildest torrents and floods of selfishness. In the time of Socrates, among men only of worn-out instincts, old conservative Athenians who let themselves go—"for the sake of happiness," as they said; for the sake of pleasure, as their conduct indicated —and who had continually on their lips the old pompous words to which they had long forfeited the right by the life they led, *irony* was perhaps necessary for greatness of soul, the wicked Socratic assurance of the old physician and plebeian, who cut ruthlessly into his own flesh as into the flesh and heart of the "noble," with a look that said plainly enough: "Do not dissemble before me! here—we are equal!" At present, on the contrary, when throughout Europe the herding animal alone attains to honours, and dispenses honours, when "equality of right" can too readily be transformed into equality in wrong: I mean to say into general war against everything rare, strange, and privileged, against the higher man, the higher soul, the higher duty, the higher responsibility, the creative plenipotence and lordliness—at present it belongs to the conception of "greatness" to be noble, to wish to be apart, to be capable of being different, to stand alone, to have to live by personal initiative; and the philosopher will betray something of his own ideal when he asserts: "He shall be the greatest who can be the most solitary, the most concealed, the most divergent, the man beyond good and evil, the master of his virtues, and of superabundance of will; precisely this shall be called *greatness:* as diversified as can be entire, as ample as can be full." And to ask once more the question: Is greatness *possible*—nowadays?

CHAPTER VII

OUR VIRTUES

221

"It sometimes happens," said a moralistic pedant and trifle-retailer, "that I honour and respect an unselfish man: not, however, because he is unselfish, but rather because I think he has a right to be useful to another man at his own expense. In short, the question is always who *he* is, and who the *other* is. For instance, in a person created and destined for command, self-denial and modest retirement, instead of being virtues would be the waste of virtues: so it seems to me. Every system of unegoistic morality which takes itself unconditionally and appeals to every one, not only sins against good taste, but is also an incentive to sins of omission, an *additional* seduction under the mask of philanthropy—and precisely a seduction and injury to the higher, rarer, and more privileged types of men. Moral systems must be compelled first of all to bow before the *gradations of rank;* their presumption must be driven home to their conscience—until they thoroughly understand at last that it is *immoral* to say that "what is right for one is proper for another."—So said my moralistic pedant and *bonhomme.* Did he perhaps deserve to be laughed at when he thus exhorted systems of morals to practise morality? But one should not be too much in the right if one wishes to have the laughers on *one's own* side; a grain of wrong pertains even to good taste.

CHAPTER IX

WHAT IS NOBLE?

257

Every elevation of the type "man," has hitherto been the work of an aristocratic society and so it will always be—a society believing in a long scale of gradations of rank and differences of worth among human beings, and requiring slavery in some form or other. Without the *pathos of distance,* such as grows out of the incarnated difference of classes, out of the constant outlooking and downlooking of the ruling caste on subordinates and instruments, and out of their equally constant practice of obeying and commanding, of keeping down and keeping at a distance—that other more mysterious pathos could never have arisen, the longing for an ever new widening of distance within the soul itself, the formation of every higher, rarer, further, more extended, more comprehensive states, in short, just the elevation of the type "man," the continued "self-surmounting of man," to use a moral formula in a supermoral sense. To be sure, one must not resign oneself to any humanitarian illusions about the history of the origin of an aristocratic society (that is to say, of the preliminary condition, for the elevation of the type "man") : the truth is hard. Let us acknowledge unprejudicedly how every higher civilization hitherto has *originated!* Men with a still natural nature, barbarians in every terrible sense of the word, men of prey, still in possession of unbroken strength of will and desire for power, threw themselves upon weaker, more moral, more peaceful races (perhaps trading or cattle-rearing communities), or upon old mellow civilizations in which the final vital force was flickering out in brilliant fireworks of wit and depravity. At the commencement, the noble caste was always the barbarian caste: their superiority did not consist first of all in their physical, but in their psychical power—they were more *complete* men (which at every point also implies the same as "more complete beasts").

259

To refrain mutually from injury, from violence, from exploitation, and put one's will on a par with that of others: this may result in a certain rough sense in good conduct among individuals when the necessary conditions are given (namely, the actual similarity of the individuals in amount of force and degree of worth, and their co-relation within one organisation). As soon, however, as one wished to take this principle more generally, and if possible even as *the fundamental principle of society,* it would immediately disclose what it really is— namely, a Will to the *denial* of life, a principle of dissolution and decay. Here one must think profoundly to the very basis and resist all sentimental weakness: life itself is *essentially* appropriation, injury; conquest of the strange and weak, suppression, severity, obtrusion of peculiar forms, incorporation, and at the least, putting it mildest, exploitation;—but why should one for ever use precisely these words on which for ages a disparaging purpose has been stamped? Even the organisation within which, as was previously supposed, the individuals treat each other as equal—it takes place in every healthy aristocracy—must itself, if it be a living and not a dying organisation, do all that towards other bodies, which the individuals within it refrain from doing to each other: it will have to be the incarnated Will to Power, it will endeavour to grow, to gain ground, attract to itself and acquire ascendency—not owing to any morality or immorality, but because it *lives,* and because life *is* precisely Will to Power. On no point, however, is the ordinary consciousness of Europeans more unwilling to be corrected than on this matter; people now rave everywhere, even under the guise of science, about coming conditions of society in which "the exploiting character" is to be absent:—that sounds to my ears as if they promised to invent a mode of life which should refrain from all organic functions. "Exploitation" does not belong to a depraved, or imperfect and primitive society: it belongs to the *nature* of the living being as a primary organic function; it is a consequence of the intrinsic Will to Power, which is precisely the Will to Life.—Granting that as a theory this is a novelty—as a reality it is the *fundamental fact* of all history: let us be so far honest towards ourselves!

260

In a tour through the many finer and coarser moralities which have hitherto prevailed or still prevail on the earth, I found certain traits recurring regularly together, and connected with one another, until finally two primary types revealed themselves to me, and a radical distinction was brought to light. There is *master-morality* and *slave-morality;*—I would at once add, however, that in all higher and mixed civilisations, there are also attempts at the reconciliation of the two moralities; but one finds still oftener the confusion and mutual misunderstanding of them, indeed, sometimes their close juxtaposition—even in the same man, within one soul. The distinctions of moral values have either originated in a ruling caste, pleasantly conscious of being different from the ruled—or among the ruled class, the slaves and dependents of all sorts. In the first case, when it is the rulers who determine the conception "good," it is the exalted, proud disposition which is regarded as the distinguishing feature, and that which determines the order of rank. The noble type of man separates from himself the beings in whom the opposite of this exalted, proud disposition displays itself: he despises them. Let it at once be noted that in this first kind of morality the antithesis "good" and "bad" means practically the same as "noble" and "despicable";—the antithesis "good" and *"evil"* is of a different origin. The cowardly, the timid, the insignificant, and those thinking merely of narrow utility are despised; moreover, also, the distrustful, with their constrained glances, the self-abasing, the dog-like kind of men who let themselves be abused, the mendicant flatterers, and above all the liars:—it is a fundamental belief of all aristocrats that the common people are untruthful. "We truthful ones"—the nobility in ancient Greece called themselves. It is obvious that everywhere the designations of moral value were at first applied to *men,* and were only derivatively and at a later period applied to *actions;* it is a gross mistake, therefore, when historians of morals start with questions like, "Why have sympathetic actions been praised?" The noble type of man regards *himself* as a determiner of values; he does not require to be approved of; he passes the judgment: "What is injurious to me is injurious in itself"; he knows that it is he himself only who confers honour on things; he is a *creator of values.* He honours whatever he recognizes in himself: such morality is self-glorification. In the foreground there is the feeling of plenitude, of power, which seeks to overflow, the happiness of high tension, the consciousness of a wealth which would fain give and bestow:—the noble man also helps the unfortunate, but not—or scarcely —out of pity, but rather from an impulse generated by the superabundance of power. The noble man honours in himself the powerful one, him also who has power over himself, who knows how to speak and how to keep silence, who takes pleasure in subjecting himself to severity and hardness, and has reverence for all that is severe and hard. "Wotan placed a hard heart in my breast," says an old Scandinavian Saga: it is thus rightly expressed from the soul of a proud Viking. Such a type of man is even proud of *not* being made for sympathy; the hero of the Saga therefore adds warningly: "He who has not a hard heart when young, will never have one." The noble and brave who think thus are the furthest removed from the morality which sees precisely in sympathy, or in acting for the good of others, or in *désintéressement,* the characteristic of the moral; faith in oneself, pride in oneself, a radical enmity and irony towards "selflessness," belong as definitely to noble morality, as do a careless scorn and precaution in presence of sympathy and the "warm heart."—It is the powerful who *know* how to honour, it is their art, their domain for invention. The profound reverence for age and for tradition—all law rests on this double reverence,—the belief and prejudice in favour of ancestors and unfavourable to newcomers, is typical in the morality of the powerful; and if, reversely, men of "modern ideas" believe almost instinctively in "progress" and the "future," and are more and more lacking in respect for old age, the ignoble origin of these "ideas" has complacently betrayed itself thereby. A morality of the ruling class, however, is more especially foreign and irritating to present-day taste in the sternness of its principle that one has duties only to one's equals; that óne may act towards beings of a lower rank, towards all that is foreign, just as seems good to one, or "as the heart desires," and in any case "beyond good and evil": it is here that sympathy and similar sentiments can have a place. The ability and obligation to exercise prolonged gratitude and prolonged revenge—both only within the circle of equals,—artfulness in retaliation, *raffinement* of the idea in friendship, a certain necessity to have enemies (as outlets for the emotions of envy, quarrelsomeness, arrogance—in fact, in order to be a good *friend*): all these are typical characteristics of the noble morality, which, as has been pointed out, is not the morality of "modern ideas," and is therefore at present difficult to realize, and also to unearth and disclose.—It is otherwise with the second type of morality, *slave-morality*. Supposing that the abused, the oppressed, the suffering, the unemancipated, the weary, and those uncertain of themselves, should moralize, what will be the common element in their moral estimates? Probably a pessimistic suspicion with regard to the entire situation of man will find expression, perhaps a condemnation of man, together with his situation. The slave has an unfavourable eye for the virtues of the powerful; he has a scepticism and distrust, a *refinement* of distrust of everything "good" that is there honoured—he would fain persuade himself that the very happiness there is not genuine. On the other hand, *those* qualities which serve to alleviate the existence of sufferers are brought into prominence and flooded with light; it is here that sympathy, the kind, helping hand, the warm heart, patience, diligence, humility, and friendliness attain to honour; for here these are the most useful qualities, and almost the only means of supporting the burden of existence. Slave-morality is essentially the morality of utility. Here is the seat of the origin of the famous antithesis "good" and "evil":—power and dangerousness are assumed to reside in the evil, a certain dreadfulness, subtlety, and strength, which do not admit of being despised. According to slave-morality, therefore, the "evil" man arouses fear; according to master-morality, it is precisely the "good" man who arouses fear and seeks to arouse it, while the bad man is regarded as the despicable being. The contrast attains its maximum when, in accordance with the logical consequences of slave-morality, a shade of depreciation—it may be slight and well-intentioned—at last attaches itself to the "good" man of this morality; because, according to the servile mode of thought, the good man must in any case be the *safe* man: he is good-natured, easily deceived, perhaps a little stupid, *un bonhomme*. Everywhere that slave-morality gains the ascendancy, language shows a tendency to approximate the significations of the words "good" and "stupid."—A last fundamental difference: the desire for *freedom*, the instinct for happiness and the refinements of the feeling of liberty belong as necessarily to slave-morals and morality, as artifice and enthusiasm in reverence and devotion are the regular symptoms of an aristocratic mode of thinking

and estimating.—Hence we can understand without further detail
why love *as a passion*—it is our European specialty—must absolutely
be of noble origin; as is well known, its invention is due to the Provençal poet-cavaliers, those brilliant, ingenious men of the *"gai sabre,"*
to whom Europe owes so much, and almost owes itself.

265

At the risk of displeasing innocent ears, I submit that egoism belongs to the essence of a noble soul, I mean the unalterable belief that
to a being such as "we," other beings must naturally be in subjection,
and have to sacrifice themselves. The noble soul accepts the fact of
his egoism without question, and also without consciousness of harshness, constraint, or arbitrariness therein, but rather as something that
may have its basis in the primary law of things:—if he sought a designation for it he would say: "It is justice itself." He acknowledges
under certain circumstances, which made him hesitate at first, that
there are other equally privileged ones; as soon as he has settled this
question of rank, he moves among those equals and equally privileged
ones with the same assurance, as regards modesty and delicate respect,
which he enjoys in intercourse with himself—in accordance with an
innate heavenly mechanism which all the stars understand. It is an
additional instance of his egoism, this artfulness and self-limitation
in intercourse with his equals—every star is a similar egoist; he honours
himself in them, and in the rights which he concedes to them, he has
no doubt that the exchange of honours and rights, as the *essence* of
all intercourse, belongs also to the natural condition of things. The
noble soul gives as he takes, prompted by the passionate and sensitive
instinct of requital, which is at the root of his nature. The notion of
"favour" has, *inter pares,* neither significance nor good repute; there
may be a sublime way of letting gifts, as it were, light upon one from
above, and of drinking them thirstily like dew drops; but for those
arts and displays the noble soul has no aptitude. His egoism hinders
him here: in general, he looks "aloft" unwillingly—he looks either
forward, horizontally and deliberately, or downwards—*he knows that
he is on a height.*

QUESTIONS AND STATEMENTS FOR DISCUSSION

(Beyond Good and Evil)

1. "In spite of all the value which may belong to the true, the positive, the unselfish, it might be possible that a higher and more fundamental value for life generally should be assigned to pretence, to the will to delusion, to selfishness and cupidity." (*Beyond Good and Evil,* Chap. I, section 2.) "The falseness of an opinion is not for us any objection to it. . . . The question is how far an opinion is life-furthering." (Section 4). Can the "advantages" thus sought be described as values? Can falsehood ever be truly described as "life-furthering"?

2. In Chap. II, section 36, he asserts the right to define all active force unequivocally as *Will to Power.* "We believe that severity, violence, slavery, danger in the street, and in the heart, secrecy, stoicism, tempter's art and deviltry of every kind—that everything wicked, terrible, tyrannical, predatory, and serpentine in men, serves as well for the elevation of the human species as the opposite." (Section 44.) Is will to power, in your judgment, as strong as love, interest, or even the creative imagination? Does the animal trainer use violence or kindness in animals capable of affection?

3. In Chap. III, sections 61, 62, he places religion in the role of aiding in the subjection of peoples, and states that it is the cause of the deterioration of Europe. What evidence is there that the teaching of social justice, moral integrity, and good-will by religion has caused the deterioration of Europe? May the deterioration be due to failure to live up to these ideals?

4. Evaluate the arguments against democracy in Chap. V, section 2.

5. What values might be destroyed by the experimentation suggested in Chap. VI, section 210?

6. In the world of modern communication, how many rulers could there be under the "egoism of the noble soul"? (Chap. IX, sections 257, 259, 260, 265.) Is it true that "every elevation of the type 'man' requires slavery in some form?"

(The Genealogy of Morals)

7. In *The Genealogy of Morals,* Essay I, section 10, Nietzsche identifies "unfortunate" with "bad." Is there a similarity between this philosophy and that of Job's friends? You suffer, therefore you are a great sinner.

8. Can the Nietzschean claim that what is goodness in the aristocrat is badness in the masses or "foreigners," be defended, and on what principles? May the idea of "the Blonde Beast" as "the core of all aristocratic races" account for the contempt of the British as

"a nation of shop-keepers"? (Section 11.) Read also *Beyond Good and Evil*, section 221.

9. Is the assumption that the sense of morality is due to suffering, tenable? Does your sense of moral obligation to your parents arise from their cruelty, or from your love? Which of these is the stronger influence?

10. In what sense, if any, is it true that "The sight of suffering does one good, the infliction of suffering does one more good"? (Section 6.)

11. Does the beginning of the state in violence (if it can be established) necessarily prove that it must also continue in violence as an example of "progress"?

(Zarathustra)

12. In Zarathustra, Part I, Chap. X, peace is presented as desirable only as a means to new wars. Is this concept of progress by war in any way accountable for the present world situation? Can you recall any philosophical or scientific ideas that have fostered the notion?

13. Chap. XVIII. Is the notion "The happiness of man is 'I will', the happiness of woman is 'He will'," defensible on the basis of the sanctity of the personality? Why is the latter important to the happiness of both sexes as well as to the future of society? Read also in this connection: Chap. VII, section 239 of *Beyond Good and Evil*.

14. Can you solve the logic of the writer who declares that the commands not to rob and not to slay are dissuaders from life? How do you think Nietzsche justified such a position in his own mind? Was he serious or merely spilling paradoxes?

15. As he writes in *Zarathustra*, Chap. LVII, of "eternal recurrence," so in Chap. LVI, section 2, we find "everything straight lieth. . . . All truth is crooked; time itself is a circle." Is there any empirical evidence of recurrence? Would recurrence have any meaning to one who had no real memory of a previous existence? Why is Nietzsche's statement, in another section, that recurrence is impossible the truth of the matter?

Suggested Supplementary Readings:

Thomas: *Living Biographies of Great Philosophers.* Pp. 275-294.

Nietzsche: *Beyond Good and Evil* ⎱ Modern Library, New
          Thus Spake Zarathustra ⎰ York (Giant Series).
          The Genealogy of Morals

Hitler: *Mein Kampf.*

Brinton: *Nietzsche.* Harvard University Press, Cambridge.

Morgan: *What Nietzsche Means.* Harvard University Press, Cambridge.

Singer: *Modern Thinkers and Present Problems.* Henry Holt, New York. Chap. VII.

Chapter 13

PASTEUR: THE SCIENTIFIC QUEST FOR VALUE

Introduction
The Modern Confidence in the Power of Science

I
The Bases of Science

II
Scientific Obligation

III
Obstructions to Scientific Inquiry

IV
The Life of Pasteur as Illustrative of the Scientific Spirit

Chapter 13

PASTEUR: THE SCIENTIFIC QUEST FOR VALUE

To understand the peculiarities of our own time is not easy, for the time-spirit is something in which we live and move and have our being. This makes us unaware of the greatness as well as of the weakness of our own era. Borne up by new discovery, lapped in the luxury of a life made easy by scientific invention, we enjoy comforts as matter-of-fact while we are unmindful of the sacrifices by which they have been achieved. The processes that dull by ease of possession also lead us to overestimate the character of future scientific advances, until we come to think there are no problems that science alone cannot solve. We trust that our enigmas, social, political, economic, or religious, can be solved in the laboratory. The extent of these beliefs is indicated in the phraseology of the day. A half century ago there were still many philosophies. Today these are nearly all called sciences. Political philosophy of yesterday is now dubbed political science; moral philosophy has become the science of human behavior; sociology becomes social science; psychology, without even so much as a change of name, claims a place among the sciences. Natural philosophy is now the science of physics, while some of our philosophers, not willing to be submerged by the scientific washout, turn logic into a science of words and symbols and call it the science of semantics.

The moment of gravest danger to any theory is often the moment of general acceptance. By the same token, the present is a period of disillusionment respecting the moral, social, and political contributions of science. Discoveries intended for the benefit of men have been turned into engines of wholesale destruction, in which man's most prized works, arts, and cultures sink in the maelstrom. The outcome of our scientific progress now threatens to be the destruction of civilization, and will accomplish this unless we can raise against it the barriers of spiritual and moral achievement. If civilization is not to collapse, if science and the scientific order of living are to survive, it can only be as we look beneath the superficialities of the age, and distinguish beyond the cries of quack and charlatan those deeper voices which are the real sources of scientific strength and progress. To turn from the make-believe to the real, from the accidental and fleeting to the intrinsic and abiding, is to get at the real meaning of science, for in its search for truth at all costs, in its spirit of integrity, in its ofttimes sacrificial order of living, science can easily come to possess many of the aspects of religion.

Let us begin by considering the bases, obligations, and obstructions attending scientific inquiry, and close with such actual illustrations as are furnished by the life of one of the greatest of modern scientists, Louis Pasteur.

I

The Bases of Science

Misunderstanding as to what may be expected or demanded from science arises from the failure to reflect upon its nature and method, and the characteristic limitations of the scientific field. The task of science is the observation of phenomena, the description of events and not the explanation of ultimate causes. It sets out to learn what can be learned respecting the order and succession of events in a space-time world. Since this is in its field, its facts are measurable in terms of movement, mass, energy, space, and time. Out of many observations it comes quite safely to state predictable successions in natural phenomena. These successions and uniformities are called the "laws of nature," but are essentially the habitual ways of nature so far as they can be observed. Where experimentation can be controlled, much can thus be learned about the nature of the world, because a knowledge of activities is also a knowledge of the nature of things. The scientist approaches the sphere of knowledge to learn what can be ascertained about reality by weighing and measuring. This means that scientifically he is limited to such realities as are called material, or which yield to controlled experimentation, and which give exact physical results. If he assumes that there are no other realities except these, he speaks unscientifically, since he should make no affirmation where he does not know. If he is criticized for being a materialist, he can rightfully answer that the physical event is the only reality which as a scientist he pretends to investigate. There may be realities, however, that are more important, which cannot be brayed in a mortar, heated in a test-tube, or filtered in his laboratory, but which are outside his realm. With such realities he is not, as a scientist, concerned. It may be claimed that there are other sciences that are immaterial, like psychology, sociology, and education, but these are of mixed order. They can be called sciences only by courtesy. They attempt to discover the norms of human action but they are susceptible to reversal in any given human will.

II

Scientific Obligation

To say that the scientist is, as a scientist, limited to the domain of physical observation, is not to say that he is thereby released from moral obligation as a member of society. As a scientist he is under obligation to tell the truth, the whole truth, and nothing but the truth as far as he can see it, remembering that with the most conscientious devotion he must frequently make mistakes of interpretation and observation, due to partial experimentation, warped hypothesis, personal prejudice, or human limitation. No human being can justly claim to be free from these. The field of science is nevertheless important to human values. Its discoveries may be so freighted with results to human life and happiness that the highest moral and spiritual character is called for in the scientist. He may become the discoverer of powers that can be used immorally, and hence he has an obligation to society.

He is bound, moreover, to a meticulous care in his observations. He dare not neglect any one of the phenomena involved in a given experiment. He must slay every temptation to stop short of complete knowledge, to be warped by prejudice, hypothesis, expectancy, or opinion, or to be turned aside by selfish interests or external threats. He must be prepared at times to destroy his own intellectual children when they are found false. In the interest of truth he may be called upon to neglect personal advantage. Such an order of honesty and integrity partakes of religious devotion which frequently puts to shame the professedly religious. Religious devotees have at times indeed confirmed their own irreligion by committing some of the world's most deeply religious scientific souls to ostracism, neglect, calumny, and even to poison, torture, and flame. Some of the outstanding conquests of disease have been won by a kind of martyrdom, as in the case of yellow fever, cholera, and various infections. Let no one declare such martyrdom to be less than religious. Sometimes to the man who with his life at stake attempts to "read God's thoughts after Him," the standards of piety set up by the formally religious must seem a bit wanting in red blood, and removed from reality.

The moral bearings of science and the moral obligation of the scientist cannot be escaped, for it is not a social obligation alone. His own standing and genuineness as a scientist is involved. To be a real scientist he must be wholly devoted to the truth, to love it more than his opinion, or theory, or predilection, or what he would like to believe, or in spite of any prejudice, or pride of discovery.   The attitude toward facts, demanded of a thoroughgoing scientist, is an attitude essentially religious in character.

The religious nature of the highest devotion to scientific truth and of its importance to scientific discovery has been admirably stated by the great Thomas Huxley :[1]

> Science seems to me to teach in the highest and strongest manner the great truth which is embodied in the Christian conception of entire surrender to the will of God. Sit down before a fact as a little child, be prepared to give up every preconceived notion, follow humbly wherever and to whatever abysses nature leads, or you shall learn nothing.

III

Obstructions to Scientific Inquiry

Contrary to popular opinion, the chief obstructions to scientific progress have not come primarily from religious sources but rather from a human desire to maintain the *status quo*. Established institutions of every kind will, in the nature of the case, fight to ward off discoveries that seem to threaten their domination. Such obstruction of scientific discovery is not peculiar to religion. It is often political or social, as when the Emperor of China put a ban on any deviation from accepted shapes of kitchen utensils under penalty of death, or when another Emperor executed the Chinese discoverer of alcohol as a dangerous and subversive person, or when Nazism set out to control scientific investigation for political ends. Organized medicine, law, theology, or even science itself sometimes set up standards of professional orthodoxy for self-protection and frequently discriminate against the innovator. Business often buys up in order to suppress inventions that endanger investments, and thus delays social progress and is ruining to the inventor.   There is no reason to name religion as the chief foe of scientific advance. Visalius, pioneer anatomist, came into conflict with the church only indirectly. His real opponents were certain medical men who feared the loss of practice through the results of

[1] Quoted by Professor Arthur H. Compton in *Science and Man*, p. 129.

his investigations in human anatomy and who raised the religious issue as an easy way to destroy him. The objections to and ridicule of Copernicus, Galileo, Newton, and Pasteur came largely from the ranks of their professional colleagues. A resort to the newspaper files of some twenty years ago will disclose how Einstein was, in our own time, the expressed object of scorn on the part of certain scientific leaders. This sort of thing happens when intrenched privileges, opinions, or institutions are threatened with compulsory readjustments. Nothing is more common than the reluctance with which the well-cared-for welcome new or disturbing ideas. The hold of totalitarianism was an example of the incapacity for thinking, or the unwillingness to think. It is easier to be dictated to than to meet and conquer new problems for one's self. This unsettling capacity is perhaps the chief benefit which science presents to society, but the capacity for innovation is one for which science has to fight within its own ranks, as elsewhere.

IV

The Life of Pasteur as Illustrative of the Scientific Spirit

To illustrate the points already mentioned, take the case of Louis Pasteur, our greatest scientific benefactor, for it did not differ essentially from the experience of other great scientists from Protagoras to Einstein.

Pasteur was meticulously clear with respect to the limitation of the scientific field to the observation of phenomena, and his refusal to draw therefrom philosophical, theological, or political conclusions. In an address[2] before the French Academy, he declared that in its investigations science must not be anxious about the philosophical results of its discoveries. But this was not to be interpreted as assuming that practical science fulfils the whole of man's needs. There was within him another set of interests, which kept him from believing that this life was all. He believed that there was a force within him that could not die, and which gave him hope of meeting again his dead children, but the two realms of science and religion must not be allowed to trespass on each other. His belief in the immortality of the soul was wholehearted and often expressed as strong, perhaps, as was his belief in the reality of matter, though not reached in the same way.

[2] See Vallery-Radot, *The Life of Pasteur,* Doubleday-Doran, New York, 1937, pp. 125, 244.

The sense of scientific obligation was very marked in Pasteur. He lived and died in comparative poverty while others made fortunes by reason of his discoveries. He feared that financial advantage would influence his scientific rectitude. His first work was for the wine-growers, who had not mastered the proper preservation of their wine because of their ignorance of the ferments that either bettered or destroyed them. A like service was performed for the brewers. The silk industries of France were saved through his studies in silk-worm diseases. The foot-and-mouth disease in sheep, and the hog cholera, sources of immense loss to agriculture, were conquered by him. He turned these same studies and discoveries to the conquest of human diseases, such as cholera, rabies, and small-pox. Yet with many opportunities to enrich himself he steadfastly refused, believing that the acceptance of monetary rewards would warp and contract his scientific disinterestedness, believing that there can be no greater disorder of the mind than to let the will influence the belief.[3] So wholesome was his distrust of hypotheses that he declared them dangerous when they became fixed ideas. In order to test the vaccine for cholera, it became necessary to inoculate himself and his laboratory assistants with the blood of cholera victims and when his courage was remarked upon he asked, "What about duty?"[4]

With respect to the sources of obstruction to scientific advance, the life of Pasteur furnishes abundant illustration. He had a lifelong struggle with the scientists, who were bound against the evidence to maintain the doctrine of spontaneous generation. The popularity of this hypothesis was due to certain materialistic prejudices against the belief in the existence of Deity. They thought spontaneous generation would show that a Creator was unnecessary. Yet in setting forth this doctrine there were put forward suppositions as ridiculous as any that the most imaginative theologian has ever mustered. Von Helmont, in the sixteenth century, gave this celebrated recipe for the spontaneous generation of mice: put some dirty linen in a receptacle with a few grains of wheat and a piece of cheese, and let stand and Presto! Mice! Buonani, the Italian scientist, declared that certain wood rotted in the sea produced worms that engendered butterflies, and these in turn became birds. While the scientists of Pasteur's time had advanced beyond such crudity, they fought with every weapon at their command—ridicule, slander, and persecution—Pasteur's claim that such things as ferments,

[3] *Ibid.*, p. 214.
[4] *Ibid.*, p. 126.

fevers, and infections came from micro-organisms that had a definite life-history. One contemporary denied the bacillar and contagious character of tuberculosis and asserted that in surgical operations it was only necessary to keep down putrid odors to avoid septi-
cemia. This same physician announced himself as unalterably opposed to the cleanliness of instruments, hands, and dressings, for
which Pasteur contended. At the same time, the French Academy
of Medicine declared that Physiology could be of no practical use
in medicine. The mere mention of the nature of these criticisms
shows that they arose more from personal animus against Pasteur
or from prejudice rather than from any scientific interest.   One
wonders how much such affirmations in the interest of filth were
dictated by pride in out-worn medical information, how much by
jealousy of the new science, and how much by fear that the profits
of the profession would be endangered by the discovery of wholesale specifics for disease.

Among the stiffest of all battles was the fight he was compelled
to wage against people who thought their financial interests were
endangered by his discoveries. For instance, he was slandered and
abused by the purveyors of silk-worm eggs, who thought if the disease which destroyed most of the eggs was stopped, they would lose
their market. They made every effort to neutralize or spoil his experimentation. In his experiments on cattle and sheep afflicted with
anthrax he had to withstand all but mob violence. The veterinari-
ans of France arranged what they expected would be a hopeless
fiasco that would forever end his scientific influence. This they did
by calling on him to demonstrate under untoward conditions his
mastery in sheep of splenic fever before which they were confessedly
powerless. When at long last it was belatedly proposed in the
French Parliament to honor Pasteur for his great discoveries, one
parliamentarian arose to declare him only a plagiarist and fraud
because the parliamentarian's father had, at one time, stated, without demonstration, his belief that a fungus growth was responsible
for what we now call athlete's foot.

Quite contrary to the popular belief that most scientists are
agnostic, most of the leading scientists are believers in religion. Pasteur was no exception. He declared that science brings men nearer
God,[5] and that positivism, which was the philosophy of materialism, took no account of things that were most important, namely,
the moral and spiritual values. At the very moment that the agnosticism of the French Enlightenment had reached its highest ex-

[5] *Ibid.,* pp. 148, 343.

pression, and scientists were proclaiming the complete dominance of materialism, this greatest scientist of them all, the man whose discoveries outstripped all others in practical benefits to society, bowed before the mystery of the Universe and proclaimed the supremacy of the spiritual realities within the soul. Thus he loved to proclaim the religious nature of the scientific life to a cavilling age, proud of its disbeliefs, affirming the pure heart, the search for truth and reality, devotion which cannot be bought off, indifference to rewards and opinions, the sacrifice of life as necessary to find supreme values. These are gifts without which no truly great scientist can work. But they are separated far from the beliefs of materialism that science alone deals with reality and that in scientific technique, spiritually unassisted, lies the social, mental, and political rehabilitation of civilization. The presence in any scientist of religious cynicism will as inevitably warp his scientific judgment, and mislead him in the interpretation of reality, as would the contrasting bigotry of the narrow theologian. Both extremes must be avoided, for the scientist himself must be ruled by the cold realism of facts. Among the misleading factors are the temptations to which he is as much subject as other men, temptation to prostitute his powers to financial gain, to easy publicity and false fame, to slipshod thinking and premature scientific announcement, to carelessly performed experiment and incomplete analysis, to *ex cathedra* utterances outside his field, to the misuse of his discoveries for the destruction of men and values. Weaknesses of character will unwaveringly affect his work and discovery. To prevent this he must be moved by convictions so strong, so deep, as to take on a religious significance. More important than all else is the necessity for an inner consciousness of the eternal nature of truth and a conformity with it which works an inner unity enabling him to withstand the allurements of time and sense. This is why science in certain privileged individuals takes on the character and devotion of religion in the achievement of value.

READINGS

(Chapter 13)

ARTHUR H. COMPTON: *WHAT YOU AND I NEED MOST*. From *This Week* Magazine*.

Our country is growing richer. Not alone in the gold buried at Fort Knox. More in the influx of brains and genius from all the world. The refugees of a shattered civilization seek sanctuary in a land where worship of God and human freedom go hand in hand.

Albert Einstein and Thomas Mann, Sigrid Undset and Jules Romains, Franz Werfel and Maurice Maeterlinck are among those who have seen in the Statue of Liberty its true meaning—a meaning that the turmoil of a world crash is now resurrecting.

We have been fascinated and obsessed by invention and research which have given us airplanes that fly 400 miles an hour, radio that carries the human voice 10,000 miles through space, and scores of other wonderful things.

Inventive genius has provided innumerable slaves to work for us; science has brought us a greater material advancement in the last half-century than in the previous 2,000 years.

Yet what have we gained? One half of the civilized world is plunged back into the jungle, and the other half is now threatened. How plain it is that genius does not suffice, that science is not enough!

Even our very freedom, which we have taken for granted as much as the air we breathe, has the fingers of death at its throat. And no achievements of science alone, no matter how wonderful, will be enough to save it. The test tube and the scales, the microscope and mathematics cannot reach those intangible, yet real, qualities of life in which is rooted human freedom.

I speak of the virtues by which man lives and progresses, on which civilization is built and by which alone it can endure. I speak of the spiritual elements of love and sacrifice, justice and honor, integrity, equality, and good-will. Call them intangibles if you will—yet they are real and they are indispensable. They are the qualities on which democracy and freedom are built. They are the qualities which must be strengthened if we would safeguard our liberty and our civilization.

These qualities in turn are rooted deep in religion. To strengthen them we must strengthen our faith, for faith is the cornerstone of religion.

There is a story about the late Thomas A. Edison that illustrates the kind of faith I am talking about. A newspaperman once asked the famous scientist: "What is electricity?"

"I do not know," Edison answered. "I only understand some of the things it will do."

"But how do you explain it?" the reporter persisted.

Edison's voice became even more humble as he answered. "I can't explain it," he said. "It just seems to me God has given it to the world to demonstrate His power. I simply take it on faith and go on working."

Without an abiding, dynamic faith, there can be no freedom; no incentive for further experiment or study; no impulse to progress. In physics there have been times when many scientists thought the limits of new discovery had been reached. But others, with greater faith, went on working, only to have strange truths revealed and whole continents opened for exploration! Faith that something lay ahead broke down the barriers.

What is faith? And how can it be strengthened?

For myself, faith begins with the realization that a Supreme Intelligence brought the universe into being and created Man. It is not difficult for me to have this faith, for it is incontrovertible that where there is a plan there is intelligence—and an orderly, unfolding universe testifies to the truth of the most majestic statement ever uttered: "In the beginning, God. . . ." When man achieves this Faith he finds a key to greater happiness and progress.

Through the centuries men of science have demonstrated their faith. "A little philosophy inclines man to atheism, a depth of philosophy brings him to religion," said Francis Bacon. Sir Isaac Newton was a man of profound religious faith as well as of science. Louis Pasteur was very devout.

Today such great scientists as Kirtley Mather, the geologist; Sir Arthur Eddington, the astronomer; Edwin Grant Conklin, the biologist; Robert A. Millikan—all find that the facts on which their scientific knowledge is based clash in no way with their faith in God.

The realization that a Supreme Intelligence brought the universe into being is the first step in the growth of Faith. The second is the understanding that God, who created life, has given it a meaning and a destiny. There is a purpose for our being and doing, and faith in that purpose spurs man to struggle and to progress.

Here is no room for cynicism, for defeatism, for frustration. True, there is chaos in parts of the world, but in the midst of that chaos we see human progress. Hospitals and colleges, asylums and orphanages gird the world, founded on the impulse given by the cardinal element of religious faith: the Fatherhood of God and the Brotherhood of Man. Science and religion join hands in the battle against ignorance, superstition, disease, poverty, and underprivilege.

Religious faith exalts man and gives him freedom. It spurs progress because it teaches an unfolding destiny for every man, woman, and child, with opportunity for all. These concepts are the heart and soul of democracy, in which governments become the servants of men.

Totalitarianism debases man and regiments him for the state. It makes men the tools of government. It may beget efficiency, but it destroys liberty.

If religion fades, freedom and democracy wither. If religious faith is reborn, we have the first guarantee of the perpetuation of our democracy. Every church and every synagogue becomes a sentinel of liberty. A strong church is the defender of freedom because it breeds the faith that makes men free.

FLEWELLING: *SCIENTIFIC DATA AND SPIRITUAL FACT. The
Personalist,* Vol. XXIV, No. 4, 1943, pp. 342-348.

Scarcely any comment on our civilization could be more enlightening
than a statement of the ideas that spring spontaneously into the minds
of nearly everyone who today hears these two expressions, "scientific
data" and "spiritual fact." Not only would the average hearer think of
them as being opposed and contradictory, but many would consider
"spiritual fact" to be the wishful expression of a nonexistent, while
"scientific data" would pass as something perfectly clear and beyond
cavil or question.

There is no purpose here to discredit the one at the expense of the
other, but rather to call attention to the illusory notion that the two can
be separated or held as mutually contradictory in the world of human
experience. It is a world that shows alarming signs of sticking together
and being of one piece in spite of the efforts of scientific or theological
specialists to separate them into opposing camps. In the final analysis,
all experience of any kind is experience which depends for its verification
upon the possibility of its being common-to-all. Experience is always in
and of an intimately coordinated world, which cannot be separated in
reality but only ideologically for purposes of academic discussion.
We can separate the tree from the earth to consider its botanic aspects,
but in reality the tree is a part of the earth, and the earth, of the tree.
Any opposition we set up between them is academic, and may be illusory.

Two classes are likely to find offence in this principle as applied to
science and religion: the man who considers that in scientific knowledge
alone we grasp reality, and the man who, in his interpretation of Divine
Revelation, imagines a world of nature at war with spiritual facts and
principles. Such a person is logically committed to a belief in the dia-
bolical origin and character of the world of nature, a universe with a
double source, which can never be brought together, in which the devil
will always be able to hold out, since he is the lord of nature as opposed
to the supernatural. Both of these conceptions rest upon an inherited
theological dogma, however contradictory they may seem, but against
them the world of reality reveals itself. No other fact is more obvious
than that we live, not in a disjointed, but in a closely coordinated universe in which neither scientific data nor spiritual fact can be taken as
natural enemies nor, at the worst, as more than the complementary
aspects of a single natural order. There is, then, every reason for mutual understanding and sympathy between the two inseparable companions of reality.

I

The Importance of Scientific Data

At first hand, it will not occur to any reader that it is necessary to plead the importance of scientific data. This is the commonplace assumption of the time. Evidently, if we are to gain control over the world of nature, we must learn the laws that govern the succession of its phenomena. By "law" we can mean nothing more than the regularity of such succession unless we wish to enter the realm of conjecture. We judge there is a reality behind the phenomenal order, but all we can know about the nature of that reality is what we can read from its activities. If these activities are widely coordinated so that they cooperate in the far-flung universe, we can justly conclude to cosmic unity. If that coordination is in keeping with our own intelligence, cooperative with our own reason, we can as justly conclude that the reality behind is, itself, intelligent as well as intelligible. Intelligence is seen to be of the very nature of reality. Such a conclusion borders on a religious character, yet it cannot be disputed without making doubtful all knowledge, including scientific knowledge. Scientific data are then important, both to the physicist and the theologian, as reflecting the nature of the world and giving us the key to its control and its meaning.

There is, moreover, a further fact seldom taken into account by the opposing parties. The importance of all scientific data depends on nothing which they possess in and for themselves but only on their relations to human beings. Sun, moon, and stars may not have been ordained for the transitory biped called man, as some love to remind us, but it is impossible to show any other reason for their existence. The old theologians may have seemed immodest in their exaltation of man but they have been more nearly right than the materialists.

The meaning of scientific data is a meaning relative to persons, and all the king's horses and all the king's men can make no more out of it than this. Nature is important in that she provides the basis, the field and the opportunity for immortal spirits, and we cannot scientifically arrive at any higher interpretation. Such may be an anthropomorphic conclusion, but anthropomorphic conclusions are the only ones possible to *Anthropos*, the man.

We must conclude then that scientific data are important, primarily because they have relation to human persons, are translatable into language of personal meaning, help man to understand himself, his fellows, and his surroundings, and contribute to the control and betterment of the human condition. Any man or party who builds up a concept of nature hostile to man or unrelated to his welfare, whether physicist or theologian, is indulging in unreal imaginings.

II

ASSUMED SUPERIORITY OF SCIENTIFIC DATA, THE MODERN ILLUSION

The assumption that scientific data are the most important of all the phenomena of experience rests, first, upon the easy desire for physical satisfaction and second, upon a mental laziness that would forego both mental and spiritual labor. Even more cogent than these two is an unwillingness to acknowledge the moral and spiritual demands that every man feels, even if he refuses to admit it. The way to the highest mental and spiritual experience is rigorous and most prefer not to take it. The challenge that not more than a dozen men could understand Einstein's all-important theory of relativity was answered by a few keen minds who came to realize that its principles were open to the most average of intelligences. Not only so, they were seen to be necessary to the commonest of operations. The unintelligibility attached itself rather to the mathematical formulae by which Einstein set out to prove what in principle every farmer, hunter, or sportsman puts daily into practice. The man in the street even yet can find a jest in Einstein in his own scant care for mathematics. However, mathematical demonstration was essential to establish Einstein's scientific orthodoxy.

We are so prone to assume with the old-time school teacher, who used to knock his pupils' heads together, that the objectivity of physical impact holds superiority over more subjective ways of learning. The actual impact of falling bricks on human heads is more impressive than the prophetic equations of Einstein. What happens to our bodies seems more demonstrable and more important than what happens to our minds and spirits. This is the great illusion of the present day.

If we have a mind to realities and think deeply enough, we shall discover that physical nature herself seems in many cases to work on the side of morality and to be at least friendly to the higher life. She punishes the glutton with the grossness of his fat, deprives him of mental alertness, and afflicts him with disease that shortens his stay in the land. At the same time she blesses the abstemious with health and mental clearness. Can it be doubted that the man of violence, who wickedly overrides his fellows, is bound for other than a violent end? If he escapes the assassin's bullet or the hangman's noose, he suffers the growing contempt of his fellows, even harder to bear. Witness the last insane days of Napoleon on St. Helena. The liar cannot ultimately cheat the universe. Soon his lies receive no further credence and his truths are not received. He creates a complex or attitude of a life of make-believe in which he deceives himself most of all. The man who hopes to achieve his ends by betrayal betrays himself more deeply than he does his victim. The unsocial or anti-social man cuts himself off from the very society he would most enjoy. He who hates surrounds himself with a whole complex of hateful responses and false judgments that turn all the brightness of life into darkness. The law-breaker, if he has the luck to escape jail, cannot avoid that deeper bondage which arises from fear of the police, fear of discovery and disgrace. This bondage causes him to start at shadows. He is no longer free, and often such a man, in a desperate bid for freedom, chooses rather to give himself over to the authorities, preferring the bondage of prison to the greater bondage of mind. Every evil-doer cuts off the fuller functioning of life, and the expression and realization of his personality to the degree of his sin. These laws of human nature are as inevitable as the functioning of plants and animals, or the law of gravitation, or the diffusion of light, or the swing of the planets. Spiritual law may act in a higher realm but it is no less certain in its results. These spiritual facts are a part of our nature and of the world of nature from which we cannot divorce ourselves by any illusion of physical objectivity. The thirty pieces of silver in the hands of Judas turned out to be worthless, finding their way at last into the temple collection plate. But even the priests, hardened in mendacity, refused to receive their own, back again, and turned it to the charity of the Potter's Field: *a place to bury future Judases.*

III

The Reality of Spiritual Fact

If we ask ourselves the question of what matters most in our human existence, we soon hit upon the undeniable reality of spiritual fact. In a humdrum world we seem to be living for a very material set of values, such as the acquirement of wealth, or power, or fame, or learning as evidenced by possessions, place, or degrees, but whatever sacrifices we are willing to make to these false and ostensible goods, we are really seeking these things in the hope of coming by deeper satisfactions. What we really hope is that these objectives, achieved, will supply us with a sense of fulfillment, a satisfaction which is met only in the praise and recognition of our fellows. We hope for the deeper reward of love from wife, or children, or companions, or even the confusion of our enemies and detractors. These accomplishments turn to dust and ashes, if, when won at last, there is no friend with whom to enjoy them. We grind at the mill of life but, whether or not we will it or know it, our grinding has for its ultimate fruitage and crown a spiritual satisfaction to which these objectives are only the means. After all, we can be happy with poverty if we are rich in love. We can suffer privation with a cheerful spirit if the end in view is noble. Fires and fagots are the martyr's triumph. The lads of yesteryear that, flirting with death, went cheering into danger were upheld by a cause that seemed worth dying for. Any great living must rise to this higher level, which is the realm of the spirit. Justice, righteousness, liberty, are these but vague generalities about which totalitarians can jest? In the final test they are stronger than goose-step, blitz, or TNT.

PLANCK: *THE PHILOSOPHY OF PHYSICS*. W. W. Norton & Company, Inc., New York. Pp. 27-35.

It is wholly absurd to maintain that an intellectual experiment is important only in proportion as it can be checked by measurement; for if this were so, there could be no exact geometrical proof. A line drawn on paper is not really a line but a more or less narrow strip, and a point a larger or smaller spot. Yet nobody doubts that geometrical constructions yield a rigorous proof.

The intellectual experiment carries the mind of the investigator beyond the world and beyond actual measuring instruments and enables him to form hypotheses and to formulate questions which, when checked by actual experiment, enable him to perceive new laws even when these do not admit of direct measurement. An intellectual experiment is not tied down to any limits of accuracy, for thoughts are more subtle than atoms or electrons, nor is there any danger that the event which is measured can be influenced by the measuring instrument. An intellectual experiment requires one condition only for its success, and this is the admission of the validity of any non-self-contradictory law governing the relations between the events under observation. We cannot hope to find what is assumed not to be existent.

Admittedly an intellectual experiment is an abstraction; an abstraction, however, as essential to the experimenter and to the theorist as the abstract assumption that there is a real external world. Whenever we observe an event taking place in nature we must assume that something is happening independently of the observer, and conversely we must endeavor to eliminate as far as possible the defects of our senses and of our methods of measurement in order to grasp the details of the event with greater perfection. There is a kind of opposition between these two abstractions: while the real external world is the object, the ideal spirit which contemplates it is the subject. Neither can be logically demonstrated and hence no *reductio ad absurdum* is possible if their existence is denied. The history of physics bears witness, however, that they have played a decisive part throughout its development. The choicest and most original minds, men like Kepler, Newton, Leibniz, and Faraday, were inspired by the belief in the reality of the external world and in the rule of a higher reason in and beyond it.

It should never be forgotten that the most vital ideas in physics have this two-fold origin. In the first instance the form which these ideas take is due to the peculiar imagination of the individual scientist: in course of time, however, they assume a more definite and independent form. It is true that there have always been in physics a number of erroneous ideas on which a quantity of labor was wasted: yet on the other hand many problems which were at first rejected as meaningless by keen critics were eventually seen to possess the highest significance. Fifty years ago positivist physicists considered it meaningless to ask after the determination of the weight of a single atom—an illusory problem not admitting scientific treatment. Today the weight of an atom can be stated to within its ten-thousandth part, although our most delicate scales are no more fit to weigh it than a weigh-bridge is to determine milli-grammes. One should therefore beware of declaring meaningless a problem whose solution is not immediately apparent; there is no criterion for deciding *a priori* whether any given problem in physics has a mean-ing or not, a point frequently overlooked by the positivists. The only means of judging a problem correctly consists in examining the conclu-sions to which it leads. Now the assumption that there are rigid laws applicable to physics is of such fundamental importance that we should hesitate before we declare the question whether such laws are applicable to atomic physics to be a meaningless one. Our first endeavor, on the contrary, should be to trace out the problem of the applicability of laws in this field.

Our first step should be to ask why classical physics fails in the ques-tion of causality when the interference arising from the measuring in-strument and the inadequate accuracy of the latter are both insufficient to explain this failure. Plainly we are forced to adopt the obvious but radical assumption that the elementary concepts of classical physics cease to be applicable in atomic physics.

Classical physics is based on the assumption that its laws are most clearly revealed in the infinitely small; for it assumes that the course of a physical event anywhere in the universe is completely determined by the state prevailing at this place and its immediate vicinity. Hence such physical magnitudes relating to the state of the physical event as posi-tion, velocity, intensity of the electric and magnetic field, etc., are of a purely local character, and the laws governing their relation can be com-pletely expressed by spatial-temporal differential equations between these magnitudes. Clearly, however, this will not suffice for atomic physics, so that the above concepts must be made more complete or more uni-versal. In which direction, however, is this to be done? Some indica-tion may perhaps be found in the recognition, which is daily spreading wider, that the spatial-differential equations do not suffice to exhaust the content of the events within a physical system and that the liminal conditions must also be taken into consideration. This applies even to wave mechanics. Now the field of liminal conditions is always finite and its immediate interference in the causal nexus is a new manner of look-ing at causality and one hitherto foreign to classical physics.

The future will show whether progress is possible in this direction and how far it will lead. But whatever results it may ultimately reveal, it is certain that it will never enable us to grasp the real world in its totality any more than human intelligence will rise into the sphere of ideal spirit: these will remain abstractions which by their very defini-tion lie outside actuality. Nothing, however, forbids us to believe that we can progress steadily and without interruption to this unattainable goal; and it is precisely the task of science with its continual self-correction and self-improvement to work in this direction without ceasing once it has been recognized that it is a hopeful direction. This progress will be a real one and not a hopeless zigzag, as is proved by the fact that each new stage reached enables us to survey all the previous stages, while those which remain to be covered are still obscure; just as a climber trying to reach higher altitudes looks down upon the distance he has covered in order to gain knowledge for the further ascent. A scientist is happy, not in resting on his attainments but in the steady acquisition of fresh knowledge.

I have so far confined myself to physics; but it may be felt that what has been said has a wider application. Natural science and the intellectual sciences cannot be rigorously separated. They form a single interconnected system, and if they are touched at any part the effects are felt through all the ramifications of the whole, the totality of which is forthwith set in motion. It would be absurd to assume that a fixed and certain law is predominant in physics unless the same were true also in biology and psychology.

We may perhaps here deal with free will. Our consciousness, which after all is the most immediate source of cognition, assures us that free will is supreme. Yet we are forced to ask whether human will is causally determined or not. Put in this way the question, as I have frequently tried to show, is a good example of the kind of problem which I have described as illusory, by which I mean that, taken literally, it has no exact meaning. In the present instance the apparent difficulty is due to an incomplete formulation of the question. The actual facts may be briefly stated as follows: From the standpoint of an ideal and all-comprehensive spirit, human will, like every material and spiritual event, is completely determined causally. Looked at subjectively, however, the will, in so far as it looks to the future, is not causally determined, because any cognition of the subject's will itself acts causally upon the will, so that any definitive cognition of a fixed causal nexus is out of the question. In other words we may say that looked at from outside (objectively) the will is causally determined, and that looked at from inside (subjectively) it is free. There is here no contradiction, any more than there was in the previous debate about the right- and left-hand side, and those who fail to agree to this overlook or forget the fact that the subject's will is never completely subordinate to its cognition and indeed always has the last word.

In principle therefore we are compelled to give up the attempt to determine in advance the motives guiding our actions on purely causal lines, i.e., by means of purely scientific cognition; in other words, there is no science and no intellect capable of answering the most important of all the questions facing us in our personal life, the question, that is, how we are to act.

It might thus be inferred that science ceases to play a part as soon as ethical problems arise. Yet such an inference would be wrong. We saw above that in dealing with the structure of any science, and in discussing its most suitable arrangement, a reciprocal inter-connection between epistemological judgments and judgments of value was found to arise, and that no science can be wholly disentangled from the personality of the scientist. Modern physics has given us a clear indication pointing in the same direction. It has taught us that the nature of any system cannot be discovered by dividing it into its component parts and studying each part by itself, since such a method often implies the loss of important properties of the system. We must keep our attention fixed on the whole and on the inter-connection between the parts.

The same is true of our intellectual life. It is impossible to make a clear cut between science, religion, and art. The whole is never equal simply to the sum of its various parts.

BAKER: *SCIENCE AND THE PLANNED STATE.* By permission of
The Macmillan Company, New York. Chap. II, pp. 25-38; Chap. V,
pp. 83-91.

CHAPTER II

THE VALUES OF SCIENCE

SCIENTISTS DO NOT WORK ONLY FOR MATERIAL ENDS

There is not any necessary connection between the material usefulness and intrinsic interest of a scientific discovery. "We can declare
without the least hesitation," says Szent-Györgyi, the famous biochem-
ist, "that to judge scientific research by its usefulness is simply to kill it.
Science aims at knowledge, not utility." It is extremely unlikely that
every discovery will serve man in a material way before the inevitable
extinction of human life. Some of the most profound truths probably
will not be used practically. Professor G. H. Hardy has made this point
neatly for mathematics. He cites some easily understood mathematical
proofs, whose beauty and general significance are apparent to everyone
who follows them. Having won the reader's willing assent to their
value, he goes on to prove that they not only are not, but cannot be used
by the practical man. Euclid's proof that the number of prime numbers
is infinite is so masterly and economical that everyone who follows it,
mathematician or not, acclaims its value; but as Professor Hardy points
out, it is more than sufficient for the engineer to know that the number
of primes less than 1,000 million is 50,847,478, for practical men never
work to more significant figures than this. In science we can never say
that a discovery will never be used to promote material welfare, but we
can and must say that scientists are interested in discoveries apart from
the possibility of their producing food, shelter, health, etc.

The pretence that science only serves humanity by giving us food,
health, and shelter leads to nonsense; for it means that we live only for
food, health, and shelter, instead of requiring them so as to live for something else. Why do we feed and protect ourselves and others? Is it so
that we and they may live to feed and protect others, so that they may
do the same for yet others, and so on interminably and senselessly?
"Have we nothing eventually in view more admirable than the abolition
of want and the securing of comfort for everyone, ends which at present
bulk so large in our programs?" The question is put by the distinguished
American physicist, Professor P. W. Bridgman. "Will we be permanently satisfied with these, or will something more be necessary to give dignity and worth to human activity?"

There must be something else for which people want to live. Great
music, art, and imaginative literature, it may be suggested, are examples
of valid ends. If a scientist makes that answer it is necessary for him
to say that he practices science so that the applications of what he dis-

covers may keep people alive, so that they may appreciate music, art, and literature, which are the real ends in life which make him practice science. This house-that-Jack-built rigamarole is nonsense. The scientist may indeed value these subjects highly, and they are certainly ends in themselves; but if this dominant impulse were not scientific he would be a poor scientist. Science is as much an end in itself as music or art or literature. ". . . . if ever there are ends in themselves or goods in themselves," Professor Bridgman has written, "then surely the gratification of the craving for understanding is one of them."

People engaged in practical pursuits have often advanced science, and this fact is sometimes made the basis of a claim that science had its origin in a desire to satisfy the material wants of ordinary human life. From that premise it is argued that scientists should devote themselves to the satisfaction of those wants. Even if the claim were justified, the conclusion could not be logically deduced from it; but the claim itself is not justifiable. We cannot know anything for certain about the earliest beginnings of science, but we do know that modern savages are interested in natural objects and phenomena apart from their material usefulness. Science as we know it today may be said to have originated about the eighteenth century, for although there were scientific geniuses before then, the spirit of the subject was confined to a small number of people, and their discoveries were somewhat isolated. During that century there was a wonderful blossoming forth of science. Magnificent work was done, especially in biology. The best of that work was inspired by nothing but an intense desire for knowledge for its own sake.

The scientist of today is often cynically indifferent to the early history of his subject. He knows that people used to make fantastic concoctions intended to cure human ailments, and he recognizes no connection between such activities and his own. He is right, but he has missed the point. The men who were struggling solely to give practical help to mankind often made little or no contribution to knowledge; but those who had an intense desire for knowledge for its own sake were doing research which is comparable with the very best that is being done today.

Just over two centuries ago Réaumur published a memoir on the reproduction of aphids, and Trembley a book on the natural history and response to experimental procedures of the little fresh-water polyp, *Hydra*. I challenge anyone who is cynical about old-time science to point out any modern work that provides a better example of scientific method than those studies of Réaumur and Trembley. Réaumur's memoir was devoted to the question whether aphids can reproduce without sexual union. The way in which he tackled this question, in free collaboration with Bonnet, Bazin, Trembley, and Lyonet, provides an example to be copied by modern scientists. The clear introductory statement of what was already surmised on the subject, the scrupulous care and accuracy of the work, the elaborate attention to detail, the unwillingness to accept anything without stringent proof, the avoidance of unnecessary hypotheses—all these are models for all time. Réaumur and his friends established beyond question that aphids can reproduce without sexual union. Trembley's book on *Hydra* is, of course, a classic. It contains not only an excellent description of the form and natural history of the various species, but also a full account of the studies on regeneration, which may be said to mark the origin of experimental zoology. Indeed, these experiments are quoted in modern text-books, not as historical curiosities, but as our best information on the subject. Trembley's description of how he turned the minute organism inside out and how it survived this extraordinary operation was for long disbelieved; but recently Mr. R. L. Roudabush has succeeded in repeating Trembley's experiment and confirmed the survival of the reversed animals. The whole of Trembley's book, like Réaumur's memoir, is a model of scientific method. *In neither is there any indication that the author was striving to satisfy the material wants of man*. Their spirit was that which has been the chief animating influence ever since.

The scientist of today opens a text-book and takes what he reads there as though it had arrived on those pages as a matter of course. What an eye-opener it would be if he could glimpse, even vaguely, the history of the knowledge contained in a single sentence chosen at random! Even if the sentence dealt with a modern subject, its history would go far back along the ages; and he would see a succession of the men who brought the knowledge contained in it into being. They were not just names in a history-book of science: they were real, live people, diverse in many ways, but nearly all united in belief in the value of science as an end in itself.

THE BORDERLAND BETWEEN THE MATERIAL AND THE IMMATERIAL VALUES OF SCIENCE

There are certain values of science which stand half-way between the crudely material values on the one hand and the immaterial values on the other. Knowledge of the facts of equal inheritance from both parents (apart from the genes borne on the sex-chromosomes) is important in framing people's general social outlook, but it does not directly provide them with food, health, or shelter. The relative status of man and woman would be different from what it is if people believed that inheritance were wholly maternal (as the Trobriand Islanders, for instance, are said to believe) or wholly paternal (as some biologists once thought). Again people's social outlook is affected by their beliefs on the scientific question whether what are popularly called "acquired characters" are inherited. The function of science in reducing superstition comes into this category of values.

The Appreciation of Science as an End in Itself

We must now analyze the immaterial or spiritual values of science.

The history of science suggests that many great investigators have accepted the value of science as an end in itself as something so obvious as not to require analysis. Einstein has well expressed what are probably the inarticulate feelings of many people who value science as an end. "The satisfaction of physical needs," he writes, "is indeed the indispensable pre-condition of a satisfactory existence, but in itself it is not enough. In order to be content, men must also have the possibility of developing their intellectual and artistic powers to whatever extent accords with their personal characteristics and abilities."

There are reasons for thinking that science is potentially the greatest achievement of the human mind. Optimists may look for that greatest achievement in ethical perfection. They may be right and I hope they are; but life among savages has shown me that if civilization and religion have improved men morally, then the improvement that has occurred has been too small to give reason for much optimism about the future. In most intellectual fields we cannot look forward with confidence of progress. There is no reason to suppose that historians of the future will tower above those of the present day. Philosophy has given the world some of its greatest geniuses, but the history of the subject contradicts the idea of a gradual approximation toward a consensus of opinion on philosophical subjects. We cannot guess the future of music, but at least it may be said that the world today has no composer who will bear comparison with the geniuses of the past. It is sometimes argued that geniuses are not recognized in their own times, and that we may even now have a genius of musical composition in our midst; but the fallacy of this argument is apparent to anyone who is acquainted with the history of music. The same considerations apply to pictorial art, and there is no sure ground for thinking that we are merely experiencing a phase of relative inactivity which will be followed by a new outburst of progress. In science, on the contrary, the present state of affairs and the prospect of the future are both very good. The standard of excellence is as high as it ever was. We have genius to rank with the greatest of all time (in physics alone we have Bohr, Dirac, Einstein and Schrödinger, and have only recently lost Rutherford and J. J. Thomson). If science be left free to expand, its expansion is inevitable, for science grows by accretion.

The unimportant composer or artist does nothing permanent to make his subject greater. The unimportant scientific research worker, on the contrary, places his brick firmly in position, and on it every subsequent worker in the same field—geniuses included—will build again. The knowledge that every step forward is an advance in a gigantic undertaking is an inspiration to the scientist, for he may legitimately feel that he is playing his part in the greatest adventure of the human mind. This knowledge is one of the supreme values of science to the investigator.

It is impossible to read the biographies of the greatest scientists without realizing the high value which they have attributed to science apart from its material benefits, but they seldom analyze their appreciation very explicitly. It is unquestionable that a pleasurable excitement in approaching the unfamiliar is part of the reason for their appreciation, an attitude of mind which is shared with the geographical explorer. A pleasure in finding order where previously disorder seemed to reign is another component of the scientific attitude. This has been stated quite unequivocally by the Danish genius of physics, Niels Bohr, who writes that the deepest foundation of science is "the abiding impulse in every human being to seek order and harmony behind the manifold and the changing in the existing world." T. H. Huxley wrote in his *Method and Results* that the research worker is inspired by "the supreme delight of extending the realm of law and order ever farther towards the unattainable goals of the infinitely great and the infinitely small, between which our little race of life is run." Some scientists, again, are animated by a component of that special awareness of the natural environment and feeling of community with nature and joy in natural beauty which also animate the poet and artist in their respective fields. This was clearly understood by the great German scientist, Alexander Humboldt, who wrote of "that important stage of our communion with the external world, when the enjoyment arising from a knowledge of the laws, and the mutual connection of phenomena, associates itself with the charm of a simple contemplation of nature."

Humboldt was a person of extraordinarily wide interests. As a young man he was a successful mining technologist, but his passion for travel drew him into wider and wider fields of study until it might be said of him if ever there was such a person as a general scientist, it was he. Few men if any have ever made such substantial contributions to so many diverse branches of science; and it was not only science that engaged his attention, for he was also a diplomat of high rank and a political economist. The extraordinary breadth of outlook of this great man enabled him to see science as a whole, and he expressed very vividly what he saw. In thirteen words of the utmost simplicity he expressed a truth which our modern materialists cannot shake: "other interests", he wrote, "besides the material wants of life, occupy the minds of men". He instanced "the desire of embellishing life by augmenting the mass of ideas, and by multiplying means for their generalization. . . . The higher enjoyments yielded by the study of nature depend upon the correctness and the depth of our views, and upon the extent of the subjects that may be comprehended in a single glance." These words are strikingly similar to those written by the philosopher, Alexander, not much less than a century later: "The greatest truths are perhaps those which being simple in themselves illuminate a large and complex body of knowledge." Such truths, when grasped, unquestionably bring pleasure to the mind; and it would be fantastic to deny the existence of this kind of pleasure or to assess it lower than crude or material kinds. "In considering the study of physical phenomena," said Humboldt, "we find its noblest and more important result to be a knowledge of the chain of connection by which all natural forces are linked together, and made mutually dependent upon each other; and it is the perception of these relations that exalts our views and ennobles our enjoyments."

The enjoyments appear subjectively to be of the same kind as those caused by the perception of artistic beauty, combined with wonder or even a pleasurable astonishment. Professor J. B. S. Haldane has stressed the beauty of science in a particularly concrete way. "As a result of Faraday's work," he wrote, "you are able to listen to the wireless. But more than that, as a result of Faraday's work scientifically educated men and women have an altogether richer view of the world: for them, apparently empty space is full of the most intricate and beautiful patterns. So Faraday gave the world not only fresh wealth but fresh beauty." These simple words express a profound truth, which can be denied only as a tone-deaf man can deny the spiritual value of music. They are a distinguished investigator's flat contradiction of the materialist concept of science. Darwin expresses his feeling of beauty and wonder in the final words of *The Origin of Species:* "There is grandeur in this view of life, with its several powers, having been originally breathed by the Creator into a few forms or into one; and that whilst this planet has gone cycling on according to the fixed law of gravity, from so simple a beginning endless forms most beautiful and most wonderful have been, and are being evolved."

The finding of a kind of wonder or awe in the majesty and apparently infinite complexity of the universe has led some of the greatest scientists—among them Boyle, Hooke, Newton, and Trembley—to ascribe the value of science to its giving us an insight into the mind of God. The great Swiss-born American zoologist, Louis Agassiz, for instance, expressed this idea unequivocally: "If I mistake not, the great object of our museums should be to exhibit the whole animal kingdom as a supreme manifestation of the Supreme Intellect." This seems to be related to the subtler feeling of some of the greatest mathematicians that mathematical reality lies outside human beings, and that in their apparently creative work they are actually only observing and recording.

The scientist is able to construct a sort of scale of scientific values and to decide that one thing or theory is relatively trivial and another relatively important, quite apart from any question of practical applications. There is, as Poincaré has well said, *"une hiérarchie des faits."* Most scientists will agree that certain discoveries or propositions are more important because more widely significant than others, though around any particular level on the scale of values there may be disagreement. Thus, every scientist will agree that the discovery of atoms and cells was important, and that the discovery of a new species of beetle, not markedly unusual in any way, is unimportant. So also with theories and "laws". A law, says Poincaré, *"sera d'autant plus précieuse qu'elle sera plus générale."* Professor G. H. Hardy has shown how mathematicians value their ideas by generality and depth, and how they universally value general and deep theorems above mere isolated curiosities, such as the fact that 8712 and 9801 are the only four-figure numbers that are integral multiples of themselves written backwards ($8712 = 2178 \times 4$ and $9801 = 1089 \times 9$). A general theorem is one of wide significance, and a deep theorem one requiring a first understanding of a simpler theorem. Both these ideas are continually being used, consciously or unconsciously, whenever one scientist says that another has done a "good" bit of work.

The existence of amateur scientists is a proof that science is appreciated as an end. The amateur plays a smaller part in scientific research than he did in the eighteenth and nineteenth centuries, but excellent work is still done by amateurs in geology and biology. Apart from those who are sufficiently interested to rank as amateur scientists, there is a mass of people who possess the same sort of feelings as the great investigator but in lesser degree. For instance, a markedly strange animal of any kind arouses great public interest in both savage and civilized communities, and no sharp dividing line can be drawn between this sort of interest and that which inspires the zoologist, though the latter's interest is, of course greater and more lasting. One has only to think of the interest taken by the most diverse people in the microscopical discoveries of van Leeuwenhoek to realize how widespread is an interest in unfamiliar natural objects. When it was discovered by Abraham Trembley almost exactly two hundred years ago that an organism exists (we now call it *Hydra*) which feeds like an animal but buds like a plant, and reorganizes itself into two or more individuals if cut into bits with scissors, the interest aroused was such that polyps became, in the words of an anonymous eighteenth century writer, *"à la mode."* Interest in the unfamiliar is abundantly illustrated by the history of science. Even in modern times, when people tend to be less enthusiastic than they were two or three centuries ago, the discovery of a living fish belonging to a group thought to have been extinct for some sixty million years caused great excitement, and a popular weekly journal devoted a large double page entirely to the event.

Just as the unfamiliar attracts the interest of both layman and scientist, so also does the orderly. In a low form one sees the appreciation of the orderly exhibited in a collection of butterflies systematically arranged by a collector who understands little of the life-processes of what he collects. No sharp line of separation can be drawn between the simple arrangement of natural objects in an orderly fashion and the systematic presentations of natural knowledge by great scientists. I found this out many years ago when demonstrating to a class of students preparing for the final Honours examination in zoology at Oxford. We were studying the anatomy of certain marine worms, and I noticed that one of the women-students had a book beside her, open at a coloured plate showing the external characters of some of the animals that we were studying. The book was unfamiliar to me and I stooped down to look at it. The name gave me a surprise that I have not forgotten. I learnt a useful lesson in modesty that day, which I should be happy to share with any scientist who thinks himself a different kind of being than the layman. The student preparing for the highest examination in zoology at a great university, was using *The Seashore shown to the Children.*

There is a widespread belief in the "worth-whileness" of finding out. The community as a whole appears to approve of the setting apart of a limited number of talented people for the express purpose of discovery, without requiring that all research should be directed towards material ends. The public expects as almost a matter of course that someone or other should concern himself with all branches of natural knowledge. This was forcibly brought home to me some years ago when I was one of the three or four people in the world who were making systematic studies of the causes of breeding seasons. When I remarked to unscientific friends that the environmental causes which regulate the breeding seasons of animals were not known—that no one knew what makes the blackbird breed in early spring—I was met by frank incredulity. "Oh, *some one* knows," I was assured; "The experts *must* know." It seemed intolerable that a community which maintains people expressly for the purpose of getting all sorts of knowledge should not be able to obtain information on such a very straightforward and familiar subject.

There is one particular kind of knowledge which both the scientist and the layman place high up on the scale of values. This is the knowledge that throws light on man's place in the universe. The discoveries of Copernicus and Darwin caused a ferment of excitement which shook and changed the outlook of the whole civilized world, quite apart from any application to material human welfare. Again, one's whole outlook on the universe is changed and broadened by the knowledge that great groups of animals, some of them of gigantic bulk, have arisen in the distant past, evolved, persisted for millions of years, and then become totally extinct millions of years before man, or even his ape-like ancestors, appeared on earth.

The Appreciation of Appreciation

One of the values of science to the scientist is of a kind that is so generally understood in all fields of human activity that it is only mentioned here for the sake of completeness. The successful investigator appreciates the appreciation of others, provided that the others are qualified to judge. The extent to which scientists are affected by the desire for the approval of others varies widely. One of the greatest, Henry Cavendish, was so little affected by it that he did not bother to publish some of his most marvellous discoveries. Most scientists, however, naturally like their colleagues to think well of them, and they value science partly because it is an activity in which they can earn the approval of others.

Has Truth Intrinsic Excellence?

So far we have been considering value as equivalent to the existence of conscious appreciation. Another aspect of the value of science, attractive to the intuitions of many people, may be illustrated by an imaginary event.

Let us suppose that a group of psychologists, having armed themselves with a marvellous new invention which enables them to assess happiness objectively, accompanies a scientific expedition which sets out to explore two islands. When they analyze their data, they find that the average happiness or general contentment of the people on the two islands is exactly the same. Meanwhile the anthropologists of the expedition have been studying the native's outlook on the universe. On the one island thunder is ascribed to the anger of the tribal ancestors, boiling springs are regarded as giants' cooking vessels, the birth of twins is regarded as indicating that the agricultural crops will be prolific, etc. On the other island these and other natural phenomena are interpreted in accordance with the scientific ideas with which we are familiar. In both islands the phenomena are regarded with interest, which is equal in the two cases. Which is the better civilization (apart from future prospects)?

There may be skeptics who will deny that a balance can be held between the two islands. Others may consider that if one island's civilization is better than the other, that is solely because some external observer appreciates the one civilization more highly, for in the absence of an external observer no difference exists. Most people, however, are likely to say that the civilization in which there is true knowledge is the better. Truth, in fact, has intrinsic excellence, apart from its effects. This belief, for it seems impossible to prove or disprove in any formal way the statement that truth has or is a value—has been a mainspring of scientific research, particularly plainly exhibited in the lives of such scientific geniuses as Charles Darwin and T. H. Huxley, but animating also many much lesser men and women.

Diametrically opposite to these ideas stand those of the rulers of totalitarian states. Some general remarks on the subject are attributed to Hitler: "There is no such thing as truth. Science is a social phenomenon, and like every other social phenomenon is limited by the benefit or injury it confers on the community." Himmler has applied these principles to a particular case, when attacking German scholars who refused to acknowledge the genuineness of a forged document on German archaeology. It surprised him that anyone should make a fuss as to whether it were true. "The one and only thing that matters to us," he is reported to have said, "and the thing these people are paid for by the state, is to have ideas of history that strengthen our people in their necessary national pride." As the Nazi professor of philosophy at Heidelberg announced, "We do not know of or recognize truth for truth's sake." For Hitler and Himmler and the Nazi professor it seemed nonsense to worry whether a given statement is true or not: the only thing that matters is how that statement affects the community. It is probable that few first-rate scientists would assent to what they regarded as an untruth, even if they could be persuaded that such assent would be materially beneficial to the community. It is apparent that the orderly structure and dependability of science would become transformed into chaos if Hitler's and Himmler's ideas were accepted by scientists as a whole; and scientists have always been accustomed to place a very high value upon truth, generally without considering the philosophical background of the position that they adopt.

(Pp. 25-38)

CHAPTER V

THE DUTIES OF SCIENTISTS TO SOCIETY

INTRODUCTION

Science is necessarily a social activity. It is true that the research worker is often rather a retiring person, finding little pleasure in the kinds of social life that mean so much to others. Nevertheless, that his work is social is shown by the necessity for demonstrable proofs. This necessity presupposes the interest and participation of others. The person who makes a systematic collection of natural objects simply for his own satisfaction, without adding to the common store of knowledge or infusing others with his interests, is not a scientist. It is true that the scientist's motives may be and often are mixed. Unless he has an intense internal urge to find out, to try to satisfy an insatiable curiosity, he will not be much of a research worker. Still, his work must be presented in a form in which it will influence the opinion of others.

Although no one should be forced to disclose his results before he has satisfied himself that they are fit for publication, yet there ought to be no private property in demonstrable knowledge. If a scientist keeps his discoveries to himself, his activities are unsocial and indefensible; for knowledge is good, and it is better for many than for one person to possess it. Every scientist lives a vastly fuller life just because generations of other scientists have not kept their discoveries to themselves. To profit from the work of others without making the return that is within one's power is indefensible.

Newton has often been charged with secretiveness, but perhaps his case has been rather misrepresented. It is true that he did not hurry to get his discoveries printed, but this was largely because of his great dis-

like of controversy.   He was elected a Fellow of the Royal Society at
the age of twenty-nine.   Five days before his election he wrote to the
Secretary saying that if elected "I shall endeavor to testify my gratitude
by communicating what my poor and solitary endeavours can effect
towards the promoting your philosophical designs."   He was by no
means slow in keeping his promise.   Exactly a month later he sent to the
Secretary his famous paper on the composition of white light, which he
showed to be made up of a spectrum of different colors, which were re-
fracted by glass to different degrees.   It was the reception of this paper
that turned him in upon himself and made him so secretive.   Professor
Linus of Liége, failing to understand Newton's experiments, criticized
them stupidly in a paper published in the *Philosophical Transactions* of
the Society.   Unfortunately, the Secretary pressed Newton to reply.
The matter dragged on for years, Newton refusing to answer because
he thought that Linus had not taken the trouble to understand what was
clearly explained in the original paper.   Finally Newton became ex-
asperated.   "I see that I have made myself a slave to philosophy," he
wrote to the Secretary, "but if I get free of Mr. Linus's business I will
resolutely bid adieu to it eternally, excepting what I do for my private
satisfaction, or leave to come out after me; for I see a man must
either resolve to put out nothing new, or to become a slave to defend it."
Newton did not stick to his threat, but this incident certainly made him
more secretive; and science would have profited even more generously
than it did from his genius if he had been readier to publish his discoveries.

The primary duty of the research scientist, as such, is to make the
greatest possible public contribution to demonstrable knowledge. He generally requires no advice from anyone on the subject of his primary
duty, for he knows better than others how his own particular qualities
can be used most effectively. There are some pitfalls, however, which may
be regarded as of a moral kind, even in the accomplishment of his primary duty.   He must be on his guard against lazily drifting into trivial
work, limited in significance and unlikely to open new fields of investigation or help others in their research.   Although he must make full use
of working hypotheses, yet he must avoid the fascination of idle speculations.   He must never depart from truth for convenience, as when a
systematic biologist leaves unchanged a classification of organisms which
he knows to be unnatural, simply because a particular grouping is usual
or convenient.   He must avoid the temptation to follow a course simply
because it is fashionable, or likely to bring him praise because it is immediately connected with practical affairs, when he knows that his own
particular talents enable him to discharge his primary duty better in another way.

The discharge of this duty is something in which the investigator
finds pleasure.   It may therefore be asked whether any extra or secondary duties are owed by the scientist to the community in return for

being allowed to do what he likes doing; for many people have uncongenial employments which they would give up at once if they were made financially independent.

It must be remembered that the research scientist has often obtained his position in society by voluntarily giving up highly prized pleasures in order to devote himself to laborious study. No scientist is likely to get far whose spare time is all spent in frivolous amusement, or whose study is always devoted to those subjects that are immediately attractive to him. He knows that he must master certain difficult subjects, although he finds them unattractive, in order that he may understand better the subject of his choice. He voluntarily disciplines himself to study while others seek ephemeral amusement, and devotes himself to hard and uncongenial tasks. This discipline he imposed on himself when young, even while still a boy; if he had not done so, he would probably not be a research scientist. The recurring disappointments of research and the unavoidable tedium of certain parts of it must also be remembered. The community, then, should not thoughtlessly demand extra services of the scientist. Nevertheless, he often asks himself what services he can render to the community as a whole, apart from his primary duty; and the general congeniality and liberty of his task under the conditions of free science make him ask himself this the more insistently. The teacher of science, whose primary duty is to instil the spirit of science and to convey factual knowledge, will ask himself the same question.

When confronted with this ethical problem, the scientist may reach either of two conclusions. On the one hand, he may decide that his best contribution to human welfare may be made privately in the circle of his own acquaintance. He may believe that social evils will continue as long as people rely on politics and propaganda for human betterment, and that the only hope for progress lies in the voluntary improvement of the relations between those who come into direct contact in the ordinary course of their lives. He may have been impressed by the low moral standards of many politicians and propagandists, and by the solid good done inconspicuously by good men and women. On the other hand, he may consider that his special qualities as a scientist give him the privilege of a wider and special scope for good.

It is for the scientist himself to judge between the two courses. His temperament must be the deciding factor. If he chooses to limit himself to private action the decision is perfectly proper, and it would be an impertinence to deny him the right to make it. In that case there is no advice that a scientist can offer. If, however, he decides that he will use his special qualifications directly for the public good, apart from his primary duty, then certain observations may be offered, which will occupy the rest of this chapter. These observations are intended to indicate some of the accessory ways in which the scientist can serve his fellow-creatures. Anyone who makes suggestions on this subject lays himself open to the charge of being an unqualified moralist, and the task is not undertaken without diffidence. Nevertheless, it is urgent that someone should undertake it, and the very defects in what I shall write may prompt better-qualified people to improve on my suggestions. Those who think that science should be centrally planned are undeterred by doubts as to their qualifications to give advice on ethical subjects. They have spread powerful propaganda intended to make scientists believe that they have three social obligations : to devote all their energies to the solution of the problems of man's material wants, to accept central planning in their own subject, and to press for the adoption of central planning of society as a whole. This, so far as one can make out, is what is meant by the social responsibilities of scientists, as the term is usually used. Scientists who have other ideas about their social responsibilities have not yet bothered to challenge the propaganda, which is effective because it is not answered.

SCIENCE AND EVIL

The scientist is often charged with being responsible for much of the misery and unhappiness in the world, because his discoveries help the engineer to devise and construct the weapons of modern war. When people reflect on human miseries, they are apt to think first of those of war, and it would be futile to seek to minimize them; yet it is doubtful whether they are the most intense. The person bereaved, wounded, or dying in war has the moral support, the fellow-feeling of his compatriots. The sufferer from incurable disease, again, has at least the relief that comes from the knowledge that friends, doctor, nurses— all with whom he is in contact—strive hard to lessen the suffering. Far more intense is the misery of those who are persecuted by authority for racial or political reasons. The concentration or penal camp, the activities of the secret police (whether it be Gestapo, Ochrana, or Ogpu), the totalitarian purge—these are surely the greatest evils of mankind, by which individual human beings, because their beliefs and ideas differ from those of a central planning authority, are taken away from everyone whom they hold dear, kept under conditions of appalling cruelty, repeatedly subjected to questionings and to threats directed at relatives, and finally, in many cases, either executed after a so-called trial, shot in prison without even that, or killed through exposure to intolerable conditions. These evils are the greater because of the huge number of people who have suffered them. They are probably the greatest evils known to man, and no part of them can be ascribed to the discoveries of science.

Man's deliberate inhumanity to man, which is probably the chief cause of intense suffering, is something for which the scientist is not responsible; though as knowledge of psychology grows he may become able to lessen it. Ruthlessness is a characteristic of totalitarian but not of democratic states, and psychologists may one day be able to prevent ruthless cruelty by discovering the causes that make people accept totalitarian government. Again, cruelty is often the result of hate engendered in childhood, and a better understanding of child psychology may reduce the amount of hate in the world.

Scarcely anyone will deny that modern war is a terrible evil, and there are those who would charge scientists with the responsibility. It is suggested that an urgent duty of scientists is to make sure that their discoveries are not used for destructive purposes, especially in war. This, however, would make scientific research impossible. Professor P. W. Bridgman, of Harvard University, has stressed this point. If, as he says, the scientist were required to make only those discoveries which could not wilfully be perverted to harmful uses, he would almost certainly feel himself so restricted that he would make no discoveries at all. It is impossible to foresee all the consequences or to balance the good consequences against the bad. There is no mechanism by which the scientist can control the consequences of his discoveries. As Professor Bridgman says, it is society as a whole that is in a position to provide the mechanism of control rather than the individual discoverer.

Again, the fact that greater numbers of people are killed in modern than in ancient wars is due not so much to the greater effectiveness of modern offensive weapons (for defensive devices are evolved to meet them), as to modern methods of sanitation and transport, which enable vast numbers of people to congregate together in cities or armies and to be killed in huge numbers. Even if technologists did not invent explosives, and soldiers relied on clubs and swords, huge numbers of people would nevertheless be killed in modern war. Nearly everyone, incidentally, would rather be wounded or killed by a bullet or shell than by a bayonet or sword. The person who condemns science because of its relation to war must be prepared to abandon modern sanitation and transport, the chief causes of huge casualties.

SOME SECONDARY DUTIES

So much for the negative aspect of the problem. We have discussed the evils for which the scientist cannot be held responsible. What good can he foster and what evils can he prevent?

First comes the preservation of our scientific heritage. . . . We have seen that knowledge has been built up by people who valued it as an end. Some of our younger scientists, affected by propaganda, are ready to let central planning and a crudely materialistic outlook supplant the freedom and idealism that have made science great. Our scientific heritage is threatened. Let us understand that science is not our private fortune, to squander as we will. It is a heritage that is entailed to future generations, and we should preserve it and add to it as much as we can before we pass it on.

Science is not simply a mass of demonstrable knowledge about nature recorded in books and journals. That is not in danger, for there is no threat to burn our scientific records. The part of our heritage that is threatened is the spirit of science. Little has been written about that spirit. As Professor Michael Polanyi has remarked, it is something that cannot easily be communicated except by personal example. It is only a few centuries old, apart from vague beginnings such as we see among present-day savages and sporadic appearances in concrete form throughout the historical period. There is no certainty that it is immortal. Only ignorant and thoughtless people can take it for granted, or imagine that they would have possessed much of it if they had not received it from others. Here is a field in which research workers, as well as students and teachers of science in schools and universities, can render a great service to the community. We can all work to maintain and enlarge the belief in the value of science as an end.

We can do much to preserve our scientific heritage. We can dispute openly with those who profess to see nothing in science except an easier supply of food, shelter, health, and leisure. As we saw in Chapter II, it is fantastic to suppose that while music and art are ends, science is not. We should urge young scientists with real aptitude for science itself to resist the higher salaries that will be held out to tempt them into technology. We should do everything within our power to make as many people as possible understand that science is an end.

This brings us to our second social responsibility. If science is good, then the greater the number of people who enjoy it, the better. There is scope for the encouragement of amateur by professional science, a subject to which I have devoted a chapter of another book. The amateur, by definition, is one who values science as an end and thus possesses the scientific spirit. In the past the contributions of amateurs to scientific knowledge have been enormous, and even in modern times excellent research is carried out by amateurs, especially in biology and geology. There are amateur scientific societies of high standing, such as the Quekett Microscopical Club, and the Malacological and Conchological Societies. Amateur science presents a field in which suitable professionals can help both amateurs and themselves, to the advantage of science; though it must be admitted that certain pitfalls present themselves. If the professional who finds happiness in the direction of others cooperates with amateurs merely by collecting round him a group of unpaid helpers who like being told what to do, there may be satisfaction of various psychological urges on both sides, but little progress in science is likely to come of it. The professional who wants to cooperate genuinely in this movement must put aside feelings of authority and condescension, and be as ready to learn as to teach and direct.

(Pp. 83-91.)

QUESTIONS AND STATEMENTS FOR DISCUSSION

1. "We live not in a disjointed, but in a closely coordinated universe in which neither scientific data nor spiritual fact can be taken as natural enemies."

2. "Intelligence is of the very nature of reality."

3. "The liar cannot ultimately cheat the universe."

4. Justice, righteousness, liberty, are these but vague generalities about which totalitarians can jest? In the final test they will be found stronger than the goose-step, blitz, or T.N.T. In what sense could this be true?

5. Justify or condemn Pasteur's statement that the researches of science have nothing to do with primary causes but only with such phenomena as it can demonstrate.

6. Are the chief opponents of progress such as Pasteur named: prejudice, petty jealousy, and even indolence?

7. Was Pasteur's assumption that a scientist would complicate his life, disorganize his thought, and paralyze his inventive faculties through monetary rewards for his discoveries a correct one?

8. What do you think of Pasteur's statement that the cultivation of science is necessary to the moral condition of the nation?

9. Why do you think Pasteur considered allowing the will to direct the belief to be the greatest disorder of the mind?

10. Professor Bridgman is quoted as asking, "Have we (the scientists) nothing eventually in view more admirable than the abolition of want and the securing of comfort for everyone. . . ? Will we be permanently satisfied with these, or will something more be necessary to give dignity and worth to human activity?" Enumerate what the "something more" might include.

11. Does the assumption of indefinite scientific progress, along with a depreciation of philosophy, music, and art in Baker's discussion on "The Appreciation of Science as an End in Itself" strike you as a scientific conclusion? Why or why not?

12. What virtues derive from assuming the intrinsic value of truth?

13. Discuss the natural restrictions to free inquiry. Should artificial hindrances ever be imposed? Cite instances, if any.

14. To what extent does the scientist owe a duty to society?

15. "The test-tube and the scales, the microscope and mathematics, cannot reach those intangible yet real qualities of life in which is rooted human freedom." (Compton, *What You and I Need Most.*)

16. "Without an abiding dynamic faith, there can be no freedom; no incentive for further experiment or study; no impulse to progress." (Compton, *ibid.*)

17. "In dealing with the structure of any science . . . a reciprocal interconnection between epistemological judgments and judgments of value was found to arise, and that no science can be wholly dis-

entangled from the personality of the scientist." (Planck, *ibid.*)
Illustrate pro and con.

18. "While the real external world is the object, the ideal spirit which
contemplates it is the subject. Neither can be logically demonstrated, and hence no *reductio ad absurdum* is possible if their existence is denied. . . . The choicest and most original minds, men
like Kepler, Newton, Leibnitz, and Faraday, were inspired by the
belief in the reality of the external world and in the rule of a higher
reason in and beyond it." (Planck, *The Philosophy of Physics.*)
Discuss the necessity of both assumptions.

19. Evaluate the statement (Baker, *Science and the Planned State*):
"The pretence that science only serves humanity by giving us food,
health, and shelter, leads to nonsense." What must be added "to
give dignity and worth to human activity"?

20. Is the argument that history, art, and music have reached their
final development, in contrast with a science which may expect indefinite progress, sound? Yes or no. Why?

21. Enumerate as many as possible of the values of science, beyond
those of mere utility.

22. Discuss the effect on scientific progress of the control of science
by the state.

23. Does the social obligation implied in the statement: "To profit
from the work of others without making the return that is within
one's power is indefensible," apply in other fields than that of
science?

24. To what degree, if any, is the scientist responsible for the social
misuse of his discoveries? Is he bound to release all information
without regard to moral effects? As, for instance, means to crime,
without any balancing benefits?

25. In the matter of the destruction of human life, have the benefits
of science outweighed its ills? Compare the destruction by ancient
devastations of plague. Can anything be said for the use of the
"A" bomb over Hiroshima? If so, what?

Suggested Supplementary Readings:

Sir Henry Roscoe: *The Life-Work of a Chemist.* Smithsonian
Institution, Washington, D. C.

De Kruif: *Microbe Hunters.* Harcourt, Brace, New York.

Vallery-Radot: *The Life of Pasteur.* Sun Dial Press, New York.

Eddington: *The Philosophy of Science.* Macmillan, New York.

Planck: *The Philosophy of Physics.* Norton, New York.

Millikan: *Time, Matter and Values.* University of North Carolina Press, Chapel Hill, N. C.

Compton: *The Freedom of Man.* Yale University Press, New Haven.

Compton: *The Human Meaning of Science.* University of North Carolina Press.

PART IV

SELF-REALIZATION AS VALUE

"What doth it profit a man if he gain the whole world
and forfeit himself?"

—JESUS OF NAZARETH

Chapter 14

SELF-REALIZATION AS WORLD-VALUE

I
The Subjective Nature of Values

In the last analysis human beings are the judges and interpreters of values. From this standpoint, truth, honor, goodness, justice, freedom are seen as superior realities, since they promote creative self-expression.

II
The Existence of Values Implies a Corresponding World

Since values are personal and persons are a part of nature, such values must be of the nature of things. Facts indicating this are: (a) the response of nature to human inventions, such as radio, television, airplane; (b) moral, the unnatural and self-defeating nature of immorality.

III
A World of Values Implies Unity

Success in the truest sense springs out of the cooperation with environment. A natural life can be lived only in accordance with one's highest and most typical nature.

IV
Evolutionary Process Demands Purpose

An evolutionary process is meaningless apart from creative intelligence. The creative power of this concept in human society and achievement.

Chapter 14

SELF-REALIZATION AS WORLD-VALUE

The time has come to make some sort of résumé of the ground covered in this book.

We began by a consideration of the meaning of the term "value." We decided that there was a sense in which anything that we wanted was a value. But we shortly discovered that such a conclusion would be an oversimplification of the term, because there were various kinds and degrees of worth. Some things desired were more satisfying than others, some were only ephemeral and quickly turned to disgust, some were even degrading, while the realization of others might keep us back from reaching those more desirable. On the other hand, we saw that some treasures grew richer and more satisfying with possession and paved the way for still more coveted achievements. We have seen also how the things we steadfastly desire and work after become the center about which we organize our lives, and indicate the final nature of our accomplishment. In view of these reflections, an understanding of the problems of value appeared to be the most important of all insights which come with a liberal education. We have learned that worth must be judged, not by artificial standards, but by the satisfactions of human needs, their accord with the nature of the world, and the proper functioning of the human spirit. We discovered three main types of effort by which men have sought to come by a knowledge of the value and reality of the world. These efforts were, first, those of scientific discovery and experiment with a rigid adherence to truth; second, the way of philosophical consistency, or the logical coherence of facts in a system of reason; third, the way of religious insight into the nature and reality of moral and spiritual facts and truths. These were seen, not as giving contradictory results, but rather as giving differing viewpoints from which to look at the world of fact and experience. These varying ways of looking at life were seen to be important, because they become the organizing centers of life and dictate our life success or failure.

Our concept of what is to be desired, then, determines our actual achievement, makes us what we are and are yet to become. Since our choice of values is bound up with our character, and constitutes us creative beings, self-realization is seen at last as the supreme consideration of all. It is this creative power which resides in some measure in each of us and which makes our lives of moment to the rest of the world and also provides us with the most enduring satisfactions. Our most important task is, then, to cultivate these inner sources of desire and action, our ideals, imagination, and moral self-respect, because these, rather than any external sources, bring usefulness and happiness. These inner resources are open to everyone, and no organization of society can be effective in the fullest degree if it denies to anyone opportunity for the completest self-development and self-expression in keeping with the common welfare.

Next in our study we took up Five World-Concepts of Human Values, segregating them into classes because of their widely prevailing acceptance, or because they represented principal types of contrasting views. While they differed widely in method, we discovered similarity in objectives sought which were such an adjustment to the world of nature, and such use of one's powers as would yield the greatest peace and happiness. We found this objective as prevalent in the Golden Mean of Confucius' "gentleman" as in the effort of Buddha to achieve an unperturbed calm and a complete self-mastery by shutting out the clamors of the world. Both Stoic and Epicurean, as we saw, sought the same objective, the one by a self-control superior to every misfortune through living the life of Reason, the latter by satisfaction with such simple pleasures as were easily his. The Judaeo-Christian effort after happiness was conceived to be the discovery of the will of God and conformity with it.

We then considered six interpretations of human values which were made by outstanding individuals in the progress of Western society. To Socrates the supreme value lay in self-knowledge and the results that sprang from it; to Boethius, in the practice of a philosophic attitude toward life, made possible by a belief in the supremacy of the human spirit over misfortune; to Dante, in the emancipation of that spirit through love, love of the good; to Rousseau, in the freedom of the life of nature; to Nietzsche, through the casting off of moral obligations and the exercise of the will to power; to Pasteur, in an utter devotion of the mind to truth.

The most casual examination of these various ways of arriving at human values convinces the student of history of certain underlying concepts common to them all. If in the beginning we had any doubts about either the reality or place of human values, we can now scarcely deny their existence in personal ideals, activities, and achievements. In other words, anything to be of worth must offer some satisfaction to the individual. Values are to be judged by the satisfaction they provide the person, and their cogency in creating in him an aptitude and love for still higher accomplishment. The highest satisfaction of all is to be the kind of man or woman which in his heart one knows he ought to be. Self-realization is the supreme value.

I
The Subjective Nature of Values

A moment's reflection on the nature of values ought to convince us of their dominantly subjective character. The aptest illustration may perhaps be found in the hoard of gold recently possessed by the American Government. It represented what might fairly be termed the world's supply of gold. We have thought of gold as one of the most precious of the world's commodities, yet we discover that its worth lies largely in its use as the basis of the world's monetary systems. As such it can be exchanged for whatever is currency and used to supply our wants of food, clothing, or luxury. No longer convertible into currency, its value would be reduced to that of one of the metals used in technical processes. Thus the importance of gold depends on its recognized use by a society of persons. Nothing seemed more outlandish to the Peruvian Indians than the avidity of their Spanish conquerors for gold, which they held only in minor esteem. It is apparent that values are created by personal wants, needs, and desires.

If this is true, and who can deny it, all those things that contribute comfort, pleasure, and well-being to society must be recognized as values. But the greatest contributions to the comfort, pleasure, and well-being of society are made by the existence of truth, honor, goodness, justice, and freedom. These are the things worth while. Without them life and physical satisfactions, however great, are as nothing. They are the essence of human satisfactions. I can endure hardship with fortitude if I have the sympathy and approval of those around me. Even poverty can become an interesting game with circumstance if I am surrounded by loving friends. For mere applause and the honor of Alma Mater, men whom we all admire will readily run the risk of maiming for life. For the sake of very immaterial freedoms, justices, and rights, men find it sweet and appropriate to die, and the last terror of all is robbed of its horror. Not only do we have such values as we are at present come by, but it is possible for persons to create new ones. Whoever paints a masterpiece, or invents a laborsaving device, or provides a dynamic philosophy, or opens new avenues of religious insight, becomes a creator of worth, and may be more important to society than the miner who discovers gold. In this higher creativeness lies the fashioning of character, which is the greatest of all earthly goods.

Such a consideration of values demands, first, an external world which responds to human endeavor, and, second, human beings so created that they can function with respect to that world.

II
The Existence of Values Implies a Corresponding World

It has been quite popular to look on man and mind as some fantastic contradiction in a universe which was nothing but matter, force, and motion. But Nature has produced mind, and the ground of personal choices, just as surely as she has produced mountains and seas. Mind, reflection, thinking, wishing, and willing, then, must be accorded at least an equal, and by all human measurements a superior, place in the reality of things. The fact that we can coöperate with Nature, discover her laws and bend them to our wills, as we have done in the invention of telephone, telegraph, television, radio, electric lighting, airplanes, and a million other creations which Nature could not by herself achieve, shows how closely the world of nature is related to persons and personal accomplishment. It also discloses the superiority of these internal and personal possessions over the world of matter. This is because it holds within its power to make the material world the servant of its desires. To say, then, that the imaginings, good purposes, religious and moral convictions, dreams of the human soul, are mere fog and vapor, illusions lacking reality and powerless for results, is to deny the supreme facts of existence. For these personal achievements are also of the nature of things. Nature is only waiting for our coöperation to carry our whisperings over land and sea, to perform our heavy labor, or to convey us on the wings of the wind. Who shall say that she was not made for human voices, and human minds? Nature has made us for herself and we are her offspring, but in a deeper sense, since we must not reverse values, she is made for us and is our servant.

Not only does Nature prove herself part and parcel of our human fabric by responding to the inventive genius of mind, but she shows moral sympathies for those who do well, who love right-

eousness, justice, and peace. The profligate she deprives of health
and strength; the violent she makes the victim of violence; for the
good man she makes goodness the normal atmosphere of life and
sets a premium on love; but she causes the deceiver to deceive himself; she betrays the betrayer; she delivers over the dishonest and
wicked to the torment of his own self-recriminations; she destroys
the creative imagination of the evil-minded, both by giving him
over to a sense of inferiority, and by making him the prey of his
own misjudgments, thus putting a limit on his power for evil. For
the children of her love she provides that her harsher decrees of
suffering, pain and death, shall not have compulsion over the inner
spirit. For Nature, the normal life is the good life, and abnormalities of every kind are ultimately self-destructive. Thus the system
of human needs rests on the great moral facts of the universe. All
sins are sins against Nature. Whenever a man steals, lies, does
unjustly, is unsympathetic against his neighbor, he really takes arms
against Nature herself and, not only so, he betrays also his own
deepest significance. Human abnormalities, digressions from the
path of virtue, become the natural means of destroying not only
man's satisfactions, but his creative genius, his powers, his personality itself.

III
A World of Values Implies Unity

If we grant the foregoing premises, it becomes evident that for
personal success, the fullest achievement of possibilities, we must
work in harmony with the external world. There is a unity which
must be achieved between ourselves and Nature. It will never do
to run in the face of Nature by defying her laws, or to expect her
to respond to the erratic moods that seize us. Success lies in our
cooperation with Nature; nor does this mean our lower nature.
Our distinction from the beasts, and our capacity for success, lie
along the direction of our higher capacities. The power of self-
conscious reflection lends a moral quality to every human act. The
beast is never immoral, because he cannot reflect upon the significance of his deed. But man is endowed with a moral self-consciousness, and if he does not live up to it, he becomes unnatural
and, as we say, "lower than the beasts." Our highest possibilities
are as much a part of the cosmic order as our bodies, and we must
expect life to deal with our moral abnormalities with the same unerring equity that she visits on all unnatural things. For man, the
life of nature is the life of his highest nature. The plant achieves

its functions by the fullest response to the soil and the sun, and the natural life of man is the highest of which he is morally capable.

Cooperation with the universe, decision to "accept" it, as Margaret Fuller expressed it in the famous epigram, is not, however, the whole of the story. We may "accept" the universe and still be crushed. The far more positive and difficult thing is to achieve an inner unity which will make us acceptable to ourselves. The greater number of failures is not to be attributed to difficult circumstances, but to a weakness within the self. Men suffer from the entertainment of cross-purposes, indefiniteness of aim, unclearness of thinking, conflicting ideals, unwillingness to concentrate, and to persist. From these springs lack of self-control, and the individual becomes like a ship without direction because it has lost its rudder.

In the journal of a young flying officer, missing in action, were found these words:

> An individual is only justifying himself fully if he is doing the work toward which he has an inclination, to which he is best suited. In this way is his work not only better done but its accomplishment gives rise to the maximum feeling of creative achievement. And I think a man is forced to be half empty if he is forced to spend his waking energies on what is not, for him, creation.[1]

Commenting on these words, Editor Schimanski speaks of the necessity of according to every man the right to follow the vocation nearest his heart, because "man's dignity is rooted in freedom, not in expediency."

> There are those who have died, not blindly throwing life away, so that we might live. But there are those among the living who are afraid of life, afraid of man, afraid of freedom and who, out of the depths of their fear, plan for the future.

These, he contends, are the enemies we must oppose, and who deny the interpretation of life given by the young pilot, "for a man who may not work except under orders does not create." The most fundamental of human rights is the right to choose a vocation, for without this freedom a man cannot realize himself and his creative powers.

> Without creative activity, there cannot be integrity of the spirit; without spiritual integrity, there cannot be an integrity of the person; without integrity of the person, the integrity of the community, its all-togetherness, is inconceivable. It can lead only into one direction —the segregation of men into masters and slaves. . . . Harmony within the individual heart can come only from that center which is at

[1] Quoted by Stefan Schimanski in *Transformation* No. 3, Lindsay Drummond Ltd., London.

peace with itself if it moves by means of creative acts, for activity is reality—the reality of the wholeness of living. . . . His [man's] ultimate freedom lies in his power to transfigure within himself the given situation; in his progressive discovery of life's spiritual principle; in the evolutionary unification of all his activities; and in the final integration of all his creative principles in the dynamic life-source of his self-found vocation.

This integration within himself is what distinguishes the individual from the person. An individual may be chiefly a freak, full of idiosyncrasies and oddities, at war with all the world, and most of all, with himself. He is made up of mental and moral confusions and contradictions, the battleground between good and evil, torn between forces of integration and dissolution.

The person, in contrast, is a final, complete entity; a unit unto himself; a spiritual and creative being with his own set of values, his own self-imposed responsibilities and censorships who has resolved the contradictions within himself.[2]

To imagine the possible results in human living when men generally live in conformity with their highest capacities and in unity with their world staggers the farthest flight of human fancy. Nature has forces in the offing, ready to put at our command as soon as we can be trusted to use them for the general good and not for the general destruction. It may be that we are prevented chiefly by our moral blindness from coming into possession of powers yet undreamed. Certainly if there is any truth in psychological inhibitions, this is believable. Civilization can get on no faster than its moral achievements.

IV

The Evolutionary Process Demands Purpose

If there is in existence an evolutionary process by which creation has advanced from the simple to the complex, from the lower to the higher, it must be conceded that the universe is no chance or chaotic accident. There must be residing within it or behind it some order or purpose which is striving for self-expression. It may be no more than an urge in a cell toward some completer life, or the inspiration in an atom to move in a meaningful direction, or it may be what is much easier to conceive, that there is a Mind within or behind all these activities, expressing Itself through them in some way analogous to that by which our choices are expressed through the movements of our hands. Or, as Max Planck, the great physicist,

[2] All above quotations quoted from work cited above, pp. 10-13.

has expressed it: "We must assume the existence of an ideal and omniscent spirit if a strict causality is to be upheld in physical events."[3]

A significant thing about the evolutionary process is that it requires time, duration, the sustaining of a self-conscious purpose. In things themselves there is no permanence. Permanence lies only in a sustained will toward things that are in constant change. Matter unattended by consciousness has no power to bind together momentary facts into meaningful connection. Relationship between forces that spread through time are established by something which is itself, in some measure, above the temporal flow. When we discover where this can occur we find it in but one place and condition. We as persons are able to gather past, present, and future into one enduring order of meaning. We are the continuing subjects of experience. Any reality that involves time as a process can be a reality only to remembering, reflective beings as the more permanent subjects of experience. Time is our method of uniting in a single meaning, events of experience, some of which no longer exist, some of which we are not conscious, and some which do not yet exist but which we anticipate. If we live in a world in which there is connection between events or which is an unfolding evolutionary process, it can only be because the moving force, the vital energy within or behind it, bears some relation to our own creative energies, is itself time-transcending, creative, mental, and personal. If so, the highest character our world can assume is a personal character, and every development of human worth, such as growing intelligence, keener appreciation of the meaning of selfhood, more widespread eagerness for justice, righteousness, freedom, and democracy, is to be viewed as a step in the evolutionary process. The values we have been considering are not only as real as the world of matter, they are of supreme importance in a world of evolution and of changing meaning. They are the realities about which we should principally concern ourselves.

Once the significance of these facts becomes apparent and an accepted concept of society, there is no conceivable limit to the powers of enjoyment, well-being, and personal achievement which might be possible. Working in unity with Nature herself we may move to the realization of aims which Nature dimly entertains but the achievement of which wait upon man's active and intelligent cooperation.

(For Readings see Chapter 15, page 497.)

[3] *The Philosophy of Physics,* W. W. Norton & Company, New York, p. 79.

Chapter 15

SELF-REALIZATION AS INTRINSIC VALUE

I
Belief in the Intrinsic Worth of the Individual Basic to the Democratic Process

1. The basic conviction of democracy that each person presents an intrinsic value
2. Any "forgotten man" may become a menace to the whole social order

II
"Personal Liberty" to Do Right

1. Deviation from righteousness a breaking of Nature's inexorable laws
2. Eventual slavery and loss of freedom by wrongdoers
3. Freedom in the State possible only on similar terms

III
Self-Expression and the Creative Imagination

1. Personal achievement and emotional control
2. Creative imagination and self-expression

IV
Making a Living or Making a Life

Chapter 15

SELF-REALIZATION AS INTRINSIC VALUE

It seemed established in the preceding chapter that there is the closest connection between values and personality—that is, that values are the particular creation of persons. If this be so, neither the advances of science, nor the mastery of physical nature, nor some fortunate organization of society can ever insure the existence of the higher values, such as widespread happiness, justice, and social well-being. To secure these there must be back of science, back of government, men and citizens who are possessors of the highest values. There must be men who will not abuse the power put into their hands. Otherwise every scientific advance will only deepen the slavery imposed by those who are in authority and can seize the power. The common welfare is secure only when there is in the individual citizen a strong devotion to the immaterial goods, such as love of freedom, justice and morality, good-will toward other citizens and states, willingness to share, and, when necessary, to suffer for the common defense. It must be evident that the foundation of all well-ordered society lies in the cultivation and prevalence of those values which the person alone can create.

I

Belief in the Intrinsic Worth of the Individual Basic to the Democracy Process

The concept of democracy has been the peculiar development of Western society. It has been a plant of slow growth and rooted in various sources. The linear theory of history, of history moving on to better and higher conditions, was given to Western society by Hellenism, Judaism, and Christianity, and is indigenous to the concept of democracy. Science also lent a great share by its emphasis on a reality made up of small parts each of which was necessary to the whole. Likewise, if each citizen was important to the whole, then each must bear within himself some intrinsic worth, the possibility of some essential contribution to the common weal. As this came to be more clearly seen, it was discovered necessary to give individuals ever-widening powers of participation in the state. The movement toward democracy began with the leading families, expanded to include the so-called upper classes, was extended to the master craftsmen in the medieval guilds, and came finally to universal suffrage. These were the steps by which democratic society has come to recognize the intrinsic value of each citizen.

This basic assumption of democracy carries with it certain implications. If every citizen is important to the state, he must be protected in his just rights. His capacity to earn a decent living, to be secure in his justly earned possessions, to be assisted in the wholesome outworking of his life, is a matter of public concern. Furthermore, to have an enlightened state, it is necessary to have opportunity for education within the reach of all, both in culture and in skills. And in the last analysis, no state can rest securely in its liberties without encouraging the free exercise of religion and training in morals. All these objectives have been in general the goal of the democracies. But since the world-wide abolition of slavery, one factor has often been overlooked: this is the contribution which every citizen must make to the common good if democracy is to succeed. For each citizen must be considered the potential bearer of some unique gift, some place that can be filled by him alone, if all are to prosper. No state, democratic or otherwise, can rest on firm foundations if one person remains deprived of his just rights to best self-fulfilment. For every such man weakens the morale of the state.

II

"Personal Liberty" to Do Right

This freedom for self-fulfilment raises the much discussed problem of "personal liberty." There is great misunderstanding of this much abused term. To many, personal liberty means the right to do anything one pleases. But obviously unrestrained liberty would be possible only in a state made up of but one individual, and he would find himself restrained in many ways by the nature of the world. In a society of two or more, one must consult not only his own wants, he has in some measure to be governed by the wants of others. The more complex society becomes, the more liberty of action must be surrendered by each. Indeed, the strange paradox of freedom is this, that man can be free only as he exercises self-restraint. The measure of his freedom is also the measure of his self-control. As he rules himself rigidly within bounds, respecting the rights of others, he has a right to claim protection from their encroachments on his liberty. The democratic way of life is thus a give-and-take proposition, and personal liberty means the liberty to behave one's self in a decent society. There never can be a just claim for liberty to invade the rights, welfare, and comfort of others.

These facts are not made by constitutions or social contracts, but exist in man's own nature and in the nature of human associations. There are certain inexorable laws of human intercourse which make civilized society possible. Personal liberty can never be rightfully granted if it means the introduction of influences that are degrading to the morals, ideals, physical health, comfort, or enjoyment of society as a whole. The wise democracy will prohibit whatever is seen to be against the common welfare, or whatever forms a special temptation to those whose immaturity, or weakness of character renders them easily susceptible. All this the democracy has the right to do for its own preservation, since it can survive only by guarding the rights of all, and can flourish only by the co-operation of all toward a common good. The same principle is discoverable in nature, which has so constructed human beings that wrong-doing, indifference to social obligations, is invariably followed by a sense of inferiority and shortcoming that reduces the individual to some bodily or mental slavery in which he is no longer free, but is the prey of abnormal emotions, conceits of evil, and unsocial desires.

III

Self-Expression and the Creative Imagination

Having launched the proposition that all values are human values and that each man has a unique and essential contribution to make to society, let us further consider the creative nature of human personality. Here we are at the very center of the domain of value, the fount and citadel of all.

We hope your consent has been obtained to the fact and existence of values: that *honesty* in the acquisition of money or other goods is quite as important as their acquirement; that a society in which every man is a thief would be a less desirable place to live than one in which all were honest; that *ideals* of education are as important as education; that *love* of wife, husband, and children are as essential and real to a happy family life as the presence of food; that willingness to risk one's life and possessions for the good of the fatherland, that immaterial value known as *patriotism*, is as

important to the state as military power. Once we grant these assumptions, it will appear that the source of the most important
values that have to do with human happiness and success is in
human character. Let us think of the person then as the creator of
important values, and let us ask ourselves how we may successfully
achieve them.

The most significant fact about man is his power to create. By
powers within himself he can determine destinies, change the direction of nature, command the activity of body and mind, and make
the physical world around him his servant. This he is able to do
because of a peculiar capacity for self-consciousness and reflection
of which, in the world order, he alone is the possessor. By reflection he can bring to bear upon the present and the future the wisdom of past experiences in creative action. He is thus able to visualize future possibilities and to make them real. This capacity lies
within the realm of the creative imagination. The first step toward
any future activity or achievement is the objectifying of that possibility as an accomplished fact. What one thus visualizes to himself,
if strongly willed and followed up with the appropriate action, is
already on the way to accomplishment. Such pictured activities
gain a power over our unconscious activity, so that the drive of life
takes the direction of what we have strongly wished and willed.
It springs up between intervals of attention like a hand guiding us
to some distant goal. It rules the thinking which does go on in
moments of slumber, bringing its contribution to our waking efforts. How important are imaginative concepts that are followed
up with action! Such dreams are the particular product of youth.
How important, then, are the dreams of accomplishment which may
present themselves to you, and how essential that they should be
noble, worthy, and daring! Let us not be afraid to dream of doing
what men declare impossible, for the great contributors to civilization have in that way reached their goal. Achievement once pictured in the mind and set by activity makes a man an inventor, a
poet, a philosopher, a painter, a musician, an administrator, a creator of human values. As one by one he turns his dreams into
action, the power to dream and the power to accomplish grow, until
the whole drive of life is set toward the desired accomplishment,
which seems so easy to the world around that they call it good luck.
But make no mistake at this point! Such accomplishments do not
arise except at the cost of laborious preparation and practice of
technique, for which the individual has to pay all there is to pay.
Intense action, painful acquirement of technique, rigid self-control,

limitation to definite objectives, these form the inner price that one must pay, and beside all these there must be both emotion and emotional control, if one is to become truly creative.

At long last, the man who follows such a program comes to high self-realization. There is no way to make the goal by short cuts or easy stages. It is useless to expect to be an accomplished musician without the drudgery of practice. Back of the one hour of a Paderewski concert lay whole days and months of finger exercises persisted in so long as he followed his profession. The artist must make many failures on which to ground success. The inventor must run down many false clues. But when the technique is mastered, the pianist no longer thinks in terms of white and black keys, nor his hands, nor even his instrument, but finds it possible to express his dreams directly in sound and symphony. This is what it means to become a creator. Any important creative work demands a background something like this, and the higher the results the greater the price we must pay. The main objective of a college career, as I see it at least, is to provide something of a cultural background on which later to specialize to good advantage. But beware of specialization before the background is achieved.

There is one further point, however, to which attention has not yet been drawn. A true creator is ruled by something higher than his selfish interests, be that fame, money, or social standing. The fire of a great emotion comes only with an objective on which a man can feel he can worthily spend his life. This was the reason that Pasteur refused the monetary rewards that might have come to him from his discoveries. He feared that the love of personal gain might lower his scientific standards, as it undoubtedly would have. Had he been less religious in his devotion to truth, or had he turned his interests toward personal profits, he could not have been so great a scientist. It is this willingness to give all to a great cause which is of the very essence of religion. Pasteur's experience has been that of all the great creators of values. The supreme philosophic statement of this truth is: "He that seeketh to save his [own] life shall lose it, but he that loseth his life [in self-forgetfulness to a worthy task] shall keep it unto life eternal."

Perhaps the whole matter of the relation of the creative imagination to the outcome of life has never been better put than in the following words by James Allen:

As you think, you travel, as you love, you attract. You are today where your thoughts have brought you; you will be tomorrow where your thoughts take you. You cannot escape the result of your thoughts, but you can endure and learn, can accept and be glad. You will realize the vision (not the idle wish), of your heart, be it base or beautiful, or a mixture of both, for you will always gravitate toward that which you secretly most love. Into your hands will be placed the exact result of your thoughts; you will receive that which you earn; no more, no less. Whatever your present environment may be, you will fall, remain, or rise with your thoughts, your vision, your ideal. You will become as small as your controlling desire; as great as your dominant aspiration.

IV

Making a Living or Making a Life

In view of these reflections, what then should a man strive after? The world's great majority spend their energy on making merely a living. Many lives go out in a dull drudgery, measured almost wholly in value by the size of a paycheck. The degree of such success may be indicated by the quantity of food on the table, a growing waist-line, or the presence of gadgets on the parlor shelf. In many cases this is so because society, remiss in its duty, has furnished the individual little alternative. Sometimes it is due to the hardness of the common lot, sometimes to the limitations of education or environment, more often to an almost utter lack of vision, an incapacity to understand what is worth while. In many minds there has been no stirring of the finer spiritual aspirations that characterize true religion. Whatever the cause, the individual may find himself in middle life in a treadmill of circumstance which becomes with the passage of years more and more difficult to break. These results are not in early life so apparent. To this group has been given a little respite of college years in which to take bearings and to learn something of human values. The college group will be inexcusable if, having seen the vision, it drops down to the lesser ideal of making a living, instead of embracing the glorious opportunity of making a life. To make a living is to rise or fall on a single throw of the dice, to measure success in terms of food and raiment; to make a life is to place one's self above the accidents, the good or evil fortunes of the world, and whatever happens, to provide one's self with undying satisfactions which neither time nor tide of luck can take away.

We who have pursued this course are about to take an examination in the problems of human values. Not the one most readily envisioned, which is marked down in the University schedules. The examination in values of deepest consequence will be carried on out in the chaotic world, and how we conceive of values and how we stick by them will determine our success or failure. The ideals of which we now dream and which we seek will, at times, be the sole anchorage to hold us fast in the storm. These hopes will not betray us. We can go forth with something of the assurance which the younger Channing expressed in the one great line of poetry he achieved: "If my bark sink, 'tis to a wider sea." If we will not allow failure and disappointment to floor us, every frustration can and will become the schooling to some higher and wider success, the emergence from a narrower to a wider sea. And through it all, let us not be too much disturbed by the turbulence of the world, for we may carry calm and happiness in our hearts, and it may be our portion to overcome the world.

READINGS

(Chapters 14 and 15)

FLEWELLING: *CREATIVE PERSONALITY,* The Macmillan Company, New_York. 1926. Chaps. XXV, XXX, XXXII.

≈≈≈

CHAPTER XXV
THE COSMIC REALITY OF HUMAN VALUES

In almost any other period of history than our own an attempt to justify or demonstrate the claim for the cosmic reality of human values would have seemed ridiculous or absurd. To coming generations again it will doubtless seem a perverted outlook on reality that made such demonstration appear necessary. Our heads are turned with the new wine of discovery and invention, so that we worship the material and the sensual as the only realities, while those deeper fires which burn within the soul, which makes possible all inspiration to creative art, to literature, to social and spiritual achievement, are quite likely to be passed over as morbid manifestations demanding the attention of the psychoanalyst. The curious fact is that we are able to live alongside so deep an inconsistency without sensing it. However much we relegate these experiences of the soul to the limbo of unreality, the existence of which we scientifically deny, they persist as the deeper objects of all our striving. Calling them unreal, we present the rather sorry spectacle of still living for and by them, and whatever of satisfaction and richness is left in life abides through a clinging loyalty to them.

The claim is frequently made for science that, while religion and philosophy possess the weakness of foundation principles by starting with a preconception, science starts from the single and only worthy principle of search for facts. Thus it is held that an inherent weakness for preconceptions invalidates the conclusions of religion and philosophy, while science, alone devoted to facts, moves on triumphantly. Such a conclusion could be drawn only through a rather arrogant oversight of the "facts" which have to do with the foundations of scientific theory. A science which was nothing but "facts" or even knowledge of facts could lay little claim to the name of science. The value of science lies in its generalization and relation of fact to fact by means of which the mind builds a universe of sequences and connections, applying these generalizations to the needs of life. Frequent reference is made to the mistakes and absurdities of philosophy and religion. The change, for instance, from the conception of God as lustful, revengeful, and

497

malicious to that of a God of tenderness, love, righteousness, and truth
is mentioned as militating against all claims for the truth of religion.
No very extended knowledge of history is required, however, to recall many instances in which science with unabashed confidence has
been positive, but incorrect, in its assertions. No one twenty-five years
out of college but has had abundant necessity to revise the theories
of physics, biology, and chemistry which were taught him as facts.
This is due to the theoretical implications through which all facts must
be interpreted. They are never so simple as they seem to the unphilosophical. Facts never stand alone nor unsupported. They are
always in relation to other facts and cannot be considered apart from
their relations without removing something of their factuality. Thus
is shown the exceeding dependence of science upon hypotheses of relation. Far from accepting as true the claim of science that it starts
without preconceptions, we are faced at the very beginning of science
with the preconception of unity, of universal and uniform laws, and
unalterable sequences. Without these preconceptions there could be
no science,[1] and instead of raising the primary claim that all science is
therefore invalidated, we rejoice in any verification of such general
hypotheses as serve to give us working insight into the nature of reality.
If science can get nowhere in the ascertainment of facts, except upon
the hypothesis of the solidarity of the universe, and must in the end
justify its hypotheses by the pragmatic test of values, how much deeper
is the demand that in philosophical and religious thinking we should
start with the hypothesis of moral and spiritual solidarity in the cosmos,
the universal reality of mental, moral, and spiritual values in the experience of man. If we are to consider life as it is there is no other
way. As there can be no scientific thought without the scientific assumption of universal law, so there can be no true explanation, religion,
or philosophy of life without the assumption of the universal reality
of human values. It is certainly bad taste if not bad faith to cling to
an assumption as the foundation of science, and to deny to religion the
fundamental religious assumption of the existence of God, or to philosophy the assumption of intelligent world-ground as a starting-point.

The denial of the reality of human values has arisen from an exaggerated notion of the certainty of scientific demonstration. Extreme
claims have been made that scientific demonstration provides the only
basis of certainty. From this the easy assumption is made that all
experience resting on any other ground is false or illusory. Such con-

[1] We speak here from the empirical standpoint of science itself rather than
from that of philosophy. From the standpoint of philosophy, law bears with it no
necessity, but may be looked upon as a uniformly acting creative will. Even under
this view, the uniformity is essential to scientific practice. If the forces of nature
were capricious and the phenomenal orders of succession were frequently reversed,
or if it were impossible to state the causal order, scientific knowledge would be
impossible. It seems clear that science is dependent upon the assumption of order
somewhere.

fidence could never have arisen if there had been a thoughtful criticism of the nature of scientific proof. At best, scientific demonstration is limited to appearances. It cannot enter into the essence or nature of things. If it be said that things have no essence but only activities, then the most that science can affirm is that these activities are thus and so, under certain conditions, but it has no right to declare that there are no facts other than these activities. In truth, while denying it, science does assume reality beyond the activity, and many who profess conscientious adherence to scientific fact are perfectly satisfied so long as the essence behind the activity is assumed to be non-purposive, unintelligent matter. If some one asserts the "essence" behind the activity to be purposive intelligence, then there is a great outcry against what is declared to be unsupported fact. The scientist, indeed, has no more right to be a materialist than an idealist. Neither of the foregoing presuppositions is scientific; both are philosophical.

The field of scientific demonstration, when understood, is limited then to "activities and relations" rather than to essences, or at least to what can be learned about the essence of anything from its activity and relation. When we come into the field of human values, demonstration of this kind is impossible. We get the activity of electricity, for instance, through the overcoming of resistance, the work it will do. We are thus permitted to express it in a term of relation, that is, in foot-pounds of energy. All the demonstration that is required is lifting power. But when we come to such human values as honor, integrity, justice, truth, patriotism, love of family, and social values, we have not the same means of demonstration at hand. This is not to overlook our friends who would reduce all these, as psychic reactions, to terms of foot-pounds of energy, chemisms, and affinities. The main difficulty with such terms, even though we get them, is that they are not uniform nor universal, nor related to scientific fact, and are therefore of doubtful value. One is not interested in discovering the number of foot-pounds of energy represented in the love of a little child; to do so would be to forfeit the love and to miss its significance altogether. To show the scientifically undemonstrable character of the human values is not to show them unreal or illusory, but simply to designate them as in another field of demonstration. Though not demonstrable scientifically, they gather and prove their value out of life and experience.

However undemonstrable human values may be from a scientific standpoint, yet they are the values that give worth and meaning to life. They are the supreme interests in spite of every effort to ignore them. The finer loyalties in the world in which we live are forever superior to the most startling of scientific facts. The heart of a friend means more as an earthly possession than all physical wealth without it. The mere opportunity to work, to take and fill our place in the social order— for what physical consideration would a real man barter it? There

are those who will betray friendship for a price, but we esteem their
lot lower than that of the beasts that perish. Patriotism may be thought
a mere sentiment, but to the greater number of living men and women
it is more important than selfish gain, however great.

Upon such loyalties, such integrities and sentiments, is the whole
social structure built. It makes possible political institutions that protect the individual in his rights and maintain for all an equal chance.
Any oversight of the practical reality of these values impoverishes life
and so divests it of meaning as to make it undesirable to live. The
loss of life itself is felt to be a slight matter as compared with the loss
of character. Ours is a time when these facts by which we live, for
which we stand ready to die, and which alone survive the passing and
changing order should be set forth in their deep significance. The
progress of civilization is not measured by scientific discoveries, by
the skill of artisans, or by its complexity and wealth of physical possessions, but rather by the esteem in which are held these finer values.
For these are supreme and mark the heights of human achievement.
They are not supreme merely for a moral content, great as that is, but
they are supreme as furnishing the only adequate ground for civilization, for society, and even for the preservation of knowledge, education, and the results of science itself. There are a host of people who,
while gladly seizing the benefits which accrue to them through the provision made by the common faith in religion and these human values,
waste much of their energy decrying those very things upon which
the significant blessings of their days depend. It is quite time that men
at large should come to a better mood.

And, after all, there is another consideration: scientific "facts"
are meaningful and real to us largely from the standpoint of value.
They are themselves values of a lesser order. Scientific facts are of
moment to us, first, because of their utility in enabling us to master our
world and thus adding to the usefulness and joy of living, and, second,
because of the insight they give regarding the common relations under
which we live. That men should give long hours of toil and endure
real sacrifices in the interests of scientific discovery—for science has
its martyrs no less surely than religion—is entirely unjustifiable except from the standpoint of the human values to be achieved. It is
forever to the honor and glory of science that along its way has shone
the bright hope of human betterment. It is because of the loftiness
of this ideal that men have felt the call to scientific research, sometimes
from motives as lofty as ever came to any of the saints. The absence
of such ideals from scientific research would not only impoverish the
history of science, but would render its future advance problematic.
Without the presence of moral insight the advance of science becomes
the menace of humanity. Morally untempered, it promises only universal destruction to that fragile plant which we call human life and
civilization. It is needless to point out that, though facts might re-

main after such devastation, science itself would be destroyed, if not forever, at least until the birth of a new race whose moral achievement should walk hand in hand with their scientific progress.

If this be true, and who can doubt it, the dependence of science upon the final test of the human quality of its values becomes complete. Here lies, it seems to some, the true "reconciliation" between science and religion, for both must pass through the same little door of social and moral justification. A science which works and lives unmindful of human society would be a menace to the common life and welfare. Science, like religion, must be forever on trial, and must justify itself by its contribution to the common welfare. Even facts have a profound moral significance in a personal world. They possess relational value. They are powers for moral use. Religion, too, cannot avoid the ethical test; with every new generation it must continually prove its validity, not by citing historic authorities and past revelation, but by its ability to contribute to the social order. A science and a religion which make life more worth living will abide forever, and if either science or religion, falsely so called, does not stand this test, they must pass away under the exigencies of life itself.

CHAPTER XXX

THE SELF-RESTRAINT OF FREEDOM

No word of social and political life is more commonly abused and misunderstood than the term freedom. Like other much used terms such as "orthodoxy," its definition is not standard but is made by every man after his own mind and thoughts. Thus freedom has been turned from its uses and made to stand for license, for looseness, for illegality and disorder, for tyrannies the most complete because the most irresponsible. Despite all this there is a widespread and profound feeling that freedom is the basis of law, politics, art, knowledge, religion, and life. Only because it holds so elemental a place could it have survived its numerous and time-honored perversions.

Experiments unnumbered indicate that the only lasting power in politics and government is based upon the principle of freedom. Autocrat and aristocrat, plutocrat and class democrat, each has felt that safety lay in enforcing his will as against all others. All have this in common, that each in its turn has insisted upon its right to rule the others. It is a perversion to call that a state of freedom where one class rules to the disadvantage of another. A benevolent despotism may be more tolerable than an intolerant class democracy. In the long run, whatever kind of government has been tried has been found unstable to just the degree that it denied the largest measure of freedom consistent with the general or largest good. But it has likewise been found that no government can long exist which does not have the cooperative self-restraint of its citizens. Laws cannot be enforced apart from the desire of law-abiding citizens, and it is the preponderance of these that makes permanent the institutions of freedom.

Freedom is similarly the backbone of creative art. Trammel it to unreasonable convention and you have destroyed it. On the other hand, it would be a mistake to consider unrestrained freedom the mother of creative art. Art, like politics, achieves freedom through self-restraint. The beauty of the circle lies perhaps in the fact that it represents the greatest freedom under the most perfect restraint. No line of beauty can ever be gotten into mere wildness.

As in art, so in religion and life, freedom and self-restraint march together. No man can be made religious by outward constraint, whether it be of a political character commanding him to worship, or whether it be that more subtle form of constraint to an authorized creed which other minds have laid down for him. Any constraint which deprives him of the full right to come unprejudiced to his own conclusions denies to him the very possibility of religion. On the other hand, religious freedom does not involve the entertainment of loose opinion. The religious thinker is bound to self-restraint, he cannot discard the religious wisdom of other men and other ages according to his whim. He must give reasons for change. He must ever keep in mind what we fear has often been forgotten in the framing of theologies, the bearing of his belief on practical ethical values. Not he who is cut loose from all conventions is best fitted to achieve religious freedom but he who feels most deeply the obligation to consider the past and the opinions of other men as well as his own.

Neither can there be true intellectual achievement without freedom. There was a day when the advance of knowledge was hindered by all sorts of statutory provisions, political and ecclesiastical. Men of the established order have usually feared the unsettling effect of discovery. Today, intellectual achievement is hindered principally by its own dogmatic prejudices. Science advances only by the setting forth of hypotheses which really constitute a cosmic philosophy. If these hypotheses prove valuable for purposes of classification they are frequently assumed as facts rather than more or less artificial classifications of fact. They then become a retarding influence in the field of knowledge until they are overcome and displaced by more accurate generalizations. Any science thus hampered cannot make fullest progress. There must be complete freedom from institutional domination if we are to know the truth. There must also be complete freedom from the preconceptions of science itself. At the same time there is a self-restraint demanded of scientific effort as important in its way as freedom. It lies in the respect of the individual scientist for the opinions and hypotheses of others which keeps him from ill-considered conclusions.

One common thread runs through the freedom in these widely separated realms of which we have been thinking. The restraint necessary to the achievement of true freedom is in all fields alike, not a restraint put on from above, but a restraint which springs from the self-consciousness of the individual, from within. If this be true, then freedom becomes a truly human value which cannot be divested of moral meaning. It does not exist apart from free individuals nor apart from self-restraint. Let us consider for a moment the effect of unrestraint on freedom. Applied to the artist, the unrestrained line means lack of form and the death of art itself; applied to government, freedom for every man to follow his own pleasure implies the destruction of organized society; applied to science, it causes us to drop from strictly ascertained fact to opinion, for no one would feel the necessity for checking his opinion by the general body of knowledge. In religion, it would bring the descent to a mere emotionalism of an unethical character, having no deeper content than the religious exercises of the whirling dervishes of India. In ethical action, the loosening of restraint brings the decay and atrophy not only of ethical power but of ethical sensitiveness, and a loss of power for freedom. The individual as he yields to the abnormal, which is sinful, becomes less and less his own master, until at last he is under a galling slavery to evil. This is because freedom is not a physical possession but one of moral activity. This being so, the highest freedom is consonant only with the highest ethical achievement. Anything short of complete good will, of perfect holiness, and of God is something less than perfect freedom. Which is to say there cannot be perfect freedom unless there is perfect goodness.

We live in an age to which self-restraint is hateful. Our emphasis is placed on achievement. Restraint without achievement is nothing, but achievement without restraint is worse. What we need is achievement through restraint. The main characteristic of life in our age is too likely to be the lack of reserve power. We are disposed to expend all our energies, all our devices, all ingenuity on the problem of the passing moment. We are too inclined to cut ourselves loose from the wisdom of the past. We lack that calm which abides ever where there are strong reserve forces. We feel so competent within ourselves that a Martian looking at our mental attitude might judge us to be the first of our race. We are restless at lessons of history, and we despise the thought of other days. Moreover, we act as if our age were going to be the last; as if anything which could not be completed within our short span were not worth attempting. We have ceased to look at things from the aspect of eternity. We are living continually upon the verge of intellectual, social, and moral bankruptcy. We shall not be able to bring about the golden day of literature, art, government, and religion until we come to a new realization of the moral self-restraint which girds the sinews of freedom.

The discussion should not close without asking the question as to whether this freedom is anything more than a human value. Has it any right to be called cosmic? Is it found only in the exercise of human wills, or has it a basic place in the world-order? No problem is perhaps more perplexing today in the joint fields of philosophy and science. Is there contingency in the world-order? Is the succession in phenomena laid down automatically, and if so why? Are the laws of nature self-executing and inexorable? It is easy to say they are. But one takes the stand only by paying a great price. To commit one's self to non-contingency in the world-order is to vacate altogether the assumptions of evolution. Are the uniformities which we call natural laws established by accident? Then there is no purpose or end and there can be no freedom. Freedom, having no place in the cosmic order, would have to be viewed as unnatural. If we can assume contingency, an intelligence supreme to but working through self-prescribed uniformities, then and only then can we provide rational accounting for a world of evolving species and growing adaptation to environment.

Moreover, this Cosmic Intelligence, being free, must likewise be moral and can find its perfect freedom only through perfect holiness. Thus much is the reasonable assumption of freedom. We meet with insuperable difficulties and embarrassments in any defense of freedom which does not assume it as a cosmic reality. Freedom in the individual argues freedom in the world-order and in God. If we deny cosmic freedom we cannot logically refuse to go the full limit of materialism and deny its reality in ourselves.

CHAPTER XXXII

CREATIVE IMAGINATION AND LIFE

Creative imagination is part and parcel of one's power to reflect upon his own conscious moods and is therefore the unique possession of man. The importance of simulation or play to the human being has long been known. The child in his play prepares in advance for the activities and situations which will form a part of his workaday world. During World War I it was found that the football experience of the men provided significant aid to their efficiency just as by creative imagination it does undoubtedly help to prepare the man for the ex-igencies contingent upon success and failure in the realm of peaceful vocations. By means of play the youth imagines himself in new situations and prepares mind and body to act when the situation actually occurs. Usually the lawyer, the doctor, the minister, the artist, the entertainer, the farmer, or the mechanic is given the bent of his life in the creative imagination long before his years of serious activity. When the church is the dominant interest in the community and the mother's dream of honorable service is the work of the ministry, a large proportion of the youth will have been so moved in early years that they will naturally seek that calling. When business success is exalted in the home the natural dreams of children will center on that, and we shall have a larger proportion entering business. There are many evidences to indicate that early surroundings and suggestions of artistic, musical, or literary nature are of vastly more moment to the future of the child than physical heredity of the highest type. Without a strongly stimulated creative imagination, original or creative work is impossible. This fact accounts for the necessity of well-appointed leisure to the artist or the writer. There must be time for imaginative self-development. The close relation sustained between the imagination and the subconscious is now psychologically well established. Involuntary movements, bodily functionings, the great field of activities laid down by habit until they become instinctive, all these are more or less influenced by or dependent upon what we call, for want of a better term, the unconscious mind.[2] Because of the fatigueless character of such effort, knowledge of how to turn over work to the unconscious or subconscious mind is of the utmost importance. It may very well be that the absence of fatigue from such operations is largely due to the absence of attention. The creative imagination might almost be called the gateway to the control of this subconscious mental life. All have had opportunity to observe the continuous and lightning-like rapidity of the mental imaginings. Only occasionally is our conscious attention directed upon it, but we are aware that the picturing faculties are going on continually in reveries, in the dreams of sleep, and even in the midst of directed mental effort. Concentration is simply the power to overcome or to command the picturing faculty in the interest of directive mental achievement. The pictures drawn by creative imagination have a tendency to usurp the subconscious mental life and to get into external action. It is essential then that the imagination should be set in the direction which we wish the outward life to take. If the imagination goes in one direction while we try to send external acts in the other, there will be serious conflict, and the imagination is very likely to win. Pictures of the imagination take up their place in the unconscious activities of the mind. The man who wills and who wills strongly to direct his life to certain desired activities finds his life strangely tending toward his subconscious dreams. If in addition to the stimulation of his imagination in the subconscious he directs his conscious efforts in preparation for the desired activity, he will almost surely find his dreams coming to fulfillment. Frequently the fulfillment will have been so unconsciously prepared for that its coming will seem unaccountable to the individual himself. Thus the creative imagination has the task of preparing mind and body for the necessary and desirable work of life.

In order that the creative imagination shall be utilized, it must be directed into avenues of activity and must not drop off into mere daydreaming. The creative imagination can easily become destructive to effort. If constantly indulged with no attempt at outward expression,

[2] Here again there is question of the proper word. Both subconscious and unconscious are applied to what might in the writer's judgment be more properly called the marginal consciousness.

it inevitably leads to loss of control and to confusion of interest. The would-be poet or artist who dreams of writing or sketching but never puts pen or pencil to paper is not preparing to profit by his imagination. The very effort to write forms lanes of interest which both stimulate and direct the creative imagination so that it grows not only inwardly but in the direction of self-realization. The individual has his laborious task to perform, calling often for the utmost exercise of will. He must start activities in the direction of fulfillment. He must clear away obstructions from his path. He must learn, by doing, how to master both his material and himself. Creative effort will be distinguished from non-creative, originality from imitation, by passing from the stage of merely mechanical and physical operation into the emotional and imaginative. This fact finds frequent illustration. One cannot become a creative musician until he has mastered technique. This means that the mechanical and physical—fingers, arms, and keyboard, or voice-placing, breathing, or standing—have been by practice placed entirely in the realm of habit, consigned to the subconscious. So long as the instrumentalist is conscious of his instrument, the vocalist of his breathing, the painter of his brush, the versifier of his vocabulary, there cannot be truly creative work. The creative imagination will have too many and great obstructions in the way of self-expression. Creative effort can never be labored, but the paths over which creative effort can move are laid down by the most exacting toil. Much of educational theory, at least the theory that rules the lay mind, has overlooked this important fact. The school does not make the genius. The genius may lay down therein by diligent toil the ways which may later be utilized for creative and original effort. Frequently also work must be indulged which seems wide of the mark. The greatest artist will be the one with the widest and most sympathetic background. History, language, the cultural treasures of the race, philosophy, mathematics, the sciences, all are needed. To put all the training upon the vocal chords is to limit that deeper training which will have power profoundly to move the souls of men. Teaching genius cannot be created by a knowledge of pedagogy and breaks down, though done according to the most scientific methods, without the background of cultural knowledge. Technique of rhyming may produce rhymesters, but it cannot produce poets. Technique properly includes not only the more obvious tools of the artist, but his own power of mental, physical, and moral self-control as well. One's training can never therefore be too broad or too deep.

The relation of the creative imagination to the subconscious has already been suggested. The imaginative powers are continually in action, asleep or awake. The task of achievement is in great part the task of learning to turn them to definite ends. The imagination is continually playing upon whatever interests us, and we will either direct it or it will direct us. This is the real difference between the truly educated and the uneducated man. The truly educated man both mentally and morally is he who has learned to control his imagination and to drive it in the direction of accomplishment. The really uneducated man may or may not be a college graduate, but his distinguishing characteristic is that he is controlled by his imagination and is thus the victim of his own emotions. By frequent and continuous effort the latent forces of the subconscious may be turned to use in the achievement of creative work. It is possible to have the great power of the picture life within the soul turned to aid the main drive of life, to have it active in sleep as in waking moments, to have access to its resources so that at the moment of awaking we can profit by solutions worked out during sleep. This drive or push of the subconscious, the utilization of sleeping hours, is possible only through the direction of the creative imagination. If there is complete unity within the self, mental, moral, and spiritual, so that one is free from fears, inhibitions, and conflicts, so that one grasps situations through the "single eye" of pure motives, then is developed the greatest power of achievement. At this point the question arises as to how we may avoid conflicts between these two minds, the unconscious or imaginative and the conscious. In achieving the desired unity only brief mention of factors involved is necessary. Reflection is one of the main elements in securing unity of outer and inner self, as is keeping on good terms with all men of good will, so that in so far as may be compatible with self-respect and righteous conduct one is at peace with all men. Most and greatest of all in securing this unity of self, is the influence of genuine religious faith realized through prayer.

The creative imagination if pursued and directed may become eventually overpowering to the will. Recalling the old though simple illustration used by Emil Coué, one has no difficulty walking a plank raised two inches above the floor. If, however, the same plank should span a chasm a thousand feet deep, the influence of the imagination would in many cases, if not in most, prove overpowering to the will of the person attempting to walk the plank so placed. He would fall from the plank as the result of his imagination dwelling upon the depth, the possibility of falling, and the result of falling. Picturing himself as falling would very likely be able to overwhelm both judgment and will. It must be admitted that there is much of truth in his illustration. Many a man thinks he can live a double life and not have it affect his business or his art, but any disloyalty in his social life, in his heart life, in his emotional life, even disloyalty to his employer, introduces a conflict which will cause inevitable deterioration and keep him back from the fullest success. For in the long run our external and our internal life must be in harmony or the internal and secret one will be the master of the other. We live our external lives of conventional habits and manners and sometimes a very different internal life of deep-seated desires. The deep-seated desires dwell in the creative

imagination and in the time of unusual opportunity, crisis, or temptation they will rise and sweep all in destruction before them. The imagination must be held often to provide the factor of conviction. In most
of the affairs of life it provides the convincing factor in decision. Where
then is the privileged place for the exercise of the will? In the control of the imaginative faculty. One can walk a height very well if
instead of willing not to fall one turns the attention of the imagination
to other matters. . The reason the spiritual Master of Men turned the
thought toward the inner sources of control is because the will really
gets in its work and makes its decisions before the imagination begins.
To imagine one's self sinning is really to will to sin. The will and the
imagination are mutually stimulative, and the sinner finds himself
borne on the tide of action which he cannot apparently stop because,
in fact, his will has already been committed in the deepest recesses of
his being. That is the reason that Jesus sought out the secret place
of the creative imagination as the point of moral danger. The creative
imagination is easily diverted and controlled in the beginning. Allowed
to grow it gathers with it all the subconscious forces of life in the direction either of good or of evil. It is still quite true that out of the heart
are the issues of life.

The power and place of suggestion in all creative effort is thus clearly
shown. Nearly all individuals need the encouragement which should
come of parents' and teachers' assuring them of faith in their ability
to achieve. Most frequently the disclosure by parent or teacher of
latent powers comes as a revelation to the individual and turns the whole
after course of life. Some day we shall realize that the greatest value
of the teacher to a community lies not in his mastery of method nor in
the marks which the schools have placed upon him, but in the possession
of moral and spiritual character and humanness which give him sympathetic contacts with his pupils. His supreme value to the community
lies not so much in the method or content of his teaching as in his ability
to discover students to themselves. By the power of suggestion he
sends individuals out to the careers for which they are fitted. The
possession of highest spiritual and religious qualities is involved if
individuals are to be directed into channels of greatest value to the
community. The teacher who has not these will merely send his students in the direction of a low and a dead vocationalism. The state
has plenty of skilled artisans. What it needs is moral and spiritual
leaders. He who has managed to capture one boy or girl from the
levels of mere vocationalism to fitness for moral and spiritual leadership, to artistic and literary genius may well be considered as justifying
his own right to recognition. No task in the community is more important than the discovery of genius to itself, and genius is not so rare
a possibility as is sometimes thought, being simply interest with power
to concentrate imagination and effort on a given end. The reason that
so much faithful work in the world lacks the touch of genius and origi-

nality is because the individual has not achieved harmony within himself. He has not learned to tie up his dreaming with his doing. His work lacks that spontaneity, freshness, and spirit which launch into new channels because he does not properly profit by these hidden and almost exhaustless resources. The output of life is comparable to that of a factory. The factory that runs three shifts a day will in the nature of the case put out three times the product of a one-shift establishment. The man who sets his subconscious mind working toward a directed end will not only increase his output but greatly improve the quality of it. For it is this fatigueless effort that is the source of our highest enthusiasm and gives to work the mark of genius.

The creative imagination will be found in close alliance with mysticism in religion and in art in the power it possesses for unlocking unsuspected creative faculties. The emotional life of the individual is all bound up with the imaginative. "No imagination, no emotion" is fairly a truism. No imagination, no emotion, no creative achievement, might no less surely be added. Here lies, it would seem, the psychological reason for religion. It is needed to bring harmony in emotion, imagination, subconscious willing, self-direction, and effort. Lack of harmony here will inevitably discolor and confine the springs of creative effort. Here we hit likewise upon the reason for worship in religion. There must be a religious ideal so great, so ennobling, as to command the best powers of man. Moments of worship, of self-conscious communion with the divine, are necessary to religious living. On exactly the same basis artist and writer, statesman and inventor must have leisure for reflection and communion. It is so in scholarship and in all creative occupations. The unusual place which religion takes in creative work furnishes ample reason why art, literature, and life reach their highest expression only through the spiritual motive. A profound reverence for beauty as pure, as human, and as intelligent, amounting to worship of the highest, must have inspired the devoted soul of the sculptor who carved the Venus di Milo. It could never have been accomplished by a cheap and irreverent soul. It is the element of worship that lies behind the inspiration of the Gothic architecture and made possible the work of the greatest artists. Art is not true art until it gathers about the central core of reverence and worship. Great literature and great lives spring equally from the same sources. And the heart of all reverential feeling is prayer. It tunes the creative imagination to the most exalted note and may truly be called the *sine qua non* of all creative work. Prayer has its place in all creative achievement. Prayer not for selfish benefits to be received, but prayer for power of highest expression is what is here meant. Prayer as an exhibition of pious mendicancy has been of no service to the world. The heart of achievement lies in that type of prayer which unifies all dreams and desires and powers of self-expression in the man, all moral and spiritual aspirations, in the direction of a great and noble aim.

Whether the result be a Rembrandt, a Beethoven, a Rheims Cathedral, or a Cross of Calvary, it is inspired, and its worth for the advancement of civilization, its value as creative effort, is to be measured by the completeness of its religious devotion. This is the story of history and of life. Again and again along the dusty way, the sordid and uninteresting life has been lifted into power and achievement by the shock of religious experience. And this will continue to be the case so long as the creative imagination of man has so profound a place in all creative work.

MUMFORD: *THE CONDITION OF MAN*. Harcourt, Brace & Company, New York. Pp. 391-394, 398-399, 400, 412, 415-417, 419, 422-423.

≈≈≋≈≈

"THE BASIS OF RENEWAL"

1 : THE EXTERNAL CRISIS

Henry Adams was right: the last thirty years have been witnessing the active disintegration of Western civilization. In a disintegrating society, decay is its form of life; and all the dynamic forces that are available have worked either to corrupt the human fiber or to multiply the agents of physical destruction. If we go further along the same route we shall fare worse. On our courage in facing this fact and on our promptness in meeting it, all plans for the renewal of personality and community depend. "Bombs educate vigorously," Adams observed, "and even wireless telegraphy or airships might require the reconstruction of society."

Has the destruction yet gone far enough to promote a genuine renewal—or has it already gone so far that it will prevent it? No one can yet answer this question. But only the ability to put the question to ourselves will provide an effectual answer in life and action.

The makers of the New World idolum confidently expected that the older part of the human heritage would disappear: science and technics seemed thoroughly able not merely to reconstruct man's institutions and his personality, but to displace any older forms of art, thought, or practice. If anything, the utilitarians would have been surprised at the persistence of institutions that were manifestly at odds with the utilitarian way of life. But they forgot that the moral and intellectual traditions of Judaea, Greece, and Rome were essential to the development of the New World ideology itself: so that, with the ebbing away of this older tide of culture, the insufficiency of their own creed as a guide to life would become plain. A science that disclaimed all interest in human values, except the satisfaction of curiosity and the increase of manipulative skill, cannot be useful even in its own limited sphere when the general dissolution of values leads to a contempt for science and a deliberate perversion of its results.

Modern civilization has been arrested in mid-flight: its technical advances in saving labor, perfecting automatism, mechanizing the daily processes of life, multiplying the arts of destruction, and dehumanizing the personality have been responsible for this arrest. The rise of the machine and the fall of man are two parts of the same process: never before have machines been so perfect, and never before have men sunk so low, for the sub-human conduct that the Nazis have exhibited in the torture and extermination of their victims drops below any level of merely animal brutality. That degradation is shared by those who passively condone this sub-human conduct, by belittling its horror and denying its terrible significance.

This catastrophe and this debasement have no parallels in earlier history; for now, for the first time, the entire world is involved. All consolations that are based on past recoveries are meaningless. What happened to Greece, Rome, China, or India has no parallel in the world today: When those civilizations collapsed, they were surrounded by neighbors that had reached nearly equal levels of culture, whereas if Western civilization should continue its downward course it will spread ruin to every part of the planet; and its going will consume the very forces and ideas within its own tradition that might have given a start to its successor.

The present crisis has long been visible. Jacob Burckhardt observed its early stages in the middle of the nineteenth century: in the series of brilliant essays, now published in English under the title, *Force and Freedom,* he not merely diagnosed the malady but accurately predicted its outward manifestations. In a letter written to Henry Osborn Taylor in 1905, Henry Adams remarked: "At the present rate of progression since 1600, it will not need another century or half century to tip thought upside down. Law, in that case, would disappear as theory or *a priori* principle and give place to force. Morality would become police. Explosives would reach cosmic violence. Disintegration would overcome integration." Henry Adams did not live to observe fascism: he anticipated it. He knew that the detonators of violence and destruction were present in every part of the social structure of Western society.

Like the die-hards of fourth century Rome, most of our contemporaries are still unaware of the dimensions of the present catastrophe. They were so completely self-hypnotized by pride in man's control over nature that they overlooked all the palpable evidence of the fact that this control did not extend to his own self and his own very life: they were unprepared to believe that a fiendish barbarism could arise in the midst of an advanced scientific country like Germany; and they were unable to analyze in their own reactions to this the characteristic symptoms of decay: a moral inertia, a flight from reality, an unwillingness to face danger or hardship on behalf of an ideal cause. The democratic peoples, inheritors of a universal culture that had actually spread throughout the globe, were willing to barter all their advances for the sake of "peace." When they finally found that the choice was not in their hands, they made ready to fight—but skeptically, reluctantly, stupidly, as men answer an alarm clock when still thick with sleep. This feeble response to the challenge of barbarism was as much a sign of disintegration as the barbarism itself.

The war itself has shocked people into facing the grimmest of realities; but is not in itself sufficient to promote an understanding of the forces that have promoted this world catastrophe. In its later phases, the war has caused people to accept unthinkable sacrifices: but they have yet to accept the hardest sacrifice of all, and that is, to give up their illusions about this civilization. Modern man is the victim of the very instruments he values most. Every gain in power, every mastery of natural forces, every scientific addition to knowledge, has proved potentially dangerous, because it has not been accompanied by equal gains in self-understanding and self-discipline. We have sought to achieve perfection by eliminating the human element. Believing that power and knowledge were by nature beneficent or that man himself was inherently good when freed from external obligations to goodness, we have conjured up a genius capable of destroying our civilization. The disproportionate development of the sciences themselves only hastens this malign end.

The physical victory over the barbarian in war is no answer to the problem that the barbarian's existence has conjured up: it merely clears the way for an answer. Even if valor and skill in war give the democratic peoples a temporary military ascendancy, that in itself will not be sufficient either to secure a lasting peace or to raise up this battered civilization. For the disease that threatens us is an organic one: it is no localized infection that can be lanced, cleaned, bandaged; on the contrary, it requires a reorientation of our whole life, a change in occupation, a change in regimen, a change in personal relationships, not least, a change in attitude and conscious direction: fundamentally, a change in religion, our total sense of the world and life and time. If we seek salvation more cheaply, we shall not be ready to undertake the heroic feats and sacrifices, the spiritual and practical efforts that will be necessary to create a life-sustaining community and a life-directed personality. To make use of our vitalities and energies—and potentially these were never greater—we must reassert once more the primacy of the person.

The obstacle to renewal does not merely lie in the fact that in so many parts of society the agents of destruction have gained the upper hand, and the organization of destruction has been forced upon us by the barbarian's attempt at world enslavement. Worse than that: organization has become in itself destructive of human values: everywhere the machine holds the center and the personality has been pushed to the periphery: a process which remains sinister even when the intention is benign—as it undoubtedly is, for example, in our overorganized institutions for teaching the young or for healing disease. The only way to renew the forces of life is to begin once again with the repressed and displaced elements: to dismantle a large part of the physical structure, to loosen up the automatisms of habit, to challenge even successful forms of routine, to give time, thought, attention, to all those changes which do not, in their first stages, require the collaboration and support of existing institutions. Our society is now at the stage where conversion—an inner change and redirection—must precede every outer change or transformation.

Here is the benign moment of disintegration: the moment when the old life is sufficiently shattered and broken to make a new life conceivable. When this moment of germination comes, the individual's experience of renewal, or at least his radical readiness for renewal, widens into a collective act. Such a change took place in classic civilization during the fourth century: it occurred again on a similar scale throughout the Western world in the eighteenth century: in both cases responses to disintegration. That inner change, under the pressure of a powerful experience, universally shared, is the prelude to every significant outer change. If rational demonstration cannot bring such a change about, it can nevertheless hasten it and clarify its goals once the personality has made itself ready and the conditions favoring it have come into being.

. . . . .

3 : THE END OF EXPANSION

The world crisis that has existed for the lifetime of a whole generation indicates that a radical shift in the direction of social movement has taken place: this shift began during the last quarter of the nineteenth century and now, directly and indirectly, has affected almost every institution. The crisis has two aspects: an external and an internal one. Here I shall deal mainly with the causes of the external crisis. The external change may be summed up in a brief sentence: an age of expansion is giving place to an age of equilibrium. The achievement of this equilibrium is the task of the next few centuries.

So far this change has been a blind and blundering one. Not merely have the underlying causes themselves been ignored, but the interests and attitudes that were formed by the tradition of expansion have kept every community from meeting by rational means the new conditions of life that open up. Those that have accepted the premises of stabilization have attached the movement itself to regressive purposes and have cut it off from its creative mission. Those who have resisted stabilization have striven to perpetuate a past that is beyond recall: a past that would not be worth recalling even if that were possible. Both the tempo and the direction of our life are about to undergo a profound change: this will prove a change for the better provided we can throw off the fatal temptation to worship our dead selves and perpetuate our past mistakes.

The present period is a painful transition between two eras. The first I have traced in some detail since the fourteenth century: it is associated with the rise of capitalism, militarism, scientism, and mechanization: likewise with the counter-movements of protestantism, romanticism, and democracy. All of these institutions made positive contributions to human culture: even militarism. The total effect of the era of expansion, however, was to increase man's power over nature, and in particular Western man's power over the more amiable or more feebly armed peoples that inhabited the rest of the planet; but the civilization that resulted has been rent by internal conflicts and contradictions which have nullified many of its real triumphs.

The outlines of the period of humanization that approaches are not so easy to describe: many of the characters have still to be invented and their lines have still to be written: at best, some of their costumes and a few odd parcels of scenery indicate what the play is to be about. But by way of broad contrast one may characterize the approaching period as one of dynamic equilibrium, such an equilibrium as the human body maintains at every stage in its growth. The theme for the new period will be neither arms and the man nor machines and the man: its theme will be the resurgence of life, the displacement of the mechanical by the organic, and the re-establishment of the person as the ultimate term of all human effort. Cultivation, humanization, co-operation, symbiosis: these are the watchwords of the new world-enveloping culture. . . .

The era of Western expansion had three overlapping and interacting phases: land expansion, population expansion, and industrial expansion. All three phases have usually been treated as if they were constant phenomena in any healthy society; whereas they were extremely unusual and highly localized changes that had a definite beginning and an inevitable terminus. In our time the whole process has come to an end, or very nearly approaches an end. Other peoples who a hundred years ago existed on a primitive level have fast become masters of Western machines and weapons, producers in their own right. Such people will no longer consent to being treated as packbearers and servants: they properly claim their place as partners, and they reinforce their claim with the Christian doctrine of the infinite worth of the individual, and the democratic doctrine of the freedom and equality of all men as men. We cannot disown either doctrine without betraying our own precious heritage. World trade, world production, world intercourse must now be based upon equivalent advantages for all the regions concerned: it must now be a two-way process: consciously and deliberately so. Meanwhile, equally radical changes are under way in the other departments where expansion has prevailed.

. . . . .

6: POPULATION EQUILIBRIUM

. . . the dream that man can make himself godlike by centering his energies solely on the conquest of the external world has now become the emptiest of dreams: empty and sinister. If anything should be plain by now it is the fact that man must build his culture about the complete human personality. Not only that: but he must compensate for his contemptuous neglect of the values that were not embraced by the machine by giving to his biological and psychological functions, to his values and his ideals, a fuller measure of his interest and attention.

An active knowledge of the social environment and of the behavior of men in social partnership, their needs, their drives, their impulses, their dreams, is just as indispensable for working out the new social order as reading, writing, and arithmetic were for those trained to capitalism. And so equally for the arts of society: the art of politics, the arts of enlightened behavior and orderly communication, must become the main field of new inventions. A world language is more important for mankind at the present moment than any conceivable advance in television and telephony: the pathetic provincialism of our present efforts at universal linguistics, from Esperanto to Basic English, proves the need here for moral self-examination and discipline, as well as semantic and linguistic skill. What we need today is not so much a moratorium on mechanical invention as a large-scale transfer of interest and personal talent to the fields of community and personality.

. . . . .

7 : THE INTERNAL CRISIS

. . . many of the plans and projects that seemed like mere escapist dreams in the nineteenth century have become conditions for renewal; indeed only those who are aware of the importance of man's higher needs will be capable even of providing intelligently for bare food and shelter. This is one of those periods when only the dreamers are practical men. By the same token, the so-called practical men have become makers and perpetuators of nightmares: for it is their attempt to crawl back into the crumbled wreckage of the immediate past that has condemned our society to frustration, to sterility, to savage barbarism.

The inner crisis in our civilization must be resolved before the outer crisis can be effectively met. Our first duty is to revamp our ideas and values and to reorganize the human personality around its highest and most central needs. If we ask ourselves as we face the future, not how to keep our old institutions and organizations running in their accustomed grooves, but how to keep life itself running, with or without the aid of these institutions, our problem immediately clarifies itself. There is no wealth, as Ruskin said, but life; and there is no consummation of life except in the perpetual growth and renewal of the human person: machines, organizations, institutions, wealth, power, culture, cities, landscapes, industries, are all secondary instruments in that process. Whatever nourishes the personality, humanizes it, refines it, deepens it, intensifies its aptitude and broadens its field of action is good: whatever limits it or thwarts it, whatever sends it back into tribal patterns and limits its capacity for human co-operation and communion must be counted as bad. Nothing that man has created is outside his capacity to change, to remold, to supplant, or to destroy: his machines are no more sacred or substantial than the dreams in which they originated.

In the end, all our contrivances have but one object: the continued growth of human personalities and the cultivation of the best life possible. What sort of personality must we now seek to foster and nourish? What kind of common life? What traits and disciplines are needed in an age of stabilization, co-operation, and balance? What is the order of value in our life needs: do we put babies above motor cars, art above plumbing, the well-being of the worker above the mechanical efficiency or cheapness of his product? If so, we must create a different ego-ideal from that which was the norm in a capitalistic and mechanical civilization: our mode of education and our plan of life must be directed to more humane ends than those that have hitherto governed us.

· · · · ·

8: The Need for Human Balance

As our culture developed during the last five centuries, its center lay more and more outside the human personality: hence a fragment of the personality displaced the whole. In attempting to restore balance in the community and in the personality, we need not be troubled by references to the undoubted existence of individual differences or to the fact, as true in society as in the individual organism, that all equilibrium is necessarily unstable and is constantly upset by the continued act of growth. The first condition makes the effort to achieve a fuller and more balanced development necessary: the second makes it an ideal goal—one always to be aimed at but never, in the nature of things, fully achieved.

Differences in temperament, capacity, aptitude, and interest, differences that have their origin in diversities of biological inheritance, characterize all men, as they characterize the same men at successive moments in life: Who would doubt it? Who would change it? These differences are the inexhaustible source of the richness of human experience. But no man is an island: every age has a common ideal of personality which represents the goals of living toward which the whole community is more or less set. To the extent that an individual shares in this personality, he is fit for his daily tasks and can co-operate freely with his fellows and make the fullest use of his culture. The more representative the common type, the more it meets the claims of its historic moment, the fewer repressions must be exercised over those whose inner tendency is to depart from it.

If the era of stabilization is to be one devoted to the intensive but balanced cultivation of our natural and social resources, balance and intensity are equally, I believe, the key to the sort of personality that is needed to work effectively within this culture and to create the necessary changes in our disrupted institutions. The age of mechanical specialization produced a quite different ideal: that of the one-sided specialist, the piece-worker, the operative conditioned by repetition and reward, as Dr. E. L. Thorndike puts it: the end product of a long period of mechanization in which one by one the higher attributes of

the personality have disappeared or have been reduced to mere whims
and hobbies. The fatal results of this process were pointed out by Comte
a full century ago. "If we have been accustomed to deplore the spectacle, among the artisan class, of a workman occupied during his whole
life in nothing but making knife handles or pinheads, we may find something quite as lamentable in the intellectual class, in the exclusive employment of the human brain in resolving equations or classifying insects.
The moral effect is, unhappily, analogous in the two cases. It occasions a
miserable indifference about the general course of human affairs as long
as there are equations to resolve or pins to manufacture."

One of Comte's most able successors in sociology, Dr. Karl Mannheim, has carried this observation even further : he notes the growing
irrationality of the personality engaged in production in proportion to the
technical refinement and "rationalization" of the process. The dismem-
bered man, whether as engineer or workman, as organizer or salesman,
needs less directive insight and intelligence once he is geared to the whole
machine than the carpenter or the weaver needed in his workshop. The
behaviorist man, with his slot-machine mind, responding mechanically
to external stimuli, passive until acted upon, incapable of taking the
initiative or choosing his destination, is the typical by-product of current society : fascist minds are thus more common than the conscious
philosophy of fascism. Indeed our whole civilization has put a premium
upon this primitive kind of automatism and compulsion : the very humanity that quickens the life-like machine leaves the person depleted
and empty.

Dr. Mannheim has well pointed out that the chief element in our
inner crisis today is the disproportionate development of human faculties : "individuals as well as historical and social groups may, under
certain circumstances, suffer from the danger of disintegration because
their capacities fail to develop equally and harmoniously." This observation has been reinforced by an experienced psychiatrist and a profound
reader of the modern soul, Dr. C. G. Jung, who has sought to combat
this unfortunate lopsidedness and disparity by counseling his patients
to cultivate their weaker sides. None of our dominant institutions
today correct this lack of balance : on the contrary, they encourage it
in the name of efficiency, an efficiency which fosters a single function
at the expense of the whole life that finally supports it. Only by making
the personality itself central, and by drawing forth its repressed or
thwarted capacities, can this mischief be cured : balance and autonomy
go together. . . .

The task for our age is to decentralize power in all its manifestations.
To this end, we must build up balanced personalities, personalities that
will be capable of drawing upon our immense stores of energy, knowledge, and wealth without being demoralized by them. On this point,
Plato's words in *The Laws* cannot be improved : "If anyone gives too
great power to anything, too large a sail to a vessel, too much food to the

body, too much authority to the mind, and does not observe the mean, everything is overthrown, and in the wantonness of excess runs in the one case to disorders, and in the other to injustice, which is the child of excess."

If we are to control machines and organizations, then, we must make men; and our first task is that of self-examination, self-education, self-control. Those who fail at this point will be incapable of contributing to the political, economic, and social transformations that are now so long overdue.

9: THE ORGANIC PERSON

The ideal personality for the opening age is a balanced personality: not the specialist but the whole man. Such a personality must be in dynamic interaction with every part of his environment and every part of his heritage. He must be capable of treating economic experiences and esthetic experiences, parental experiences and vocational experiences, as the related parts of a single whole, namely, life itself. His education, his discipline, his daily routine must tend toward this wholeness. To achieve this, he must be ready to spurn easy successes that come, in a dying culture, through self-mutilation.

Such a dynamic balance is not easily achieved: its consummations are precious and its stability is precarious: it demands a vigilance and an athletic readiness for new shifts and stresses that more specialized vocations do not habitually achieve. . . .

Only in one place can an immediate renewal begin: that is, within the person; and a remolding of the self and the super-ego is an inescapable preliminary to the great changes that must be made throughout every community, in every part of the world. Each one, within his or her own field of action—the home, the neighborhood, the city, the region, the school, the church, the factory, the mine, the office, the union— must carry into his immediate day's work a changed attitude toward all his functions and obligations. His collective work cannot rise to a higher level than his personal scale of values. Once a change is effected in the person, every group will record and respond to it.

Today our best plans miscarry because they are in the hands of people who have undergone no inner growth. Most of these people have shrunk from facing the world crisis and they have no notion of the manner in which they themselves have helped to bring it about. Into every new situation they carry only a fossilized self. Their hidden prejudices, their glib hopes, their archaic desires and automatisms— usually couched in the language of assertive modernity—recall those of the Greeks in the fourth century B.C. or those of the Romans in the fourth century A.D. They are in a powerdive and their controls have frozen. By closing their eyes they think they can avoid a crash.

Those who look for swift wholesale changes to take place in our

institutions under-rate the difficulties we now face: the inroads of barbarism and automatism, those twin betrayers of freedom, have been too
deep. In their impatience, in their despair, such people secretly long
to cast the burden of their own regeneration upon a savior: a president,
a pope, a dictator—vulgar counterparts of a divinity debased or a corruption deified. But such a leader is only the mass of humanity writ
small: the incarnation of our resentments, hates, sadisms, or of our
cowardices, confusions and complacencies. There is no salvation through
such naked self-worship: God must work within us. Each man and
woman must first silently assume his own burden.

We need not wait for bombs and bullets actually to strike us before
we strip our lives of superfluities: we need not wait for events to bend
our wills to unison. Wherever we are, the worst has already happened
and we must meet it. We must simplify our daily routine without
waiting for ration cards; we must take on public responsibilities without
waiting for conscription; we must work for the unity and effective
brotherhood of man without letting further wars prove that the current
pursuit of power, profit and all manner of material aggrandizement is
treason to humanity: treason and national suicide. Year by year, we
must persevere in all these acts, even though the restrictions are lifted
and the urgencies of war have slackened. Unless we now rebuild our
selves all our external triumphs will crumble.

There is no easy formula for this renewal. It is not enough for us
to do all that is possible: we must do that which seems impossible. Our
first need is not for organization but for orientation: a change in direction and attitude. We must bring to every activity and every plan a
new criterion of judgment: we must ask how far it seeks to further the
processes of life-fulfillment and how much respect it pays to the needs of
the whole personality.

More immediately we must demand: What is the purpose of each
new political and economic measure? Does it seek the old goal of expansion or the new one of equilibrium? Does it work for conquest or
co-operation? And what is the nature of this or that industrial or
social achievement—does it produce material goods alone or does it
also produce human goods and good men? Do our individual life-plans
make for a universal society, in which art and science, truth and beauty,
religion and sanctity, enrich mankind? Do our public life-plans make
for the fulfillment and renewal of the human person, so that they will
bear fruit in a life abundant: ever more significant, ever more valuable,
ever more deeply experienced and more widely shared?

If we keep this standard constantly in mind, we shall have both a
measure for what must be rejected and a goal for what must be achieved.

In time, we shall create the institutions and the habits of life, the rituals, the laws, the arts, the morals that are essential to the development of the whole personality and the balanced community: the possibilities of progress will become real again once we lose our blind faith in the external improvements of the machine alone.   But the first step is a personal one: a change in direction of interest *towards* the person. Without that change, no great betterment will take place in the social order. Once that change begins, everything is possible.

Questions and Statements for Discussion

(Chapters 14 and 15)

(Creative Personality)

1. "If science can get nowhere in the ascertainment of facts, except upon the hypothesis of the solidarity of the universe, and must in the end justify its hypothesis by the pragmatic test of values, how much deeper is the demand that in philosophical and religious thinking, we should start with the hypothesis of the moral and spiritual solidarity in the Cosmos, the universal reality of mental, moral, and spiritual values in the experience of man." (Flewelling, *Creative Personality,* Chap. XXV, p. 217.)

2. "That men should give the long hours of toil and endure such sacrifices in the interests of scientific discovery . . . is unjustifiable, except from the standpoint of human values to be achieved." (Chap. XXV, p. 221.)

3. "The only lasting power in politics and government is based upon the principle of freedom." (Chap. XXX, p. 254.)

4. "Freedom and self-restraint march together." (Chap. XXX, p. 225.)

5. "Creative imagination . . . is the unique possession of man. . . . It is essential that the imagination should be set in the direction which we wish the outward life to take." (Chap. XXXII, pp. 273, 274.)

6. "Creative effort will be distinguished from noncreative, originality from imitation, by passing the stage of merely mechanical and physical operation into the emotional and imaginative." (Chap. XXXII, p. 275.)

7. "The creative imagination . . . may become eventually over-powering to the will." (Chap. XXXII, p. 277.)

(The Condition of Man)

8. How could "wireless telegraphy or airships require the reconstruction of society"?

9. Discuss the result: "When man's control over nature [does] not extend to his own self and his own way of life."

10. What does Mumford describe as a greater necessary sacrifice than the unthinkable sacrifices of war?

11. Cite and consider the obstacles to renewal and their removal.

12. Consider the truth of the sentence: "Inner change, under the pressure of powerful experience, universally shared, is the prelude to every significant outer change."

13. Meaning of the sentence: "The theme for the new period . . . will be the resurgence of life, the displacement of the mechanical by

the organic, and the reestablishment of the person as the ultimate term of all human effort." How do you think it might be brought about?

14. Discuss the relation of scientific invention, and the doctrine of the infinite worth of the individual to a new demand for democracy, among belated peoples.

15. "A world language is more important for mankind at the present moment than any conceivable advance in television." If so, why?

16. "Differences are the inexhaustible source of the richness of human experiences." How is this compatible with peace and democracy?

17. Discuss the effect of "piece-work" on personal values and on civilization.

18. Why is it essential for us to develop our "weaker sides"? And how is such development treated in modern education?

19. A man's "collective work cannot rise higher than his scale of values."

Suggested Supplementary Readings:

Flewelling: *Creative Personality*. Macmillan, New York.

Compton: *The Freedom of Man*. Yale University Press, New Haven. Chap. V.

Wilson: *The Self and Its World*. Macmillan, New York.

Vaughan: *The Significance of Personality*. Macmillan, New York.

Berdyaev: *Freedom and the Spirit*. Scribner's, New York.

INDEX

Note: Titles of books are printed in italics.